GOD CHAS

ExTREME

NEW TESTAMENT

GOD CHASERS
ExTREME
NEW TESTAMENT

(The International English® Bible translation)

Foreword by Tommy Tenney

Destiny Image® Publishers, Inc.
P.O. Box 310
Shippensburg, PA 17257-0310

"Speaking to the Purposes of God for This Generation
and for the Generations to Come"

ISBN 0-7684-2112-8

(Previously published as The Simple English™ Bible, New Testament
ISBN 0-937830-02-X)

For Worldwide Distribution
Printed in the U.S.A.

This book and all other Destiny Image, Revival Press, MercyPlace, Fresh Bread, Destiny Image Fiction, and Treasure House books are available at Christian bookstores and distributors worldwide.

For a U.S. bookstore nearest you, call **1-800-722-6774**.
For more information on foreign distributors, call **717-532-3040**.
Or reach us on the Internet: **www.reapernet.com**

Contents

Foreword

"You are always searching the Scriptures...you will find eternal life in them" (John 5:39).

I love the Scriptures! They are the road map and inspiration for my daily chase for the presence of God. Over the years I have discovered some important keys that have helped me unlock powerful truths, many of which are contained in my writing.

One of these keys is that *preparing your spirit to receive the Word is very critical*. It is in the attic of our spirit that God's Word shines like a light. If our spirits are jammed with junk, the light cannot penetrate into our spirits and make its truths known. Shadows and fleeting doubts appear. Clean out the attic! We carry nothing in our minds that cannot be washed by His Word.

Another key is understanding that reading your Bible is not revelation—rather, *reading prepares the way for revelation*. It is very important to maintain a regular discipline of reading the Scriptures. My father calls it "grazing" the Word! The methods you use may vary. You might want to make it a practice to read through the entire Scriptures on a regular basis. At other times you will feel constrained to read a certain portion. Sometimes a particular issue will grab your attention, and you will find yourself searching out Scriptures related to that topic. The important thing is that you are regularly reading the Word.

Once the Word seeps into my spirit, I let it incubate there as I ponder its meaning and implications. Mary, the mother of our Lord, provides a great example of this truth. "Mary was keeping all these things in her heart; she continued to think about them" (Luke 2:19). I am cautious not to be too quick to share the discoveries I have made. The meditative process is so important in the development of the Word in us. We must take time to carefully think through every aspect of that Word.

As I ponder and meditate, I often see a facet of the truth that others may have overlooked. Revelation isn't new information. It is, very simply, newly discovered old information. The reality of that truth was always there, but our eyes were distracted and we missed it. I am like the proverbial Indian scout. My eyes have been sensitized to see broken branches and disturbed dust. Spiritual perceptiveness will enable you to effectively track Him as you read, meditate, and study His Word. You will find, over time, that your sensitivity will be sharpened and refined.

It is very important to guard well this sensitivity. I am careful about the things that I allow to enter into my spirit. I am cautious about what movies I see and what books I read, so that nothing will disrupt my sensitivity. Even good movies and enjoyable books can distort the lens of my spirit. I don't want my spirit to become muddled and distracted by the wrong kind of information.

During this process God will give me appropriate and effective words that enable me to clearly communicate the truths I have seen. Those words are formed in the chambers of my heart as God inscribes His words on my soul. Those words become "phrases of destiny" for me. Landmarks from past revelation to biblical writers and heroes provide direction for me.

You cannot take any shortcuts. The hard work you do in the private place will reap its rewards in the public place. Reading God's Word is the training ground for eternal athletes—pursuers of His presence!

Now open the Book and get on with the chase!

Tommy Tenney
Author, GodChaser

Introduction

The Bible is the message of God. It is the inspired, infallible, written record of God's will. Through the Bible, God speaks to mankind. In order for all people to easily understand what God wants, it is extremely important that the Holy Scriptures be accurately translated into many languages, one of which is contemporary English.

The New Testament was originally written in the Greek language. It was not the Classical Greek of Aristotle nor was it even couched in the literary Greek of the first century (with a few exceptions). It is noteworthy that the entire New Testament was written in Koine (common) Greek—an everyday language which was used by almost everyone in conversation and commerce throughout the Roman Empire. Jesus talked plainly to people, the way we would talk to one another every day. Today the widespread use of English (Koine English), especially on the Worldwide Web, parallels the dominance of Hellenistic Greek in the time of Jesus.

A good translation should produce the same effect today as the original text did on those who first heard it. How would the New Testament have been written in English if English had been the original language instead of Greek? That is the degree of normality that was sought—to reclothe the meaning of the original in the words and structure of modern English. God's message should be conveyed in today's mode of speech, not yesterday's. His Word ought to be expressed in the same form which people use every day, in a style which seems so natural to them that they are generally not aware that they are even reading a translation.

Jesus, the master Teacher, was very careful not to give people more than they could grasp. According to Mark 4:33, "...Jesus was telling them the message—but only as much as they were able to understand." Jesus did not try to impress people with big words, yet he was still able to reach their hearts. We are trying to re-capture that level of communication.

Using profound illustrations, Jesus was able to communicate clearly, even with children. He attracted them, because they could feel His love (Matthew 19:13-14). In fact, Jesus said we ought to become humble like little children (Matthew 18:1-6). Jesus Himself *is* the Message (John 1:1).

There is no single translation for everyone, but *The International English® Bible* may be the most useful one for a majority of English speakers. This new translation was designed primarily to communicate to a wide spectrum of people all over our small planet. We believe that *The International English® Bible* can be understood by 20 percent of the world! There is still room for an appropriately-pitched translation which can communicate throughout the world to masses of people who speak English, the *lingua franca* of modern times. And, it is imperative that these people have a fresh, reliable translation which is both easy to understand and accurate.

To reach the greatest number of people *The International English® Bible* uses only easy phrase structures and a vocabulary of about 3,000 words. Sentences are purposely kept short, transparent, and uncomplicated to promote greater understanding. Complex sentence structures are often unnecessary anyway. Because of our approach, portions of Scripture which have formerly been difficult to understand are now much easier to comprehend. The style coincides nicely with spoken grammar. Try reading the text aloud and you will find that it flows easily off the tongue. Like a conversation, it is easy to listen to.

In translating the original words of the Holy Spirit, great care was taken to find those exact English words which tell God's message both simply and precisely. Also, because some traditional "religious" words (e.g. saints, baptism, church, justification, redemption, etc.) do *not* teach the root meanings of the original Greek text, a special effort was made to translate these terms into expressions which can be understood by everyone, especially by those who have never read the Bible.

Not only must a translation make sense, but it must at the same time conform to the meaning of the original message. We wanted the text to communicate as clearly as possible without giving up accuracy. Painstaking effort was exercised not to deviate from the best available Greek manuscripts. Several technical editions were consulted. It was an eclectic approach, letting each variant reading stand on the evidence presented for it individually.

The International English® Bible is smooth, but it is not a loose rendering. It is *not* a paraphrase, but a meticulously constructed translation which expresses the original Greek meaning accurately in natural English equivalents. Nothing is added or taken away merely for the sake of style. Every piece of meaning can be accounted for through established linguistic methodology.

Italics indicate words or phrases which are only implied in the original Greek text. In some cases where confusion might result (e.g. four different Herods or two Antiochs), italicized words have been incorporated into the text to clarify referents (e.g. Herod *the Great* in Matthew 2:1). Occasionally, **bold face** is used for emphasis. Asterisks (*) are used to indicate the presence of footnotes. Footnotes include: further concise explanations, more literal renderings, cross-references, textual variants, historical notes, and alternative translations.

All translations of the Bible are made by uninspired men who make some mistakes. None are more painfully aware of this fact than they. Though perfection is always the goal, imperfections persist. However, the help and wisdom of God were constantly sought in prayer. We all are indebted to hundreds of anonymous scribes down through the centuries. They have transmitted the ancient texts to us with great fidelity, long before the modern age of printing. And, much is owed to the insights of the thousands of Biblical scholars who have preceded us.

We are so thankful to God for His help and the strength that He alone could give to accomplish such a task. What a joy and a privilege! Our earnest prayer today is that *The International English® Bible* may be used by the Lord to bring salvation to many, so that every person on earth can know what God's will is and obey it.

Our deep appreciation also goes out to all who helped in countless ways, small and great. We implore you to continue pointing out needed corrections. Your suggestions for future improvements are sincerely invited. We commend this translation to the considerate judgment of all students of God's Word.

Achieving understanding of Scripture is a worthy goal, but a far more important aim is to apply what we learn from Scripture to our daily lives. *That* is the ultimate translation!

—THE BIBLE TRANSLATION COMMITTEE

MATTHEW

Chapter 1

Jesus' Family Tree

1 This is the record of the family names of Jesus Christ,* a descendant of David, a descendant of Abraham:

2 Abraham fathered Isaac;
Isaac fathered Jacob;
Jacob fathered Judah and his brothers.

3 Judah fathered Perez and Zerah by Tamar;
Perez fathered Hezron;
Hezron fathered Ram.

4 Ram fathered Amminadab;
Amminadab fathered Nahshon;
Nahshon fathered Salmon.

5 Salmon fathered Boaz by Rahab;
Boaz fathered Obed by Ruth;
Obed fathered Jesse.

6 Jesse fathered David, the king;
David fathered Solomon by the *wife* of Uriah.

7 Solomon fathered Rehoboam;
Rehoboam fathered Abijah;
Abijah fathered Asa.

8 Asa fathered Jehoshaphat;
Jehoshaphat fathered Jehoram;
Jehoram fathered Uzziah.

9 Uzziah fathered Jotham;
Jotham fathered Ahaz;
Ahaz fathered Hezekiah.

10 Hezekiah fathered Manasseh;
Manasseh fathered Amon;
Amon fathered Josiah.

11 Josiah fathered Jehoiachin and his brothers when *Israel* was carried away to Babylon.

12 After *Israel* was carried away to Babylon,
Jehoiachin fathered Shealtiel;
Shealtiel fathered Zerubbabel.

13 Zerubbabel fathered Abiud;
Abiud fathered Eliakim;
Eliakim fathered Azor.

14 Azor fathered Zadok;
Zadok fathered Achim;
Achim fathered Eliud.

15 Eliud fathered Eleazar;

1:1   or, the Messiah

Eleazar fathered Matthan;
Matthan fathered Jacob.
16 Jacob fathered Joseph, Mary's husband.
Mary gave birth to Jesus, the one called the
Messiah.

17 There was a total of 14 generations from *the time of* Abraham until David's *time.* There were 14 generations from *the time of* David until *Israel* was carried away to Babylon. And there were 14 generations from *the time when Israel* was carried away to Babylon until *the time of* the Messiah.

Birth Announcement

18 This is how the birth of Jesus Christ* occurred: Mary, the mother of Jesus, was engaged to be married to Joseph, but before they were married, it was discovered that she was pregnant (by the Holy Spirit)! 19 However, Joseph, her husband-to-be, was a fair man; he did not want to disgrace her. So he decided to quietly call off the marriage. 20 He was thinking deeply upon these things when, suddenly, an angel of the Lord appeared to him in a dream, saying, "Joseph, descendant of David, don't be afraid to take Mary to be your wife. The baby inside her comes from the Holy Spirit. 21 She will give birth to a son. You will name him Jesus,* because he will save his people from their sins. 22 The Lord spoke about this through the prophet *Isaiah.* All these things occurred to make this come true:

23 'Listen! The virgin will be pregnant
and give birth to a son.
They will name him Emmanuel   *Isaiah 7:14*
(which means, God is with us).' "   *Is iah 8:8*

24 When Joseph woke up from sleeping, he did as the angel of the Lord had ordered him to do; he took *Mary* to be his wife. 25 He did not have sexual relations with her,* until she gave birth to the little boy. Joseph named him Jesus.

Chapter 2

Three God Chasers

1 Jesus was born in Bethlehem, a town in Judea, during the time of King Herod *the Great.* Some wise men from the east traveled to Jerusalem. 2 They asked, "Where is the one who was born to be king of the Jews? We saw his star in the east, and we came to worship him."

3 When King Herod heard this, he was disturbed. Everyone else in Jerusalem was too. 4 He gathered all of the most important priests and teachers of the law from the people and asked them where the Messiah would be born. 5 They answered, "In the town of Bethlehem in Judea, because this was written by the prophet *Micah*:

6 'And you, Bethlehem, in the land of Judea,
you are surely not the least *important*
among the leading *towns* of Judea,
because a Leader will come out from you.
He will shepherd my people, Israel.' "   *Micah 5:2*

1:18   or, the Messiah
1:21   "Jesus" comes from a Hebrew word which means "Yahweh (God) is salvation."
1:25   literally, know her (in a sexual way). See Genesis 4:1.

7 Then, in secret, Herod called for the wise men. From them he added up the exact time when the star appeared.   **8-10** "Go, search very carefully for *information* about the child. When you find him, report to me, so that I, too, may come to worship him." After they had listened to the king, they left; Herod sent them to Bethlehem.

Suddenly, the star which they had seen in the east was leading them. When they saw the star, they were very, very happy. It finally stopped above the place where the child was.   **11** They went into the house and saw the child with Mary, his mother. They bowed down to worship him. They opened their treasures and brought him gifts—gold, perfume, and precious spices.

12 But God used a dream to warn them that they should not return to Herod. So they returned to their country by a different road.

Get Up and Go!

13 After they had gone, an angel of the Lord suddenly appeared to Joseph in a dream. The angel said, "Get up! Take the child and his mother and escape to Egypt. Stay there until I speak to you *again*. Herod is about to begin searching for the child to kill him."   **14** So, Joseph got ready. He took the child and his mother at night and left for Egypt.   **15** He stayed there until Herod died, to make what the Lord *God* had said through the prophet come true:

"I called My Son out of Egypt."   *Hosea 11:1*

Herod Kills the Baby Boys

16 When Herod realized that the wise men had made a fool out of him, he was very angry. He ordered *his men* to kill all the little boys in and around the town of Bethlehem— the boys who were two years old or younger (the exact time which Herod had figured out from the wise men).   **17** Then what God had said through Jeremiah the prophet came true:

18 "A sound was heard in the town of
Ramah,* crying and loud screaming.
Rachel is crying for her children:
She will not let anyone comfort
her, because the children are dead."   *Jeremiah 31:15*

Get Up and Go Back!

19 After Herod died, an angel of the Lord suddenly appeared to Joseph in a dream in Egypt.   **20** The angel said, "Get ready! Take the child and his mother and go to the land of Israel. The people who were trying to kill the child have died."   **21** So, Joseph got ready. He took the child and his mother and entered the land of Israel.   **22** Joseph heard that *Herod* Archelaus was ruling Judea, instead of his father, Herod *the Great*. Joseph was afraid to go back there, but, in a dream, God told him to leave for the land of Galilee.   **23** So, he went and lived in a town called Nazareth, so that what God had said through the prophets would come true:

"He will be called a Nazarene."

Chapter 3

Preach It and They Will Come

1 During those days, John (the one who immersed people) was preaching in the desert in the land of Judea.   **2** He said, "Change your hearts! The kingdom of heaven

---

2:18   Bethlehem

3

is very near!" **3** This is the man whom God talked about through the prophet Isaiah:
"There is a voice crying out in the desert:
'Prepare the Lord's road.
Make His paths straight.' "   *Isaiah 40:3*
4 John always wore clothes made of camel hair. He had a leather belt around his waist.
He ate grasshoppers and wild honey.   **5** People from Jerusalem and all over the land
of Judea and all the area around the Jordan River continued coming to John.   **6** They
were admitting that they had sinned. John immersed them in the Jordan River.

7 When John saw many Pharisees and Sadducees coming to his immersions, he said
to them, "You are like poisonous snakes! Who told you to run away from *God's* punishment which is coming?   **8** You must do the things which will show that you really
have changed your hearts!   **9** Don't think this to yourselves: 'Abraham is our father!'
I tell you that God could make children for Abraham from these rocks here.   **10** The
ax is now ready to cut the trees down. Every tree which does not produce good fruit is
being cut down and thrown into fire.

11 "Whenever you change your hearts, I immerse you in water. But there is one
coming later who is more important than I am. I am not worthy to carry his shoes. **He**
will immerse you in the Holy Spirit and in fire!

Get Ready for the Chase!

12 He will come ready to clean the grain. He will separate the good grain from the
straw. He will put the good part of the grain into his barn. Then he will burn the straw
with a fire which cannot be put out."

John Immerses Jesus

13 Then Jesus traveled from the land of Galilee to the Jordan River where John was,
so that John could immerse him,   **14** but John was trying to stop him. John said, "I
need you to immerse **me**, yet **you** are coming to me?"

15 Jesus answered him, "Allow this for now, because this is the proper way for us to
fulfill all righteousness." Then John did so.   **16** After Jesus was immersed, he came up
from the water immediately. Suddenly, the sky was opened for him. He saw the Spirit
of God coming down on him like a dove.   **17** Suddenly, a Voice came from heaven and
said, "This is My Son, and I love him, I am very pleased with him!"

Chapter 4

Jesus Passes the Test

1 Then the Spirit led Jesus into the desert to be tempted by the Devil.   **2** Jesus did
not eat anything for 40 days and nights. After this, Jesus was very hungry.   **3** The
Devil* came and said to Jesus, "Since you are the Son of God, command these rocks to
become food."

4 Jesus answered, "It is written:
'A person does not live on food alone. Instead, he lives on every word which comes
from the mouth of God.' "   *Deuteronomy 8:3*
5 Then the Devil took Jesus into the holy city, *Jerusalem*, and put him on a very high
place of the temple.   **6** He said to Jesus, "Since you are the Son of God, jump off!
Because it is written:

4:3   literally, the tempter

4

'God will command His angels to take care of you.'   *Psalm 91:11*

and,

'Their hands will catch you, so that
   you will not hit your foot against a rock.' "   *Psalm 91:12*

7 Jesus answered him, "But this is also written:
   'You must not test the Lord your God.' "   *Deuteronomy 6:16*

8 Suddenly, the Devil took Jesus to a very tall mountain and showed him all the kingdoms of the world and the glory which was in them.   9 The Devil said to Jesus, "I will give you all of these things, if you will only bow down to worship me."

10 Then Jesus said to the Devil, "Go away, Satan, because it is written:
   'You must worship the Lord your God. Serve only Him.' "   *Deuteronomy 6:13*

11 Then the Devil left Jesus. Immediately, angels came and helped him.

Get Ready for the Chase

12 When Jesus heard that John had been arrested,* he went away to Galilee. 13 After leaving Nazareth, he went and lived in Capernaum, beside Lake *Galilee* , in the Zebulun and Naphtali area.   14 *He did this* to fulfill what God had said through the prophet Isaiah:

15 "Land of Zebulun, land of Naphtali,
       the way to the *Mediterranean* Sea
   across the Jordan River,
       Galilee of the nations.
16 The people who live in darkness have seen a great light.
       The light has dawned upon the people who live in that country and in the fear
       of death."   *Isaiah 9:1-2*

17 From then on Jesus began to preach: "Change your hearts, because the kingdom of heaven is very near!"

God Chasers: Peter, Andrew, James, and John

18 While Jesus was walking beside Lake Galilee, he saw two brothers. They were Simon (called Peter) and Andrew, his brother. They were fishermen and they were throwing their nets into the lake.   19 Jesus said to them, "Follow me and I will make you fishermen—of **people**!"   20 They left their nets immediately and followed him.

21 Jesus went farther and saw two more men. They were brothers—James and John—sons of Zebedee. They were in a boat with Zebedee, their father, preparing their nets. Jesus called them also.   22 Immediately they left the boat and their father to follow Jesus.

Very Good News

23 Jesus was going all around Galilee, teaching the Good News of the kingdom in their synagogues. Jesus was healing people of all types of diseases and sicknesses.

24 The news about Jesus went all over the land of Syria. They brought him all the people who were sick. These people had all kinds of diseases; they were suffering with much pain. Some of them had demons inside them. Some were epileptics* and some were paralyzed. Jesus healed them all.

4:12   Herod Antipas arrested John because John had accused Herod Antipas of illegally marrying his half-brother's wife. (See Matthew 14:3.)

4:24   Epilepsy is a disease that violently affects the central nervous system by loss of muscular control and loss of consciousness.

25 Large crowds followed him, coming from the land of Galilee, from the area of the Ten Towns,* from Jerusalem, from the land of Judea, and from the area across the Jordan River.

Chapter 5

The "Sermon on the Mount"

1 When Jesus saw the crowds, he went up on a mountain and sat down. His followers came to him.   **2** This is what he started teaching them:

Be Happy

3 "The people who are broken in spirit are happy,
  because the kingdom of heaven belongs to **them**.
4 The people who are crying now will be happy,
  because **they** will be comforted.
5 Humble people are happy,
  because the earth will be given to **them**.
6 People who are hungry and thirsty for what is right are happy,
  because **they** will be filled.
7 People who give mercy *to others* are happy,
  because **they** will receive mercy.
8 People who have pure hearts are happy,
  because **they** will see God.
9 People who make peace are happy,
  because **they** will be called the sons of God.
10 The people who have been persecuted
    because they were doing right are happy,
  because the kingdom of heaven belongs to **them**.
11 "You will be happy when people insult you, persecute you, and tell all kinds of lies against you because of me.   **12** You should be full of joy and be very glad, because you will have great rewards in heaven. This was the way *your ancestors* persecuted the prophets before you."

Be Salt and Light

13 "You are the salt of the earth, but if the salt loses its salty taste,* then *it is no good.* You cannot make it salty again. It is good for nothing. It is thrown outside where people walk on it.
14 "You are light for the world. It is not possible to hide a city which is sitting on a hill.   **15** No one lights a lamp and then puts it under a basket. Instead, *he puts the lamp* on a lamp table, and it shines for everyone in the house.   **16** So, let your light shine in front of people, so that they will see the good things you do. Then they will give glory to your Father, who is in heaven."

4:25   literally, the Decapolis, a defense confederation which originally consisted of ten cities. Eventually, they became an entire Roman province.
5:13   In Jesus' day, salt was often stored inside bags made of animal skin. This salt contained impurities which absorbed moisture during damp weather. The pure salt would dissolve and leak through the bags, leaving only saltless residue. Thus, salt eventually lost its qualities.

The Importance of the Law and the Prophets

17 "Do not think I came to destroy the law or the prophets. I did not come to destroy them. *I have come* to give them their full meaning. **18** I am telling you the truth: While heaven and earth are standing, not even the smallest letter—or part of a letter—can be changed in the law until everything is completed. **19** Anyone who disobeys even one of the smallest commands and teaches this way to others will not be important in the kingdom of heaven. But, anyone who obeys and teaches *the right way* will be important in the kingdom of heaven. **20** I tell you, if your 'righteousness' is no better than that of the Pharisees and the teachers of the law, you will not enter the kingdom of heaven."

"Altar" Your Heart

21 "You have heard that this was said to the people long ago: 'Do not murder. Anyone who commits murder will be punished.' **22** But **I** tell you that anyone who is angry with his brother will be punished. Anyone who says 'You idiot!'* to his brother must answer to the Jewish Council. Anyone who says, 'You fool!' will be punished in hell fire. **23** Suppose you are bringing your gift *to God* at the altar. While there, you remember that your brother has something against you. **24** Leave your gift right there in front of the altar. The important thing is to go and make friends with your brother. When you come back, offer your gift *to God*. **25** When someone is trying to sue you, settle things out of court quickly. Do this while you are still with him *on the way* to court, or he might give you to the judge. And the judge might give you to the officer and then you might be thrown into jail. **26** I am telling you the truth: You may never get out of there, until you pay off the last penny."

Where Sin Begins

27 "You have heard this said: 'You must not commit adultery.' **28** But **I** am telling you that when any man continues looking at a woman because he wants her sexually, he has already, in his heart, committed adultery with her. **29** If your right eye is making you sin, take it out and throw it away from you! You would be better off to destroy one part of your body than to have your whole body thrown into hell. **30** Or, if your right hand is making you sin, cut it off and throw it away from you! You would be better off to destroy one member of your body than for your whole body to go off into hell."

Divorce and Remarriage

31 "This has been said: 'A man who divorces his wife must give her divorce papers.' **32** But **I** am telling you, unless the reason is *her* sexual sin, any man who divorces his wife causes her to commit adultery, and anyone who marries a divorced woman commits adultery, too."

Say What You Mean and Mean What You Say

33 "Again, you have heard that this was said to the people long ago: 'Do not break your vow by God; do what you promised!' **34** But **I** am telling you this: Do **not** make vows by God! Don't make a vow by heaven, because heaven is God's throne.

5:22   a very unkind word (raka). It attacks the humanity of a person. It is the same as calling someone empty-headed, stupid, and good-for-nothing—a judgment which only God can make. We are made in God's image (Genesis 1:26).

7

35 Don't do it by the earth, because the earth is God's footstool. Don't do it by Jerusalem, because that is the city of the great king.   36 Don't do it by your head, because you are not able to change one hair to be white or black.   37 Your yes answer should mean 'yes,' and your no answer should mean 'no.' Saying any more than this is bad."

Overcome Evil With Good

38 "You have heard that this was said: 'Get back an eye for an eye. Get back a tooth for a tooth.'   39 But I am telling you this: Do not fight back against evil. Instead, if a person hits you on the right side of your face, turn the other side to him, too! 40 If someone wants to sue you in order to take your shirt, let him have your robe, too!   41 If someone forces you to go one mile,* go two miles with him!   42 Give to every person who asks you. When someone wants to borrow something, lend it to him."

Very Radical Love

43 "You have heard that this was said: 'Love your friend* and hate your enemy.' 44 But I say this to you: Love your enemies! Pray for those who are cruel to you, 45 so that you will become sons of your Father, who is in heaven. God's sun shines* upon good people and bad people. It rains upon the people who do right **and** upon those who do wrong.   46 If you love only those people who love you, then you are not any better than anyone else. Even tax collectors do the same thing!   47 If you greet only your brothers, what more are you doing? Even people without God do the same thing! 48 You must be mature, as your Father in heaven is."

Chapter 6

Care About What God Thinks of You

1 "Be careful not to do your good deeds in front of people, so that they will notice you. If you do that, you will not receive a reward from your Father who is in heaven.

2 "When you help poor people, don't sound a trumpet before you.* The hypocrites* act like that in the synagogues and on the streets, so that people will praise them. I am telling you the truth: They have received their reward.   3 Instead, when you are helping poor people, don't let your left hand know what your right hand is doing,   4 so that it will be in secret. Your *heavenly* Father secretly sees this; He will repay you."

How to Pray

5 "And when you pray, don't be like the two-faced people.* They love to stand praying in the synagogues and on the street corners, so that other people will see them. I am telling you the truth: They have received their reward.   6 Instead, when you pray, go into your private room and close the door. Then pray secretly to your *heavenly* Father. He sees this in secret; He will repay you.

5:41   A Roman mile (4,854 feet) was shorter than today's mile (5,280 feet).
5:43   literally, neighbor
5:45   literally, rises
6:2   make a religious show
6:2   those who act as though they are good when they are not
6:5   hypocrites

7 "When you pray, don't use words without thinking, as people in the world do. They think that by saying many words they will be listened to.   8 Don't be like them. Your *heavenly* Father knows the things you need, even before you ask Him.

9 "This is the way you should pray:
'Father in heaven, may Your name always be kept holy.

10 May Your kingdom come.
May what You want done be done.
May it always be here on earth as it is in heaven.

11 Give us the food we need each day.

12 Forgive us of the sins we have committed, as we forgive everyone who has done wrong to us.

13 Keep us away from temptation.
Rescue us from the evil one.'*

14 "If you forgive people of the things they have done wrong to you, your heavenly Father will also forgive you.   15 However, if you do not forgive people, then your Father will not forgive the wrong things which you have done."

True Fasting

16 "And when you fast,* do not wear a sad face as the hypocrites do. They make their faces look serious, so that people will realize that they are fasting. I am telling you the truth: They are receiving their reward.   17 Instead, when you fast, comb your hair and wash your face,   18 so that people will not realize that you are fasting. Your *heavenly* Father sees it in secret; He will repay you openly."

Don't Trust in Money

19 "Do not store your treasures on the earth, where moths and rust destroy and where robbers dig through to steal.   20 Instead, store your treasures in heaven where moths and rust do not destroy and where robbers cannot dig through to steal.   21 The place where your treasure is will also be the place where your heart is."

Be a Light for the World

22 "Your eye is like a lamp for the body. If your eye can see clearly, then the whole body is made bright.   23 But if your eye is dark *with sin*, then your whole body is made dark. If the light in you becomes dark, how great is that darkness!"

Chase God, Not Money

24 "No one can serve two masters *at the same time*. He will either like one and not like the other or he will be more loyal to one and not care about the other. You cannot serve God and Money *at the same time*.   25 Because of this, I am telling you, you should not worry about what you will eat* to stay alive. *Don't worry* about what clothes you will wear. Living is more important than eating, and the body is more important than clothes.   26 Look at the wild birds of the sky. Birds do not plant seeds or harvest them or gather them into barns, but your heavenly Father takes care of them. Are you not worth so much more than birds? Of course!   27 None of you can grow 18 inches

---

6:13   the Devil
6:16   to go without food for a period of time, usually for spiritual reasons
6:25   Many manuscripts add: "or what you will drink."

taller by worrying about it.　**28**　And why worry about clothes? Learn from the way the wild flowers grow. They do not work hard or make threads for clothes.　**29**　I tell you, even Solomon, with all his beautiful clothes, was not dressed as well as one of these flowers.　**30**　Look how well God clothes the grass in the fields! But the grass is here today and thrown into the oven tomorrow to be burned. Will not God dress you so much better? Oh, you have so little faith!

31　"So, don't worry, thinking to yourself, 'What will we eat?' or, 'What will we drink?' or, 'What will we wear?'　**32**　People without God put all these things first. Your heavenly Father knows you need all these things.　**33**　So, put first God's kingdom and what is right. Then all the *things you need* will be given to you.　**34**　Don't worry about tomorrow, because tomorrow will have its own worries. There is enough trouble in just one day."

Chapter 7

Look at Yourselves First

1　"Don't pass judgment *on others*. Then you won't be condemned.　**2**　You will be judged by the standard which you use to judge others. You will be measured by the measure you use to measure others.　**3**　Why do you see the small speck which is in your brother's eye, but you don't notice the wooden pole which is in your own eye?　**4**　Or, how can you say this to your brother: 'Let me take that little speck out of your eye!'? When, look, there is a wooden pole in your own eye!　**5**　*You are a* hypocrite!* First, take the pole out of your own eye. Then you will see clearly to take the speck out of your brother's eye.

6　"Don't give what is holy to dogs. Don't throw your pearls in front of pigs. They might walk on them, then turn and attack you!"

Keep Asking

7　"So, I tell you, continue asking, and it will be given to you. Keep on searching and you will find. Be knocking, and the door will open for you.　**8**　You will receive, if you will always ask. You will find, if you continue looking. And the door will open for you, if you continue knocking.　**9**　Do any of you have a son? What would you do if your son asked you for bread? Would you give him a rock?　**10**　What if he asked you for a fish? Would you give him a snake?　**11**　You are evil people, and yet you know how to give good gifts to your children. Surely your heavenly Father knows how to give good things to those people who ask Him.

12　"Do for other people all the things which you want them to do for you. This is the meaning of the law and the prophets."

Broad Versus Narrow

13　"Go through the narrow door *which leads to eternal life*. The door is wide and the road is broad which leads to destruction. Many people are entering through it. **14**　The door is small which leads to life and the road is narrow. Only a few people are finding it."

Fruit Proof

15　"Be careful of false prophets. They come to you wearing clothes to make them look like sheep, but they are actually fierce wolves.　**16**　They can be recognized by the things

---

7:5　　those who act as though they are good when they are not

10

they produce. Do people get grapes from thorn bushes? Do they gather figs from thorny weeds?   **17** So, every tree which is a good tree produces good fruit. But a rotten tree produces bad fruit.   **18** It is not possible for a good tree to yield bad fruit. A rotten tree cannot yield good fruit.   **19** Every tree which does not produce good fruit is chopped down and thrown into fire.   **20** Therefore, you can recognize them by what they produce."

Don't Be a Loser

21 "Not everyone who says to me, 'Lord! Lord!' will enter the kingdom of heaven. Only the person who does what my heavenly Father wants *will enter it*.   **22** On that Day many people will say this to me: 'Lord! Lord! Isn't it true that we have prophesied, using your name? We threw out demons with your name. And, by your name, we performed many miracles.'   **23** But then I will say this openly to them: 'You people who are doing wrong, go away from me, because I never knew you!' "

A House That Really Rocks

24 "Every person who listens to my words and obeys them is like a wise man who built his house upon rock.   **25** It rained and the river overflowed. The winds blew hard against that house, but the house did not fall, because it was founded upon rock!   **26** However, every person who listens to my words and does not obey them is like a foolish man; he built his house upon sand.   **27** The rain came down and the river overflowed. The winds blew hard against that house and it fell down. It was a terrible fall!"

Jesus Taught With Authority

28 And when Jesus finished saying these things, the crowds were greatly amazed at his teaching.   **29** Jesus was teaching them as one having authority, not like the teachers of the law.

Chapter 8

Jesus WANTS to Heal

1 When Jesus came down from the mountain, large crowds followed him.   **2** Then a man with leprosy* came to him. He bowed down in front of Jesus. The leper said, "Lord, you can heal me, if you want to."

3 Jesus said, "I **do** want to heal you—be healed!" Then Jesus stretched out his hand and touched the man. Immediately the man's leprosy was healed.   **4** Jesus said to him, "Don't tell anyone what happened. Go show yourself to the priest. Then give a gift to God, because you have been healed. This is what the law of Moses commands. It will prove to the priests that you are healed."

Jesus Heals a Servant Boy

5 Jesus went into the town of Capernaum. A *Roman* army officer came to him, begging him, saying,   **6** "Lord, my servant is at home, sick in bed. He is crippled and suffering badly."

7 Jesus said to him, "I will go heal him."

8 The army officer answered, "Lord, you don't need to come into my house. I am not good enough to be with you. You only need to give the order and my servant boy

---

8:2   a very bad skin disease which destroys the flesh

will be healed.   **9** I, too, am a person under authority. And, there are soldiers below me whom I command. I can say to one, 'Go!' and he goes. I can say to another man, 'Come!' and he will come. Or, if I say to my servant, 'Do this!' he will do it.''

10 When Jesus heard this, he was surprised. Jesus *turned* to the people who were following him and he said, "I am telling you the truth: I have not found this much faith anywhere—not even in Israel!   **11** I tell you, many people will come from the east and the west and sit down with Abraham, Isaac, and Jacob in the kingdom of heaven. **12** Those who were sons of the kingdom will be thrown out into the dark. In that place there will be screaming and grinding of teeth."   **13** Then Jesus said to the army officer, "Go, it will happen for you as you believed." The servant boy was healed in that same hour.

Jesus Heals Peter's Mother-in-law

14 As Jesus came into Peter's house, he saw Peter's mother-in-law. She was sick in bed with a fever.

15 Jesus touched her hand and the fever left her. She got up and began to serve Jesus.

16 When it was late, they brought many people with demons to Jesus. With one word, he threw out the spirits. He healed all the people who were sick,   **17** so that what God had said through the prophet Isaiah would come true:

"He took our sicknesses

and carried away our diseases."   *Isaiah 53:4*

Following Jesus

18 When Jesus saw that there was a crowd around him, he ordered, "Let us go across *the lake*."   **19** A teacher of the law came near and said to him, "Teacher, I will follow you wherever you go!"

20 Jesus said to him, "The foxes have holes to live in. The wild birds have nests in which to live, but I* have no place where I can rest my head."

21 Another follower said to Jesus, "Lord, let me go and bury my father first."

22 But Jesus said to him, "Follow me! Let the 'dead' bury their own dead!"

Asleep in the Storm

23 Jesus got into a boat and his followers did, too.   **24** Soon there was such a big storm on the lake that the waves were getting into the boat, but Jesus was asleep. **25** The followers went to Jesus and woke him up. They said, "Lord, save us! We are going to die!"

26 Then Jesus said to them, "Why are you so afraid? Oh, you have so little faith!" Then Jesus got up and gave an order to the wind and *the waves of* the lake. The lake became very calm.   **27** The men were amazed. They said, "What kind of man is this? Even the wind and the lake obey him!"

Going Whole Hog

28 Jesus arrived on the other side *of the lake* in the country of the Gadarene people.* Two men met him. They had demons in them. These men came out of the graveyard. They were so fierce that no one could pass by on that road.   **29** They yelled, "What do

---

8:20   literally, the Son of Man
8:28   Some ancient copies have "Gergesenes"; others have "Gerasenes."

you want with us, Son of God? Did you come here to punish us ahead of time?"
30 A long way off there was a large herd of pigs that was feeding. **31** The demons were begging Jesus, "Since you must throw us out, send us into the herd of pigs."

32 Jesus said to them, "Go!" And they came out and went into the pigs. Suddenly, the whole herd ran down the cliff and into the lake. They drowned. **33** Some men had been taking care of the pigs. They ran away. When they came into the town, they told the whole story about the two men with demons. **34** Then the whole town came out to meet Jesus. When they saw him, they begged him to leave their area.

Chapter 9

Get Up and Go

1 Jesus got into a boat and went back across *the lake*. He came to his own home town. **2** There was a man who was paralyzed. He was lying on a small bed and some men were carrying him. When Jesus saw that these men believed, he said to the paralyzed man, "Be strong, friend, your sins are forgiven."

3 Some of the teachers of the law thought to themselves, "This man is speaking as if he were God!" **4** Jesus knew what they were thinking. He said, "Why are you thinking evil thoughts in your hearts? **5** Which is easier: to say, 'Your sins are forgiven,' or to say, 'Stand up and walk'? **6** I will prove to you that, on earth, I* have the authority to forgive sins." Then Jesus said to the paralyzed man, "Stand up! Pick up your bed and go home!"

7 Then the man stood up and went home.

8 When the crowds saw this, they had great respect *for Jesus*; they praised God for giving such power to men.

God Chaser: Matthew

9 As Jesus was leaving that place, he saw a man named Matthew sitting at the tax office. Jesus said to him, "Follow me!" Matthew got up and followed him.

10 While Jesus was having dinner at Matthew's house, many tax collectors and sinful people came and joined Jesus and his followers for dinner. **11** Some Pharisees saw this. They asked Jesus' followers, "Why does your teacher eat with tax collectors and sinful people?"

12 When Jesus heard about it, he said, "Healthy people don't need a doctor, but sick people do. **13** Go and learn what this means:
'I want mercy more than I want animal sacrifices.'   *Hosea 6:6*
I came to invite sinners, not 'righteous' people."

Fasting

14 Then the followers of John came to Jesus, asking, "Why do we and the Pharisees fast,* but your followers do not fast?"

15 Jesus asked them, "Would it be right for the friends of the groom to be sad* while he is still with them? But the time will come when the groom will be taken away from them. Then his friends will fast.

9:6   literally, the Son of Man
9:14   to go without food for a period of time, usually for spiritual reasons
9:15   literally, fast

New Wine

16 "No one sews a piece of cloth which has never been washed onto an old robe because it would *shrink and* tear away from the robe and the hole would become worse.
17 No one puts new wine into old wine bags. If they did, the old wine bags would break open, the wine would spill out, and the wine bags would be ruined. Instead, people put new wine into new wine bags and both are preserved."*

The Daughter of Jairus

18 While Jesus was talking to them, suddenly a ruler *of the synagogue* came near and began to bow down in front of Jesus. The man said, "My daughter has just died! But, if you come and put your hand on her, she will come back to life."
19 Jesus stood up and started to follow him. Jesus' followers did too.   **20** But there was a woman who had an open sore. (It had been bleeding for twelve years.) She went behind Jesus and touched the tassel of his robe.*   **21** She was thinking to herself, "If only I can touch his robe, then I will be made well!"
22 But Jesus turned around and saw her. He said, "Be strong, dear woman, you are made well because you believed." And, from that moment on, the woman was made well.
23 When Jesus came to the ruler's house, he saw the men playing flutes and the crowd making noise.*   **24** Jesus said again and again, "Go away! The little girl did not die; she is only sleeping." But they laughed at him.   **25** When the crowd had been put outside, Jesus went in and took her hand, and the little girl stood up.   **26** And the news about this went out all over that land.

Two Blind Men See

27 As Jesus was leaving that place, two blind men followed him. They were shouting, "Son of David! Please help us!"   **28** After Jesus had gone into a house, the blind men came to him. Jesus said to them, "Do you believe that I can do this?"
They said to him, "Yes, Lord."
29 Then Jesus touched their eyes. He said, "May this happen to you because you believed!"   **30** And their eyes were opened. Jesus warned them, "Don't tell anyone about this!"   **31** But they went out and spread the news about him all over that whole area.

Look out, Devil!

32 While they were leaving, they brought a man to Jesus. The man could not talk. He had a demon.   **33** After the demon had been thrown out, the man who had not been able to talk began to talk. The crowds were amazed. They said, "No one has ever seen anything like this happen in Israel!"
34 However, the Pharisees continued to say, "Jesus makes demons go away by using *the power of* the ruler of the demons!"

Pray for Workers

35 Jesus went around all the towns and villages, teaching in their synagogues and preaching the Good News about the kingdom. He was healing all kinds of sicknesses

---

9:17   In those days, the wine bottles were made of animal skins. The grape juice would ferment and stretch the wine bags. If new wine were put into an old wine bag (one which was already stretched to the limit), the fermentation process would break it open. A new wine bag still had room to stretch.
9:20   A true Israelite wore tassels on the four corners of his outer garment. (See Numbers 15:38-39.)
9:23   They were probably mourners who were paid to perform this function.

and diseases.   **36** When Jesus saw the crowds, he felt sorry for them, because they were worried and helpless, like sheep that didn't have a shepherd.   **37** Then Jesus said to his followers, "There is a big harvest, but there are not many workers.   **38** So, pray that the Owner of the harvest will send more workers into the harvest field."

Chapter 10

Jesus Chooses Twelve God Chasers

1 Jesus called his twelve followers. He gave them the authority to throw out evil spirits and to heal every kind of disease and sickness.   **2** These are the names of the twelve apostles:

First there was Simon (called Peter);
Andrew (Peter's brother);
James (the son of Zebedee);
John (James' brother);
3 Philip;
Bartholomew;
Thomas;
Matthew (the tax collector);
James (the son of Alphaeus);
Thaddaeus;
4 Simon the Revolutionary*;
Judas Iscariot (He turned against Jesus.).

Jesus Sends Out the Twelve God Chasers

5 Jesus sent out these twelve men with these orders: "Don't go off into any non-Jewish area. Don't go into any Samaritan town.   **6** Instead, go to the lost sheep—the people of Israel.   **7** As you are going, preach this: 'The kingdom of heaven is very near!'   **8** Heal sick people. Raise people from death. Make lepers well. Throw out demons. You received freely; give freely.   **9** Don't take along any gold, silver, or copper in your money belts.   **10** Don't take a bag for the trip, an extra suit of clothes, shoes, or a walking cane. A worker should be given his pay.   **11-13** When you enter a town or a village, find someone there who is worthy. When you go into his house, give your greeting to it. If the household is worthy, let your greeting of peace be upon it. Stay there until *it is time* to leave. However, if the household is not worthy, let your greeting of peace come back to you.   **14** Whenever someone does not welcome you or listen to your words, go outside that town or house and shake the dust off your feet.*   **15** I am telling you the truth: On the Judgment Day, God will punish the people of that town more than He will punish the people of Sodom and Gomorrah!"

Watch Out!

16 "Listen! I am sending you like sheep into a pack of wolves. Be wise like snakes, yet as gentle as doves.

10:4   The Zealots were a group of Jewish men—fanatics. They claimed to uphold the law of Moses, even if they had to become violent to do so. They favored revolt against Rome.

10:14   A Jewish custom showing rejection of non-Jews. Here it is used toward those who reject the Good News.

15

17 "Watch out for people! They will betray you to the local courts. They will whip you in their synagogues. **18** Men will take you *to be judged* before governors and kings because you are associated with me. You can tell them and the nations of the world all of the things you have seen me do. **19** When they turn against you, don't worry about what or how you will speak. At that time what you should say will be given to you. **20 You** will not be doing the talking; it will be the Spirit of your *heavenly* Father who will be speaking through you.

21 "A brother will hand over his own brother—to put him to death! A father will do the same thing to his child. Children will rebel against their parents and have them put to death. **22** Everyone will hate you because of me, but the person who endures to the end will be saved. **23** When they persecute you in one town, quickly go to another town. I am telling you the truth: I* will come before you finish *working in* the towns of Israel.

24 "A student is not higher than the teacher. A servant is not higher than his master. **25** The student should be satisfied to become like his teacher. The servant should be satisfied to become like his master. Since they called the owner of the house 'Beelzebul,'* they will call the members of the owner's family by names which are even worse."

Don't Be Afraid

26 "Don't be afraid of people, because everything which is hidden will be found out and everything which is secret will be made known. **27** What I am telling you in the dark you must tell in the light. What you hear whispered you must announce from the top of the houses.

28 "Don't be afraid of people. People can kill the body, but they cannot kill the soul. Instead, you should fear the One who can destroy both soul and body in hell. **29** Two sparrows are sold for only a small coin and yet, not one sparrow falls to the ground without your *heavenly* Father *knowing it.* **30** God even knows how many hairs you have on your head. **31** Don't be afraid. **You** are worth more than many sparrows."

Don't Be Ashamed

32 "If anyone confesses, in front of other people, that he believes in me, then I will speak for him in front of my Father in heaven. **33** But if anyone is ashamed of me in front of people, then I will be ashamed of him in front of my Father in heaven."

Chase God—No Matter What

34 "Don't think that I came to give peace to the world. No, I came to make war. **35** I came to divide:

'a man against his father,
  a daughter against her mother,

36 a daughter-in-law against her mother-in-law.

  The enemies of a person might be the members of his own family.' *Micah 7:6*

37 "The person who loves his father or mother more than me is not worthy of me. The person who loves his son or daughter more than me is not worthy of me. **38** The person who does not accept his cross* and follow me is not worthy of me. **39** The

---

10:23   literally, the Son of Man
10:25   literally, lord of the flies, a name given to the Devil
10:38   responsibility from God

person who finds his life will lose it, but the person who gives his life away because of me will find it."

Prophet or Non-Prophet

40 "The person who welcomes you welcomes **me**. The person who is welcoming me is welcoming the One who sent me. **41** The person who welcomes a prophet as a true prophet will receive a prophet's reward. A person who receives a good man as a truly good man will receive a good man's reward. **42** If anyone gives one of these precious ones a drink of cold *water* because he is my follower, I tell you the truth, that person will certainly not lose his reward."

Chapter 11

Now, About John

1 When Jesus finished giving these orders to his twelve followers he left there to teach and to preach among their towns.

2 John was in prison.* He heard about the things which the Messiah was doing. So he sent his followers to ask Jesus this question: **3** "Are **you** the one who is coming, or should we expect someone else?"

4 Jesus answered them, "Go tell John the things you see and hear. **5** The blind people can see again. Crippled people can walk. People with leprosy are made well. The deaf can hear. Dead people are given life. And the Good News is given to the poor people. **6** The person who is not ashamed of me is truly happy!"

7 After these men left, Jesus began to tell the crowds about John: "What did you people go into the desert to see? A stalk *of grass* being blown by the wind? **8** Why did you go out there? Did you go to see a man dressed in fine clothes? Listen, the people who wear fine clothes *live* in palaces. **9** Really, what did you go out to see? A prophet? Yes, I tell you, John is even more than a prophet. **10** This was written about John:

'Listen! I am sending my messenger
    to go ahead of you.
He will prepare the way for you!'   *Malachi 3:1*

11 I am telling you the truth: John (the one who immersed people) is greater than any man ever born, but the person who is least important in the kingdom of heaven is greater than John. **12** From the time when John *appeared* until now, the kingdom of heaven is being attacked; violent men are trying to capture it. **13** Until the time of John, the law *of Moses* and all the prophets prophesied about it. **14** And, if you are willing to accept it, John **is** the Elijah who was to appear.* **15** The person who has ears to hear with should use them.

16 "Now, I will compare the people of this time to something else: What are they like? The people of this time are like little children sitting in the marketplaces, **17** calling to each other:

'We played a happy song, but you did not dance.
We played a sad song, but you did not cry!'

11:2   Herod Antipas had put John in prison, because John accused Herod Antipas of illegally marrying his
          half-brother's wife. (See Matthew 14:3.)
11:14   See Malachi 4:5,6.

18 John came neither eating *normal food* nor drinking *wine*. And they say, 'He has a demon inside him!' **19** I* came eating and drinking. And they say, 'Look, he eats too much and drinks too much wine! He is the friend of tax collectors and other sinful people!' *True* wisdom is shown to be right by the things it does."*

People Who Won't Join the Chase

20 Then Jesus began to criticize the towns where most of his miracles had occurred. The people had not changed their hearts. **21** "It will be horrible for you, O town of Chorazin! It will be horrible for you, Bethsaida! Many miracles have occurred in you. If these same miracles had occurred in the cities of Tyre and Sidon, then those people in Tyre and Sidon would have changed their hearts and actions* long ago. **22** But on the Judgment Day, God will punish **you** more than the people of Tyre and Sidon. **23** And you, Capernaum, do you think you will be lifted up to heaven? You will be thrown down to Hades!* Many miracles have occurred in you. If these same miracles had occurred in Sodom, that city would still be standing today. **24** But on the Judgment Day, God will punish you more than He will punish the people of Sodom!"

Jesus' Prayer

25 At that time, Jesus said, "Father, Lord of heaven and earth, I praise You because You have hidden these teachings from the 'wise' and 'intelligent' people, but You show Your teachings to little children. **26** Yes, Father, I praise You, because this is what You really wanted to do.

27 "My Father has given me all things. Only the Father knows who the Son is. And only the Son knows who the Father is. The only people who will know about the Father are those people whom the Son chooses to tell.

A Rest

28 "You are tired and have heavy loads. If all of you will come to me, I will give you rest. **29** Take the job* I give you. Learn from me because I am gentle and humble in heart. You will find rest for your lives. **30** The duty I *give you* is easy. The load I *put upon you* is not heavy."

Chapter 12

Jesus Is Lord Over the Sabbath Day

1 At that time, Jesus was traveling through a field of grain on a Sabbath day. His followers were hungry. They began to pick the grain and eat it. **2** The Pharisees saw this and said to Jesus, "Look! Your followers are doing what is not right to do on the Sabbath day!"

3 Jesus said to them, "Do you remember reading about what David did when he and his men were hungry? **4** David went into the house of God. They ate the holy loaves of bread. The law did not permit David or his men to eat them—only the priests could eat them. **5** You have read in the law *of Moses* that every Sabbath day the priests in

---

11:19   literally, the Son of Man
11:19   literally, Wisdom is made right by her works.
11:21   or, repented
11:23   the world of the dead
11:29   literally, the yoke (responsibility)

the temple courtyard disobey the laws of the Sabbath. And yet, they have no guilt. **6** But, I'm telling you, there is one here who is more important than the temple! **7** Have you read this:

'I want mercy more than I want animal sacrifices.'? *Hosea 6:6*

If you had read this, you would not have condemned innocent people! **8** I* am Lord over the Sabbath day."

Jesus Heals a Man on the Sabbath Day

9 Jesus moved away from that place. He went into their synagogue. **10** A man with a crippled hand was there. They asked Jesus, "Is it right to heal people on the Sabbath day?" (They wanted to accuse Jesus *of doing something wrong.*)

11 Jesus said to them, "Suppose one of you has a sheep and it falls into a pit on the Sabbath day. Wouldn't you grab it and pull it out? **12** A human being is so much more important than a sheep. So it is right to do good on the Sabbath day."

13 Then Jesus said to the man, "Stretch out your hand!" The man did this. His hand was made as healthy as his other hand. **14** The Pharisees left. They made plans to kill Jesus.

Jesus: The Ultimate God Chaser

15 When Jesus learned about this, he left that place. Many people followed him. Jesus healed them all. **16** Jesus warned them not to tell anyone about him. **17** What God said through the prophet Isaiah came true:

18 "Look at My special servant!
He is the one I have chosen.
I love him and I am very pleased with him.
I will put My Spirit upon him.
He will announce justice for the nations, too.
19 He will not argue or yell.
No one will hear his voice in the streets.
20 He will not break the stem of a plant that has been bent.
He will not even put out the flame of a wick which is barely burning,
until he causes justice to win.
21 The nations will put their hope in his name." *Isaiah 42:1-4*

The Power of God

22 Then they brought a man with a demon to Jesus. This man was blind and he could not talk. Jesus healed him. The man was able to speak and see. **23** All the crowds were amazed. They kept saying, "This man is not the son of David, is he?"

24 But when the Pharisees heard this, they said, "This man throws demons out only by using the power of Beelzebul,* the ruler of demons!"

25 Jesus knew what they were thinking. He said to them, "Every kingdom which is divided against itself will be ruined. Every town or family which is divided against itself will not hold together. **26** If Satan were throwing out Satan, then he would be divided against himself. How could his kingdom stay together? **27** But if I throw out demons by using the power of Beelzebul,* then whose power do your own people use

---

12:8 Jesus
12:24 literally, the lord of the flies, a name given to the Devil
12:27 the Devil

to throw them out? This is why your own people prove you are wrong!   **28** However, if it is true that **I** use the Spirit of God to throw out demons, then God's kingdom has come upon you!

29 "How can someone go into a strong man's house and take away his possessions? He must first tie up the strong man. Then he can rob the strong man's house.

30 "If a person is not with me, he is against me. The person who does not gather with me scatters.   **31** This is why I am telling you that people may be forgiven of any sin or any evil thing said against God. But they cannot be forgiven of saying evil things against the *Holy* Spirit!   **32** If someone says something against me,* he can be forgiven. However, if someone says something against the Holy Spirit, he cannot be forgiven—not in this age nor the next one."

What's Inside Comes Out

33 "Either call the tree good and its fruit good, or call the tree rotten and its fruit rotten. A tree can be known by its fruit.   **34** You are like poisonous snakes. You are evil. How can you say good things? A person speaks what flows out of his heart.   **35** A good man brings good things out of the good treasure of his heart, but an evil man brings out evil things from an evil treasure.   **36** I tell you, sometimes people talk without thinking. On the Judgment Day they will be held responsible for every word. **37** Your words can make you right with God or your words can condemn you."

Give Us Proof!

38 Then some of the teachers of the law and the Pharisees answered Jesus, "Teacher, we want to see you do a miracle."

39 Jesus answered them, "The people living today are very evil. They are not faithful *to God*. They ask for a proof from God, but no proof will be given to them. The only proof will be the miracle *which God worked for* Jonah the prophet.   **40** Jonah was in the belly of the big fish for three days and three nights. In the same way, I* will be in the heart of the earth for three days and three nights.   **41** On the Judgment Day the men from the city of Nineveh will condemn the people of this time. Why? Because when Jonah preached to them, they changed their hearts. Listen! **I** am greater than Jonah.   **42** The Queen of Sheba* will rise up on the Judgment Day with *the men* of this time and she will condemn them. Why? Because she came a very long way to listen to the wisdom of Solomon. Listen! **I** am greater than Solomon!"

Don't Let It Rest

43 "When an evil spirit comes out of a man, it goes through dry places looking for a place to rest. If the spirit does not find a place,   **44** it says, 'I will go back to the house* from which I came.' So, it goes and finds that house empty, cleaned up, and in order.   **45** Then the evil spirit goes and brings seven other spirits worse than itself, and they go into that man and live there. And that man has even more trouble than he had before. The evil people of this time will be the same way."

12:32   literally, the Son of Man
12:40   literally, the Son of Man
12:42   literally, the queen of the south (See 1 Kings 10:1-10; 2 Chronicles 9:1-12.)
12:44   the meaning of house here is "body."

Jesus' Family Ties

46 While Jesus was speaking to the crowds, suddenly, his mother and his brothers stood outside. They were wanting to speak with him.   **47** Someone said to him, "Your mother and your brothers are standing outside; they want to speak with you."

48 Jesus answered that person, "Who is my mother? Who are my brothers?" **49** Then Jesus pointed to his followers and said, "Look, *all these people are* my mother and my brothers!   **50** If a person does what my Father in heaven wants him to do, **he** is my brother, my sister, or my mother!"

Chapter 13

The Story of the Seed

1 That day Jesus left the house, and he was sitting beside the lake *of Galilee.* **2** There were so many people who came to Jesus that he had to get into a boat. He sat in the boat and all the crowd stood on the shore.   **3** Jesus used many examples to speak with them: "A farmer went out to plant his seed.   **4** While he was planting, some seeds fell along the road. The wild birds ate them up.   **5** Some other seeds fell on rocky soil. There was not much soil there. The little plants grew up quickly, because the soil was not deep.   **6** But when the sun came up, the plants were burned, because their roots dried up.   **7** Some more seeds fell among thorny weeds. But the thorny weeds came up and killed them off *later.*   **8** And some seeds fell on good soil. Some were producing fruit 100 times more, some were producing 60 times more, and some 30 times more.   **9** The person who has ears must use them!"

Ears to Hear

10 Jesus' followers came and asked him, "Why do you use examples to speak to us?"

11 Jesus answered, "You have been chosen to learn the secrets of the kingdom of heaven, but these secrets have not been given to others.   **12** The person who has something will get more. However, what will happen to the one who has *almost* nothing? Even what he has will be taken away from him!   **13** This is why I use stories when I talk with them, so that they look, but do not see, and they listen, but they do not understand.   **14** They have made Isaiah's prophecy come true:

'You will certainly hear, but you won't understand!
You will certainly see, but you won't understand!
15 The heart of this people has become hard.
They have ears, but they do not listen.
They have shut their eyes.
Otherwise, they would
    see with their eyes,
    hear with their ears,
    understand with their minds,
    and then turn.
I would heal them.' *Isaiah 6:9-10*

16 "You are very blessed to see what you now see, and to hear what you now hear. **17** I am telling you the truth: Many prophets and good men wanted to see what you now see, but they did not see it. And they wanted to hear what you now hear, but they did not hear it."

21

The Meaning of the Story

18 "Listen to *the meaning of* the example about the farmer: **19** A person hears the message about the kingdom, but he does not understand it. Then the evil one* comes and takes away what was planted in the person's heart. This is *the meaning of* what was planted along the road.   **20** What was planted on rocky soil is the person who hears the message and accepts it with gladness right away.   **21** However, he does not have deep roots in himself; he doesn't last long. When, because of the message, trouble or persecution comes, he soon gets discouraged and gives up.   **22** That which was planted among the thorny weeds is the one who hears the message, but the worries of this age and deceiving riches choke out the message. It never produces fruit.   **23** What was planted on good soil is the one who listens to the message and understands it. He produces fruit—some of it is 100 times more, some is 60 times more, and some is 30 times more."

The Story of Wheat and Weeds

24 Jesus used another story. He said, "The kingdom of heaven is like this: A man planted some good wheat seed in his field.   **25** While his men were sleeping, the man's enemy came and planted some weeds among the wheat. Then he went away. **26** When the wheat came up and started making heads of wheat, the weeds appeared, too.   **27** The servants went to the owner and said to him, 'Lord, you planted good *wheat* seed in your field. Where did the weeds come from?'

28 The man said to them, 'An enemy did this!'

The servants said to him, 'Do you want us to go out and collect the weeds?'

29 He said, 'No, because while you are collecting the weeds, you might tear up the wheat which is next to the weeds.   **30** Let the wheat and the weeds grow together until harvest time. At that time, I will tell the workers to gather up the weeds first. Then they can tie them together in bundles to burn them, but they will gather the wheat into my barn.' "

A Mustard Seed

31 As Jesus was talking to them, he used another story: "What is the kingdom of heaven like? *It is like* the seed of the mustard plant. A person plants the seed in his garden.   **32** It is one of the smallest seeds of all. But when it grows up, it is the largest garden plant—it becomes a tree. The wild birds build nests in its branches."

Yeast

33 Jesus spoke to them with another example: "The kingdom of heaven is like yeast which a woman mixes into a tub* of flour to make the bread rise."

Wanna Know My Secrets?

34 Jesus used examples to say all these things to the crowds. He always spoke to them with a story.

35 What God said through the prophet came true:

"When I open my mouth *to speak* , I will use examples.

I will tell things which have been hidden since the world was created."

Psalm 78:2

13:19   the Devil
13:33   literally, three satas; about 40 quarts (about four and a half pecks)

The Meaning of the Wheat/Weed Story

36 Then Jesus left the crowds and went into the house. His followers came to him and said, "Tell us plainly *the meaning of* the story about the weeds in the field."

37 Jesus answered, "I* am the one who planted the good seed.   **38** The field is the world. The good seeds are the sons of the kingdom. The weeds are the sons of the evil one.*   **39** The enemy who sowed the weeds is the Devil. Harvest time is the end of the age. And the workers are angels.   **40** The weeds will be collected and burned in fire. It will be like this at the end of the age.   **41** I* will send my angels. They will collect everything which makes people sin and the people who do wrong, and put them out of his kingdom.   **42** The angels will throw them into a hot oven. In that place there will be screaming and grinding of teeth.   **43** Then the good people will shine as brightly as the sun in the kingdom of their Father. The person who has ears should use them!"

A Buried Treasure

44 "The kingdom of heaven is like a buried treasure. A man finds it buried in a field. He is so happy that he goes and sells everything he owns and buys that field."

A Very Beautiful Pearl

45 "Again, the kingdom of heaven is like a businessman who is always looking for good pearls.   **46** *One day* he found a very beautiful pearl. He went and sold everything he owned and bought that pearl."

A Large Net

47 "Again, the kingdom of heaven is like a big net which is thrown into the lake. It catches every kind *of fish*.   **48** When the net is full, the men pull it onto the shore. Then they sit down and pick out the good fish. They throw the good fish on the beach, but they throw the worthless fish away.   **49** It will be like this at the end of the age. The angels will come and separate the good people from the bad people.   **50** The angels will throw the bad people into a hot oven. In that place there will be screaming and grinding of teeth."

Old and New

51 *Jesus said*, "Do you understand all these things?"
They said to him, "Yes."
52 Jesus said to them, "Every teacher of the law who becomes trained for the kingdom of heaven is like a man who is the head of his house. He brings new things and old things out of his treasure."

Not Believing = Not Seeing

53 When Jesus finished all these examples, he left that place.   **54** He came to his home town. He was teaching them in their synagogue. They were greatly amazed at him. They asked, "Where did Jesus get this wisdom and these miraculous powers?   **55** Isn't it true that he is the son of *Joseph*, the woodworker, and that his mother's name is Mary? His brothers are: James, Joseph, Simon, and Judas.   **56** His sisters are here with us, too. So, where did he get all these things?"   **57** They were offended at Jesus.

13:37   literally, the Son of Man
13:38   the Devil
13:41   literally, the Son of Man

23

But Jesus said to them, "A prophet is not accepted in his own home town or by his own family." **58** So, because they did not believe, Jesus did not perform many miracles there.

Chapter 14

John the God Chaser Dies

1 At that time, Herod *Antipas*, the ruler, heard the report about Jesus. **2** He said to his servants, "This is John (the one who immersed people)! He has come back to life! That is why these powers are working in him."

3 *Before this time*, Herod had ordered his men to arrest John, tie him up, and put him in prison. He did this because of Herodias, his brother Philip's* wife. **4** John had been saying to Herod, "It is not right for you to have her!" **5** Herod wanted to kill John, but he was afraid of the crowd. (The people thought of John as a prophet.) **6** When it was Herod's birthday, the daughter of Herodias danced in front of everyone. She pleased Herod. **7** He vowed to give her anything she asked for. **8** Her mother suggested this to her: "Give me, here on a plate, the head of John!" **9** The king was very sad, but, because of the vow and the guests, Herod ordered that it be done. **10** He sent *some men* to the prison to cut off John's head. **11** His head was brought on a plate and given to the girl. She gave it to her mother. **12** John's followers came and carried the body away and buried it. Then they went to tell Jesus about it.

Jesus Does Lunch With a Bunch (5,000+ People)

13 When Jesus heard this, he left there in a boat to be all alone. He went to a place where no one lived. However, the crowds found out where Jesus had gone and, on foot, they followed him from the towns. **14** When Jesus got out *of the boat*, he saw a large crowd; he felt sorry for them. He healed their sick people.

15 Since evening was coming, Jesus' followers came to him and said, "No one lives in this place and it is already late. Tell the people to go away. They need to buy food for themselves in the villages *around here*."

16 Jesus said to them, "They don't need to go away. **You** give them something to eat!"

17 But they said to him, "We have only five loaves of bread and two fish."

18 Jesus said, "Bring them here to me."

19 Jesus ordered the people to sit down on the grass. He took the five loaves of bread and two fish. Then he looked up to heaven. He thanked God for the food and divided it. Then he began giving the loaves of bread to his followers and they gave it to the people. **20** Everyone ate and was full. They gathered up all the pieces of the food which were left over. They filled twelve large baskets with this food. **21** (There were about 5,000 men who were eating, not including the women and children.)

Who Needs a Boat?

22 Soon Jesus made his followers get into the boat. He wanted them to go on ahead of him across *the lake*, while he sent the people away. **23** After Jesus sent the people away, he went up to a mountain to be alone and to pray. It was evening and Jesus was

---

14:3   This was not Philip the tetrarch, ruler of Iturea and Trachonitis (Luke 3:1), but he was another half-brother of Herod Antipas by the same name.

the only one there.   24 The boat was already a long way from the shore. The waves were beating against the boat; they were heading into the wind.   25 It was after three o'clock in the morning when Jesus came to them. He was walking **on** the lake. 26 When Jesus' followers saw him walking on the lake, they were alarmed. They shouted with fear, "It's a ghost!"   27 Immediately, Jesus spoke to them, "Be strong! It is I. Don't be afraid."

28 Peter answered him, "Lord, if it is really you, tell me to come to you on the water!"

29 Jesus said, "Come!" Then Peter got down from the boat and went toward Jesus, walking on the water.   30 But when Peter saw the way the wind was blowing, he was afraid. He began to sink. Peter cried out, "Lord, save me!"

31 Immediately, Jesus stretched out his hand and caught him. Jesus said to him, "Oh, you have so little faith; why did you doubt?"   32 When they climbed into the boat, the wind stopped.   33 They all worshiped him, saying, "You really are the Son of God!"

One Touch Healing

34 After they crossed over, they came to the shore at Gennesaret.   35 The men from that place recognized Jesus. They sent people all over that area, bringing all of their sick people to Jesus.   36 The people were begging him; they only wanted to touch the tassel of his robe.* And all those who did touch it were made well.

Chapter 15

What Rules Do God Chasers Follow?

1 Then some teachers of the law and some Pharisees from Jerusalem came to Jesus. They asked,   2 "Why are your followers breaking the old rules of the elders? When your followers eat, they do not wash their hands."

3 Jesus answered them, "Why do **you** break God's command for the sake of old rules of your own?   4 God said,

'You must love and obey your father and mother.'   *Exodus 20:12*
and

'The person who curses his father or mother must die.'   *Exodus 21:17*
5 But **you** say if anyone says to his father or mother, 'Whatever you might have gotten from me, I have given *to God* instead!'   6 So, he will never respect his father or his mother. Because of your tradition you are taking away the authority of God's teaching! 7 Hypocrites!* How right Isaiah was when he prophesied about you:

8 'These people respect me with their lips,
   but their heart is far away from Me.

9 It does no good for them to worship Me.
   They teach rules made by men, *not God.*' "   *Isaiah 29:13*

What Goes in Will Come Out

10 Jesus called the crowd. He said to them, "Listen, and understand!   11 What goes into the mouth does not make a person unholy. No, it's what comes out of the mouth that makes a person unholy."

14:36   Tassels were worn on four corners of a robe to remind the people of the law (Numbers 15:38-40).
15:7   those who act as though they are good when they are not

12 Then Jesus' followers came to him and asked, "Do you know that the Pharisees were insulted when they heard this teaching?"

13 Jesus answered, "Every plant which was not planted by my heavenly Father will be pulled up by the roots. **14** Leave them alone! They are blind guides. If a blind man guides another blind man, both of them will fall into a pit."

15 Peter said to Jesus, "Explain this story to us."

16 Jesus said, "Do you still not understand? **17** You know that everything which goes into the mouth goes into the stomach. Then it comes out as waste. **18** But the things which are coming from the mouth are really coming from the heart—these things make a person unholy. **19** These things come from the heart:

evil thoughts,
murder,
adultery,
sexual sin,
stealing,
lying,
slander.

20 These are the things which make a person unholy. Eating with unwashed hands does **not** make a person unholy!"

God Chaser: a Canaanite Woman

21 Jesus left there and went to the area of the cities of Tyre and Sidon. **22** A Canaanite woman from that area came out *to Jesus*. She shouted, "Lord! Son of David! Please help me! My daughter has a demon inside her; she is suffering terribly!"

23 But Jesus did not say a word to her. His followers came begging him, "Send her away! She is always following us around, shouting."

24 Jesus answered *her*, "I was sent only to the lost sheep of the family of Israel."

25 But she came to Jesus and bowed down in front of him. She said, "Lord, help me!"

26 Jesus answered, "It is not good to take the children's bread and throw it to the puppies."

27 But the woman said, "Yes, Lord, but even the puppies eat the crumbs which fall from their masters' table."

28 Then Jesus answered her, "Woman, you have a strong faith. What you want will be done for you!" At that moment her daughter was healed.

29 Jesus went away from there and came to Lake Galilee. He went up a mountain and sat down there. **30** Many people came to him. They had their sick people with them: the lame, the blind, the crippled, the deaf, and many others. They laid them at Jesus' feet and he healed them all. **31** The crowd was amazed when they saw the deaf talking, crippled people healthy, the lame walking, and blind people seeing. They praised the God of Israel.

Jesus Does Lunch With More Than 4,000 People

32 Jesus called his followers. He said to them, "I feel sorry for the people. For three days they have stayed with me without eating anything. I don't want to send them away hungry; they might faint along the road."

33 His followers said to him, "Where can we get enough bread in this remote place to satisfy such a large crowd?"

34 Jesus said to them, "How many loaves of bread do you have?"
They answered, "Seven... and a few little fish."
35 Jesus ordered the crowd to sit down on the ground.   36 He took the seven loaves of bread and the fish. After he thanked God, he divided the food and began giving it to his followers who then gave it to the crowd.   37 Everyone ate and was full. They gathered up all the pieces of food which were left over. With this food, they filled seven small baskets.   38 (There were 4,000 men who ate, not including the women and children.)   39 Jesus sent the crowds away. Then he climbed into the boat and he came to the Magadan area.

Chapter 16

Understanding the Times

1 The Pharisees and Sadducees came to Jesus. They were trying to make Jesus prove to them that he came from heaven.   2 Jesus answered them, "When evening begins, you say, 'It will be good weather *tomorrow* , because the sky is red.'   3 And, in the morning, you say, 'Today it will be stormy, because the sky is red and dark.' You can understand changes in the sky which show a change in the weather, but you cannot understand the signs of change of this time in history.   4 The people who are living today are evil and not faithful *to God*. They ask for a proof from God, but no proof will be given to them except the Jonah miracle." Then Jesus left them and went away.

Watch What You Follow

5 When Jesus' followers went across *Lake Galilee* , they forgot to bring along some bread.   6 Jesus said to them, "Be careful! Watch out for the yeast* of the Pharisees and the Sadducees."
7 They started thinking to themselves, " *Jesus must have said this* because we didn't bring along any bread."
8 Jesus knew *what was on their minds*. He said, "Oh, you have so little faith! Why are you thinking to yourselves, '. . . that you have no bread'?   9 Do you still not understand? Do you remember the five loaves of bread *which fed* the 5,000 men? Do you remember how many large baskets *of leftovers* you picked up?
10 "Do you remember the seven loaves of bread *which fed* the 4,000 men? Do you remember how many small baskets *of leftovers* you picked up?   11 Why could you not understand what I was saying to you? When I said, 'Watch out for the yeast of the Pharisees and the Sadducees,' I was not talking about bread."
12 Then they understood that Jesus was not wanting them *to stay* away from the yeast used for bread. Instead, he wanted them *to stay* away from the teaching of the Pharisees and the Sadducees.

Who Do You Say I Am?

13 When Jesus came to the area of Caesarea Philippi, he began to ask his followers, "Who do people say I* am?"
14 They answered, "Some people say you are John (the one who immerses people). Other people say you are Elijah. And some people say you are Jeremiah or one of the prophets."
15 Jesus asked them, "But who do **you** say I am?"

16:6   Here "yeast" means influence.
16:13   literally, the Son of Man

16 Simon Peter answered, "You are the Messiah, the Son of the living God!"

17-18 "Upon this rock foundation,"* Jesus answered, "I will build my community—those called out by God. Death* will not overpower them. Blessed are you, Simon, son of John. My Father in heaven, not man, showed that to you. You are Peter.* **19** I will give you the keys of the kingdom of heaven. Whatever you bind on earth will have already been bound in heaven. And whatever you loosen on earth will have already been loosened in heaven." **20** Then Jesus warned his followers not to tell anyone that he is the Messiah.

God's Ways Are Not Our Ways

21 From then on, Jesus began to show his followers that he must go away to Jerusalem; that the Jewish elders, the most important priests, and the teachers of the law would make him suffer many things; that he would be killed, but on the third day, he would rise from death.

22 But Peter came to him and began to correct him, "This will never happen to you, Lord!"

23 Jesus turned around and said to Peter, "Get behind me, Satan! You are thinking something which might cause me to sin. You are not thinking the way that God thinks, but as man thinks."

24 Then Jesus said to his followers, "If anyone wants to follow me, he must carry his cross* and follow me. He must say no to himself. **25** The person who wants to save his life will lose it, but every person who gives his life for me will find it. **26** What good is it, if a person gains the whole world, but wrecks his own soul? What can a person use to trade for his soul? **27** I* am ready to come with my angels in the glory of my Father. I will repay every person according to the kind of life he lived. **28** I am telling you the truth: There are some people standing here who will see me* coming into my kingdom."

Chapter 17

A Mountain Top Experience

1 After six days, Jesus took along Peter and the two brothers, James and John. He went up on a tall mountain to be alone. **2** Jesus' appearance began to change in front of them. His face was shining like the sun. His clothes became white as light. **3** Suddenly, Moses and Elijah appeared to them. They were talking with Jesus.

4 Peter said to Jesus, "Lord, it is good that we are here. If you wish, I will make three holy tents here; one for you, one for Moses, and one for Elijah."

5 While Peter was still speaking, a bright cloud came all around them. Suddenly, a Voice spoke from the cloud, saying, "This is My Son, and I love him. I am very pleased with him. He is the one you must listen to!"

6 When Peter, James, and John heard this, they fell to the ground and bowed. They were very frightened. **7** Jesus came to them and touched them. He said, "Get up. Don't be afraid." **8** They looked up. They saw no one else but Jesus.

16:17-18 The Greek word is "petra" (feminine gender).
16:17-18 literally, the gates of Hades
16:17-18 The Greek word is "petros" (masculine gender).
16:24 suffering
16:27 literally, the Son of Man
16:28 literally, the Son of Man

9 As they were going down the mountain, Jesus gave them this command, "Don't tell anyone about this vision until after I* rise from death."

10 They asked Jesus, "Why do the teachers of the law say that Elijah must come before *the Messiah?*"

11 Jesus answered, "Elijah comes and makes all things right.   **12** But, I am telling you, Elijah has already come! They did not acknowledge him. Instead, they treated him as they wished. In the same way, I* am about to suffer many things from them."

13 Then the followers understood that Jesus was talking to them about John (the one who immersed people).

Jesus Heals a Boy With an Evil Spirit

14 When they got to the crowd, a man came up to Jesus. Kneeling down,   **15** he said, "Lord, please help my son. He has a very bad case of epilepsy.* Many times he falls into the fire. Often he falls into the water.   **16** I brought him to your followers, but they could not heal him."

17 Jesus answered, "You people are a generation with no faith. You are warped. How long must I be with you and put up with you? Bring your son here to me."

18 Jesus gave an order and the demon came out of him. The boy was healed from that moment on.

19 Then Jesus' followers came to him alone. They asked, "Why were **we** not able to throw out the demon?"

20 Jesus answered them, "Because you have so little faith. I am telling you the truth: If your faith were the size of the small seed of the mustard plant, then you could say to this mountain, 'Move from here to there!' and the mountain would move. Nothing would be impossible for you."   **21** *

Jesus Tells About His Death

22 When they gathered together in the land of Galilee, Jesus said to them, "I* am about to be handed over to some men.   **23** They will kill me." (This made the followers feel very sad.) "However, on the third day, I will rise *from death.*"

Jesus Pays the Temple Tax

24 They came to the town of Capernaum. The temple* tax collectors came to Peter and said, "Your teacher pays the temple tax, doesn't he?"

25 Peter said, "Yes."

When Peter went into the house, before Peter could say anything, Jesus spoke, "Simon, what do you think? From whom do kings on earth take their taxes or tariffs? From their own sons or from other people?"

26 Peter said, "From other people."

Jesus said to him, "So their sons are free *from being taxed.*   **27** However, we don't want to offend them. Go to the lake and throw in your hook. Take the first fish that

---

17:9   literally, the Son of Man
17:12   literally, the Son of Man
17:15   a disease that violently affects the central nervous system by loss of muscular control and loss of consciousness
17:21   Many manuscripts include verse 21: "This kind does not go out except by prayer and fasting." (See Mark 9:29.)
17:22   literally, the Son of Man
17:24   Jews were commanded to support the temple's upkeep.

comes up. When you have opened its mouth, you will find a coin. Take it and use it to pay the temple tax for you and me."

Chapter 18

The Most Important God Chasers—Kids

1 At that time, the followers came to Jesus. They asked, "Who is the most important in the kingdom of heaven?" **2** So Jesus called for a little child and placed the child in the middle of them. **3** He said, "I am telling you the truth: If you don't change and become like little children, you will never enter the kingdom of heaven. **4** The person who humbles himself like this little child is the most important one in the kingdom of heaven. **5** The person who, in my name, welcomes a little child such as this one welcomes **me**."

Be Careful With Kids

6 "If someone causes one of these little ones who believe in me to sin, it would be better for him to have a large rock hanging around his neck and to be drowned in the deep ocean. **7** It will be horrible for the world, because of the things which cause people to sin. Things will surely happen which will cause people to sin. But it will be horrible for the person who causes this to happen. **8** If your hand or your foot causes you to sin, cut it off and throw it away from you! It would be better for you to enter *eternal* life injured or crippled than to be thrown into eternal fire with two hands or two feet. **9** If your eye causes you to sin, take it out and throw it away from you! It would be better for you to enter *eternal* life with one eye than to be thrown into hell fire with two eyes."

Children Have Friends in High Places

10 "Don't treat one of these little ones as if they were not important. I tell you, their angels in heaven are always looking at my heavenly Father's face. **11** *

Each One Is Precious

12 "What do you think? Suppose a man has 100 sheep, but one of them wanders away. Then he will leave the other 99 on the mountain and go out and look for the sheep that wandered away. **13** I am telling you the truth: When he finds it, he will be happier about it than the 99 sheep that did not wander away. **14** In the same way, your heavenly Father doesn't want any of these little ones to be lost."

People Who Hurt the Chase

15 "If your brother *or sister* does something wrong, go *to him or her*. Give that person a private warning, just between you and that person. If he *or she* listens to you, you have won a brother *or sister*. **16** But if he *or she* will not listen to you, take one or two people along with you because:

'The testimony of two or three people is true.'   *Deuteronomy 19:15*

17 If that person doesn't want to listen to them, then tell the congregation. And, if he *or she* won't listen to the congregation, have nothing to do with them. Treat him like tax collectors or unbelievers are treated."

18:11   Many manuscripts include verse 11: "For the Son of Man came to save that which was lost." (See Luke 19:10.)

Agree to Ask

18 "I am telling you the truth: Whatever you bind on earth will have already been bound in heaven. Whatever you loosen on earth will have already been loosened in heaven. **19** Again, I am telling you, if two people on earth agree to ask *God* for anything, my heavenly Father will make it happen for them. **20** Wherever two or three people have gathered in my name, I am there."

Seven Times Seventy

21 Then Peter came to Jesus and said, "Lord, how many times must I forgive my brother when he sins against me? Seven times?"

22 Jesus said to him, "I am not saying seven, but seven times seventy!* **23** The kingdom of heaven is like a man who is ruling. He wanted to make his servants give an account. **24** When the audit began, a man who owed the ruler several million dollars* came to him. **25** The man could not repay. So, the master ordered that his wife, children, and everything he owned be sold to pay *the debt*. **26** The servant fell down and began bowing to him. He said, 'Be patient with me! I will pay you back everything!' **27** The master felt sorry for that servant. He canceled his debt and allowed him to leave. **28** However, the same servant went out and found another servant who owed him three months' wages.* He grabbed that servant and began to choke him, saying, 'Pay me what you owe me!' **29** The servant fell down and began to beg him, 'Be patient with me! I will pay you back!' **30** But he wouldn't do it. Instead, he went and threw the servant in jail until he could repay what he owed. **31** When the other servants saw what had taken place, they felt very sad. They went and told the whole story to their master. **32** Then the master of the *first* servant came to him and said, 'You evil servant! You begged me, so I canceled your whole debt. **33** You should have given mercy to your fellow servant as I did to you!' **34** The master became very angry. He handed the servant over to some men to punish him, until he paid back everything he owed. **35** My heavenly Father will treat you the same way, if each of you does not forgive his brother *or sister* from his heart."

Chapter 19

Divorce and Re-Marriage

1 When Jesus finished *saying* these words, he left Galilee. He went to the part of Judea which is on the other side of the Jordan River. **2** Large crowds followed him. Jesus healed some of them there.

3 Some Pharisees came to Jesus. They were testing him with this question: "Is it all right for a man to divorce his wife for any reason?"

4 Jesus answered, "You have read this:
'In the beginning, when God created people, he made them male and female.'
Genesis 1:27

5 He said,
'A man will leave his father and mother and be joined to his wife.
The husband and wife will become one flesh.'
Genesis 2:24

18:22   The numbers 7 and 10 were considered to be perfect (complete) numbers. 70 is a multiple of both numbers. The meaning here is: Forgive your brother every time he sins against you.

18:24   literally, 10,000 talents. It would take a workman about 1,000 weeks to earn one talent.

18:28   literally, 100 silver coins

6 So, they are no longer two, but one flesh. Man must not separate what God has joined together."

7 The Pharisees said to Jesus, "Then why did Moses give this command:
'A man who divorces his wife must give her divorce papers'?"

Deuteronomy 24:1

8 Jesus said to them, "Your hearts were hard, so Moses allowed you to divorce your wives, but it was not like that from the very beginning. 9 I am telling you, unless *her* sexual sin is the reason, if a man divorces his wife and marries another woman, he is committing adultery."

10 Jesus' followers said to him, "If this is the true relationship between a husband and his wife, it would be better not to marry!"

11 But Jesus said to them, "Not everyone can accept this teaching—only those to whom it has been given. 12 There are some men who cannot have sexual relations; they were born like this. Others were made that way by man. And some did this to themselves because of the kingdom of heaven. Let the person who is able to accept it accept it."

Let the Children Come

13 Then some people brought their small children to Jesus, so that he could put his hands on them and pray. But his followers told the people not to do this. 14 Jesus said *to his followers*, "Let the little children come to me. Don't stop them, because the kingdom of heaven belongs to people who are like these children." 15 Then Jesus placed his hands on them. *Later* he left there.

The Poor Rich Man

16 A man came to Jesus and asked, "Teacher, what good thing must I do to get eternal life?"

17 Jesus said to him, "Why are you asking me about goodness? *God* is the only One who is good. Since you want to enter *eternal* life, obey the commands *of God.*"

18 The man said to Jesus, "Which commands?"

Jesus said,

" 'You must not commit murder.'
'You must not commit adultery.'
'You must not steal.'
'You must not lie.'

19 'You must love and obey your father and your mother.'   *Exodus 20:12-16*
'You must love other people the same way you love yourself. . . .' "

Leviticus 19:18

20 However, the young man said to Jesus, "But I have obeyed all these things! What do I still need to do?"

21 Jesus answered him, "If you want to be all *that God wants you to be*, go sell everything you have and give the money to the poor people. Then you will have a treasure in heaven. Then come, follow me!"

22 When the young man heard these words, he went away sad, because he owned many things *and he wanted to keep them.*

23 Jesus said this to his followers, "I am telling you the truth: It will be hard for a person with lots of money to enter the kingdom of heaven! 24 I am telling you again: It will be easier for a camel to go through the eye of a needle than for a rich man to enter the kingdom of God."

25 When Jesus' followers heard this, they were very surprised. They asked, "Then who can be saved?"

26 Jesus looked into their eyes and said, "For men, this is impossible, but for God, all things are possible!"

27 Then Peter answered Jesus, "Look, we have left everything and followed you! What will there be for us?"

28 Jesus said to them, "I am telling you the truth: You have followed me. At the time when things will be made right, when I* sit on my glorious throne, you will also sit on twelve thrones. You will judge the twelve tribes of Israel.   **29** Every per-son who has left his home, brothers, sisters, father, mother, children, or fields, because of my name, will receive many rewards and, *after that person dies*, he will receive eternal life *with God*.   **30** Many people who seem as if they are not important now will be important at that time. Those who seem important now will not be important then."

Chapter 20

The Story of the Vineyard Workers

1 "The kingdom of heaven is like the man who owned some land. He went out early in the morning to hire some workers for his vineyard.   **2** He agreed to pay them one silver coin per day. Then he sent them into his vineyard.   **3** At about nine o'clock in the morning, he went out again and saw some men standing around in the marketplace. They were not working.   **4** He said to them, 'You go into my vine-yard, too. I will pay you whatever is fair.'   **5** So they went. In the same way, the owner went out about noon and again around three o'clock in the afternoon.   **6** About five o'clock in the afternoon, he went out and found some more men standing around. He asked them, 'Why have you been standing around here all day long? Why weren't you working?'   **7** They answered him, 'Because no one hired us.' He said to them, 'You go into my vineyard, too.'   **8** When evening came, the owner of the vineyard said to his manager, 'Call the workers and give them their pay.' He began *paying the ones who came to work* last before the ones *who came* first.   **9** The men who came *to work* at five o'clock received one silver coin each!   **10** The men who came *to work* first thought they would be paid more *than a silver coin*, but they also received only one silver coin. **11** They took the money, but they began to complain against the owner of the farm. **12** They said, 'The men who came last worked only one hour. You are paying them the same amount as us! We did most of the work all day long—and it was hot, too!' **13** But the owner said to one, 'Friend, I was not unfair to you. You agreed *to work* for me for one silver coin.   **14** Take this coin. It belongs to you. Go! I want to give to this man *who came to work* last the same amount that I gave to you.   **15** It is not wrong for me to do what I desire with what's mine! Do you have a jealous eye because I am gen-erous?'   **16** The people who seem as though they are not important now will be impor-tant *later*. Those who seem important now will not be important then."

Jesus Will Rise From Death

17 Jesus was ready to go up to Jerusalem. Along the road he took the twelve *fol-lowers* aside. He said to them,   **18** "Listen! We are going up to Jerusalem. The most

---

19:28   literally, the Son of Man

33

important priests and the teachers of the law will turn against me.* They will condemn me to death.   19 Then they will give me to non-Jewish men who will laugh at me, beat me with whips, and nail me to a cross. However, I will rise from death on the third day."

How to Be Really Great

20 Then the mother of the sons of Zebedee, *James and John*, came to Jesus with her sons. She bowed down and asked him for something.

21 Jesus said to her, "What do you want?"

She said to him, "Promise me that these two sons of mine will sit *on thrones* in your kingdom, one at your right side and one at your left side."

22 Jesus answered them, "You don't know what you are asking. Can you drink the cup *of suffering* which I am about to drink?"

They said to Jesus, "We are able."

23 Jesus said to them, "Yes, you will drink from the cup *of suffering* which I will drink, but the *privilege of* sitting at my right side or my left side is not mine to give. Instead, those places belong to those for whom my Father prepared them."   24 When the other ten *apostles* heard about this, they were very angry with the two brothers. 25 Jesus called for them and said, "You know that the rulers of the world lord it over their people. Important men use their authority over them,   26 but you must not think that way. Instead, if one of you wants to be great, that person should be your servant. 27 If one of you wants to be important, he should be your slave.   28 I* did not come to be served. Instead, I came to serve and to give my life to pay the price for many people's *sins*."

Jesus Heals Two Blind Men

29 As they were coming out of Jericho, a large crowd was following Jesus.

30 Two blind men were sitting beside the road. When these men heard that Jesus was passing by, they shouted, "Lord! Son of David! Please help us!"

31 Some of the people told them to be quiet. But they shouted even louder, "Lord! Son of David! Please help us!"

32 Jesus stopped there and called for them. He asked, "What do you want me to do for you?"

33 They answered, "Lord, *heal us* ! Let us be able to see again!"

34 Jesus felt sorry for them, so he touched their eyes. Immediately, the men were able to see again. They followed Jesus.

Chapter 21

Jesus Draws a Crowd

1 When they came near Jerusalem, they went into the town of Bethphage on Olive Mountain. Then Jesus sent two of his followers on ahead.   2 He said to them, "Go into the village just ahead of you. You will soon find a donkey tied up. A young donkey will be with her. Untie them and bring them to me.   3 And if anyone says anything to you, say, 'The Lord, their owner, needs them.' Then he will send them right away."

4 This took place to make what God said through the prophet come true:

20:18   literally, the Son of Man
20:28   literally, the Son of Man

5 "Tell this to the city of Jerusalem:*
'Listen! Your King is coming to you.
He is gentle; he is riding on a donkey
even upon a young donkey, born of a work animal.' "   *Zechariah 9:9*

6 The two followers went into town. They did exactly as Jesus told them.   **7** They brought the mother donkey and her young colt. They put their robes on top of the donkeys. Jesus took his seat upon the robes.   **8** A very large crowd spread their robes on the road *for Jesus*. Other people began to cut down branches from trees and to spread them on the road.   **9** The crowds were shouting. Some people were in front of Jesus and some were behind him. They said, "Hosanna* to the son of David! Give praise to this one who is coming with the authority of the Lord *God*. Hosanna to God!"*

10 When Jesus came into Jerusalem, the whole city was excited, asking, "Who is this man?"

11 The crowds continued to say, "He is Jesus, the prophet from the town of Nazareth in Galilee."

Keep Things Pure

12 Jesus went into the temple courtyard. He threw out all the people who were selling and buying things there. He turned the money-exchangers' tables upside down. He also turned over the chairs of the people who were selling pigeons.   **13** Jesus said to them, "It is written,
'My house will be called a place for praying.'   *Isaiah 56:7*
but **you** have changed it into a hiding place for thieves!"*

14 Blind people and crippled people came to Jesus in the temple courtyard. He healed them.   **15** The most important priests and teachers of the law became very angry. They saw the amazing things which Jesus did. They saw children crying out in the temple courtyard, "Hosanna* to the son of David!"   **16** The most important priests and teachers of the law asked Jesus, "Do you hear what they are saying?"

Jesus answered them, "Yes! Have you not read this:
'I will make praise complete by using the words of small children and babies.' "
          Psalm 8:2

17 Then Jesus left them and went outside of Jerusalem to the town of Bethany where he spent the night.

A Fig Tree

18 Early the next morning, when Jesus was going back into Jerusalem, he was hungry.   **19** He saw a fig tree next to the road. He went to it, but found no fruit on it—only leaves.* Then Jesus spoke to the tree, "May no fruit ever come from you!" The fig

---

21:5   literally, daughter of Zion
21:9   literally, "Help!" "Please save!" This expressed great religious enthusiasm.
21:9   literally, in the highest places
21:13   The merchants and money-exchangers were providing a service for foreign Jews who needed to buy animals for sacrifice and exchange their foreign money, but they should not have been conducting such business in the temple courtyard. Also, they should not have charged such high prices for their services.
21:15   an Aramaic expression of praise meaning, "Save, I pray."
21:19   Although it was not time to gather figs, edible figs should have been present, along with the leaves. This tree would never produce figs; it was deceptive.

tree soon dried up. **20** When Jesus' followers saw this, they were amazed. They asked, "How could the fig tree dry up so quickly?"

21 Jesus answered them, "I am telling you the truth, if you have faith and don't doubt, you will be able to perform this, too! You can even say to this mountain, 'Pick yourself up and throw yourself into the sea!' and it will happen. **22** If you believe, then you will receive everything you ask for in prayer."

Where Does Your Authority Come From?

23 Jesus went into the temple courtyard. He was teaching the people. The most important priests and some of the Jewish elders came to him. They asked, "What sort of authority do you have to do these things? Who gave you this authority?"

24 Jesus answered them, "I will ask **you** a question, too. If you answer me, I will tell you what sort of authority I have to do these things: **25** Where did John's immersion come from? Was it from God* or from man?"

They began thinking to themselves: "If we say, 'From God,'* then he will say this to us: 'Why didn't you believe John?' **26** But if we say, 'From man,' we are afraid of the people. All of them thought of John as a prophet."

27 They answered Jesus, "We don't know."

Jesus said to them, "Then I am not telling you what sort of authority I have to do these things."

The Story of Two Sons

28 *Jesus said to them,* "What do you think? A man had two sons. The man came to the first son and said, 'Son, go work in the vineyard today.' **29-31** He answered, 'Yes sir,' but he did not go. Then the man went to the second son and said the same thing. The son answered, 'I don't want to!' but later he changed his mind and went. Which of the two sons did what their father wanted?"

The Jewish leaders answered, "The second one."

Jesus said to them, "I am telling you the truth: The tax collectors and prostitutes will go into the kingdom of God before you ever do! **32** John came to you *preaching* the way of righteousness, but you did not believe him, but the tax collectors and prostitutes believed him. You saw this, but you did not change your mind later to believe what John was saying."

The Story of the Vineyard

33 "Listen to another story: There was a man who owned some land. He planted a vineyard. He put a wall around it, dug a hole for the wine press, and built a lookout tower. Then he rented the land to some farmers and went away on a trip. **34** When harvest time was near, he sent his servants to the farmers to receive his part of the grapes. **35** But the farmers grabbed his servants. They beat one and killed another. They threw stones at another servant until he died. **36** Again the owner sent servants, more than before, but they did the same thing to those servants. **37** Finally, the owner sent his son to them, thinking, 'They will respect my son.' **38** But when the farmers saw the son, they thought to themselves, 'When the owner dies, his son will own the vineyard. Come, let us kill him and we will get his field!' **39** So they took the son,

21:25   literally, heaven
21:25   literally, heaven

threw him out of the vineyard, and killed him.   40 When the owner of the vineyard comes, what will he do to those farmers?"

41 The Jewish leaders answered Jesus, "He will kill those evil men! After that, he will give the field to some other farmers who will share the fruits with him at harvest time."

42 Jesus said to them, "You have read this in the Scriptures:
'The stone that the builders did not want will become the cornerstone.
The Lord *God* makes this happen.
It is a wonderful thing for us to see.'   *Psalm 118:22-23*
43 This is why I am telling you that the kingdom of God will be taken away from you and given to a people who will make it produce fruit.   44 Everyone who falls on that stone will be broken. If that stone falls on you, it will crush you!"*

45 When the most important priests and the Pharisees heard these stories, they knew that he was talking about them.   46 They wanted to arrest Jesus, but they were afraid of what the crowds might do to them, because the people believed that Jesus was a prophet.

Chapter 22

The Story of the Wedding Banquet

1 Again Jesus used an example to answer them: 2 "The kingdom of heaven is like a king who gave a wedding party for his son.   3 The king sent his servants to invite the guests to the wedding party, but the guests didn't want to come.   4 Again, the king sent more servants saying, "Tell the guests, 'Look, I have prepared the dinner—the steers and fattened calves have been killed—everything is ready!' 5 However, the guests didn't care. They left. One went to his field. One went to his business.   6 The others grabbed the king's servants, insulted them, and killed them.   7 The king was very angry. He sent his army to destroy those murderers and to burn their city.   8 Then the king said to his servants, 'The wedding party is still ready, but the guests were not worthy enough *to come.*   9 So, go to the street corners and invite whomever you can find to the wedding party.'   10 Those servants went out to the streets and gathered up everyone they could find, good people and bad people. Then the wedding hall was filled with guests.   11 The king entered and looked at the guests. He saw a man there who was not wearing wedding clothes.   12 The king said to him, 'Friend, how did you get in here without wedding clothes?' The man had nothing to say.   13 Then the king said to the servants, 'Tie his hands and feet and throw him outside in the dark. In that place there will be screaming and grinding of teeth.'   14 Many people are invited, but few people are chosen."

Give to Caesar What Is Caesar's

15 Then the Pharisees came. They had made a plan to trap Jesus with a question. 16 The Pharisees sent some of their followers and the followers of Herod *Antipas* to him. They said, "Teacher, we know that you are true and you teach God's true way. It does not matter to you what people think. You don't pay attention to how important someone is.   17 So, tell us, what do you think? Is it right that we should pay taxes to Caesar?* Yes or no?"

21:44   Some ancient copies omit this verse.
22:17   The title of the supreme Roman rulers. "Caesar" became the title of each emperor.

18 But Jesus knew their evil plan. He said, "You hypocrites!* Why are you trying to trap me?   **19** Show me the coin for the tax." They brought a silver coin.   **20** Jesus said to them, "Whose name and picture is on it?"

21 They answered, "Caesar's."

Jesus said to them, "Then give to Caesar the things which are Caesar's, and give to God the things which belong to God."   **22** When they heard this, they were amazed. They left him and went away.

The God of the Living

23 That same day some Sadducees came to Jesus. (Sadducees believed that no one will rise from death.) They asked Jesus,   **24** "Teacher, Moses said that if someone has no children and he dies, his brother must marry the widow. Then they will have children for the *dead* brother.   **25** There were seven brothers among us. The first one got married, but died. He left his wife with no children.   **26** In the same way, the second brother, the third brother—all seven brothers— *died without having children.*   **27** Last of all, the woman died.   **28** All seven men had married her. So, when this woman rises from death, whose wife will she be?"

29 Jesus answered them, "You are wrong. You don't know the Scriptures or God's power.   **30** When people rise from death, they don't marry one another. Instead, they are like angels in heaven.   **31** Do people rise from death? I know you have read what God said *to Moses* :

32 'I am the God of Abraham, the God of Isaac, and the God of Jacob.'

Exodus 3:6,15,16

God is not a God of dead people; He is the God of people who are alive!"   **33** When the crowds heard this, they were very surprised at his teaching.

The Most Important Commandment

34 When the Pharisees heard that Jesus had silenced the Sadducees, they gathered together.   **35** One of them, an expert on the law *of Moses*, tried to trap Jesus. He asked,   **36** "Teacher, what is the most important command in the law?"

37 Jesus answered him,

" 'You must love the Lord your God,
    with all your heart,
    with all your soul,
    and with all your mind.'   *Deuteronomy 6:5*

38 This is the most important command.   **39** The second most important command is like it:

'You must love other people the same way you love yourself.'   *Leviticus 19:18*

40 These two commands support the whole law and the prophets."

Is the Messiah the Son of David?

41 When some Pharisees gathered, Jesus asked them,   **42** "What do you think about the Messiah? Whose son is he?"

They answered Jesus, "David's son."

43 Jesus asked them, "Then why did the Spirit (through David) call the Messiah 'Lord'? *David wrote* :

22:18   those who act as though they are good when they are not

38

44 'The Lord *God* said to my Lord:*
  Sit at My right side until I put your enemies under your feet.'*

Psalm 110:1

45 Since David called him 'Lord,' how could Messiah be David's son?"   46 No one was able to answer Jesus. From that time on, no one dared to ask him any more *trick* questions.

Chapter 23

True Greatness

1 Then Jesus spoke to the crowds and to his followers.   2 He said, "The teachers of the law and the Pharisees sit on Moses' seat *of authority.*   3 Therefore, do everything they tell you. Obey them. But don't act as they do, because they say one thing and do another.   4 They bind heavy loads and put them on people's shoulders, but they don't want to lift a finger to *help* move them.   5 Everything they do, they do so that people will notice them. They show off their phylacteries* and they make their tassels* long.   6 They like to have the best seats at the dinners and the most important seats in the synagogues.*   7 They like the greetings *of respect* which people give them in the marketplaces. They like people to call them, 'Rabbi.'*   8 You should not be called 'Rabbi,' because there is only one teacher for you. You are all brothers.   9 On earth, you should not be called 'Father,' because you have only one Father—the heavenly Father.   10 You should not be called, 'Leader' because the Messiah is your only Leader.   11 The most important one among you will be your servant.   12 Every person who acts as though he is important will be made ashamed, but every person who truly humbles himself will be made important."

White-Washed Tombs

13 "It will be horrible for you, teachers of the law and Pharisees. You hypocrites!* You shut *the door to* the kingdom of heaven in people's faces. You will not go in, and you stop those who are trying to get in.   14 *

15 "It will be horrible for you, teachers of the law and Pharisees. You hypocrites! You travel all over the world* to make one convert. And when you convert him, you make him twice as much a child of hell as you are!

16 "It will be horrible for you, you blind guides who say, 'It is not important if someone makes a vow to God by the temple sanctuary. But, if someone makes a vow to God by the gold in the temple sanctuary, he is guilty!'   17 You are foolish and blind! What

---

22:44   In the Hebrew text of this psalm, the first "Lord" is *Yahweh*; the second "Lord" is *Adonai,* referring to the Messiah.

22:44   in his control

23:5   These leather boxes contained verses of Scripture and were strapped to their arms or foreheads while praying.

23:5   Tassels were worn on four corners of a robe to remind the people of the law (Numbers 15:38-40).

23:6   on a raised platform where speakers stood, overlooking the congregation

23:7   It means "my master" or "my teacher." It became a title of respect for Jewish leaders.

23:13, 14, 15, 23, 25, 27, 29   those who acted as though they were righteous but they were not righteous

23:14   Some manuscripts include verse 14: "It will be horrible for you, teachers of the law and Pharisees. You are hypocrites, because you rob widows' houses while you make long prayers for a show. You will receive greater condemnation." (See Mark 12:40; Luke 20:47.)

23:15   literally, travel over land and sea

is more important? The gold or the temple sanctuary which makes the gold holy? 18 You also say, 'If someone vows to God by the altar, it does not matter. But, if someone vows to God by the gift on the altar, he is guilty!' 19 You blind men! Which is more important? The gift or the altar which makes the gift holy? 20 The person who vows to God by the altar vows to God by the altar and everything on the altar. 21 The person who vows to God by the temple sanctuary vows by the sanctuary and by the One who dwells there. 22 The person who vows to God by heaven vows to God by God's throne and the One who sits upon it.

23 "It will be horrible for you, teachers of the law and Pharisees. You hypocrites! It is true that you give God ten percent of everything you have. You even give him ten percent of your spices—mint, dill, and cummin. But you forget about more important things in the law: being fair to other people, giving mercy, and faith. You should always tithe, but you must remember to do the more important things, too. 24 You blind guides! You strain out the gnat,* but you swallow the camel!

25 "It will be horrible for you, teachers of the law and Pharisees. You hypocrites! You wash the outside of the cup or the bowl. But inside, there are the things you got by cheating other people and pleasing yourselves. 26 Blind Pharisees! Make the inside of the cup clean first, so that the outside of it will be clean, too.

27 "It will be horrible for you, teachers of the law and Pharisees. You hypocrites! You are like tombs which have been painted white. They seem to be very beautiful outside, but inside they are full of all kinds of filth and the bones of dead people. 28 You are the same way. Outside you seem good to people, but inside you are full of hypocrisy* and sin."

You Murderers!

29 "It will be horrible for you, teachers of the law and Pharisees. You hypocrites! You build tombs for the prophets. You make the graves of good people beautiful. 30 You claim, 'If we had lived in the time of our ancestors, we would not have helped them kill the prophets.' 31 So, you are admitting you are the sons of the men who murdered the prophets! 32 You are finishing what your ancestors started.

33 "You snakes! You are from a family of poisonous snakes! How will you escape the judgment of hell? 34 Look! I am sending you prophets, wise men, and teachers of the law. You will kill some of them and you will nail others to crosses. You will whip some of them in your synagogues. You will chase them from town to town. 35 You will have to answer for the death of every good person who has been killed on earth. You will have to answer for all the spilled blood from the murder of Abel to the murder of Zechariah, the son of Barachiah.* You murdered Zechariah between the temple sanctuary and the altar. 36 I am telling you the truth: All these things will happen to the people of this generation!"

Jerusalem, Jerusalem

37 "O Jerusalem, Jerusalem! You kill the prophets. *God* sent you His men, but you stoned them to death. I have often wanted to gather up your people, as a hen gathers up her baby chicks under her wings, but you refused. 38 Listen! Your house is

---

23:24   The Pharisees strained out drinking water to avoid ceremonially unclean insects. (See Leviticus 23:4-8.)
23:28   they were not sincere
23:35   See Second Chronicles 24:20,21.

completely abandoned. **39** I tell you, you will never see me again until you say, 'Praise to the one who is coming with the authority of the Lord *God*.' "

Chapter 24

The Destruction of the Temple and the Last Days

1 Jesus left the temple courtyard. While he was walking away, his followers came to him to show him the beautiful things of the temple area. **2** Jesus said to them, "Do you see all these things? I am telling you the truth: Everything *you see* here will be destroyed. No stone will stay on top of another. Everything will be completely destroyed!"

Things Will Get Tough

3 While Jesus was sitting on Olive Mountain, his followers came to him alone. They asked, "Tell us, when will these things happen? How will we know when it is the time for you to return? When will the end of the age be?"

4 Jesus answered them, "Be careful! Don't let anyone fool you. **5** Many people will come *to you* using my name. They will say, 'I am the Messiah!' And, they will fool many people. **6** You will hear about wars and wars that are about to begin. Be sure that you don't get upset. These things must happen, but the end will come later. **7** One country will fight against another country. Kingdoms will fight against other kingdoms. There will not be enough food to eat. Everywhere there will be earthquakes, **8** but all these things are only the beginning of the pain.

9 "Then they will hand you over to some men for torturing. They will kill you. All people will hate you, because of my name. **10** Then many people will feel disgraced; they will turn against one another. They will hate each other. **11** Many false prophets will appear. They will fool many people. **12** Because the influence of sin will be so strong, the love of many people will grow cold. **13** But the person who endures until the end will be saved. **14** This Good News about the kingdom will be preached in the whole world, so that all nations may hear the truth. And then the end will come."

Run Away!

15 "When you see what God talked about through Daniel the prophet—'The Abomination of Desolation'—standing in the holy place (let the reader note the meaning*), **16** then those people who are in the land of Judea must run away to the mountains. **17** The person who is on top of his house must not come down to carry things in the house away with him. **18** The person who is in the field must not turn back to get his robe. **19** At that time, it will be horrible for pregnant women and nursing mothers. **20** Pray that the time when you escape will not be during winter or on a Sabbath day. **21** There will be great suffering. Never has there been such suffering since the beginning of the world until the present time and there will never be such suffering in the future. **22** If that period of time were to last any longer, then no one would be left alive. But those times will be cut short because of the people chosen *by God*.

23 "At that time, if someone says to you, 'Look, here is the Messiah!' or, 'There he is!' don't believe him. **24** False messiahs and false prophets will appear. They will perform such great proofs and miracles to fool people—even *God's* chosen people, if that were possible. **25** Listen! I am telling you ahead of time. **26** If they say this to

---

24:15   See Daniel 9:27; 11:31; 12:11.

you, 'Look, he is in the desert!' don't go out there! or, 'He is in secret rooms!' don't believe them!   **27** I* will return. On the day when I come, I will shine, as lightning flashes across the sky, from the east to the west.   **28** People can always know where a dead body is—they can see the vultures gathering.' "

Gathering Time

29 "Soon after the trouble of those times,
   'The sun will become dark.
      The light of the moon will not be seen.'   *Isaiah 13:10*
   'The stars will fall from the sky.
      The powers in the universe will be moved.' "   *Isaiah 34:4*
30 "Then my* sign will appear in the sky: All people on earth will see me coming on the clouds with power and great glory; they will mourn.   **31** I will use a loud trumpet to send out my angels. From all directions the angels will gather together my chosen people."

The Story of the Fig Tree

32 "Learn from the story about the fig tree: When its branches start to become soft and green, and new leaves begin to grow, you know that summer is near.   **33** In the same way, when you see all these things *happening*, you will know that the time is very, very near.   **34** I am telling you the truth: All these things will happen in this generation."

Be Ready at All Times

35 "The world* will be destroyed, but my words will **never** be destroyed!   **36** No one knows when that exact time will be. The angels of heaven don't know it. The Son doesn't know it. Only the *heavenly* Father knows.   **37** When I* come, it will be just as it was in Noah's time.   **38** People were eating, drinking, getting married, giving their daughters away in marriage—even on the day when Noah entered the ark.   **39** The people did not know *the truth*, until the flood came and swept them all away. That is how it will be when I* come.   **40** At that time, there will be two men in the field; one will be taken and one will be left.   **41** Two women will be grinding grain; one will be taken and the other will be left.   **42** So, watch! You don't know on what day your Lord is coming.   **43** Know this: If a homeowner knew what time of night a robber was coming, he would watch for the robber and not let him break into his house.   **44** This is why you must be ready. I* will come at a time when you are not expecting me."

Be Trustworthy

45 "Who is the wise and trusted servant? Who is the servant whom the master can choose to take care of the master's family and the other servants by giving them food at the right time?   **46** When the master comes and finds that servant doing the work he

---

24:27   literally, the Son of Man
24:30   literally, the Son of Man
24:35   literally, the sky and the earth
24:37   literally, the Son of Man
24:39   literally, the Son of Man
24:44   literally, the Son of Man

gave him, that servant will be very happy.   **47** I am telling you the truth: The master will choose that servant to take care of everything which the master owns. **48** However, if that servant thinks his master will not come back soon,   **49** then he may begin to beat the other servants. That servant may also eat all the food and get drunk with other men.   **50** Then the master of that servant will come when that servant is not ready, at a time when that servant is not expecting him.   **51** Then the master will punish that servant and send him away. This is what the master does to all the servants he cannot trust. In that place there will be screaming and grinding of teeth."

Chapter 25

Be Ready!

1 Jesus said, "At that time, the kingdom of heaven will be like ten virgins. They took their lamps and went out to meet the groom.   **2** Five of them were foolish and five were wise.   **3** The foolish ones took their lamps, but they did not take extra oil with them.   **4** The wise virgins took extra oil in their jars with their lamps.   **5** The groom was late. All of the virgins became sleepy. They fell asleep.   **6** About midnight there was a shout: 'Look, the groom! Go out and meet him!'   **7** Then all ten virgins got up and prepared their lamps.   **8** But the foolish virgins said to the wise virgins, 'Give us some of your oil, because our lamps have almost gone out.'

9 "The wise virgins answered, 'No! There would not be enough for all of us. Instead, go to the store and buy some more oil.'   **10** While these virgins were gone to buy some more oil, the groom came. The *wise virgins*, who were ready, went inside with him to the wedding party. And the door was shut.   **11** Later, the other virgins came and said, 'Master, master, open the door for us!'

12 "But the master answered, 'I am telling you the truth: I don't know you.' **13** So, watch! You don't know the day or the exact hour *when I will come*."

Use Your Talents

14 *"The kingdom of heaven* will be like a man leaving on a trip. He called his servants and turned his property over to them.   **15** He gave five talents* to one, two talents to one, and one talent to another. Each man *received* what he was able *to manage*. Then the man went on the trip.   **16** The man with five talents went out immediately and earned five more talents.   **17** In the same way, the man with two talents earned two more talents.   **18** But the man with one talent went off, dug a hole in the ground, and buried his master's money.   **19** After a long time, the master of those servants came back. He made them give an account.   **20** The man who had received five talents came and brought five more talents, saying, 'Master, you turned five talents over to me, but, look, I earned five more talents!'

21 "His master said to him, 'Fine! You are a good and faithful servant. I see that I can trust you with small things. Therefore, I will put you in charge of important things. Come and share your master's happiness.'

22 "The man with two talents came and said, 'Master, you turned two talents over to me, but, look, I have earned two more talents!'

23 "His master said to him, 'Fine! You are a good and faithful servant. I see that I can trust you with small things. Therefore, I will put you in charge of important things.

25:15   It would take a workman 1,000 weeks to earn one talent.

Come and share your master's happiness.' 24 Then the man who had received one talent came. He said, 'Master, I knew you were a hard man. You take money which you didn't earn and you gather food which you didn't grow. 25 So I was afraid. I went off and hid your talent in the ground. Look, here is your talent.'

26 "His master answered, 'You evil, lazy slave! You knew that I take money which I didn't earn and gather food which I didn't grow. 27 Therefore, you should have put my money in the bank. Then when I returned, I could have my money, with interest, too. 28 Take the talent away from him and give it to the man who has ten talents. 29 The person who uses what he has will get more, but the person who doesn't use what he has will have everything taken away from him. 30 Throw this useless slave outside into the dark.' In that place, there will be screaming and grinding of teeth."

Be a Sheep

31 "When I* come with my glory and all my angels, then I will sit on my glorious throne. 32 All the people in the world will be gathered in front of me. I will separate them from one another, as a shepherd separates the sheep from the goats. 33 I will put the sheep on the right side and the goats on the left side. 34 Then I* will say to the people on the right side, 'You are blessed by my Father. Come, take what belongs to you—the kingdom which was prepared for you since the beginning of the world. 35 I was hungry and you gave me something to eat. I was thirsty and you gave me something to drink. I was a stranger and you took me into your home. 36 I had no clothes, so you gave me some clothes. I was sick and you took care of me. I was in jail and you came *to visit* me.'

37 "Then the good people will answer him, 'Lord, when did we see you? When did we feed you when you were hungry? When did we give you something to drink when you were thirsty? 38 When did we see you as a stranger and take you into our homes? When did you need clothes and we gave you some clothes? 39 When were you sick or in jail? When did we come to you?'

40 "I* will answer them, 'I am telling you the truth: Since you treated some of my *so-called* "unimportant" brothers this way, you did it to me!'

41 "Then I* will say to the people on the left side, 'Go away from me into eternal fire. You are condemned! The fire has been prepared for the Devil and his angels. 42 I was hungry and you gave me nothing to eat. I was thirsty and you gave me nothing to drink. 43 I was a stranger and you didn't take me into your homes. I had no clothes and you didn't give me any. I was sick; I was in jail, but you didn't take care of me.'

44 "Then they will answer, 'Lord, when did we see you? When were you hungry, thirsty, a stranger, without clothes, sick, or in jail and we didn't help you?'

45 "Then I will answer them, 'I am telling you the truth: Since you didn't treat one of these *so-called* "unimportant" people *with kindness*, you didn't do it to me, either.'

46 "Then these people will go off into eternal punishment, but the good people will go into eternal life."

25:31   literally, the Son of Man
25:34   literally, the king
25:40   literally, the king
25:41   literally, he

Chapter 26

The Plot

1 When Jesus finished saying all these things, he said this to his followers, 2 "You know that the day after tomorrow is the Passover* Festival. I* will be handed over to be nailed to a cross."

3 Then the most important priests and the Jewish elders of the people gathered together at the high priest's house. His name was Caiaphas. 4 They planned to use a trick to arrest Jesus and kill him, 5 but they said, "*Let us* not *do it* during the Passover Festival, so that there will be no trouble among the people."

The Perfume

6 Jesus was in the town of Bethany in Simon's house. (Simon was a leper.*) 7 A woman came to Jesus. She had an alabaster* jar of some very expensive perfume. While Jesus was sitting at the table, she poured it on his head. 8 When Jesus' followers saw this, they became very angry. They asked, "Why waste this? 9 This could have been sold for a lot of money and given to poor people!"

10 Knowing what they were saying, Jesus said to them, "Why are you bothering this woman? She has done a good thing to me. 11 You will always have poor people with you, but you will not always have **me** ! 12 When she put this perfume on my body, she did it for when I will be buried. 13 I am telling you the truth: The Good News will be preached in the whole world. Wherever they tell it, what she did will be mentioned to remember her."

The Price

14 Then one of the twelve *apostles*, the one called Judas Iscariot, went to the most important priests. 15 He said, "If I were to hand Jesus over to you, what would you pay me?" They agreed with him *on the price* —30 silver coins.* 16 From that time on, Judas was looking for the best time to give Jesus to them.

The Passover

17 On the first day of the Feast of Unleavened Bread,* Jesus' followers came to him. They asked, "Where do you want us to prepare the Passover meal?"

18 Jesus answered, "Go into the city to the host. Tell him, 'The Teacher says, "My time is near. My followers and I will have the Passover meal with you." ' "

19 Jesus' followers did exactly as Jesus told them. They prepared the Passover meal. 20 When evening came, Jesus sat down at the table with his twelve followers. 21 While they were eating, Jesus said, "I am telling you the truth: One of you will turn against me!"

22 They began to feel very sad. Each one of them said to Jesus, "Lord, I am not the one, am I?"

26:2   A yearly feast reminding the Jews of the death angel that had "passed over" their homes in Egypt (Exodus 12:21-28).

26:2   literally, the Son of Man

26:6   a person who had a very bad skin disease which destroyed the flesh

26:7   Jars were sometimes made of alabaster, a soft, cream-colored stone.

26:15   about one month's pay

26:17   A yearly feast when unleavened bread (no yeast to make the bread rise) was eaten. It lasted seven days. (See Leviticus 23:4-8.)

23 Jesus answered, "The person who dipped his hand in the same dinner bowl with me will turn against me. 24 I* will die just as it is written about me.* But, how horrible it will be for that man who turns against me.* It would be better if that man had never been born!"

25 Judas (the one who turned against him) answered, "Rabbi, I am not the one, am I?"

Jesus answered Judas, "Yes, you are."*

The Proclamation

26 While they were eating, Jesus took bread and gave thanks. He broke off some of the bread and gave it to his followers. He said, "Take it and eat it. This bread is* my body." 27 Then he took a cup. He gave thanks to God for it and gave it to them. He said, "All of you, drink from it. 28 This is* my blood which I am pouring out for many people for the forgiveness of sins. *It shows* the *new* agreement which God has made with men. 29 I tell you, from now on, I will never drink this fruit of the vine again, until the day when I drink it new with you in my Father's kingdom." 30 Then they sang a song of praise and went out to Olive Mountain.

31 Then Jesus said to them, "Tonight all of you will be ashamed of me. This is written:

'I will strike the shepherd and the flock of sheep will be scattered.'

Zechariah 13:7

32 However, after I rise from death, I will go ahead of you to the land of Galilee."

The Prediction

33 Peter answered him, "Everyone else may be ashamed of you, but **I** will never be ashamed of you!"

34 Jesus said to Peter, "I am telling you the truth: Before the rooster crows in the morning, you will say you don't even know me three different times!"

35 Peter answered him, "Even if I must die with you, I will always be loyal to you!" All of Jesus' followers said the same thing.

The Prayer

36 Then Jesus and his followers went to a place called Gethsemane. Jesus said to them, "Sit here while I go over there and pray."

37 He took Peter and the two sons of Zebedee with him. He began to feel sad and depressed. 38 Then he said to them, "My soul is full of sorrow; I am going to die. Stay here and be watchful with me." 39 Then Jesus went forward a short distance and bowed down to pray. He said, "My Father, if it is possible, take this cup *of suffering* away from me—but what You want is more important than what I want."

40 Then Jesus came to his followers. He found them sleeping. He asked Peter, "Were you not strong enough to stay awake with me for just one hour? 41 Watch and pray for strength against temptation. The spirit is willing, but the body is weak."

42 Jesus went away the second time. He prayed, "My Father, if this must happen and I must drink the cup *of suffering*, if this is what You want, let it be." 43 Again, Jesus

---

26:24   literally, the Son of Man
26:25   literally, "You are saying it"; a statement meaning: "I agree with what you are saying."
26:26   represents
26:28   represents

came and found them sleeping. Their eyes were very tired. **44** He left them again. The third time he prayed the same prayer. **45** Then Jesus came to his followers and asked them, "Are you still sleeping and resting? Listen, the time has come—I* am now being handed over into the hands of sinful men. **46** Get up, we must go. Look! The one who turned against me is near!"

The Panic

47 While Jesus was still speaking, Judas, one of the twelve *apostles*, came. There was a large crowd with him. They had come from the most important priests and the elders of the Jewish people. They had sticks and swords. **48** Judas had given them the signal to arrest the one he would kiss. **49** Judas went immediately to Jesus and said, "Greetings, Rabbi!" Then Judas kissed him.

50 But Jesus said to him, "Friend, do what you came for!" Then the men who came *with Judas* reached out and took hold of Jesus. **51** Suddenly, one of the men with Jesus reached for his sword and pulled it out. He struck the high priest's slave, cutting off his ear. **52** Then Jesus said, "Put your sword back in its place! Everyone who uses violence will be violently destroyed. **53** Don't you think I could call on my Father *for help* ? He would bring more than twelve legions* of angels here! **54** But how could the Scriptures come true, if this did not happen?" **55** At that moment, Jesus said this to the crowd: "Why did you come out here to get me with swords and sticks? Do you think I am a criminal? I was sitting in the temple courtyard every day teaching. You did not arrest me there. **56** All this happened to make the writings of the prophets come true." Then all of Jesus' followers left him. They ran away.

The Priest

57 After they arrested Jesus, they brought him to Caiaphas, the high priest. The teachers of the law and the Jewish elders were gathered there. **58** Peter was following Jesus, but he did not come near Jesus. He came as far as the high priest's courtyard. Later, he went inside. He was sitting with the guards. He wanted to see what would happen. **59** The most important priests and the whole Jewish Council were trying to find some men who would give false evidence against Jesus, so that they could put him to death. **60** But they didn't find many people to come forward to tell lies. Finally, two men came forward. **61** They claimed, "This man said, 'I am able to destroy God's temple sanctuary and build it again in three days!' "

62 The high priest stood up and asked Jesus, "Will you give no answer to what they say against you—is it true?" **63** Jesus continued to be silent. The high priest said to him, "By the living God, I hereby force you: You **must** answer! Tell us if you are the Messiah, the Son of God!"

64 Jesus said to him, "Yes, I am.* Nevertheless, I tell you, from now on, you will see me:*

'sitting at the right side of God.'*	*Psalm 110:1*
'I* will be coming on the clouds of the sky.' "	*Daniel 7:13*

26:45	literally, the Son of Man
26:53	In the Roman army a legion numbered about 5,000 men.
26:64	literally, "You are saying it"; a statement meaning: "I agree with what you are saying."
26:64	literally, the Son of Man
26:64	literally, the Power
26:64	literally, the Son of Man

65 Then the high priest ripped his clothes* and he cried out, "He has said an evil thing! Why do we need any more witnesses? Listen, you have just heard him say this evil thing!   **66** What do you think?"

They answered, "He is guilty! He must die!"   **67** Then they spit in Jesus' face. They hit him with their fists. Some of them slapped him.   **68** They said, "Prophesy for us, you Messiah! Let God tell you which one of us hit you!"

Peter

69 Peter was sitting outside in the courtyard. A servant girl came to him. She said, "You, too, were with Jesus, the one from Galilee!"   **70** But, in front of everyone, Peter said that this was not true. He said, "I don't know what you're talking about!"

71 Later, Peter went out to the gate. Another girl saw him. She said to the men there, "This man was with Jesus from Nazareth!"

72 Again Peter denied it. This time he said, "I swear, I don't know the man!"

73 After a little while, the men who were standing there came to Peter and said, "Surely you are one of Jesus' group! It is clear that you have a *Galilean* accent!"

74 Peter began to curse and swear, "I don't know the man!" Immediately the rooster crowed.   **75** Then Peter remembered that Jesus had said, "Before the rooster crows, you will say, three different times, that you don't even know me." Peter went outside and cried bitterly.

Chapter 27

Too Late for Judas

1 It was early in the morning. The most important priests and the Jewish elders of the people made the decision to put Jesus to death.   **2** They tied him up. Then they brought him and handed him over to Governor Pilate.

3 Judas, the one who turned against Jesus, saw that Jesus had been condemned. Judas changed his mind and brought back the 30 silver coins to the most important priests and the Jewish elders.   **4** He said, "I have done wrong! I handed over an innocent man to die!"

They answered, "We don't care! That's your problem!"   **5** Then Judas threw the silver coins toward the temple sanctuary and left. He went off and killed himself by hanging.

6 The priests picked up the coins and said, "Since this is blood money, it would not be right to put this into the treasury."   **7** So they decided to use it to buy a potter's field for burying strangers.   **8** Today that field is called Blood Land.   **9** Then what God had said through Jeremiah the prophet came true:

"They took 30 silver coins.
This was the value that the sons of Israel put on him.

10 They used the money to buy the potter's field,
as the Lord *God* ordered me."

Zechariah 11:12-13

Jesus to Pilate

11 Jesus stood before the governor. The governor asked him, "Are you the King of the Jews?"

Jesus answered, "Yes."*

26:65   a sign of grief or outrage
27:11   literally, "You are saying it"; a statement meaning: "I agree with what you are saying."

12 The most important priests and the Jewish elders accused Jesus, but Jesus gave no answer. **13** Then Pilate said to him, "Don't you hear how many charges they are bringing against you?"

14 But Jesus didn't even say a word. The governor was very surprised.

Crown of Thorns

15 Every year at the *Passover* Feast, the governor always set one prisoner free, whomever the people wanted. **16** This time they had a well-known prisoner named Jesus Barabbas. **17** Therefore, when the people gathered, Pilate said to them, "Who do you want me to set free? Jesus Barabbas or the Jesus who is called Messiah?" **18** (Pilate knew that they had handed Jesus over to him because of jealousy.) **19** While Pilate was sitting on the judgment seat, his wife sent *a message* to him. It said, "Have nothing to do with this innocent man! Last night in a dream I suffered many things because of him!"

20 The most important priests and the Jewish elders persuaded the crowds to ask *Pilate* for Barabbas. They wanted to destroy Jesus. **21** The governor asked them, "Which of the two men do you want me to set free?"

They answered, "Barabbas!"

22 Pilate asked them, "What should I do with Jesus, the one who is called Messiah?"

They all answered, "Nail him to a cross!"

23 But Pilate asked, "Why? What crime has Jesus done?"

But they continued yelling even more, "Nail him to a cross!"

24 Pilate saw that he was getting nowhere—only more trouble. He took some water and washed his hands in front of the crowd.* He said, "I am not responsible for this man's death— **you** are!"

25 The whole crowd answered, "We accept that responsibility for us and for our children!"

26 Then he set Barabbas free for them. After beating Jesus with whips, Pilate handed him over to be nailed to the cross.

27 The governor's soldiers took Jesus to the *Roman* fortress. The whole group gathered around Jesus. **28** They took off his clothes and dressed him with a long red robe. **29** They used thorny branches to make a crown. Then they put it on his head. They put a stick in his right hand. They kneeled down before him and made fun of him, saying, "Hail, King of the Jews!" **30** They spit on him. They took the stick and began to hit him on the head. **31** When they finished making fun of him, they took off the long robe and dressed him with his own clothes. Then they led him away to nail him to the cross.

On the Cross

32 As they were going out *of Jerusalem*, they found a man from the city of Cyrene. His name was Simon. They forced him to carry Jesus' cross. **33** They came to a place called Golgotha. (This means 'The Place of the Skull.') **34** They gave Jesus some wine. (A drug for pain was mixed with it.) When he had tasted it, he refused to drink it. **35** Then they nailed him to the cross. The soldiers gambled to see who would get Jesus' clothes. **36** They sat there watching him. **37** At the top of the cross they wrote the reason for his punishment in these words:

THIS IS JESUS, THE KING OF THE JEWS.

27:24   a sign claiming innocence (Deuteronomy 21:6,7; Psalm 26:6)

38 Along with Jesus, two criminals were nailed to crosses. One was on his right side. The other was on his left. **39** The people who were passing by shook their heads and said terrible things to Jesus. **40** They said, "You are the one who was going to destroy the temple sanctuary and build it again in three days! Since you are the Son of God, save yourself! Come on down from the cross!"

41 In the same way, the most important priests, the teachers of the law, and the Jewish elders made fun of Jesus. They continued to say, **42** "He saved other people, but he cannot save himself! He is the King of Israel; let him come down from the cross now! Then we will believe in him! **43** He trusts in God; let **God** rescue him now if He wants him. Jesus did say, 'I am the Son of God.' "

44 Even the criminals who were nailed to the other crosses did the same thing—they kept insulting Jesus.

Jesus Dies

45 There was darkness over the whole land from noon until three o'clock in the afternoon. **46** At about three o'clock, Jesus shouted this loudly: "Eli, Eli, lema sabakthani?" (This means: "My God, my God, why did you abandon me?") **47** Some of the men standing there heard this. They said, "This man is calling for Elijah."*

48 One of them quickly ran and got a sponge. He soaked it in some sour wine. Then he put it on the end of a long stick and gave Jesus a drink. **49** The other men said, "Leave him alone. Let's see if Elijah will come and save him!"

50 Again, Jesus cried out very loudly. Then he died.

51 The curtain in the temple sanctuary was split into two parts—from the top to the bottom.* The earth shook. Large rocks broke apart. **(52-53** Tombs were opened. After Jesus rose from the grave, many holy people who had died were raised from death, too. They left their tombs and went into Jerusalem* and appeared to many people.)

54 There was a *Roman* army officer and some of his men guarding Jesus. When they saw the earthquake and the other things that happened, they were very frightened. They said, "This man really was God's Son."

55 There were many women there. They had helped Jesus and followed him from the land of Galilee. They were far away, watching. **56** Some of them were:

Mary (from the town of Magdala);
Mary (the mother of James and Joseph);
the mother of the sons of Zebedee.

The Rich Man's Grave

57 Since it was getting late, a rich man named Joseph from the town of Arimathea (He was also a follower of Jesus.) **58** came to Pilate to ask for the body of Jesus. Then Pilate gave an order to give the body to him. **59** So Joseph took the body and wrapped it in a clean sheet. **60** Then he put Jesus' body into his own new tomb which he had cut out of *solid* rock. He rolled a large stone to cover the door of the tomb. Then Joseph left. **61** Mary (the one from Magdala) and the other Mary were there. They were sitting in front of the grave.

27:47 "Eli" may have sounded like "Elijah" in his language.
27:51 Jesus, our High Priest, had entered the most holy place on our behalf. (See Hebrews 9:11,12.)
27:52-53 literally, the holy city

Sealed Tight

62 That day was called Preparation Day.* The next day,* the most important priests and the Pharisees had a meeting with Pilate. **63** They said, "Sir, we remember what that liar said while he was still alive: 'After three days I will rise from death.' **64** So, give an order to make the grave secure until the third day. Otherwise, his followers might come, steal him, and tell the people: 'Jesus came back to life!' Then this last lie will be even worse than the first lie."

65 Pilate said to them, "You have a guard. Go and make it as secure as you know how." **66** So they went and protected the grave. They put a seal on the stone and they stationed a guard.

Chapter 28

The Empty Tomb

1 After the Sabbath day, when Sunday* morning was dawning, Mary (the one from Magdala) and the other Mary were on their way to look at the grave. **2** Suddenly, there was a great earthquake. An angel of the Lord came down from heaven. He went to the large stone and rolled it away. Then the angel sat on top of it. **3** His appearance was *shining* like lightning. His clothes were as white as snow. **4** The men who were guarding the tomb acted as if they were dead men; they trembled with fear.

5 The angel said to the women, "Don't be afraid. I know you are looking for Jesus who was nailed to the cross. **6** He is not here! He was raised from death, just as he said. Come, look at the place where he lay. **7** Go quickly and tell his followers: 'Jesus has been raised from death! Listen, he will go ahead of you to the land of Galilee. You will see him there.' Remember, I told you."

8 The women left the tomb quickly. They were afraid, yet very happy. They ran to tell Jesus' followers. **9** Suddenly, Jesus met them. He said, "Greetings!" They went to him, held onto his feet, and worshiped him. **10** Then Jesus said to them, "Don't be afraid. Go tell my brothers that they must leave for Galilee. They will see me there."

The Soldiers Tell a Lie

11 While the women were going, some of the guards went into Jerusalem. They told the most important priests everything which had happened. **12** The priests had a meeting with the Jewish elders. They decided to give the soldiers some money *to lie.* **13** They said to the soldiers, "Say this: 'While we were sleeping, the followers of Jesus came at night and stole his body.' **14** If the governor hears about this, we will make him believe **us**. We will fix it; don't worry." **15** So, the soldiers took the money and did as they were told. This rumor has spread among Jewish people until this very day.

The "Great Commission"

16 The eleven followers went to a mountain in Galilee where Jesus had told them to meet him. **17** When they saw him, they worshiped him, but some had doubts. **18** Jesus came to them and said, "All authority in heaven and on earth has been

---

27:62   Friday
27:62   The Jews considered sundown to be the beginning of the day.
28:1   literally, the first day of the week

given to me. **19** Therefore, after you've gone out, make followers *for me* from all nations.* Immerse them by the authority of the Father, the Son, and the Holy Spirit. **20** Teach them to obey everything I commanded you. Remember, I will always be with you even until the end of time!"

28:19   every cultural group

MARK

Chapter 1

Prepare for the Chase

1 This is how the Good News about Jesus Christ,* God's Son,* began: **2** It was like what Isaiah the prophet wrote:

"Listen! I am sending My messenger to go ahead of you.
He will prepare the way for you."   *Malachi 3:1*

3 "There is a voice crying out in the desert:
'Prepare the Lord's road. Make His paths straight.' "   *Isaiah 40:3*

John the (God Chaser) Baptist

4 In the desert, John was immersing people. He was preaching *this message*: "Change your hearts and be immersed for the forgiveness of sins!" **5** Everyone in Jerusalem and from the land of Judea was going out to John. They were admitting that they had sinned. Then he was immersing them in the Jordan River.   **6** John always wore clothes made of camel hair. He had a leather belt around his waist. He ate grasshoppers and wild honey.   **7-8** John preached, "I immersed you in water, but there is one coming later who is more important than I am. I'm not worthy to bend down to untie his shoelace. **He** will immerse you in the Holy Spirit."

John Immerses Jesus

9 At that time, Jesus came from the town of Nazareth in Galilee. John immersed him in the Jordan River.   **10** Suddenly, as Jesus was coming up from the water, he saw the sky separate. The Spirit was like a dove coming down to Jesus.   **11** A Voice came from heaven, saying, "This is My Son, and I love him. I am very pleased with him!"

The Devil Tries to Stop the Chase

12 Immediately, the Spirit made Jesus go into the desert.   **13** Satan was testing Jesus for 40 days in the desert. Jesus was with the wild animals, but the angels were helping him.

Very Good News

14 After John was arrested, Jesus went to the land of Galilee. He was proclaiming the Good News about God: **15** "The time is ripe. The kingdom of God is very near! Change your hearts and believe in the Good News!"

God Chasers: Peter, Andrew, James, and John

16 While Jesus was walking beside Lake Galilee, he saw Simon and Andrew, his brother. They were fishermen. They were throwing their nets into the lake.   **17** Jesus said to them, "Follow me and I will make you fishermen—of **people**!"   **18** Immediately, they left their nets and followed him.

19 Jesus went a little farther and saw James and his brother, John. They were in a boat preparing their nets. They were sons of Zebedee.   **20** Suddenly, Jesus invited

---

1:1   or, the Messiah
1:1   Some ancient copies do not have "God's Son."

them, too. They left their father, Zebedee, in the boat with the hired workers. And they followed Jesus.

With Authority

21 They went into the town of Capernaum. On the Sabbath day, when Jesus went into the synagogue, he began to teach the people right away. **22** They were amazed at what he taught. Jesus was teaching them as one with authority—not as the teachers of the law.

23 There was a man in their synagogue with an evil spirit. Suddenly, he shouted, **24** "Jesus of Nazareth! What do you want with us? Did you come here to destroy us? I know who you are—the Holy One of God!"

25 But Jesus stopped the evil spirit. Jesus said, "Stop talking and come out of the man!" **26** The evil spirit jerked the man around. He shouted loudly and came out of the man.

27 The people were shocked. They started asking one another, "What is this? A new teaching? With authority Jesus commands evil spirits, and they obey him." **28** And so, the news about Jesus went out immediately to the whole area around the land of Galilee.

Jesus Heals a Woman

29 After Jesus left the synagogue, he went immediately into Simon and Andrew's house with James and John. **30** Simon's mother-in-law was very sick with a fever. They soon talked to Jesus about her. **31** He went to her, took her hand, and raised her up. The fever left her and she began to serve them.

32 When it was late, after the sun had gone down, they brought to Jesus all the sick people and people with demons. **33** The whole town was gathered at the door. **34** Jesus healed the many people who had many types of diseases. He also threw out many demons. He would not allow the demons to talk, because the demons knew who he was.

The Way of Prayer

35 It was very early the next morning. Jesus got up and went out to a place where people did not live. There he was praying *to God*. **36** Simon and the men with him searched for Jesus. **37** They found him and said to him, "Everyone is looking for you."

38 Jesus said to them, "We must go to other villages near here. I must preach there, too. This is why I came."

39 Jesus went everywhere in the land of Galilee, preaching in their synagogues and throwing out demons.

Jesus Heals a Sick Man

40 A man with leprosy* came to Jesus. He bowed down and begged Jesus, "You can heal me, if you want to."

41 He felt sorry for him. So, he reached out and touched the man. Jesus said to the man, "I do want to heal you—be healed!" **42** Immediately the leprosy left him; he was healed. **43** Jesus made him go away immediately. He gave him a strong warning, **44** "Don't tell anyone about what happened, but go show yourself to the priest. Then

---

1:40   a very bad skin disease which destroys the flesh

give a gift to God, because you have been healed. This is what the law of Moses commands. This will prove to the priests *that you are healed*."

45 But the man went out and began to tell all about it. He spread the news so far that Jesus was no longer able to go into a town openly. Instead, Jesus stayed out in places where people did not live. From everywhere the people were coming to him.

Chapter 2

Jesus Heals a Crippled Man

1 A few days later, Jesus went back to the town of Capernaum. The people heard this: "He's home!" **2** So many people gathered there that there was no room—not even at the door. Jesus was giving them a lesson. **3** There was a man who was paralyzed. Four men came there carrying him. **4** But, because of the crowd, they were not able to get to Jesus. So, they went up on the roof of the house where Jesus was. They dug a hole and lowered the paralyzed man through the hole, lying on his bed. **5** Jesus saw that these men believed. He said to the paralyzed man, "Friend, your sins are forgiven."

6 Some of the teachers of the law were sitting there. In their hearts they were thinking, **7** "How can this man talk like this? He is saying an evil thing. Only **God** can forgive sins!"

8 Immediately Jesus knew in his spirit that they were thinking like this to themselves. Jesus said to them, "Why are you thinking these things in your heart? **9** Which is easier: to say, 'Your sins are forgiven,' or to say, 'Stand up, pick up your bed and walk?' **10** *I* will prove to you that I* have the right to forgive sins on earth." So, Jesus said to the paralyzed man, **11** "I tell you, stand up! Take your bed and go home!"

12 Immediately the man stood up, picked up his bed, and left in front of all of them. All the people were completely amazed. They began to praise God. They said, "We have never seen such things!"

Hey, Levi—Chase Me!

13 Jesus went back again to Lake *Galilee*. All the people were coming to him and he was teaching them. **14** As Jesus was walking along, he saw Levi, *the son* of Alphaeus, sitting at the tax office. Jesus said to him, "Follow me." Then Levi got up and followed him.

15 While Jesus was having dinner at Levi's house, many tax collectors and sinful people joined Jesus and his followers for dinner. Many of them were beginning to follow Jesus, too. **16** Some of the Pharisees' teachers of the law saw that Jesus was eating with sinful people and tax collectors. These teachers continued to ask Jesus' followers, "Why does Jesus eat with tax collectors and sinful people?"

17 When Jesus heard about this, he said to them, "Healthy people don't need a doctor, but sick people do. I didn't come to invite 'good' people, but sinners!"

Fasting

18 The followers of John and the Pharisees were fasting.* Some people came and said to Jesus, "Why do John's followers and the followers of the Pharisees fast, but your followers do not fast?"

2:10   literally, the Son of Man
2:18   going without food for a period of time, usually for spiritual reasons

19 Jesus said to them, "Would it be right for the friends of the groom to be sad while the groom is still with them? As long as they have the groom with them, they cannot fast. **20** But the time will come when the groom will be taken away from them. Then his friends will fast.

21 "No one sews a piece of cloth which has never been washed onto an old robe. If he does, it will *shrink and* tear away from the robe. Then the hole will become worse. **22** No one puts new wine into old wine bags. If they do, the old wine bags will break open. The wine will spill out and the wine bags will be ruined. Instead, people put new wine into new wine bags."*

Jesus Is Lord Over the Sabbath Day

23 Once, on a Sabbath day, Jesus was traveling through a field of grain. His followers began to make a path by picking the grain *to eat.*

24 The Pharisees said to Jesus, "Look! Why are they doing what is not right on the Sabbath?"

25 Jesus said to them, "Do you remember reading about what David did when he needed something? He and his men were hungry. **26** During the time when Abiathar was high priest, David went into the house of God. He took the holy loaves of bread and ate them. The law *of Moses* says only priests could eat them, but David gave some to his men." **27** Jesus was saying this to the Pharisees, "The Sabbath was made for man. Man was not made for the Sabbath! **28** I* am Lord, even of the Sabbath day."

Chapter 3

Jesus Heals a Man on the Sabbath Day

1 Again Jesus went into a synagogue. A man with a crippled hand was there. **2** *Some Jewish leaders* were waiting to see if Jesus would heal the man on the Sabbath day. They wanted *to see Jesus do something wrong*, so that they could accuse him. **3** Jesus said to the man with the crippled hand, "Stand in the middle." **4** Then Jesus said *to the Jewish leaders*, "I ask you, which is right on the Sabbath day, to do good or to do evil? Is it right to save a life or to destroy one?" But they wouldn't answer. **5** Jesus looked around at all of them. He was angry, but he was sad, too, because their hearts were hard. He said to the man, "Stretch out your hand!" The man stretched it out. His hand was restored.

6 Immediately, the Pharisees and the followers of Herod *Antipas** left. They began to make a plot to kill Jesus.

People Came From Everywhere

7 Jesus and his followers went away to Lake *Galilee.* A large group followed him from the land of Galilee, from the land of Judea, **8** from Jerusalem, from the land of Idumea, from the area across the Jordan River, and from the cities of Tyre and Sidon. They heard about the things Jesus was doing. So, they came to him.

2:22　　In those days, the wine bottles were made of animal skins. The grape juice would ferment and stretch the wine bags. If new wine were put into an old wine bag (one which was already stretched to the limit), the fermentation process would break it open. A new wine bag still had room to stretch.

2:28　　Jesus

3:6　　literally, the Herodians. They were a Jewish political group who favored Roman rule.

9 To keep the crowd from pushing up against Jesus, he told his followers to get a boat ready for him.   10 The people were trying to get as close to Jesus as they could, because he had healed many people. People with diseases wanted to touch him. 11 When people with evil spirits saw Jesus, they fell down in front of him and shouted, "You are the Son of God!"   12 But Jesus warned them not to tell who he was.

Twelve God Chasers Line Up

13 Jesus went up on a mountain. He called for the ones he wanted. They came to him.   14 He appointed twelve and named them "apostles."* He wanted them to be with him and to send them out to proclaim.   15 They would have authority to throw out demons.   16 These are the twelve men whom Jesus chose:
　　Simon (Jesus called him Peter.);
17 James, *the son* of Zebedee;
　　John, James' brother (Jesus gave them the name Boanerges; this means "sons of thunder.");
18 Andrew;
　　Philip;
　　Bartholomew;
　　Matthew;
　　Thomas;
　　James (*the son* of Alphaeus);
　　Thaddaeus;
　　Simon the Revolutionary;*
19 and Judas Iscariot (the one who turned against Jesus).

The Power of God

20 Jesus came home. Again, such a crowd came together that they didn't even have time to eat.   21 When Jesus' family heard this, they went out to get Jesus. They were saying, "He's crazy!"
22 The teachers of the law who came down from Jerusalem were saying, "Jesus has Beelzebul.* Jesus uses the prince of demons to throw out demons!"
23 Jesus called them and began to speak to them with stories: "How could Satan throw out Satan?   24 If a kingdom is divided and fights against itself, that kingdom will not be able to stand.   25 If a family is divided and fights against itself, that family will not be able to stand.   26 And, if Satan is fighting against himself then he is divided. How can he last? He has lost.
27 "No one can go into a strong man's house to rob him, unless he ties up the strong man first. Then he will rob his house.
28 "I am telling you the truth: Every sin and terrible thing which people say may be forgiven.   29 But the person who says evil things against the Holy Spirit will never receive forgiveness—not ever. Instead, he is guilty of eternal sin!"   30 *Jesus said this,* because they were saying, "Jesus has an evil spirit!"

The True Family of Jesus

31 Jesus' mother and his brothers came. They were standing outside. They sent someone inside to Jesus to call him.   32 A crowd was sitting around Jesus. They

---

3:14　special messenger, one sent
3:18　literally, Zealot. This was a term used for Jews who favored a revolt against Rome.
3:22　literally, lord of the flies. This was a name which the Jews gave to the Devil.

57

said to him, "Listen, your mother and your brothers are outside; they want *to talk to* you."

33 Jesus answered them, "Who is my mother? Who are my brothers?" 34 Jesus looked around at the people who were surrounding him. He said, "Look, my mother and my brothers! 35 The person who does what God wants is my brother, my sister, or my mother."

Chapter 4

Four Kinds of Ground

1 Again, Jesus began to teach beside Lake *Galilee*. A very large crowd gathered around him. So, Jesus got into a boat on the lake and sat down. The whole crowd was on the shore, at the edge of the lake. 2 Jesus was teaching them with many stories. While he was teaching, he said, 3 "Listen! A farmer went out to plant his seed. 4 While he was planting, some seeds fell along the road. The wild birds came and ate them up. 5 Some seeds fell on rocks where there was not much soil. The seeds grew up fast there, because the ground was not deep. 6 But when the sun came up, the little plants were burned, because their roots dried up. 7 Some more seeds fell among thorny weeds, but the thorny weeds came up and killed them off *later*. They did not produce fruit. 8 And some seeds fell on good soil. They came up, grew, and produced a crop—some 30 times more, some 60 times more, and some 100 times more." 9 Jesus said, "The person who has ears to hear with should use them!"

God's Got a Secret

10 When Jesus was alone, the twelve *apostles* and some other people around Jesus asked him about *the meaning of* the stories. 11 Jesus said, "You have been chosen to learn the secrets of the kingdom of God. All these secrets are given to outsiders in stories, 12 so that:
'They will certainly see, but they won't understand;
and they will certainly hear, but they won't understand.
Otherwise, they might turn and be forgiven!' "   *Isaiah 6:9-10*
13 Jesus said to them, "Since you don't understand this story, how can you understand any of the stories? 14 The farmer was planting *God's* message. 15 The message was planted like seeds along the road. When those people hear it, Satan comes quickly and takes away the message which was planted in them. 16 Some people are like the seeds which were planted on rocks. When they hear the message, they accept it immediately with gladness. 17 However, they don't have deep roots in themselves; they don't last long. When trouble comes or persecution comes because of the message, they soon get discouraged. 18 Those which were planted among the thorny weeds are the people who heard the message, 19 but the worries of this age, deceiving riches, and desires for other things come in and choke the message. It never produces fruit. 20 Those seeds which were planted on good soil are the ones who listen to the message and accept it. They produce fruit—some of it is 30 times more, some is 60 times more, and some 100 times more."

Listening

21 Jesus said to them, "Do you bring a lamp, so that you can put it under a basket or under the bed? It is supposed to go on top of a lamp table. 22 Everything that is

hidden will become clear. Every secret thing will be made known.   **23** If a person has ears to hear with, he should use them!"

24 Jesus said to them, "Be careful what you hear. You will be measured by the measure you use to measure others—even more carefully!   **25** Because the person who has something will get more. But this will happen to the person who has *almost* nothing: Even what *he thinks* he has will be taken away from him."

The Power in a Seed

26 Jesus said, "The kingdom of God is like this: A man puts seed in the ground. **27** The seed comes up and grows while he sleeps at night and when he gets up every day. The man doesn't know how this happens.   **28** The ground produces by itself. The grass comes first, then the head, then the ripe wheat in the head.   **29** When the crop is ready, the man soon cuts it with a sickle; harvest time has come."

Big Things in Small Packages

30 Jesus said, "What is the kingdom of God like? What can I compare it with? **31** It is like the seed of the mustard plant which someone puts in the ground. It is one of the smallest seeds on earth.   **32** But after it is planted and comes up, it is one of the largest garden plants. It produces great branches. Even wild birds build nests in it and are protected from the sun."

33 With many stories like these Jesus was telling them the message—but only as much as they were able to understand.   **34** Jesus always spoke to them with a story. But, when he was alone with his followers, he would explain everything.

The Power of Jesus

35 When it was evening of that same day, Jesus said to them, "Let us go across *Lake Galilee*."   **36** Jesus was in the boat. They took him and left the crowd. Other boats went with him.   **37** *Suddenly*, there was a storm—a strong wind. The waves were getting into the boat; it was about to be filled with water.   **38** But Jesus was in the back of the boat, asleep on a pillow. They woke him up, saying, "Teacher, we are going to die; don't you care?"

39 Jesus woke up and gave an order to the wind and *the waves of* the lake, "Be still! Stop!" The wind stopped blowing; it was very calm.   **40** Jesus said to them, "Why were you so afraid? Do you not yet have faith?"

41 They were very frightened. They continued to say to one another, "What kind of a man is this? Even the wind and the lake obey him!"

Chapter 5

The Man With Demons Inside Him

1 Jesus and his followers came to the other side of the lake, the land where the Gerasene* people lived.   **2** When Jesus was getting out of the boat, immediately a man with an evil spirit met him. This man came from the graveyard.   **3** His home was among the tombs. No one was able to bind him with chains anymore.   **4** His hands and feet had been bound many times, but he would always break the chains apart and smash the shackles. No one was strong enough to tame him.   **5** Day and night, he was always in the hills or among the tombs shouting and cutting himself with *sharp* stones.

5:1   Some ancient copies have "Gadarenes." Others have "Gergesenes."

6 When this man saw Jesus far away, he ran to Jesus and bowed down. **7-8** While Jesus was saying this to him, "Evil spirit, come out of this man!" the man shouted loudly, "What do you want with me, Jesus, Son of the Most High God? In the name of God, I beg you, don't punish me!"

9 Jesus asked him, "What is your name?"

He said to Jesus, "My name is Legion,* because we are many." **10** The man started to beg Jesus for many things. He wanted Jesus not to send them out of the country. **11** On that hill there was a large herd of pigs feeding. **12** They begged Jesus, "Send us into the pigs; we could go into them!" **13** Jesus allowed them. So, the evil spirits came out *of the man* and went into the pigs. (There were about 2,000 pigs.) The herd ran down the cliff and into the lake. They drowned.

14 Some men had been taking care of the pigs. They ran away. They told the story in the fields and in the town. The people came to see what had happened. **15** They came to Jesus and saw the man sitting there. The man had clothes on and he was in his right mind. This man did not have a legion* *of evil spirits* anymore. The people were afraid. **16** There were men who had seen what Jesus did to the man with demons. They told all about the pigs. **17** The people began to beg Jesus to leave their area.

18 As Jesus was getting into the boat, the man who no longer had demons continued to beg Jesus; he wanted to stay with Jesus. **19** But Jesus would not allow him to do this. Instead, Jesus said to him, "Go home to your family. Tell them what the Lord has done for you. He has given you mercy." **20** So, the man went back and began to proclaim what Jesus had done for him in the area of Ten Towns.* Everyone was amazed.

The Daughter of Jairus

21 After Jesus went back across *Lake Galilee* in the boat to the other side, a large crowd gathered together near him. It was beside the lake. **22** A man named Jairus came, too. He was one of the rulers of the synagogue. When Jairus saw Jesus, he fell down at Jesus' feet, **23** asking for many things. He said, "My little girl is dying. Please come and put your hand on her, so that she will be all right and live!" **24** Jesus left with Jairus. A large crowd was following Jesus. They were bumping up against him.

25 There was a woman who had a sore which had been bleeding for twelve years. **26** She had suffered much. Many doctors *had tried to help her*. She had spent all the money she had, but she was not getting any better—only worse. **27** She had heard things about Jesus. So, she went behind Jesus in the crowd and touched his robe. **28** She was thinking this: "If I can touch his clothes, I will be made well!" **29** Immediately, the source of her bleeding was dried up. In her body she felt that she had been healed of the disease. **30** Immediately Jesus knew within himself that power had left him. He turned to the crowd and said, "Who touched my clothes?"

31 Jesus' followers said to him, "You see the crowd. The people are pressing up against you. Yet you say, 'Who touched me?' " **32** But Jesus continued to look around to see who had done this. **33** The woman was afraid; she was trembling. She knew what had happened to her. She came and bowed down to Jesus. Then she told him the whole truth.

5:9   A legion was about 5,000 men in the Roman army.
5:15   A legion was about 5,000 men in the Roman army.
5:20   literally, Decapolis, a confederation of cities. Originally, there were ten of them.

34 Jesus said to her, "Dear woman, you are made well, because you believed. Go in peace. Be healed from your disease!"

35 While Jesus was still speaking, some people came from *the house of* the synagogue ruler. They said, "Your daughter has died! Why bother the Teacher anymore?"

36 When Jesus overheard this message, he said to the ruler of the synagogue, "Don't be afraid! Just believe!"

37 Jesus did not allow anyone to go with him—only Peter, James, and John. (James and John were brothers.) **38** They went into the synagogue ruler's house. Jesus saw that there was confusion. Many people were crying loudly and showing great sadness. **39** Jesus went and said to them, "Why are you making so much noise and crying? The child is not dead; she is only sleeping." **40** They laughed at Jesus. After he made them all leave, Jesus took the child's father and mother along and those who were with Jesus. He went into *the room* where the child was. **41** Jesus held the child's hand and said to her, "Talitha, koum!" (This means "Little girl, I tell you, get up!") **42** Immediately, the little girl stood up and began walking around. (She was twelve years old.) They were shocked. **43** Jesus gave them many strong warnings: "Don't make this known to anyone!" Then Jesus told them to give her something to eat.

Chapter 6

Jesus' Home Town

1 Jesus left there and came to his home town. His followers went along behind him. **2** When the Sabbath day came, Jesus began to teach in the synagogue. Many people were listening; they were amazed. They said, "Where did Jesus get all these things? Who gave him this wisdom? How do such miracles happen by his hands? **3** He is the one who works with wood. He is the son of Mary. His brothers are: James, Joses, Judas, and Simon. His sisters are here with us, too." They were ashamed of Jesus.

4 Jesus said this to them: "A prophet is not accepted in his own home town, or among his relatives, or in his own family." **5** Jesus was not able to perform a miracle there. He only put his hands on a few sick people and made them well. **6** He was amazed that they did not believe.

Twelve God Chasers Sent

Jesus was going around all the villages, teaching people. **7** He called for his twelve *followers*. He began to send them out in pairs, giving them authority over evil spirits. **8** Jesus ordered them: "When you travel, don't carry anything else along—no food, no bag, no money in your belt, and only one walking stick. **9** Wear a pair of shoes, but don't wear an extra shirt." **10** Jesus continued to say to them, "When you go into a house, stay there until *it is time* to leave. **11** When people in one place don't welcome you, or they won't listen to you, leave there and shake off the dust from under your feet.* This will be a warning to them." **12** So, Jesus' followers went out. They preached that people must change their hearts. **13** They were rubbing olive oil* on many sick people and healing them. They were throwing out many demons.

6:11   A Jewish custom showing rejection of non-Jews. It is used here toward those rejecting the Good News.

6:13   for medicinal purposes. (See Luke 10:34.)

A God Chaser Is Martyred

14 King Herod *Antipas* heard about Jesus. Jesus had become famous. People were saying, "John (the one who immersed people) has been raised from death! This is why miracles are working in him."

15 Other people were saying, "He is Elijah!" Some other people were saying, "He is a prophet, like one of the prophets *from long ago*."

16 When Herod heard this, he was thinking, "I cut off John's head; he must have been raised to life."

17 Herod had arrested John, tied him up, and put him in jail. He did this because of Herodias. Herod had married her, even though she was the wife of Philip, Herod's brother.* **18** John was always saying this to Herod: "It is not right for you to have your brother's wife!" **19** So, Herodias held a grudge against John. She wanted to kill him, but she was not able to, **20** because Herod was afraid of John. He knew that John was a good, holy man. So, he protected John. When Herod heard John *preach*, Herod was in doubt about many things, but Herod liked to listen to John. **21** One day *her* opportunity came. It was on Herod's birthday. He gave a dinner for his important government officials, army commanders, and leaders in the land of Galilee. **22** Herodias' daughter came in and danced. She pleased Herod and his guests. The king said to the girl, "Ask for whatever you want, and I will give it to you." **23** He vowed to her, "I will give you whatever you ask for—even half of my kingdom!" **24** She left and asked her mother, "What should I ask for?"

Herodias said, "The head of John (the one who immersed people)!"

25 Immediately the girl hurried back to the king. She demanded, "I want you to give me the head of John on a plate—**now!**"

26 The king was very sad, but because of the vow and the guests, Herod didn't want to refuse her. **27** Immediately, the king sent a guard away with orders to bring John's head. He left. He cut off John's head in the prison. **28** He brought the head on a plate and gave it to the girl. The girl gave it to her mother.

29 When John's followers heard about this, they came and carried away John's body. They put it in a tomb.

Jesus Does Lunch With a Bunch (5,000+ People)

30 The apostles came together to Jesus. They told him everything they had done and taught. **31** There were so many people coming and going that they didn't even have a chance to eat. So, Jesus said to them, "Let us go away to a quiet place to be alone. We can relax a little."

32 So, they left in a boat to be alone in a place where there were no people, **33** but many people saw them leaving and recognized them. From all the towns together they ran ahead on land to where Jesus and his followers were going. **34** When Jesus got out *of the boat*, he saw a large crowd; he felt sorry for them because they were like sheep that didn't have a shepherd. So, he began to teach them many things.

35 Since it was already getting late, Jesus' followers came to him and said, "This is a remote place and it is already very late. **36** Tell the people to go away. They need to buy something to eat for themselves in the field and villages around here."

6:17 This man was not Herod Antipas' brother called Philip, "the tetrarch" (Luke 3:1). He was a different brother with the same name.

37 Jesus answered them, " **You** give them something to eat!"
They said to him, "Should we leave and buy 200 silver coins' worth of food and give them something to eat?"
38 Jesus said to them, "How much food do you have? Go see!" They found out that they had five loaves of bread and two fish.
39 Jesus ordered the people to sit down on the green grass in groups. 40 They sat down in rows, groups of 50 or 100. 41 Jesus took the five loaves of bread and two fish. He looked up to heaven and thanked God for the food and divided the loaves of bread. Then he began giving them to his followers, so that they could distribute them to all the people. Jesus also divided the two fish for everyone. 42 Everyone ate and was satisfied. 43 They gathered up all the pieces of bread which were left over. They filled twelve large baskets with this bread and the fish. 44 (There were 5,000 men who were eating.)

Walking on Water

45 Immediately Jesus made his followers get into the boat and go on ahead to the other side *of Lake Galilee* to the town of Bethsaida. Jesus was sending the crowd away. 46 After Jesus sent the people away, he went to a mountain to pray. 47 That night the boat was in the middle of the lake. Jesus was alone on land. 48 He saw that his followers were rowing hard, because the wind was against them. It was about three o'clock in the morning. Jesus came to them; he was walking **on** the lake. He wanted to pass them by, 49 but they saw him walking on the lake. They thought that Jesus was a ghost. They cried out; 50 they all saw him. They were scared, but Jesus soon talked with them. He said, "Be strong! It is I. Don't be afraid." 51 Jesus climbed into the boat with them. The wind stopped. They were completely amazed, 52 because they did not understand *the miracle of* the loaves of bread. Their heart was hard.

Jesus Heals Some Sick People

53 After they crossed over, they came to the shore at Gennesaret. They tied up their boat. 54 After they left the boat, people recognized Jesus immediately. 55 People began running all over that area. Wherever they heard that Jesus was they brought sick people on small beds. 56 Jesus went into villages, towns, fields, and marketplaces. He always put his hands on the sick people. They were begging him to let them touch the tassel* of his robe. The people who touched him were made well.

Chapter 7

God's Command or Man's Tradition?

1 Some teachers of the law and some Pharisees came from Jerusalem to get together with Jesus. 2 They saw that some of Jesus' followers were eating with unholy (that is, unwashed) hands. 3 (The Pharisees and all the Jewish people won't eat unless they wash their hands with a ceremony. They carefully obey the old rules of the elders. 4 They won't eat anything from the marketplace, unless they wash it. They have received many other rules about washing cups, pots, and copper bowls which they must obey.) 5 The Pharisees and the teachers of the law asked Jesus, "Why are your followers breaking the old rules of the elders? They are eating bread with unholy hands!"

6:56   Tassels were worn on four corners of a robe to remind the people of the law.

63

6 Jesus said to them, "How right Isaiah was when he prophesied about you hypocrites.* As it is written:

'These people honor Me with their lips,
>   but their heart is far away from Me.
7 It does no good for them to worship Me.
>   They teach rules made by men, *not God* !'   *Isaiah 29:13*

8 You have forgotten about God's command and you are obeying the old rules of man."   **9** Jesus continued to speak to them, "You have a clever way of rejecting God's command, so that you may keep your traditions.   **10** Moses said,

'You must love and obey your father and mother.'   *Exodus 20:12*
and,
'The person who curses his father or mother must die.'   *Exodus 21:17*

11 But **you** say that if anyone says to his father or mother, 'It is Corban' (This means: 'Whatever you might have gotten from me is a gift *to God*.')   **12** then you no longer allow him to do anything for his father or mother.   **13** You are taking away the authority of God's teaching by using the traditions you have received. And you are doing many other things like this."

God Chasers: Be Good!

14 Again, Jesus called for the crowd. He said to them, "Listen and understand! **15** What goes into the mouth from outside is not able to make a person unholy. No, the things which come out of the mouth make a person unholy."   **16** *

17 Jesus went into a house away from the crowd. His followers began asking him about the story.

18 Jesus said to them, "Do you still not understand? You know that everything which goes into a person from the outside is not able to make him unholy.   **19** It does not go into his heart. No, it enters his stomach. Then it comes out as waste. (*Here Jesus was saying that* all foods are clean.)   **20** But, what comes out of *the mouth of* a person makes him unholy.   **21** These things come from the inside of man's heart:
>   evil thoughts,
>   sexual sin,
>   stealing,
>   murder,
22   adultery,
>   greed, all kinds of evil things,
>   treachery,
>   sensuality,
>   jealousy,
>   slander,
>   bragging,
>   foolishness.
23 All these evil things come from the inside; they make a person unholy."

7:6   those who act as if they are righteous when they are not
7:16   Many manuscripts include verse 16: "If any person has ears to hear with, let him use them." (See Mark 4:9, 23.)

A Determined God Chaser

24 Jesus got up from there and went away to the area near the city of Tyre. He went into a house. (Jesus didn't want anyone to know where he was, but it was not possible for him to hide.) **25** Soon a woman heard about Jesus. Her daughter had an evil spirit. The woman came and bowed down at Jesus' feet. **26** She was not a Jew. She was born in the land of Phoenicia, an area of Syria. She kept begging Jesus to throw the demon out of her daughter.

27 Jesus said to her, "Let the children eat first. It is not good to take the children's bread and throw it to the puppies."

28 But the woman answered Jesus, "Yes, Lord, but even the puppies under the table eat the crumbs from the children!"

29 Jesus said to her, "Go! The demon has come out of your daughter—because of your answer!" **30** The woman went back home and found her child lying on a bed. And the demon was gone.

A Deaf Man

31 Jesus left the area near Tyre and went through the city of Sidon to Lake Galilee and the area of Ten Towns.* **32** Some people brought a man to Jesus. They begged Jesus to put his hand on the man *to heal him.* The man was deaf. It was very hard for him to talk. **33** Jesus took the man along with him to be alone, away from the crowd. Then Jesus put his fingers into the man's ears, made some spit, and touched the man's tongue. **34** Looking up to heaven, Jesus groaned. He said to the man, "Ephphatha!" (This means "Be opened!") **35** Then the man could hear clearly and the bond on his speech was released. He began to talk plainly. **36** Jesus warned them not to tell anyone about this. But the more he warned them, the more they proclaimed it! **37** The people were shocked. They said, "He has done everything well. He causes deaf people to hear and people who could not speak to speak!"

Chapter 8

Jesus Does Lunch With More Than 4,000 People

1 During that time, there was another large crowd. They didn't have anything to eat. Jesus called his followers and said to them, **2** "I feel sorry for the people. They have stayed with me for three days without eating anything. **3** I don't want to send them away hungry; they might faint on the road. Some of them have come from a long way off."

4 Jesus' followers asked him, "Where could we get enough to satisfy these people in this far away place?"

5 Jesus asked them, "How many loaves of bread do you have?"

They answered, "Seven."

6 Jesus ordered the crowd to sit down on the ground. He took the seven loaves of bread and thanked God. He divided it and began giving it to his followers, so that they could distribute it. The followers did so. **7** They had a few fish, too. Jesus blessed the fish and told the followers to distribute them. **8** The people ate and were satisfied. They gathered up all the pieces of food which were left over. There were seven small

---

7:31   literally, Decapolis, a confederation of cities. Originally, there were ten of them.

baskets *full.* **9** (There were about 4,000 men.) Then Jesus sent them away. **10** Immediately Jesus got into a boat with his followers. He went to the Dalmanutha area.

Living Proof

11 The Pharisees came out and began to argue with Jesus. They were trying to make Jesus prove that he came from God. **12** Jesus groaned in his spirit. He said, "Why do the people living today ask for a miracle? I am telling you the truth; no proof like that will be given to them!" **13** Then Jesus left them. He got into *the boat* and went across *Lake Galilee.*

Are You Dense?

14 Jesus' followers forgot to bring along loaves of bread with them in the boat. They had only one loaf of bread. **15** Jesus warned them, "Be careful! Watch out for the yeast* of the Pharisees and the yeast of the followers of Herod *Antipas.*" **16** They began talking to one another, saying, "*Jesus said this* because we don't have any loaves of bread."

17 Jesus knew *what was on their mind.* He said, "Why are you talking about having no bread? Don't you know yet? Do you still not understand? Do you have hard hearts? **18** Do you have eyes, but do not see clearly? Do you have ears, but do not understand? Surely you remember **19** when I divided the five loaves of bread for the 5,000 men. How many large baskets full of leftovers did you pick up?"

Jesus' followers answered, "Twelve."

20 Jesus said, "When I divided the seven loaves of bread for the 4,000 men, how many small baskets full of leftovers did you pick up?"

They answered, "Seven."

21 Jesus said to them, "Do you still not understand?"

Jesus Heals a Blind Man

22 Jesus and his followers came into Bethsaida. The people were carrying a blind man to Jesus. They begged Jesus to touch him. **23** He held the blind man's hand and led him outside the village. After Jesus spit into the man's eyes, he put his hands on him. Jesus asked him, "Do you see anything?"

24 The man looked up and said, "I see people moving around; they look like trees to me!" **25** Jesus put his hands on the man's eyes again. Then the man could see; his sight came back. He could see everything clearly. **26** Jesus sent the man home with these words, "Don't go into the village!"

Just in Case You Don't Get It

27 Then Jesus and his followers went away to the villages of Caesarea Philippi. Along the road, Jesus asked his followers this question: "Who do people say I am?"

28 They answered, "*Some people say* John (the one who immersed people). Other people say you are Elijah, and others say you are one of the prophets."

29 But Jesus continued to ask them, "But who do **you** say I am?"

Peter answered Jesus, "You are the Messiah!" **30** Jesus warned them not to tell anyone about him.

8:15   Here "yeast" means influence.

Jesus Must Die

31 Jesus began to teach them, "I* must suffer many things. I will be rejected by the Jewish elders, the most important priests, and the teachers of the law. I will be killed, but after three days, I will be raised from death."   **32** Jesus was speaking this message to them very plainly.

But Peter came to Jesus and tried to correct him.   **33** Jesus turned around and looked at his followers. He warned Peter, "Get behind me, Satan! You are not thinking the way God thinks, but the way man thinks."

34 Jesus called the crowd together with his followers. He said to them, "If anyone wants to follow me, he must carry his cross and follow me. He must say no to himself. **35** The person who wants to save his life will lose it, but every person who gives his life for me and for the Good News will save it.   **36** What good is it if a person gains the whole world, but wrecks his own soul?   **37** What can a person use to trade for his soul? **38** If a person in this unfaithful, sinful generation is ashamed of me and my words, I* will be ashamed of him when I come with the holy angels in the glory of my Father."

Chapter 9
1 Jesus said to them, "I am telling you the truth: There are some people standing here who will not die, until they have seen God's kingdom come with power."

Jesus Keeps Company With Some Old Friends

2 After six days, Jesus took Peter, James, and John and brought them up to a tall mountain to be alone. Jesus' appearance began to change in front of them.   **3** His clothes became shining white—as white as white could be. (No one on earth could make them so white.)   **4** Moses and Elijah appeared to them. These two men were talking to Jesus.

5 Peter said to Jesus, "Rabbi, it is good that we are here. We will make three holy tents; one for you, one for Moses, and one for Elijah."   **6** (He didn't know what to say; they were afraid.)   **7** A cloud came all around them and a Voice came from the cloud: "This is My Son, and I love him. Listen to what **he** says!"*

8 Suddenly, they looked around. They no longer saw anyone except Jesus. He was the only one with them.

9 As they were going down the mountain, Jesus ordered them, "Don't tell anyone about what you saw until I* rise from death."

10 They obeyed and kept it to themselves. But they began to argue among themselves about what Jesus meant when he said, "...until I rise from death."

11 They began to ask Jesus, "Why do the teachers of the law say that Elijah must come before *the Messiah does*?"

12 Jesus answered, "Elijah does come first and he makes all things right. Then why is it written that the Son of Man* will suffer many things and be rejected?   **13** No, I am telling you, Elijah* does come first! They treated him the way they wanted to, as it was written about him."

8:31	literally, the Son of Man
8:38	literally, the Son of Man
9:7	Listen to Jesus, not Moses or Elijah.
9:9	literally, the Son of Man
9:12	Jesus
9:13	John (the one who immersed people)

Jesus Heals a Boy With an Evil Spirit

14 When they got *back* to the *other* followers, they saw a large crowd around them. The teachers of the law were arguing with them.   **15** As soon as the whole crowd saw Jesus, they were very surprised. They ran to him and greeted him.   **16** Jesus asked them, "Why are you arguing with them?"

17 One man in the crowd answered Jesus, "Teacher, I brought my son to you. He has a spirit that stops him from talking.   **18** It attacks him and throws him down on the ground. He foams at the mouth and grinds his teeth. His body becomes hard. I told your followers, so that they could throw out the spirit, but they were not strong enough."

19 Jesus said to them, "You people are a generation with no faith. How long must I be with you and put up with you? Bring your son here!"

20 They brought the boy to Jesus. When the *evil* spirit saw Jesus, the boy lost control of himself. He fell down on the ground and began rolling around, foaming at the mouth.   **21** Jesus asked the boy's father, "How long has he been like this?"

The father said, "Since he was a child.   **22** This spirit wants to kill him. It often throws him into fire or into water. Take pity on us! Help us, if you are able to!"

23 Jesus said to him, " 'If you are able'? All things are possible for the person who believes."

24 Immediately the boy's father cried out, "I believe! Help me when I don't believe enough!" He said this again and again.

25 When Jesus saw that a crowd was running together, he gave an order to the evil spirit, "O spirit that keeps this boy from talking and hearing, I command you—come out of him! Never go into him again!"   **26** The spirit screamed and again made the boy fall down and roll around on the ground. Then the spirit left. The boy looked as if he was dead. Many people said, "He's dead!"   **27** But Jesus took hold of his hand and raised him up. The boy was on his feet.

28 After Jesus went into a house, his followers began asking him questions when they were alone, "Why were **we** not able to throw out the spirit?"

29 Jesus answered them, "Praying is the only way that you can throw this kind out."

30 They left there and traveled through the land of Galilee. Jesus did not want anyone to know where they were,   **31** because he was teaching his followers. This is what he was telling them: "I* am being turned over to some men. They will kill me, but three days after my death, I will rise to life."   **32** They did not understand the meaning of this, but they were too afraid to ask him.

God Chasers: Take Care of the Little Ones

33 They came to the town of Capernaum. After they had gone into a house, Jesus began to ask them questions, "What were you arguing about along the road?"

34 They wouldn't answer him, because on the road, they were arguing with one another about who was the most important.   **35** Jesus sat down and called for the twelve apostles. He said to them, "If one of you wants to be number one, he should be in last place. He should serve everyone."   **36** Jesus took a small child and stood him in the middle of them. He put his arms around the child and said to them,   **37** "The person who welcomes one of the children like this one in my name welcomes **me**. And, when a person welcomes me, that person welcomes the One who sent me."

9:31   literally, the Son of Man

Someone Was Throwing Out Demons

38 John said to Jesus, "Teacher, we saw someone throwing out demons by using your name. He was not following us! We kept telling him to stop because he was not following us."

39 But Jesus said, "Don't stop him. There is no one who can perform a miracle in my name and then say something evil about me. **40** If someone is not against us, he is for us. **41** If anyone gives you a cup of water in my name because you belong to the Messiah, I am telling you the truth, that person will not lose his reward.

42 "If someone causes one of these little ones to sin who believe in me, it would be better for him to have a large rock hanging around his neck and to be thrown into the ocean. **43** If your hand makes you sin, cut it off! It would be better for you to go into *eternal* life injured than to go away with two hands into hell, where the fire cannot be put out. **44** * **45** If your foot makes you sin, cut it off! It would be better for you to go into *eternal* life crippled than to be thrown into hell having two feet. **46** * **47** If your eye makes you sin, throw it away! It would be better for you to go into the kingdom of God with only one eye than to be thrown into hell with two eyes. **48** Hell is where:

'Their maggots never die,
    and the fire never goes out.'   *Isaiah 66:24*
49 Every person will be salted with fire."

God Chasers: Be Salt

50 "Salt is a good thing, but if the salt loses its salty taste, *then it is no good*. You cannot make it salty again. Have salt* in yourselves; be at peace with one another."

Chapter 10

God Chasers: Be Pure

1 Jesus got up from there and went to the part of Judea which is on the other side of the Jordan River. Again, crowds traveled to him. Jesus was teaching them, as he always did.

2 Some Pharisees came to Jesus. They were testing him with this question: "Is it all right for a man to divorce his wife?"

3 Jesus answered them, "What did Moses command you?"

4 They said, "Moses allowed a man who was divorcing his wife to give her divorce papers."

5 Jesus said to them, "Moses wrote this command, because your hearts were hard. **6** But, in the beginning, when God created people,

'He made them male and female.'   *Genesis 1:27*
7 and,
'This is why a man will leave his father and mother.'
8 The husband and wife will become one flesh.'   *Genesis 2:24*
So, they are no longer two, but one flesh. **9** Man must not separate what God has joined together."

9:44   Some manuscripts include verse 44. It reads the same as verse 48.
9:46   Some manuscripts include verse 46. It reads the same as verse 48.
9:50   Salt was, and still is, used as a preservative. Salt was symbolic for preserving peace and for loyalty.
        Here it means to keep peace with one another.

10 When they were in the house again, Jesus' followers began to ask him about this. 11 Jesus said to them, "If a man divorces his wife and marries another woman, he is committing adultery against her. 12 If she divorces her husband *and* she marries another man, she is committing adultery."

Children Are God Chasers, Too

13 Then some people brought their small children to Jesus, so that he could touch them, but his followers told the people to stop doing that. 14 When Jesus saw this, it bothered him. He said to them, "Let the little children come to me. Don't stop them, because the kingdom of God belongs to people who are like these little children. 15 I am telling you the truth: You must accept God's kingdom as a little child accepts things, or you will never enter it!" 16 Jesus put his arms around the children. He put his hands on them and blessed them.

A Poor Rich Man

17 As Jesus was leaving, a man ran up to him and kneeled down. He asked him, "Good Teacher, what must I do to get eternal life?"

18 Jesus said to him, "Why do you call **me** good? Only God is good. 19 *But I will answer your question.* You know the commands:

'You must not murder.'
'You must not commit adultery.'
'You must not steal.'
'You must not lie.'
'You must not cheat anyone.'
'You must love and obey your father and mother.' "   *Exodus 20:12-16*

20 The man said to Jesus, "Teacher, I have obeyed all these commands since I was a boy!"

21 Jesus loved the man. He looked into his eyes and said to him, "But there is still one more thing you need to do: Go, sell **everything** you have, and give it to the poor people. Then you will have a treasure in heaven. So, come, follow me!"

22 But when Jesus said this, the man's face looked gloomy. He went away sad, because he owned many things *and wanted to keep them.*

23 Then Jesus looked around and said to his followers, "It will be hard for people who own many things to enter the kingdom of God." 24 The followers were amazed at Jesus' words. Again, Jesus said to them, "Friends, it is so hard to enter the kingdom of God. 25 It is easier for a camel to go through the eye of a needle than for a rich man to enter the kingdom of God!"

26 Jesus' followers were completely amazed. They said to one another, "Then who can be saved?"

27 Jesus looked into their eyes and said, "God can do things which do not seem possible to man. God can do anything!"

28 Then Peter began to say to Jesus, "Look, we have left everything and followed you!"

29 Jesus said, "I am telling you the truth: Every person who has left his home, brothers, sisters, mother, father, children, or fields (because of me and because of the Good News) 30 will surely be rewarded 100 times more now, in this time, with houses, brothers, sisters, mothers, children, fields—with persecutions! However, he will get eternal life in the next age. 31 Many people who seem as though they are not important now will be important at that time. Those who seem important now will not be important then."

It Will Go From Bad to Great!

32 They were on the road, going up to Jerusalem. Jesus was walking ahead of them. This surprised them. Those who were following were afraid. Then Jesus took the twelve *apostles* aside. He began to tell them what was about to happen to him. **33** "Listen! We are going up to Jerusalem. The most important priests and the teachers of the law will turn against me.* They will condemn me to death. Then they will give me to non-Jewish men. **34** Those people will laugh at me, spit on me, beat me with whips, and kill me, but I will rise from death on the third day."

James and John

35 James and John, the two sons of Zebedee, came to Jesus. They said to him, "Teacher, we want you to do us a favor."

36 Jesus said to them, "What do you want me to do for you?"

37 They said to him, "Allow us to sit *on thrones* in your glory, one at your right side and one at your left side."

38 Jesus said to them, "You don't know what you're asking. Can you drink the cup *of suffering* which I am drinking? Can you be immersed *in the trouble* in which I am being immersed?"

39 They said to Jesus, "We are able!"

Jesus said to them, "Yes, you will drink from the cup *of suffering* which I am drinking, and you will be immersed *in the trouble* in which I am immersed, **40** but *the privilege of* sitting at my right side or my left side is not mine to give. No, that belongs to the people for whom it has been prepared."

41 When the ten *apostles* heard about this, they began to be angry with James and John. **42** Jesus called for them and said, "You know there are rulers of the world who seem to rule over their people. Important men use their authority over them. **43** You must not think that way. Instead, if one of you wants to be great, he should be your servant. **44** If one of you wants to be important, he should be the slave of everyone, **45** because I* did not come to be served. Instead, I came to serve and give my life to pay for many people's *sins.*"

Bartimaeus Joins the Chase

46 They went into Jericho. Jesus, his followers, and a large crowd left Jericho later. There was a blind man named Bartimaeus (the son of Timaeus). He was sitting beside the road. He was a beggar. **47** When he heard: "It is Jesus from Nazareth!" he began to shout, "Jesus! Son of David! Please help me!" **48** Some of the people told him to be quiet, but he began shouting even louder, "Son of David! Please help me!"

49 Jesus stopped there and said, "Call him."

So they called for the blind man. They said to him, "Be strong! Get up, Jesus is calling for you!"

50 The blind man threw his robe aside and jumped to his feet. He went toward Jesus. **51** Jesus asked him, "What do you want me to do for you?"

The blind man said to Jesus, "Rabboni,* I want to see again!"

52 Jesus said to him, "Go. You are made well, because you believed." Immediately the man was able to see again. He began to follow Jesus on the road.

10:33   literally, the Son of Man
10:45   literally, the Son of Man
10:51   a form of "Rabbi," showing even greater respect

Chapter 11

Jesus Enters Jerusalem

1 When Jesus and his followers were coming near to Jerusalem, close to the towns of Bethphage and Bethany at Olive Mountain, Jesus sent two of his followers on ahead. **2** He said to them, "Go into the village just ahead of you. As you are going in, you will soon find a young donkey tied up. No one has ridden it yet. Untie it and bring it *to me.* **3** And if anyone says anything to you about why you are doing this, say, 'The Lord, its owner, needs it.' Then he will send it here immediately."

4 They went away and found the young donkey out on the street tied at the door. As they were untying it, **5** some of the people standing there asked them, "What are you doing? Why are you untying this young donkey?"

6 They answered them exactly as Jesus had told them. So, they let them go. **7** They brought the young donkey to Jesus and threw their clothes on top of it. Jesus sat on it. **8** Many people spread their clothes on the road. Other people cut down branches in the fields, *and spread them on the road, too.* **9** The people in front and in back were shouting, "Hosanna!* Give praise to this one who is coming by the authority of the Lord *God.** **10** Give praise to the future kingdom of our ancestor, David. Hosanna to God!"*

11 Then Jesus entered Jerusalem and went into the temple courtyard. He looked around at everything there, but it was already late, so he went away with the twelve *apostles* to Bethany.

A Fig Tree

12 The next day, as they were leaving the town of Bethany, Jesus was hungry. **13** Far away he saw a fig tree with *lots of* leaves. So, he went to it to find *something to eat.* But, when he came to it, he found nothing—just leaves. (It was not the season for figs.)* **14** Jesus spoke to the tree, "May no one ever eat fruit from you!" Jesus' followers were listening.

Keep God's House a Place of Prayer

15 They came into Jerusalem. Then Jesus went into the temple courtyard and he began to throw out all the people who were selling pigeons. **16** Jesus was not allowing anyone to carry a jar through the temple courtyard.* **17** Jesus was teaching them, "It is written,

'My house will be called a place of prayer for all nations.'   *Isaiah 56:7*
But **you** have changed it into a hiding place for thieves!"

18 When the most important priests and teachers of the law heard this, they continued trying to find a way to kill Jesus. They were afraid of Jesus, because the whole crowd was amazed at his teaching.

19 When evening came, Jesus and his followers left Jerusalem.

11:9   literally, "Help! Please save!" This expressed great religious enthusiasm.
11:9   Psalm 118:26
11:10   literally, in the highest places
11:13   Although it was not yet time to gather figs, edible figs should have been present along with the leaves. This tree would never produce figs; it was deceptive.
11:16   Jews who came to Jerusalem from distant places needed to buy animals to sacrifice. Also, no foreign coins were allowed in the temple. But these merchants were charging very high prices and treating God's temple only as a place to make money.

God Chasers: Have Faith

20 Early the next morning, while they were walking along, they saw the same fig tree. It was dried up at the roots.   **21** Peter remembered *what happened the day before.* He said to Jesus, "Rabbi,* look at the fig tree which you spoke to! It has dried up!"

22 Jesus answered them, "Have faith in God.   **23** I am telling you the truth: You could say to this mountain, 'Pick yourself up and throw yourself into the lake!' and it would happen for you. You must not doubt in your heart. Instead, believe that what you are saying will happen.   **24** This is why I am telling you: When you are praying and asking *God for something,* believe that you have received it, and it will happen for you.   **25** And when you stand praying, if you have something against someone, forgive him. Then your heavenly Father will forgive you of the things you have done wrong."   **26** *

Where Does Your Authority Come From?

27 They came into Jerusalem. While Jesus was walking around in the temple court-yard, the most important priests, the teachers of the law, and some Jewish leaders came to him.   **28** They were asking him, "What sort of authority do you have to do these things? Who gave you this authority?"

29 Jesus answered them, "I will also ask **you** a question. Answer me and I will tell you what sort of authority I have to do these things.   **30** Was John's immersion from God or from man? Answer me!"

31 They began thinking this among themselves: "If we say 'from God,' then he will say this to us: 'Why didn't you believe John?'   **32** But if we say, 'from man,' we are afraid of the people. All of them truly believe that John was a prophet."   **33** So they answered Jesus, "We don't know!"

Jesus said to them, "Then I am not telling you what sort of authority I have to do these things, either."

Chapter 12

Reject Me, and You're Out of the Chase

1 Then Jesus began to use examples to talk to the people. "A man planted a vine-yard. He put a wall around it, dug a hole for the wine press, and built a lookout tower. Then he rented the land to some farmers and went away on a trip.   **2** At harvest time, he sent a servant to the farmers. He wanted to receive his share of the grapes in the field from the farmers.   **3** But the farmers grabbed the servant and beat him up. They sent him away with nothing.   **4** Again, the owner sent another servant to them. They wounded this servant in the head and made fun of him.   **5** The owner sent another ser-vant. The farmers killed him. They beat up many servants and killed many servants. **6** But the owner still had one man—his precious son. So he sent him to them last of all, thinking, 'The farmers will show respect for my son.'   **7** But those farmers said to one another, 'When the owner dies, his son will get the vineyard. Come, let us kill him and we will have his field!'   **8** So they took the son, killed him, and threw him out of the vineyard.   **9** What will the owner of the vineyard do to those farmers? He will come and kill them. After that, he will give the field to some other farmers.   **10** You have read this Scripture:

11:21   It means "my master" or "my teacher." It became a title of respect for Jewish leaders.

11:26   Many manuscripts include verse 26: "But if you do not forgive others, your Father, who is in heav-en, will not forgive your sins, either." (See Matthew 6:15.)

'The stone that the builders did not want
will become the cornerstone.
11 The Lord *God* causes this to happen;
it is a wonderful thing for us to see.' "   *Psalm 118:22-23*
12 They wanted to arrest Jesus, but they were afraid of the people. They knew Jesus had told this story against them. They left him and went away.

The Jewish Leaders Try to Trick Jesus

13 They sent some of the Pharisees and followers of Herod *Antipas* to Jesus. They wanted to trap him with a question.   **14** They came to him and said, "Teacher, we know you are true. It doesn't matter to you what people think. You don't pay attention to how important someone is. Instead, you teach God's true way. Is it right that we should pay taxes to Caesar*? Yes or no? Should we pay? Or, should we not pay?"

15 But Jesus knew what they were actually trying to do.* He asked, "Why are you trying to trap me? Bring me a coin, so I can see it."   **16** They brought it. Then Jesus asked them, "Whose name and picture is on it?"

They said to him, "Caesar's."

17 Jesus said to them, "Give to Caesar the things which are Caesar's. Give to God the things which belong to God."

And they were amazed at Jesus.

God Is Not Just Alive—He Is LIFE!

18 Some Sadducees* came to Jesus. (Sadducees believe that no one will rise from death.) They were asking Jesus,   **19** "Teacher, Moses wrote this to us:
'If a brother dies and he leaves a wife behind, but no children, his brother must
marry the widow. Then they will have children for the *dead* brother.'
Deuteronomy 25:5
20 There were seven brothers. The first one got married, but he died, leaving no children.   **21** The second brother married the widow. He died too, leaving no children. The same thing happened to the third brother.   **22-23** All seven men married her. None of the seven brothers had any children. The woman was the last of all to die. Therefore, when this woman rises from death, whose wife will she be?"

24 Jesus answered them, "You are wrong! You don't know either the Scriptures or God's power.   **25** When people rise from death, they don't marry each other. Instead, they are like angels in heaven.   **26** Do people rise from death? I know you have read what it says in the book of Moses at the place about the *burning* bush,* how God said to him,
'I am the God of Abraham, the God of Isaac, and the God of Jacob.'
Exodus 3:6,15,16
27 God is not a God of dead people; He is the God of people who are alive! You are so wrong!"

12:14   The title of the supreme Roman rulers. "Caesar" became the title of each emperor.
12:15   literally, He knew about their hypocrisy.
12:18   A Jewish religious group which accepted only the first five books of Moses in the Old Testament. (See Acts 23:8.)
12:26   Before there were chapter numbers or verse numbers inserted into the Biblical text, certain sections were known by key words, for example, "bush."

God Chasers: Two Rules to Obey

28 One of the teachers of the law came to Jesus. This man had heard them arguing with Jesus. He knew that Jesus had answered them well. So he asked Jesus, "What is the most important command?"
29 Jesus answered, "This is the most important one:
'Listen, O Israel, the Lord our God is one Lord.
30 You must love the Lord your God
from all your heart,
from all your soul,
from all your mind,
and from all your strength.'   *Deuteronomy 6:4-5*
31 The second most important command is this:
'You must love other people the same way you love yourself.'   *Leviticus 19:18*
There are no commands more important than these two."
32 The teacher of the law said to Jesus, "Fine, Teacher, you spoke the truth. There is only one God; besides Him, there are no other gods.   **33** Loving God from all your heart, from all your understanding, and from all your strength, and loving other people the same way you love yourself—these are more important than all sacrifices and offerings of animals."
34 When Jesus saw that the man's answer was very wise, he said to him, "You are not far from God's kingdom." No one dared to ask Jesus another *trick* question.

Is the Messiah the Son of David?

35 While Jesus was teaching the people in the temple courtyard, he asked, "How can the teachers of the law claim that the Messiah is the son of David?   **36** By the *power of the* Holy Spirit David himself said:
'The Lord *God* said to my Lord,
"Sit at My right side until I put your enemies under your feet.*' "
                                        Psalm 110:1
37 David himself calls the Messiah 'Lord'! So, how can the Messiah be the son of David?"

God Chasers: Don't Show Off

A large crowd was gladly listening to Jesus.   **38** As he was teaching, he said, "Watch out for the teachers of the law! They want to walk around wearing clothes which make them look important. They like the greetings *of respect* which people give them in the marketplaces.   **39** They always want the most important seats in the synagogues and the best seats at the dinners.   **40** But *they are unfair* to widows; they steal their homes. Then they make themselves look good by saying long prayers. Because of all this, God will punish these men so much more."

What's Little in Our Eyes Is Big in God's Eyes

41 Jesus sat next to the temple treasury. He was watching the way the people were putting money in the box. Many people were rich; they put in a lot of money.   **42** A poor widow came. She put two small coins (worth less than a penny) in the box.
43 Jesus called his followers and said to them, "I am telling you the truth: This poor widow has put more in the box than all those rich people put there.   **44** The rich have

---

12:36   under his control

plenty; they only gave what they didn't need, but this woman gave everything she had. She needed that money to live on."

Chapter 13

There Will Be Hurdles in the Chase

1 As Jesus was leaving the temple courtyard, one of his followers said to him, "Teacher, look at the great stones! Look at the great buildings!"*

2 Jesus said to him, "Do you see all these great buildings? Everything *you see here* will be destroyed. No stone will stay on top of another. It will be completely destroyed!"*

3 When Jesus was sitting on Olive Mountain across from the temple, Peter, James, John, and Andrew asked him these private questions: **4** "Tell us, when will these things happen? How will we know when it is the time for these things to happen?"

5 Jesus began to answer them, "Be careful: Don't let anyone fool you.   **6** Many people will come *to you* using my name. They will say, 'I am the one!' And they will fool many people.   **7** You will hear about wars and wars which are about to happen. Don't become upset. These things must happen, but the end will come later.   **8** One country will fight against another country. Kings will fight against other kings. There won't be enough food to eat. Everywhere there will be earthquakes. These things are only the beginning of the pain.

9 "Watch out for yourselves! They will hand you over to the local courts. They will beat you in their synagogues. Men will take *you to be judged* before governors and kings, because you are associated with me. You will tell them the truth.   **10** The Good News must first be proclaimed to all the people in the world.   **11** When they turn against you and arrest you, don't worry about what you will say. Say whatever is given to you at that time. You are not doing the talking; it is the Holy Spirit.

12 "A brother will betray his own brother, putting him to death. A father will do the same thing to his child. Children will rebel against their parents; they will put them to death.   **13** All people will hate you because of my name. But the person who endures until the end will be saved."

Don't Be Fooled in Your Chase

14 "When you see 'The Abomination of Desolation,'* standing where it must not be (let the reader note the meaning), then those people who are in the land of Judea must run away to the mountains.   **15** The person who is on top of his house must not come down and go inside the house to carry things out with him.   **16** The person who is in the field must not turn back to get his robe.   **17** At that time, it will be horrible for pregnant women and nursing mothers.   **18** Pray that the time when you run away will not be during winter.   **19** During those days, there will be great suffering. Never has there been such suffering since the beginning of the world when God created it until the present time. And, there will never be such suffering in the future.   **20** If that period of time lasted any longer, no one would be left alive. But those times will be cut short

---

13:1   This was a magnificent group of buildings which had been built by Herod the Great in his attempt to gain favor with the Jews.

13:2   This happened in 70 A.D. when the Roman army completely surrounded the temple and destroyed the temple and the city of Jerusalem.

13:14   See Daniel 9:27; 11:31; 12:11.

because of the people *God* has chosen. **21** At that time, if someone says to you, 'Look, here is the Messiah!' or 'There he is!' don't believe him. **22** False messiahs and false prophets will appear. They will perform proofs and miracles to fool people— even *God's* chosen people, if that were possible.

23 "Be careful! I am telling you everything ahead of time."

I'll Be Back

24 "After the trouble of those times,
'The sun will become dark.
The light of the moon will not be seen.
25 The stars will fall from the sky.
The powers in the universe will be moved.'   *Isaiah 13:10; 34:4*
26 "Then they will see me* coming in the clouds with much power and glory.
27 Then I will send my angels out. They will gather together my chosen people from every place and time."*

Just So You'll Know When

28 "Learn from the story about the fig tree: When its branches start becoming soft and green, you know that summer is near. **29** In the same way, when you see all of these things happening, you will know that the time is very, very near. **30** I am telling you the truth: All of these things will happen in this generation!"

So Keep Chasing till Then

31 "The world* will be destroyed, but my words will **never** be destroyed! **32** No one knows when that exact time will be. The angels in heaven don't know it. I* don't know it. Only the *heavenly* Father knows. **33** Be careful! Watch, because you don't know when the right time will be.

34 "It will be like a man who left his house for a trip. He gave his servants authority. Each one of them had a job. He ordered the doorkeeper to watch closely. **35** So, watch! You don't know when I* am coming. It might be in the evening, at midnight, before dawn, or at sunrise. **36** If I come suddenly, you must not let me find you sleeping. **37** I am telling you and everyone else—watch!"

Chapter 14

The Plot: Kill Jesus

1 It was two days before the Passover* and the Feast of Unleavened Bread.* The most important priests and the teachers of the law were trying to find a way to kill Jesus. They planned to use a trick to arrest him. **2** They were saying this: "*Let us* not *begin* during the Passover Festival, so that there will be no trouble among the people."

13:26   literally, the Son of Man
13:27   literally, the four winds, from the farthest end of the earth to the farthest end of heaven
13:31   literally, the sky and the earth
13:32   literally, the Son of Man
13:35   literally, the lord of the house
14:1   a yearly feast reminding Jews of the death angel that had "passed over" their homes in Egypt (Exodus 12:21-28)
14:1   a yearly feast when unleavened bread (no yeast to make the bread rise) was eaten. It lasted seven days (Leviticus 23:4-8).

A God Chaser Anoints Jesus

3 Jesus was in the town of Bethany in Simon's house. (Simon was a leper.*) While Jesus was sitting at the table, a woman opened an alabaster* jar of some very expensive perfume. (It was made of pure nard.*) Then she poured it on his head. 4 Some *of Jesus' followers* were there. They were very angry, saying to one another, "Why waste this perfume? 5 This could have been sold for more than 300 silver coins* and given to poor people." They yelled angry words at her.

6 But Jesus said, "Leave her alone! Why are you bothering her? She has done a good thing to me. 7 You will always have poor people with you. When you want to, you can do good things for them, but you won't always have **me** ! 8 She did what she could. She put perfume on my body ahead of time to prepare it for when I am buried. 9 I am telling you the truth: The Good News will be proclaimed in the whole world. Wherever it is told, what she did will be mentioned to remember her."

Judas Turns Against Jesus

10 Then Judas Iscariot, one of the twelve *apostles*, went away *to talk* to the most important priests; he wanted to give Jesus to them. 11 When they heard this, they were pleased. They promised to give Judas some money. Judas was waiting for the best way to give Jesus to them.

Prepare the Passover Meal

12 On the first day of the Feast of Unleavened Bread, they were sacrificing the Passover lambs.* Jesus' followers said to him, "Where do you want us to go and prepare the Passover meal?"

13 Jesus sent two of his followers, saying to them, "Go into the city. And you will see a man carrying* a jar of water. Follow him. 14 Enter the house he enters and say this to the owner: 'The Teacher asks that you please show us the room where the Teacher and his followers may eat the Passover Feast.' 15 He will show you a large room upstairs. This room is ready. Prepare the Passover meal there." 16 So the followers left and went into the city. Everything happened just as Jesus told them. Then they prepared the Passover meal. 17 When evening came, Jesus sat down at the table with his twelve *followers*. 18 While they were sitting down and eating, Jesus said, "I am telling you the truth: One of you will turn against me. He is eating with me!" 19 They began to be sad. Each one of them asked Jesus, "I am not the one, am I?"

20 Jesus answered, "It is one of the twelve *men* who dipped *his hand* in the same dinner bowl with me. 21 I* will die, just as it is written about me. However, how horrible it will be for that man who turned against me. It would be better if that man had never been born!"

14:3   one who has a very bad skin disease which destroys the flesh
14:3   Jars were sometimes made of alabaster, a soft, cream-colored stone.
14:3   extracted from the root of the nard plant which was native to India
14:5   The perfume was worth a full year's work.
14:12   The most important act around which the feast was centered. It reminded the Jews of how God freed them from Egyptian slavery (Exodus 12:1-14).
14:13   This was unusual because women normally did this.
14:21   literally, the Son of Man

God Chasers Break Bread

22 While they were eating, Jesus took bread and gave thanks. He broke off some of it and gave it to them. He said, "Take it. This bread is* my body."   **23** Then he took a cup. He gave thanks to God for it and gave it to them. He said, "All of you, drink from it.   **24** This is* my blood for the agreement. It is being poured out for many people. **25** I am telling you the truth: I will never drink the fruit of the vine again, until the day when I drink it new in the kingdom of God."

26 Then they sang a song of praise and went out to Olive Mountain.

A God Chaser (Peter) Makes a Promise He Can't Keep

27 Then Jesus said to them, "All of you will be ashamed of me. This is written:
'I will strike the shepherd
   and the sheep will be scattered.'   *Zechariah 13:7*
28 But after I rise from death, I will go ahead of you to the land of Galilee."
29 Peter said to Jesus, "Everyone else may be ashamed of you, but not I!"
30 Jesus said to him, "I am telling you the truth: Tonight—this very night—you will say you don't even know me. You will do this three different times, before the rooster crows a second time!"
31 But Peter insisted, "Even if I must die with you, I will always be loyal to you." All of them were saying the same thing.

God Chasers: Watch and Pray

32 Then they went to a place called Gethsemane. Jesus said to his followers, "Sit here while I go pray."
33 He took Peter, James, and John along with him. He began to feel very sad and depressed.   **34** Then he said to them, "My soul is full of sorrow; I am going to die. Stay here and be watchful."   **35** Then Jesus went ahead a short distance and fell down on the ground. He was praying that, if possible, this time might pass away from him. **36** He continued to pray, "Father, dear Father, all things are possible for You. Take this cup *of suffering* away from me, but what You want is more important than what I want."
37 Then Jesus came and found them sleeping. He said to Peter, "Are you asleep, Simon? Were you not strong enough to watch one hour?   **38** Watch and pray for strength against temptation. The spirit is willing, but the body is weak."
39 Again Jesus went away. He prayed the same prayer.   **40** Once more, Jesus came and found them sleeping. Their eyes were very tired. They didn't know what to say to him.   **41** Jesus came back the third time and said to them, "Are you still sleeping and resting? That's enough! The time has come. Listen! I* am being handed over to sinful men.   **42** Get up, we must go. Look! The one who turned against me is near!"

Jesus Is Treated Like a Criminal

43 And, immediately, while Jesus was still speaking, Judas, one of the twelve *apostles*, came. There was a crowd with him. They had come from the most important priests, the teachers of the law, and the Jewish elders. They had sticks and swords. **44** Judas had given them a signal: "Arrest the man whom I kiss;* lead him away

14:22   represents
14:24   represents
14:41   literally, the Son of Man
14:44   Kissing was a form of greeting. (See Romans 16:16.)

carefully." **45** Immediately Judas came to Jesus and said to him, "Rabbi!"* Then Judas kissed him.

46 Then they reached out and grabbed Jesus. **47** One of the men standing nearby pulled out his sword. He struck the high priest's servant, cutting off his ear.

48 Jesus asked them, "Why did you come out here with swords and sticks? Do you think I am a criminal? **49** I was teaching in the temple courtyard every day. You did not arrest me there. No, *this occurred* to make the Scriptures come true." **50** Then all of Jesus' followers left him. They ran away.

51 There was a young man who was following Jesus. He was wearing only a sheet. Some men grabbed him, too. **52** He left the sheet behind and ran away naked.

The Leaders Can't Face the Truth

53 They brought Jesus to the high priest. All of the important priests, the teachers of the law, and the Jewish elders came together. **54** Peter followed Jesus from a distance. He came as far as the high priest's courtyard. He was sitting with the servants, warming himself by the fire.

55 The most important priests in the whole Jewish Council wanted to find some men who would give evidence against Jesus, so that they could kill him. But, they did not find any *real proof*. **56** Many people were telling lies against Jesus, but their testimony did not match. **57** Some men stood up and told lies against Jesus, **58** "We heard this man say, 'I will destroy this temple sanctuary built by men and build another one in three days—without human hands!' " **59** Their testimony still did not agree. **60** The high priest stood up in the center and asked Jesus, "Aren't you going to answer? What they are saying against you—is it true?" **61** Jesus continued to be silent; he gave no answers.

Again, the high priest asked Jesus, "Are you the Messiah, the Son of the Blessed One?"

62 Jesus said, "I am!

'You will see the Son of Man* sitting at the right side of God.'*   *Psalm 110:1*

'He will be coming with the clouds of the sky!' "   *Daniel 7:13*

63 Then the high priest ripped his own clothes.* He said, "Why do we need any more witnesses? **64** You heard the evil thing that Jesus said. How does it look to you?"

They all condemned him, saying, "He is guilty! He should be killed!" **65** Some of them began to spit on Jesus. They covered his face and hit him with their fists. They said to him, "Prophesy!" And when the guards took charge of him, they started beating him up.

Peter Breaks His Promise

66 While Peter was down below in the courtyard, one of the high priest's servant girls came to him. **67** She saw Peter warming himself. She looked closely at him and said, "You were with Jesus from Nazareth, too!"

68 But Peter said this was not true, "I don't know what you're talking about. I don't understand!"

14:45   It means "my master" or "my teacher." It became a title of respect for Jewish leaders.
14:62   Jesus
14:62   literally, the Power
14:63   Tearing one's clothes was a sign of grief or outrage.

Later Peter went out to the front part of the courtyard. The rooster crowed. **69** Another servant girl saw him and began to say to the men who were standing there, "This man is one of them!"

70 Again, Peter denied it. After a little while, the men who were standing there began to talk to Peter again, "Surely you are one of Jesus' group. You are from Galilee!"

71 Then Peter began to curse and to swear. He said, "I don't know this man. I don't know what you're talking about!" **72** Immediately the rooster crowed a second time. Then Peter remembered what Jesus had said to him: "Before the rooster crows twice, you will say that you don't even know me—three different times." Then Peter broke down and began to cry.

Chapter 15

They Bring Jesus to Pilate

1 It was early in the morning. The most important priests, the teachers of the law, and the Jewish elders—the whole council—were soon ready. They tied up Jesus, took him, and gave him to Pilate.* **2** Pilate asked Jesus, "Are you the king of the Jews?"

Jesus answered, "Yes."* **3** There were many important priests there accusing Jesus. **4** Again, Pilate asked him, "Won't you say something? Look at how many charges they are bringing against you!"

5 But Jesus gave no answers. Pilate was surprised.

Jesus Must Die on the Cross

6 At each *Passover* Feast, Pilate always set one prisoner free, the one whom the people wanted. **7** A man named Barabbas was arrested with some rebels. They had committed murder during a riot. **8** The crowd came up and began to ask Pilate to do the same as he always did for them.

9 Pilate answered them, "Do you want me to release the King of the Jews for you?" **10** (Pilate knew they had turned Jesus over to him because they were jealous of Jesus.)

11 The most important priests made the people excited. They wanted Pilate to set Barabbas free for them, instead *of Jesus.*

12 Again Pilate asked them, "What should I do with Jesus, the one you call 'King of the Jews'?"

13 They yelled again, "Nail him to a cross!"

14 Pilate said to them, "Why? What crime has Jesus done?"

But they continued to yell even more, "Nail him to a cross!"

15 Pilate wanted to please the people. So, he set Barabbas free for them. After beating Jesus with whips, Pilate handed him over to be nailed to the cross.

King of the Jews

16 The soldiers took Jesus inside the courtyard of the *Roman* fortress. The whole group gathered around Jesus. **17** They dressed him with a purple *robe.* They used thorny branches to make a crown. **18** Then they began to salute Jesus, saying, "Hail, King of the Jews!" **19** They hit Jesus many times on the head with a stick and they were spitting on him. They kneeled down and acted as though they were worshiping him. **20** When they finished making fun of him, they took off the purple

---

15:1   Pilate was the Roman governor. The Jews could not execute anyone without his special permission.
15:2   literally, "You are saying it"; a statement meaning: "I agree with what you are saying."

81

robe and dressed him with his own clothes. Then they led him away to nail him to the cross.

Jesus on the Cross

21 There was a man coming into the city from the fields. He was Simon, from the city of Cyrene. (He was the father of Alexander and Rufus.*) They forced him to carry Jesus' cross.*

22 They brought Jesus to the place of Golgotha. (This means 'The Place of the Skull.') **23** They gave him some wine mixed with myrrh,* but Jesus didn't drink it. **24** Then they nailed him to the cross. The soldiers gambled to see who would get Jesus' clothes. **25** It was about nine o'clock in the morning* when they nailed Jesus to the cross. **26** At the top of the cross they nailed up his crime with these words:

THE KING OF THE JEWS.

27 Along with Jesus, two criminals were nailed to crosses. One was at his right side. The other was on his left. **28** * **29** The people who were passing by shook their heads and said terrible things to Jesus. They said, "Bah! You were the one who was going to destroy the temple sanctuary and build it again in three days! **30** Save yourself! Come on down from the cross!"

31 The most important priests, together with the teachers of the law, made fun of Jesus in the same way. They continued to say, "He saved other people, but he cannot save himself! **32** He is the King of Israel, the Messiah; let him come down from the cross now, so that we can see and believe."

Even the men who were nailed to other crosses were insulting Jesus.

Jesus Dies So We Can Live

33 From noon until three o'clock in the afternoon, there was darkness over the whole land. **34** About three o'clock, Jesus cried out loudly, "Eloi, Eloi, lema sabakthani?" (This means: "My God, my God, why did You abandon me?")

35 Some of the men standing there heard this. They said, "Look! He is calling Elijah."* **36** Someone ran and soaked a sponge in some sour wine. Then he put it on the end of a long stick* and gave Jesus a drink. Someone said, "Leave him alone! Let us see if Elijah will come down for him!"

37 Jesus gave out a loud cry and died. **38** The curtain in the temple sanctuary was split from the top to the bottom into two parts.*

39 There was a *Roman* army officer standing there in front of Jesus. When he saw the way Jesus died, he said, "This man really was God's Son!"

40 Some women were there, too. They were far away, watching. Some of them were:

15:21 possibly the man named Rufus in Romans 16:13
15:21 Jesus began to carry his own cross (John 19:17), but he was not able to continue. So, they forced a man in the crowd to do it.
15:23 a sweet-smelling hardened sap used as medicine and for burial preparation
15:25 literally, the third hour
15:28 Many manuscripts include verse 28: "And the Scripture came true which says, 'He was counted with sinners.' " (See Luke 22:37.)
15:35 "Eloi" may have sounded like "Elijah" in his language.
15:36 literally, *the branch of* a hyssop plant. It was about one yard long.
15:38 Jesus, our High Priest, had entered the most holy place on our behalf. (See Hebrews 9:11,12.)

Mary (from the town of Magdala);
Mary (the mother of the younger James and Joses);
Salome.

41 These women always followed Jesus and helped him while he was in the land of Galilee. Many women had come up to Jerusalem with Jesus.

A God Chaser Takes Care of Jesus

42 It was already getting late. It was Preparation Day,* the day before the Sabbath. **43** Joseph came. He was from the town of Arimathea. He was a very important member of the Jewish Council. He was expecting the kingdom of God, too. He dared to go to Pilate and ask for the body of Jesus. **44** Pilate was surprised that Jesus had already died. He called for the army officer to ask him whether Jesus had been dead for a long time. **45** When Pilate found out from the officer that Jesus was dead, he gave the body to Joseph. **46** Joseph bought a sheet. He took the body down *from the cross* and wrapped it in the sheet. Then he put Jesus' body into a tomb which he had cut out of *solid* rock. He rolled a stone in front of the doorway of the tomb. **47** Mary (the one from the town of Magdala) and Mary (the mother of Joses) were watching where the body was placed.

Chapter 16

Where Is Jesus?

1 When the Sabbath day had passed,* Mary (the one from Magdala), Mary (the *mother* of James), and Salome bought some sweet-smelling spices. They wanted to rub this on Jesus' body. **2** It was now very early on Sunday morning.* The sun had not come up yet. They were going to the tomb, **3** saying to one another, "Who will roll away the stone for us at the doorway of the tomb?" **4** (The stone was very large.) But, they looked up and saw that the stone was already rolled away! **5** They walked into the tomb. They saw an angel* sitting on the right side. He was wearing a long white robe. They were stunned.

6 But the angel said to them, "Don't be alarmed! You are looking for Jesus from Nazareth, who was nailed to the cross. He is not here. He has risen from death! Look at the place where they put him! **7** Now, go tell his followers that he will go ahead of you to the land of Galilee. You will see him there, just as he told you. Tell Peter, too."

8 The women left the tomb. They ran away. They were trembling. They were shocked. They didn't say anything to anyone, because they were afraid.

He's Back!

9 When Jesus came back to life early Sunday morning, he appeared first to Mary (the one from Magdala; Jesus had forced seven demons to leave her.). **10** Jesus' friends were crying; they were so sad. She went and told them. **11** When they heard that Jesus was alive and that he had been seen by Mary, they didn't believe it.

15:42   Friday. According to Jewish custom, each day began at sundown.
16:1   our Saturday
16:2   literally, the first day of the week
16:5   literally, a young man

Jesus Makes a Guest Appearance

12 After this, while two more of them were walking to a field, Jesus used a different form to appear to them.   **13** They went back and told this to the other followers, but the followers didn't believe them, either.

God Chasers: GO!

14 Finally, Jesus appeared to the eleven *apostles* when they were sitting at the table. He rebuked them, because their hearts were hard and they did not have faith. They did not believe those who had seen him after he came back to life.

15 Jesus said to them, "When you have gone into the whole world, preach the Good News to all mankind.   **16** The person who believes it and is immersed will be saved, but the person who doesn't believe it will be condemned.   **17** These miracles will go with the believers:

They will use my name to throw out demons.

They will speak *inspired* languages which are new *to them*.

18 They could hold snakes.

If they drink poison, it won't hurt them.

They will put their hands on sick people

and the sick people will become well."

God Chasers Did Miracles

19 After the Lord Jesus talked with them, he was lifted up into the sky. He sat down at God's right side.   **20** They left and preached everywhere. And miracles went with them. The Lord used these miracles to prove that the message was true. He was working with them.*

16:20   Verses 9-20 do not appear in two important Greek manuscripts.

LUKE

Chapter 1

Luke Says "Hi" to Theo

1 Since many people have tried to give a history of the certainties which have taken place among us   **2** and some have handed it down to us having seen those things from the beginning and preached the story *of Jesus*,   **3** I, too, thought, after I studied everything carefully from the beginning, your Excellency, that I should write it down for you. Therefore, I put it in order *in a book*,   **4** so you may be sure that the words you have been taught are true.

A God Chaser Is Coming

5 During the time when Herod *the Great* ruled Judea, there was a Jewish priest named Zechariah. He belonged to Abijah's section.* His wife came from the family of Aaron. Her name was Elizabeth.   **6** They were truly righteous before God, doing everything which was right and everything the Lord *God* commanded. They were *spiritually* spotless,   **7** but they had no children; Elizabeth could not have a baby. Both of them were very old, too.   **8** Zechariah was serving as a priest before God for his section.   **9** The other priests chose him to offer the incense.* So he went into the *holy place* of the temple sanctuary* of the Lord *God*.   **10** There was a large group of people outside. They were praying at the time the incense was being offered.   **11** Then, standing on the right side of the incense table, an angel of the Lord *God* appeared to him.   **12** When Zechariah saw the angel, he was disturbed and overcome with fear. **13** But the angel said to him, "Zechariah, don't be afraid. Your prayer has been heard. Your wife, Elizabeth, will give birth to a son. You will name him John.   **14** You will be very, very happy. Many people will rejoice because of his birth.   **15** John will be a great man in the presence of the Lord *God*. He will never drink wine or liquor.* Even at the time when he is being born, he will be filled with the Holy Spirit.   **16** *He will help* many Jewish people turn back to the Lord their God.   **17** John himself will go ahead of the Lord in a powerful way, like Elijah.* He will have the same forceful spirit that Elijah had. He will make peace between fathers and their children. He will bring those people who are not obeying God back to the right way that people should think. He will make ready a people for *the coming of the* Lord."

At a Loss for Words

18 Zechariah said to the angel, "How can I be sure of this? I am an old man, and my wife is old, too."

19 The angel answered him, "I am Gabriel. I stand before God. God sent me to talk to you and to tell you this good news.   **20** Now, listen! You won't be able to talk until the day when these things occur. You will lose your speech, because you didn't believe what I told you. Nevertheless, these things will come true in their proper time."

1:5   See 1 Chronicles 24:1-4; 23:6. They divided the Jewish priests into 24 groups.
1:9   This was a powder that smelled nice when it was burned.
1:9   the overall temple complex
1:15   Refers to the Nazarite vow. (See Numbers 6:3.)
1:17   Elijah was the great prophet. (See Malachi 4:5-6.)

21 *Outside*, the people were still waiting for Zechariah. They were surprised that he was staying so long inside the temple sanctuary.*   22 Then he came outside, but he could not speak to them. Then the people realized that he had seen a vision inside the holy place. Zechariah couldn't speak; he could only make signs to the people. 23 When his time of service was over, he went home.

24 Later, Elizabeth, Zechariah's wife, became pregnant. So, she didn't go out of her house for five months. She said,   25 "Look what the Lord *God* has done for me! My people were ashamed* of me, but now the Lord *God* has taken that shame away."

Mary's Surprise Guest

26-27 During *Elizabeth's* sixth month of pregnancy, the angel Gabriel was sent from God to a virgin *who lived* in Nazareth, a town in Galilee. The virgin girl was engaged to marry a man named Joseph, from the family of David. Her name was Mary. 28 The angel came to her and said, "Greetings! The Lord *God* is with you. He has blessed you."

29 But Mary was very disturbed about what the angel said. She wondered, "What does this mean?"

30 The angel said to her, "Don't be afraid, Mary, because God has blessed you. 31 Listen! You will become pregnant and give birth to a son. And you will name him Jesus.   32 He will be great. People will call him the Son of the Highest One. The Lord God will give him the authority of King David, his ancestor.   33 Jesus will rule over the people of Jacob forever. His kingdom will never end."

34 Mary said to the angel, "How will this happen? I have no sexual relations with any man."

35 The angel said to Mary, "The Holy Spirit will come upon you and the power of the Highest One will cover* you. The holy baby will be called God's Son.   36 Now listen to this: *You know that* Elizabeth, your relative, is very old, but she is already pregnant with a son. The woman who could not have a baby has been pregnant for six months!   37 With God, nothing is impossible!"

38 Mary said, "I am the servant girl of the Lord *God*. Let what you said happen to me!" Then the angel went away.

39 Mary got up and went quickly to a town in the hill country of Judea.   40 She went into Zechariah's house and greeted Elizabeth.   41 When Elizabeth heard Mary's greeting, the unborn baby kicked inside Elizabeth's body.   42 Then Elizabeth said with a loud voice, "Mary, you have been blessed more than any other woman. The baby to which you will give birth has also been blessed.   43 You are the mother of my Lord, and you have come to me! How could something *this good* happen to me?   44 When I heard your voice, the baby inside me jumped for joy.   45 You are happy, because you believed that what the Lord *God* said to you would actually take place."

Mary Praises the Lord God

46 Then Mary said,
"My soul praises the Lord *God* ;
47 my heart is happy, because God is my Savior.
48 Though I am not important,

1:21   the very holy place
1:25   Jewish people believed that God was punishing a woman if she could not have a baby.
1:35   literally, overshadow

God has looked upon me,
His servant girl.
Listen! From now on, all generations will be happy for me,
49 because the Powerful One has done great things for me.
His name is holy.
50 God will always give His mercy to those who worship Him.
51 His arm is strong.
He scatters those who are proud and boastful.
52 He pulls men down from their thrones and He raises up the humble.
53 He fills hungry people with good things,
but He sends rich, *selfish* people away with nothing.
54 He has always helped His people* who served Him.
He always gave them His mercy.
55 It was just as God said to our ancestors,
to Abraham and to his children forever."
56 Mary stayed with Elizabeth for about three months, then Mary returned home.

John's Chase Begins

57 When it was time for Elizabeth to give birth, she had a son. **58** Her neighbors and relatives heard that the Lord *God* had been very good to her. They rejoiced with her. **59** Eight days later, they came to circumcise* the child. They wanted to name him Zechariah, because this was his father's name. **60** But his mother said, "No! He will be called John, instead."

61 The people said to Elizabeth, "But no one in your family is named John!" **62** Then they began to make signs to his father, asking, "What would you like to name him?"

Zechariah's Speaking Engagement

63 Zechariah asked for something to write on. Then he wrote, "His name is John." All of the people were surprised. **64** Then Zechariah could talk again. He began to praise God. **65** All of their neighbors became afraid. Throughout the hill country of Judea, people continued to talk about all these events. **66** All of the people who heard about these things wondered about them. They thought, "What will this little child become *when he grows up?" The people could see that* the Lord *God's* hand was with this child

67 Then Zechariah, John's father, was filled with the Holy Spirit. He told them what was going to take place:

68 "Praise the Lord God of Israel.
He watches over His people
and He has given them freedom.
69 He has given us a powerful Savior
from the family of David, His special Servant.
70 God's holy prophets who lived long ago
said that He would do this.

1:54   literally, His son (Israel)
1:59   to cut off the foreskin of the male sex organ, as a sign of God's agreement with Israel. (See Genesis 17:9-14.)

71 He will save us from our enemies
and from the power of all those who hate us.
72 *God said* that He would give mercy to our fathers
and remember His holy promise.
73 God vowed to Abraham, our ancestor,
that He would rescue us from the
74 control of our enemies,
so that we could serve Him without fear.
75 We will be holy and righteous before God
as long as we live.
76 Now you, little boy, will be called a prophet
of the Highest One.
You will go ahead of the Lord
to make His roads ready.
77 You will make His people know
that they can be saved,
through the forgiveness of their sins.
78 With the loving mercy of our God,
a new day from heaven will shine upon us.
79 God will help those people who don't understand,
people who dread death.
He will lead us in the way which goes toward peace."

80 And so, the little boy was growing up and becoming stronger in spirit. John lived in the desert, away from other people, until the time when he came out *to preach* to Israel.

Chapter 2

Jesus Is Born

1 About that time, Augustus Caesar* sent out an order *to everyone* in the empire that everyone must register. 2 This was the first registration.* It occurred while Quirinius was governor of Syria. 3 Each person *traveled to be registered* in the town *where he was born.*

4 So Joseph left Nazareth, a town in Galilee. He went to the town of Bethlehem in Judea. This was known as David's town. Joseph went there, because he was from the family of David—a direct descendant. 5 Joseph registered with Mary, because she was engaged to marry him. (Mary was now pregnant.*) 6 While they were in Bethlehem, the time came for Mary to have the baby. 7 She gave birth to her first son and wrapped him with cloths. There were no rooms left in the hotel. So she laid the baby in a box where cattle are fed.

Shepherds Flocked to Bethlehem

8 Some shepherds were in the fields there, watching their flock of sheep that night. 9 An angel of the Lord *God* stood in front of the shepherds. The glory of the Lord

---

2:1 the title of the supreme Roman rulers. "Caesar" became the title of each emperor.
2:2 a census. The Romans wanted to count all the people and everything they owned.
2:5 Joseph did not have sexual relations with Mary until after Jesus was born (Matthew 1:24,25).

shined around them. They were very frightened. **10** The angel said to them, "Don't be afraid, because I am telling you some good news. It will make all the people very happy. **11** Today your Savior was born in David's town. He is Messiah,* the Lord. **12** This is how you will know him: You will find a baby wrapped in cloths and lying in a box where cattle are fed."

13 Suddenly, a very large group of angels from heaven joined the *first* angel. They were all praising God:

14 "Give glory to God in heaven,
    and, on earth, let there be peace
      among those who please God."

15 The angels left the shepherds and went back to heaven. The shepherds kept saying to each other, "Let us go to Bethlehem and see this event which has occurred, which the Lord *God* has revealed to us."

16 So, the shepherds went quickly and found Mary and Joseph. The baby was lying in the feeding box. **17** The shepherds saw the baby. Then they revealed what the angels had said about this child. **18** Everyone was amazed when they heard what the shepherds told them. **19** Mary was keeping all these things in her heart; she continued to think about them. **20** The shepherds went back, singing to God and praising Him for everything they had seen and heard. It was just as the angel had told them.

21 When the baby was eight days old, he was circumcised.* Then he was named Jesus. (This name was given by the angel before the baby began to grow inside Mary's womb.)

Baby Jesus at the Temple

22 The time came for Mary and the baby to be made pure,* according to the law of Moses. Joseph and Mary brought Jesus to Jerusalem, so that they could present him to the Lord *God*. **23** It is written in the law of the Lord:

"When the first male in every family is born,
    he will be called 'holy for the Lord *God*.' "   *Exodus 13:2,12,15*

24 The law of the Lord also says that the people must give a sacrifice:*
"You must sacrifice two young doves or two young pigeons."   *Leviticus 12:8*

Simeon's Wait Is Over

25 A man named Simeon lived in Jerusalem. He was a good man and very devout. Simeon was waiting for the time when *God* would comfort Israel. The Holy Spirit was upon him. **26** The Holy Spirit had revealed to Simeon that Simeon would not die before he saw the Lord's Messiah. **27** The Spirit led Simeon to the temple. The parents of the child went to the temple to do what the Jewish law said that they must do about the child. **28** Simeon held the baby in his arms and thanked God:

2:11   Christ, "the anointed one," one especially chosen by God. The people were expecting this special one to come.

2:21   They cut off the foreskin of the male sex organ of every Jewish baby boy. It was a sign of God's agreement with Israel. (See Genesis 17:9-14.)

2:22   See Leviticus 12:2-8. A Jewish woman had to be cleansed by a special ceremony 40 days after she had given birth to a boy.

2:24   a gift offered to God

29 "Now, Master, You can let me, Your servant
      die in peace, just as You said.
30 I have seen Your Salvation* with my own eyes.
    31 You prepared him before all people everywhere.
32 He is light for all the people
    of the world to see
    and honor for Your people, Israel."

33 Jesus' father and mother were surprised at what Simeon said about him. **34** Then Simeon blessed them and said to Mary, the baby's mother, "Many Jewish people will fall and many will rise because of this boy. He will be a proof from God which some people will not accept. **35** The things which people think in secret will be revealed. The things which will happen will slice through your heart."

Anna's Wait Is Over

36 Anna, a prophetess, was there at the temple. She was from the family of Phanuel in the Asher tribe. Anna was very old. She had been married for seven years. **37** She had been a widow for 84 years. Anna was always at the temple; she never left. She worshiped God day and night by fasting* and praying. **38** Anna was standing there at that same moment, thanking God. She began to talk about Jesus to everyone who was waiting for *God* to bring salvation to Jerusalem.

Back to Nazareth

39 Joseph and Mary finished doing everything which the law of the Lord commanded. Then they returned home to Nazareth, their own town in Galilee. **40** The little boy began to grow up. He became stronger and wiser. God's gracious love was upon him.

When Jesus Was Twelve

41 Every year Jesus' parents traveled to Jerusalem for the Passover Festival.* **42** When Jesus was twelve years old, they went up *to Jerusalem to the feast*, as they always did. **43** When the *feast* days were over, they were returning home, but the boy Jesus stayed behind in Jerusalem. His parents didn't know about it. **44** Joseph and Mary traveled for a whole day. They thought that Jesus was with them in the caravan. They began to look for him among their relatives and close friends, **45** but Joseph and Mary didn't find *Jesus*. So, they went back to Jerusalem to look for him there. **46** After three days, they found him. Jesus was sitting in the temple courtyard among the teachers, listening to them and asking them questions. **47** Everyone heard him. They were amazed at his understanding and *wise* answers. **48** When Jesus' parents saw him, they were very surprised. His mother said to him, "Son, why did you treat us like this? Your father and I were very worried about you. We were looking *everywhere* for you."

49 Jesus asked them, "Why did you have to look for me? You should have known that I must be where my Father's *house* is!" **50** But they did not understand the meaning of what he said to them.

2:30   Here Simeon was referring to Jesus. "Jesus" means salvation.
2:37   to go without food for a period of time, usually for spiritual reasons
2:41   a yearly feast which reminded Jews of the time when the death angel "passed over" their homes in Egypt. (See Exodus 12:21-28.)

51 Jesus went down with them and came to Nazareth. He always obeyed them. His mother was still thinking about all of these things. **52** Jesus grew taller and continued to learn more and more. People liked him, and he pleased God.

Chapter 3

John the (God Chaser) Baptist

1-2 While John, Zechariah's son, was in the desert, the message of God came to him. This occurred during the 15th year of the rule of Tiberius Caesar.* These men were ruling *for Caesar* : Pontius Pilate ruled Judea; Herod *Antipas* ruled Galilee; Philip,* Herod's brother, ruled Iturea and Trachonitis; Lysanias ruled Abilene. Annas and Caiaphas were high priests* at that time. **3** John went through the whole area around the Jordan River. He was preaching to the people: "Change your hearts and be immersed for the forgiveness of sins." **4** As the words in the book of Isaiah the prophet are written:

"There is a voice shouting in the desert:
'Prepare the Lord's road.
  Make His paths straight.
5 Every valley will be filled
  and every mountain and hill will be flattened.
Crooked roads will become straight
  and rough roads will become smooth.
6 Everyone will see
  the salvation of God!' "   *Isaiah 40:3-5*

7 People were coming to be immersed by John. John said to them, "You are like poisonous snakes! Who told you to run away from *God's* punishment which is coming? **8** You must do the things which will show that you have really changed your hearts. Don't start thinking this to yourselves: 'Abraham is our father.' I tell you, God could make children for Abraham from these rocks here. **9** The ax is now ready to cut down the trees.* Every tree which does not produce good fruit is cut down and thrown into fire."

10 The people asked John, "What should we do?"

11 John answered, "If you have two shirts, share with the person who doesn't have one. If you have food, share that, too."

12 Even the tax collectors* came to John. They wanted to be immersed. They asked John, "Teacher, what should we do?"

13 John answered them, "Don't take more *taxes* from anyone than you have been ordered to take."

14 The soldiers asked John, "What about us? What should we do?"

3:1-2   the title of the supreme Roman rulers. "Caesar" became the title of each emperor.

3:1-2   Herod Antipas had two half brothers with the name of Philip. The Philip mentioned here is not the Philip who had a wife whom Herod married.

3:1-2   The Romans allowed only one high priest each year. The old Annas was the real power behind that office. Caiaphas, Annas' son-in-law, was the official high priest that particular year. Before this, each of Annas' five sons had been high priest.

3:9   This refers to Jewish people who would not accept Jesus.

3:12   These were Jews hired by the Romans to gather taxes for the Romans. They often cheated their fellow countrymen. They were considered traitors.

John said to them, "Don't force people to give you their money. Don't tell lies about anyone. Be happy with the pay you receive."

15 All of the people were hoping *for the Messiah to come*, and they were wondering about John. They thought, "Perhaps he is the Messiah?"

16 John answered everyone, "I immerse you in water, but there is one coming who is more important than I am. I am not worthy to untie his shoe. He will immerse you in the Holy Spirit and in fire. **17** He will come ready to clean the grain, separating the good grain from the straw. He will put the good part into his barn. Then he will burn the part which is not good. He will burn it with a fire which cannot be put out!"*

18 John continued to preach the Good News, saying many different things to encourage the people. **19** (*Later* John denounced Herod *Antipas*, the ruler, by saying, " *You were wrong to marry* Herodias. Herodias is your brother's wife!" John also rebuked Herod for the many other evil things which Herod had done. **20** Then Herod did another evil thing (it was the worst thing of all)—he put John in prison).

John Immerses Jesus

21 *Before John was put in prison* all the people were immersed by him. Then Jesus came and was immersed, too. While Jesus was praying, the sky opened up. **22** The Holy Spirit came down upon him in a physical form, like a dove. Then a Voice came from heaven and said, "You are My Son, and I love you. I am very pleased with you!"

Relatively Speaking

23 Jesus was about 30 years old when he began *to teach.*
People thought that Jesus was Joseph's son.
> Joseph was Eli's son.
24 Eli was Matthat's son;
Matthat was Levi's son;
Levi was Melchi's son;
Melchi was Jannai's son;
Jannai was Joseph's son.
25 Joseph was Mattathias' son;
Mattathias was Amos' son;
Amos was Nahum's son;
Nahum was Esli's son;
Esli was Naggai's son.
26 Naggai was Maath's son;
Maath was Mattathias' son;
Mattathias was Semein's son;
Semein was Josech's son;
Josech was Joda's son.
27 Joda was Joanan's son;
Joanan was Rhesa's son;
Rhesa was Zerubbabel's son;
Zerubbabel was Shealtiel's son;
Shealtiel was Neri's son.
28 Neri was Melchi's son;
Melchi was Addi's son;

3:17   hell

Addi was Cosam's son;
Cosam was Elmadam's son;
Elmadam was Er's son.

29 Er was Joshua's son;
Joshua was Eliezer's son;
Eliezer was Jorim's son;
Jorim was Matthat's son;
Matthat was Levi's son.

30 Levi was Simeon's son;
Simeon was Judah's son;
Judah was Joseph's son;
Joseph was Jonam's son;
Jonam was Eliakim's son.

31 Eliakim was Melea's son;
Melea was Menna's son;
Menna was Mattatha's son;
Mattatha was Nathan's son;
Nathan was David's son.

32 David was Jesse's son;
Jesse was Obed's son;
Obed was Boaz' son;
Boaz was Salmon's son;
Salmon was Nahshon's son.

33 Nahshon was Amminadab's son;
Amminadab was Admin's son;
Admin was Arni's son;
Arni was Hezron's son;
Hezron was Perez' son;
Perez was Judah's son.

34 Judah was Jacob's son;
Jacob was Isaac's son;
Isaac was Abraham's son;
Abraham was Terah's son;
Terah was Nahor's son.

35 Nahor was Serug's son;
Serug was Reu's son;
Reu was Peleg's son;
Peleg was Eber's son;
Eber was Shelah's son.

36 Shelah was Cainan's son;
Cainan was Arphaxad's son;
Arphaxad was Shem's son;
Shem was Noah's son;
Noah was Lamech's son.

37 Lamech was Methuselah's son;
Methuselah was Enoch's son;
Enoch was Jared's son;
Jared was Mahalaleel's son;
Mahalaleel was Cainan's son.

38 Cainan was Enos' son;
Enos was Seth's son;
Seth was Adam's son;
Adam was God's son.

Chapter 4

Jesus Knows the Book

1 Jesus returned from the Jordan River. He was full of the Holy Spirit. The Spirit was leading Jesus into the desert. 2 The Devil tempted Jesus for 40 days. Jesus didn't eat anything during that time. When those days were over, Jesus was very hungry.

3 The Devil said to him, "Since you are the Son of God, command this rock to become food."

4 Jesus answered him, "It is written:

'A person does not live on food alone.' "   *Deuteronomy 8:3*

5 The Devil took Jesus and showed him in a moment of time all of the kingdoms of the world. 6 The Devil said to him, "I will give you all of these kingdoms and all the power and glory which is in them. It has all been given to me. I may give it to anyone I want. 7 It will all belong to **you**, if you will only bow down in front of me."

8 Jesus answered him, "It is written:

'You must worship* the Lord God. Serve only Him!' "   *Deuteronomy 6:13-14*

9 The Devil led Jesus to Jerusalem and stood him on a very high place of the temple. He said to Jesus, "Since you are the Son of God, jump off,   10 because it is written:

'*God* will command His angels to take care of you.'   *Psalm 91:11*

11 *It is* also *written*:

'Their hands will catch you,
so that you won't hit your foot on a rock.' "   *Psalm 91:12*

12 Jesus answered him, "But it also says:
'You must not test* the Lord your God.' "   *Deuteronomy 6:16*

13 The Devil finished tempting Jesus and went away from him to wait until a better time.

Very Good News

14 Jesus went back to Galilee with the power of the Holy Spirit. Stories about Jesus went all over the area around Galilee.   15 He began to teach in their synagogues. All of the people were praising him.

16 Jesus came to Nazareth, the town where he grew up. On the Sabbath day he went into the synagogue. That is what Jesus always did. He stood up to read.   17 The book of Isaiah the prophet was given to him. Jesus opened the scroll and found the place where this was written:

4:8   literally, bow down
4:12   or, doubt

18 "The Spirit of the Lord *God* is upon me.

He chose me to tell the Good News to poor people.

He sent me to proclaim freedom to captives.

and to help blind people see again.

He sent me to lift up broken-hearted people

19 and to announce the welcome year of the Lord *God*." *Isaiah 61:1-2*

20 Jesus rolled up the scroll and gave it back to the keeper. Then Jesus sat down. Every person in the synagogue was watching Jesus very closely. **21** Jesus began to speak to them. He said, "While you heard me reading these words just now, the words were coming true!"

22 All of the people were saying good things about Jesus. They continued to be amazed at the beautiful words which were coming from his mouth. The people asked, "Isn't Jesus the son of Joseph?"

23 Jesus said to them, "Surely you will tell me this old saying: 'Doctor, heal yourself.' *You would like to say*, 'We have heard about some of the things you did in Capernaum. Do those things here in your own home town, too!' " **24** Then Jesus said, "I am telling you the truth: A prophet is not accepted in his own home town. **25** I am telling you the truth: During Elijah's time,* it did not rain in Israel for 3¹/₂ years. There was very little food anywhere in the whole country. There were many widows in Israel during that time, **26** but Elijah was sent to none of those widows. He was sent only to a widow in Zarephath, a town in the land of Sidon. **27** And there were many people with leprosy* living in Israel during the time of the prophet Elisha.* However, **not one** of those people was healed; the only one was Naaman. And Naaman was from the country of Syria, *not from Israel*."

28 All the people in the synagogue heard these things. The people became very, very angry. **29** Their town was built on a hill. They got up and forced Jesus out of town, bringing Jesus to the edge of the cliff. They wanted to throw him over, **30** but Jesus walked through the middle of them and went away.

Jesus Stops an Evil Spirit

31 On the Sabbath day Jesus went down to Capernaum, a town in Galilee. Jesus was teaching the people. **32** They were amazed at what he taught; this message had authority. **33** In the synagogue there was a man who had an evil spirit inside him. The man shouted with a loud voice, **34** "Bah! Jesus of Nazareth! What do you want with us? Did you come here to destroy us? I know who you are—God's Holy One!" **35** But Jesus stopped the evil spirit. Jesus said, "Stop talking and come out of the man!" The demon threw the man down on the ground in front of all the people. Then the evil spirit left the man without hurting him.

36 The people were shocked. They continued to ask each other, "What does this mean? With such authority and power Jesus commands evil spirits and they come out!" **37** And so, the news about Jesus was spreading to every place in the whole area.

Jesus Heals Peter's Mother-in-law

38 Jesus left the synagogue. He went into Simon's* house. Simon's mother-in-law was very sick. She had a high fever. They asked Jesus to do something to help her.

4:25   the great prophet who lived about 800 years before Christ. (See 1 Kings 17:1,7; 18:1.)

4:27   a very bad skin disease which destroys the flesh

4:27   See Second Kings 5:1-14.

4:38   His other names were Peter and Cephas.

39 Jesus stood very close to her and commanded the fever to leave her. It left her immediately. She got up and began to serve them.

Many People Are Made Well

40 When the sun went down, the people brought their sick friends to Jesus. They had many different kinds of sicknesses. He put his hands on every one of them and healed them. **41** Demons were coming out of many people, shouting, " **You** are the Son of God!" But Jesus wouldn't let the demons say anything more; the demons knew that Jesus was the Messiah.*

Spread the Word

42 The next day Jesus traveled to a place to be alone. The people were looking for Jesus. When they found him, they wouldn't let him leave. **43** But Jesus said to them, "I must tell the Good News about God's kingdom to other towns, too. This is why I was sent."

44 Then Jesus began to preach in the synagogues of Judea.

Chapter 5

Jesus Finds Followers

1 Jesus stood beside Lake Gennesaret.* Many people pushed to get all around him. They wanted to hear the message of God. **2** Jesus saw two boats at the shore of the lake. The fishermen were washing their nets. **3** Jesus climbed into the boat which belonged to Simon.* He asked Simon to push away from the shore a little. Then Jesus sat down and, from the boat, continued to teach the people on the shore.

4 Jesus finished speaking. He said to Simon, "Take the boat into the deep water. If all of you will drop your nets into the water, you will catch some fish."

5 Simon answered, "Teacher, we worked hard all night long trying to catch fish, but we caught nothing. But you say I should lower the nets into the water, so I will do it." **6** The fishermen dropped their nets into the water. They caught so many fish that their nets were beginning to rip. **7** They called to some friends in another boat to come and help them. The friends came and both boats were filled so full of fish that they were almost sinking.

8-9 The fishermen were shocked because of the *large number of* fish that they caught. When Simon Peter saw this, he fell down in front of Jesus and said, "Go away from me, Lord. I am a sinful man!" **10** James and John, the sons of Zebedee, were amazed, too. (James and John were partners with Simon.)

Jesus said to Simon, "Don't be afraid. From now on, you will catch **people**, *instead of fish*!"

11 The men brought their boats to the shore. They left everything and followed Jesus.

One Touch

12 Once Jesus was in a town. There was a man who was covered with leprosy.* When the man saw Jesus, he bowed down in front of Jesus and begged him, saying, "Lord, you can heal me, if you want to."

4:41   Christ, "the anointed one," one especially chosen by God. The people were expecting this special
        one to come.
5:1   the same as Lake Galilee
5:3   Peter (Cephas)
5:12   a very bad skin disease which destroys the flesh

13 Jesus said, "I **do** want to heal you—be healed!" Then Jesus stretched out his hand and touched the man. The leprosy disappeared immediately. 14 Then Jesus said, "Don't tell anyone about what happened. Instead, go show yourself to the priest.* Then offer a gift *to God*, because you have been healed. This is what *the law of* Moses commands. This will prove to the priests that you are healed."

15 But the news about Jesus was spreading more and more. Many people were coming to listen to him and to be healed of their sicknesses. 16 Often Jesus went away to other places to be alone, so that he could pray.

A Crippled Man

17 One day, Jesus was teaching the people. The Pharisees and teachers of the law were sitting there, too. They had come from every village in Galilee and from Judea and Jerusalem. The Lord *God* was giving Jesus the power to heal people. 18 There was a man who was paralyzed. Some men carried him on a small bed. The men were trying to bring him and put him down in front of Jesus, 19 but there were so many people that the men couldn't find a way to get to Jesus. So, the men went up on top of the roof. They lowered the crippled man on his small bed down through a hole in the ceiling *into the room* in front of Jesus. 20 Jesus saw that these men believed. He said *to the sick man*, "Friend, your sins are forgiven!"

21 The teachers of the law and the Pharisees began to think to themselves, "Who is this man? He speaks such an evil thing! Only **God** can forgive sins!"

22 But Jesus knew what they were thinking. He answered them, "Why are you reasoning in your hearts? 23 Which is easier to say: 'Your sins are forgiven,' or to say, 'Stand up and walk'? 24 I will prove to you that I* have the authority to forgive sins on earth." So Jesus said to the paralyzed man, "I tell you, stand up! Pick up your bed and go home!"

25 Immediately, the man got up in front of all of them. He took his bed and went home, praising God. 26 All of the people were completely amazed. They began to praise God. They were filled with awe. They said, "Today we have seen amazing things!"

God Chaser: Levi

27 After this, Jesus went out and saw a tax collector sitting at the tax office. His name was Levi. Jesus said to him, "Follow me!" 28 Levi got up, left everything, and started to follow Jesus.

29 Then Levi in his own home gave a big feast in honor of Jesus. At the table there were many tax collectors and some other people. 30 The Pharisees and those men who taught the law for the Pharisees began to complain to the followers of Jesus, saying, "Why do you eat and drink with tax collectors and sinners?"

31 Jesus answered them, "Healthy people do not need a doctor, but sick people do. 32 I have not come to ask 'righteous' people to change their hearts; I have come to call sinners."

Jesus Will Die

33 They said to Jesus, "John's followers often fast* and pray, the same as the Pharisees, but **your** followers are always eating and drinking!"

5:14   Leviticus 14:2-32 said that the priests were to act as medical examiners. The priests were the ones to declare whether a person was cured or not.

5:24   literally, the Son of Man

5:33   to go without food for a period of time, usually for spiritual reasons

34 Jesus said to them, "Can the friends of a groom* be sad* while he is still with them? 35 However, the time will come when the groom will be taken away from them. Then his friends will fast* during that time."

The New and the Old

36 Jesus told this example: "No one takes cloth off a new robe to cover a hole in an old robe. If he does, the new piece of cloth will *shrink and* tear and not match the old cloth. 37 No one puts new wine into old wine bags.* If he does, the old wine bags will break open. The wine will spill out and the wine bags will be ruined. 38 Instead, new wine should be put inside new wine bags. 39 No one who drinks old wine wants new wine, because he says, 'The old is better.' "

Chapter 6

Jesus Is Lord Over the Sabbath

1 Once on a Sabbath day, Jesus was passing through a field of grain. His followers were picking some of the grain, rubbing it in their hands, and eating it. 2 Some of the Pharisees asked, "Why are you doing this? You are doing what is not right to do on the Sabbath day."

3 Jesus answered them, "Do you remember reading about what David did when he and his men were hungry? 4 David went into the house of God. He took the holy loaves of bread and ate them. The law says that only the priests can eat them, but David gave some to his men." 5 Then Jesus said to the Pharisees, "I* am Lord over the Sabbath day."

Do Good or Evil on the Sabbath?

6 On another Sabbath day, Jesus went into the synagogue to teach the people. A man with a crippled right hand was there. 7 The teachers of the law and the Pharisees were waiting to see whether Jesus would heal on the Sabbath day. They wanted *to see Jesus do something wrong*, so that they could accuse him. 8 But Jesus knew what they were thinking. He said to the man with the crippled hand, "Arise and stand in the middle." The man got up and stood there. 9 Then Jesus said to them, "I ask you, which is right on the Sabbath day—to do good or to do evil? Is it right to save a life or to destroy one?" 10 Jesus looked around at all of them and said to the man, "Stretch out your hand!" The man did this; his hand was restored. 11 The Pharisees and the teachers of the law became very, very angry. They started saying to each other, "What can we do to Jesus?"

Jesus Chooses Twelve God Chasers

12 At that time, Jesus went out to a mountain to pray. He stayed there all night long praying to God. 13 When morning came, Jesus called his followers and chose twelve of them and named them "apostles." They were:

5:34   literally, the sons of the groom
5:34   literally, fast
5:35   to go without food for a period of time, usually for spiritual reasons
5:37   These were bags made of animal skins. In the wine fermentation process, which produces gases, the bags would be stretched. If new wine were to be put into an old bag, which was already stretched, the fermentation process would cause the old bag to break open.
6:5   literally, the Son of Man

14 Simon (Jesus named him Peter.);
   Andrew (Peter's brother);
   James;
   John;
   Philip;
   Bartholomew;
15 Matthew;
   Thomas;
   James (*the son* of Alphaeus);
   Simon (He was named The Revolutionary.*);
16 Judas (*the son* of James);
   Judas Iscariot (the one who turned against Jesus).

Jesus Healed Them All

17 Jesus and the apostles came down from the mountain. Jesus stood on a level place. A large group of his followers were there. Also, there were many, many people from all around Judea, Jerusalem, and the seacoast cities of Tyre and Sidon. 18 They all came to listen to Jesus and to be healed of their diseases. Jesus healed those people who were troubled by evil spirits. 19 All of the people were trying to touch Jesus, because power was coming out of him. Jesus healed them all!

Be Happy!

20 Jesus looked up at his followers and began to speak:
"Poor people, be happy,
      because God's kingdom belongs to **you**!
21 You who are hungry now, be happy,
      because you will be satisfied.
   You who are crying now, be happy,
      because you will laugh.
22 "Be happy when people hate you and are cruel to you. Be happy even when they pull away from you and throw you out because you are my friend.* 23 At that time, you should jump for joy, because you will have a great reward in heaven. Their ancestors treated the prophets the same way that these people treat you.
24 "Nevertheless it will be horrible for you,
      you rich *and selfish* people,
   because you've had your comfort.
25 It will be horrible for you,
      you people who are full now,
      because you will be hungry.
   It will be horrible for you people
      who are laughing now,
   because you will mourn and cry aloud.

6:15   literally, Zealot. The Zealots were a group of Jewish men—fanatics—who claimed to uphold the law of Moses, even if it meant violence. They favored revolt against Rome.
6:22   literally, because of the Son of Man

26 "How horrible it is when everyone says good things about you. Their ancestors always did that to the false prophets!"

Love Your Enemies

27 "However, I say to you people who are listening to me, love your enemies. Do good to those who hate you. **28** Bless those people who curse you. Pray for those people who are cruel to you. **29** If a person hits you on one side of your face, offer the other side, too. If someone takes away your robe, let him have your shirt, too. **30** Give to every person who asks you. When a person takes something that belongs to you, don't ask for it back. **31** Treat other people the way you want them to treat you. **32** If you love only those people who love you, then you are no better than anyone else. Even sinners love those who love them! **33** If you do good only to those who do good to you, you are no better than anyone else. Even 'sinners' do that! **34** If you lend something to someone, always hoping to get something back, what good have you done? Even 'sinners' lend to other 'sinners,' so that they may get the same amount back! **35** So, love your enemies, do good to them, and lend to them without hoping for anything back. God is good, even to the people who are full of sin and who are not thankful. If you do these things, you will have a great reward. You will be sons of the Highest One. **36** Give love and mercy, as your *heavenly* Father gives love and mercy."

Give and You Will Get

37 "Don't pass judgment *on other people*, and you won't be judged. Do not condemn other people, and you will not be condemned. Forgive and you will be forgiven. **38** Give to others, and it will be given to you. You will be given much. It will be poured into your hands, shaken, and pressed down—more than you can hold. It will be so much, that it will spill over into your lap. The measure you use to measure will be used to measure back to you."

39 Jesus gave them this example: "Can a blind man guide a blind man? Both of them will fall into a pit. **40** A student is not higher than his teacher. However, when the student has learned, he will be like his teacher.

41 "Why do you see the speck of dust which is in your brother's eye, but do not notice the wooden pole which is in your own eye? **42** How can you say to your brother, 'Brother, let me take that speck out of your eye,' while you still have that pole in your own eye? Can't you see it? You hypocrite!* First, take the pole out of your own eye. Then you will see clearly to take the speck out of your brother's eye."

What's Inside Comes Out

43 "A good tree does not produce rotten fruit, neither does a rotten tree produce good fruit. **44** Each tree can be known by its fruit. Do people gather figs from thorny weeds? Do people get grapes from bushes? **45** A good man brings good out of the good treasure of his heart, but an evil man brings out evil from an evil treasure. A person speaks what flows out of his heart."

A House That Really Rocks

46 "Why do you call me, 'Lord! Lord!' yet you do not obey what I say? **47** Everyone who comes to me and listens to my words and obeys them **48** is like a man

---

6:42   or, "You act as though you are good, but you're really not."

building a house. He digs down deep and builds his house on *strong* rock. Then the floods come, and the water tries to wash the house away, but the flood cannot move the house, because it was built well.   **49** However, the person who hears my words and does not obey them is like a man who does not build his house on rock. There is no *solid* foundation. When the floods come, the house quickly falls down, and that house is completely destroyed."

Chapter 7

Jesus Heals a Servant Boy

1 Jesus finished saying all these things to the people. Then he went into Capernaum. **2** The servant of a *Roman* army officer was very sick—near death. The officer loved that servant very much.   **3** When the officer heard about Jesus, he sent some Jewish elders to him to ask Jesus to come and save the life of his servant.   **4** When the men came to Jesus, they begged him earnestly, "This officer deserves to have your help. **5** He built the synagogue for us; he loves our people."

6 So Jesus went with the men. He was coming near to the officer's house when the officer sent friends to say, "Lord, don't bother to come into my house. I am not worthy to be with you.   **7** That is why I did not come to you myself. Just give the order and my servant will be healed.   **8** I, too, am a person under authority and I have soldiers below me *whom I command.* I can say to one, 'Go!' and he goes. I can say to another, 'Come!' and he comes. Or, if I say to my servant, 'Do this!' he does it."

9 When Jesus heard this, he was surprised. Jesus turned to the crowd that was following him. He said, "I tell you, I have not found this much faith anywhere—not even in Israel!"

10 The group that was sent to Jesus went back to the house. They found that the servant was made well.

Jesus Heals a Widow's Son

11 The next day Jesus went to a town called Nain. His followers and a large group of people were traveling with him.   **12** When Jesus came near the town gate, he saw *a funeral procession.* A mother had lost her only son. She was also a widow. A large crowd from the town was there with the mother while the dead son was being carried out.   **13** When the Lord *Jesus* saw her, he felt very sorry for her. He said to her, "Don't cry."   **14** Jesus came near the coffin and touched it. The men who were carrying it stopped. Jesus said, "Young man, I tell you, get up!"   **15** Then the dead son sat up and began to talk. Jesus gave him to his mother.

16 All of the people felt much respect. They were praising God. They said, "A great prophet has come to us!" and, "God is taking care of His people."

17 This news about Jesus spread into all Judea and throughout all the places around there.

Now, About John

18 John's followers told John about all of these things. He called for two of his followers.   **19** John sent them to the Lord *Jesus* to ask, "Are **you** the one who is coming, or should we look for someone else?"

20 So, the men came to Jesus. They said, "John (the one who immerses people) sent us to you with this question: 'Are you the one who is coming, or should we wait for another person?'"

21 At that time, Jesus healed many people of their sicknesses, diseases, and evil spirits. He gave sight to many blind people. **22** Then Jesus said to John's followers, "Go tell John the things you have seen and heard. Blind people can see again. Crippled people can walk. Those with leprosy* are made well. The deaf can hear, dead people are given life, and the Good News is given to the poor people. **23** The person who is not ashamed of me is truly happy!"

24 After John's messengers left, Jesus began to tell the crowds about John: "What did you people go out into the desert to see? A stalk *of grass* being blown by the wind? **25** Why did you go out there? Did you go to see a man dressed in fine clothes? The people who have fine, nice clothes live in palaces. **26** Really, what did you go out to see? A prophet? Yes, I tell you, John is even more than a prophet. **27** This was written about John:

'Listen! I am sending my messenger to go ahead of you.
He will prepare the way for you.'

Malachi 3:1

28 I tell you, John is greater than any man ever born. However, the person who is the least important in God's kingdom is greater than John!"

(**29** All of the people and the tax collectors who heard this agreed that God's *command* was good; they had allowed themselves to be immersed by John. **30** But the Pharisees and teachers of the law refused to obey God's plan; they did not allow themselves to be immersed by John.)

31 *Then Jesus said*, "Now, I will compare the people of this time to something. What are they like? **32** The people of this time are like little children sitting in the marketplace, calling to each other,

'We played a happy song, but you wouldn't dance.
We played a sad song, but you wouldn't cry.'

33 John (the one who immersed people) came, not eating *normal food* or drinking wine, and you say, 'He has a demon!' **34** I* came eating and drinking, and you say, 'Look, he eats too much, and he drinks too much wine! He is the friend of tax collectors and other sinners!' **35** *True* wisdom is shown to be right by all the things it does."*

Forgiven Much = Love Much

36 One of the Pharisees asked Jesus to eat with him. Jesus went into the Pharisees's house and sat down at the table. **37** At that time, there was a sinful woman in town. She knew that Jesus was having dinner at the Pharisee's house. So, the woman brought some expensive perfume. **38** She stood crying at Jesus' feet. Then she began to wash his feet with her tears and to dry them with her hair. She kissed his feet again and again and rubbed them with perfume. **39** The Pharisee who had invited Jesus saw this. He thought to himself, "If Jesus really were a prophet, he would **know** that the woman who is touching him is a sinner!"

40 Then Jesus said to the Pharisee, "Simon, I have something to say to you."
Simon said, "Say it, teacher."

41 Jesus said, "There were two men. Both men owed money to the same moneylender. One man owed him 500 silver coins. The other man owed him 50 silver coins.

7:22 a very bad skin disease which destroys the flesh
7:34 literally, the Son of Man
7:35 literally, Wisdom is justified by all her children.

42 The men didn't have any money to pay back the moneylender. So, the moneylender told the men that they didn't have to pay him. Which one of them will appreciate the moneylender more?"

43 Simon answered, "I think it would be the one who owed him the most money."

Jesus said to him, "You are correct." **44** Then Jesus turned to the woman and said to Simon, "Do you see this woman? When I came into your house, you provided me with no water for my feet,* but **she** washed my feet with her tears and dried them with her hair. **45** You didn't give me the kiss *of friendship*, but **she** has not stopped kissing my feet since I came in! **46** You did not rub my head with oil, but **she** rubbed my feet with perfume. **47** Because of her great love, I tell you, her many sins are forgiven. The person who feels only a little need to be forgiven will feel only a little love when he is forgiven."

48 Then Jesus said to her, "Your sins are forgiven."

49 The guests sitting at the table began to think to themselves, "Who does Jesus think he is? How can **he** forgive sins?"

50 Jesus said to the woman, "Because you believed, you are forgiven. Go in peace."

Chapter 8

Women Who Joined the Chase

1 Later, Jesus was traveling through each town and village. He was preaching and telling the Good News about God's kingdom. The twelve *apostles* were with him. **2** There were also some women with him. Jesus had healed these women of evil spirits and sicknesses. One of the women was Mary, from a town called Magdala. Seven demons had come out of her. **3** Also, there were: Joanna, the wife of Chuza (Herod *Antipas'* business manager), Suzanna, and other women. These women used their own money to help Jesus and his apostles.

The Story of the Seed

4 Many people came together. People came to Jesus from every town. He gave the people this example:

5 "A farmer went out to plant his seed. While he was planting, some seeds fell along the road. People walked on the seeds, and the wild birds ate them up. **6** Some seeds fell on rocky soil. They began to grow, but they died, because they did not have any water. **7** Some other seeds fell among thorny weeds. They grew, but the weeds choked them off *later*. **8** And some seeds fell on good soil. They grew and produced fruit a hundred times more."

After saying these things, Jesus called out, "The person who has an ear to hear with should use it."

9 Jesus' followers asked him, "What does this story mean?"

10 And Jesus said, "You have been chosen to know the secrets of the kingdom of God. However, these secrets are given to other people in stories, so that

'They will see, but they won't understand!

They will hear, but they won't understand!' *Isaiah 6:9*

11 "This is what the story means: The seed is God's message. **12** Those along the road are the people who hear, but then the Devil comes and takes away the message from their hearts, so that those people cannot believe it and be saved. **13** The seeds

---

7:44   A polite host always provided water for his guest's feet.

which fell on rocky soil are like the people who hear the message and accept it gladly, but they do not have deep roots. They believe for a while, but, in time, temptation comes and they turn away *from God.*   **14** The seeds which fell among the thorny weeds are like the people who heard *God's* message, but they are gradually choked by the worries, riches, and pleasures of life. They never produce fruit.   **15** But, the seeds which fell on good soil are like the people who when they listen to the message with a good, honest heart, obey it and patiently produce fruit."

Use What You Have

16 "No one lights a lamp and then covers it with a basket or hides it underneath a bed. Instead, he puts the lamp on a lamp table, so that the people who come in will have enough light to see by.   **17** Everything which is hidden will become clear. Every secret thing will be made known.   **18** So, be careful how you listen, because the person who has something will get more. But this will happen to the person who has *almost* nothing: Even what he thinks he has will be taken away from him!"

Who Is Related to Jesus?

19 Jesus' mother and brothers came *to visit* him. They could not get to him, because there were so many people.   **20** Someone told Jesus, "Your mother and your brothers are standing outside. They want to see you."

21 Jesus answered them, "My mother and my brothers are those people who listen to God's message and obey it!"

Jesus Calms a Storm

22 One day Jesus and his followers climbed into a boat. He said to them, "Let us go across the lake." And so, they sailed.   **23** While they were sailing, Jesus was asleep. Then a big storm blew down on the lake. The boat began to fill with water. They were in danger.   **24** The followers went to Jesus and woke him up. They said, "Teacher! Teacher! We are going to die!"

Jesus woke up and gave an order to the wind and the waves. Everything stopped. The lake became calm.   **25** He asked his followers, "Where is your faith?"

The followers were afraid and amazed. They asked each other, "What kind of man is this? Even wind and water obey him!"

Legion

26 Jesus and his followers sailed across the lake from Galilee. They reached the land where the Gerasene* people lived.   **27** When Jesus went ashore, a man from the town met him. This man was full of demons. For a long time he had worn no clothes. He was living in the graveyard, not in a house.   **28-29** He had often been taken, put in jail, and tied with chains and shackles, but the man would always break the bonds and the demon *inside him* would force him to go out to the desert places. Then Jesus commanded the evil spirit to come out of this man. The man fell before Jesus and shouted, "What do you want with me, Jesus, Son of the Most High God? Please, don't punish me!"

30 Jesus asked him, "What is your name?"

8:26   Some manuscripts have "Gergasenes." Others have "Gadarenes."

He said, "Legion"* (because many demons had gone into him).   31 The demons begged Jesus not to send them into the bottomless *pit*.   32 On that hill there was a large herd of pigs feeding. The demons begged Jesus to allow them to go into the pigs. So, Jesus let them.   33 Then the demons came out of the man and went into the pigs. The herd ran down the cliff into the lake and drowned.

34 Some men had been taking care of the pigs. When they saw what happened, they ran away. They told the story in the fields and in the town.   35 People went out to see what had occurred. They came to Jesus and found the man sitting there at Jesus' feet. The man had clothes on and he was in his right mind—the demons were gone. The people became afraid.   36 The men who saw these things happen told the other people all about how Jesus had healed the man with demons.

37 All the people of the surrounding Gerasene area asked Jesus to go away from them. They were all very frightened. So, he climbed into a boat and went back *to Galilee*.   38 The demon-free man begged to stay with Jesus.

But Jesus sent the man away, saying,   39 "Go back home and tell what God did for you."

So the man went all over town proclaiming what Jesus had done for him.

Jesus Raises a Little Girl From Death

40 When Jesus returned *to Galilee*, a crowd of people welcomed him. Everyone was waiting for him.   41 A man named Jairus came, too. He was a ruler of the synagogue.* He bowed down at Jesus' feet and kept begging him to come to his house.   42 Jairus had only one daughter. She was twelve years old, and she was dying.

While Jesus was going *to Jairus' house*, the crowds were pressing in upon him.   43 There was a woman who had a sore which had been bleeding for twelve years. She had spent all of her money on doctors, but no one was able to heal her.   44 She went behind Jesus and touched the tassel* of his robe. At that moment, her bleeding stopped.   45 Then Jesus asked, "Who touched me?"

Everyone denied touching Jesus. Peter said, "Teacher, the people are all around you and they are pressing against you."

46 But Jesus said, "Someone **did** touch me! I *felt* it when power left me."   47 When the woman saw that she could not hide, she came forward trembling. She bowed down before Jesus. While all the people listened, she told why she touched Jesus and how she was healed immediately.   48 Jesus said to her, "Dear woman, you are made well because you believed. Go in peace."

49 While Jesus was still speaking, someone came from *the house of* the synagogue ruler and said, "Your daughter has just died! Don't bother the Teacher anymore."

50 When Jesus heard this, he said to Jairus, "Don't be afraid! Just believe and your daughter will be well again."

51 Jesus came to the house. He allowed only Peter, John, James, and the girl's father and mother to go with him. He did not allow anyone else inside.   52 Everyone was

8:30   In the Roman army a legion numbered about 5,000 men.
8:41   A synagogue is a place where Jews gather to read the law and to worship.
8:44   Tassels were worn on four corners of a robe to remind the people of the law.

crying and showing great sadness because of the girl. But Jesus said, "Stop crying, because she is not dead; she is only sleeping!"

53 They laughed at Jesus, because they knew that the girl was dead. **54** But Jesus held her hand and called to her, "Little girl, get up!" **55** Her spirit came back into her and she stood up immediately. Jesus said, "Give her something to eat." **56** The girl's parents were amazed. Jesus warned them not to tell anyone about what had occurred.

Chapter 9

Jesus Sends Out the Twelve God Chasers

1 Jesus called the twelve *apostles* together. He gave them authority over all demons and power to heal sicknesses. **2** Jesus sent them to proclaim God's kingdom and to heal sick people. **3** He said to them, "When you travel, don't carry a *walking* staff. Also, don't carry a bag, food, or money. Don't even bring an extra suit of clothes. **4** When you go into a house, stay there until *it is time* to leave that town. **5** If the people there won't welcome you, go outside the town and shake off the dust from your feet.* This will be a warning to them."

6 So the apostles went out, traveling through each village. They told the Good News and healed people everywhere.

Herod Wonders About Jesus

7 Herod *Antipas*, the ruler, heard about all these things which were happening. He was confused, because some people said, "John has come back to life!" **8** Others said, "Elijah has appeared!" And some others said, "One of the prophets from long ago has risen from death!" **9** Herod said, "I cut off John's head. So, who is this man I hear such things about?" Herod kept trying to see Jesus.

Jesus Does Lunch With a Bunch (5,000+ People)

10 The apostles came back. They told Jesus what they had done *on their trip*. Then Jesus took them away to a town called Bethsaida where they could be all alone. **11** But the crowds found out where Jesus had gone and they followed him. Jesus welcomed them and began to talk with them about God's kingdom. He healed the people who were sick.

12 Late in the afternoon, the twelve *apostles* came to Jesus and said, "No one lives here. Send the people away. They need to find food and places to sleep in the farms and small towns around here."

13 But Jesus said to them, " **You** give them something to eat."

They said, "We have only five loaves of bread and two fish. Do you want us to go buy some food for all these people?" **14** (There were about 5,000 men there.)

Jesus said to his followers, "Have them sit down in groups of about 50."

15 So, the followers did this and all the people sat down. **16** Then Jesus took the five loaves of bread and two fish. He looked up to heaven. Jesus thanked God for the food and divided it. Then he began giving the food to the followers. The followers gave it to the crowd. **17** Everyone ate and was satisfied. They gathered up all the pieces of food which were left over. They filled twelve large baskets with them.

9:5   a gesture meaning that one would have no more to do with those people

Who Do You Say I Am?

18 One time when Jesus was all alone praying, his followers came together. Jesus asked them, "Who do the crowds say that I am?"

19 The followers answered, "Some people say you are John (the one who immersed people). Others say you are Elijah. And some people say you are one of the prophets from long ago who has come back to life."

20 Then Jesus said to his followers, "But who do **you** say I am?"

Peter answered, "You are God's Messiah."

21 Jesus warned them not to tell this to anyone. Then Jesus said, **22** "I* must suffer many things. I will be rejected by the Jewish elders, the most important priests, and the teachers of the law. I will be killed. However, after three days, I will be raised from death."

23 Jesus kept saying to all of them, "If anyone wants to follow me, he must carry his cross* every day. He must say no to himself and follow me. **24** The person who wants to save his life will lose it, but every person who gives his life for me will save it. **25** What good is it, if a person gets the whole world, but loses or wrecks his own soul? **26** If a person is ashamed of me or my words, then I* will be ashamed of him when I come with my glory and the glory of my Father and the holy angels. **27** I am telling you the truth: There are some people standing here who will see the kingdom of God before they die!"

A Mountain Top Experience

28 After saying these things, about eight days later, Jesus took Peter, James, and John and went up on top of a mountain to pray. **29** While Jesus was praying, his appearance began to change. His clothes became as bright as a flash of lightning. **30** Suddenly, two men were talking with Jesus. They were Moses and Elijah. **31** Moses and Elijah were shining brightly, too. They were talking with Jesus about his death* which was about to be fulfilled in Jerusalem. **32** Peter and the others were deep in sleep, but they woke up and saw the glory of Jesus. They also saw the two men who were standing with Jesus. **33** As Moses and Elijah were about to leave, Peter said, "Teacher, it is good that we are here. We will set up three holy tents—one for you, one for Moses, and one for Elijah." (Peter didn't know what he was saying.)

34 While Peter was saying these things, a cloud came all around them. Peter, James, and John became afraid when the cloud covered them. **35** A Voice came from the cloud, saying, "This is My Son; he is My chosen one. Listen to what **he** says!"

36 When the Voice finished, only Jesus was there. Peter, James, and John said nothing. At that time, they told no one about what they had seen.

Jesus Heals a Boy With a Demon

37 The next day they came down from the mountain. A large group of people met Jesus. **38** A man from the crowd cried out to Jesus, "Teacher, please come and look at my son. He is the only child I have. **39** An *evil* spirit gets hold of my son, and suddenly he shouts. He loses control of himself and he foams at the mouth. It hurts him and

---

9:22   literally, the Son of Man
9:23   suffering
9:26   literally, the Son of Man
9:31   literally, departure

it will almost never leave him. **40** I begged your followers to make it leave him, but they were not able to."

41 Jesus answered, "You people are a generation with no faith. You are warped. How long must I be with you and put up with you?" Then Jesus said to the man, "Bring your son here."

42 While the boy was coming, the demon threw him on the ground. The boy lost control of himself. Jesus gave a command to the evil spirit and healed the boy. Then Jesus gave him back to his father. **43** All of the people were shocked at the great power of God.

Jesus Tells About His Death

The people were still amazed about all of the things which Jesus was doing. Jesus said to his followers, **44** "Remember these words: I* am about to be handed over to some men." **45** But the followers did not know what Jesus meant. The meaning was hidden from them, so that they couldn't understand it, but they were afraid to ask Jesus about what he had said.

True Greatness

46 The *apostles* began to have an argument about which one of them was the most important. **47** Jesus understood what the argument was about. He knew what was in their hearts. So, he took a little child and stood the child beside him. **48** Then Jesus said to them, "The person who welcomes this little child in my name welcomes **me**. And when a person welcomes me, this person welcomes the One who sent me. The one who is the most humble among you is the most important person."

For or Against

49 John answered, "Teacher, we saw someone who was throwing demons out by using your name. We kept telling him to stop, because he is **not** one of your followers, as we are."

50 Jesus said to him, "Don't stop him, because if someone is not against you, he is for you."

A Samaritan Town

51 The time was coming near when Jesus *would leave and* go back up to heaven. He traveled toward Jerusalem. **52** Jesus sent some men ahead of him. The men went into a village in Samaria to make everything ready for Jesus. **53** But the people there would not welcome him, because he was heading toward Jerusalem. **54** James and John, the followers of Jesus, saw this. They asked, "Lord, do you want us to call fire down from heaven and burn up these people?"*

55 But Jesus turned and reprimanded them.* **56** They all went to another village.

God's Kingdom Must Be First

57 As they were all traveling along the road, someone said to Jesus, "I will follow you wherever you go!"

9:44   literally, the Son of Man
9:54   Here some Greek copies of Luke add: ". . . as Elijah did."
9:55   Some ancient manuscripts have: "Jesus answered, 'You don't know what kind of spirit that you have. The Son of Man did not come to destroy the souls of men, but to save them.'"

58 Jesus said to him, "The foxes have holes *to live in*. The wild birds have nests. I* have no place where I may rest my head."

59 Jesus said to another man, "Follow me!"

But the man answered, "Lord, let me first go and bury my father."

60 But Jesus said to him, "Let the 'dead' bury their own dead! **You** must go and tell about the kingdom of God."

61 Another man said, "I will follow you, Lord, but first let me go and say good-bye to my family."

62 Jesus said, "If anyone begins to plow a field, but then looks back, he is not qualified for the kingdom of God."

Chapter 10

Jesus Sends Out More God Chasers

1 After this, the Lord *Jesus* chose 72* more men. He sent the men out in pairs ahead of him into every town and place where he was planning to go. **2** Jesus said to them, "The harvest is great, but there are not many workers. Pray that the Owner of the harvest will send more workers out into the harvest field. **3** So, you may go now. But listen, I am sending you like lambs into a pack of wolves. **4** Don't carry a pack, a bag, or *extra* shoes. Don't stop to talk with people along the road. **5** Before you go into a house, say, 'Peace be to this home.' **6** If a peaceful man lives there, your blessing of peace will stay upon him. However, if he is not peaceful then your blessing of peace will come back upon you. **7** Stay in the peaceful house. Eat and drink what the people there give you. A worker should be given his pay. Don't move from that house to stay in another house. **8** If you go into a town and the people welcome you, eat what they give you. **9** Heal the sick people who live there. Then tell them: 'The kingdom of God is very near to you!' **10** But, if you go into a town and the people don't welcome you, then go out into the streets of that town and say: **11** 'Even the dust from your town which sticks to our feet we wipe off against you.* But know this: The kingdom of God is very near!' **12** I tell you, on the *Judgment* Day, God will punish the people of that town more than He will punish the people of Sodom!"*

People Who Won't Join the Chase

13 "How horrible it will be for you, O town of Chorazin! How horrible it will be for you, Bethsaida! Many miracles have occurred in you. If these same miracles had occurred in Tyre and Sidon,* then those people in Tyre and Sidon would have changed their hearts* and actions long ago. **14** But on the Judgment *Day*, God will punish **you** more than the people of Tyre and Sidon. **15** And you, Capernaum, do you think you will be lifted up to heaven? You will be thrown down to Hades!

9:58   literally, the Son of Man

10:1   Many early manuscripts have 70.

10:11   a gesture meaning that they would have nothing more to do with those people

10:12   See Genesis 19:24-25.

10:13   See Isaiah 23; Ezekiel 26—28; Joel 3:4-8; Amos 1:9-10; Zechariah 9:2-4

10:13   literally, would have worn sackcloth and put ashes on themselves to show that they were sorry for their sins

16 "When a person listens to what you say, he is really listening to **me**. When a person rejects you, **I** am the one he is rejecting. When a person rejects me, he is actually rejecting the One who sent me."

A Reason to Be Happy

17 When the 72* men returned, they were very happy. They said, "Lord, when we used your name, even the demons obeyed us!"

18 Jesus said to them, "I was watching Satan fall, as lightning falls from the sky. **19** Listen! I have given you the authority to walk on *dangerous* snakes and scorpions— even more power than the enemy* has. Nothing will ever hurt you!   **20** The *evil* spirits obey you. This is true, but don't be happy for that reason. Instead, be happy because your names are written in heaven."

Jesus' Prayer

21 In that hour the Holy Spirit made Jesus feel very happy. Jesus said, "Father, Lord of heaven and earth, I praise You, because You have hidden these teachings from the 'wise' and 'intelligent' people yet You reveal Your teachings to little children. Yes, Father, I praise You, because this is what You really wanted to do.

22 "My Father has given me all things. Only the Father knows who the Son is. And only the Son knows who the Father is. The only people who will know about the Father are those whom the Son chooses to tell."

23 Then Jesus turned to his followers who were there alone with him. Jesus said, "You are very blessed to see what you now see!   **24** I tell you, many prophets and kings wanted to see what you now see. And many prophets and kings wanted to hear what you now hear, but they didn't."

The Story of the Good Samaritan

25 Then a teacher of the law stood up. (He was trying to test Jesus.) He asked Jesus, "Teacher, what must I do to get eternal life?"

26 Jesus said to him, "What is written in the law? What do you read there?"

27 The man answered, " 'You must love the Lord your God from all your heart, with all your soul, with all your strength, and with all your mind.'* Also, 'You must love your neighbor* the same way you love yourself.' "*

28 Jesus said to him, "You have answered correctly. Do this and you will have life *forever.*"

29 But the man wanted to make himself look good. So, he said to Jesus, "But who is my neighbor?"

30 Jesus understood what the man meant. So, Jesus said, "A man was going down the road from Jerusalem to Jericho. Some bandits surrounded him. They tore off his clothes and beat him up. Then they left him lying there on the ground. He was almost dead.   **31** By chance, a Jewish priest was going down that *same* road. When the priest saw the man, he just walked away.   **32** Next, a Levite* came to the spot, too. The

---

10:17   Many early manuscripts read 70.
10:19   the Devil
10:27   Deuteronomy 6:5
10:27   other people
10:27   Leviticus 19:18
10:32   Levites helped Jewish priests. Both were from the tribe of Levi. (See 1 Chronicles 23:28-32.)

110

Levite saw him, but he went around him; he also walked away.   33 A Samaritan* man was traveling down the road. He came to the place where the man was lying. When he saw the man, he felt sorry for him.   34 The Samaritan went to him and poured olive oil and wine* on his wounds. Then he bandaged the man's wounds. The Samaritan had a donkey. He put the man on his donkey and took him to a hotel where he took care of him.   35 The next day, the Samaritan brought out two silver coins and gave them to the person who worked at the hotel. The Samaritan said, 'Take care of this man. If you spend any more money on him than this, I'll pay you back when I return.' "

36 Then Jesus said, "Which one of these three men do you think was a **real** neighbor to the one who was hurt by the thieves?"

37 The teacher of the law answered, "The one who showed mercy to him."

Jesus said to him, "Then **you** go and do the same thing!"

Martha, Martha

38 While Jesus and his followers were traveling, Jesus went into a village. A woman named Martha welcomed him.   39 Martha had a sister named Mary. Mary was sitting at Jesus' feet and listening to his message, but her sister Martha was doing the housework.   40 Martha became angry, because she had so much work to do. She went in and said, "Lord, don't you care that my sister has left me alone to do all the housework? Tell her to help me!"

41 But the Lord answered her, "Martha, Martha, you are getting worried and upset about too many things.   42 Only **one** thing is important. Mary has made the right choice; and this will never be taken away from her."

Chapter 11

How to Pray

1 One time Jesus was somewhere praying. When he stopped, one of his followers said to him, "John taught his followers how to pray. Lord, please teach us how to pray, too."

2 Jesus said to them, "When you pray, pray like this:
'Father, may Your name always be kept holy.
   May Your kingdom come.
3 Give us the food we need each day.
4 Forgive us of the sins we have committed;
   because we, too, forgive everyone who has done wrong to us.
And keep us away from temptation.' "

Keep Asking

5-6 Then Jesus said to them, "Suppose one of you went to your friend's house in the middle of the night and said to him, 'A friend of mine has come into town to *visit* me, but I have nothing for him to eat. Please give me three loaves of bread.'   7 Your friend inside the house answers, 'Go away! Don't bother me! The door is already locked. My children and I are in bed. I cannot get up and give it to you.'   8 I tell you, perhaps friendship is not enough to make him get up to give you the bread. However, he will

---

10:33   Samaritans and Jews hated each other. Samaritans had become mixed with non-Jews in marriage, custom, and religion.

10:34   These had a cleansing effect on the wounds. Compare James 5:14.

surely get up to give you what you need, because you are not ashamed to continue asking. **9** So, I tell you, continue asking, and it will be given to you. Keep searching, and you will find. Knock, and *the door* will open for you. **10** You will receive, if you will always ask. You will find, if you keep looking. And *the door* will open for you, if you continue knocking. **11** Do any of you have a son? What would you do if your son asked you for a fish? Would any father give his son a snake? No, you would give him a fish. **12** Or, if your son asks for an egg, would you give him a scorpion? **13** You are evil men, yet you know how to give good gifts to your children. Surely your heavenly Father knows how to give the Holy Spirit to those people who ask Him."

The Finger of God

14 One time Jesus was throwing a demon out of a man who couldn't talk. When the demon came out, the man was able to speak. The crowds were amazed. **15** But some of the people said, "Jesus throws demons out by using the power of Beelzebul,* the ruler of demons."

16 Other people were trying to make Jesus prove that he came from God. **17** But Jesus knew what they were thinking. He said to them, "Every kingdom which is divided against itself will be ruined. And a family that does not work together will break apart. **18** So, if Satan is *fighting* against himself, then he is divided. How could his kingdom stay together? You claim that I throw out demons by using the power of Beelzebul, **19** but if I throw out demons by using the power of Beelzebul, then by whose power do your own sons throw them out? Because of this, your own people prove you are wrong. **20** However, if it is true that I use the finger of God to throw out demons, then God's kingdom has come upon you!

21 "When a strong man guards his own house with many weapons, his house is safe. **22** But, suppose a stronger man comes and defeats him. The stronger man will take away the weapons in which the first man had trusted to keep his house safe. Then the stronger man will keep the things he wants.

23 "If a person is not with me, he is against me. The person who does not work with me scatters."

Seven Times Worse

24 "When an evil spirit comes out of a man, it goes through dry places looking for a place to rest. If the spirit does not find a place, it says, 'I will go back to the house from which I came.' **25** And so, it goes and finds that house cleaned up and orderly. **26** Then the evil spirit goes and brings seven other spirits *worse* than itself. They go into that man and live there. And that man has even more trouble than he had before. "

Obedience = Happiness

27 When Jesus said these things, a woman from the crowd spoke up, "Your mother, who gave birth to you and nursed you, must be very happy!"

28 But Jesus said, "The people who hear the message of God and keep it are the ones who are truly happy!"

Jesus Is the Greatest

29 The group of people grew larger and larger. Jesus said, "The people living today are evil. They ask for proof from God, but no proof will be given to them except the

---

11:15   literally, lord of the flies, a name given to the Devil by the Jews

Jonah miracle.   30 Jonah's coming was a warning to those people who lived in the city of Nineveh. It is the same with me.* I *will judge* the people of this time.   31 The Queen of Sheba* will rise up on the Judgment Day with the men of this time and she will condemn them. Why? Because she came a very long way to listen to the wisdom of Solomon, yet I am greater than Solomon!   32 On the Judgment Day, the men from the city of Nineveh will condemn the people of this time, because when Jonah preached to them, they changed their hearts. I am greater than Jonah!"

Be a Night Light

33 "No one puts a light under a basket and hides it. Instead, a person puts the light on the lamp table, so that everyone who comes in may see.   34 Your eye is like a lamp for the body. When your eye sees clearly, the whole body is made bright. However, if your eye is dark *with sin*, then your whole body is dark.   35 So, be careful! Don't let the light in you become dark.   36 If your whole body is bright, and none of it is dark, then you will shine brightly as lightning does."

Jesus Didn't Wash His Hands

37 While Jesus spoke, a Pharisee asked Jesus to eat with him. So Jesus came and sat at the table.   38 But the Pharisee was surprised when he saw that Jesus didn't wash *his hands*before the meal.   39 The Lord *Jesus* said to him, "You Pharisees clean the outside of the cup and the dish, but inside you are greedy and full of evil.   40 You are foolish! The same One who made the outside of you also made the inside.   41 The next time you give to the poor people, give your heart, too. Then, you will be completely clean.   42 But it will be horrible for you, you Pharisees! It is true that you give God ten percent of *everything you have*. You even give Him ten percent of all the little plants in your gardens—mint, rue, or other seasoning herbs, but you forget to give Him love and you forget to be fair to other people. You should always tithe, but you must remember to do the more important things, too.   43 It will be horrible for you, you Pharisees, because you love to have the most important seats in the synagogues. You love to have the respect that people give you in the marketplaces.   44 It will be horrible for you, because you are like hidden graves. People walk on them without knowing it."

The Religious Experts

45 One of the teachers of the law said to Jesus, "Teacher, when you say these things *about the Pharisees*,* you are insulting our group, too."

46 Jesus answered, "It will be horrible for you, too, you teachers of the law! You put heavy loads* on people which are hard for them to carry, but you yourselves don't even begin to help people carry those loads.   47 It will be horrible for you, because you build tombs* for the prophets, but these are the same prophets whom your *ancestors*

11:30   literally, the Son of Man
11:31   literally, the queen of the south (See 1 Kings 10:1-10; 2 Chronicles 9:1-12.)
11:38   This was a Jewish religious custom which was thought to be very important by the Pharisees (separated ones).
11:45   a Jewish religious group which was very strict about observing the law of Moses and traditions of their ancestors
11:46   very strict religious rules
11:47   elaborate monument to honor them outwardly

killed! **48** And now you show everyone that you agree with what your fathers did. They killed the prophets, and you build tombs for the prophets! **49** This is why the wisdom of God said, 'I will send prophets and apostles* to them. Some of my prophets and apostles will be killed by evil men. Others will be hunted down.' **50** But you people will have to answer for the deaths of all the prophets who were killed since the beginning of the world. **51** You will have to answer for everything from the murder of Abel to the murder of Zechariah.* (Zechariah was killed between the altar and the temple.)

52 "It will be horrible for you, you teachers of the law! You have hidden the key to learning *about God*. You yourselves would not learn, and you also stopped others from learning."

53 As Jesus was leaving, the teachers of the law and the Pharisees began to give him a lot of trouble. They asked Jesus questions about many other things. **54** They hoped that Jesus *would say something wrong*. They were trying to trap him with something that he might say.

Chapter 12

Everything Will Be Found Out

1 Many thousands of people came together. There were so many people that they were stepping on each other. Before Jesus began to speak *to the people, he said* to his followers, "Be careful of the yeast* of the Pharisees—they act as if they are good men, but they are not.* **2** Everything which is hidden will be found out, and everything that is secret will be made known. **3** The things you say in the dark will be heard in the light. The things you whisper in secret rooms will be proclaimed from the tops of houses."

Don't Be Afraid

4 "I tell you, my friends, don't be afraid of people. People can kill the body, but after that, they can do nothing more to hurt you. **5** I will show you the One to fear. You should fear **God**, who has authority over you to throw you into hell after you die. Yes, I tell you, **He** is the One you should fear.

6 "Five sparrows are sold for only a few small coins, but God doesn't forget about any of them. **7** Yes, God even knows how many hairs you have on your head. Don't be afraid. **You** are worth much more than many sparrows."

Don't Be Ashamed

8 "I tell you, if anyone says he believes in me in front of other people, then I* will speak for him in front of the angels of God. **9** But, if anyone denies me in front of people, then I will deny him in front of the angels of God.

10 "If a person says something against me,* he may be forgiven. However, a person who says evil things against the Holy Spirit will **not** be forgiven.

11:49   special messengers
11:51   The books of the Hebrew Scriptures were in a different order from our Old Testament. Abel was the first man to die (Genesis 4:1-8) and Zechariah was the last man to die in the Hebrew Bible (2 Chronicles 24:20,21).
12:1   Here "yeast" means influence.
12:1   literally, hypocrites
12:8   literally, the Son of Man
12:10   literally, the Son of Man

11 "When men bring you into the synagogues before the leaders and other men with authority, don't worry about how you will answer their questions. Don't worry about what you will say. 12 At that time, the Holy Spirit will teach you what you must say."

The Poor Rich Man

13 One of the men in the crowd said to Jesus, "Teacher, tell my brother to share my father's money with me!"
14 But Jesus said to him, "Friend, no one chose me to be a judge between you two."
15 Then Jesus said to them, "Be careful and guard against all kinds of greed. A person's life is not measured by the things he owns."
16 Then Jesus used this example: "There was a rich man who had some land which grew a very good crop. 17 The rich man was thinking to himself, 'What will I do? I have no place in which to keep all my crops.' 18 Then the rich man said, 'I know what I will do. I will tear down my barns and build bigger ones! I will put together all of my wheat and good things in my new barns. 19 Then I can say to myself, "I have many good things stored. I have saved enough for many years. Relax, eat, drink, celebrate!" ' 20 But God said to that man, 'Foolish man! Tonight you will die. So, what about the things you prepared? Who will own those things now?'
21 "This is how it will be for the one who saves things only for himself. To God he is not rich."

Chase God, Not Money

22 Jesus said to his followers, "I say this to you, because you shouldn't worry about what you will eat to stay alive. You shouldn't worry about what clothes you will wear. 23 You shouldn't worry, because life is more important than food. The body is more important than clothes. 24 Notice the crows. They don't plant seeds or harvest them. Birds do not store their food in barns, yet God takes care of them. And, **you** are worth so much more than birds. 25 None of you can grow 18 inches taller by worrying about it. 26 If you cannot do a little thing like that, then why worry about the big things? 27 Notice how the wild flowers grow. They don't work or make clothes for themselves. But, I tell you, even Solomon, with all his beautiful clothes, was not dressed as well as one of these flowers. 28 Why do you have so little faith? Look at how well God clothes the grass in the fields, but the grass is here today and thrown into the oven tomorrow to be burned. Wouldn't God dress you so much better? You are much more important than the grass in the fields. Don't have so little faith! 29 So don't be wondering or worrying about what you will eat or what you will drink. 30 People without God put all these things first, but your *heavenly* Father knows you need these things. 31 So, put His kingdom first, and all of the things *you need* will be given to you."

Heavenly Treasures

32 "Don't be afraid, little flock, your *heavenly* Father wants to give you the kingdom. 33 Sell the things you have and give that money to people who need it. Money does not last, so don't trust in it. Let your riches be the treasure which is in heaven, where it will never be stolen or destroyed.* 34 The place where your treasure is will also be the place where your heart is."

12:33 literally, Provide money-bags for yourselves which do not get old.

115

Ready for the Chase

35 "Be ready; be completely dressed and have your lights lit.   **36** Be like servants who are waiting for their master to come home from a wedding party. The master comes and knocks. The servants open the door for the master.   **37** Those servants will be blessed when their master comes home, because he sees that his servants are ready for him. I am telling you the truth: The master will dress *for work* and tell the servants to sit at the table. Then the master will come and serve *them*.   **38** Those servants might have to wait all night long* for their master, but they will be happy when their master comes in and finds them still waiting.   **39** Pay attention to this: Suppose a man has a house. If the man knew the exact time a thief would come *to rob him*, the man would not allow the thief to break into his house.   **40** So, be ready! I* will come at a time when you don't expect me!"

The Story of the Trusted Servant

41 Peter said, "Lord, did you give this example for us or for everyone?"

42 The Lord *Jesus* said, "Well, who is the wise and trusted servant? Who is the servant whom the master can choose to take care of the master's family and the other servants, to give out the proper amount of food at the right time?   **43** When the master comes and finds him doing the work he gave him, that servant will be very happy.   **44** I am telling the truth: The master will choose him to take care of everything the master owns.   **45** But, if that servant thinks that his master will not come back soon, then he will begin to beat the other servants, both men and women. He will also eat too much and get drunk.   **46** Then the master of that servant will come when he is not ready, at a time when he is not expecting the master. Then the master will punish him and send him away. This is what the master does to all of the servants he cannot trust.

47 "That servant knew what his master wanted him to do, but he didn't try to do it. So, he will be punished with a hard whipping!   **48** What about the servant who didn't know what his master wanted? Although the servant did things which deserve punishment, he will get less punishment. Any person who has been given much will be responsible for much. Much more will be expected from the person who has been given more."

Chase God – No Matter What

49 "I came to set the world on fire; I wish it were already burning!   **50** I must be immersed with *one more* immersion; how hard pressed I feel until it is finished!   **51** Do you think I came to bring peace to the world? No! I came to divide the world!   **52** From now on, a family with five people will be divided, three against two, and two against three.

53 A father and son will be divided:
The son will be against his father.
The father will be against his son.
A mother and her daughter will be divided:
The daughter will be against her mother.
The mother will be against her daughter.
A mother-in-law and her daughter-in-law will be divided:

12:38   literally, whether it is at the second watch or the third watch
12:40   literally, the Son of Man

The daughter-in-law will be against her mother-in-law.
The mother-in-law will be against her daughter-in-law."

Signs of the Times

54 Then Jesus said to the crowds, "When you see clouds in the west growing bigger, immediately you say, 'A rainstorm is coming.' And soon it starts to rain. **55** When you feel the wind begin to blow from the south, you say, 'It will be a hot day.' And it happens. **56** You hypocrites!* You can understand the weather, but you don't know the importance of this time in history."

Settle Out of Court!

57 "Can't you decide for yourselves what is right? **58** When a person is suing you, and you are going with him to court, try hard to settle it on the way to court. If you don't, then he may take you to the judge, and the judge will throw you in jail.* **59** And you will never get out of there until they have taken everything you have."*

Chapter 13

Turn Back to God!

1 At that time, some were there with Jesus. They told Jesus about what had happened to some people from Galilee: Pilate had killed those people while they were worshiping, mixing their own blood with the blood of the animals that they were sacrificing. **2** Jesus answered, "Do you think this happened to those Galileans because they were more sinful than all others from Galilee? **3** No, they were not! However, I am telling you, if all of you don't change your hearts, then you will be destroyed as they were! **4** What about those 18 people who died when the tower of Siloam fell on them? Do you think those people were more sinful than all others who live in Jerusalem? **5** They were not! But I tell you, if all of you don't change your hearts, then you will be destroyed, too!"

The Story of the Fig Tree

6 Jesus gave this example: "A man had a fig tree. He planted the tree in his field. The man came looking for some fruit on the tree, but he found none. **7** So, the man said to his servant who took care of the field, 'Listen, I have been looking for fruit on this fig tree for three years, but I never find any. Chop it down! Why should it waste the ground?' **8** But the servant answered, 'Master, let the tree have one more year to produce fruit. Let me dig up the dirt around it and put on some fertilizer. **9** Perhaps the tree will yield fruit next year. If it still does not produce, then you can chop it down.' "

Jesus Heals a Woman on the Sabbath Day

10 Jesus was teaching in one of the synagogues on the Sabbath day. **11** In that synagogue there was a woman who had a spirit that made her sick for 18 years. Her back was always bent; she couldn't stand up straight. **12** When Jesus saw her, he called to her, "Woman, your sickness has left you!" **13** Jesus put his hands on her. Immediately she was able to stand upright. She began to praise God.

12:56   literally, those who act as though they are good when they are not
12:58   literally, to the judge and the judge hands you over to the bailiff and the bailiff throws you in jail.
12:59   literally, your last small coin, a lepta (worth less than a penny)

14 The synagogue leader was angry, because Jesus had healed on the Sabbath day. The leader began to say to the crowds, "There are six days for work. So, come to be healed on one of those days. Do **not** come for healing on the Sabbath day!"

15 The Lord *Jesus* answered, "You hypocrites!* All of you untie your ox or your donkey from the stall and lead them to drink water every day—even on the Sabbath day! **16** This woman whom I healed is our Jewish sister,* but Satan has held her for 18 years. Why can't **she** be untied from her sickness on the Sabbath day?" **17** When Jesus said this, all the people who were opposing him felt ashamed of themselves. The whole crowd was happy. They were thanking God for the wonderful things Jesus was doing.

The Story of the Mustard Seed

18 Then Jesus said, "What is God's kingdom like? With what can I compare it? **19** God's kingdom is like the seed of the mustard plant.* A person plants this seed in his garden. The seed grows and becomes a large tree. The wild birds build nests among its branches."

20 Again, Jesus said, "With what can I compare God's kingdom? **21** It is like yeast* which a woman puts into a tub* of flour to make the bread rise."

I Don't Know You

22 Jesus was teaching in every town and village. He continued to travel toward Jerusalem. **23** Someone asked Jesus, "Lord, how many people will be saved? Only a few?"

Jesus said, **24** "Try hard to get through the narrow door! I tell you, many people will try to get in, but most of them won't be strong enough to enter. **25** If a man locks the door of his house, then you can stand outside and knock on the door, but he won't open it. You can say, 'Master! Open the door for us!' But the man will answer, 'I don't know where you come from!' **26** Then you will begin to say, 'We ate and drank with you. You taught in the streets of our town.' **27** Then he will say to you, 'Where do you come from? I don't know you. Go away from me! All of you are troublemakers!' **28** You will see Abraham, Isaac, Jacob, and all of the prophets in God's kingdom, but you won't be allowed to come in. Then you will scream and grind your teeth. **29** People will come from the east, west, north, and south. They will sit down at the table in the kingdom of God. **30** Those who seem as though they are not important now will be important at that time. Those who seem important now will not be important then."

Jerusalem, Jerusalem

31 At that time some Pharisees came to Jesus and said, "Go away from here and hide! Herod *Antipas* wants to kill you!"

32 Jesus said to them, "Go tell that fox:* 'Listen, today and tomorrow I am throwing out demons and finishing my work of healing. Then, the next day, the work will be finished. **33** After that, I must go, because all prophets should die in Jerusalem.'

13:15   literally, those who are two-faced
13:16   literally, a daughter of Abraham
13:19   The seed from the mustard plant is very small. However, the plant can sometimes grow taller than a man.
13:21   something added to the dough to make it rise before being baked into bread
13:21   literally, three satas; about 40 quarts (four and a half pecks)
13:32   Herod. A fox was thought to be a sly, destructive, worthless animal.

34 "O Jerusalem, Jerusalem! You kill the prophets. *God* sent you His men, but you stoned them to death. I have often wanted to gather up your people like a hen gathers her baby chicks under her wings, but you wouldn't let me.   **35** Listen! Your house is completely empty. I tell you, you will never see me again until you say, 'Praise be to the one who is coming with the authority of the Lord *God*.' "

Chapter 14

Jesus Heals a Man on the Sabbath Day

1 During a Sabbath day, Jesus went to the home of an important Pharisee to eat with him. The Pharisees were all watching Jesus very closely.   **2** A man had a swelling disease. He was put before Jesus.   **3** Jesus asked the Pharisees and the teachers of the law, "Is it right or wrong to heal on the Sabbath day?"   **4** But they kept quiet. So, Jesus took the man and healed him. Then he sent the man away.   **5** Jesus said to them, "If your son or ox falls into a well on the Sabbath day, *you know that* you would quickly pull him out."   **6** The Pharisees and teachers of the law were not able to say anything against what Jesus said.

The Most Important Seat

7 Then Jesus noticed that some of the guests were choosing the best places to sit. So, Jesus gave this example: **8** "When a person invites you to a wedding, don't sit in the most important seat. He may have invited someone more important than you.   **9** If you do sit in the most important seat, then the one who invited you may come to you and say, 'Give this man your seat!' Then you will start to move down to the last place. And you will be very embarrassed.   **10** Instead, when a person invites you, go sit in the seat which is least important. The one who invited you will come to you and say, 'Friend, move up here to a more important seat!' Then all of the other guests will respect you. **11** Every person who acts as if he is important will be made ashamed, but every person who truly humbles himself will be made important."

They Can't Pay You Back

12 Then Jesus said to the Pharisee who had invited him, "When you give a luncheon or a dinner, don't invite only your friends, brothers, relatives, and rich neighbors. They will just invite you back to eat with them. Then you will have your reward. **13** Instead, when you give a party, invite the poor people, the crippled, the lame, and the blind.   **14** Then you will be happy, because these people cannot pay you back. They have nothing. However, you will be rewarded when the righteous rise from death."

Excuses, Excuses

15 One of the men sitting at the table with Jesus heard these things. The man said to Jesus, "A person who eats bread in God's kingdom will be very happy!"
16 Jesus said to him, "A man was giving a big dinner. He invited many people. **17** When it was time to eat, the man sent his servant to tell the guests, saying, 'Come! *Dinner* is ready!'   **18** But all the guests said they couldn't come. Each man gave an excuse. The first man said to him, 'I have just bought a field; I must go out and see it. Please excuse me.'   **19** Another man said, 'I have just bought five pair of oxen; I must go and try them out. Please excuse me.'   **20** A third man said, 'I have just gotten married; I can't come.'   **21** So, the servant returned. He told his master what had

happened. Then the master became angry and said, 'Hurry! Go into the streets and alleys of the town. Bring me the poor people, the crippled, the blind, and the lame.' **22** *Later* the servant said to him, 'Master, I did what you told me to do, but we still have room for more people!' **23** The master said to the servant, 'Go out to the highways and country roads. Make them come. I want my house to be full! **24** I tell you, none of those men I invited first will ever eat with me!' "

Count the Cost

25 Many people were traveling with Jesus. He turned around and said to them, **26** "If someone comes to me, yet that person loves his father, mother, wife, children, brothers, or sisters more than he loves me, he cannot be my follower. A person must love me more than he loves himself! **27** The person who does not carry his own cross* cannot be my follower. **28** If you wanted to build a building, you would sit down first and add up how much it would cost, to see if you had enough money to finish the job. **29** If you didn't do that, you might begin the work, but you wouldn't be able to finish it. Then all of the people watching you would laugh at you. **30** They would say, "This man began to build, but he wasn't able to finish!"

31 "If a king is going to fight against another king, first he will sit down and plan. If the king has only 10,000 men, he will see if he is able to defeat the other king who is opposing him with 20,000 men. **32** If he cannot defeat the other king, then he will send a group of men to ask for terms of peace from the other king while he is far away. **33** In the same way, all of you *must first plan*. You must give everything you have. If you don't, you cannot be my follower!"

When Good Changes to Bad

34 "Salt is a good thing, but if the salt loses its salty taste, *then it is no good.** You cannot make it salty again. **35** You can't even use it for dirt or fertilizer. People just throw it away.*

"The person who has ears to hear with should use them!"

Chapter 15

The Story of the Lost Sheep

1 Tax collectors and "sinners" all came near to listen to Jesus. **2** Then the Pharisees and the teachers of the law began to complain, "This man welcomes sinners! He even **eats** with them!"

3 Then Jesus gave them this example: **4** "Suppose a man has 100 sheep, but he loses one of them. He will leave the other 99 sheep in the open country, and go out and look for the lost one. The man will continue to search for the lost sheep until he finds it. **5** And when he finds the sheep, the man is very happy. The man carries it home on his shoulders. **6** He goes to his friends and neighbors and says to them, 'Rejoice with me, because I found my lost sheep!' **7** I tell you, there is much joy in heaven when

---

14:27   suffering

14:34   In Christ's day, salt contained certain impurities which are not present in our salt today. The salt was stored in skin bags, and during damp weather, the impurities in the salt would absorb water which would dissolve the pure salt and it would escape from the bag. The residue thus lost its saltiness and it was therefore no longer any good for anything.

14:35   literally, it is unfit. People just throw it out.

one sinner changes his heart. There is more joy for that one sinner than there is for 99 good people who don't need to change their hearts.'"

The Story of the Lost Coin

8 "Suppose a woman has ten silver coins, but she loses one of them. The woman gets a light and sweeps the house. She will look carefully for the coin until she finds it. **9** And when she finds the lost coin, she will call her friends and neighbors and say to them, 'Rejoice with me, because I have found the coin which I lost!' **10** In the same way, I tell you, there will be joy before the angels of God when one sinner changes his heart."

The Story of the Lost Son

11 Then Jesus said, "A man had two sons. **12** The younger son said to his father, 'Father, give me my part of all our holdings!' So, the father divided the property with his two sons. **13** Not long afterward, the younger son gathered up all that he had and left. He traveled far away to another country. There the son wasted his money like a fool; **14** he spent everything he had. Then the land became very dry, and it did not rain. There was not enough food to eat anywhere in that country. He began to starve. **15** So, he went and got a job with one of the important men of that country. The man sent him into the fields to feed pigs. **16** The boy was so hungry, that he wanted to stuff himself with the food which the pigs were eating. No one was giving him anything. **17** Finally, the boy realized that he had been very foolish. He thought, 'All of my father's servants have plenty of food, yet here I am about to die, because I have nothing to eat. **18** I will get up and go to my father. I will say to him: "Father, I sinned against God* and in front of you. **19** I'm not worthy to be called your son anymore. Treat me as one of your paid servants.' " **20** So, the son got up and went to his father."

"While the son was still a long way off, his father saw him coming. He felt sorry for his son. So, the father ran to him. He hugged and kissed his son. **21** The son said, 'Father, I sinned against God* and in front of you. I'm not worthy to be called your son anymore.' **22** But the father said to his servants, 'Hurry! Bring the best robe and dress him. Put a ring on his finger and *good* shoes on his feet, too. **23** Bring our fattened calf. We will kill it and have plenty to eat. Then we can have a party! **24** My son was dead, but now he is alive again. He was lost, but now he is found!' So, they began to celebrate."

The Other Brother

25 "The older son was in the field. As he came closer to the house, he heard the sound of music and dancing. **26** So, the older son called to one of the servant boys and asked, 'What does all this mean?' **27** The servant said, 'Your brother has come back. Your father killed the fattened calf *for him to eat. Your father was happy*, because your brother came back home safely!' **28** The older son was angry and wouldn't go inside to *join* the party. So, his father went out to beg him to come in. **29** But the son said to his father, 'Look, I have served you like a slave for many years! I have obeyed every one of your commands, but you never even killed a goat for me, so that I could have a party with my friends. **30** But this other son of yours has wasted all of your

---

15:18   literally, heaven; Jewish people often avoided direct references to God because of their deep respect for Him.

15:21   literally, heaven

121

money on whores. Then he comes home and you kill the fattened calf for him!'
31 But the father said to him, 'Son, you are always with me. All that I have is yours.
32 We must be happy and celebrate, because your brother was dead, but now he is
alive. He was lost, but now he is found!' "

Chapter 16

The Story of the Shrewd Manager

1 Jesus said to his followers, "Once there was a rich man who hired a manager to
take care of his business. Later the rich man learned that his manager was cheating him.
2 So, he called in the manager and said to him, 'I have heard some bad things about
you. Give me a report of what you have done with my money. You're fired!'   **3** Later
the manager thought to himself, 'What will I do? My master is taking my job away from
me! I'm not strong enough to dig ditches, and I'm too proud to beg.   **4-5** I know what
I will do! I will do something, so that, when I lose my job, other people will welcome
me into their homes.' So, the manager called in each person who owed the master some
money. He said to the first one, 'How much do you owe my master?'   **6** The man
answered, 'I owe him 800 gallons of olive oil.' The manager said to him, 'Here is your
bill; hurry, sit down and change it to 400 gallons.'   **7** Then the manager said to another man, 'How much do you owe my master?' The man answered, 'I owe him 1,000
bushels of wheat.' Then the manager said to him, 'Here is your bill; change it to 800
bushels.'   **8** The master learned about this later. The master thought the dishonest
manager had done a shrewd thing. Worldly people use their knowledge about worldly
things better than spiritual people do.

9 "I ask you, should you make friends for yourselves with dishonest money? When
the money is all gone, can they welcome you into homes which last forever?   **10** I tell
you, if a person can be trusted with small things, he may also be trusted with big things.
If a person is dishonest in little things, then he will be dishonest in big things, too.
11 If you cannot be trusted with worldly money, no one will trust you with true wealth.
12 And, if you cannot be trusted with the things which belong to someone else, then no
one will give you things for yourself."

For the Love of Money

13 "No servant can serve two masters *at the same time*. The servant will like one but
not like the other. Or, he will be more loyal to one and look down on the other. You cannot serve God and Money *at the same time*."

14 The Pharisees were listening to all these things. They were criticizing Jesus,
because they all loved money.   **15** Jesus said to the Pharisees, "You make yourselves
look good in front of people, but God knows what is really in your hearts. The things
which are very important to people are worthless to God."

The Law and the Kingdom of God

16 "Until the time of John, there was the law and the prophets. Since then, the Good
News about the kingdom of God is being told. Everyone is trying hard to get into the
kingdom of God.

17 "Even the smallest part of the law cannot be changed. It would be easier for the
world* to pass away.

16:17   literally, the sky and the earth

18 "If a man divorces his wife and marries another woman, he is committing adultery. And the man who marries a divorced woman is also committing adultery."

The Story of Lazarus and the Rich Man

19 Jesus said, "There was a rich man who always dressed up in the finest clothes. He was so rich that he was able to feast and have a party every day.   **20** There was also a beggar named Lazarus. His body was covered with sores. He was often put at the rich man's gate.   **21** Lazarus only wanted to eat the crumbs which fell from the rich man's table. Instead, the dogs came and licked his sores!   **22** After a while, Lazarus died. The angels took Lazarus and placed him in the arms of Abraham.* The rich man also died and was buried.   **23** He was *sent to* Hades* and was in much pain. The rich man saw Abraham far away, with Lazarus in his arms.   **24** He called out, 'Father Abraham, have mercy on me! Send Lazarus to me, so that he may dip the tip of his finger in water and cool my tongue. I am suffering in this fire!'   **25** But Abraham said, 'My child, do you remember when you lived *on earth* ? You had all the good things in life, but all the bad things happened to Lazarus. Now he is comforted here, and you are suffering.   **26** Also, there is a great canyon established between you and us. No one can cross over to help you; and no one can come over here from there.'   **27** The rich man said, 'Then father Abraham, please send Lazarus to my father's house on earth!   **28** I have five brothers. Lazarus could warn my brothers, so that they won't come to this place of pain.'   **29** But Abraham said, 'They have Moses and the prophets *to read*; let them learn from that!'   **30** But the rich man said, 'No, father Abraham! If only someone could come back to them from death, then they would change their hearts.'   **31** But Abraham said to him, 'No! If your brothers won't listen to Moses and the prophets, then they wouldn't be persuaded by anyone who might come back from death!' "

Chapter 17

Be Careful With the Kids

1 Jesus said to his followers, "Things will surely occur which will cause people to sin, but it will be horrible for the person who causes this to happen.   **2** If he causes one of these little ones to sin, it would be better for him to drown with a big rock tied to his neck.

3 "Be careful! If your brother sins, tell him he is wrong, but if he changes his heart, forgive him.   **4** If your brother does something wrong to you seven times in one day, but each time he says that he is sorry, then you should forgive him."

Mustard Seed Faith

5 The apostles said to the Lord *Jesus*, "Give us more faith!"

6 The Lord said, "If your faith were the size of the seed of the mustard plant, then you would say to this mulberry tree, 'Dig yourself up and plant yourself in the ocean!' and the tree would obey you."

I've Only Done My Duty

7 "Suppose one of you has a slave who has been *working* in the field, plowing the ground or caring for the sheep. When the slave comes in, what would you say to him? Would you say, 'Hurry, come in! Sit down to eat!'?   **8** No, you would say this to your

16:22   To a Jew it was a wonderful thought to think of being that close to his greatest ancestor.
16:23   the Greek word for the unseen world of the dead

servant: 'Prepare something for me to eat. Then get dressed up and serve me. When I finish eating and drinking, then you may eat.'   **9** The slave does not get any special thanks for doing his job. He is only doing what his master told him to do.   **10** It is the same with you, too. When you do all of the things you are told to do, you should think: 'We are not good slaves; we have only done our duty and nothing more.' "

One Out of Ten

11 Jesus was traveling to Jerusalem, going from Galilee through Samaria.   **12** He came into a village. Ten men met him there. These men did not come close to Jesus, because they all had leprosy.*   **13** But the men shouted to Jesus, "Jesus! Teacher! Take pity on us!"

14 When Jesus saw the men, he said, "Go and show yourselves to the priests."

As the ten men were going to the priests, they were healed.   **15** When one of the men saw that he had been healed, he went back to Jesus and praised God with a loud voice.   **16** He bowed down at Jesus' feet and thanked Jesus. (This man was a Samaritan.*)   **17** Jesus answered, "Ten men were healed; where are the other nine?   **18** Is this Samaritan man the only one who came back to give glory to God?"   **19** Then Jesus said to him, "Stand up! You may go. You were healed, because you believed."

God's Kingdom Is Inside You

20 Some of the Pharisees asked Jesus, "When will the kingdom of God come?"

Jesus answered, "God's kingdom is not coming in such a way that you will be able to watch it.   **21** People will not say, 'Look, God's kingdom is here!' or, 'There it is!' No, God's kingdom is inside of you."

22 Then Jesus said to his followers, "The time will come when you will want very much to re-live one of the days of the Son of Man,* but you will not be able to."   **23** People will say to you, 'Look, there it is!' or, 'Look, here it is!' Stay where you are; don't go away and search."

When Jesus Comes Again

24 "I* will come again. On the day when I come, I will shine, as lightning flashes across the sky.   **25** But first, I* must suffer many things and be rejected by the people of this time.   **26** When I come again, it will be the same as it was when Noah lived. **27** In the time of Noah, people were eating, drinking, getting married, and giving their daughters away in marriage—even on the day when Noah entered the ship.* Then the flood came and killed everyone else.   **28** It will be just like it was in the time of Lot.* Those people were eating, drinking, buying, selling, planting, and building houses. **29** The people were doing these things even on the day when Lot left Sodom. Then fire and sulfur rained down from the sky and killed them all.   **30** This is exactly how it will be when I come again.*

17:12   a very bad skin disease which destroys the flesh
17:16   Samaritans were distantly related to the Jews. They had married non-Jews. (See 2 Kings 17:24.) There was much hatred between the Jews and the Samaritans.
17:22   Jesus
17:24   literally, the Son of Man
17:25   literally, the Son of Man
17:27   ark
17:28   See Genesis 19:1-29.
17:30   literally, the Son of Man is revealed

31 "On that day, if a man is on his roof, he won't have time to go inside and get his things. If a man is in the field, he must not go back home. **32** Remember Lot's wife.*

33 The person who tries to save his life will lose it, but the person who gives his life away will save it. **34** I tell you, when I come again, there may be two men sleeping in one room; one man will be taken and the other man will be left. **35** There may be two women working* together; one woman will be taken and the other will be left." **36** *

37 The followers asked Jesus, "Where will this be, Lord?"

Jesus answered, " *People can always tell* where a dead body is; *they can see* the vultures gathering."

Chapter 18

Never Give Up

1 Then Jesus used this story *to teach* the followers that they should always pray and never give up:

2 "Once there was a judge in a town. He didn't fear God. The judge didn't care what people thought about him, either. **3** In that same town, there was a woman who was a widow. The woman was always coming to this judge and saying, 'There is a man who is trying to ruin me. Give me my rights!' **4** The judge didn't want to help the woman. However, after a long time, the judge thought to himself, 'Even though I don't fear God, and I don't care what people think, **5** this woman is beginning to bother me. If I give her what she wants, then she will leave me alone. If I don't give her what she wants, she will keep coming back until I get sick!' "

6 The Lord *Jesus* said, "Listen to what the bad judge said. **7** God's chosen people cry out to Him night and day. God will always give them what is right; He will not be slow to answer His people. **8** I am telling you, God will soon help His people! Nevertheless, when I* come again, will I find people on earth who believe in me?"

The Story of a Pharisee and a Tax Collector

9 There were some who were sure that they were righteous. They acted as if they were better than other people. Jesus gave this example *to teach*: **10** "Once there was a Pharisee and a tax collector.* They both went up into the temple courtyard one day to pray. **11** The Pharisee stood there alone. He was praying like this: 'O God, I thank Thee that I am not like other people. I am not like men who steal, cheat, commit adultery, or even like this tax collector. **12** I fast* twice a week and I give ten percent of everything I make!'

13 "The tax collector stood alone, too. However, when he prayed, he wouldn't even look up to heaven. The tax collector felt very humble before God. He said, 'O God, have mercy on me. I am a sinner!' **14** I am telling you, when **this** man went back home,

---

17:32   See Genesis 19:26

17:35   literally, grinding grain

17:36   Some manuscripts have verse 36: "There will be two men in the field; the one will be taken and the other will be left." (Compare Matthew 24:40.)

18:8   literally, the Son of Man

18:10   These were Jews hired by the Romans to gather taxes for the Romans. They often cheated their fellow countrymen. They were considered traitors.

18:12   to go without food for a period of time, usually for spiritual reasons

he was right with God; the Pharisee was not right with God. Every person who acts as if he is important will be made ashamed, but every person who humbles himself will be made very important."

Like a Child

15 Some people were bringing their small children to Jesus, so that he could touch them. When his followers saw this, they told the people not to do this. **16** But Jesus called the little children to him and said *to his followers*, "Let the little children come to me. Don't stop them, because the kingdom of God belongs to people who are like these children. **17** I am telling you the truth: You must accept God's kingdom as a little child accepts things, or you will never enter it!"

The Poor Rich Man

18 A *rich* leader asked Jesus, "Good Teacher, what must I do to get eternal life?"

19 Jesus asked him, "Why did you call **me** good? Only God is good! **20** *But I will answer your question.* You know the commands:

'You must not commit adultery.'
'You must not commit murder.'
'You must not steal.'
'You must not lie.'
'You must love and obey your father and mother . . . .' "   *Exodus 20:13-16*

21 But the leader said, "I have obeyed all these commands since I was a boy!"

22 When Jesus heard that, he said to the leader, "But there is still one more thing you need to do. Sell everything you have and distribute it to the poor people. Then you will have a treasure in heaven. Then come, follow me!" **23** But when the man heard this, he was very sad. (The man was very rich *and wanted to keep his money.*)

24 When Jesus saw that the man was very sad, he said, "It will be so hard for people with a lot of money to enter the kingdom of God! **25** It would be easier for a camel to go through the eye of a needle than for a rich man to enter the kingdom of God!"

We've Left Everything!

26 When the people heard this, they asked, "Then who can be saved?"

27 Jesus answered, "God can do things which don't seem possible to human beings!"

28 Peter said, "Look, we have left everything we had and followed you!"

29 Jesus said, "I am telling you the truth: Every person who has left his home, wife, brothers, parents, or children because of God's kingdom **30** will surely be rewarded many times in this time, and, in the age to come, with eternal life."

Jesus Will Come Back From Death

31 Then Jesus took the twelve *apostles* aside. He said to them, "Listen! We are going up to Jerusalem. Everything which God told the prophets to write about me* will take place! **32** God's people will turn against me and give me to the non-Jewish men. They will laugh at me and spit on me, and insult me. **33** They will beat me with whips and

---

18:31   literally, the Son of Man

then kill me! But, on the third day *after my death*, I will rise." **34** The apostles tried to understand this, but they could not; the meaning was hidden from them. They did not know what Jesus was talking about.

35 Jesus came near the city of Jericho. There was a blind man sitting beside the road. The man was begging people for money. **36** When this man heard the crowd coming down the road, he asked, "What's happening?"

37 The people told him, "Jesus, the one from Nazareth, is coming here."

38 The blind man became excited and cried out, "Jesus! Son of David! Take pity on me!"

39 The people who were in front leading the group told the blind man to be quiet, but he shouted even louder, "Son of David! Take pity on me!"

40 Jesus stopped there and said, "Bring that man to me!" When the blind man came near, Jesus asked him,

41 "What do you want of me?"

The blind man said, "Lord, *heal me*! Let me be able to see again."

42 Jesus said to him, "See again! You are made well, because you believed."

43 Immediately, the man was able to see again. He followed Jesus, giving glory to God. All of the people who saw this praised God for what had occurred.

Chapter 19

Zacchaeus Went Out on a Limb

1 Jesus was going through the city of Jericho. **2** In Jericho there was a man named Zacchaeus. He was a very important, rich tax collector.* **3** He wanted to see Jesus, but there were also many other people, and Zacchaeus was too short to see over them.

4 So he ran ahead to a place where he knew Jesus would pass. Then he climbed a sycamore-fig tree, so that he could see Jesus. **5** When Jesus came to that spot, he looked up. Jesus said to him, "Zacchaeus, hurry! Come down! I must stay at **your** house today!"

6 Then Zacchaeus came down quickly. He was so happy to have Jesus in his house. **7** All of the people saw this. They began to complain, saying, "Look at the type of person Jesus stays with. Zacchaeus is a sinner!"

8 Zacchaeus stood up and said to the Lord *Jesus*, "Lord, I am now giving half of my money to the poor. If I have cheated anyone, I am now paying him back four times more!"

9 Jesus said, "This man is a son of Abraham. Today salvation has come to this house! **10** I* came to find lost people and to save them."

The Story of Wise Investments

11 Jesus traveled closer to Jerusalem. Some of the people thought that God's kingdom would soon appear. *Jesus knew* that the people thought this, so, while the people were listening to these things, he continued with a story: **12** "A very important man was preparing to go to a faraway country to be made a king. After that, the man planned to return home *and rule*. **13** So, the man called ten of his servants together. He gave a gold coin to each servant. The man said, 'Do business with this money until I come

---

19:2   These were Jews hired by the Romans to gather taxes for the Romans. They often cheated their fellow countrymen. They were considered traitors.

19:10   literally, the Son of Man

back.' **14** But the people in his kingdom hated the man. So the people sent a group of their men to follow the man to the other country. There these men said, 'We don't want that man to rule over us!'

15 "However, he **did** become king. When he came home, he said, 'Call those servants who have my money. I want to know how much more money they earned with it.' **16** The first servant came and said, 'Sir, I earned ten gold coins with the coin you gave me!' **17** The king said to the servant, 'Fine! You are a good servant. I see that I can trust you with small things. So **now** I will let you have authority over ten of my cities!' **18** The second servant said, 'Sir, with the one gold coin which belongs to you, I earned five coins!' **19** The king said to this servant, 'You may rule over five cities!' **20** Then another servant came in. The servant said to the king, 'Sir, here is your gold coin. I hid it in a piece of cloth. **21** I was afraid of you; you are a hard man. You take money which you didn't earn and gather food you didn't even grow!' **22** Then the king said to the servant, 'You evil servant! I will use your own words to condemn you. You said that I am a hard man. You said I take money which I didn't earn and gather food I didn't even grow. **23** If this is true, then you should have put my money in the bank. Then, after I came back, my money would have earned some interest.' **24** Then the king said to the men who were watching, 'Take the gold coin away from this servant and give it to the servant who earned ten coins.' **25** The men said to the king, 'But sir, that servant already has ten gold coins!' **26** The king said, 'The person who uses what he has will get more, but the person who doesn't use what he has will have everything taken away from him! **27** Now where are my enemies? Where are the people who didn't want me to rule over them? Bring my enemies here and kill them. I will watch them die!' "

Jesus Enters Jerusalem

28 After Jesus said these things, he continued traveling upward toward Jerusalem. **29** He came near to Bethphage and Bethany, villages close to Olive Mountain. Jesus sent two of his followers on ahead. **30** He said, "Go into that village over there. You will find a young donkey tied there that has not been ridden. Untie it and bring it to me here. **31** If someone asks you why you are taking the donkey, you will say, 'The Lord, its owner, needs it.' "

32 The two followers went into town. They found the donkey exactly as Jesus had told them. **33** The followers untied the donkey, but its owners *came out*. They asked the followers, "Why are you untying our donkey?"

34 Jesus' followers answered, "The Lord, its owner, needs it." **35** Then the followers brought it to Jesus. They put some of their clothes on the donkey's back. Then they helped Jesus get on top of it. **36** While Jesus was riding along the road *toward Jerusalem*, the followers were spreading their robes on the road in front of him.

37 Jesus was coming close *to Jerusalem*. He was already near the bottom of Olive Mountain. The whole group of followers were happy. They were very excited and they praised God for all the powerful things they had seen. They said,

38 "Give praise to this king who is coming
    with the authority of the Lord *God*!
  Let there be peace in heaven
    and glory to God!"*

Psalm 118:26

19:38   literally, in the highest places

39 From the crowd some of the Pharisees said to Jesus, "Teacher, tell your followers not to say such things!"

40 But Jesus answered, "I am telling you, these things must be said. If my followers don't say them, then these rocks will shout!"

Know the Time of the Chase

41 Jesus came near to Jerusalem and saw it. He began to cry over the city. **42** Jesus spoke to Jerusalem, "I wish you knew today what would bring you peace, but it is hidden from your eyes!   **43** A time is coming when your enemies will build a wall around you. Your enemies will hold you in on all sides.   **44** They will completely destroy you and all of your children. Not one stone will remain on top of another. All this will happen, because you didn't know the time when God came to save you."*

Jesus Threw Them Out

45 Jesus went into the temple courtyard. He began to throw out the people who were selling things there.   **46** Jesus said, "It is written,
'My house will be a place for praying.'   *Isaiah 56:7*
But **you** have changed it into a hiding place for thieves!"*

47 Every day Jesus was teaching the people in the temple courtyard. The most important priests, the teachers of the law, and some of the leaders of the people were trying to kill Jesus,   **48** but they didn't know how they could do it, because all of the people were listening closely to Jesus. The people were very interested in what Jesus had to say.

Chapter 20

Question for Question

1 One day Jesus was in the temple courtyard, teaching the people. Jesus told them the Good News. The most important priests, teachers of the law, and Jewish elders came.   **2** They said to Jesus, "Tell us! What sort of authority do you have to do these things? Who gave you this authority?"

3 Jesus answered, "I will also ask **you** a question. Tell me: **4** When John immersed people, did that come from God or from man?"

5 They all talked about this. They said to each other, "If we answer, 'From God,' then Jesus will say, 'Then why didn't you believe John?'   **6** But if we say, 'It was from man,' then all of the people will stone us to death, because they believe John was a prophet."   **7** So they decided to give this answer: "We don't know where John's immersion came from."

8 So Jesus said to them, "Then I won't tell **you** what sort of authority I have to do these things!"

The Story of the Vineyard

9 Then Jesus began to give this example to the people: "A man planted a vineyard. He rented the land to some farmers. Then he went away on a trip for a long time. **10** At harvest time, the man sent a servant to those farmers. They were supposed to give

---

19:41-44   This prophecy was fulfilled in every detail when the Romans destroyed Jerusalem in 70 A.D.
19:46   These men were taking advantage of Jews from other countries who had come to Jerusalem to worship by selling them animals necessary for their sacrifices at very high prices.

the owner of the land some of the grapes, but the farmers beat the servant and sent him away with nothing. **11** So the man sent a different servant. They also beat this servant. They showed no respect for him and sent the servant away with nothing. **12** The man sent a third servant to the farmers. The farmers wounded this servant and kicked him out. **13** The owner of the vineyard said, 'What will I do now? I will send my precious son. Perhaps the farmers will show respect for him!' **14** When the farmers saw the son, they began to think to themselves, 'This is the owner's son. If we kill him, then this field will be ours!' **15** So the farmers kicked the son out of the field and killed him.

"What do you think the owner of this field will do to those farmers? **16** He will come and destroy them! After that, he will give the field to some other farmers."

They Wanted to Have Jesus Arrested

The people heard this story. They said, "No! May this never happen!" **17** But Jesus looked into their eyes and said, "Then what does this verse mean:

'The stone that the builders did not want
 became the cornerstone.'?* *Psalm 118:22*

18 Everyone who falls on that stone will be broken. If that stone falls on you, it will crush you!"

19 The Jewish leaders *heard this*. They knew that this story was about them. They wanted to arrest Jesus right then, but they were afraid of what the people would do to them if they did. **20** So the teachers and priests waited for the right time.

They sent some men to Jesus and told them to act as if they were good men. They wanted to find something wrong with the things that Jesus said. (If they found anything wrong, then they could hand Jesus over to the high priest and the governor to be punished.) **21** So the men asked Jesus, "Teacher, we know what you say and teach is right. You don't care how important or unimportant a person is. You always teach the truth about God's way. **22** Now, *tell us*, is it right that we should pay taxes to Caesar* or not?"

23 But Jesus knew that these men were trying to trick him. Jesus said to them, **24** "Show me a coin. Whose name and picture is on it?"

They said, "Caesar's."

25 Jesus said to them, "Then give to Caesar the things which are Caesar's. And give to God the things which belong to God."

26 The men were amazed at his *wise* answer; they could say nothing. The men were not able to trick Jesus in front of the people.

No Marriage in Heaven

27 Some Sadducees* came to Jesus. (Sadducees believe that no one will rise from death.) They asked Jesus, **28** "Teacher, Moses wrote to us that if a married man dies and he did not have children, his brother must marry the widow. Then they will have children for the *dead* brother. **29** Now there were seven brothers. The first one got married, but died. He had no children. **30-31** Then the second brother also married

---

20:17   This was the first and most important stone in constructing a building.
20:22   The title of the supreme Roman rulers. "Caesar" became the title of each emperor.
20:27   The Sadducees were a Jewish religious sect and political group. Many priests, including the high
        priests, belonged to this party. See Acts 4:6; 23:8.

her and he died. They also had no children. The same thing happened with all the other brothers. 32 The woman was the last to die. 33 All seven men had married her. So, when this woman rises from death, whose wife will she be?"

34 Jesus answered the Sadducees, "During this age, people marry each other. 35 Some people will be declared worthy enough to be raised from death and live again after this life. However, in that life, they will not marry or give in marriage. 36 They cannot die anymore, because they will be like angels. When they rise from death, they will be the children of God. 37 Moses clearly showed that people are raised from death. When Moses wrote about the *burning* bush,* he said that the Lord is the God of Abraham, the God of Isaac, and the God of Jacob.* 38 *This means that* the Lord *God* is not a God of dead people; He is the God of people who are alive! To God, everyone is alive."

39 Some of the teachers of the law said, "Teacher, your answer was very good." 40 No one dared to ask him another question.

Jesus Asks a Hard Question

41 Then Jesus said to them, "How can they claim that the Messiah* is the son of David? 42 In the book of Psalms, David himself says:

'The Lord *God* said to my Lord:*
 "Sit at my right side
  43 until I put your enemies under your feet." '*   *Psalm 110:1*

44 Therefore, David is calling the Messiah 'Lord.' So, how can the Messiah be the son of David?"

Watch Out for the Experts!

45 While all of the people were listening to Jesus, he said to his followers, 46 "Watch out for the teachers of the law. They want to walk around wearing clothes which make them look important. They like the greetings *of respect* which people give them in the marketplaces. They always want the most important seats in the synagogues and the best seats at the dinners, 47 but *they cheat* widows and steal their homes. Then they make themselves look good by saying long prayers. Because of all this, God will punish these men so much more."

Chapter 21

Who Gave More?

1 As Jesus looked up, he saw some rich people putting their gifts for God into the temple money box.* 2 Then Jesus saw a widow who was very poor. She put two small coins into the box. 3 Jesus said, "I am telling you the truth: This poor widow has given more than all those rich people. 4 The rich people have plenty; they only

---

20:37   Before the Bible had chapter and verse numbers, sections were known by key words. In this case, it was "bush."

20:37   In other words, if He is still their God, they must not be dead.

20:41   Christ, God's chosen one whom the Jewish people expected to come to save them

20:42   In the Hebrew text of Psalms, the first "Lord" is Yahweh; the second "Lord" is Adonai, referring to Christ.

20:43   in his control

21:1   See Joshua 6:19-24; 1 Kings 7:51. (Compare Mark 12:41.)

gave what they didn't need, but this woman gave everything she had. She needed that money to live on."

The Temple Will Be Destroyed

5 Some of the followers were talking about the temple. They said, "This is a beautiful temple. It has the best stones. Look at the many good gifts which have been offered to God!"*

But Jesus said, 6 "The time will come when everything you see here will be destroyed. Not one stone will stay on top of another. This will be completely destroyed!"

First Things First

7 Some followers asked Jesus, "Teacher, when will these things occur? How will we know* when it is the time for these things to happen?" 8 Jesus said, "Be careful! Don't be fooled. Many people will come to you using my name. They will say, 'I am the one!' and, 'The right time has come near!' But don't believe them. 9 When you hear about wars and riots, don't be afraid. These things must happen first. The end will come later."

10 Then Jesus said to them, "One country will fight against another country. Kingdoms will fight against other kingdoms. 11 There will be great earthquakes, sicknesses, and other terrible things in many places. In some places there will be no food for the people. Great wonders and amazing proofs will come from heaven.

12 "But before all of these things happen, men will arrest you and persecute you. They will hand you over to their synagogue courts and throw you in jail. Men will lead you to kings and governors because you are associated with my name. 13 But this will give you an opportunity to tell about all of the things you have seen me do. 14 Don't worry about how you will answer them or what you will say. 15 I will give you the ability to speak well, with much wisdom. None of your enemies will be able to show that you are wrong. 16 Even your parents, brothers, relatives, and friends will turn against you. They will have some of you put to death. 17 All people will hate you because of my name, 18 but not one hair on your head will be harmed. 19 By enduring all of these things, you will keep your souls."

Tough Times

20 "You will see armies all around Jerusalem. Then you will know that the time for the destruction of Jerusalem is very near.* 21 At that time, the believers in Judea should run away to the mountains. Those inside Jerusalem must leave quickly. If you are near the city, don't go in! 22 The prophets wrote many things about the time when God will punish His people. This is the time when all of these things must occur. 23 At that time, it will be horrible for pregnant women and nursing mothers, because very hard times will come to this land. God will be angry with the Jewish people. 24 Some of the people will be killed by soldiers. Other people will be made prisoners and taken to every nation. The holy city of Jerusalem will be walked on by people of the world until their time is completed."

21:5   This was the magnificent temple which Herod the Great had built in his attempt to gain favor from the Jews.
21:7   literally, what sign will there be
21:20   The temple and the city of Jerusalem were completely destroyed by the Romans in 70 A.D.

Jesus Will Return

25 "Amazing things will occur with the sun, moon, and stars. On earth people without God will feel trapped. The oceans will be upset and the people will not know why. **26** Men will become so afraid that they will faint. They will be very worried about the things which will happen to the whole world. The powers in the universe will be moved. **27** Then people will see me* coming on a cloud with power and great glory. **28** When these things begin to happen, *don't be afraid*. Stand straight and lift up your heads! *The time* is near when God will save you!"

The Story of the Fig Tree

29 Then Jesus gave them this story: "Look at all of the trees. The fig tree *is a good example.* **30** When you see it turning green, no one needs to tell you that summer is near. **31** In the same way, you will see all of these amazing things occur. Then you will **know** that God's kingdom is coming very soon.

32 "I am telling you the truth. All of these things will occur while the people of this time are still alive! **33** The world* will be destroyed, but my words will **never** be destroyed!"

Ready for the Chase

34 "Be careful! Otherwise, your hearts will become burdened with drinking, getting drunk, and the worries of this life. That day may come suddenly, when you are not ready. **35** It will come as a surprise* to all people who live on earth.

36 "So, be ready all the time. Pray that you will be strong enough to endure all of these things when they occur and to stand before me."*

37 During the day Jesus was teaching the people in the temple courtyard. At night he went out of the city and stayed all night on Olive Mountain. **38** Every morning all of the people got up early to go listen to Jesus in the temple courtyard.

Chapter 22

Betrayed by a Friend

1 It was almost time for the Feast of Unleavened Bread, called the Passover Festival.* **2** The most important priests and teachers of the law were trying to find a way to kill Jesus, but they were afraid of the people.

3 One of Jesus' twelve *apostles* was named Judas Iscariot. Satan entered Judas. **4** He went off and talked with the most important priests and some of the soldiers *who guarded the temple*. Judas talked to them about a plan he had to hand Jesus over to them. **5** They were pleased. They agreed to give Judas some money. **6** Judas said, "Yes." He waited for the best time to give Jesus to them—when there was no crowd around *to see it*.

Jesus' Last Supper

7 The day came for the Passover Feast.* This was the day when *the priests* sacrificed the Passover lambs.* **8** Jesus sent Peter and John, saying, "Go and prepare the Passover meal for us to eat."

21:27 literally, the Son of Man
21:33 literally, the sky and the earth
21:35 literally, snare or trap
21:36 on the Judgment Day
22:1 A yearly feast which reminded Jews of the time when the death angel "passed over" their homes in Egypt (Exodus 12:21-28).
22:7 literally, the Day of Unleavened Bread
22:7 animals sacrificed during the Passover Festival (Exodus 12:21)

9 Peter and John said to Jesus, "Where do you want us to prepare the meal?"

Jesus said to them, 10 "Listen! After you go into Jerusalem,* you will see a man carrying a jar of water.* Follow him. He will go into a house. Go inside with him. 11 Say this to the owner of that house: 'The Teacher asks that you please show us the room where the Teacher and his followers may eat the Passover Feast.' 12 Then he will show you a large upstairs room. This room is ready. Prepare the Passover meal there."

13 So, Peter and John left. Everything happened just as Jesus had told them. Then they prepared the Passover meal.

Remember Me

14 The time came *for them to eat the Passover meal*. Jesus and the apostles were sitting around the table. 15 Jesus said to them, "I wanted very much to eat this Passover meal with you before I die. 16 I tell you, I will never eat another Passover meal until it is given its true meaning in the kingdom of God."

17 Then Jesus took a cup. He gave thanks to God for it. Then he said, "Take this cup and give it to everyone here. 18 I tell you, I will never drink from the fruit of the vine again until God's kingdom comes. "

19 Then Jesus took bread and gave thanks. He broke off some of the bread and gave it to them. Then he said, "This bread is* my body which I am giving for you. Eat this to remember me." 20 In the same way, after supper, Jesus took a cup and said, "This cup is* *God's* new agreement in my blood which is being poured out for you."*

Who Will Turn Against Jesus?

21 Jesus said, "Listen! One of you will turn against me. He is sitting with me at this table now! 22 I* will do what God has planned, but how horrible it will be for the man who hands me over."

23 Then the apostles began to ask each other, "Which one of us would do such a thing to Jesus?"

The Way Up Is Down

24 Later the apostles began to argue about which one of them was the most important. 25 But Jesus said to them, "The kings of the nations rule over their people. Men who have authority over other people are called 'benefactors.'* 26 But you must not think that way. The greatest person among you should be like a younger person. Leaders should be like servants. 27 Who is more important? A man who is sitting at the table or the one who is serving him? You may think it is the one sitting at the table, but **I** am like a servant among you!

28 You men have stayed with me through many struggles. 29 My Father has given me a kingdom. I also give you authority to rule with me. 30 In my kingdom you will eat and drink at my table. You will sit on thrones and judge the twelve tribes of Israel."

22:10   literally, the city
22:10   This was unusual, because women normally did this.
22:19   represents
22:20   represents
22:20   Some manuscripts do not have the words in verse 19 following ". . . gave it to them" nor verse 20.
22:22   literally, the Son of Man
22:25   those who do good to others

Peter Thinks He Is Strong

31 "O Simon, Simon *Peter*. Listen! Satan has asked to sift* all of you like a farmer sifts his wheat.   **32** I have prayed that you will not lose your faith! When you come back to me, help your brothers be stronger."

33 But Peter said to Jesus, "Lord, I am ready to go to jail with you. I will even **die** with you!"

34 But Jesus said, "Peter, I tell you, before the rooster crows in the morning, you will say that you don't even know me three different times!"

35 Then Jesus said to the apostles, "I sent you *to preach to the people* without a bag, money, or extra shoes. Did you need anything?"

The apostles said, "Nothing."

36 Jesus said to them, "But **now** if you have a bag or money, carry that with you. If you don't have a sword, sell your robe and buy one.   **37** The Scripture says:

'They classed him with the criminals.'   *Isaiah 53:12*

I tell you, this verse must come true; it was written about me, and it is being fulfilled now."

38 They said, "Look, Lord, here are two swords!"
He said to them, "Two will be enough."

Watch and Pray

39-40 Jesus went out of Jerusalem to Olive Mountain. His followers went with him. (Jesus often went there.) He said to his followers, "Pray for strength against temptation."
41 Then Jesus went about 50 yards away* from them. He kneeled down and began to pray,   **42** "Father, if it is in Your plan, then take this cup *of suffering* away from me. However, what You want is more important than what I want."   **43** Then an angel from heaven appeared. The angel *was sent* to help Jesus.   **44** Jesus was full of deep concern; he struggled hard in prayer. Sweat dripped from his face to the ground as though he were bleeding.*   **45** When Jesus finished praying, he went to his followers. They were asleep. (Their sadness had made them very tired.)   **46** He said to them, "Why are you sleeping? Get up and pray for strength against temptation."

The Kiss of Betrayal

47 While Jesus was speaking, a crowd came. One of the twelve *apostles* was leading them. His name was Judas. He came near Jesus, so that he could kiss him.
48 But Jesus said to him, "Judas, are you using the kiss *of friendship* to betray me?"*   **49** The followers of Jesus were standing there, too. They saw what was going to happen. They asked him, "Lord, shall we use our swords?"   **50** And one of the followers **did** use his sword. He cut off the right ear of the high priest's servant.
51 Jesus answered, "Stop!" Then Jesus touched the servant's ear and healed him.

22:31   test
22:41   literally, about as far as one could throw a stone
22:43-44 Many manuscripts do not have verses 43-44.
22:48   literally, the Son of Man

135

52 A group came to arrest Jesus. They were the important Jewish priests, the Jewish elders, and the soldiers *who guarded* the temple. Jesus asked them, "Why did you come out here with swords and sticks? Do you think I am a criminal? 53 I was with you every day in the temple courtyard. Why didn't you try to arrest me there? But this is your time—the time when darkness* rules."

Peter Wasn't Strong

54 They arrested Jesus and took him away. They brought him into the high priest's* house. Peter was following from a distance. 55 The soldiers started a fire in the middle of the yard and sat together. Peter sat with them. 56 Because of the light from the fire, a servant girl saw Peter sitting there. The girl looked closely at Peter's face. Then she said, "This man was also with Jesus!"

57 But Peter said that this was not true. He said, "Lady, I don't know him." 58 After a little while, a different person saw Peter and said, "You, too, are one of the men *who follow Jesus*."

But Peter said, "Mister, I am **not**!"

59 About an hour later, another man kept insisting, "It is true! This man **was** with Jesus. He is from Galilee!"

60 But Peter said, "Man, I don't know what you are talking about!"

Immediately, while Peter was still speaking, a rooster crowed. 61 Then the Lord *Jesus* turned and looked into Peter's eyes. And Peter remembered what the Lord had said to him: "Before the rooster crows in the morning, you will say that you don't even know me three times." 62 Then Peter went outside, and cried bitterly.

Jesus Is Ridiculed

63-64 Some men were guarding Jesus. This is the way they made fun of Jesus: They covered his eyes, so that he couldn't see them. Then they hit him and said, "Prophesy for us! Let God tell you which one of us hit you!" 65 The men were saying many terrible things to Jesus.

Believe What I Say

66 When morning came, the elders of the people, the most important priests, and the teachers of the law came together. They led Jesus away to the Jewish Council.* 67 They said, "Since you are the Messiah, **tell** us that you are!"
Jesus said to them, "If I were to tell you I am the Messiah, you wouldn't believe me. 68 And if I ask you, you won't answer. 69 But I* will sit at the right side of God's throne—from now on."

70 They all asked, "Then you are the Son of God?" Jesus said to them, "Yes I am."* 71 They said, "Why do we need witnesses now? We ourselves heard it from his own lips!"

22:53   sin
22:54   The high priest was the most important Jewish leader.
22:66   literally, the Sanhedrin, the highest court
22:69   literally, the Son of Man
22:70   literally, "You are saying it." A statement meaning: "I agree with what you are saying."

Chapter 23

Not Guilty!

1 Then the whole group stood up and led Jesus to Pilate.   **2** They began to accuse Jesus. They said, "We caught this man telling things which were confusing our people. He says we should stop paying taxes to Caesar.* He calls himself the Messiah, a king."

3 Pilate asked Jesus, "Are you the King of the Jews?"

Jesus answered, "Yes."*

4 Pilate said to the most important priests and to the crowds, "I find nothing wrong with this man."

5 They said again and again, "But Jesus is making trouble with the people! He teaches all over Judea. He began in Galilee and now he is here!"

Jesus Does Not Perform

6 Pilate heard this and asked if Jesus were from Galilee.   **7** Pilate learned that Jesus was under the authority of Herod *Antipas*. Herod was in Jerusalem at that time. So, Pilate sent Jesus to him.   **8** When Herod saw Jesus, he was very glad. Herod had heard all about Jesus. For a long time, he had wanted to meet Jesus. Herod wanted to see a miracle. He was hoping that Jesus would work one.   **9** Herod asked Jesus many questions, but Jesus wouldn't answer him.   **10** The important priests and teachers of the law stood there. They continued to accuse Jesus. They were very excited.   **11** Then Herod and his soldiers laughed at Jesus. They made fun of him by dressing him in royal clothes. Then Herod sent Jesus back to Pilate.   **12** In the past, Pilate and Herod had always been enemies, but on that day Herod and Pilate became friends.

Barabbas Is Free

13 Pilate called everyone together. He called the most important priests, the leaders, and the people.   **14** He said to them, "You brought this man Jesus to me. You said he was making trouble among the people. But, listen, I judged him before all of you. I found nothing wrong with him. Jesus is not guilty of the things you are saying against him.   **15** Herod *Antipas* found nothing wrong with him, either; he sent him back to us. Look, Jesus has done nothing wrong. He shouldn't be killed.   **16** So, after I give him some punishment, I will let him go free."   **17** *

18 But all of the people yelled, "Kill him! Set Barabbas free for us!"   **19** (Barabbas was a man who was thrown into prison because of a riot which took place in the city, and for murder.)

20 Pilate really wanted to let Jesus go free. So, Pilate appealed to them again.   **21** But they yelled again, "Kill him! Nail him to a cross!"

22 A third time Pilate said to them, "Why? What crime has Jesus done? He is not guilty. I can find no reason to kill him. So I will set him free, after I give him a little punishment."

23 But the people continued to yell. They demanded that Jesus be killed on a cross. Their yelling became so loud that   **24-25** Pilate decided to give them what they wanted. The people wanted Barabbas to go free. (Barabbas was the man who had been

---

23:2   The title of the supreme Roman rulers. "Caesar" became the title of each emperor.

23:3   literally, "You are saying it." A statement meaning: "I agree with what you are saying."

23:17   Many manuscripts have verse 17: "Now he was required to release one to them at the feast" (Compare Matthew 27:15.)

thrown into jail because of a riot. He was a murderer.) Pilate let Barabbas go free, but Pilate gave them Jesus *to be killed*. This is what the people wanted.

Carrying the Cross

26 The *soldiers* led Jesus away *to be killed*. At that same time, there was a man coming into the city from the fields. His name was Simon. He was from the city of Cyrene. The *soldiers* forced him to carry Jesus' cross and to walk behind Jesus.*

27 A very large crowd was following Jesus. Some of the women were crying and mourning for Jesus. They felt so sorry for him, **28** but Jesus turned and said to the women, "Women of Jerusalem, don't cry for **me** —cry for yourselves and also for your children! **29** Listen, the time is coming when people will say, 'Happy are the women who cannot have babies! Happy are the women who have never had children to care for.' **30** Then the people will begin to say to the mountains, 'Fall on us!' The people will say to the hills, 'Cover us!'* **31** If people do things like this now when life is good, what will happen when bad times come?"*

32-33 There were also two criminals led out with Jesus. Jesus and the two criminals were led to a place where they would be killed. The people called this place "The Skull." There some men nailed Jesus to his cross. They also nailed the criminals to their crosses; Jesus' cross was between the crosses of the two criminals.

Father, Forgive Them

34 Jesus said, "Father, forgive these people. They don't know what they are doing."*
The soldiers gambled to see who would get Jesus' clothes.

35 The people stood there watching. The Jewish leaders were laughing at Jesus. They said, "Since he is God's chosen one, the Messiah, let him save himself! He saved other people, didn't he?"

36 Even the soldiers made fun of him. They came to Jesus and offered him some sour wine. **37** The soldiers said, "If you are the King of the Jews, save yourself!"

38 At the top of the cross these words were written:

THIS IS THE KING OF THE JEWS.

39 One of the criminals who was hanging there began to say awful things to Jesus: "Aren't you the Messiah? Then save yourself! And save us, too!"

40 But the other criminal stopped him. He said, "You should fear God! All of us are about to die! **41** You and I are guilty; we **should** be killed, because we did wrong. But this man Jesus has done nothing wrong!" **42** Then he said to Jesus, "Jesus, remember me when you come into your kingdom!"

43 Then Jesus said to him, "I am telling you the truth: Today you will be with me in Paradise!"*

Jesus Dies

44 It was about noon, but the whole area became dark until three o'clock in the afternoon. **45** There was no sun! The curtain hanging *between the holy place and the most*

23:26   Jesus started to carry the cross himself, but it was probably too heavy for him in his weakened condition (John 19:17).
23:30   Hosea 10:8
23:31   literally, "If they do these things in a tree full of sap, what will happen in the dry (tree)?"
23:34   A few early copies of Luke do not contain these words of Jesus.
23:43   a happy place where righteous people go after they die

holy place in the temple was torn right down the middle.   46 Jesus shouted, "Father, I put my spirit into Your hands." After Jesus said this, he died.

47 The *Roman* army officer saw what happened. He was giving glory to God, saying, "This man was truly righteous!"

48 Many people had come out of the city to see this event. When the people saw it, they felt deep sorrow and left.   49 The people who were close friends of Jesus were there. Also, there were some women who had followed Jesus from Galilee. They all stood far away *from the cross* to watch.

The Rich Man's Grave

50-51 There was a man from Arimathea, a Judean town. His name was Joseph. He was a good, righteous man. He was looking for the kingdom of God. Joseph was a member of the Jewish Council, but he did not vote when the priests decided to kill Jesus.   52 Joseph went to Pilate to ask for the body of Jesus.   53 So Joseph took the body down from the cross and wrapped it in a sheet. Then he put Jesus' body into a cave which was cut out of *solid* rock. This tomb had never been used before.   54 This was late on a Friday afternoon.* (When the sun went down, the Sabbath day would begin.*)

55 The women who had come from Galilee with Jesus followed Joseph. They saw the tomb. Inside they saw where the body of Jesus was placed.   56 Then the women left to prepare some sweet-smelling things *to put on Jesus' body.*

They rested on the Sabbath day, according to *God's* command.

Chapter 24

The Empty Tomb

1 Very early on Sunday* morning, the women came to the tomb. They brought the sweet-smelling things they had prepared.   2 But the women found that the rock was rolled away from the tomb.   3 They went in, but they didn't find the Lord Jesus' body. 4 While they were wondering about it, suddenly two angels* stood beside them in shining clothes.   5 The women were frightened; they bowed their heads down to the ground. The two men said to the women, "Why are you looking here for a living person? This is a place for dead people!   6 Jesus is not here. He has risen from death! Do you remember what he said in Galilee?   7 Jesus said that he* must be handed over to evil men, be killed on a cross, and rise from death on the third day."*   8 Then the women remembered Jesus' words.

9 The women left the tomb and went to the eleven apostles and the other followers. The women told them everything which had occurred at the tomb.   10 The women were: Mary of Magdala, Joanna, Mary, the *mother of* James, and some other women. These women told the apostles everything that had happened,   11 but the men didn't believe what the women said. It sounded crazy.   12 However, Peter got up and ran to

---

23:54	literally, Preparation Day
23:54	The Jews considered sundown to be the beginning of the day.
24:1	literally, the first day of the week
24:4	literally, men
24:7	literally, the Son of Man
24:7	It was customary for Jews to count a part of a day as one day. Thus, Friday evening, Saturday, and Sunday morning were equivalent to three days.

the tomb. He bent down and looked in, but the only things he saw were the grave clothes. Peter went off by himself, wondering what had taken place.

Jesus Appears

13 That same day, two of Jesus' followers were going to a village named Emmaus. (It was about seven miles from Jerusalem.) **14** They were talking about everything which had happened. **15** While they were discussing these things, Jesus himself came near and walked along with them. **16** (But the two men were not allowed to recognize Jesus.) **17** *Jesus walked with them for a while.* Then he said, "What are these things you are talking about as you walk?"

They stood still. Their faces looked very sad. **18** The one named Cleopas answered, "You must be the only man in Jerusalem who doesn't know what has just happened there!"

19 Jesus asked them, "What are you talking about?"

The men said to him, "It is about Jesus, the one from Nazareth. He was a prophet from God to all the people. He said and did many powerful things. **20** Our leaders and important priests gave him away to be judged and killed. They nailed Jesus to a cross, **21** but we were hoping that Jesus was about to bring salvation to Israel. Besides all this, it has been three days since this happened. **22** And today some of our women told us some amazing things. Early this morning the women went to the tomb, **23** but they didn't find Jesus' body there. They came and told us that, in a vision, they had seen two angels. The angels said that Jesus was alive! **24** Some of our group also went to the tomb. They found that it was just as the women had said, but none of us saw him."

25 Then Jesus said to the two men, "You are foolish and slow to realize what is true. You should believe everything the prophets said: **26** The Messiah must suffer these things before he enters his glory." **27** Then Jesus began to explain everything which had been written in the Scriptures about him. Jesus started with the books of Moses and then he talked about what the prophets had written about him.

28 They came near the village of Emmaus, their destination, and Jesus acted as though he didn't plan to stop there. **29** They begged him, "Stay with us. It is late; it is almost night." So, he went in to stay with them.

30 Jesus sat down with them and took some bread. He gave thanks for the food and broke off some of it. Then he gave it to them. **31** At that time, the men were allowed to recognize Jesus. They saw who he really was, but he disappeared. **32** They said to each other, "While Jesus was talking to us on the road, it felt like a fire burning in us when he explained *the true meaning of* the Scriptures."

33-34 During that same hour, they got up and returned to Jerusalem. There they found *the followers of Jesus* meeting together. The eleven apostles and those people who were with them said, "The Lord *Jesus* has actually come back to life! He appeared to Simon *Peter.*"

Jesus Appears Again

35 Then the two men gave a report about the things which had happened on the road. They talked about how they recognized Jesus when he broke off some of the bread.

36 While they were saying these things, Jesus himself stood among them. He said to them, "Peace to you."

37 They began to be filled with fear. They were terrified. They thought they were seeing a ghost. **38** But Jesus asked, "Why are you disturbed? Why do you doubt what you see?   **39** Look at my hands and my feet. It is really **me**! Touch me. You can see that I have a living body; a ghost doesn't have a body like this."

40 After Jesus told them this, he showed them *the holes in* his hands and feet. **41** They were amazed and very, very happy to see that he was alive. They still couldn't believe it. So Jesus asked them, "Do you have any food here?"   **42** They gave him a piece of cooked fish.   **43** While they watched, Jesus took it and ate it.

44 Jesus said to them, "Do you remember when I was with you before? I said that everything written about me must come true—everything written in the law of Moses, *the books of* the prophets, and the Psalms."

45 Then Jesus explained the Scriptures. He helped them to understand the things which had been written *about him*.   **46** Then Jesus said to them, "It is written that the Messiah would be killed and come back to life on the third day.   **47-48** You saw these things happen. You must go and tell all nations* that their sins can be forgiven. Tell them that they must change their hearts. You must start from Jerusalem and preach these things with my authority.   **49** Listen, I am sending my Father's promise upon you, but you must stay in Jerusalem until you are clothed with that power from heaven."

Up, Up, and Away

50 Jesus led them out of Jerusalem, almost to the town of Bethany. He raised his hands and blessed them.   **51** While Jesus was blessing them, he was separated from them and carried up into heaven.   **52** They worshiped him. Then they went back to Jerusalem. They were very happy.   **53** They were always in the temple courtyard, praising God.

24:47-48   every cultural (ethnic) group

JOHN

Chapter 1

Meet Jesus

1 In *the* beginning was the Word,* and the Word was with God, and the Word was God.* **2** He was with God in the beginning. **3** Through him everything was made. Without him nothing which has happened would have happened. **4** He was the Source of life. That life was light for people. **5** The light shines in the darkness; the darkness can never put it out!

6 There was a man named John. He had been sent from God. **7** This man came to give proof about the light, so that through him, everyone would believe. **8** John was not the light; *he came* to tell the truth about the light. **9** The true light was coming into the world. He gives light to every person.

10 He was in the world. Through him the world was made, but the people of the world did not acknowledge him. **11** He came to what was his, but his own people would not accept him. **12** But he gave the right to become God's children to those who did accept him, to those who believe in his name. **13** They were born, not in a human way, from the natural human desire of men, but born of God.

14 The Word* became human and lived among us for a while. We saw his glory, the kind of glory like that of *the* Father's one and only* *Son*—full of gracious love and truth. **15** John was telling the truth about him. John cried out, "This is the man I talked about: 'The one who is coming behind me has been ahead of me,' because he was alive before I was."

16 We have all received one blessing after another from the fullness of his gracious love. **17** Though the law was given through Moses, gracious love and truth have come through Jesus Christ.* **18** No one has ever seen God,* but Jesus,* who is in the arms of the Father, **he** unfolded the story.

John the (God Chaser) Baptist

19 The Jewish leaders from Jerusalem sent some priests and Levites to ask John this question: "Who are you?" This is the proof that John gave:

20 John did not refuse to answer; he spoke freely. He clearly said, "I am not the Messiah!"

21 They asked him, "Who are you? Are you Elijah?"

John said, "No, I am not Elijah."

They asked, "Are you the Prophet?"

John answered, "No."

1:1 or, the Logos (Expression, Message)

1:1 or, Deity, Divine (which is actually a better translation, because the Greek definite article is *not* present before this Greek word)

1:14 or, the Logos (Expression, Message)

1:14 or, only begotten

1:17 or, Jesus the Messiah

1:18 or, Deity (which does *not* have the definite article before this Greek word)

1:18 literally, (the) only one, Deity. Some early manuscripts have "the only Son."

22 Then they asked him, "Who are you? We must give an answer to the men who sent us here. What do you say about yourself?"

23 John said,

"I am 'a voice shouting in the desert:
Prepare the Lord's road,'
just as Isaiah the prophet said."

Isaiah 40:3

24 (They had been sent from the Pharisee group.)

25 They asked John, "If you are not the Messiah, Elijah, or the prophet, why are you immersing people?"

26 John answered them, "Yes, I immerse people in water, but there is another one among you whom you don't know about. **27** He is coming later. I am not worthy to untie his shoelace."

28 This happened in the town of Bethany (the one across the Jordan River). John was immersing people there.

Here's the One John's Chasing

29 The next day, John saw Jesus coming toward him. John said, "Look, God's Lamb who will take away the world's sin! **30** This is the one I was talking about: "The man who is coming behind me has been ahead of me, because he was alive before I was.' **31** I didn't know him. Why did I come, immersing people in water? To show him to the people of Israel."

32 This is the proof that John gave: "I saw the Spirit coming down like a dove from the sky, hovering above him. **33** I didn't know him, but the One who sent me to immerse people in water said to me, 'If you see the Spirit coming down and staying upon someone, **this** is the one who immerses in the Holy Spirit.' **34** I have seen it! I am telling you the truth. **He** is the Son of God!"

Some of the First God Chasers

35 Again, on the next day, John stood there with two of his followers. **36** He looked at Jesus walking by. John said, "Look, God's Lamb!"

37 When the two followers heard John say this, they followed Jesus.

38 Jesus turned around and saw them following him. He said to them, "What are you looking for?"

39 They asked him, "Where do you live, Rabbi? (This word means 'Teacher')."

Jesus said to them, "Come and see."

So, they went and saw where Jesus was staying. They spent the rest of the day with him. (It was about four o'clock in the afternoon.)

40 Andrew (Simon Peter's brother) was one of the two men who heard John and followed Jesus. **41** The first thing that Andrew did was to find his own brother, Simon. Andrew said to him, "We have found the Messiah!" (This word means "Christ."*) **42** Then Andrew led Peter to Jesus. When Jesus looked at Peter, he said, "You are Simon, John's son. You will be called Cephas." (Translated into Greek, this name means "Peter."*)

1:41   from a Greek word meaning "the anointed one." God selected a man and this choice was shown by anointing (rubbing with oil). See 1 Samuel 10:1; 16:1-3. It was like crowning someone as king.

1:42   It means "a small stone."

Philip and Nathaniel Join the Chase

43 The next day, Jesus decided to leave for the land of Galilee. He found Philip and said to him, "Follow me!"   **44** Philip was from Bethsaida, the same town where Andrew and Peter lived.   **45** Philip found Nathanael and told him, "We have found the one of whom Moses wrote in the law. The prophets wrote about him, too! He is Jesus, the son of Joseph, from Nazareth."

46 Nathanael said to him, "Is it possible for anything good to come from Nazareth?"
Philip said to him, "Come and see *for yourself*!"

47 Jesus saw Nathanael coming toward him. Jesus said this about Nathanael: "Look, here is a real man of Israel! There is nothing false about him!"

48 Nathanael asked Jesus, "From where do you know me?"
Jesus answered him, "Before Philip called you *to come here*, I saw you under that fig tree!"

49 And Nathanael answered Jesus, "Rabbi, **you** are the Son of God! **You** are the king of the people of Israel!"

50 Jesus answered him, "Do you believe because I told you that I saw you under a fig tree? You will see even greater things than this.   **51** I am telling you the truth: You will all see heaven open and God's angels coming down and going up from me."*

Chapter 2

The First Miracle

1 On the third day, in the town of Cana in Galilee, there was a wedding. Jesus' mother was there.   **2** Jesus and his followers were invited to the wedding.   **3** When the wine was gone, Jesus' mother said to him, "They have no more wine!"

4 Jesus asked her, "What do you want with me, woman? My time has not yet come."

5 His mother said to the servants, "Do whatever he tells you."

6 There were six stone water jars sitting there. (Jewish people used them to make things *ceremonially* pure.) Each water jar could hold about 20 to 30 gallons.   **7** Jesus said to them, "Fill the jars with water." They filled the jars to the top.   **8** Jesus said to the servants, "Now, pour some of this and take it to the master of ceremonies." They did it.   **9** He didn't know where it came from, but the servants who had gotten the water knew. When the master of ceremonies tasted the water which had been changed into wine, he called for the groom.   **10** He said to the groom, "Everyone serves the good wine first, and when the people have had plenty to drink, he serves the cheaper wine. But you have reserved the good wine until now!"   **11** This was the first miracle which Jesus performed. It was in the town of Cana in Galilee. Jesus revealed his glory, and his followers believed in him.

12 After this, Jesus, his mother, his brothers, and his followers went down into the town of Capernaum. They stayed there for a few days.

"Get out of My Father's House!"

13 The time for the Jewish Passover Festival* was near. Jesus went up to Jerusalem.
14 He found some men in the temple courtyard. They were selling cattle, sheep, and

1:51   literally, the Son of Man
2:13   spring time

pigeons. The money-exchangers were also sitting there.* **15** Jesus made a whip from some ropes. He forced all of them to leave the courtyard—even the cattle and the sheep. He turned the money-exchangers' tables over and scattered their coins. **16** He said to the men who were selling pigeons, "Get those things out of here! Don't turn my Father's house into a place of business." **17** His followers remembered that this verse was in the Scriptures:

"The fire which I feel for Your house* burns within me!" *Psalm 69:9*

18 The Jewish leaders asked Jesus this question: "What proof do you give to show us *that you have the authority to* do these things?"

19 Jesus answered them, "Destroy this temple sanctuary and I will raise it in three days!"

20 Then the Jewish leaders said, "It took 46 years to build this temple sanctuary—and you would build it again in three days?" **21** (Jesus was talking about his body.* **22** After Jesus was raised from death, his followers remembered that he always used to say this. They believed the Scripture and what Jesus had said.)

23 While Jesus was in Jerusalem during the Passover Festival, many believed in his name. They saw the miracles from God which he was doing. **24–25** Jesus knew what people were like. He didn't need anyone to tell him about men; he always knew what was in man. So, Jesus was not committing himself to them.

Chapter 3

Nick at Night

1 There was a man named Nicodemus. He was a Jewish leader, one of the Pharisees. **2** This man came to Jesus at night. Nicodemus said to him, "Rabbi, we know you are a teacher who has come from God. No one could do these miracles which you are performing, if God were not with him."

3 Jesus answered him, "I am telling you the truth: If a person is not born again, he cannot see the kingdom of God!"

4 Nicodemus asked him, "When a man is already old, how can he be reborn? It is not possible for him to go inside his mother's womb the second time and be born!"

5 Jesus answered, "I am telling you the truth: If a person is not born from water and the Spirit, he cannot enter the kingdom of God! **6** What has been born from men is human. And what has been born from the Spirit is spiritual. **7** Don't be surprised because I said this to you: 'You must be born again.' **8** The wind blows wherever it wishes. You hear the sound of it, but you don't know where it comes from or where it is going. It is the same way with everyone who has been born from the Spirit."

9 Nicodemus answered Jesus, "How can these things happen?"

10 Jesus answered him, "Are you a teacher of the people of Israel, and you don't know these things? **11** I am telling you the truth: We are talking about what we know. We are telling the truth about what we have seen. But you are not accepting our truth. **12** Since I am talking to you about things on earth and you are not believing them, if I

2:14   Jews who came to Jerusalem from distant places needed to buy animals to sacrifice. Also, no foreign coins were allowed in the temple. But these merchants were charging very high prices and treating God's temple only as a place to make money.

2:17   temple

2:21   literally, the temple sanctuary of his body

were to tell you about heavenly things, how could you believe? **13** I* am the only one who ever came down from heaven; no one else has ever gone up to heaven. **14** Moses lifted up the *brass* snake in the desert *for the people*. In the same way, I* must be lifted high, **15** so that everyone who commits himself to me will have eternal life."

16 God loved the people of the world so much that He gave up His one and only* Son. Every person who commits himself to Jesus will not be destroyed. Instead, that person will have eternal life. **17** God did not send His Son into the world to judge it. God sent Jesus, so that the people of the world could be saved through him. **18** The person who commits himself to Jesus is not condemned, but the one who does not commit himself to Jesus has already been condemned, because he has not believed in the name of God's one and only* Son.

19 This is the verdict: Light has come into the world, but people loved darkness more than they loved light because the things which they were doing were evil. **20** Everyone who does evil hates the light. He does not come toward the light. He doesn't want his evil deeds to be exposed. **21** But the person who is living the truth comes toward the light. He wants his actions to become clear, because he did them for God.

Jesus Is Greater Than John

22 After this, Jesus and his followers went to the land of Judea. He stayed there with them and he was immersing some people. **23** John was immersing people in the town of Aenon (which is not far from the town of Salim) because there was plenty of water there. People continued coming to be immersed. **24** (John had not yet been thrown into prison.)

25 There was an argument between some of John's followers and a Jewish man about making things pure. **26** They came to John and said to him, "Rabbi, the man you have endorsed, who was with you on the other side of the Jordan River, look, he is immersing people, too. Everyone is coming to him!"

27 John answered, "No one can receive anything if heaven has not given it to him. **28** You yourselves know that I told the truth when I said, 'I am not the Messiah!' I have been sent ahead of him. **29** The groom is the one who will get the bride. The best man is the one who stands by and listens. He is glad when he hears the groom's voice. This is **my** joy; it is now complete. **30** Jesus must become more important; I will become less important."

Jesus Comes From God

31 The one who comes from above is greater than all things. The person who comes from the earth belongs to the earth and talks about the earth. The one who comes from heaven is the most important. **32** He tells the truth about what he has seen and heard, but no one accepts his proof. **33** The person who does accept his proof confirms that God is real. **34** God sent Jesus. Jesus speaks the words of God, because God gave him the Spirit without limit. **35** The Father loves the Son and has put everything in the Son's control. **36** The person who commits himself to the Son has eternal life, but the person who does not obey the Son will not see eternal life. Instead, God's punishment stays on that person.

3:13   literally, the Son of Man. See Numbers 21:5-9.
3:14   literally, the Son of Man. See Numbers 21:5-9.
3:16   or, only begotten
3:18   or, only begotten

Chapter 4

A Samaritan Woman

1 The Pharisees heard that Jesus was making more followers and immersing more people than John. **2** (Jesus was really not the one who performed the immersion; his followers did it.) **3** Jesus left Judea and went back to the land of Galilee.

4 Jesus needed to go through the land of Samaria. **5** He came to a town in Samaria called Sychar. It was near the property which Jacob had given to Joseph, his son.* **6** Jacob's well was there. Jesus was tired because of traveling. So, he sat down for a while at the well. It was about noon.

7 A Samaritan woman came to get some water. Jesus said to her, "Please, give me a drink of water." **8** (His followers had gone into town to buy some food.)

9 The Samaritan woman said to Jesus, "You are a Jewish man and I am a Samaritan woman. Why are you asking me for a drink of water?" (Jewish people don't want to associate with Samaritans.)

10 Jesus answered her, "If you knew about God's gift and who I really am,* **you** would ask me to give you a drink of living* water!"

11 The woman said to Jesus, "Mister, you don't even have a bucket and the well is deep. Where are you going to get this living water? **12** You are not greater than Jacob, our ancestor, are you? Jacob's flocks and herds, his sons, and Jacob himself drank from this well. He gave it to us!"

13 Jesus answered her, "Any person who drinks this water will become thirsty again, **14** but if anyone drinks the water which I will give him, he will never be thirsty again. The water which I give him will become a spring inside him, welling up to eternal life."

15 The woman said to Jesus, "Mister, give me some of this water, so that I won't get thirsty and won't have to come back here again and again to get water."

16 Jesus said to her, "Go, call your husband. Then come back here."

17 The woman answered him, "I don't have a husband."

Jesus said to her, "So true! **18** You have had five husbands, and the man you have now is not your husband. You spoke the truth."

19 The woman said to him, "Sir, I now understand that you are a prophet. **20** Our ancestors worshiped on this mountain,* but you *Jews* say that Jerusalem is the place where people must worship."

21 Jesus said to her, "Believe me, woman, the time is coming when you won't worship the Father on this mountain or in Jerusalem. **22** You *Samaritans* are worshiping that which you don't understand, but we *Jews* are worshiping what we know. Salvation comes from the Jewish people. **23** But the time is coming and has now come when the true worshipers will worship the Father in the true, spiritual way. The Father is searching for this kind of people to worship Him. **24** God is spirit. The people who worship God must worship Him in the true way and with the *right* spirit."

25 The woman said to Jesus, "I know that the Messiah (the one called Christ) is coming. When he comes, he will tell us about everything."

26 Jesus said to her, "I am the one!"*

4:5	See Genesis 50:24-25; Exodus 13:19; Joshua 24:32.
4:10	literally, who is talking to you
4:10	fresh (Compare John 7:38.)
4:20	Mount Gerazim. The Samaritans had built a temple there about 130 years before, but the Jews destroyed it.
4:26	literally, That person is talking to you right now. I am *the Messiah.*

27 Just then, Jesus' followers came. They were amazed that Jesus was talking with a woman.* However, not one of them asked, "What do you want?" or "Why are you talking with her?"

28 Then the woman left her water bucket and went back into town. This is what she said to people: 29 "Come, see a man who told me everything I've ever done. He must be the Messiah!" 30 So they left town and they were coming to him.

31 Meanwhile Jesus' followers were encouraging Jesus *to eat something*. They said, "Rabbi, eat!"

32 But Jesus said to them, "I have some food to eat which you don't know about." 33 The followers said to one another, "No one brought Jesus anything to eat, did they?"

34 Jesus said to them, "I must obey what God wants; He sent me. I must finish His work. **That** is food for me!

35 "You say, 'Four months more and then the time for harvest comes.' But, listen, I am telling **you** to look up and see the fields. They are ready for harvest now. 36 The person who gathers the harvest receives his pay; he gathers the crops for eternal life. The person who plants and the person who gathers will be happy at the same time. 37 This saying is true: 'One person plants and another person gathers.' 38 I sent you to gather the harvest for which you have not worked. Other men worked hard; you are gaining from their work."

39 Many Samaritan people in that city believed in Jesus, because of the woman's word. She testified, "He told me everything I ever did!" 40 When the Samaritan men came to Jesus, they were begging him to stay with them. Jesus stayed there for two days. 41 Many more people believed because of Jesus' message. 42 They said to the woman, "We believe, not only because of what you said, but also because we ourselves have heard *Jesus*. We know that he is truly the Savior of the world!"

Jesus Heals an Official's Son

43 After two days, Jesus left there to go to the land of Galilee. 44 Jesus himself said that this was true: "A prophet is not accepted in his own home town." 45 When he came to Galilee, the people of Galilee welcomed him. They had seen all the things he did in Jerusalem at the Passover Festival.* (They also went to the feast.)

46 Again, Jesus went to the town of Cana in Galilee, where he had changed the water into wine. There was a government official there. He had a son who was sick in the town of Capernaum. 47 This man heard that Jesus had arrived in Galilee from the land of Judea. The man came to Jesus and begged him to go down to *Capernaum* and heal his son. (The son was about to die.) 48 Jesus said to the man, "You people must see proofs from God and miracles or you will never believe."

49 The government official said to Jesus, "Lord, please go down to *Capernaum* before my little boy dies!"

50 Jesus answered him, "Go, your son lives." The man believed. He took Jesus at his word and left. 51 While the man was going down to *Capernaum*, his servants met him. They said, "Your child lives!" 52 Then the man began asking them questions about the exact time when the boy got better. They answered, "The fever left him yesterday at one o'clock in the afternoon." 53 The father knew that this was the exact time when Jesus had said, "Your son lives!" The man and his whole family believed.

54 This was the second proof that Jesus performed, after he came to Galilee from the land of Judea.

4:27   The rabbis taught that a man should not talk with a woman in public.
4:45   one of the most important Jewish holidays. It celebrated deliverance from Egypt.

Chapter 5

Pick up Your Bed and Walk!

1 Later there was another Jewish festival. Jesus went up to Jerusalem. **2** Near the Sheep Gate in Jerusalem there is a pool that is called Bethzatha in the Aramaic language. It has five porches. **3** A crowd of people used to lie around among the porches. Some of them were sick, blind, lame, or crippled. **4** * **5** One man had been there for 38 years with his sickness. **6** When Jesus saw the man lying there, he knew that the man had been there a long time. Jesus asked him, "Do you want to be well?"

7 The sick man answered Jesus, "Mister, I don't have anyone to put me into the pool when the water stirs. While I am going, someone else goes ahead of me."

8 Jesus said to him, "Get up! Pick up your small bed and walk!" **9** Immediately, the man got well. He picked up his bed and began walking around. (This happened on a Sabbath day.)

10 The Jewish leaders were saying to the man who had been healed, "It is the Sabbath day! It is not right for you to carry your bed."

11 The man answered them, "The one who made me well told me to pick up my bed and walk."

12 They asked him, "Who is the man who told you to pick up your bed and walk?"

13 The man who was healed didn't know who Jesus was, because Jesus had slipped away in the crowd which was there.

14 Later Jesus found the man in the temple courtyard. Jesus said to him, "Look, you have been made well. Stop sinning, so that something worse won't happen to you."

15 The man went and told the Jewish leaders that Jesus was the one who had made him well. **16** Because of this, the Jewish leaders were persecuting Jesus—he was doing these things on the Sabbath day.

17 Jesus answered them, "My Father always works and I must work, too."

18 Because of this, the Jewish leaders were trying even harder to kill Jesus. *They* thought that Jesus was not only breaking *the rules about* the Sabbath day, but he was also claiming that God was his own Father, thus putting himself on the same level with God.

I Do What I See the Father Doing

19 So Jesus answered them, "I am telling you the truth: The Son can do nothing on his own. He can only do what he sees the Father doing. Whatever the Father may do, the Son will do the same thing. **20** The Father loves the Son. The Father shows him everything He is doing. The Father will show him even greater deeds than these, so that **you** will be amazed. **21** Just as the Father raises dead people and makes them live again, in the same way the Son gives life to whom he wishes. **22** The Father does not judge anyone. Instead, He has given the Son the *right* to judge everything, **23** so that everyone will honor the Son as they honor the Father. The person who does not honor the Son is not honoring the Father who sent the Son. **24** I am telling you the truth: The person who listens to my teaching and believes in the One who sent me has eternal life. That person is not under condemnation. Instead, he has passed from death over to life. **25** I am telling you the truth: The time is coming—the time has already come—when dead

---

5:4 Many late manuscripts have all or part of the following: "waiting for the moving of the water, 4 because an angel of the Lord went down at certain times into the pool and stirred up the waters. The first one into the pool after the waters were stirred up was healed of whatever disease that he had."

people will hear the voice of the Son of God. And when they hear it, they will live again! **26** The Father has life in Himself. In the same way, He gave life to the Son to have in himself. **27** The Father gave the Son authority to judge, because he is the Son of Man. **28** Don't be surprised at this, because the time is coming when everyone in the graves will hear the voice of the Son of God. **29** They will come out of the graves. Those who lived right will rise to life, but those who did evil things will rise for judgment."

John Told the Truth

30 "I cannot do anything on my own. I judge on the basis of what I hear. Since I am not seeking my own will, my decision is fair. I am seeking the will of the One who sent me. **31** If I were giving proof about myself, my proof would not be valid. **32** But there is another man* who is giving proof about me. I know that the proof he gives for me is valid.

33 "You *sent some men* to him and he has told the truth. **34** I don't accept proof from human beings. But I am saying these things, so that you can be saved. **35** John was a light that burns and shines. You were willing to enjoy his light for a while. **36** But I have more proof than John's—the deeds that I do. The deeds prove that the Father sent me! **37** The One who sent me is the Father; He has given proof about me. You have never heard God's voice. You have never seen His shape. **38** And you don't have His teaching staying in you. You don't believe in the one whom God sent. **39** You are always searching the Scriptures, because you think you will find eternal life in them. But the Scriptures are giving proof about **me**! **40** You don't want to come to me, so that you may have life.

41 "I don't accept praise from man, **42** but I know you—you don't have love for God in your hearts. **43** I have come with the authority of my Father and you are not accepting me. If someone else comes with his own authority, you will accept him. **44** How can you believe? You accept praise from one another. You are not looking for praise from the only *true* God. **45** Don't think that I will accuse you to your father. Moses is the one you trust. **He** is accusing you! **46** If you believed Moses, you would have believed **me** because he wrote about me. If you won't believe in what he wrote, how can you believe in **my** words?"

Chapter 6

Jesus Does Lunch With the 5,000

1 After this, Jesus went back across Lake Galilee (Lake Tiberias). **2** A large crowd of people was following him, because they saw him perform miracles on sick people. **3** Then Jesus went up on a hill and sat down with his followers. **4** The time for the Jewish Passover Festival* was near. **5** Jesus looked up and saw that a large crowd was coming toward him. He said to Philip, "Where can we buy *enough* food to feed so many people?" **6** (Jesus said this to test Philip; Jesus knew what he was going to do.)

7 Philip answered him, "200 silver coins' worth of food would not be enough—even if each person had only a small amount!"

5:32   John (the one who immersed people)
6:4   spring time

8 One of Jesus' followers, Andrew, Simon Peter's brother, said to Jesus, **9** "Here is a little boy who has five small loaves of barley bread and two fish, but how long would that last among so many people?"

10 Jesus said, "Have the people sit down." (There was a lot of grass in that spot.) There were about 5,000 men. They sat down. **11** Then Jesus took the loaves of bread and gave thanks *to God* for them. He divided them among those who were sitting down. He did the same thing with the fish. They had as much as they wanted. **12** When they were full, Jesus said to his followers, "Gather up the leftovers, so that nothing will be wasted." **13** So, they gathered them up and filled twelve large baskets with the left-over pieces from the five small barley loaves.

14 The people saw this miracle that Jesus performed. They began saying, "Surely this is the prophet *we were expecting* to come into the world." **15** Jesus knew they were about to come and take him, so that they could make him a king. So, he left again for the mountains to be alone.

Who Needs a Boat?!

16 When it was evening, Jesus' followers went down to the lake. **17** They climbed into a boat and started across the lake, *heading* for the town of Capernaum. It was already dark and Jesus had not yet come to them. **18** A strong wind was blowing and *the waters of* the lake became rough. **19** Jesus' followers had rowed between 3 and 3½ miles when they saw Jesus. He was walking **on** the lake. He was coming closer to the boat. They were afraid. **20** But Jesus said to them, "Don't be afraid. It is I!" **21** They wanted to take him into the boat, but the boat soon came to the shore where they were heading.

Looking for Jesus

22 The next day the crowd which had stood on the other side of the lake saw that only one boat was still there. *They knew* that Jesus did not get into that boat with his followers; they had left by themselves. **23** Some more boats from Tiberias came near the place where the people had eaten the bread for which the Lord had given thanks. **24** So, when the crowd realized that Jesus and his followers were not there, they got into some boats and went to Capernaum to look for Jesus.

The Forever Kind of Food

25 When the people found Jesus on the other side of the lake, they asked him, "Rabbi, when did you come here?"

26 Jesus answered them, "I am telling you the truth: You are looking for me, not because of the miracles but because you ate the food and were filled! **27** Don't work for the kind of food which spoils. Instead, work for the kind of food *which gives you* life forever. I* will give you this kind of food. God the Father puts His stamp of approval on me."

28 They asked Jesus, "What should we do, so that we may work God's works?"

29 Jesus answered them, "This is God's work—you must commit yourselves to the one whom God sent!"

30 They said to him, "What miracle will you do, so that we may see it and commit ourselves to you? What will you do? **31** Our ancestors ate manna* in the desert. It is written: 'He gave them food to eat from heaven.'"

6:27   literally, the Son of Man
6:31   food miraculously supplied to the people of Israel on their journey through the desert (See Exodus 16:13-21; Numbers 11:7-9.)

32 Jesus said to them, "I am telling you the truth: Moses did not give you food from heaven. My Father is the One who gives you the true food from heaven. **33** God's food comes down from heaven and gives life to the world."

34 Then they said to Jesus, "Sir, **always** give us this food!" **35** Jesus said to them, " **I** am the food *which gives* life. The person who comes to me will never be hungry. The one who commits himself to me will **never** be thirsty. **36** I told you, 'Though you have seen me, yet you still do not believe.' **37** All that the Father gives to me comes to **me**. I will never throw out the person who comes to me. **38** Why did I come down from heaven? It was not to do what I want to do, but to do the will of the One who sent me. **39** This is the will of the One who sent me: I must not lose anything that God has given to me. I must restore it *to God* on the last day. **40** This is what my Father wants: Every person who sees the Son and commits himself to him will have eternal life. I will restore that person on the last day."

41 The Jewish leaders were complaining about Jesus, because he said, "I am the food which came down from heaven."

42 They said, "This is Jesus, Joseph's son. We know his father and mother. Why is he now saying, 'I have come down from heaven?' "

43 Jesus answered them, "Stop complaining among yourselves. **44** No one can come to me, unless the Father who sent me draws him. On the last day I will raise that person *from death*. **45** One of the prophets wrote this:

'All people will be taught by God.' *Isaiah 54:13*

Everyone who listens to the Father and learns *from Him* comes to me. **46** No one has seen the Father. The only one who has seen the Father is the one who was with God. **47** I am telling you the truth: The person who believes has eternal life. **48** I am the food *which gives* life. **49** Our ancestors ate manna* in the desert, but they died. **50** There is a *type of* food which comes down from heaven. If someone eats it, he will not die. **51** **I** am the food which comes down from heaven; *it gives* life. If anyone eats this food, he will live forever. The food which I will give is my flesh. I want the people of the world to live."

52 The Jewish leaders started arguing strongly with each other, "How can Jesus give us his flesh to eat?"

53 Jesus said to them, "I am telling you the truth: If you don't eat my* flesh and you don't drink my blood, you do not have life in you! **54** The person who eats my flesh and drinks my blood has eternal life. I will raise him *from death* on the last day. **55** My flesh is real food and my blood is real drink. **56** The person who eats my flesh and drinks my blood stays in me and I stay in him. **57** The living Father sent me. I live because of the Father. In the same way, the person who feeds on me will live because of **me**. **58** This is the food which came down from heaven. The person who eats this food will live forever. This food is not what our ancestors ate and then died." **59** These are the things which Jesus said while teaching in the synagogue at Capernaum.

Some People Quit Chasing Jesus

60 Many of Jesus' followers heard these things and said, "This is a hard teaching. Who can obey it?"

6:49 food miraculously supplied to the people of Israel on their journey through the desert (See Exodus 16:13-21; Numbers 11:7-9.)

6:53 literally, the Son of Man's

61 Jesus knew that his followers were complaining about this. He asked them, "Does this offend you? **62** Suppose you were to see me* going up to where I was before? **63** The Spirit is life-giving; physical things are not worth very much. The words I have spoken to you are Spirit and life, **64** but some of you don't believe." (From the very beginning Jesus knew who didn't believe and which one would turn against him.) **65** Jesus said, "This is why I told you that no one could come to me if he were not allowed to come by my Father."

66 Because of this, many of Jesus' followers turned back. They were not walking with him anymore. **67** Jesus said to the twelve *apostles*, "You don't want to go away, too, do you?"

68 Simon Peter answered him, "Lord, who else is there to go to? **You** have the words of eternal life! **69** We have believed and know that you are God's holy one." **70** Jesus answered them, "Did I not choose all twelve of you? But one of you is a devil!" **71** Jesus was talking about Judas, the son of Simon Iscariot. Judas, one of the twelve *apostles*, was about to turn against Jesus.

Chapter 7

Show Yourself to the World!

1 After this, Jesus was traveling around in the land of Galilee. He didn't want to go to the land of Judea, because the Jewish leaders were trying to kill him. **2** The time for the Jewish Festival of Tents* was near. **3** Jesus' brothers said to him, "Get away from here and go to Judea, so that your followers may see the miracles you are doing. **4** If someone wants to be famous, he doesn't hide the things he is doing. Since you are doing these things, show yourself to the world!" **5** (Even Jesus' brothers did not believe in him.)

6 Then Jesus said to them, "It is not yet the right time for me. There is always a good time for you. **7** The people of the world cannot hate you. They hate me because I tell the truth about them—their lives are evil! **8** You should go on up to the feast *in Jerusalem*. I am not going up to this feast just yet. The time is not yet ripe for me." **9** After he said these things, Jesus stayed in the land of Galilee.

Jesus Comes to Jerusalem

10 After Jesus' brothers went up *to Jerusalem* for the feast, Jesus also went up there, but Jesus did it secretly. **11** The Jewish leaders were looking for him at the festival. They continued to ask, "Where is Jesus?"

12 Many people in the crowd were arguing about Jesus. Some were saying, "He is a good man." Others were saying, "No, he fools the people!" **13** But no one was talking about Jesus openly because they were afraid of the Jewish leaders.

14 The festival was already half over when Jesus came up *to Jerusalem* to the temple. Jesus began to teach the people. **15** The Jewish leaders were amazed. They asked, "How did this man learn so much? He never went to school!"

16 Then Jesus said to them, "What I am teaching does not belong to me; it comes from the One who sent me. **17** If anyone wants to do what God wants, that person will find out whether my teaching comes from God or if I am speaking on my own. **18** The person who speaks on his own is trying to get glory for himself, but the person who

---

6:62   literally, the Son of Man
7:2   the fall. Each year the Jews lived in tents for seven days. (See Leviticus 23:39-43.)

wants glory *to go* to the One who sent him is honest. There is nothing wrong with him.
19 Moses gave you the law, but not one of you is obeying the law. Why are you trying
to kill me?"

20 The crowd answered, "You are crazy! Who is trying to kill you?"

21 Jesus answered them, "I did one miracle *on the Sabbath day* and all of you are
amazed. **22** Yet you will circumcise* a child on the Sabbath day. Moses gave you circumcision! Actually, circumcision did not come from Moses, but from our ancestors.
23 Since a child can receive circumcision on the Sabbath day, so that the law of Moses
won't be broken, why are you so angry with me? I made a man completely well on the
Sabbath day. **24** Don't judge by the way things look! Judge fairly."

Where Does the Messiah Come From?

25 Some of the people of Jerusalem were saying, "This is the man whom the Jewish leaders are trying to kill. **26** And look, he speaks in the open and they are saying
nothing to him about it. Is it possible that the leaders know he **is** the Messiah? **27** But
we know where this man comes from. When the Messiah comes, no one will know
where he comes from!"

28 While Jesus was teaching the people in the temple courtyard, Jesus cried out, "Do
you know me? Do you know where I come from? I have not come on my own. However, the One who sent me is true. You don't know Him! **29** But I know Him, because
I was with Him. He sent me!"

30 Then they tried to arrest Jesus. But no one laid a hand on him, because his time
had not yet come. **31** Many people in the crowd believed in Jesus. They said, "When
the Messiah comes, will he do more miracles than this man has done?"

Where Will Jesus Go?

32 The Pharisees heard the crowd arguing these things about Jesus. The most important priests and the Pharisees sent some guards to arrest Jesus. **33** Then Jesus said,
"I will be with you a little while longer, but then I must go to the One who sent me.
34 You will look for me, but you won't find me. I will be where you cannot come."

35 Then the Jewish leaders thought to themselves, "Where is he about to go, so that
we cannot find him? He wouldn't go to the Jews who live in the Greek cities, would he?
Would he teach non-Jewish people there? Surely not! **36** What is the meaning of
what he said: 'You will look for me, but you won't find me' and, 'Where I am, you cannot come'?"

Are You Thirsty?

37 On the last and most important day of the festival, Jesus stood and cried out, "If
you are thirsty, come to me and drink! **38** The person who believes in me will be like
the Scripture which says:

'A river of fresh* water will flow from his body.' "

Proverbs 18:4; Isaiah 58:11

39 (Here Jesus was talking about the Spirit whom the believers were about to receive.
The Spirit had not yet *been given*, because Jesus had not yet been *raised* to glory.)

7:22   Each Jewish boy received a physical mark—cutting off the foreskin. This was a sign of the agreement which God had made with Abraham (Genesis 17:9-14).

7:38   or, living

Who Did You Say Jesus Was Again?

40 Some of the people in the crowd heard these words. They said, "Surely he is the prophet!"

41 Other people said, "This man is the Messiah!"

Still others said, "The Messiah does not come from the land of Galilee! **42** The Scripture said that the coming Messiah would be from David's family and from Bethlehem, the village where David lived." **43** So, the people in the crowd were divided because of Jesus. **44** Some of them were wanting to arrest him, but no one laid a hand on him.

Nicodemus Again

45 Later the guards came back to the most important priests and Pharisees. They asked the guards, "Why didn't you bring back Jesus?"

46 The guards answered, "No man ever spoke like this!"

47 The Pharisees answered them, "You haven't been fooled, have you? **48** None of the Jewish leaders or the Pharisees have believed in Jesus, have they? **49** This crowd is ignorant of the law. They should be condemned!"

50 Nicodemus was one of the Pharisees. (*Remember*, he had come to Jesus before.*) He said to them, **51** "Our law does not condemn a man without hearing from him first. We must find out what he is doing."

52 They answered Nicodemus, "Are you also from Galilee? Search the *Scriptures* and you will see that no prophet comes from Galilee."*

[**53** Then each one of them went home.

Chapter 8

Finger Pointing

1 Jesus went to Olive Mountain. **2** Early the next morning Jesus went back to the temple courtyard. All the people were coming to him. He sat down and began teaching them. **3** The teachers of the law and the Pharisees brought a woman *to Jesus*. They had caught her committing adultery. They made her stand in the center. **4** They said to Jesus, "Teacher, this woman was caught in the very act of committing adultery. **5** In the law Moses commanded us to stone such people to death. What do **you** say about her?" **6** (They were saying this to test Jesus. They wanted to get something which they could use to accuse him.)

Jesus bent down and wrote something on the ground with his finger. **7** They continued to ask Jesus questions. Jesus stood up and said to them, "The one among you who has not sinned should throw the first stone at her!" **8** Jesus bent down again and continued writing on the ground.

9 When they heard this, they began to leave one by one from the oldest on down. Jesus was the only one left. The woman was still standing there, too. **10** Jesus stood up and said to her, "Woman, where are they? Is anyone condemning you?"

11 She answered, "No one, Lord."

Jesus said, "I am not condemning you, either. Go, and from now on, don't sin anymore!"]

7:50   See John 3:1-13.

7:52   Most ancient manuscripts do not have John 7:53–8:11. In many copies it was found at the end of the Gospel of John. Others have it at John 7:36, John 7:44, or Luke 21:38.

Night Light

12 Jesus spoke to the people again. He said, "I am the light for the people of the world. The person who follows me will never walk in darkness. Instead, he will have the living light."

13 Then the Pharisees said to Jesus, "You are testifying on your own behalf; your proof is not valid!"

14 Jesus answered them, "Even though I am testifying on my own behalf, my proof is *still* valid, because I know where I came from and where I am going. But you don't know where I came from or where I'm going.   **15** You judge in a human way; I am not judging anyone *now*.   **16** But if I were to judge, my decision would be right, because I am not alone—the Father who sent me is with me, too.   **17** And in your law this is written,

'The testimony of two people is valid.'   *Deuteronomy 17:6*
18 So, I am testifying on my own behalf and the Father who sent me is testifying for me, too."

19 The Pharisees asked Jesus, "Where is your father?"

Jesus answered, "You don't know me or my Father. If you knew me, you would know my Father."

20 Jesus spoke these words, while he was teaching in the temple courtyard. He was near the place where the offering boxes were placed. No one arrested Jesus, because his time had not yet come.

What Do You Mean, I Can't Go With You?!

21 Then Jesus said to them again, "I am going away and you will look for me, but you will die in your sins. You cannot come where I am going."

22 The Jewish leaders asked, "Will he kill himself? He said, 'You cannot come where I am going.'"

23 Jesus said to them, "You come from below. I come from above. You come from this world. I do not come from this world.   **24** I told you that you would die in your sins. If you don't believe that I am the one, you will die in your sins."

25 Then they asked, "Who are you?"

Jesus answered them, "I am what I have been telling you all along!   **26** There are many things I have to judge and to say about you. However, the One who sent me is true. I tell the people in the world only what I have heard from my Father."

27 They did not understand that Jesus was talking to them about the *heavenly* Father. **28** So Jesus said this to them: "You will know that I am the one when you raise me* high. I do nothing on my own. I am only saying the things which the Father teaches me. **29** The One who sent me is with me. He has not left me alone, because I always do what is pleasing to Him."   **30** While Jesus was speaking, many people believed in him.

The Truth Frees You

31 Jesus was talking with the Jews who had believed in him, saying, "If you stay with my teaching, you are truly my followers.   **32** You will find out the truth, and the truth will set you free."

33 They answered him, "We are Abraham's descendants. We have never been slaves. How can you say, 'You will be free'?"

8:28   literally, the Son of Man, meaning when Jesus would be raised onto the cross

34 Jesus answered them, "I am telling you the truth: Every person who continues to sin is a slave of sin.   35 A slave does not live in the house forever, but a son will always live there.   36 If the Son sets you free, you are truly free.   37 I know that you are descendants of Abraham, but you are trying to kill me because you cannot find room in your hearts for my teaching.   38 I talk about the things which I saw while I was with the Father. You do the things which you hear from your father.*

39 They answered Jesus, "Abraham is our father!"

Jesus said to them, "If you were Abraham's children, you would be doing the things that Abraham did.   40 Abraham would not have done this, but now you are trying to kill me. I have told you the truth which I heard when I was with God.   41 You are doing the things your father does."

They said to Jesus, "The only Father we have is God; we are not illegitimate!"

42 Jesus said to them, "If God were your Father, you would love me. I am here now and I came from God. I didn't come on my own; God sent me.   43 Why do you not understand what I am saying? You cannot obey my teaching.   44 You come from your father, the Devil. You want to do the sinful things that your father wants. The Devil was a murderer from the very beginning. He does not stand with the truth, because there is no truth in him. When he tells a lie, he is only talking naturally, because he is a liar and the father of lies.

45 "But I am telling you the truth and that is why you don't believe me.   46 Can one of you prove that I am guilty of sin? Since I *always* tell the truth, why do you not believe me?   47 The person who comes from God listens to God. This is why you won't listen—you are not from God!"

I Lived Before Abraham Did

48 The Jewish leaders answered, "How right we are when we say that you are a Samaritan; you are crazy!"

49 Jesus answered, "I am not crazy. I honor my Father, but you don't honor me. 50 I'm not looking for glory for myself, but there is One who is looking for *glory for me*; He is the Judge.   51 I am telling you the truth: If anyone obeys my teaching, he will **never** die!"

52 Then the Jewish leaders said to Jesus, "Now we **know** that you are crazy! Abraham and the prophets died. Yet you say, 'If anyone obeys my teaching, he will **never** die.'   53 You are not more important than Abraham, our ancestor, are you? He died. The prophets died, too. Just who do you think you are?"

54 Jesus answered, "If I *were trying* to get glory for myself, my glory would be *worth* nothing. The One who is giving me glory is my Father. You are saying, 'He is our God!'   55 But you don't know Him. I know Him. If I were to say that I do not know Him, I would be like you—a liar! But I really do know Him and I obey His teaching. 56 Abraham, your ancestor, was very happy to see my day; he saw it and was glad."

57 Then the Jewish leaders said to Jesus, "You are not yet 50 years old—and you have seen Abraham?"

58 Jesus said to them, "I am telling you the truth: I was alive before Abraham was born!"

59 They picked up stones to throw at Jesus, but he left the temple courtyard and kept out of sight.

8:38   meaning, Their father was the Devil. (See John 8:44.)

Chapter 9

A Man Born Blind

1 As Jesus was walking along, he saw a man who had been born blind. **2** Jesus' followers asked him, "Rabbi, who sinned, this person or his parents, to cause him to be born blind?"

3 Jesus answered, "This person did not sin; his parents did not sin. No, *this occurred,* so that God's deeds might be shown in this man'*s life.* **4** We must do the tasks of the One who sent me while it is still daytime. Night is coming. No one can work then. **5** I am light for the people of the world while I am in the world."

6 After Jesus said these things, he spit on the ground and made some mud with it. Then he rubbed it on the blind man's eyes. **7** Jesus said to him, "Go, wash yourself in the pool of Siloam." (This word means "Sent.") Then the blind man went away and washed himself and came back with sight!

8 Then the people who used to see him before (when he was a beggar) and his neighbors were saying, "This is the man who used to sit and beg!"

9 Other people were saying, "It's him!" Still others were saying, "No, but he looks like him." But the man himself continued to say, "I'm the one!"

10 They asked again and again, "How come you can see?"

11 The man answered, "A man called Jesus made some mud and rubbed it on my eyes. Then he told me, 'Go to Siloam and wash yourself.' So I went there and washed myself, and now I can see!"

12 They asked him, "Where is Jesus?"

The blind man answered, "I don't know."

Who's Really Blind?

13 They brought the man who was once blind to the Pharisees. **14** (Jesus had made the mud and opened the blind man's eyes on the Sabbath day.) **15** Again, the Pharisees kept asking the blind man how he could see. The man said to them, "He put mud on my eyes, I washed myself, and I can see."

16 Some of the Pharisees were saying, " This man is not from God because he does not keep the Sabbath day!"

But others were asking, "How could a sinful man perform such miracles?" They were divided among themselves.

17 They asked the man again, "What do you say about Jesus? *Do you believe* he opened your eyes?"

The man answered, "He is a prophet."

18 The Jewish leaders didn't believe that the man had really been blind and could now see, until they called the man's parents. **19** The leaders asked them, "Is this man your son? Do you claim that he was born blind? How come he now sees?"

20 Then his parents answered, "We know he is our son and that he was born blind, **21** but we don't know how he can see now. We don't know how he opened his eyes. Ask him. He is a grown man; he can speak for himself." **22** (The man's parents said these things, because they were afraid of the Jewish leaders. The Jewish leaders had already agreed that if anyone said that Jesus was the Messiah, that person would be thrown out of the synagogue. **23** That is why his parents said, "He is an adult; ask him.")

24 Then, a second time, the Jewish leaders told the man (who had been blind), "Give glory to God! We know that this man is a sinner."

25 The man answered, "Maybe he is a sinner. I don't know. But one thing I do know, I was blind and now I can see."

26 They asked him, "What did he do to you? How did he open your eyes?"

27 The man answered, "I have already told you and you didn't listen. Why do you want to hear it again? You don't want to become his followers, do you?"

28 Then they insulted the man saying, "You are Jesus' follower. We are Moses' followers. **29** We **know** that God has spoken to Moses. But we don't know where this Jesus comes from."

30 The man answered them, "That is amazing! You don't know where Jesus comes from, and yet he opened my eyes! **31** We know that God does not listen to sinners, but God will listen to anyone who respects Him and obeys His will. **32** Since time began, no one has ever heard of anyone opening the eyes of a man born blind. **33** If Jesus did not come from God, he could not do anything."

34 They answered him, "You were totally born in sin; you cannot teach us!" And they threw him out.

I Know Who's Blind

35 Jesus heard that the Jewish leaders had thrown the man out. Jesus found him and asked him, "Do you believe in the Son of Man?*"

36 The man answered, "Sir, who is he, so that I may believe in him?"

37 Jesus said to him, "You have seen him and he is speaking to you right now!"

38 The man said, "Lord, I believe." And he worshiped Jesus.

39 Jesus said, "I came into this world, so that there can be a Judgment *Day*, so that the people who cannot see may see and those who *think they* can see may become blind."

40 Some Pharisees who were with Jesus heard this. They said to him, "You don't think **we** are blind, too, do you?"

41 Jesus said to them, "If you were blind,* you would be innocent, but, you are now claiming you can see.* So, your guilt remains."

Chapter 10

Jesus Is the Good Shepherd

1 "I am telling you the truth: If a man does not get into the sheep pen through the gate, but climbs in by some other way, he is either a robber or a bandit. **2** The one who comes through the gate is the shepherd of the sheep. **3** The man who guards the gate opens the gate for him. The sheep know the shepherd's voice. The shepherd calls the name of each one of his sheep and leads them out. **4** After he has brought all his own sheep out, he walks ahead of them and the sheep follow him because they know his voice. **5** They would never follow a stranger; they would run away from him. They would not recognize a stranger's voice." **6** Jesus used this example *about sheep*, but the people didn't understand what he was talking about.

9:35   Jesus
9:41   without understanding
9:41   know what you are doing

Abundant Life

7 Therefore, Jesus spoke again, "I am telling you the truth: **I** am the gate for the sheep. **8** All those who came before me were either robbers or bandits, but the sheep didn't listen to them. **9** **I** am the gate. If anyone will go through me, he will be saved. He may come and go *as he pleases* and find plenty to eat. **10** Why does the robber come? Only to steal, kill, and destroy. I came, so that they might have life—to the fullest!

11 "I am the good shepherd. The good shepherd gives his own life for the sheep. **12** A man who has been hired is not really a shepherd. The sheep do not belong to him. When he sees a wolf coming, he leaves the sheep and runs away. The wolf catches them and scatters them. **13** The man doesn't care about the sheep, because he is a hired man. **14** **I** am the good shepherd. I know my *followers*, and my *followers* know me, **15** just as my Father knows me and I know my Father. I will give my life for the sheep. **16** But I have some other sheep that are not in this flock. I must lead them, too. They will listen to my voice. Then they will be one flock and one shepherd. **17** *Do you know* why my Father loves me? Because, I will give my life, so that I may take it back. **18** No one takes it away from me. I am giving it of my own free will. I have the authority to give it and I have the authority to take it back. I received this order from my Father."

19 Again, the Jewish people were divided because of these words. **20** Many of them were saying, "He is crazy! He's insane! Why are you listening to him?"

21 Others were saying, "These words don't *sound like* the words *of a crazy person.* Could a crazy man open the eyes of a blind man?"

They Hate Jesus

22 It was winter. The time came for the Feast of Dedication* in Jerusalem. **23** Jesus was walking in the temple courtyard next to Solomon's Porch. **24** Some Jews gathered around him. They kept asking him, "How much longer will you make us wait? If you are the Messiah, tell us clearly!"

25 Jesus answered them, "I told you, but you didn't believe. I am doing miracles with my Father's authority. These are telling the truth about me, **26** but you don't believe, because you are not my sheep. **27** My sheep listen to my voice. I know them. They follow me. **28** I give them eternal life. They will **never** be lost. No one will snatch them out of my hand.

My Father and I Are Tight...Real Tight

29 My Father is stronger than anyone. No one can snatch them from my Father's hand. He has given me all things. **30** My Father and I are united."

31 Again, some Jews picked up stones to throw at Jesus and kill him. **32** Jesus answered them, "I have shown you many good works from my Father. For which good work are you stoning me?"

33 They answered him, "We are going to throw rocks at you, not for any good work, but because you said some evil things against God! You are only a man, yet you are making yourself God."

34 Jesus answered them, "This is written in your law:
'I said that you are gods.'

Psalm 82:6

10:22   Hanukkah, a festival which celebrates the rededication of the temple after Judas Maccabaeus was victorious over Syria (164 B.C.).

35 The message of God came to them, and since he said 'gods'—and the Scripture cannot be broken— 36 why are you claiming I am saying evil things against God when I said, 'I am God's Son'? The Father selected me and sent me into the world. 37 If I am not performing miracles from my Father, don't believe in me. 38 But, if I **am** doing them, even though you may not believe in me, believe in *the evidence* of the miracles. You must know, once and for all, that the Father is in me and I am in the Father."

39 Once again, they were trying to arrest Jesus, but he slipped through their hands.

40 Jesus went back across the Jordan River to the place where John was first immersing people. Jesus stayed there. 41 Many people came to him. They said, "John did not perform any miracles, but everything he said about Jesus is true." 42 Many people there believed in Jesus.

Chapter 11

Lazarus Is Sick to Death

1 A man named Lazarus was sick. He and his sisters, Mary and Martha, were from the village of Bethany. 2 (Mary was the one who rubbed the Lord *Jesus*' feet with perfume and dried them with her hair.*) Lazarus, the brother, was very sick. 3 The *two* sisters sent *a message* saying, "Listen, your friend, *Lazarus*, is very sick!"

4 When Jesus heard this, he said, "This sickness will not end in death. Instead, it will be for God's glory. This will be used to give glory to the Son of God."

5 Jesus loved Mary, Martha, and Lazarus. 6 When Jesus heard that Lazarus was sick, he stayed where he was for two days. 7 After that, Jesus said to his followers, "Let us go back to the land of Judea."

8 Jesus' followers said to him, "But Rabbi, the Jewish leaders are now trying to stone you to death! Do you want to go there again?"

9 Jesus answered, "There are twelve hours in a day. Someone who is walking in the daytime does not stumble; he sees the light in this world. 10 But a person may stumble when he walks at night because he has no light."

11 After Jesus said these things, he told them this: "Our friend Lazarus is asleep, but I will go wake him up."

12 Then Jesus' followers said to him, "Lord, he will be all right if he's asleep."

13 (Jesus was talking about the death of Lazarus. They thought Jesus was talking about natural sleep.)

14 Then Jesus told them plainly, "Lazarus has died! 15 For your sakes, I'm glad I was not there *when he died*. I want you to believe. Let us go to him."

16 Thomas (called The Twin) said to the other followers, "Let us go, too, so we can die with him!"

Jesus Comes

17 When Jesus came, he found that Lazarus had been put in the grave four days before. 18 The village of Bethany was near Jerusalem, less than two miles away. 19 Many Jews had come to Martha and Mary to comfort them over their brother's death. 20 When Martha heard that Jesus was coming, she went to meet him, but Mary continued to sit in the house. 21 Martha said to Jesus, "Lord, my brother would never have died, if you had been here. 22 But, even now, I know if you ask God, He would give you anything."

11:2   See John 12:3.

23 Jesus said to her, "Your brother will rise from death."

24 Martha said to Jesus, "I know that Lazarus will rise from death, when all people are raised on the last Day."

25 Jesus answered her, "I am the resurrection and the life. The person who commits himself to me will live, even though he may die. 26 Every person who lives and commits himself to me will **never** die! Do you believe this?"

27 Martha said to him, "Yes, Lord. I still believe that **you** are the Messiah, the Son of God, who comes into the world."

Jesus Calls for Mary

28 After Martha said these things, she went back and secretly called Mary, her sister, telling her, "The Teacher is here; he is calling for you."

29 When Mary heard this, she got up quickly and went to Jesus. 30 Jesus had not yet come into the village. He was still at the place where Martha had met him. 31 Some Jews were with Mary in the house, comforting her. When they saw Mary stand up quickly and leave, they followed her. They thought she was going to Lazarus' grave, to cry *some more* there. 32 When Mary came to where Jesus was and saw him, she fell down at Jesus' feet. She said, "Lord, if you had been here, my brother would not have died!"

33 Jesus saw her crying and the Jews who had come with her crying, too. He felt very sorry and upset. 34 Jesus said, "Where have you put Lazarus?"

They said to him, "Lord, come and see." 35 Tears came to his eyes.

36 Then the Jews said, "Look how Jesus loved Lazarus!"

37 But some of them said, "This man was able to open the blind man's eyes.* Couldn't he have kept Lazarus alive?"

A God Chaser Is Back on the Chase

38 When Jesus came to the grave, again he was deeply moved in his heart. It was a cave with a large stone placed in front of it. 39 Jesus said, "Take the stone away!"

Martha, the dead man's sister, said to him, "Lord, this is the fourth day; there is already a bad smell!"

40 Jesus said to her, "I told you that if you would believe, you would see the glory of God." 41 Then they took the stone away. Jesus looked up to heaven and said, "Father, I am thankful that you are listening to me. 42 I know that you always listen to me, but I said this because of the crowd which is standing here. I want them to believe that You sent me." 43 After Jesus said this, he cried out with a loud voice, "Lazarus! Come out!" 44 The dead man came out. Lazarus' hands and feet were bound with pieces of cloth. His face was wrapped with a handkerchief. Jesus said to them, "Untie him and let him go."

45 Many Jews had come to visit Mary. They saw the things which Jesus did. They believed in him. 46 But some of them went off to the Pharisees and told them what Jesus had done. 47 The most important priests and the Pharisees called a meeting. They asked each other, "What are we going to do? This man is performing many miracles! 48 If we let him go on like this, everyone will believe in him. Then the Romans will come and take us away—our *holy* place and our nation." 49 One of them was Caiaphas. He was the high priest that year. He said to them, "You know nothing! 50 Don't you think it would be better for one man to die for the people, than for the whole nation to be destroyed?" 51 (Caiaphas did not say this on his own. But, since he was the high priest that year, he prophesied that Jesus was about to die for

11:37   See John 9:6-7.

162

the Jewish nation.   **52** And not only for them, but also so that *all* God's scattered children might be gathered together into one people.)   **53** From that day forward, they plotted to kill Jesus.

54 So, Jesus was not moving around among the Jews openly anymore. Jesus left there for an area which was near the desert. It was a town called Ephraim. Jesus stayed there with his followers for a while.

55 The time for the Jewish Passover Festival was near. Many people went from the country up to Jerusalem before the Passover began. They wanted to make themselves pure.   **56** These people were standing in the temple courtyard looking for Jesus. They were asking one another, "What do you think? Will Jesus come to the festival or not?" **57** The most important priests and Pharisees had given an order: "If anyone knows where Jesus is, he must tell us, so that we may arrest him."

Chapter 12

Mary Prepares Jesus for Burial

1 Six days before the Passover Festival,* Jesus came to the town of Bethany. Lazarus was there—the one whom Jesus had raised from death.   **2** They gave a dinner for Jesus. Martha was helping and Lazarus was one of the guests with Jesus.   **3** Mary brought in about a pint of a very expensive perfume—pure nard.* She rubbed it on Jesus' feet. Then she dried his feet with her hair. The house was filled with the smell of perfume.

4 One of Jesus' followers was ready to turn against Jesus. This was Judas Iscariot. He said,   **5** "Why wasn't this perfume sold for 300 silver coins and given to some poor people?"   **6** (Judas did not say this because he cared about poor people. Judas was a thief; he was the one who was always carrying the *group's* bag of money.)

7 Then Jesus said, "Leave her alone. She must do this for the day when I am buried. **8** You will always have the poor with you, but you will not always have **me**!"

A God Chaser Draws a Crowd

9 A large crowd of Jews knew that Jesus was there. They came not only because they wanted to see Jesus, but also because of Lazarus, who had been raised from death.   **10** The most important priests planned to kill Lazarus, too.   **11** Many people were going away from the Jewish leaders because of Lazarus. They were beginning to believe in Jesus.

Jesus Enters Jerusalem

12 The next day, a large crowd came to the festival. When they heard that Jesus was coming to Jerusalem,   **13** they took branches from palm trees and went out to meet him. They were shouting,

"Hosanna! Give praise to the king of Israel who is coming with the authority of the Lord *God.*"

14 Jesus found a young donkey and rode on it, as it is written:

15 "Don't be afraid, city of Jerusalem.*
Look, your King is coming,
sitting on a young donkey." *Zechariah 9:9*

12:1   one of the most important Jewish holidays. It celebrated deliverance from Egypt.
12:3   a very expensive perfume made from a plant
12:15   literally, daughter of Zion

16 At first, Jesus' followers didn't understand these things, but later, when Jesus was *raised to life* in glory, they remembered that these things had been written about him and that they had done these things for him.

17 There was a crowd with Jesus. They were always telling people about how Jesus called Lazarus from the grave, how he raised him from death. 18 This is why a crowd met Jesus. They heard that Jesus had performed this miracle. 19 Then the Pharisees said to one another, "Look! Nothing we do does any good. Everyone is following Jesus!"

Jesus Must Die So We May Live

20 Some non-Jewish people had come up *to Jerusalem* to worship *God* at the festival. 21 They came to Philip, who was from the town of Bethsaida in Galilee. They kept saying to him, "Sir, we want to meet Jesus."

22 Philip went and told Andrew. Andrew and Philip came and spoke to Jesus. 23 Jesus answered them, "The time has come for me* to receive glory. 24 I am telling you the truth: If one grain of wheat does not fall into the ground and die, it will always be just one grain of wheat, but if the grain dies, it will produce a large cluster. 25 The person who loves his own life is destroying it, but the person who does not value his life in this world will keep his life forever. 26 If anyone serves me, he must follow me. My servant will be where I am. If anyone serves me, the Father will honor that person."

Jesus Prays to His Father

27 "My soul is very troubled now. What should I say: 'Father, save me from this time *of suffering*'? No, the reason I came was for this time. 28 Father, bring glory to Your name!"

Then a Voice spoke from heaven, saying, "I have brought glory to it and I will bring glory to it again."

29 There was a crowd standing there. They heard the Voice, too. Some of them were saying, "It thundered!"

Others were saying, "An angel has spoken to him!"

30 Jesus answered, "This Voice did not speak for my sake—but for your sake. 31 The time has come for this world to be judged. The time has come for the ruler of this world* to be thrown out. 32 When I am lifted high above the earth,* I will attract everyone to me." 33 (Jesus was saying this to show what kind of death he was about to suffer.)

34 The crowd answered him, "In the law, we have heard that the Messiah will live forever. How can you say that the Son of Man must be nailed to a cross?* Who is this 'Son of Man'?"

35 Jesus said to them, "The light is with you only for a little while longer. Travel while you have the light, so that darkness will not catch you. A person who is walking around in the dark doesn't know where he is going. 36 Believe in the light while you have the light. You must be sons of light."

12:23   literally, the Son of Man
12:31   the Devil
12:32   meaning, when Jesus was raised onto the cross
12:34   literally, lifted high

God Chasers Aren't Afraid of What People Think

When Jesus had finished speaking, he went away and kept out of sight.   37 People did not believe in Jesus, even though such proofs from God* were in front of them.
38 The message of Isaiah the prophet has come true:

"Lord, who believed our report?
To whom did the Lord God show His power?"   *Isaiah 53:1*

39 They could not believe for the reason given by Isaiah:
40 "Their eyes are blind because of God.
Their hearts are hard because of God.
Otherwise, they could see with their eyes
and understand with their hearts and turn.
Then I could heal them."   *Isaiah 6:10*

41 Isaiah said these things, because he saw Jesus' glory. Isaiah was talking about Jesus.
42 Many people, even some of the leaders, believed in Jesus. But they would not say that they believed, because they were afraid of the Pharisees. They didn't want to be thrown out of the synagogues.   43 They loved praise from man more than praise from God.

To Chase God You've Got to Believe in Jesus

44 Jesus cried out, "The person who believes in me is not only believing in **me**, but also in the One who sent me.   45 The person who sees **me** sees the One who sent me.
46 I have come like light into the world, so that every person who believes in **me** will not stay in the darkness.   47 If someone hears my words and does not obey them, I am not the one who judges him *now*. I came to save the world, not to judge it.   48 The person who rejects **me** and does not accept my words has something to condemn him—the very message which I spoke. That message will condemn him on the last day.   49 I have not spoken on my own. The Father Himself sent me. He told me what to say.   50 I know that His command is eternal life. I am saying exactly what the Father said to me."

Chapter 13

Jesus Washes Their Feet

1 Just before the Passover Festival,* Jesus knew that his time had come; He must pass from this world to the Father. Jesus loved his own people in the world; he loved them to the very end.
2 It was time for the evening meal. The Devil had already put it in Judas' heart to turn against Jesus. (Judas Iscariot was the son of Simon.)   3 Jesus knew that the Father had put everything into his hands. He knew that he had come from God and that he was going back to God.   4 Jesus got up from the evening meal and laid his clothes aside. He took a towel and wrapped it around his waist.   5 Then Jesus put water into a pan. He began to wash his followers' feet. He dried their feet with the towel which was around his waist.   6 Then Jesus came to Simon Peter. Peter asked him, "Lord, are **you** going to wash my feet?"
7 Jesus answered him, "You may not understand what I am doing now, but you will understand it later."

12:37   literally, miracles or signs
13:1   one of the most important Jewish holidays. It celebrated deliverance from Egypt.

8 Peter said to him, "You will **never** wash my feet!"

Jesus answered him, "If I don't wash you, you are not sharing with me."

9 Simon Peter said to Jesus, "Lord, wash not only my feet; wash my hands and head, too!"

10 Jesus said to him, "The person who has already had a bath needs only to wash his feet *when they get dirty*; his whole body is clean. You are clean—but not all of you!" **11** Jesus knew who was turning against him. That is why Jesus said, "Not all of you are clean!"

12 After Jesus had washed their feet, he put on his clothes and sat down at the table again. He asked them, "Do you know what I have just done to you? **13** You call me 'Teacher' and 'Lord.' You are right, because I **am** the Teacher and the Lord. **14** Since I, the Lord and Teacher, washed your feet, you ought to wash one another's feet. **15** I have given you an example. You should do things *for others* as I have done for you. **16** I am telling you the truth: A slave is not more important than his master. A messenger is not more important than the one who sent him. **17** Since you know these things, you will be happy if you practice them. **18** I am not talking about all of you. I know the ones whom I have chosen. The Scripture must come true:

'The person who was eating my food turned against me.'   *Psalm 41:9*

19 I am telling you now, before it happens, so that when it does happen, you may believe that I am *the Messiah*. **20** I am telling you the truth: If anyone accepts someone whom I send, he is accepting **me**, too! The person who accepts me is accepting the One who sent me." **21** After Jesus said these things, he was very troubled in his spirit. He told them openly, "I am telling you the truth: One of you will turn against me!"

Judas Sells Out

22 Jesus' followers began looking at one another. They were wondering which one he was talking about. **23** One of his followers, (the one whom Jesus loved)* was sitting very close to Jesus. **24** Simon Peter signaled to this follower. Peter wanted him to ask Jesus, "Which one are you talking about?" **25** So, that follower moved very close to Jesus and whispered to him, "Lord, who is it?" **26** Jesus answered, "After I dip this piece of bread in the sauce, I will give it to that person." Then Jesus dipped a piece of bread into the sauce and gave it to Judas Iscariot, the son of Simon. **27** When this happened, Satan went into Judas. Then Jesus said to him, "Do what you plan to do quickly!" **28** None of the guests knew why Jesus said this to him. **29** Since Judas kept the *group's* bag of money, some were thinking that Jesus meant: "Buy what we need for the feast." or "Give something to the poor people." **30** So, Judas took the piece of bread and went out immediately. And it was night.

God Chasers Care about Each Other

31 After Judas left, Jesus said, "Now I* am given glory and, in me,* God is given glory. **32** Since God is given glory in me,* God will give me* glory for myself; He will do it immediately. **33** Little children, I am still with you a little while longer. Just as I said to the Jewish leaders, 'You will look for me, but where I am going you cannot

13:23   probably John the apostle
13:31   literally, the Son of Man...in him
13:31   Jesus was nailed to the cross. (Compare John 3:14.)
13:32   literally, the Son of Man.
13:32   Jesus was nailed to the cross. (Compare John 3:14.)

come.' I am saying the same thing to you now.   **34** I am giving you a new command—love one another. You must love one another, just as I loved you.   **35** You must have love for one another. This is how everyone will know that you are **my** followers."

Peter Thought He Was Strong

36 Simon Peter said to Jesus, "Lord, where are you going?"

Jesus answered him, "I am going where you cannot follow now, but you will follow later."

37 Peter said to him, "Lord, why can't I follow you now? I would give up my life for you!"

38 Jesus answered, "Would you give up your life for me? I am telling you the truth: Before the rooster crows *tomorrow morning*, you will say that you don't even know me. You will do it three different times!"

Chapter 14

I'll Go on Ahead

1 "Don't let your heart be troubled. You trust in God; trust in me, too.   **2** There are many rooms in my Father's house. I would have told you, if that were not true. I am taking a trip to prepare a place for you.   **3** Since I am leaving to prepare a place for you, *you can be sure that* I will come back and take you with me, so that you will be where I am.   **4** You know the road to where I am going."

5 Thomas said to Jesus, "Lord, we do not know where you are going. How can we know the way?"

6 Jesus said to him, "**I** am the way and the truth and the life! The only way anyone can come to the Father is through **me**!   **7** If you had known me, you would have known my Father. But even now, you do know Him and you have seen Him."

8 Philip said to Jesus, "Lord, show us the Father; that would be enough for us."

9 Jesus asked him, "Philip, have I been with you such a long time and you have not known me? The person who has seen **me** has seen the Father! How can you say, 'Show us the Father'?   **10** You believe that I am in the Father and the Father is in me, don't you? The words which I am using to speak to you are not words I use on my own. The Father performs His miracles; He stays in me.   **11** Believe me, I am in the Father and the Father is in me. At least believe, because of these miracles.   **12** I am telling you the truth: The person who believes in me will do the same deeds that I am performing. He will do even greater things than these. I am going to the Father.   **13** I will do whatever you ask for in my name. The Father will receive glory in the Son.   **14** If you ask me for something in my name, I will do it."

The Holy Ghost Comforter

15 "If you love me, obey my commands.   **16–17** I will ask my Father and He will give you another Comforter—the Spirit of truth. He will be with you forever. The people of the world cannot accept him, because they don't see him or know him, but you know him because he stays with you—he is in you.   **18** I will not abandon you, as though you were orphans. I am coming to you.   **19** A little longer and the people of the world will not see me anymore. However, **you** will see me. You will live, because **I** live.   **20** At that time, you will know that I am in my Father, you are in me, and I am in you.   **21** The person who accepts my commands and obeys them is the one who truly loves me. My Father will love the person who loves me, and I will love him and make myself known to him."

22 Judas (not Judas Iscariot) said to Jesus, "Lord, what has happened that you are ready to reveal yourself to **us**, but not to the people of the world?"

23 Jesus answered him, "If anyone loves me and obeys my teaching, my Father will love him. We will come and live with him. **24** The person who does not love me will not obey my teachings. The message you are hearing is not mine; it belongs to the Father who sent me.

25 "I have said these things to you while I am staying with you. **26** The Comforter will teach you everything. He will cause you to remember everything I have told you. He is the Holy Spirit. The Father will send him with my authority. **27** I am leaving peace with you. I am giving you my peace. This peace that I am giving you is not like *the type that* the world gives. Don't let your heart be troubled or afraid.

28 "You have heard me say: 'I am leaving, but I will come back to you.' If you really loved me, you would be glad that I am traveling to the Father. The Father is greater than I am. **29** Now I have told you before it happens, so that when it happens, you will believe. **30** I will not say many more things while I am with you. The ruler of the world* is coming. He can do nothing to me. **31** I must do as my Father ordered me, so that the people of the world may know that I love the Father. Get up! Let us go away from here."

Chapter 15

God Chasers Produce Fruit

1 "I am the true vine. My Father is the farmer. **2** My Father takes away any branch in me which is not producing fruit. My Father trims each branch which is producing fruit, so that it will produce more fruit. **3** You are already clean, because of the message I have spoken to you. **4** Stay in me and I will stay in you. No branch can produce fruit on its own; it must stay on the vine. In the same way, you cannot *produce*, unless you stay in **me**. **5** I am the vine; you are the branches. Who will produce much fruit? The person who stays in me and in whom I stay. You can do nothing without me! **6** If someone does not stay in me, he is like a branch which is thrown away. He dries up. People gather *dead* branches and throw them into the fire, and they burn up. **7** If you stay in me and my words stay in you, then you may ask for whatever you want and it will happen for you. **8** You must produce much fruit and be my followers. This is how my Father gets glory. **9** I love you, just as the Father loves me. Stay in my love. **10** I have obeyed my Father's commands and I stay in His love. If you obey my commands, you will stay in my love.

11 "I have said these things to you, so that my joy may be in you and your joy may be complete. **12** This is my command: Love one another, as I have loved you. **13** Suppose someone gives up his life for his friends. No one has a greater love than this.

14 "You are my friends, if you do what I tell you to do. **15** I am no longer calling you 'slaves,' because a slave doesn't know what his master is doing. I am calling you 'friends,' because I have revealed to you everything which I have heard from my Father. **16** You did not choose me; I chose you! I have appointed you to go and produce fruit. Your fruit will last. My Father will give you whatever you ask for in my name. **17** Love one another! I am ordering you to do this."

14:30   the Devil

168

The World Will Hate You, Too!

18 "If the people of the world hate you, remember that they hated **me** first.   **19** If you were from the world, the people of the world would love their own people. I chose you from out of the world. You are not in the world *anymore*. That is why the people of the world hate you.   **20** Do you remember the lesson I taught you: 'No slave is more important than his master'? Since they persecuted me, they will persecute you. Since they obeyed my teaching, they will obey your teaching.   **21** The people of the world will do all these things to you, because of my name; they didn't know the One who sent me.   **22** If I had not come and talked to them, they would not be so guilty, but now, they have no excuse for their sin.   **23** A person who hates **me** hates my Father, too.   **24** They would not be so guilty if I had not performed deeds among them which no one has ever done. But they have now seen *the miracles*. They have hated me and my Father.   **25** *It was necessary* for this verse written in their law to come true:

'They have no reason to hate me.'   *Psalm 35:19*

26 "I will send you the Comforter from the Father. He is the Spirit of truth who is coming out from the Father. When he comes, he will tell the truth about me.   **27** You will testify, too, because you were with me from the very beginning."

Chapter 16

They'll Throw You Out!

1 "I have said these things to you, so that you will not be led into sin.   **2** They will throw you out of the synagogues. The time is coming when each person who kills you will think he is offering service to God.   **3** They don't know the Father or me. That is why they will do these things.   **4** But I have told you these things, so when the time comes, you will remember that I warned you.

"I did not tell you this in the beginning because I was with you,   **5** but now I am going to the One who sent me. Not one of you is asking me, 'Where are you going?'   **6** You feel very sad, because I have told you these things.   **7** But I am telling you the truth; if I leave, it is really better for you. If I don't leave, the Comforter won't come to you. However, if I go away, I will send him to you.   **8** He will prove that the people of the world* are wrong about sin, wrong about what is right, and wrong about judgment: **9** about sin, because they are not believing in me;   **10** about what is right, because I am going to the Father and you will not see me anymore;   **11** about judgment, because the ruler of this world* has been condemned.

12 "I still have many things to tell you, but you cannot take it right now.   **13** When the Spirit of truth comes, he will guide you into all truth. He will not speak on his own *authority*. He will say whatever he hears. He will tell you about things to come.   **14** He will give me glory. He will take what I am saying and will tell it to you.   **15** Everything that belongs to my Father belongs to me, too. This is why I said, 'He will take what I am saying and tell it to you.'"

How Long Is "a Little While"?

16 *Jesus said*, "In a little while, you will not see me anymore, but then, after a little while, you will see me!"   **17** Some of Jesus' followers said to one another, "What is

---

16:8   those who have turned away from God
16:11   the Devil

the meaning of what he told us: 'In a little while, you will not see me anymore, but then, after a little while, you will see me,' and 'I am going to the Father'? **18** What does this 'little while' mean? We don't know what he is talking about!"

19 Jesus knew that they were wanting to ask him a question. He said to them, "Were you arguing with one another about what I said: 'In a little while, you won't see me anymore, but then, after a little while you will see me'? **20** I am telling you the truth: You will cry and be sad, but the people of the world will be glad. You will be full of sorrow, but your sorrow will change into joy. **21** When a woman is giving birth, she has much pain. Her time has come. But, after the child is born, she no longer remembers the suffering; she is so happy that a human being is born into the world. **22** You may have pain now, but I will see you again. Your heart will be glad. No one will be able to take your joy away from you. **23** At that time, you will ask me no questions. I am telling you the truth: The Father will give you whatever you ask for in my name. **24** So far, you have not asked for anything in my name. Ask *now*, and you will receive. Your joy will be complete."

Jesus Is Going Home

25 "I have used symbolic examples* to tell you about these things. The time is coming when I will no longer use examples like that. I will speak plainly to you. I will tell you about the Father. **26** At that time, you will use my name to ask for things. I am not saying that I will ask the Father for your sake. **27** The Father Himself loves you, because you have loved me and have believed that I came from God. **28** I did come from the Father and I have come into the world. But now, I am leaving the world and going back to the Father."

29 Jesus' followers said, "Listen, now you are talking plainly. You are not using figurative language anymore. **30** Now we **know** that you know everything! There is no need for anyone to ask you more questions. This is why we believe that you came from God."

31 Jesus asked them, "Do you believe now? **32** Listen, the time is coming—it's already here—when you will all be scattered, every man for himself. You will abandon me. However, I am really not alone; the Father is with me. **33** I have said these things to you, so that you may have peace in me. You will have trouble in the world, but be strong; I have conquered the world."

Chapter 17

Jesus' Prayer

1 After Jesus said these things, he looked up to heaven and said, "Father, the time has come. Bring glory to Your Son, so that Your Son may bring glory to You. **2** You have given him authority over all mankind. To each one that You have given the Son You will give eternal life. **3** This is eternal life: that they may know You, the only true God, and Jesus Christ, the one whom You sent. **4** I have brought You glory on the earth. I finished the work which You gave me to do. **5** Now, Father, give me glory— the glory I had with You when I was with You before the world existed.

6 "I have revealed Your name to men. You gave these men to me from the world. They were Your people and You gave them to me. They have obeyed Your teaching.

16:25   figurative language

7 They now know that everything You have given me comes from You.   8 I have given them the words which You gave me. They have received them. They knew I really did come from You. They believed that You sent me.

9 "I am praying for them, not for the world. I am praying for those men You have given me, because they belong to You.   10 Everything that is mine is Yours. Everything that is Yours is mine, too. In them I have received glory.   11 I am not in the world anymore, but my apostles are in the world. I am coming to You. Holy Father, keep them in Your name, the name which You have given me. May they be united, as we are.   12 When I was with them, I was always keeping them in Your name, the name You have given me. I have protected them. Not one of them was lost—only the child of destruction. The Scripture must come true.   13 Now I am coming to You. I am saying these things in the world, so that these men may have my complete joy in them.   14 I have given them Your message. The people of the world hated them, because they don't come from this world. I am not from this world, either.   15 I do not pray that You take them out of the world—just keep them from the evil one.*   16 I don't come from the world; they don't come from the world, either.   17 Your message is the truth. May the truth make them holy!   18 I sent them into the world, just as You sent me into the world.

19 "I keep myself holy for them, so that they will be holy by the truth.

20 "I pray not only for my apostles, but also for the people who believe in me through their teaching.   21 May all of them be united, just as You are in me and I am in You. I pray that they will be in us, so that the people of the world may believe that You sent me.   22 I have given them the glory that You have given me. May they be united, as we are;   23 I in them and You in me. May they be completely united, so that the people of the world will know that You sent me and that You loved them as You loved me.

24 "Father, You loved me before the world was created. You have given me glory. I want them to see it. I want them to be with me, where I will be.

25 "Righteous Father, the people of the world do not know You, but I know You. These men here know that You sent me.   26 I revealed Your name to them and I will reveal it. I want them to have Your love in them, the same love that You have for me. I want to be in them, too."

Chapter 18

Betrayed by a Friend

1 After Jesus had said these things, he and his followers went across Kidron Creek, where there was a garden. They went into the garden.   2 Judas (the one who turned against Jesus) also knew the place. Jesus often met there with his followers.   3 Then Judas took a group of soldiers and some *temple* guards sent by the most important priests and Pharisees. They had torches, lanterns, and weapons.   4 Jesus knew everything which was going to happen to him. He stepped forward and said to them, "Who are you looking for?"

5 They answered him, "Jesus from Nazareth."

Jesus said to them, "I am the one."

Judas (the one who turned against Jesus) was standing there with them.   6 When Jesus said, "I am the one," they drew back and fell to the ground.   7 Jesus asked them again, "Who are you looking for?"

They said, "Jesus from Nazareth."

17:15   the Devil

8 Jesus answered, "I told you that I am the one. Since you are looking for **me**, let these men go free." **9** (Jesus said that to make this come true: "I have not lost one of those You have given me."*)

10 Simon Peter had a sword. He struck the high priest's servant, cutting off his right ear. (The servant's name was Malchus.) **11** Then Jesus said to Peter, "Put your sword back into its place! My Father has given me this cup *of suffering.* Shouldn't I drink it?"

They Arrest Jesus

12 The commanding officer, his group of soldiers, and the Jewish *temple* guards arrested Jesus and tied him up. **13** They brought him first to Annas who was Caiaphas' father-in-law. Caiaphas was the high priest that year.* **14** (He had advised the Jewish leaders that it would be better for one man to die for all of the people.*)

Peter Wasn't As Strong As He Thought He Was

15 Simon Peter and another follower went along behind Jesus, but the high priest knew the other follower. This man went with Jesus into the high priest's courtyard. **16** Peter stood outside at the gate. The other follower, the one known to the high priest, went outside and told the gatekeeper to let Peter come in. **17** The girl who was the gatekeeper said to Peter, "**You** are one of this man's followers, aren't you?"

Peter answered, "I am not."

18 The servants and the guards were standing there. They had made a fire, because it was cold. They were warming themselves. Peter stood with them and warmed himself, too.

19 The high priest asked Jesus about his followers and about his doctrine. **20** Jesus answered him, "I have spoken plainly to the world. I always taught where Jewish people gather—in *the* synagogues and in the temple courtyard. I have said nothing secretly. **21** Why ask me? Ask those who heard me. Look, they know what I said." **22** When Jesus said this, one of the guards who was standing there struck Jesus. This man asked, "Is that the way to answer the high priest?"

23 Jesus answered him, "If I said something wrong, show me what it was. If it was good, then why did you hit me?"

24 Then Annas sent Jesus down to Caiaphas.

25 Simon Peter was still standing there warming himself. Then they said to him, "**You** are one of Jesus' followers, aren't you?"

Peter said it was not true. He said, "I am not!"

26 One of the high priest's servants said, "**I** saw you with Jesus in the garden." (This man was a relative of Malchus. Peter had cut off Malchus' ear.)

27 Again, Peter denied it. Immediately the rooster crowed.

They Bring Jesus to Pilate

28 Then they took Jesus from Caiaphas to the *Roman* fortress. It was early in the morning. They didn't go into the fortress. They didn't want to be made unclean, so that they could not eat the Passover lamb.* **29** So Pilate went outside where they were. He asked, "What charge are you making against this man?"

18:9   See John 17:12.
18:13   Annas was high priest (retired). All five of his sons had been high priests for short periods of time. Caiaphas was his son-in-law.
18:14   See John 11:49-52.
18:28   During the Festival, Jews were commanded to sacrifice a lamb to remember the blood which protected their ancestors. (See Exodus 12.)

30 They answered Pilate, "If he were not a criminal, we would not be giving him to you."

31 Pilate said to them, "**You** take him and judge him by your own law."

Then the Jewish leaders said to him, "*Under Roman law*, it is not legal for us to execute anyone." **32** (The Jewish leaders said this, so that what Jesus said would come true. This was showing what kind of death Jesus was about to suffer.)

33 Pilate went back into the fortress. He called for Jesus and asked him, "Are **you** the King of the Jews?"

34 Jesus answered, "Are you saying this on your own, or did someone else tell you this about me?"

35 Pilate answered, "I am not a Jew, am I? The leading priests and your own people turned you over to me. What have you done?"

36 Jesus answered, "My kingdom does not come from this world. If it did, my servants would be fighting to keep the Jewish leaders from giving me to you. My kingdom is not from here."

37 Pilate said to him, "So then, you **are** a king!"

Jesus answered, "You say that I am a king. The reason I was born, the reason why I have come into the world is to give evidence for the truth. Every person who listens to my voice comes from *the* truth."

38 Pilate asked, "What **is** truth?"

After this, Pilate went back out to the Jewish leaders. He said to them, "I find nothing to charge this man with. **39** You have a custom that I set one *prisoner* free at each Passover time. You decide; should I set the King of the Jews free?"

40 They yelled, "No! Not this man! Set Barabbas free." (Barabbas was a criminal.)

Chapter 19

The Crown of Thorns

1 Then Pilate took Jesus and had *them* whip him. **2** The soldiers made a crown out of thorny branches. They put it on Jesus' head and put a purple* robe on him. **3** They kept coming up to Jesus and saying, "Hail! O King of the Jews!" They hit him many times.

4 Pilate went back out and spoke to them, "Look, I am bringing him out to you, so that you will know that I find nothing wrong with him." **5** Then Jesus came out. He was wearing the thorny crown and the purple robe. Pilate said to them, "Look at the man!"

6 When the most important priests and the *temple* guards saw Jesus, they shouted, "Nail him to a cross! Nail him to a cross!"

Pilate said to them, "**You** take him and nail him to a cross! I find nothing wrong with him."

7 But the Jewish leaders answered him, "We have a law. According to the law, he must die, because he made himself God's Son!"

8 When Pilate heard this statement, he was even more afraid. **9** So Pilate went back into the fortress and asked Jesus, "Where do you come from?" Jesus did not give him an answer.

10 Then Pilate said to him, "Aren't you speaking to me? Surely you must know I have authority to set you free and I have authority to nail you to a cross!"

19:2   signifying royalty. They were mocking Jesus in this case.

11 Jesus answered Pilate, "You have no authority over me at all, unless it has been given to you by God! That is why the man who gave me to you has even more guilt."

12 From this time on, Pilate tried hard to set Jesus free.

But the Jewish leaders continued to yell, "If you set this man free, you are not Caesar's friend! Anyone who makes himself a king is against Caesar!"

13 When Pilate heard these words, he brought Jesus outside. Pilate sat down on the judge's seat. He was at a place called The Stone Pavement. (In the Aramaic language the name was Gabbatha.)   14 It was about noon on the day before the Passover. Pilate said to the Jewish leaders, "Look, your King!"

15 They yelled, "Take him away! Take him away! Nail him to a cross!"

Pilate said to them, "Should I nail your King to a cross?"

The most important priests answered, "The only King we have is Caesar!"
16 Then Pilate turned Jesus over to them to be nailed to the cross. So they took hold of Jesus.

Jesus on the Cross

17 Jesus was carrying his own cross. He went out to a place which was called Skull Place. (In Aramaic it is Golgotha.)

18 This is where they nailed him to the cross, along with two other men. Jesus' cross was between the crosses of the other two men.

19 Pilate made a sign and put it on Jesus' cross. It read:
JESUS FROM NAZARETH, THE KING OF THE JEWS

20 Many Jewish people read this sign. This place was near the city of *Jerusalem*. The sign was written in Aramaic, Latin, and Greek.   21 The most important Jewish priests kept saying to Pilate, "Don't write, 'The King of the Jews'! Instead, you should write, 'This man **said**, "I am the King of the Jews."'"

22 Pilate answered, "What I have written stays written!"

23 After the soldiers had nailed Jesus to the cross, they took his clothes and divided them into four parts—one for each soldier but the robe *remained*. This robe was seamless—completely made of one piece of woven cloth.   24 They said to one another, "Let's not tear it. Let's gamble for it, to see who will get it!" *This happened* to make this Scripture come true:

"They divided my clothes among them.
They gambled for my clothing."   *Psalm 22:18*
That is what the soldiers did.

25 Jesus' mother, his mother's sister, Mary the *wife* of Clopas, and Mary, from the town of Magdala, stood near the cross.   26 Jesus saw his mother and the follower whom he loved standing there. He said to his mother, "Woman, look at your son."*   27 Then Jesus said to that follower, "Look at your mother."* From that moment on, that follower accepted Mary as his own mother.

It Is Finished!

28 After this, when Jesus knew that everything was finished, he said this to make the Scripture come true: "I am thirsty."   29 There was a jar full of sour wine nearby. So they soaked a sponge in it and put it on a long stick.* Then they brought this to Jesus'

19:26   probably John the apostle
19:27   meaning, Mary. Here John is being told to take care of Mary, to adopt her as his own mother.
19:29   literally, *the branch of* a hyssop plant. It was about one yard long.

mouth.   **30** After Jesus drank some of it, he said, "It is finished!" Then he bowed his head and died.

31 The Jewish leaders did not want the bodies to stay on the crosses during the Sabbath day. This Sabbath was a very important one. So, since it was Friday,* they asked Pilate to *hurry their death* by breaking their legs. Then they could carry them away. *Pilate allowed it.*   **32** The soldiers came to the first man and broke his legs, and then to the other man who had been nailed to a cross, too.   **33** But when they came to Jesus, they saw that Jesus was already dead. They did not break his legs,   **34** but one of the soldiers did plunge his spear into Jesus' side. Immediately, blood and water flowed out. **35** The person who saw it has given proof. His testimony is true. You know he is speaking the truth. **You** must believe, too.   **36** These things happened to make this Scripture come true:

"Not one of his bones will be broken."   *Exodus 12:46*

37 Another Scripture says,

"They will look upon the one they wounded."   *Zechariah 12:10*

Joseph of Arimathea

38 After this, Joseph, a man from the town of Arimathea, asked Pilate if he could take Jesus' body away. Joseph was a secret follower of Jesus, because he was afraid of the Jewish leaders. Pilate allowed Joseph to do this. Then Joseph came and took Jesus' body away.   **39** Nicodemus came, too. (Earlier he had come to Jesus at night.*) He mixed myrrh and aloes* together and brought about 75 pounds of it.   **40** The two men took Jesus' body and wrapped it in sheets with the sweet-smelling spices. (This is the way Jews bury their dead.)   **41** The place where Jesus was nailed to the cross was next to a garden. The garden had a new tomb in it. No one had been put there yet.   **42** *There was not much time*—it was Friday.* So, because the tomb was near, they placed Jesus in it.

Chapter 20

The Empty Tomb

1 It was very early on Sunday morning. It was still dark. Mary (the one from Magdala) came to the tomb. She saw the stone moved away from the tomb.

2 Then she ran and came to Simon Peter and the other follower whom Jesus loved. She said to them, "They have taken away the Lord *Jesus* from the tomb! We don't know where they put him!"

3 Then Peter and the other follower left. They went to the tomb.   **4** Both of them were running, but the other follower outran Peter. He arrived at the tomb first.   **5** He bent down and saw the sheets, but he did not go inside.   **6** Then Simon Peter came, following. Peter went into the tomb. He also saw the sheets lying there.   **7** But the handkerchief which had been on Jesus' face was not lying with the sheets. Instead, it was all alone, folded in one place.   **8** Then the other follower, who had come to the tomb first, also went in. He saw and he believed.   **9** (They did not yet know the Scripture which said that Jesus must rise from death.)   **10** The two followers went back home.

19:31   literally, Preparation *Day*

19:39   See John 3:1-13.

19:39:   a substance from a plant which smells sweet. It was used both as a medicine and for perfume.

19:42   literally, the Jewish Preparation Day. The Sabbath would begin at sunset.

Jesus Appears to Mary

11 Mary was standing outside the tomb, crying while she was praying. She bent down and looked *into the tomb.* **12** She saw two angels dressed in white. They were seated where Jesus' body had been lying—one at the head and one at the foot. **13** They asked her, "Woman, why are you crying?"

She answered them, "They took my Lord away. I don't know where they put him."

14 After she said this, she turned around. She saw Jesus standing there, but she didn't know that it was Jesus.

15 Jesus said to her, "Woman, why are you crying? Who are you looking for?"

Thinking that Jesus was the gardener, she said to him, "Mister, if you carried him off, tell me where you put him and I will take him away."

16 Jesus said to her, "Mary!"

She turned and said to Jesus in Aramaic, "Rabboni!" (This word means *"My Teacher!"*)

17 Jesus said to her, "Don't cling to me; I have not yet gone up to the Father. Go to your brothers and tell them this: 'I am going to my Father and your Father, to my God and to your God.'"

18 Mary (the one from Magdala) went and told the followers, "I have seen the Lord *Jesus*!" She told them that he had talked with her.

Jesus Appears to the Disciples

19 It was late that same Sunday. The doors were locked where the followers were gathered. They were afraid of the Jewish leaders. Jesus came and stood in the middle of them. He said to them, "Peace be to you." **20** After Jesus said this, he showed them his hands and his side. When the followers saw the Lord *Jesus*, they were happy. **21** Then Jesus said to them again, "Peace to you. I am sending you just as the Father has sent me." **22** After Jesus said this, he breathed on them* and said, "Receive the Holy Spirit. **23** If you say some people are forgiven, then they are forgiven. But, if you say that the sins of some people are not forgiven, then they are not forgiven."

Jesus Appears to Thomas

24 Thomas, (the one called The Twin) was one of the twelve *apostles*. He was not with them when Jesus came.

25 The other followers continued to tell him, "We have seen the Lord *Jesus*!"

Thomas said to them, "I will never believe it, unless I see the marks of the nails in his hands, unless I put my finger into the marks of the nails, unless I put my hand into his side!"

26 A week later, Jesus' followers were inside again. Thomas was with them, too. The doors were locked, but Jesus came and stood in the middle of them and said, "Peace to you." **27** Then Jesus said to Thomas, "Look at my hands! Put your finger here. Bring your hand here and put it in my side. Stop doubting, and start believing!"

28 Thomas answered Jesus, "My Lord and my God!"

29 Jesus said to him, "You have believed, because you have seen me. The happy ones are those who have not seen me and yet who believe."

20:22   Here the prophet Jesus was demonstrating inspiration.

In Case You Weren't Sure

30 Jesus showed many more proofs from God in front of his followers, but these are not written in this book. **31** These proofs have been written, so that you, the reader, might believe this: Jesus is the Messiah, the Son of God. If you believe this, you will have *eternal* life by his name.

Chapter 21

Jesus Does Breakfast With the Disciples

1 Later Jesus showed himself again to the followers at Lake Tiberias. This is the way he showed himself:

2 Simon Peter, Thomas (the one called The Twin), Nathanael (the one from the town of Cana in Galilee), the sons of Zebedee, and two more followers were all together. **3** Simon Peter said to them, "I am going fishing."

They said to him, "We are coming with you." They went out and got into a boat. They caught nothing that night. **4** It was now early in the morning. Jesus stood on the shore, but the followers didn't know that it was Jesus. **5** Jesus said to them, "Young men, you haven't caught anything, have you?"

They answered, "That's right."

6 Jesus said to them, "Throw your net on the right side of the boat and you will find *some fish*." They did so. There were so many fish that they were no longer able to pull *the net into the boat*. **7** Then the follower whom Jesus loved said to Peter, "That is the Lord *Jesus*!" When Simon Peter heard this, he put on his clothes (he was stripped) and he jumped into the lake. **8** They were near the shore, about 100 yards away. The other followers came in the boat, dragging the net full of fish. **9** When they got to shore, they saw hot coals, with some fish and bread *cooking* on them. **10** Jesus said to them, "Bring some of the fish you just caught."

11 Simon Peter got into the boat and dragged the net to shore. The net was full of big fish—153 of them! As large as they were, the net was still not torn.

12 Jesus said to them, "Come, have breakfast!" None of the followers dared to ask Jesus, "Who are you?" They **knew** that he was the Lord. **13** Jesus went and got some bread and fish. He gave it to them. **14** This was now the third time that Jesus showed himself to the followers after he was raised from death.

Do You Love Me Enough to Chase Me Anywhere?

15 After they had eaten breakfast, Jesus asked Simon Peter, "Simon, *son of* John, do you love me more than these?"

Peter answered him, "Yes, Lord, you know that I like you."

Jesus said to him, "Feed my lambs."

16 Jesus asked Peter the second time, "Simon, *son of* John, do you love me?"

Peter said to him, "Yes, Lord, you know that I like you."

Jesus said to him, "Be a shepherd to my sheep."

17 Jesus asked him the third time, "Simon, *son of* John, do you like me?"

Peter was sad, because the third time Jesus asked, "Do you **like** me?" Peter said to Jesus, "Lord, you know everything. You know that I like you!"

Jesus said to him, "Feed my sheep. **18** I am telling you the truth, *Peter*, when you were young, you tied your own belt and you walked where you wanted to go. But when you get old, you will stretch out your hands and someone else will tie you. They will carry you where you don't want to go." **19** (Jesus said this to show what kind of death would be used to bring glory to God.) After Jesus said this, he said to Peter, "Follow me!"

Jesus Talks About John

20 Peter turned and saw the follower coming behind them. (This was the man whom Jesus loved, the one who had been sitting at the table very close to Jesus who asked, "Lord, who is the one who is turning against you?") **21** When Peter saw this man, he said to Jesus, "Lord, and what about this man?"

22 Jesus said to him, "If I want him to stay alive until I come, what business is it of yours? **You** follow me!" **23** So this rumor went out to the brothers: "That follower will not die." But Jesus did not say to him that he would not die. Jesus said, "If I want him to stay until I come, what business is it of yours?"

24 He is the follower who wrote these things. He is the one who is giving proof about these things. We know that his testimony is true.

Not Enough Space

25 There are many things which Jesus did. If each one of them were written down, I suppose that the whole world could not hold the books which could be written.

ACTS

Chapter 1

Dear Theo

1 *Dear* Theophilus,
The first book which I wrote was about everything that Jesus did and taught, **2** from the beginning until the day when he was carried up *into heaven*. He talked to the apostles whom he had chosen. Through the Holy Spirit, Jesus told them what they must do. **3** After his death, he showed that he was alive. Jesus proved this by doing many convincing things. The apostles saw him several times during 40 days. Jesus was talking about the kingdom of God. **4** Once when he was together with them, he ordered them not to leave Jerusalem. He said, "Wait here for the Father's promise that you heard me talk about.* **5** John immersed people in water, but in a few days **you** will be immersed in the Holy Spirit."

The Holy Spirit Will Come

6 The apostles were all together. They asked Jesus, "Lord, is this the time for you to rebuild the kingdom for Israel?"
7 Jesus said to them, "The Father is the only One who has the authority to decide such dates and times. It is not for you to know these things. **8** However, when the Holy Spirit comes upon you, you will receive power. You will be my witnesses in Jerusalem, in all of Judea, in Samaria, and to the farthest parts of the world."

Jesus Goes Back to Heaven

9 After Jesus said these things, he was lifted up *into the sky*. While the apostles were watching, Jesus went into a cloud; they couldn't see him anymore. **10** As Jesus was going away, the apostles were staring into the sky. Suddenly, two angels* stood beside them. They were dressed in white clothes. **11** The two angels said, "Men from Galilee, why are you standing here looking into the sky? This Jesus who was carried away from you into heaven will return in the same way that you saw him go."

Chasing God in the Upper Room

12 Then the apostles went back to Jerusalem from Olive Mountain. (This mountain is about three-quarters of a mile* from Jerusalem.) **13** The apostles entered the city. They went to the place where they were staying; this was in an upstairs room. The apostles were:
Peter,
John,
James,
Andrew,
Philip,

1:4 the Holy Spirit. (See John 14:26; 16:13.)
1:10 literally, men
1:12 literally, a Sabbath day's journey. (See Exodus 16:29; Numbers 35:5; Joshua 3:4.)
1:13 literally, Zealot. The Zealots were a group of Jewish men—political fanatics—who claimed to uphold the law of Moses, even if it meant violence. They favored revolt against Rome.

Thomas,
Bartholomew,
Matthew,
James (*the son* of Alphaeus),
Simon (known as the Revolutionary*),
Judas (*the son* of James).

14 They were all together. They were constantly praying with the same purpose. Jesus' brothers, some women, and Mary (the mother of Jesus) were also there.

Someone Needed to Replace Judas Iscariot

15 During those days there was a meeting. (There were about 120 people present.) Peter stood up among them and said, **16-17** "Brothers *and sisters*, the Scriptures must come true which the Holy Spirit spoke ahead of time through David's lips. He was talking about Judas *Iscariot* who was one of our group; he had a part in this work. The Spirit said that Judas would guide men to arrest Jesus. **18** Judas was paid money for doing this. (However, Judas fell on his head, and his body broke open in the middle. All of his intestines poured out.) His dishonest money was used to buy a field for his body. **19** All of the people who lived in Jerusalem learned about this. That is why they named that field Akeldama. (In their language Akeldama means 'Blood Land.') **20** In the book of Psalms, this is written *about Judas*:

'People should not go
   near his *property* ;
No one should live there!'   *Psalm 69:25*
and,

'Let another man take his work of overseeing.'   *Psalm 109:8*

21-22 "So now another man must join us and be a witness that Jesus arose *from death*. This man must be one of those men who was part of our group during the whole time that the Lord Jesus was among us. It is necessary that this man has been with us from the time when John started to immerse people, until the day when Jesus was carried away from us *to heaven*."

23 They found two men. One was Joseph Barsabbas. (He was also called Justus.) The other man was Matthias.

24-25 The apostles prayed, "Lord, You know the hearts of all people. Show us which one of these two men You choose to be an apostle and to do this work. Judas turned away from it and went where he belongs." **26** Then the apostles gave the two men lots.* The lots showed that Matthias was the one. So, he became an apostle like the other eleven.

Chapter 2

Chasing the Wind

1 When the day of Pentecost* came, they were all together in one place. **2** Suddenly, a noise came from the sky. It sounded like a strong wind blowing. This noise filled the whole house where they were sitting. **3** They saw something which looked like flames of fire separating and staying over each one of them. **4** They were all

---

1:26   a reverent way of seeking God's help in this decision (See Proverbs 16:33.)
2:1   Pentecost (a Sunday), a yearly Jewish feast of the wheat harvest, held 50 days after Passover

filled with the Holy Spirit and they began to speak different *inspired* languages; the Spirit was giving them the power to do this.

5 There were some devout Jewish men staying in Jerusalem at this time. These men were from every country in the world. **6** A large group of them came together because they heard the noise. They were confused. The apostles were speaking, and every man heard in his own language. **7** The Jewish people were all amazed at this. They didn't understand how the apostles could do this. They said, "Look! These men whom we hear speaking are all from Galilee!* **8** But each of us is hearing them in our own native language. *We are* :

9 Parthians,
   Medes,
   Elamites,
   those living in Mesopotamia,
   from Judea,
   from Cappadocia,
   from Pontus,
   from Asia,*
10 from Phrygia,
   from Pamphylia,
   from Egypt,
   from parts of Libya around Cyrene,
   visitors from Rome,
11 Cretans,
   Arabians.

Some of us *were born* Jews. Others are converts *to Judaism*. We can hear these men in our own languages! We can all understand the wonderful things they are saying about God." **12** The people were all amazed but confused. They asked each other, "What does this mean?" **13** Other people were laughing at the apostles. They were claiming that the apostles were drunk.

Peter's Power-Filled Preaching

14 Then Peter stood up with the other eleven apostles. He spoke loudly:* "My Jewish brothers and all of you who are staying in Jerusalem, listen to me. I will tell you something you need to know. Listen carefully. **15** These men are not drunk, as you think; it is only nine o'clock in the morning! **16** This is the *same* thing which *God* said through the prophet Joel:

17 "God says: 'In the last days,
   I will pour out My Spirit upon all people.
   Your sons and your daughters will prophesy.
      Your young men will see visions.
      Your old men will have special dreams.
18 At that time, I will pour out My Spirit
   upon My servants, both men and women,
   and they will prophesy.
19 I will show amazing things in the sky above.

2:7   These were natives of Palestine who would not be expected to know many languages.
2:9   This is not the modern continent of Asia. It is the country of Turkey.
2:14   literally, raised his voice

> I will do miracles on the earth below.
> There will be blood, fire, and thick smoke.
> **20** The sun will be changed into darkness,
>> and the moon will become *red like* blood.
> Then the great and glorious day of the Lord will come.
> **21** And every person who trusts in the name of the Lord
>> will be saved.'   *Joel 2:28-32*

22 "Men of Israel, listen to these words: Jesus from Nazareth was a very special man. God clearly showed this to you. God proved this by the powerful and amazing things which He did through Jesus among you. You **know** this is true.   **23** You killed this man Jesus by handing him over to lawless men. They nailed him to a cross. But God knew ahead of time that all this would occur; it was part of His plan which He made long ago.   **24** Jesus suffered the pains of death, but God set him free. God raised Jesus up from death. It was impossible for death to hold him.   **25** This is what David said about Jesus:

> 'I always saw the Lord before me,
>> because He is at my right side
>>> to keep me secure.
> **26** So, my heart was glad
>> and my mouth spoke with joy.
> Yes, even my body will live with hope,
> **27** because You won't abandon my soul in death.*
>> You will not allow the body of Your holy one
>>> to decay in the grave.
> **28** You taught me how to live.
> You came near me,
>> and I felt great joy.'   *Psalm 16:8-11*

29 "My Jewish brothers, I can tell you plainly about David, our ancestor. He died and was buried. His grave is still here with us today.   **30** David was a prophet. God vowed to David that one of his descendants would sit upon David's throne.   **31** David knew this before it took place. That is why David said this:

> 'He will not be left in death.*
> His body will not decay in the grave.'   *Psalm 16:10*

David was talking about the Messiah rising from death.   **32** So Jesus, *not David*, is the one whom God raised from death! We are all eye-witnesses of this!   **33** Jesus was lifted up *to heaven*. Now Jesus is with God—at His right side. The Father has now given the promise of the Holy Spirit to Jesus. So now, Jesus poured out this which you see and hear.   **34** David did not go up to heaven. *It was Jesus*. David himself said:

> 'The Lord *God* said to my Lord.*
>> "Sit at My right side
>>> **35** until I put your enemies under your feet." '*   *Psalm 110:1*

36 "Therefore, all the people of Israel can be sure of this one thing: God has made Jesus both Lord and Messiah, this man whom **you** nailed to the cross!"

2:27   literally, Hades, the Greek word for the unseen world of the dead
2:31   literally, Hades, the Greek word for the unseen world of the dead
2:34   In the Hebrew text of Psalms, the first "Lord" is Yahweh; the second "Lord" is Adonai, referring to Christ.
2:35   in your control

37 When the people heard this, they felt a sharp, cutting pain in their conscience. They asked Peter and the other apostles, "What should we do, brothers?"

38 Then Peter answered, "Change your hearts and each one of you must be immersed by the authority of Jesus the Messiah,*so that your sins may be forgiven. Then you will receive the gift of the Holy Spirit. **39** This promise is for **you** and for your children. It is also for people who are far away,* for everyone whom the Lord our God may call."

40 Peter was warning them with many other words; he was encouraging them, saying, "Be saved from this twisted generation of people!" **41** Then those people who accepted what Peter said were immersed. On that day, about 3,000 people were added *to the group of believers*. **42** After this, the believers dedicated themselves to learning the teaching of the apostles, to sharing with each other, to eating *the supper of the Lord*,* and to prayer.

Chasers Share and Share and Share

43 God was using the apostles to do many powerful and amazing things; every person felt great respect for God. **44** All of the believers stayed together. They shared everything. **45** They sold their *property* and the things they owned and they were dividing the money, giving it to anyone who needed it. **46** Every day the believers met together with the same purpose in the temple courtyard. They ate together in their homes, eating their food with joyful hearts. They were very happy. **47** The believers were praising God. All of the people liked them. More and more people were being saved every day; the Lord was adding them to the congregation.

Chapter 3

Wasn't There a Cripple Over There?

1 One day Peter and John went up to the temple courtyard. It was three o'clock in the afternoon. (This was the time for prayer.) **2** A man was there who had been crippled all his life. He couldn't walk, so some *friends* carried him to the temple every day. They put him beside one of the gates outside the temple. It was called Beautiful Gate. There the man begged for money from the people who were going into the temple area. **3** When he saw Peter and John about to go in, he began to ask them for money. **4** They looked straight at the crippled man and answered, "Look at us!" **5** He looked at them, thinking that they might give him some money. **6** But Peter said, "I don't have any silver or gold, but I do have something else I can give you: By the authority of Jesus the Messiah* from Nazareth—walk!" **7** Then Peter took hold of the man's right hand and lifted him up. Immediately, the man's feet and legs became strong. **8** He jumped up and stood on his feet and he began to walk around. He went into the temple courtyard with them. He was walking and jumping and praising God. **9-10** All of the people recognized him. The people knew he was the beggar who always sat by the temple's Beautiful Gate. Now they saw him walking and praising God. They were shocked and amazed. They couldn't understand how this could have happened.

2:38   or, Jesus Christ
2:39   See Ephesians 2:13.
2:42   literally, "to the breaking of bread," an idiom usually referring to the Lord's supper
3:6   or, Jesus Christ

Don't Chase US—Chase HIM!

11 The man was holding onto Peter and John. All of the people were stunned. They ran to Peter and John at Solomon's Porch.* **12** When Peter saw this, he said to the people, "Men of Israel, why are you surprised at this? You are staring at us as though **our** power made this man walk. Do you think this was done because we are good? **13** No! *God did it*! He is the God of Abraham, of Isaac, and of Jacob—the same God of all our ancestors. He gave glory to Jesus, His special servant, but **you** handed Jesus over *to evil men*. You rejected him in front of Pilate after Pilate had already decided to let him go free. **14** Jesus was holy and innocent, but you said you didn't want him. You told Pilate to give you a murderer* instead of Jesus. **15** And so, you killed the one who gives life, but God raised him from death. We saw this with our own eyes. **16** It was the authority of Jesus which made this crippled man well. This happened because we trusted in the power of Jesus. You can see this man and you know him. He was made completely well because of trusting in Jesus. You all saw it happen!

17 "My brothers, I know you did those things *to Jesus*, because you didn't know what you were doing. Your leaders did not understand, either. **18** God said that these things would happen. All of the prophets who spoke for God long ago said that His Messiah would suffer and die. I have told you how God made this happen. **19** So, change your hearts! Come back to God, so that He may wipe out your sins. **20** Then the Lord will give you times of spiritual rest. He will send you the Messiah—Jesus. **21** But Jesus must stay in heaven until the time when all things will be made whole again. God told about these things long ago when He spoke through His holy prophets. **22** Moses said,

'The Lord your God will raise up a prophet for
you who is like me. He will come from among
your own people. You must obey everything
he tells you. **23** If any person does not obey that
prophet, he will die, cut off from God's people.' *Deuteronomy 18:15,16,19*
24 Samuel and all of the other prophets after Samuel who spoke for God talked about **these** days. **25** You are the sons of the prophets. You have received the agreement which God made with your ancestors. God said to Abraham, your ancestor,

'I will bless all nations of the earth. I will use
one of your descendants to do this.' *Genesis 22:18*
26 God has raised up His special servant.* God sent him to you first, to bless you by turning each one of you away from doing evil things."

Chapter 4

Didn't You Want Him to Be Healed?

1 While Peter and John were speaking to the people, some men came to them. There were some Jewish priests, the officer of the temple *police*, and some Sadducees. **2** They were upset, because the two apostles were teaching the people. Peter and John were preaching that people can rise from death through the power of Jesus. **3** They arrested Peter and John and put them in jail. It was already evening, so they kept Peter and John in jail until the next day. **4** But, many of the people who had heard Peter and

---

3:11   a covered court on the east side of the temple complex. The Beautiful Gate opened to it.
3:14   Barabbas
3:26   Jesus. See Isaiah 53:11; 42:1; Matthew 12:15-21.

John preach believed the things that they said. There were now about 5,000 men in the group of believers.

5 The next day the Jewish leaders, the elders, and the teachers of the law met in Jerusalem. **6** Annas (who was the high priest), Caiaphas, John, Alexander and everyone from the high priest's family were there. **7** They made Peter and John stand in the center. The Jewish leaders asked them again and again, "How did you make this crippled man well? What name did you use? By whose authority did you do this?"

8 Then Peter was filled with the Holy Spirit. He said to them, "You elders and leaders of the people: **9** Are you questioning us today about the good thing which was done to this crippled man? Are you asking us who made him well? **10** We want all of you and all the people of Israel to know that this man was made well by the authority of Jesus from Nazareth, the Messiah!* Although you nailed him to the cross, God raised him from death. This man who was crippled is now well and able to stand here before you because of **Jesus**! **11** Jesus,

'the stone* which you builders thought was worthless,
has become the cornerstone.' *Psalm 118:22*

12 Jesus is the only one who can save people. His authority is the only power given to the world by which we can be saved."

13 The Jewish leaders saw that Peter and John were not afraid to speak. They were amazed because they understood that the two men had no education or training. Then they realized that Peter and John had been with Jesus. **14** When they saw the man standing there beside the two apostles—that he was healed—they could find nothing to say against the apostles. **15** So, the Jewish leaders ordered them to go outside. The Jewish Council wanted to talk among themselves. **16** They asked, "What shall we do with them? Everyone who lives in Jerusalem knows that these men have performed a great miracle! That is clear. We cannot deny it. **17** However, we must make them afraid to talk to anyone about this man. Then this problem will not spread among the people."

18 So, the Jewish leaders called Peter and John in again. They warned the apostles not to say anything or to teach anything by the authority of Jesus. **19** But Peter and John answered them, "What do you think is right? What would God want? Should we obey you or God? **20** We are not able to be silent. We must tell people about the things we saw and heard." **21-22** The Jewish leaders could not find a way to punish the apostles, because all of the people were praising God for what had been done. (This miracle was a proof from God. The man who was healed was more than 40 years old!) So, the Jewish leaders threatened them again and then let them go free.

Power-Filled Praying

23 Peter and John left the meeting of the Jewish leaders and went to their own group. They told the group everything which the most important priests and the Jewish elders had said to them. **24** When they heard this, they prayed to God with one purpose, "Master, You are the One who made the land, the sea, the sky, and everything in the world. **25** Our ancestor, David, was Your servant. With the help of the Holy Spirit he wrote these words:

'Why were the nations so mad?
Why did the people of the world

4:10   or, Jesus Christ
4:11   This refers to Jesus.

> plan things *against God*?
> That is hopeless!
26 Why did the kings and the rulers of the earth,
> come together against the Lord God and against His
> Messiah?'   *Psalm 2:1-2*

27 "These words came true when Herod *Antipas*, Pontius Pilate, the nations of the world, and the Jewish people all 'came together' against Jesus here in Jerusalem. Jesus is Your holy servant, the one You made Messiah.   28 These people who 'came together' against Jesus made Your plan come true; it happened because of Your power and Your will.   29 And now, Lord, listen to what they are saying. They are trying to make us afraid! Lord, we are Your servants. Help us to speak the things You want us to say without fear.   30 Show your power: make sick people well, give proofs, and cause miracles to take place by the power of Jesus, Your holy servant."

31 After the believers prayed, the place where they were meeting shook. They were all filled with the Holy Spirit and they began to speak God's message without fear.

God Chasers Don't Lie

32 The group of believers were joined in their hearts and they were united in spirit. No one in the group said that the things he had were his own. Instead, they shared everything.   33 The apostles used great power to give evidence that the Lord Jesus has been raised from death. All of the believers felt very thankful for God's great blessings.   34 They all received the things they needed. Everyone who owned fields or houses sold them. Then they brought the money   35 and gave it to the apostles. Each person was given the things he needed.

36 One of the believers was named Joseph. The apostles called him Barnabas. (This name means "a person who encourages others.") He was a Levite,* born in Cyprus.   37 Joseph owned a field. He sold it and brought the money and gave it to the apostles.

Chapter 5

1 There was a man named Ananias. His wife's name was Sapphira. Ananias sold some land which he had   2 and, from the sale, he gave some of the money to the apostles. But, he kept back part of the money for himself. His wife knew this.*   3 Peter asked him, "Ananias, why did you let Satan fill your heart? You lied to the Holy Spirit. You misused the sale price of the land.   4 Before you sold the field, it belonged to you. Even after you sold it, you could have used the money any way you wanted. Why did you think of doing this evil thing? You lied to God, not to men!"   5-6 When Ananias heard these words, he fell down and died. Some young men came and wrapped up his body. Then they carried it out and buried it. Everyone who heard about this was filled with fear.

7 About three hours later, the wife of Ananias came in, but she did not know what had happened to her husband.   8 Peter said to her, "Tell me, how much money did you receive for your field? Was it this much?"*

Sapphira answered, "Yes, that was all we got for the field."

4:36   a member of the tribe of Levi. It included the priests and their helpers.
5:2   She conspired with her husband. Ananias wanted everyone to think he and his wife had given all the
        money.
5:8   giving the amount Ananias had said. Then Peter would know if Sapphira were lying.

9 Peter asked her, "Why did you and your husband agree to test the Spirit of the Lord? Listen! *Do you hear* those footsteps? The men who buried your husband are at the door! They will carry you out in the same way." **10** At that moment Sapphira fell down at Peter's feet and died. The young men came in and saw that she was dead. The men carried her out and buried her next to her husband. **11** The whole congregation and all of the other people who heard about these things were filled with fear.

Shadow Healing

12 The apostles did many miracles and powerful things among the people. The apostles were together in Solomon's Porch;* they all had the same purpose. **13** None of the other *believers* dared to join the apostles, but all of the people were saying good things about them. **14** And more and more people were added to the *group of* believers. **15** People began to bring their sick into the streets. They put their sick on little beds and mattresses for Peter's shadow to touch them when he came by.* **16** They were coming from all the towns around Jerusalem. They brought their sick and those who were bothered by evil spirits. All of these people were healed.

Under Arrest Again

17 The high priest and all of his friends (a sect called the Sadducees) became very jealous. **18** They grabbed the apostles and put them in the public jail, **19** but, during the night, an angel of the Lord opened the gates of the jail. The angel led the apostles outside and said, **20** "Go and stand in the temple courtyard. Tell the people everything about this new life *in Jesus*." **21** When the apostles heard this, they went into the temple courtyard. It was early in the morning. The apostles began to teach the people.

The high priest and his friends came *together*. They called a meeting of the Jewish leaders and all the important older men of the sons of Israel. They sent some men to the jail to bring the apostles to them. **22** When the guards came to the jail, they couldn't find the apostles there. So, they went back and told this to the Jewish leaders. **23** They said, "The jail was shut and locked. The guards were standing at the gates, but when we opened the doors, no one was in there!" **24** The captain of the temple *guards* and the most important priests heard this. They were confused. They wondered, "What will happen because of this?" **25** Then another man came and told them, "Listen! The men you had put in jail are standing in the temple courtyard. They are teaching the people!" **26** Then the captain and his men went out and brought the apostles back. However, the soldiers did not use force, because they were afraid of the people. The people might *become angry* and kill the soldiers with stones.

27 The soldiers brought the apostles to the Jewish Council and made them stand before their leaders. The high priest questioned the apostles. **28** He said, "We warned you never to teach with this man's authority, but look what you've done! You have filled Jerusalem with your teaching. You are trying to put the blame on us for the death of this man *Jesus*."

29 Peter and the other apostles answered, "We must obey God, not men! **30** The God of our ancestors raised up Jesus *from death*. He is the one you killed, having hung him upon *a cross of* wood. **31** Jesus is the one whom God raised to His right side to

---

5:12   the temple of Herod the Great

5:15   They thought that if the sick could be close enough to Peter's shadow, this would be enough to heal them.

be our Leader and Savior. God did this, so that Israel could have the opportunity to change their hearts. Then God could forgive their sins. **32** We saw all of these things happen. The Holy Spirit has shown you that we are telling you the truth! God has given the Spirit to those who obeyed Him."

33 When the Jewish leaders heard these words, they became very angry. They started to make plans to kill the apostles. **34** One of the Pharisees in the Jewish Council stood up. His name was Gamaliel. He was a teacher of the law, and all of the people respected him. He ordered *the men* to take the apostles outside for a few minutes. **35** Then he said to them, "Men of Israel, be careful of what you are about to do to these men! **36** Remember when Theudas appeared? He *claimed* that he was an important man. About 400 men joined him, but he was killed. And all of the men who followed him were scattered. They were never able to do anything. **37** Later, a man named Judas came from Galilee. It was at the time of the registration.* He also led a group of followers away but he was destroyed and all his followers were scattered. **38** So now I tell you: Stay away from these men! Leave them alone. If this plan or this effort comes from human beings, it will fail. **39** But if this is from God, then you will not be able to stop them. You might even be fighting against God Himself!"

The Jewish leaders then agreed with what Gamaliel said. **40** They called in the apostles again. They whipped the apostles and commanded them not to talk to the people ever again about the name of Jesus. After that they let them go free. **41** The apostles left the Jewish Council, but they were happy, because they were given the honor of suffering dishonor for the name *of Jesus*. **42** The apostles didn't stop teaching people. They kept on telling the people the Good News that Jesus is the Messiah. Every day they did this in the temple courtyard and in each home.

Chapter 6

Seven Faithful God Chasers

1 More and more people were becoming followers *of Jesus*. But during this same time, the Greek-speaking Jewish followers had an argument with the Aramaic-speaking followers. They claimed that their widows were not getting their share of the things which the widows received each day. **2** The twelve *apostles* called the whole group of followers together. They said to them, "It is wrong for us to quit teaching God's message to serve tables instead. **3** So, brothers, pick out seven of your own men. They must be known to be full of wisdom and full of the Spirit. We will confirm them to be over this work. **4** Then we will use all of our time to pray and to teach the message of God."

5 The whole group liked this idea. So, they chose these men:
Stephen (a man of great faith and full of the Holy Spirit),
Philip,
Prochorus,
Nicanor,
Timon,
Parmenas,
Nicolas (a man from Antioch who had become a Jew).
6 Then they put these men before the apostles, who prayed and placed their hands on them.*

5:37   See Luke 2:2.
6:6   a common practice when appointing people to special duties (Numbers 27:22-23)

7 God's message was influencing more and more people. The group of followers in Jerusalem became larger and larger. Even many of the Jewish priests were obedient to the faith.

Stephen: God Chaser Extraordinaire

8 Since Stephen was full of *God's* favor and power, he was working miracles among the people to show great proofs from God.   **9** But, some Jews stood up and argued with Stephen. They were from a synagogue called "A Synagogue for Freed Men."* (This synagogue was also for Jews from the cities of Cyrene and Alexandria.) Jews from Cilicia and Asia were with them. They all came and argued with Stephen, **10** but the Spirit was helping Stephen speak with wisdom. His words were so powerful that the Jews could not argue with him.   **11** So they secretly paid some men to say, "We heard Stephen say some evil things against Moses and against God!"   **12** In this way, they stirred up the people, the Jewish elders, and the teachers of the law. They became so angry that they came and grabbed Stephen. Then they took him to the Jewish Council.   **13** They brought some men into the meeting. These men were told to tell lies about Stephen. The men said, "This man always says things against this holy place* and against the law *of Moses.*   **14** We heard him say that Jesus from Nazareth will destroy this place. He also said that Jesus will change the customs which Moses passed down to us."   **15** Everyone sitting in the Jewish Council stared at Stephen. They saw that his face looked like the face of an angel.

Chapter 7

God Chaser Archives: Chasing God Since Abraham

1 Then the high priest asked Stephen, "Are these things true?"

2 Stephen answered, "My Jewish fathers and brothers, listen to me. Our glorious God appeared to Abraham, our ancestor, while he was in Mesopotamia. This was before he lived in Haran.   **3** God said to Abraham,

'Leave your country and your relatives!
Go to another country.
I will show you where to go.'   *Genesis 12:1*

4 So Abraham left the country of Chaldea and went to live in Haran. After Abraham's father died, God sent him to this same land where you live now.   **5** But God did not give Abraham any of this land—not even a foot of it! God promised that in the future He would give this land to Abraham and his descendants; it would belong to them. (This was before Abraham had any children.)   **6** This is what God said to him: 'Your descendants will live as strangers in another country. The people there will make them slaves and do evil things to them for 400 years.*   **7** I will judge that nation which will make them slaves.' And God also said,

'After those things happen, your children will come
out of that country to worship Me in **this** place.'   *Exodus 3:12*

8 God made an agreement with Abraham; *the sign* was circumcision.* And so, when Abraham had a son, Abraham circumcised him when he was eight days old. His son's

---

6:9   freedmen or sons of men freed from slavery
6:13   the temple
7:6   Stephen was using round numbers here. The total time was actually 430 years. (See Exodus 12:40,41; Galatians 3:17.)
7:8   cutting off the foreskin of the male sex organ, as a sign of God's agreement with Israel. (See Genesis 17:9-14.)

name was Isaac. Isaac also circumcised his son Jacob, and Jacob did the same for *his sons. These sons later became* the twelve fathers.*

9 "These fathers, Joseph's brothers, became jealous of him. They sold Joseph to be a slave in Egypt. But God was with him. **10** Joseph had many troubles there, but God rescued him from them all. Pharaoh, the king of Egypt, liked Joseph and respected him, because of the wisdom which God gave Joseph. Pharaoh gave Joseph the job of being governor of Egypt. He even allowed Joseph to rule over all the people in Pharaoh's house. **11** But the whole land of Egypt and the land of Canaan became dry. It became so dry that crops couldn't grow there. This made the people suffer terribly. Our ancestors could find nothing to eat. **12** But Jacob heard that there was wheat *stored* in Egypt. So he sent our ancestors* there. (This was their first trip to Egypt.) **13** Then they went there a second time. On this visit, Joseph told his brothers who he was. And, Pharaoh learned about Joseph's family. **14** Then Joseph sent some men to invite Jacob, his father, to come to Egypt. He also invited all of his relatives (75 persons altogether). **15** So Jacob went down to Egypt. He and our ancestors died there. **16** Later their bodies were moved to Shechem. They were placed in a grave there. (It was the same grave in Shechem that Abraham had bought from the sons of Hamor. He paid them with silver.)

17 "In Egypt our nation grew larger in number. (The promise which God made to Abraham was soon to come true.) There were more and more of our people in Egypt. **18** Then a different king began to rule over Egypt. He knew nothing about Joseph. **19** This king cheated our people. He persecuted our ancestors; he forced them to put their babies outdoors to die. **20** During this time, Moses was born. He was no ordinary baby. For three months they took care of Moses in his father's house. **21** When they put Moses outside, Pharaoh's daughter took him in. She raised him as if he were her own son. **22** The Egyptians taught Moses everything they knew. He was powerful in the things he said and did.

23 "When Moses was about 40 years old, he thought it would be good to visit his brothers, the sons of Israel. **24** *One day* Moses saw an Egyptian man doing wrong to a Hebrew brother. So, he defended him. Moses punished the Egyptian for hurting that brother. Moses hit the Egyptian so hard that the man died. **25** Moses was thinking his brothers would understand that God was using him to save them, but they did **not** understand. **26** The next day Moses saw two of the sons of Israel fighting. He tried to make peace between them. He said, 'Men, you are brothers! Why are you doing wrong to one another?' **27** The man who was doing wrong to the other man pushed Moses away. He said to Moses, 'Who made you our ruler and judge? **28** Do you want to kill me, as you killed the Egyptian man yesterday?' **29** When Moses heard him say this, he ran away from Egypt. He went to live in the land of Midian where he was a stranger. While he lived there he had two sons.

30 "After 40 years, Moses was in the desert on Mount Sinai. An angel appeared to him in the flame of a burning bush. **31** When Moses saw this, he was amazed. He went nearer to look at it more closely. He heard a Voice; it was the Lord's. **32** The Lord *God* said, 'I am the same God of your ancestors—the God of Abraham, of Isaac, and of Jacob.' Moses began to shake with fear. He was afraid to look *at the bush.* **33** The Lord said to him, 'Take off your shoes, because the place where you are now

---

7:8   literally, patriarchs
7:12   See Gen. 42:1-3.

standing is holy ground.   **34** I have seen My people suffer much in Egypt. I have heard My people moaning. I have come down to rescue them. And now, Moses, I am sending you back to Egypt.'

35 "This Moses was the same man the people of Israel had rejected. They had asked him, 'Who made you a ruler and judge *over us*?' Moses is the same man whom God sent to be a ruler and deliverer. God sent Moses with the help of an angel. This was the angel that Moses saw in the *burning* bush.   **36** So, Moses led the people out. He did powerful things and miracles in Egypt, at the Red Sea,* and in the desert for 40 years. **37** This is the same Moses who said these words to the sons of Israel: 'God will raise up for you a prophet who is like me. He will come from among your own brothers.'   **38** This is the same Moses who was with the congregation in the desert at Mount Sinai. He was with the angel that spoke to him and with our ancestors. There at Mount Sinai, Moses received commands *from God* which still live. Moses gave us these commands.

39 "But our ancestors didn't want to obey Moses. They rejected him. In their hearts, they wanted to go back to Egypt.   **40** Our ancestors said to Aaron, 'Make us some gods to lead us! Moses brought us out of Egypt, but we don't know what has happened to him.'   **41** So, the people made an idol which looked like a calf. Then they brought sacrifices to it. The people were very happy with what they had made with their own hands!   **42** But God turned against them. He stopped trying to change their hearts. They were worshiping the sun, the moon, and the stars. This is what is written in the writings of the prophets; *God says*:

'People of Israel, you killed animals
        and offered sacrifices in the desert for 40 years,
    but these sacrifices were not for Me.
43 You carried with you the tent for Moloch and the image of the star of your god
        Rephan—statues which you made to worship.
    So, I will send you away beyond Babylon.'   *Amos 5:25-27*

44 "God spoke to our ancestors in a special tent; it was with the people in the desert. God commanded Moses how to make this tent. He made it like the pattern which God showed him.   **45** Later Joshua led our fathers to capture the lands of the other nations. Our people went in and God drove those people out. When our people went into this new land, they took this same tent with them. They had received it from their ancestors. They kept it until the time of David.   **46** God was very pleased with David. David asked God to allow him to build a house for Him, the God* of Jacob,   **47** but Solomon was the one who actually built it.

48 However, the Highest One does not live in houses which men build with their hands. This is what the prophet *Isaiah* wrote:
49 'The Lord *God* says, "Heaven is My throne.
        The earth is a place to rest My feet.
    What kind of house could you build for Me?
        There is no place where I need to rest!
50 Remember, I made all these things!" ' "   *Isaiah 66:1-2*

51 *Stephen continued speaking*: "You stubborn leaders! Your hearts are not circumcised! You won't listen to God! You are always against what the Holy Spirit is trying to tell you. Your ancestors did this, and you are just like them!   **52** Your ancestors

7:36   Sea of Reeds
7:46   Many manuscripts have "house" instead of "God."

191

persecuted every prophet who ever lived. Those prophets said long ago that the righteous one* would come, but your ancestors killed the prophets. And now, you have turned against this righteous one and murdered him. **53** You are the people who received the law *of Moses*, the commands which God gave through the angels—but you don't obey the law!"

Stephen Dies for the Chase

54 When the Jewish leaders heard Stephen say these things, they became very angry. They were so mad that they were grinding their teeth at Stephen. **55** Stephen was full of the Holy Spirit. He looked up into the sky and saw the glory of God, and Jesus standing at God's right side. **56** He said, "Look! I see heaven open. And, I see the Son of Man* standing at God's right side!"

57 Then they all shouted with a loud voice. They covered their ears *with their hands.* Together they all ran at Stephen. **58** They took him out of the city to stone him to death. The men, who told lies against Stephen, gave their robes to a young man named Saul.* **59** Then they began to throw stones at Stephen, but Stephen was praying. He said, "Lord Jesus, receive my spirit!" **60** He fell on his knees and shouted this: "Lord, don't blame them for this sin!" After Stephen said that, he died.

Saul approved of the killing of Stephen.

Chapter 8

The Good News Goes Everywhere

1-3 Some good men buried Stephen. They cried very loudly for him.* On that day there was a fierce attack on the congregation in Jerusalem. Saul was also trying to destroy them. He even went into their homes. He dragged out men and women and put them in jail. All of the believers had to leave Jerusalem; only the apostles stayed there. The believers went to different places in Judea and Samaria. **4** They were scattered everywhere. And everywhere the believers went, they told people* the Good News *about Jesus.*

Miracles—Not Magic!

5 Philip* went to the city of Samaria. He was preaching about the Messiah. **6** The crowds there heard Philip and they saw the miracles that he was doing. With a single purpose, they all listened very carefully to the things Philip said. **7** Many of these people had evil spirits. The spirits came out of them; they made a loud noise. There were also many paralyzed and crippled people. Philip healed them. **8** This made the people in that city very happy.

9 However, there was in that city a man named Simon who did magic tricks before Philip came. He amazed all the people of Samaria with these tricks. Simon boasted and called himself a great man. **10** All of the people—the least important and the most

---

7:52   Jesus
7:56   Jesus
7:58   Paul
8:1-3 It was a custom in Palestine to cry long and loud when someone died. (See Jeremiah 9:17-20.)
8:4   In the beginning, they thought that the message was given only to Jewish believers (including Samaritans and converts to Judaism).
8:5   not the apostle Philip, but rather, one of the seven men mentioned in Acts 6

important—had listened closely to Simon. The people said, "This man is the power of God which is called 'The Great Power'!" 11 Simon had amazed the people with his magic tricks for so long that the people became his followers. 12 But, Philip told the people the Good News about the kingdom of God and the authority of Jesus the Messiah.* Men and women believed Philip and were immersed. 13 Simon himself also believed and was immersed. Simon stayed near Philip. He saw the miracles and the very powerful things which Philip did. Simon was amazed.

14 The apostles were still in Jerusalem. They heard that the people of Samaria had accepted God's message. So, the apostles sent Peter and John to the people in Samaria. 15 When Peter and John arrived, they prayed for the Samaritan believers to receive the Holy Spirit. 16 (These people had been immersed by the authority of the Lord Jesus, but the Holy Spirit had not yet come down on any of them.) 17 The two apostles put their hands on the people. Then the people received the Holy Spirit.

18 Simon saw that *the gifts of* the Spirit were given to people when the apostles put their hands on them. So, Simon offered the apostles some money. 19 Simon said, "Give **me** this power so that when I put my hands on a person, he will receive the Holy Spirit."

20 Peter said to Simon, "You and your money should both be destroyed! You thought you could **buy** God's gift with money. 21 Your heart is not right before God. You cannot have a part with us or a share in this work. 22 Change your heart! Turn away from this evil thing which you have done. Pray to the Lord *God*. Perhaps He will forgive you for thinking this in your heart. 23 I can see that you are full of bitter jealousy and bound by sin."

24 Simon answered, "Both of you pray to the Lord *God* for me! Pray that the things you have said will not happen to me!"

25 Then the two apostles told the people the things which they had seen *Jesus do*. The apostles preached the message of the Lord. Then they went back to Jerusalem. On the way, they went through many Samaritan villages and preached the Good News to the people.

Divine Appointment

26 An angel of the Lord spoke to Philip. The angel said, "Get ready and go south. Go to the road which leads down to the town of Gaza from Jerusalem—the road that isn't used much now." 27 So Philip got ready and went. On the road he saw a man from the country of Ethiopia. This man was an important officer* in the service of Candace, the queen of the Ethiopians. He was responsible for taking care of all her money. This man had gone to Jerusalem to worship. 28 Now he was on his way home. He was sitting in his chariot and reading *from the book* of Isaiah, the prophet. 29 The Spirit said to Philip, "Go to that chariot and stay near it." 30 So Philip ran toward it, and he heard the man reading aloud. He was reading from the prophet Isaiah. Philip asked him, "Do you understand what you are reading?"

31 The man answered, "How can I understand? I have no one to explain it to me!" Then he invited Philip to climb in and sit with him. 32 He was reading this part of Scripture:

"He was like a sheep when it is taken away to be killed.
He was like a lamb which makes no sound when someone cuts off its wool.

8:12   or, Jesus Christ
8:27   literally, a eunuch

33 He was shamed;
   all his rights were taken away.
   His life on earth was ended.
   There will be no story about his descendants."   *Isaiah 53:7-8*

34 The officer asked Philip, "Please, tell me, who is the prophet talking about? Is he talking about himself or about someone else?"   35 Philip began to speak. He started with this same Scripture and told the man the Good News about Jesus.

36 While they were traveling down the road, they came to some water. The officer said, "Look! Here is water! What is stopping me from being immersed?"   37 *
38 Then the officer gave a command for the chariot to stop. Both Philip and the officer went down into the water, and Philip immersed him.   39 When they came up out of the water, the Spirit of the Lord took Philip away; the officer did not see him. The officer continued on his way home. He was very happy.   40 Philip appeared in a town called Azotus.* He was preaching the Good News *about Jesus* in all the towns along the way from Azotus to Caesarea.

Chapter 9

Saul Sees the Light

1 *In Jerusalem* Saul was still trying to scare the followers of the Lord *Jesus*, threatening to kill them. So, he went to the high priest.   2 Saul asked him to write letters to the Jews of the synagogues in the city of Damascus. Saul wanted the authority to find people in Damascus who were followers of The Way. If he found any believers there, men or women, he would tie them up and bring them back to Jerusalem.

3 So, Saul went to Damascus. When he came near the city, a bright light from the sky suddenly shined all around him.   4 Saul fell to the ground. He heard a voice saying to him: "Saul! Saul! Why are you persecuting me?"

5 Saul asked, "Who are you, Lord?"

The voice answered, "I am Jesus. I am the one you are persecuting.   6 Get up now and go into the city. Someone there will tell you what you must do."

7 The men traveling with Saul stood there. They said nothing. The men heard the voice, but they saw no one.   8 Saul got up from the ground. He opened his eyes, but he couldn't see anything. So, the men with Saul held his hand and led him into Damascus.   9 For three days, Saul could not see; he didn't eat or drink.

10 There was a follower *of Jesus* in Damascus. His name was Ananias.* The Lord *Jesus* spoke to Ananias in a vision, saying: "Ananias!"

Ananias answered, "Here I am, Lord."

11 The Lord said to Ananias, "Get up and go to Straight Street. Find the house of Judas. Ask for a man named Saul, from the city of Tarsus. He is there now, praying.   12 In a vision, a man named Ananias came to him and put his hands on him, so that he could see again."

8:37   Some late manuscripts have : 37 "And Philip said, 'If you believe with all your heart, you may.' And he answered, 'I believe that Jesus Christ is the Son of God.'"
8:40   ancient Ashdod. It is next to the Mediterranean Sea, west of Jerusalem.
9:10   There are three different men named Ananias in Acts (5:1; 9:10; 23:2).

13 But Ananias answered, "Lord, many people have told me about this man Saul. They told me about how many terrible things he did to your holy people in Jerusalem.

14 Now he has come to Damascus. The ruling priests have given him the authority to arrest all people who trust in your name."

15 But the Lord *Jesus* said to Ananias, "Go! I have chosen Saul for an important work. He will carry my name to kings, to the Jewish people, and to other nations. **16** I will show Saul the things he must suffer for my name."

17 So Ananias left and went to the house of Judas. He put his hands on Saul and said, "Saul, my brother, the Lord Jesus sent me. He is the one you saw on the road when you came here. He sent me, so that you may see again and so that you may be filled with the Holy Spirit." **18** Immediately, something which looked like fish scales fell off Saul's eyes. Saul could see again! He got up and was immersed. **19** Then he ate some food and began to feel strong again.

Saul (Paul) Joins the Chase

Saul stayed with the followers *of Jesus* in Damascus for a few days.

20 Very soon he began to preach about Jesus in the synagogues, "Jesus is the Son of God!"

21 Everyone who heard Saul was surprised. They were saying, "This is the same man who was in Jerusalem. He was trying to destroy the people who trust in this name! He had come here to do the same thing, to arrest the followers *of Jesus* and take them back *to Jerusalem* to the ruling priests."

22 But Saul became more and more powerful. He proved that Jesus is the Messiah. His proofs were so strong that the Jewish leaders who lived in Damascus didn't know how to answer him.

The Great Escape

23 After many days, the Jewish leaders made plans to kill Saul. **24** The Jews were watching the city gates day and night. They wanted to kill him, but Saul learned about their plan. **25** One night some followers whom Saul had taught helped him leave the city. The followers put him in a basket. Then they lowered him down through a hole in the city walls.*

Saul (Paul) and Barnabas

26 Then Saul went to Jerusalem. He was trying to join the group of followers, but they were all afraid of him; they didn't believe that Saul truly was a follower *of Jesus*, **27** but Barnabas accepted him and brought him to the apostles. Barnabas told them that Saul had seen the Lord *Jesus* on the road *to Damascus*. He explained to the apostles how the Lord had spoken to Saul. Then he told them how in Damascus Saul had preached to the people in the name of the Lord without fear.

28 And so, Saul stayed with the followers. He went everywhere in Jerusalem, preaching with the authority of the Lord *Jesus* without fear. **29** Saul often talked with the Jewish people who spoke Greek. He had arguments with them. So, they were trying to kill him. **30** When the brothers learned about this, they took Saul to the city of Caesarea. From Caesarea, they sent Saul to the city of Tarsus.

9:25   Before Saul went to Jerusalem, he spent some time in Arabia where he received the gospel directly from Jesus (Galatians 1:17,18).

9:31   The Greek word is *ekklesia,* which is often translated "church."

31 Everywhere in Judea, Galilee, and Samaria, God's people* had a time of peace. With the help of the Holy Spirit, the group became stronger and stronger. The believers showed that they respected the Lord by the way they lived. Because of this, the group of believers grew larger and larger.

Make Your Bed, Aeneas!

32 Peter was traveling through all of the towns *around Jerusalem*. He visited the holy people who lived in the town of Lydda.   **33** In Lydda he met a paralyzed man named Aeneas. Aeneas had not been able to leave his bed for the past eight years. **34** Peter said to him, "Aeneas, Jesus Christ* heals you. Get up and make your bed! You can do this for yourself now!" Aeneas got up immediately.   **35** All of the people living in Lydda and on the plain of Sharon saw him. These people turned to the Lord *Jesus*.

Dorcas Gets Up for the Chase

36 In the town of Joppa, there was a follower *of Jesus* named Tabitha. (Her Greek name, Dorcas, means "a deer.") She always did good things for people. She always gave to people in need.   **37** While Peter was in Lydda, Tabitha became sick and died. They washed her body and put it in an upstairs room.   **38** The followers in Joppa heard that Peter was in Lydda. (Lydda is near Joppa.*) So, they sent two men to Peter. They begged him, "Hurry, please come quickly!"

39 Peter got ready and went with them.

When he arrived, they took him to the upstairs room. All of the widows stood around Peter. They were crying. They showed him the shirts and robes which Dorcas had made while she was still alive.   **40** Peter sent everyone out of the room. He kneeled down and prayed. Then he turned to Tabitha's body and said, "Tabitha, get up!" She opened her eyes. When she saw Peter, she sat up.   **41** He gave her his hand and helped her stand up. Then he called the holy people and the widows *into the room*. He showed them Tabitha; she was alive!

42 People everywhere in Joppa learned about this. Many of these people believed in the Lord *Jesus*.   **43** Peter stayed in Joppa for many days. He stayed with a man named Simon who was a leather-worker.*

Chapter 10

Cornelius Wants to Chase God

1 In the city of Caesarea there was a man named Cornelius. He was an officer in the "Italian" regiment *of the Roman army*.   **2** Cornelius was a good man. He and everyone who lived in his home worshiped the true God. He gave much of his money to the poor people. Cornelius always prayed to God.   **3** One afternoon about three o'clock, Cornelius clearly saw a vision. In the vision, an angel of God came to him and said, "Cornelius!"

4 Cornelius stared at the angel. He became afraid and asked, "What do you want, sir?"

The angel said to Cornelius, "God has heard your prayers. He has seen your gifts to the poor people. God has not forgotten the things you have done.   **5** Send some men now to the town of Joppa. Send for a man named Simon. He is also called Peter.

9:34   or, Jesus the Messiah
9:38   about a two and a half hour walk from Lydda to Joppa
9:43   This was an unclean occupation to very strict Jews, but this did not seem to bother Peter.

6 Simon is staying with another man named Simon, who is a leather-worker. He has a house beside the ocean." 7 The angel who spoke to Cornelius left. Then Cornelius called two of his servants and a soldier. This soldier was a good man. They always stayed close to Cornelius. 8 Cornelius explained everything to these three men. Then he sent them to Joppa.

So Peter, What's for Lunch?

9 The next day, these men came near Joppa. At that time, Peter was going up to the roof to pray. It was about noon. 10 Peter was hungry and wanted to eat. But while they were preparing the food for Peter to eat, a vision came to him. 11 He saw something coming down through the open sky. It looked like a big sheet coming down to the ground. It was being lowered to the ground by its four corners. 12 Every kind of animal was in it—animals which walk on four feet, animals which crawl on the ground, and birds which fly in the air. 13 Then a Voice said to Peter, "Get up, Peter; kill any one of these animals and eat it."

14 But Peter said, "I would never do that, Lord! I have never eaten food which is unholy or not pure."

15 But the voice said to him the second time, "God has made these things pure. Don't call them 'unholy'!" 16 This happened a third time. Then the whole thing was taken back up into the sky immediately.

17 Peter was wondering what this vision meant. Then the men whom Cornelius had sent found Simon's house. They were standing at the gate. 18 They asked, "Is Simon Peter staying here?"

19 While Peter was still thinking about the vision, the Spirit said to him, "Listen, three men are looking for you. 20 Get up and go downstairs. Go with these men and don't have any doubts. I have sent them *to you*." 21 So, Peter went downstairs to the men. He said, "I am the man you are looking for. Why did you come here?"

22 The men answered, "A holy angel told Cornelius to invite you to his house. Cornelius is a *Roman* army officer. He is a good man; he worships God. All of the Jewish people respect him. The angel told Cornelius to invite you to his house, so that he may listen to the things you have to say."

Cornelius Joins the Chase

23 Peter asked the men to come in and stay for the night.

The next day, Peter got ready and went away with the three men. Some of the Jewish brothers from Joppa went with Peter. 24 The next day they came into the city of Caesarea. Cornelius was waiting for them. He had already called in his relatives and close friends. 25 When Peter entered the house, Cornelius met him. Cornelius fell down at Peter's feet and worshiped him. 26 But Peter made him get up. Peter said, "Stand up! I am only a man, *like you*."* 27 Peter continued talking with Cornelius. Then Peter went inside and saw a large group of people there. 28 Peter said to them, "You people understand that it is forbidden for a Jewish man to associate with or visit any non-Jewish person. But God has shown me that I should not call any person 'unholy' or 'unclean.' 29 That is why I didn't argue when the men invited me to come here. Now, please tell me why you sent for me."

30 Cornelius said, "Four days ago, I was praying in my house. It was at this same time—three o'clock in the afternoon. Suddenly, there was an angel standing before me.

10:26 Compare Revelation 22:8,9.

He was dressed in shining clothes. **31** The man said, 'Cornelius! God has heard your prayer. He has seen your gifts to the poor people. God has not forgotten the things you have done. **32** So, send someone to the city of Joppa. Ask Simon Peter to come. Peter is staying in the house of another man named Simon, who is a leather-worker. His house is beside the ocean.' **33** So, I sent for you immediately. It was very good of you to come here. Now we are all here in the presence of God. We want to hear everything that the Lord has commanded you to tell us."

Every Race Can Chase

34 Peter began to speak, "Now I understand! God treats everyone the same. **35** God accepts any person who worships Him and does what is right. It doesn't matter what race a person comes from. **36** God has spoken to the sons of Israel. He sent them the Good News, that peace has come through Jesus the Messiah, who is the Lord of all people! **37** You know what occurred all over Judea. It began in Galilee after John preached to the people about immersion. **38** You know about Jesus from Nazareth. God anointed him with the Holy Spirit and power. Jesus went everywhere doing good things for people. He healed everyone who was ruled by the Devil. God was with Jesus. **39** We saw all of the things that he did in Judea and in Jerusalem. But Jesus was killed; they put him on a cross made of wood. **40** However, on the third day *after his death*, God raised Jesus to life! God allowed a few people to see him clearly. **41** Jesus was not seen by all of the people; only the witnesses whom God had already chosen—they saw him. We are those witnesses! We ate and drank with Jesus after he was raised from death. **42** Jesus commanded us to proclaim to the people. He told us to tell them that he is the one whom God chose to be the judge of all people, living or dead. **43** Every person who commits himself to Jesus will be forgiven through the authority of Jesus. All of the prophets say that this is true . . . ."

The Holy Spirit Comes Upon Them

44 While Peter was still speaking these words, the Holy Spirit came upon all those people who were listening to his speech. **45** The Jewish believers who came with Peter were amazed. They were shocked because the gift of the Holy Spirit was poured out on people who were **not** Jewish. **46** These Jewish believers heard them speaking different *inspired* languages and praising God. Then Peter said, **47** "Can we refuse to allow these people to be immersed in water? They have received the Holy Spirit the same as we did!" **48** So, Peter commanded that Cornelius and his relatives and friends be immersed by the authority of Jesus the Messiah. Then they asked Peter to stay with them for a few days.

Chapter 11

Peter Tells the Whole Story

1 The apostles and the brothers in Judea heard that non-Jewish people had also accepted God's message. **2** However, there were some Jewish believers who argued with Peter when he came *back* to Jerusalem. **3** They said, "You went into the homes of men who are not Jewish!* You even ate with them!"

4 Then Peter began to explain the whole story to them. **5** He said, "I was in the town of Joppa. While I was praying, a vision came to me. In the vision, I saw

---

11:3   It was forbidden for Jews to go into non-Jewish homes.

something coming down from the sky. It looked like a big sheet. It was being lowered to the ground by its four corners. It came down and stopped very near to me.   **6** After staring, I looked inside it and I saw animals, both tame and wild. I saw animals which crawl and birds which fly in the air.   **7** I heard a voice say to me, 'Get up, Peter. Kill *any of these animals* and eat!'   **8** But I said, 'I would never do that, Lord! I have never eaten anything that is unholy or not pure.'   **9** But the voice from the sky answered a second time, 'God has made these things pure. Don't call them unholy!'   **10** This happened a third time. Then the whole thing was pulled back up into the sky.   **11** Suddenly three men came to the house where I was staying. These three men were sent to me from the city of Caesarea.   **12** The Spirit told me to go along with them without doubts. These six brothers here also went with me. We went into the house of Cornelius. **13** Cornelius told us about the angel that he had seen standing in his house. The angel said to him, 'Send someone to Joppa. Invite Simon Peter to come.   **14** He will tell you words by which you and everyone in your group will be saved.'   **15** After I began my speech, the Holy Spirit came upon them, the same as He did upon us in the beginning.* **16** Then I remembered the words of the Lord *Jesus* when he used to say: 'John immersed people in water, but you will be immersed in the Holy Spirit!'   **17** God gave the same gift to these people that He gave to us who believed in the Lord Jesus, the Messiah. So, could I stop God?"

18 When the group heard these things, they stopped arguing. They gave glory to God and said, "Then God is allowing non-Jewish people to change their hearts and have life, too!"

Chasers Are Called Christians for the First Time

19 The believers were scattered by the persecution which occurred after Stephen was killed.* Some of the believers went to places far away, like Phoenicia, Cyprus, and Antioch *in Syria*. The believers told the message in these places, but they told it only to Jews.   **20** However, some of these believers came to the city of Antioch. They were men from Cyprus and Cyrene. These men were also talking to non-Jews,* telling them the Good News, that Jesus is Lord.   **21** The Lord was helping the believers. A large group of people believed and turned to the Lord.

22 The congregation which was in Jerusalem heard about these new believers *in Antioch in Syria*. So, the believers in Jerusalem sent Barnabas to Antioch. **23-24** Barnabas was a good man. He was full of the Holy Spirit and full of faith. When Barnabas went to Antioch, he saw how much God had blessed them. This made him very happy. He began to encourage all the believers in Antioch. He told them, "Never lose your faith. Always obey the Lord with all your hearts." A large number of people became followers of the Lord *Jesus*.

25 Then Barnabas left for the city of Tarsus. He was looking for Saul.   **26** When he found Saul, Barnabas brought him to Antioch. Saul and Barnabas taught a large crowd. For a whole year they met with the congregation. In Antioch, God called the followers *of Jesus* "Christians" for the first time.

27 About that same time, some prophets went down from Jerusalem to Antioch. **28** Agabus stood up and spoke. With the help of the Holy Spirit, he said, "A very bad time is coming to the whole world. There will be very little food for people to eat." (This

11:15 See Acts 2:1-13.
11:19 See Acts 7:59—8:3.
11:20 This was the first time this ever happened.

famine occurred during the time when Claudius *was Caesar.**)   **29** The followers of Jesus decided that they would all try to help their brothers *and sisters* who lived in Judea. Each believer planned to send them *as much as he could.*   **30** They gathered the money and gave it to Barnabas and Saul. Then Barnabas and Saul brought it to the elders *in Jerusalem.*

Chapter 12

Peter Is Put in Jail

1 During that same time, King Herod *Agrippa I* began to persecute some members of the congregation.   **2** He ordered that James be killed with a sword. (James was the brother of John.)   **3** Herod saw that the Jewish leaders liked this. So he decided to arrest Peter, too. (This happened during the time of the Feast of Unleavened Bread.*)   **4** Herod had Peter arrested and put in jail. He turned Peter over to a group of 16 soldiers to guard him. Herod wanted to wait until after the Passover Festival. Then he planned to bring Peter before the people.   **5** So, Peter was kept in jail, but the congregation was constantly praying to God for Peter.

Peter Is Touched by an Angel

6 Peter was sleeping between two of the soldiers. He was bound with two chains. More soldiers were guarding the jail entrance. It was at night, and Herod planned to bring Peter out to the people the next day.   **7** Suddenly, an angel of the Lord stood there. A light shined in the cell. The angel touched Peter on the side and woke him up. The angel said, "Hurry, get up!" Then the chains fell off of Peter's hands.   **8** The angel said to Peter, "Get dressed and put your shoes on." So Peter did this. Then the angel said, "Put on your robe and follow me."   **9** Then the angel went out and Peter followed. Peter didn't know if the angel were really doing this. He kept thinking that he might be seeing a vision.   **10** Peter and the angel went past the first guard and the second guard. Then they came to the iron gate which separated them from the city. The gate opened for them by itself. Peter and the angel went through it and walked about a block. Then the angel suddenly left.

11 Then Peter realized what had happened. He thought, "Now I know that the Lord really did send his angel to me. He rescued me from Herod and everything which the Jewish people were expecting."

12 When Peter realized this, he went to Mary's house. She was the mother of John. (John was also called Mark.) Many people were gathered there; they were all praying. **13** Peter knocked on the outside door. A servant girl named Rhoda came to answer it. **14** Rhoda recognized Peter's voice. She was so happy she *even forgot to* open the door. Instead, she ran inside and told the group, "Peter is at the door!"

15 The believers said to Rhoda, "You are crazy!" But she kept insisting that it was true. So they said, "It must be Peter's angel."

16 Peter continued to knock. When the believers opened the door, they saw Peter. They were amazed.   **17** Peter made a sign with his hand to tell them to be quiet. He

---

11:28   the title of the supreme Roman rulers. "Caesar" became the title of each emperor. This must have happened about 43-44 A.D. Claudius became emperor in 41 A.D. and ruled until 54 A.D.

12:3   a yearly feast when unleavened bread (no yeast to make the bread rise) was eaten. It lasted seven days. (See Leviticus 23:4-8.)

explained to them how the Lord led him out of jail. He said, "Tell James and the other brothers what happened." Then Peter left to go to another place.

18 The next day the soldiers were very upset. They wondered what had happened to Peter.   **19** Herod looked everywhere for Peter, but couldn't find him. Herod asked the guards many questions *and tortured* them. Then he gave the order that the guards be killed.

It's Not Nice to Take God's Glory

Later Herod left Judea. He went down to the city of Caesarea* and stayed there for a while.   **20** Herod was very angry with the people from the cities of Tyre and Sidon. However, they were able to get Blastus on their side. (Blastus was the king's personal servant.) They came to Herod with one purpose in mind: They wanted peace, because their country needed food from Herod's country.

21 Herod decided on a day to meet with them. On that day Herod was wearing a beautiful royal robe. He sat on his throne and made a speech to the people.   **22** The people shouted, "This is not the voice of a man; it is the voice of a god!"   **23** But Herod didn't give the glory to God. So, an angel of the Lord caused him to become sick. He was soon eaten by worms inside him, and he died.

24 The message of God was spreading and influencing more and more people. The group of believers became larger and larger.

25 After Barnabas and Saul finished their work in Jerusalem, they returned to Antioch. John Mark went along with them.

Chapter 13

Paul and Barnabas Get Picked

1 In the congregation at Antioch *in Syria*, there were some prophets and teachers. They were:

Barnabas,
Simeon (also called Black),
Lucius (from the city of Cyrene),
Manaen (who had grown up with Herod *Antipas*, the ruler),
Saul.

2 They were all serving the Lord and fasting.* The Holy Spirit said to them, "Appoint Barnabas and Saul for My service; I have chosen them to do a special work."

3 So, the congregation fasted and prayed. They put their hands on Barnabas and Saul* and sent them out.

Saul (Paul) and Barnabas on Tour

4 Barnabas and Saul were sent out by the Holy Spirit. They went to the city of Seleucia. Then they sailed from Seleucia to the island of Cyprus.   **5** When Barnabas and Saul came to the city of Salamis, they were preaching God's message in the Jewish synagogues. (John *Mark* went along to help them.)

12:19   After Tiberius Caesar's time, the Herods no longer headquartered in Caesarea.
13:2   going without food for a period of time, usually for spiritual reasons
13:3   Paul

6 They went across the whole island to the town of Paphos. In Paphos, they met a Jewish man who did tricks of magic. His name was Bar-Jesus. He said he was a prophet, but he was not. 7 Bar-Jesus always stayed close to Sergius Paulus, the governor. Sergius Paulus was a wise man. He asked Barnabas and Saul to come to him; he wanted to hear God's message. 8 But Elymas, the magician, opposed Saul and Barnabas. (Elymas is the name for Bar-Jesus in the Greek language.) Elymas tried to turn the governor away from the faith. 9 However, Saul was filled with the Holy Spirit. (Saul's other name was Paul.) Paul looked straight at Elymas 10 and said, "You son of the Devil! You are an enemy of everything which is right! You are full of evil tricks and lies. You always try to turn the Lord's truths into lies! 11 Now the Lord will touch you, and you will be blind. For a time, you won't be able to see the light which comes from the sun."

Then everything quickly became dark for Elymas. He walked around lost, trying to find someone to lead him by the hand. 12 When the governor saw this, he believed. He was amazed at the teaching of the Lord.

God Chaser Archives: From Moses to David

13 Paul and those who were with him sailed away from Paphos. They came to Perga, a town in Pamphylia. But John *Mark* left them; he went back home to Jerusalem. 14 They continued their trip from Perga and went to Antioch, a city in Pisidia. In Antioch, on the Sabbath day, they went into the Jewish synagogue and sat down. 15 The law of Moses and the writings of the prophets were read. Then the leaders of the synagogue sent a message to Paul and Barnabas: "Brothers, if you have something to say which will help the people here, please speak."

16 Paul stood up. He raised his hand* and said, "Men of Israel, and you other people who also worship the true God, please listen to me! 17 The God of our people, Israel, chose our ancestors. God made His people great during the time that they lived in Egypt as strangers. God brought them out of that country with great power. 18 For 40 years in the desert, God was patient with them. 19 He destroyed seven nations in the land of Canaan, giving their land to His people. 20 All of this happened in about 450 years.

"After this, God gave judges to our people, until the time of Samuel, the prophet. 21 Then the people asked for a king. God gave them Saul, the son of Kish. Saul was from the tribe of Benjamin. He was king for 40 years. 22 After God removed Saul, He made David their king. God vouched for David:

'David, the *son* of Jesse, is the man I like.
He will do all the things I want him to do.'
                                                                          1 Samuel 13:14

23 God has brought one of David's descendants to Israel to be their Savior; he is Jesus. God had promised to do this. 24 Before Jesus came, John preached to all the people of Israel. John told the people to change their hearts and to be immersed. 25 As John was finishing his work, he always used to say, 'Who do you think I am? I am not the Messiah. He is coming later. I'm not worthy to untie his shoes!'

26 "My brothers, sons in the family of Abraham, and you non-Jews who also worship the true God, *listen!* The news about this salvation has been sent to us. 27 The *Jews* living in Jerusalem and the Jewish leaders did not realize it. The words that the prophets wrote *about the Messiah* were read to the Jews every Sabbath day, but they didn't understand. The Jewish leaders condemned the Messiah. When they did this, they made the words of the prophets come true! 28 They couldn't find any real reason why

---

13:16   a common gesture calling for attention

he should die, yet they asked Pilate to kill him. **29** These Jews did all the things that the Scriptures said about him. Then they took him down from the *cross of* wood and put him in a tomb. **30** But God raised him up from death! **31** After this, for many days, Jesus was seen by the people who had gone with him from Galilee to Jerusalem. They are now his witnesses to the people. **32-33** We are telling you the Good News: God made a promise to our fathers. We are their descendants, and God has made this promise come true for us. God did this by raising Jesus from death. We also read about this in Psalm 2:

'You are My Son.
Today I have become your Father.'   *Psalm 2:7*

34 God raised Jesus from death. Jesus will never go back to the grave and decay. So God said:

'I will give you the sure and holy promises
which I made to David.'   *Isaiah 55:3*

35 But in another place God says:

'You will not let *the body of* Your holy one decay in the grave.' *Psalm 16:10*

36 But David did God's will during his own generation. Then he died. David was buried with his fathers and his body **did** decay! **37** However, the one whom God raised from death did **not** decay!

38-39 "Brothers, you must understand what we are telling you: You can have forgiveness of your sins through this man. The law of Moses could not make you right *with God*, but everyone who believes *the Good News* is made right. **40** The prophets said something would take place. Be careful! Don't let this happen to you:

41 'Look, you people who doubt!
Wonder and die!
During your time, I* will do
something which you won't believe.
You wouldn't believe it,
even if someone were to explain it to you!' "   *Habakkuk 1:5*

42 While Paul and Barnabas were leaving *the synagogue*, the people were begging them to *come back* on the next Sabbath day and tell them *more* about these things. **43** After the meeting, many converts to the Jewish faith (who worshiped the true God) and many of the Jews followed Paul and Barnabas. Paul and Barnabas were persuading them to continue living in the gracious love of God. **44** On the next Sabbath day, almost all the people in the city came together to hear the message of the Lord. **45** The Jewish leaders saw the crowds there. So, they became very jealous. They said some terrible things and argued against the words which Paul said. **46** But Paul and Barnabas were very bold. They said, "It was necessary that we speak God's message to you Jews first, but you won't listen. You are deciding that you are unworthy of having eternal life! Therefore, we will now go to the people of other nations! **47** This is what the Lord *God* commanded us to do:

'I have made you a light for other nations,

13:41   God

so that you may show the way of salvation
to people all over the world.' "   *Isaiah 49:6*

48 When the non-Jewish people heard Paul say this, they were happy. They gave honor to the Lord's message, and many of the people believed the message. These were the people appointed to have eternal life.

49 And so, the message of the Lord was spreading through the whole country. **50** But the Jewish leaders stirred up some of the important religious women and the leaders of the city to oppose Paul and Barnabas. They were angry. These people persecuted them and threw them out of town. **51** So, Paul and Barnabas shook the dust off their feet.* Then they went to the town of Iconium. **52** The followers *of Jesus in Antioch* were happy and full of the Holy Spirit.

Chapter 14

Paul and Barnabas Cause Divided Opinions

1 Then Paul and Barnabas went to the town of Iconium. They entered the Jewish synagogue. (This is what they did in every town.) They spoke to the people there in such a way that many Jews and non-Jews believed what they said. **2** However, some of the Jews did not believe. These Jews stirred up the non-Jewish people and made them persecute the brothers. **3** The Lord helped Paul and Barnabas to be bold, and they stayed in Iconium a long time. Paul and Barnabas preached about how God forgives sins. The Lord proved what they said was true; He helped them do miracles and wonders. **4** But, some of the people in the town agreed with the Jews. Other people in the town believed Paul and Barnabas. So, the town was divided.

5 Some non-Jewish people, some Jews, and their Jewish leaders tried to hurt Paul and Barnabas. These people wanted to stone them to death. **6** When Paul and Barnabas learned about this, they left that town. They went to Lystra and Derbe, towns in Lycaonia, and to the surrounding area. **7** They told the Good News there, too.

Mistaken Identity: We're Not the Ones You Are Supposed to Be Chasing

8 In Lystra there was a man whose feet were paralyzed. He had been born crippled; he had never walked. This man was sitting there **9** and listening to Paul speak. Paul looked straight at him. Paul saw that the man believed that God could heal him. **10** So, Paul shouted, "Stand up on your feet!" The man jumped up and began walking around. **11** When the crowd saw what Paul did, they shouted in their own Lycaonian language. They said, "The gods have become like men! They have come down to us!" **12** The people began to call Barnabas "Zeus."* They called Paul "Hermes,"* because he was the main speaker. **13** The temple of Zeus was near the town. The priest of this temple brought some bulls and flowers to the town gates. The priest and the crowds wanted to give an offering, to *worship* Paul and Barnabas.

14 But when the apostles,* Barnabas and Paul, understood what the people were doing, they ripped their own clothes.* Then they ran in among the crowd and shouted

---

13:51   a gesture meaning that one will have no more to do with those people
14:12   the chief god of the Greeks. Barnabas may have appeared to be the leader.
14:12   the son of Zeus, the messenger of the gods
14:14   The word means "special messengers" (from Antioch in Syria). Here it does not refer to the original twelve apostles.
14:14   a sign of grief or outrage

to them, **15** "Men, why are you doing these things? We are not gods! We have the same feelings you have! We came to tell you the Good News. We are telling you to turn away from these worthless things. Turn to the true living God. He is the One who made the land, the sea, the sky, and everything which is in them. **16** In the past, God let all the nations do what they wanted. **17** But God did things to prove that He is real: He does good things for you. He gives you rain from the sky and good harvests at the right times. He gives you plenty of food and fills your hearts with joy." **18** Paul and Barnabas told the crowds these things. The people still wanted to offer sacrifices to *worship* them, but Paul and Barnabas stopped them.

19 Then some Jews came from Antioch *in Pisidia* and Iconium. They persuaded the people *to oppose Paul*. And so, the people stoned Paul and dragged him out of the town. The people thought that they had killed him. **20** The followers *of Jesus* gathered around Paul, and he got up and went back into town. The next day he and Barnabas left and went to the town of Derbe.

On the Road Again

21 Paul and Barnabas told the Good News in the town of Derbe, too. Many people became followers *of Jesus*. Paul and Barnabas went back to the towns of Lystra, Iconium, and Antioch *in Pisidia*. **22** *In those cities* they made the followers *of Jesus* stronger. They helped them to stay in the faith. They said, "We must suffer many things on our way into God's kingdom." **23** They appointed elders for each congregation. The believers fasted* and prayed for these men. These men had put their trust in the Lord *Jesus*. So, Paul and Barnabas put them in the Lord's care.

24 Paul and Barnabas went through the country of Pisidia. Then they came to the country of Pamphylia. **25** They preached the story of Jesus in the town of Perga, and then they went down to the town of Attalia. **26** And from there Paul and Barnabas sailed away to Antioch *in Syria*. This is the city where they had begun this work. The believers here had sent them out with God's gracious love. Now their trip was over.

27 When Paul and Barnabas arrived, they gathered the congregation together. Paul and Barnabas told them all about the things which God had done with them. They said, "God opened a door so that non-Jewish people could believe too!" **28** They stayed there a long time with the followers *of Jesus*.

Chapter 15

The Law Does Not Make the Chase

1 Then some men came down *to Antioch in Syria* from Judea. They began teaching to non-Jewish brothers: "You cannot be saved if you are not circumcised.* Moses told us to do it." **2** Paul and Barnabas were very much opposed to this teaching. They argued with these men about it. So, the group decided to send Paul, Barnabas, and some other men to Jerusalem. These men were going there to talk more about this issue with the apostles and elders.

3 The congregation helped the men with what they needed for the trip. These men went through the provinces of Phoenicia and Samaria. In these countries, they told all about how non-Jewish people had turned *to the true God*. This made all the brothers very happy. **4** Paul, Barnabas, and the others arrived in Jerusalem. The apostles, the

14:23 going without food for a period of time, usually for spiritual reasons
15:1 to cut off the foreskin of the male sex organ as a sign of God's agreement with Israel

elders, and the whole congregation welcomed them. Paul, Barnabas, and the others told about all the things which God had done with them.   **5** Some of the believers *in Jerusalem* had belonged to the Pharisee sect. They stood up and claimed, "The non-Jewish believers **must** be circumcised.* We must command them to obey the law of Moses!"

6 Then the apostles and the elders gathered to study this problem.   **7** There was a long debate. Then Peter stood up and said to them, "My brothers, I know you remember what happened in the early days. At that time God chose me from among you to preach the Good News to non-Jewish people and they believed it.   **8** God knows the hearts *of all people* and He accepted these *non-Jewish* people. He showed this to us by giving them the Holy Spirit, too.   **9** God did the same thing for them that He did for us. When they made a commitment, God made their hearts pure.   **10** So now, why are you testing God? You are putting a heavy load* around the necks of the *non-Jewish* followers. Neither we nor our ancestors were strong enough to carry it!   **11** No, we believe that both we **and** these people will be saved by the gracious love of the Lord Jesus!"

12 Then the whole group became quiet. They were listening to Paul and Barnabas tell all the miracles and wonders that God did through them among non-Jewish people. **13** After a time of silence, James spoke. He said, "My brothers, listen to me. **14** Simon *Peter* has told us how God showed His love for non-Jewish people. For the first time, God accepted non-Jewish people and made them His own people.   **15** The written words of the prophets agree with this, too:

16 'I* will return later.
    I will build David's house again.
    It has fallen down,
  but I will build it up again.
    I will restore it.
17 Then all people can look for the Lord *God*.
    All the other nations will search for Him.
    They can be My people, too.
    The Lord *God* said this.'

                                                      Amos 9:11-12

"And He is the One who does all these things.   **18** These things have been known from the beginning of time.   **19** So, I think we shouldn't bother non-Jewish *brothers* who have turned to God.   **20** Instead, we should write them a letter to tell them these things:

Do not eat food which has been given to idols.
Do not commit any kind of sexual sin.
Do not eat animals which have been strangled.
Do not taste blood.

21 There are those* in every town who proclaim the law of Moses. The words of Moses have been read in the synagogue every Sabbath day for generations long past."

15:5   receive the physical mark which sealed the agreement that God made with Abraham. See Genesis
        17:9-14.
15:10 literally, yoke
15:16 God
15:21 the Jewish people

Take a Letter

22 The apostles, the elders, and the whole congregation wanted to send some men with Paul and Barnabas to Antioch *in Syria*. The group decided to choose some of their own men. They chose Judas Barsabbas and Silas. These men were respected by the brothers *in Jerusalem*. **23** The group sent the letter with these men. The letter said:

From the apostles and elders, your brothers.
To all non-Jewish brothers in the city of Antioch and in the
countries of Syria and Cilicia:

Dear Brothers,
24 We have heard that some men have come to you from our group. The things they said have troubled and upset you, but we didn't tell them to do this! **25** We have all agreed to choose some men and send them to you. They are with our dear *friends*, Barnabas and Paul. **26** Paul and Barnabas have given their lives to serve the name of our Lord Jesus Christ. **27** So, we have sent Judas and Silas with them. They will tell you the same things. **28** The Holy Spirit thinks you should have no more burdens. We agree. You only need to do these things:

29 Do not eat any food which has been given to idols.

Do not taste blood.

Do not eat any animals which have been strangled.

Do not commit any kind of sexual sin. If you stay away from these things, you will do well. Now we say good-bye.

30 So Paul, Barnabas, Judas, and Silas left *Jerusalem*. They went down to Antioch *in Syria*. They gathered the group *of believers* and gave them the letter. **31** When the believers read it, they were happy. It encouraged them. **32** Judas and Silas were prophets, too. They said many things to help the brothers and make them stronger. **33** After Judas and Silas stayed there for a while, they left with a blessing of peace from the brothers. Judas and Silas went back to the brothers *in Jerusalem* who had sent them. **34** *

35 But Paul and Barnabas were staying on in Antioch. They and many others were telling the Good News and teaching the people the message of the Lord.

Paul and Barnabas Go Their Separate Ways

36 A few days later, Paul said to Barnabas, "We spoke the Lord's message in many towns. We should go back to all of those towns to visit the brothers and see how they are doing." **37** Barnabas wanted to bring John Mark along with them, too. **38** But, *on their first trip*, John Mark had left them at Pamphylia; he did not continue with them in the work. So, Paul didn't think it was such a good idea to take him along. **39** Paul and Barnabas had a sharp disagreement about this. They separated and went different ways. Barnabas took Mark with him and sailed to the island of Cyprus. **40** Paul chose Silas to go with him. The brothers *in Antioch* put Paul into the Lord's care and sent him out. **41** Paul and Silas went through the countries of Syria and Cilicia, helping the congregations grow stronger.

15:34   Some manuscripts have: 34 "But Silas decided to stay there."

Chapter 16

Timothy: Apprentice God Chaser

1 Paul went to the towns of Derbe and Lystra. A follower *of Jesus* named Timothy was there. Timothy's mother was a Jewish believer. His father was not a Jew.*   **2** The brothers in the towns of Lystra and Iconium respected Timothy. They said good things about him.   **3** Paul wanted Timothy to travel with him, but all of the Jewish people living in that area knew that Timothy's father was not Jewish.* Therefore, Paul took Timothy and circumcised* him *to please the Jews*.   **4** Then Paul and Timothy were traveling through other towns.* They gave the believers the rules and decisions from the apostles and elders in Jerusalem. Paul and Timothy told the believers to obey these rules.   **5** So, the congregations were becoming stronger in the faith and they were growing every day.

Paul's Seeing Things

6 Paul and Timothy went through the countries of Phrygia and Galatia. The Holy Spirit did not allow them to preach the Good News in the country of Asia.*   **7** They went near the land of Mysia. They wanted to go into the country of Bithynia, but the Spirit of Jesus didn't let them go in.   **8** So they passed by Mysia and went down to the city of Troas.   **9** That night Paul saw a vision. In this vision, a man from the country of Macedonia appeared to Paul. The man stood there begging him, "Come across to Macedonia. Help us!"   **10** After Paul had seen the vision, immediately we prepared to leave for Macedonia. We* understood that God had called us to tell the Good News to those people.

Breakfast at Lydia's

11 We left Troas by ship and sailed to the island of Samothrace. The next day, we sailed to the town of Neapolis.*   **12** Then we went to Philippi. Philippi is an important city in that part of Macedonia. It is a city for Romans. We stayed there for a few days.   **13** On the Sabbath day, we went through the city gate to the river. At the river we thought we might find a special place for prayer. Some women had gathered there. So, we sat down and talked with them.   **14** There was a woman named Lydia from the city of Thyatira. Her job was selling purple cloth. She worshiped the true God. Lydia listened to Paul. The Lord opened her heart and she believed the things which Paul said. **15** She and all of the people living in her house were immersed. Then Lydia invited *us into her home*. She said, "If you think I am truly a believer in the Lord Jesus, then come stay in my house." She persuaded us.

Jailed Again

16 Once we were going to the place for prayer. A slave-girl met us. She had an evil spirit* in her. This spirit gave her the power to tell what would happen in the future. By

---

16:1	literally, His father was a Greek.
16:3	literally, a Greek
16:3	to cut off the foreskin of the male sex organ as a sign of God's agreement with Israel
16:4	where Paul had been on his first journey
16:6	modern Turkey
16:10	Luke, Paul, and perhaps others
16:11	They went from Samothrace, an island, to the port of Neapolis on the coast.
16:16	a demon. The people believed that she could predict the future by the power of Apollo, a Greek god.

doing this, she earned a lot of money for the men who owned her. **17** This girl followed Paul and us everywhere. She said loudly, "These men are servants of the Highest God! They are telling you how you can be saved!" **18** She continued doing this for many days. This bothered Paul, so he turned and said to the spirit, "By the authority of Jesus Christ, I order you to come out of her!" At that moment, the spirit came out. **19** The men who owned the slave-girl saw this. These men knew that they could no longer use her to make money. So they grabbed Paul and Silas and dragged them into the meeting place of the city. The city officials were there. **20** The men brought Paul and Silas to the leaders and said, "These men are Jews who are making trouble in our city. **21** They are telling the people to do things which are not right for us. We are Roman citizens and cannot do these things." **22** The crowd was against Paul and Silas. Then the leaders tore off the clothes of Paul and Silas and ordered *some men* to beat them with rods. **23** The men beat them many times. Then the leaders threw Paul and Silas in jail. The leaders commanded the jailor, "Guard them very carefully!" **24** The jailor heard this special order. So he put Paul and Silas into the inner prison far inside the jail. He locked their feet in wooden stocks.

Jail House Rocks

25 About midnight, Paul and Silas were praying and singing songs to God. The other prisoners were listening to them. **26** Suddenly, there was a great earthquake. It was so strong that it shook the foundations of the jail. Then all the doors of the jail quickly opened. All prisoners were freed from their chains. **27** The jailor woke up. He saw that the jail doors were open. He thought that the prisoners had escaped. So the jailor took his sword and was ready to kill himself.* **28** But Paul shouted, "Don't hurt yourself! We are all here!"

29 The jailor told someone to bring a light. Then he ran inside. He was shaking. He fell down in front of Paul and Silas. **30** Then he brought them outside and asked, "Men, what must I do to be saved?"

31 They said to him, "Commit yourself to the Lord Jesus and you will be saved— you and all the people living in your house." **32** So, Paul and Silas told the story of the Lord *Jesus* to the jailor and to all the people in his house. **33** It was late at night, but the jailor took Paul and Silas and washed their wounds. The jailor and all of his people were immersed right away. **34** After this, the jailor took Paul and Silas and gave them some food. All of the people were very happy because they now trusted in God.

35 The next morning, the leaders sent some soldiers to tell the jailor this: "Let these men go free!"

36 The jailor said to Paul, "The leaders have sent these soldiers to set you free. You may leave now. Go in peace."

37 But Paul said to the soldiers, "Your leaders did not prove that we did anything wrong, yet they beat us in public and put us in jail. We are Roman citizens.* Now the leaders want to make us go away quietly? No! The leaders must come and bring us out!"

38 The soldiers told the leaders what Paul had said. When the leaders heard that Paul and Silas were Roman citizens, they were afraid. **39** So, the leaders came and told Paul and Silas how sorry they were. The leaders led them out of jail and kept asking them to leave the city. **40** But when they came out of the jail, they went to

---

16:27   The keeper of the jail would be killed if he let even one prisoner escape.
16:37   Roman citizens could not be tortured or beaten until they had a fair trial.

Lydia's house. They saw some of the brothers there and encouraged them. Then Paul and Silas left.

Chapter 17

Jealous Jews Meet Jason

1 Paul and Silas traveled through the towns of Amphipolis and Apollonia. Then they came to the city of Thessalonica. In that city there was a Jewish synagogue. **2** According to Paul's custom, he went to them in this synagogue, and on three Sabbath days he reasoned with them from the Scriptures. **3** Paul explained and clearly showed that the Messiah must die and then rise from death. Paul said, "This Jesus, whom I announce to you, is the Messiah!" **4** Some of the Jews believed Paul and Silas and joined them. In the synagogue there were many Greeks.* They worshiped the true God. There were also many important women. They joined Paul and Silas, too.

5 But the Jews *who didn't believe* became jealous. They hired some evil men from the city to gather many people and make trouble in the city. The people went to Jason's house looking for Paul and Silas. The men wanted to bring them out to the people. **6** But the group didn't find them. So, the people dragged Jason and some of the other brothers to the leaders of the city. The people all cried out, "These men have made trouble everywhere in the world. And now they have come here, too! **7** Jason is keeping them in his house. All of them do things against the laws of Caesar.* They say that there is another king named Jesus!" **8** The leaders of the city and the crowd heard these things. They became very upset. **9** They made Jason and the other brothers post bond. Then they let them go free.

God Chasers Get Chased Out of Town

10 That same night, the brothers sent Paul and Silas to another town named Berea. In Berea, Paul and Silas went to the Jewish synagogue. **11** These Jews were better people than the ones in Thessalonica. These Jews were very happy to listen to the things which Paul and Silas said. They wanted to know whether these things were true or not. They studied the *Old Testament* Scriptures every day. **12** Many of these Jews believed. Many important Greek men and women also believed. **13** But when the Jews in Thessalonica learned that Paul was telling God's message in Berea, they came to Berea, too. The Jews from Thessalonica made the people in Berea upset and they caused trouble. **14** So the believers quickly sent Paul away to the sea,* while Silas and Timothy stayed in Berea. **15** The believers who went with Paul took him to the city of Athens. These brothers carried a message from Paul back to Silas and Timothy. It said, "Come to me as soon as you can!"

Chasers of an Unknown God

16 Paul was waiting for Silas and Timothy in Athens. Paul felt deeply troubled, because he saw that the city was full of idols. **17** In the synagogue, Paul debated with the Jews and the Greeks who worshiped the true God. Every day he also debated with some people in the business district of the city, with people who just happened to be there. **18** Some of the Epicurean and Stoic philosophers argued with him.

17:4 non-Jewish people who wanted to worship with the Jews
17:7 The title of the supreme Roman rulers. "Caesar" became the title of each emperor.
17:14 the Aegean Sea

210

Some of them said, "This man doesn't really know what he is talking about. What is he trying to say?" (Paul was telling them the Good News about Jesus rising from death.) So, they said, "He seems to be telling us about some other gods." **19** They got Paul and took him to a meeting of the Areopagus Council. They said, "Please explain to us this new idea which you have been teaching. **20** The things that you are saying are so new to us. We have never heard these things before. We want to know what this teaching means." **21** (All the people of Athens and the people from other countries who lived there always used their time to talk about any new idea.)

22 Then Paul stood before the meeting of the Areopagus Council. Paul said, "Men of Athens, I can see that you are very religious in all things. **23** I was going through your city and I saw the things you worship. I found an altar which had these words written on it:

'TO THE GOD WHO IS NOT KNOWN.'

You worship a God you don't know. **This** is the God I am telling you about! **24** He is the God who made the whole world and everything in it. He is the Lord of the heavens and the earth. He doesn't live in temples which men build! **25** This God is the One who gives all people life, breath, and everything else. He doesn't need any help from human beings; God has everything He needs. **26** God started with one man.* He made all the different people in the world to live everywhere. God decided exactly when and where they must live. **27** He wanted the people to look for Him. Perhaps they could search all around for Him and find Him—He is not far from any of us:
   28 'In Him,
        we live, we walk, we are.'
Some of your own writers have said:
   'For we are *God's* children.'*
29 Therefore, we **are** God's children. So you must not think that God is something like what man imagines or makes out of silver or stone. **30** In the past, although man didn't understand God, God ignored this, but **now**, God commands every person in the world to change his heart. **31** God has set a day when He will judge the whole world. He will be fair, using a man to do this. He chose this man a long time ago. God proved it to everyone by raising that man from death!"

32 When the people heard about *Jesus* rising from death, some of them began to laugh at Paul. The people said, "We will hear more about this from you later." **33** Paul left them. **34** However, some of the people did believe Paul and joined him. One of them was Dionysius, a member of the Areopagus Council. Another was a woman named Damaris. There were some others, too.

Chapter 18

Paul Stays Put

1 Later Paul left Athens and went to the city of Corinth. **2** In Corinth, he met a Jewish man named Aquila. Aquila was born in the country of Pontus. Aquila and his wife, Priscilla, had recently moved *to Corinth* from Italy. They left Italy, because Claudius *the Emperor* had commanded all Jews to get out of Rome. Paul went to visit

---

17:26   Adam
17:28   written by Aratus in *Phaenomena* 5

Aquila and Priscilla. **3** They were tentmakers, the same as Paul. Paul was staying there and working with them. **4** Every Sabbath day Paul debated with the Jews and Greeks in the synagogue. He tried to persuade them to believe.

5 Silas and Timothy came down from Macedonia to Paul in Corinth. After this, Paul used all his time to tell people the Good News. He showed the Jews that Jesus is the Messiah. **6** But the Jews would not accept Paul's teaching. They said some terrible things. So, Paul shook off the dust from his clothes.* He said to the Jews, "If you are not saved, it will be your own fault! I have done all that I can do! After this, I will go to non-Jewish people!" **7** Paul left the synagogue and moved into the home of Titius Justus. This man worshiped the true God. His house was next door to the synagogue. **8** Crispus was the leader of that synagogue. Crispus and all of the people who were living in his house trusted in the Lord *Jesus.* Many other people in Corinth also listened to Paul. They too believed and were immersed. **9** Paul had a vision during the night. The Lord said to him, "Don't be afraid! Keep on talking to people; don't be quiet! **10** I am with you. No one will be able to hurt you. I have many people in this city." **11** Paul stayed there for a year and a half, teaching God's message to the people.

Gallio Clears the Court

12 Some of the Jews came together with only one thing in mind—to stop Paul. They took him to court. Gallio had become the governor of the country of Achaia. **13** The Jews said to Gallio, "This man is influencing people to worship God in a way that is against our law!"

14 Paul was ready to say something, but Gallio spoke to the Jews. Gallio said, "I would listen to you Jews if you were complaining about a terrible crime or some wrong. **15** But the things you are claiming are only questions about words and names— arguments about your own law. You must solve this problem yourselves. I don't want to be a judge over these matters." **16** Then Gallio made them leave the courtroom.

17 So, they all grabbed Sosthenes. (Sosthenes was *now* leader of the synagogue.) They were beating him in front of the court house, but this didn't bother Gallio at all.

Paul Sails for Syria

18 Paul stayed with the brothers for many days. Then he left and sailed for Syria. Priscilla and Aquila were also with him. At Cenchrea, Paul cut off his hair.* *This showed that* he had made a vow to God. Then he left Priscilla and Aquila. **19** While Paul was in Ephesus, he went into the synagogue and debated with the Jews. **20** The Jews asked Paul to stay longer, but he said no. **21** As Paul was leaving them, he said, "I will come to you again, if God wants me to." And so, Paul sailed away from Ephesus.

22 Paul went down to the city of Caesarea. Then he went up and greeted the congregation *in Jerusalem.* After that, he went down to the city of Antioch *in Syria.* **23** Paul stayed in Antioch for a while. Then he left Antioch and went through the countries of Galatia and Phrygia. He traveled from town to town in these areas. He made all of the followers *of Jesus* stronger.

Apollos Helps the Chase

24 A Jewish man named Apollos came to Ephesus. Apollos was born in the city of Alexandria. He was an educated man. His knowledge of the Scriptures was very

---

18:6   a gesture meaning that one would have nothing more to do with those people
18:18   This was similar to a Nazarite vow (Numbers 6:13-21).

powerful.   **25** He had been taught the way of the Lord *Jesus*. Apollos was always very enthusiastic when he talked to people about Jesus. The things he taught about Jesus were correct, but the only immersion that he knew was the immersion which John* *taught*.   **26** Apollos began to speak very boldly in the synagogue. Priscilla and Aquila heard him speak. They took him home and helped him understand the way of God better.   **27** Apollos wanted to go to the country of Achaia. So, the brothers *in Ephesus* helped pay his expenses. They wrote a letter to the followers *of Jesus in Achaia*. In the letter, they asked them to accept Apollos. The followers *of Jesus in Achaia* had believed in Jesus through God's gracious love. When Apollos went there, he helped them very much.   **28** He argued very convincingly in public against the Jews. Apollos clearly proved that they were wrong. He used the Scriptures to show that Jesus is the Messiah.

Chapter 19

In School for Two Years

1 While Apollos was in the city of Corinth, Paul was visiting some places along the northern route to the city of Ephesus. In Ephesus, Paul found some followers *of John*. **2** Paul asked them, "Did you receive the Holy Spirit when you believed?"

These followers answered him, "We have never even heard of a Holy Spirit!"

3 So Paul asked them, "What kind of immersion did you receive?"

They said, "It was the immersion which John *taught.*"

4 Paul said, "John immersed people after they changed their hearts. John told people to trust in the one who would come after him. That person is Jesus."

5 When these followers *of John* heard this, they were immersed by the authority of the Lord Jesus.   **6** Then Paul put his hands on them* and the Holy Spirit came upon them. They began speaking different *inspired* languages and prophesying.   **7** In this group there were about twelve men.

8 Paul went into the synagogue and began to speak very boldly. Paul did this for three months. He debated with the Jews and he tried to persuade them to believe in the kingdom of God,   **9** but some of the Jews became stubborn. They refused to believe. They said some terrible things about The Way. The people heard these things. So Paul left and took the followers *of Jesus* with him. He went to a place where a man named Tyrannus had a school. There he reasoned with people every day.   **10** He did this for two years. Because of this work, every Jew and Greek in the country of Asia* heard the message of the Lord.

It's Miracles, Not Magic—Remember?

11 God was using Paul to perform some very unusual miracles.   **12** Some people carried handkerchiefs and clothes which Paul had worn. The people put these things on sick people. When they did this, the sick people were healed and evil spirits left them.

13-14 Some wandering Jews were also trying to make evil spirits go out of people. The seven sons of Sceva were doing this. (Sceva was an important Jewish priest.) These

---

18:25   See Matthew 3:1-17; Mark 1:1-11; Luke 3:1-22; John 1:6-8,15,19-34; 3:22-30.
19:6   a common practice when appointing people to special duties (Numbers 27:22-23)
19:10   modern Turkey

Jews were using the name of the Lord Jesus to do this. They all said, "By the same Jesus whom Paul proclaims, I order you to come out!"

15 One time, an evil spirit said to these Jews, "I have heard about Jesus, and I know Paul, but who are **you**?"

16 Then the man who had the evil spirit jumped on these Jews. He was much stronger than they were. He beat them up and tore off their clothes. They ran away from that house.   **17** All of the people who lived in Ephesus, Jews and Greeks,* learned about this. They all began to have great respect *for God.* The people were giving more and more honor to the name of the Lord Jesus.   **18** Many of the believers began to admit all of the evil things they had done.   **19** Some of the believers had used magic. These believers brought their books of evil magic and burned them up before everyone. Those books were worth about two million dollars.*   **20** This is how the message of the Lord was influencing more and more people in a powerful way.

Travel Plans

21 After these things, Paul made plans to go to Jerusalem. Paul planned to go through the countries of Macedonia and Achaia, and then go to Jerusalem. Paul thought, "After I visit Jerusalem, I must also visit Rome."   **22** Timothy and Erastus were two of Paul's helpers. Paul sent them ahead to the country of Macedonia, but he stayed in Asia* for a while.

God Chasers Are in the Way of Artemis

23 However, during that time, there was some bad trouble in Ephesus. It was about The Way. This is how it all happened:

24 There was a man named Demetrius, a silver-worker. He made little silver models which looked like the temple of the goddess Artemis.* The men who did work like this made lots of money from it.   **25** Demetrius had a meeting with some other men who did the same kind of work. Demetrius told them, "Men, you know that we make a lot of money from our business.   **26** But, Paul has influenced many people. He has done this in Ephesus and all over the whole country of Asia!* Look at what this man Paul is doing! Listen to what he is saying! He says that the gods which men make are fake! **27** This might turn the people against our work. But there is also another danger: People will begin to think that the temple of the great goddess Artemis is not important! Her greatness will be destroyed. Artemis is the goddess that everyone in Asia and the whole world worships."

28 When the men heard this, they became very angry. The men shouted, "Artemis, the goddess of the city of Ephesus, is great!"   **29** All the people in the city became very upset. The people grabbed Gaius and Aristarchus, men from Macedonia. (These men always traveled with Paul.) Then all the people ran together to the stadium with a single purpose.   **30** Paul wanted to go in and talk to the people, but the followers *of Jesus* wouldn't let him go.   **31** Also, some leaders of the country were friends of Paul. These leaders sent him a message, begging him not to come into the stadium. **32** Some people were yelling one thing and others were yelling something else. The

---

19:17   non-Jews
19:19   literally, 50,000 drachmas. A drachma was worth about one day's pay.
19:22   not the continent of Asia, but rather, a Roman state in Western Turkey
19:24   the Greek name given to one believed to be the mother of gods and men; her Roman name was Diana
19:26   modern Turkey

meeting was very confused. Most of the people didn't even know why they had come there.   33 The Jews had a man stand before the people. His name was Alexander. The Jews told him what to do. Alexander waved his hand, because he wanted to explain things to the people.   34 But when the people *realized* that Alexander was a Jew, they all continued shouting together for two hours. They shouted, "Great is Artemis of Ephesus! Great is Artemis of Ephesus... !"

35 Then the main city official made the crowd be quiet. He said, "Men of Ephesus, everyone knows that Ephesus is the city which keeps the temple of the great goddess, Artemis, and her holy rock.*   36 No one can say that this is not true. So, you should be quiet. You must stop and think before you do anything wrong!   37 They have not stolen anything from her temple or said anything bad about her.   38 We have courts of law and there are judges. Do Demetrius and those men who work with him have a charge against anyone? They should go to the courts! **That** is where they can accuse each other!   39 Is there anything else you want to talk about? Then come to the regular town meeting of the people. It can be decided there.   40 I say this because someone might see this trouble today and say that we were rioting. We could not explain all of this trouble, because there is no real reason for this mob."   41 After the official said these things, he told the people to go home. Then all of the people left.

Chapter 20

Paul Really Gets Around

1 When the trouble stopped, Paul invited the followers *of Jesus* to come visit him. He wanted to encourage them. Then Paul said good-bye and left. He went to the country of Macedonia.   2 He encouraged the followers in the different places on his way through Macedonia. He told the followers many things. Then Paul went to Achaia.* 3 He stayed there three months. He was ready to sail for Syria, but some Jews were planning something evil against him. So, Paul decided to go back to Syria through Macedonia.   4 Some men were with him. They were:

Sopater (*the son of* Pyrrhus, from the town of Berea),
Aristarchus and Secundus (from the city of Thessalonica),
Gaius (from the town of Derbe),
Timothy,
Tychicus and Trophimus (from Asia).*

5 These men went first, ahead of Paul. They were waiting for us in the city of Troas. 6 We sailed from the city of Philippi after the Jewish Festival of Unleavened Bread.* We met these men in Troas five days later. We stayed there for seven days.

Paul Talks All Night

7 On Sunday,* we all met together to eat the supper of the Lord.* Paul was talking with the group. He was ready to leave the next day. Paul continued his speech until

---

19:35	literally, from the sky. It was probably a meteorite.
20:2	the southern part of Greece
20:4	modern Turkey
20:6	a yearly feast when bread without yeast was eaten for seven days (Leviticus 23:4-8)
20:7	literally, the first day of the week. According to Jewish custom, the first day of the week began at sundown (when the Sabbath ended) and lasted until the next sundown.
20:7	literally, to break bread, a Greek idiom usually referring to the Lord's supper

midnight.   **8** There were many torches in the room where we were gathered. The room was upstairs.   **9** There was a young man named Eutychus sitting in the window. As Paul talked on and on, Eutychus became sleepier and sleepier. Finally, Eutychus went to sleep and fell out of the window. He fell to the ground from the third floor. When they got to him, he was dead.   **10** Paul went down to Eutychus. He kneeled down and hugged him. Paul said to the other believers, "Don't worry. He is alive now."   **11-12** They brought the young man inside. He was alive, and they were very much comforted. Paul went upstairs again. After he broke off some of the bread and ate it, Paul spoke to them a long time. When he finished talking, it was early morning.

On the Way Back to Jerusalem . . .

13 We sailed for the town of Assos. We went first, ahead of Paul. He planned to meet us in Assos and join us on the ship there. Paul told us to do this, because he wanted to walk to Assos.   **14** Later we met Paul at Assos and there he came onto the ship with us. Then we all went to the town of Mitylene.   **15** The next day, we sailed away from Mitylene and came to a place near the island of Chios. The next day we sailed to the island of Samos. A day later we came to the town of Miletus.   **16** Paul had already decided not to stop at Ephesus. He didn't want to stay in Asia* too long. He was hurrying, because he wanted to be in Jerusalem on the day of Pentecost,* if that were possible.

Fond Farewells

17 Paul sent a message back to Ephesus from Miletus. He invited the elders of the congregation in Ephesus to come to him.   **18-19** When the elders came, Paul said to them, "Do you remember when I came to you on my first day in Asia?* I stayed with you the whole time. The Jewish leaders planned evil things against me. Although this troubled me very much (sometimes I even cried), I always served the Lord. I never thought about myself first.   **20** I always did what was best for you, telling you the Good News about Jesus in public and also in your homes.   **21** I told both Jewish and non-Jewish* people to change their hearts *and turn* to God. I told them all to trust in our Lord Jesus.   **22** But now I must obey the Holy Spirit and go to Jerusalem. I don't know what will happen to me there.   **23** I only know that, in every town, the Holy Spirit warns me that troubles and even jail wait for me.   **24** My life doesn't matter. The most important thing is that I finish the race—the work which the Lord Jesus gave me to do, telling people the Good News about God's gracious love.

25 "And now, listen to me. I know that none of you will ever see my face again! During the whole time I was with you, I was preaching to you about the kingdom *of God*. **26** So, today I can tell you one thing that I am sure of: I'm not to blame, if some of you

---

20:7   literally, the first day of the week. According to Jewish custom, the first day of the week began at sundown (when the Sabbath ended) and lasted until the next sundown.

20:7   literally, to break bread, a Greek idiom usually referring to the Lord's supper

20:16   modern Turkey

20:16   a Jewish feast of the wheat harvest which was held around early June. It came in the springtime 50 days after the Passover feast. Many people would gather in Jerusalem. It would be a good opportunity to tell the Good News about Jesus.

20:18   modern Turkey

20:21   literally, Greeks

will not be saved!*   **27** I can say this, because I **know** I told you everything that God wants you to know.   **28** Watch out for yourselves and for all the people God has given you. The Holy Spirit chose you to guard this flock. You must shepherd the Lord's people whom he bought with his own blood.*   **29** I know that after I leave, some men will come into your group. They will be like vicious wolves, trying to destroy the flock.   **30** Also, men from your own group will begin to teach things which are wrong, leading some followers away from the truth.   **31** So, be alert! Always remember: I was with you for three years. During this time, I never stopped warning each one of you. I taught you night and day. I often cried over you.

32 "Now I am giving you to God. I am depending on the message of God's gracious love to make you strong. That story is able to give you the blessings which God gives to all His holy people.   **33** When I was with you, I never wanted anybody's money or fine clothes.   **34** You know I always worked to take care of my own needs and the needs of the people who were with me.   **35** I always showed you that you should work as I did and help people who are weak. I taught you to remember the words of the Lord Jesus. Jesus once said, 'You will be happier when you give than when you receive.' "

36 When Paul finished saying these things, he kneeled down and they all prayed together.   **37-38** They all cried and cried and cried. They were especially sad, because Paul had said that they would never see his face again. They hugged Paul and kept on kissing him. They went with him to the ship to say good-bye.

Chapter 21

Where There's God's Will, There's a Way

1 After we all said good-bye to the elders, we sailed away, straight for Cos Island. The next day we went to the island of Rhodes. From Rhodes we went to Patara.   **2** At Patara, we found a ship which was going to Phoenicia. We went aboard the ship and sailed away.   **3** We sailed near the island of Cyprus. We could see it on the north side, but we did not stop. We sailed to the country of Syria. We stopped at the city of Tyre, because the ship needed to unload its cargo there.   **4** In Tyre, we found some followers *of Jesus*, and we stayed with them for seven days. They warned Paul not to go to Jerusalem because of what the Holy Spirit had told them.   **5** But when we finished our visit, we left and continued our trip. All the followers *of Jesus*, including the women and children, came outside the city with us to say good-bye. We all kneeled down on the beach and prayed.   **6** Then we said good-bye to one another. We went aboard the ship, and they went back home.

7 We continued our trip from Tyre and went to the city of Ptolemais. We greeted the brothers there and stayed with them one day.   **8** The next day we left Ptolemais and went to the city of Caesarea. We went into the home of Philip and stayed with him. Philip was a preacher of the Good News. He was one of the seven *servants*.*   **9** He had four virgin daughters. These daughters had the gift of prophesying.   **10** After we had stayed there for many days, a prophet named Agabus came down from Judea.   **11** He came to us and borrowed Paul's belt. Then Agabus used the belt to bind his own

20:26   literally, "I am clean (innocent) from the blood of all."
20:28   Some manuscripts have "God" for "Lord." Some manuscripts have: "the blood of His own."
21:8   See Acts 6:3.

hands and feet. Agabus said, "The Holy Spirit tells me, 'This is how the Jewish leaders in Jerusalem will bind the man who wears this belt.* Then they will hand him over to non-Jewish people.' "

12 We all heard these words. So, we and the local followers *of Jesus* kept begging Paul not to go up to Jerusalem. **13** But Paul asked, "Why are you crying? Why are you making me so sad? I am ready to be bound in Jerusalem. I am even ready to **die** for the name of the Lord Jesus!"

14 We could not persuade him *to stay away from Jerusalem*. So, we stopped *trying* and said, "We pray that what the Lord wants will be done."

15 After this, we got ready and started on our way up to Jerusalem. **16** Some of the followers *of Jesus* from Caesarea went with us. These followers took us to the home of Mnason, a man from Cyprus. Mnason was one of the first people to become a follower *of Jesus*. They took us to his home, so that we could stay with him.

Meanwhile, Back in Jerusalem

17 Later we arrived in Jerusalem, the brothers there were very happy to see us. **18** The next day Paul went with us to visit James. All of the elders were there, too. **19** Paul greeted all of them. Then he told them exactly how God had used him to do many things among non-Jewish people. **20** When the leaders heard these things, they gave glory to God. Then they said to Paul, "Brother, you can see that thousands of Jews have become believers, and they all think it is very important to obey the law *of Moses*. **21** These Jews have heard that you tell Jews who live in other countries among non-Jews to abandon the law of Moses. They heard that you tell those Jews not to circumcise* their children and not to obey Jewish customs. **22** Therefore what should we do? The Jewish believers here will learn that you have come. **23** We advise you to do this: Four of our men have made a vow to God. **24** Take these men with you and share in their washing ceremony.* Pay their expenses, so that they may shave their heads.* Do this and it will prove to everyone that the things they have heard about you are not true. They will see that you yourself respect the law *of Moses* in your own life. **25** But, as for non-Jewish believers, we have already sent a letter. The letter said:

"Do not eat food which has been given to idols.
Do not taste blood.
Do not eat animals which have been strangled.
Do not commit any kind of sexual sin."

26 Then Paul took the four men with him. The next day Paul shared in the washing ceremony. Then he went to the temple. He *announced* the time when the days of the cleansing ceremony would be ended. On the last day, an offering would be given for each of the men.

What a Riot!

27 The seven days were almost over, but some Jews from Asia* saw Paul at the temple. They stirred up the whole crowd. They grabbed Paul **28** and shouted, "Men of

---

21:11   referring to Paul
21:21   to cut off the foreskin of the male sex organ as a sign of God's agreement with Israel (See Genesis 17:9-14.)
21:24   See Numbers 6:2-21.
21:24   A Nazarite who contacted a dead body would do this (Numbers 6:4; 19:11-19).
21:27   modern Turkey

218

Israel, help us! This is the man who is teaching things which are against the law *of Moses*, against our people, and against this place. This man is teaching these things to all people everywhere. And now he has even brought some non-Jewish* men into the temple! He has made this *holy* place unclean!"   **29** (These Jews said this, because they had seen Trophimus with Paul in Jerusalem. Trophimus was a *non-Jewish* man from the city of Ephesus. They thought that Paul had taken him into the temple.)

30 All of the people in Jerusalem became very upset. They all ran together and grabbed Paul. They dragged him out of the temple courtyard. Immediately the temple gates were closed.   **31** The people were trying to kill Paul. Then the commander of the *Roman* army *in Jerusalem* learned that there was much confusion in the whole city of Jerusalem.   **32** Right away the commander ran down to the place where the people were. He brought some officers and soldiers with him. The people saw the commander and his soldiers. Then they stopped beating Paul.   **33** The commander went to Paul and arrested him. He ordered his soldiers to bind Paul with two chains. Then the commander asked, "Who is this man? What has he done *wrong*?"   **34** Some people there were yelling one thing and other people were yelling something else. Because of all this confusion and shouting, the commander could not learn the truth about what had happened. So the commander ordered the soldiers to take Paul to the fortress.*   **35-36** All of the people were following them. When the soldiers came to the steps, they had to carry Paul. They did this *to protect him*, because the people were so wild. The people shouted, "Kill him!"

37 The soldiers were ready to take Paul into the fortress, but Paul spoke to the commander. Paul asked, "Do I have the right to say something to you?"

The commander said, "Oh! Do you speak Greek?   **38** Then you are not the man I thought you were. I thought you were the Egyptian man who started some trouble *against the government* not long ago. He led 4,000 murderers out to the desert."

39 Paul said, "No, I am a Jew from Tarsus, in the country of Cilicia. I am a citizen of that important city. Please, let me speak to the people."

40 The commander allowed Paul to speak to the people. So Paul stood on the steps. He made signs with his hands, so that the people would be quiet. The people became even quieter when Paul used the Aramaic language to speak to them.*

Chapter 22

Paul Is Never Speechless

1 Paul said, "My brothers and fathers, listen to me! I will make my defense to you now."   **2** The Jews heard Paul speaking in Aramaic,* so they became very quiet. Paul said,   **3** "I am a Jew. I was born in Tarsus in the country of Cilicia. I grew up in this city of Jerusalem. I was a student of Gamaliel.* He carefully taught me everything about the law of our ancestors. I was very serious about serving God, the same as all of you here today.   **4** I persecuted *the people who believed in* the way *of Jesus*. Some of them were killed *because of me*. I arrested men and women, and I put them in jail.

21:28   literally, Greeks
21:34   the tower of Antonio at the northwest corner of the temple courtyard. Part of the Roman army was stationed there.
21:40   a language much more dear to them than Greek, because it was their own language
22:2   the native language of the Jews
22:3   Acts 5:34

5 The high priest and the whole council of the Jewish elders can tell you that this is true! One time these leaders gave me some letters. The letters were to the Jewish brothers in the city of Damascus. I was going there to arrest *the followers of Jesus* and bring them back to Jerusalem for punishment."

How I Met Jesus

6 "However, something happened to me on my way to Damascus. It was about noon, when I came close to the city. Suddenly, a bright light from the sky shined all around me. **7** I fell to the ground. I heard a voice saying to me: 'Saul, Saul, why do you persecute me?' **8** I asked, 'Who are you, Lord?' The voice answered, 'I am Jesus from Nazareth, the one you are persecuting.' **9-10** I said, 'What should I do, Lord?' The Lord *Jesus* answered, 'Get up and go into Damascus. There you will be told about all of the things I have planned for you to do.' The men who were with me did not understand the voice, but they saw the light. **11** I couldn't see, because the bright light had blinded me. So, the men led me into Damascus.

12 *"In Damascus*, a man named Ananias* came to me. He was a devout man; he obeyed the law *of Moses*. All of the Jews who lived there respected him. **13** Ananias came to me, stood over me, and said, 'Brother Saul, you can see again!' At that moment I was able to see him. **14** Ananias told me, 'The God of our ancestors chose you a long time ago to know His plan. God wanted you to see the righteous one* and to hear words from his mouth. **15** You will be his witness to all persons. You will tell them about the things you have seen and heard. **16** Now, don't wait any longer. Rise up, get yourself immersed and get your sins washed away, trusting in his name.'

17 "Later I came back to Jerusalem. I was praying in the temple courtyard, and I saw a vision. **18** I saw Jesus, and he said to me: 'Hurry. Leave Jerusalem now! The people here won't accept the truth about me.' **19** I said, 'But Lord, the people know that I was the one who put the believers in jail and beat them. I went through all the synagogues *to find and arrest* those who believe in you. **20** The people also know that I was there when Stephen, your witness, was killed. I stood there and agreed that they should kill him. I even held the robes of the men who were killing him!' **21** But Jesus said to me, 'Leave now. I will send you far away to non-Jewish people.' "

22 The people stopped listening when Paul spoke this last sentence. They all shouted, "Kill him! Get him out of the world! A man like this should not be allowed to live!" **23** They yelled and threw off their robes. They threw dust into the air.* **24** Then the commander ordered the soldiers to take Paul into the fortress. He told the soldiers to beat Paul. The commander wanted to force Paul to tell him why the people were shouting against him like this. **25** As the soldiers were tying Paul, preparing to beat him, Paul asked an officer who was standing there, "Do you have the right to beat a Roman citizen who has not been proven guilty?"

26 When the officer heard this, he went to the commander and told him about it. The officer asked, "Do you know what you are doing? This man is a Roman citizen!"

27 The commander came to Paul and asked, "Tell me, are you really a Roman citizen?"

Paul answered, "Yes."

22:12 There are three different men named Ananias in Acts (5:1; 9:10; 23:2).
22:14 Jesus
22:23 a way of showing extreme anger
22:25 Roman citizens could not be tortured or beaten until they had a fair trial.

28 The commander said, "I paid a lot of money to become a Roman citizen." But Paul said, "I was born a citizen."

29 The men who were preparing to torture Paul moved away from him immediately. The commander was afraid, because he had already bound Paul, and Paul was a Roman citizen!

God Chasers Confront Religion

30 The next day, the commander decided to learn why the Jews were accusing Paul. So, he commanded the most important priests and the entire Jewish Council to meet together. Then he brought Paul out and took his chains off. Then he made Paul stand before their meeting.

Chapter 23

1 Paul looked straight at the Jewish Council and said, "*My Jewish* brothers, I have always lived my life before God in all good conscience, and that includes today!"
2 Ananias,* the high priest, was there. Ananias *heard Paul and* told the men who were standing near Paul to hit him on the mouth.   **3** Paul said to Ananias, "God will hit you, too! You are like a *dirty* wall which has been painted white! You sit there and judge me, using the law *of Moses*, yet you are telling them to hit me. That is against the law!"

4 The men standing near Paul said to him, "You must not talk like that to God's high priest!"

5 Paul said, "Brothers, I didn't know this man was the high priest. It is written in the Scriptures,

'You must not say evil things about a ruler of your people.' "   *Exodus 22:28*

6 Some of the men in the meeting were Sadducees and some others were Pharisees. Paul knew this. Therefore, he said to them, so that everyone could hear, "My brothers, I am a Pharisee and my father was a Pharisee! I am on trial here, because I believe that people will rise from death!"

7 When Paul said this, it caused a big argument between the Pharisees and the Sadducees. The group was divided.   **8** (The Sadducees believe after people die, they cannot live again. The Sadducees also teach that there are no angels or spirits, but the Pharisees believe in all these things.)   **9** All these Jews began shouting louder and louder. Some of the teachers of the law, who were Pharisees, stood up and argued: "We find nothing wrong with this man! Perhaps an angel or a spirit **did** speak to him *on the road to Damascus!*"

10 The argument turned into a fight. The commander was afraid that the Jews would tear Paul to pieces. So the commander ordered the soldiers to go down and take Paul away from them and put him in the fortress.

11 The next night the Lord *Jesus* came and stood by Paul. He said, "Be strong! You have told the people in Jerusalem the truth about me. You must also go to Rome to do the same thing there!"

A Plot to Kill Paul

12 The next morning some of the Jews made a plan. They wanted to kill Paul. These Jews vowed to themselves that they would not eat or drink anything until they had killed Paul!   **13** There were more than 40 Jews who plotted this.   **14** They went and talked

---

23:2   There are three different men named Ananias in Acts (5:1; 9:10; 23:2).

to the most important priests and the older Jewish leaders. These Jews said, "We have vowed to ourselves that we won't eat or drink until we have killed Paul! **15** So, this is what we want you to do: Send a message to the commander from you and the Jewish Council. Tell the commander that you want him to bring Paul out to you, as if you want to ask Paul more questions. While he is on the way here, we will be waiting to kill him."

16 But Paul's nephew heard about this plan. He went to the fortress and told Paul. **17** Then Paul called one of the officers and said to him, "Take this young man to the commander. He has a message for him." **18** So, the officer brought Paul's nephew to the commander. The officer said, "The prisoner Paul asked me to bring this young man to you. He wants to tell you something."

19 The commander led the young man to a place where they could be alone. The commander asked, "What do you want to tell me?"

20 The young man said, "The Jewish leaders have decided to ask you to bring Paul down to their council tomorrow. They want you to think that they plan to ask Paul more questions. **21** But don't believe them! There are more than 40 Jews who are hiding and waiting to kill Paul. They have all vowed not to eat or drink until they have killed him! They are now waiting for you to say yes."

22 The commander ordered him, "Don't tell anyone that you have told me this." Then the commander sent the young man away.

23 After this the commander called two officers. He said to them, "I need some men to go to Caesarea. Get 200 soldiers ready. Also, get 70 horsemen and 200 men to carry spears. Be ready to leave at nine o'clock tonight. **24** Get some horses for Paul to ride. He must be safely taken to Governor Felix." **25** The commander wrote a letter. This is what it said:

26 From Claudius Lysias

To the Most Excellent Governor Felix:

Greetings.

27 The Jews had taken this man, and they were about to kill him, but I learned that he is a Roman citizen.* I went with my soldiers and saved him. **28** I wanted to know why they were accusing him, so I brought him before their council. **29** This is what I learned: The Jews said that Paul did some things which were wrong, but these charges were about their own Jewish laws. None of these things were worthy of jail or death. **30** I was told that some of the Jews were plotting to kill Paul. Therefore, I sent him to you. I also ordered those Jews to tell you the things they have against him.

31 The soldiers did the things they were told. They got Paul and took him to the town of Antipatris that night. **32** The next day, the horsemen went with Paul to Caesarea, but the soldiers and the spearmen went back to the fortress *in Jerusalem.* **33** The horsemen entered Caesarea and gave the letter to the governor.* Then they gave Paul to him. **34** The governor read the letter. He asked Paul, "What country are you from?" He learned that Paul was from Cilicia. **35** The governor said, "I will hear your case when the Jews who are accusing you come here, too." Then the governor gave orders for Paul to be kept in the palace. (This building had been built by Herod *the Great.*)

23:27   Roman citizens could not be tortured or beaten until they had a fair trial.
23:33   Felix

Chapter 24

In Caesarea

1 Five days later, Ananias went down *to the city of Caesarea*. Ananias was the high priest. He also brought some of the older Jewish leaders and a lawyer named Tertullus. They went to Caesarea to make charges against Paul before the governor. **2** Paul was called into the meeting, and Tertullus began to make his charges.

Tertullus said, "Our people have enjoyed much peace, because you are a wise reformer,* **3** Most Excellent Felix. We are very thankful to accept these things from you, always and in every place. **4** But, I don't want to use any more of your time. So I will say only a few words. Please be patient. **5** This man Paul is a trouble-maker. He stirs up trouble among the Jews everywhere in the world. He is a ringleader of the Nazarene sect.* **6** He was also trying to make the temple unclean when we stopped him. **7** * **8** You can decide whether all of our charges are true or not. Ask him some questions yourself." **9** The other Jews agreed. They said, "These things are really true!"

10 The governor signaled for Paul to speak. So Paul answered, "*Governor Felix*, I know that you have been a judge over this nation* for many years. So I am happy to defend myself before you. **11** I went up to worship in Jerusalem only twelve days ago. You can learn for yourself that this is true. **12** These Jews who are accusing me didn't find me arguing with anyone in the temple. I wasn't stirring up a crowd. And I wasn't causing trouble or arguing in the synagogues or any place else in the city. **13** They cannot prove the things they are claiming against me now. **14** However, I will admit this to you: I worship the God of our ancestors as a follower of the way *of Jesus*. The Jewish leaders claim that The Way is a 'sect,' but I too believe everything which is taught in the law *of Moses* and everything which is written in the books of the prophets. **15** I have the same belief in God that these Jews have—the hope that all people, good and bad, will be raised from death. **16** This is why I always try to do what I believe is right before God and man.

17 I was away *from Jerusalem* for many years. I went back there to bring money to my people and to give some offerings. **18** I was doing this when some Jews found me in the temple courtyard. I had just finished the cleansing ceremony. No crowd was gathered around me. I had not caused any trouble. **19** However, some Jews from Asia* were there. They should be here, standing before you. If I have really done anything wrong, those Jews from Asia are the ones who should accuse me. **20** Ask these Jews here if they found any wrong in me when I stood before the Jewish Council *in Jerusalem*. **21** I did say one thing when I stood before them: I said, loud enough for all to hear, 'You are judging me today because I believe that people will rise from death!' "

22 Felix already understood much about the way *of Jesus*. He *stopped the hearing* *and* said, "When commander Lysias comes here, I will decide on these things later."

24:2 a good leader who brings improvement to government
24:5 Jesus grew up in Nazareth (Luke 2:39-52).
24:7 Some manuscripts have part of the last of verse 6, all of verse 7, and the beginning of verse 8: "We planned to judge him according to our own law,[7] but the commander Lysias came and, with great violence, took him from us[8] Then Lysias gave orders that his accusers should come before you."
24:10 Israel
24:19 modern Turkey
24:22 a session in which testimony is heard by a judge before a formal trial

23 Felix ordered the officer to keep Paul guarded, but he told the officer to give him some freedom and to let Paul's friends bring the things that he needed.

Paul on Call

24 After a few days, Felix came with his wife, Drusilla. She was a Jewish woman.* Felix asked for Paul to be brought to him. He listened to Paul talk about believing in Christ Jesus. 25 However, Felix became afraid when Paul spoke about such things as righteousness, self-control, and the Judgment *Day*, which will come in the future. Felix said, "Go away now! When I have time, I will call for you." 26 Felix hoped that Paul would pay him a bribe. So, Felix sent for Paul often and talked with him.

27 After two years, Portius Festus became governor. So, Felix was no longer governor, but Felix left Paul in prison, because he wanted to do something to please the Jewish leaders.

Chapter 25

On the Judgment Seat

1 So, Festus became governor, and three days later he went up from Caesarea to Jerusalem. 2 The most important priests and the important Jewish leaders made charges against Paul before Festus. 3 They asked Festus to do something for them; they wanted Festus to send Paul back to Jerusalem. They had a plan to kill Paul along the way. 4 But Festus answered, "No! Paul will be kept in Caesarea. I myself will go to Caesarea soon. 5 Some of your leaders should go down with me. They can accuse the man *there in Caesarea*, if he really has done something wrong."

6 Festus stayed in Jerusalem another eight or ten days. Then he went back down to Caesarea. The next day Festus ordered the soldiers to bring Paul before him. Festus was seated on the judgment seat. 7 Paul came into the room. The Jews who had come down from Jerusalem stood around him. They said that Paul had done many serious crimes, but they couldn't prove any of them. 8 This is what Paul said to defend himself: "I have done nothing wrong against the Jewish law, against the temple, or against Caesar!"*

9 However, Festus wanted to please the Jewish leaders. So he asked Paul, "Do you want to go up to Jerusalem? Do you want me to judge you there on these charges?"

10 Paul said, "I am standing at Caesar's judgment seat **now**. This is where I **must** be judged! I have done nothing wrong to the Jews; you know this is true. 11 If I have done anything wrong, and the law says I must die, then I agree that I should die. I don't ask to be spared from death. But if these charges are not true, then no one can give me to these Jews. No! I want Caesar* to hear my case!"

12 Festus talked about this with his advisors. Then he said, "You have asked to see Caesar, so to Caesar you will go!"

Agrippa and Bernice

13 A few days later, King *Herod* Agrippa *II* and Bernice* came to Caesarea to visit Festus. 14 They stayed there many days. Festus told the king about Paul's case. Festus said, "There is a man whom Felix left in prison. 15 When I went to Jerusalem,

---

24:24   She was the younger sister of Herod Agrippa II. (See Acts 25:13.)
25:8   The title of the supreme Roman rulers. "Caesar" became the title of each emperor.
25:11   Every Roman citizen had the right to appeal his case to the emperor in Rome.
25:13   She was another sister of Herod Agrippa II. (See Acts 24:24.)

the most important priests and the Jewish elders made charges against him. These Jews wanted me to order his death. **16** But I answered, 'When a man is accused of doing something wrong, Romans do not give the man to other people to judge. First, the man must face the people who are accusing him. Then he must be allowed to defend himself against their charges.' **17** Some Jews came here *to Caesarea* for the trial. I didn't waste any time. The next day I sat on the judgment seat and ordered that the man* be brought in. **18** The Jewish leaders stood up and accused him. They didn't accuse him of any of the crimes I thought they would. **19** They wanted to argue about their own religion and about a man named Jesus. Jesus died, but Paul said that Jesus is still alive. **20** I didn't know much about these things, so I didn't ask questions. Instead I asked Paul, 'Do you want to go to Jerusalem and be judged there?' **21** But Paul asked to be kept in Caesarea. He wants a decision from the Emperor.* So I commanded that Paul be held until I could send him to Caesar *in Rome.*"

22 Agrippa said to Festus, "I would also like to hear this man."

Festus said, "You can hear him tomorrow!"

23 The next day Agrippa and Bernice appeared. They dressed and acted like very important people. Agrippa and Bernice, the army leaders, and the important men of Caesarea went into the courtroom. Festus ordered the soldiers to bring Paul in. **24** Festus said, "King Agrippa and all of you men gathered here with us, you see this man. All the Jewish people, here and in Jerusalem, have complained to me about him. They cry out that he should not be allowed to live anymore. **25** When I judged him, I could find nothing wrong. I found no reason to order his death, but he asked to be judged by the Emperor.* So, I have decided to send him *to Rome.* **26** But, I really don't know what to tell* Caesar that this man has done. Therefore, I have brought him before all of you—especially you, King Agrippa. I hope that you will question him, and give me something to write *to Caesar.* **27** I think it is foolish to send a prisoner *to Caesar* without making some charges against him."

Chapter 26

Check Out Paul's Chase

1 Agrippa said to Paul, "You are now permitted to defend yourself."

Then Paul raised his hand* and began to speak. **2** He said, "King Agrippa, I will answer all of the charges that the Jews make against me. I think it is a privilege that I can stand here before you today and do this. **3** I am very happy to talk to you, because you know much about all of the Jewish customs and issues. Please listen to me patiently.

4 "All the Jewish people know about my whole life. They know the way I lived, from the beginning among my own people and later in Jerusalem. **5** These Jews have known me for a long time. If they want to, they can tell you that I was a Pharisee. And the Pharisees obey the laws of the Jewish faith more carefully than any other group of

---

25:17   Paul
25:21   the Greek title for "Caesar" is used here.
25:25   the Greek title for "Caesar" is used here.
25:26   literally, write
26:1   a common gesture calling for attention

Jewish people.   **6-7** Now I am on trial because I believe in God's promise which all the twelve tribes of our people hope to receive. For this hope, the Jews earnestly serve God day and night. O King, the Jews have accused me because I hope for this same promise!

8 "Why do you think it is impossible for God to raise people from death?   **9** Even I thought that I must do many things against the name of Jesus of Nazareth.   **10** And in Jerusalem I did persecute the holy people. The most important priests gave me authority to put many of these people in jail. When they were being killed, I voted for it.   **11** In every synagogue, I punished them. I tried to force them to say evil things against *Jesus*. I was so crazed against these people that I hunted them down to other towns."

Speaking of the Chase

12 "Once the most important priests gave me permission and authority to go to the city of Damascus.   **13** It was noon, O King. I was on my way to Damascus. I saw a light from the sky. It was brighter than the sun. The light shined all around me and the men who were traveling with me.   **14** We all fell to the ground. Then I heard a voice talking to me in the Aramaic language.* The voice said, 'Saul, Saul, why are you persecuting me? By fighting me you are only hurting yourself.'*   **15** I said, 'Who are you, Lord?' The Lord said, 'I am Jesus. I am the one you are persecuting.   **16** Get up. Stand on your feet! I have chosen you to be my servant. You will be my witness telling people the things that you have seen and the things I will show you. This is why I have appeared to you *today*.   **17** I will rescue you from *your own* people and from non-Jewish people to whom I am sending you.   **18** You will show the non-Jewish people the truth. They will turn away from darkness to light,* turning from the power of Satan back to God. Then they can receive forgiveness of their sins. They will have a share with those people who have been made holy by trusting in me.' "

And Then

19 *Paul continued speaking*: "King Agrippa, after I had this vision from heaven, I obeyed it.   **20** First, in Damascus, I began to tell Jews that they should change their hearts. I told them to turn back to God. I also went to Jerusalem and to the area around Judea and I said, 'Change your lives and do *good* things. This will show that you have truly changed your hearts.'   **21** This is why some Jews took hold of me and tried to kill me in the temple courtyard.   **22** But God helped me, and He is still helping me today. With God's help I am standing here today and telling *all people*, whether 'important' or 'unimportant,' the things I have seen. I am saying nothing new; I am only saying the same things which Moses and the prophets said would take place: **23** They said that the Messiah would die and be the first to rise from death; and that the Messiah would bring light to Jewish people and non-Jewish people."

Not Easily Persuaded

24 While Paul was saying these things to defend himself, Festus shouted, "Paul, are you crazy? Too much education has made you crazy!"

26:14   The Jews had a special reverence for their native language.
26:14   literally, It is hard for you to kick against the pricks.
26:18   or, from sin to righteousness

25 Paul said, "Most Excellent Festus, I'm not crazy. The things I say are true. My words are not the words of a foolish man; I am serious. 26 King Agrippa knows about these matters. I can speak freely to him. I know that he has heard about all of these things, because these things happened where everyone could see.* 27 King Agrippa, do you believe what the prophets wrote? I **know** you believe!"

28 King Agrippa asked Paul, "Do you think you can persuade me to become a Christian so easily?"

29 Paul said, "It doesn't matter whether it is easy or hard; I pray to God that not only you, but everyone who is listening to me today, could be like me—except for these chains!"

30 King Agrippa, Governor Festus, Bernice, and all of the people sitting with them got up 31 and left the room. They began to talk to each other. They said, "This man should not be killed or put in prison; he has done nothing **that** bad!" 32 And Agrippa said to Festus, "We could have let this man go free, but he has already asked to be judged by Caesar."*

Chapter 27

They Set Sail for Italy

1 It was decided that we would sail for Italy. A *Roman* officer named Julius guarded Paul and some other prisoners. Julius served in the Emperor's regiment. 2 We went aboard a ship which was from the city of Adramyttium. It was ready to sail for ports along the coast of Asia.* Then we set sail. Aristarchus went with us. He was a man from the city of Thessalonica in Macedonia. 3 The next day we came to the city of Sidon. Julius was very kind to Paul. He gave Paul freedom to go visit Paul's friends who took care of his needs. 4 We left the city of Sidon. We sailed south of the island of Cyprus, because the wind was *blowing* against us. 5 We went across the sea next to Cilicia and Pamphylia. Then we came to the town of Myra in Lycia. 6 In Myra the *Roman* officer found a ship from the city of Alexandria. This ship was going to Italy. So he put us on it.

7 We sailed slowly for many days. It was hard for us to reach the town of Cnidus, because the wind was blowing against us. We could not go any further that way. So we sailed past the south side of the island of Crete, near the town of Salmone. 8 We sailed along the coast, but sailing was hard. Then we came to a place called Safe Harbors. The town of Lasea was near there.

9 However, we had lost much time. It was now dangerous to sail, because it was after mid-September.* So Paul warned them, 10 "Men, I can see that there will be much destruction on this trip. The ship and the things on this ship will be lost. Even our lives may be lost!" 11 But the captain of the ship and its owner didn't agree with Paul. The *Roman* officer believed what they said, rather than what Paul said. 12 That harbor was not a good place for the ship to stay for the winter. Therefore, most of the men decided that the ship should leave there. The men hoped that we could go to Phoenix. The ship could stay there for the winter. (Phoenix was a city on the island of Crete. It had a harbor which faced southwest and northwest.)

26:26   literally, have not been done in a corner
26:32   The title of supreme Roman rulers. "Caesar" became the title of each emperor.
27:2   modern Turkey
27:9   literally, the Fast (Yom Kippur)

Against the Wind

13 Then a good wind began to blow from the south. The men on the ship thought, "This is the wind we wanted, and now we have it!" So they pulled up anchor. We sailed very close to the island of Crete, **14** but then a very strong wind named "the Northeaster"* came down from the island. **15** This wind took the ship and carried it away. The ship couldn't hold against the wind. So, we stopped trying to resist and let the wind blow us. **16** We went below a small island named Cauda. Then* we were able to bring in the lifeboat. (It was very hard to do this.) **17** After the men took the lifeboat in, they tied ropes around the ship to hold the ship together. The men were afraid that the ship would hit the sandbanks of Syrtis.* So they lowered the sail and let the wind carry the ship along. **18** The next day the storm was blowing us so hard that the men threw some things out of the ship* *to make the ship lighter.* **19** A day later they threw out the ship's equipment. **20** For many days we couldn't see the sun or the stars *to guide us.* The storm was very bad. We lost all hope of staying alive—we thought we would die.

21 For a long time the men didn't eat. Then one day Paul stood up before them and said, "Men, I told you not to leave Crete. You should have listened to me. Then you would not have had all of this trouble and loss. **22** But now I am telling you to cheer up. None of you will die! However, the ship will be lost. **23** Last night an angel came to me from the true God. This is the God I worship. I am His. **24** God's angel said, 'Paul, don't be afraid! You must stand before Caesar. And God *has promised* to give you something good: He will save the lives of all those sailing with you.' **25** So men, cheer up! I trust in God. Everything will happen just as His angel told me. **26** But, we will run aground on an island."

27 On the 14th night, we were floating around in the Adriatic Sea.* The sailors sensed that we were close to land. **28** They threw a rope into the water with a weight on the end of it. They found that the water was 120 feet deep. They went a little further and threw the rope in again. It was 90 feet deep. **29** The sailors were afraid that we would hit the rocks. So, they threw four anchors into the water. Then they prayed for daylight to come. **30** Some of the sailors wanted to leave the ship. They lowered the lifeboat to the water, trying to make the other men think that they were throwing out more anchors from the front of the ship. **31** But Paul told the officer and the other soldiers, "If these men don't stay in the ship, then your lives cannot be saved!" **32** So the soldiers cut the ropes and let the lifeboat fall into the water.

33 Just before dawn, Paul started persuading everyone to eat something. He said, "For the past two weeks you have been waiting and watching. You have not eaten for 14 days. **34** Now, I beg you, eat something! You need it to stay alive. Not one of you will lose even one hair of your head." **35** After he said this, Paul took some bread and, in front of them all, thanked God for it. He broke off a piece and began to eat. **36** All of the men felt better. They all started to eat, too. **37** (There were 276 people on the ship.) **38** We ate all we wanted. Then we began to make the ship lighter by throwing the wheat into the sea.

27:14   literally, Euraquilo
27:16   while the island protected them from the strong wind
27:17   an area off the African coast where many ships sank
27:18   They threw the cargo overboard.
27:27   literally, Adria, the central part of the Mediterranean Sea

The Ship Was a Wreck

39 When daylight came, the sailors saw land, but they did not know where we were. We saw a bay with a beach. The sailors wanted to sail the ship to the beach, if they could. **40** So the men cut the ropes to the anchors and left the anchors in the sea. At the same time, the men untied the ropes which were holding the rudders. Then the men raised the front sail into the wind and sailed toward the beach, **41** but the ship hit a sandbank and the front of the ship stuck there; the ship could not move. Then the big waves began to break up the back of the ship.

42 The soldiers decided to kill the prisoners, so that none of the prisoners could swim away and escape, **43** but the officer wanted to let Paul live. Therefore, he didn't allow the soldiers to kill the prisoners. Julius ordered the people who could swim to jump into the water and swim toward land. **44** Others used wooden boards or pieces from the ship. This is how all of the people got to land. No one died.

Chapter 28

On Malta

1 When we were safe on land, we realized that the island was called Malta. **2** It was very cold and raining. The people who lived there were very kind to us. They made a fire for us and welcomed us all. **3** Paul picked up a pile of sticks for the fire. He was putting the sticks on the fire. Then, because of the heat, a poisonous snake came out and bit him on the hand. **4** The people living on the island saw the snake hanging from Paul's hand. They said to each other, "Surely this man is a murderer! He didn't die in the ocean, but Justice* will not permit him to live." **5** However, Paul shook off the snake into the fire. He was not hurt. **6** The people expected him to swell up or to suddenly fall down dead. For a long time the people waited and watched him, but nothing bad happened to him. So the people changed their minds and they began to say, "He is a god!"

7 There were some fields around that same area. A very important man on the island owned these fields. His name was Publius. He welcomed us into his home. Publius was very kind to us. We stayed in his house for three days. **8** Publius' father was very sick. He had a fever and dysentery, but Paul went to him and prayed for him. Paul put his hands on the man and healed him. **9** After this occurred all the other sick people on the island began to come to Paul. Paul healed them, too. **10-11** The people on the island gave us many honors. We stayed there three months. When we were ready to leave, the people gave us the things we needed.

On the Home Stretch

We got on a ship from the city of Alexandria. The ship had stayed on the island of Malta during the winter. On the front of the ship was the sign for the twin gods.* **12** We stopped at the town of Syracuse and stayed there for three days. **13** Then we came to the town of Rhegium. The next day, a wind began to blow from the southwest, so we were able to leave. A day later we came to the town of Puteoli. **14** We found some brothers there. They asked us to stay with them seven days. Finally, we came *near* to Rome. **15** The believers in Rome heard that we were there. They came out to meet us at the Market of Appius and at the Three Inns. When Paul saw these believers, he felt better. He thanked God.

28:4 blind fate. Here it is personified.
28:11 literally, Dioscuri, sons of Jupiter (Castor and Pollux) who were believed to protect sailors

Paul Helps Others Join the Chase

16 Then we went to Rome. In Rome, though Paul was allowed to live alone, a soldier stayed with Paul to guard him.

17 Three days later Paul sent for some of the most important Jewish leaders. When they came together, Paul said to them, "My Jewish brothers, I have done nothing against our people or against the customs of our ancestors, yet I was arrested in Jerusalem and handed over to the Romans. **18** The Romans asked me many questions, but they couldn't find any reason why I should be put to death. They wanted to let me go free. **19** However, the Jewish leaders there didn't want me to go free. So, I was forced to ask to have my trial before Caesar *in Rome.** I am not accusing my people of anything wrong. **20** This is the reason I wanted to see you and talk with you. I am bound with this chain, because I believe in the hope of Israel."*

21 These Jews answered Paul, "We have received no letters from Judea about you. None of our Jewish brothers who have traveled from Judea brought any news about you or told us anything bad about you. **22** We do want to hear your ideas. We know that people everywhere are speaking against this sect."

23 Paul and the Jewish leaders set a day for a meeting. On that day many more of these Jews met with Paul at his house. Paul spoke to them all day long. He explained to them the truth about the kingdom of God. Using the law of Moses and the writings of the prophets, Paul tried to persuade them about Jesus. **24** Some of the Jews believed the things that Paul said, but others did not believe. **25** They disagreed among themselves. The Jewish leaders were ready to leave, but Paul said one more thing to them: "The Holy Spirit spoke the truth to your ancestors through the prophet Isaiah. He said:

26 'Go to this people and tell them:

You will certainly hear, but you won't understand!

You will certainly see, but you won't understand!

27 The heart of this people has become hard.

They have ears, but they don't listen.

They have shut their eyes.

Otherwise, they would

see with their eyes,

hear with their ears,

understand with their minds,

and then turn.

I would heal them.'

Isaiah 6:9-10

28 "I want you Jewish leaders to know that God has sent His salvation to non-Jewish people. **They** will listen!" **29** *

30 Paul stayed two full years in his own rented house. He welcomed everyone who came to visit him. **31** Paul was preaching about the kingdom of God and teaching about the Lord Jesus Christ. He was very bold. No one tried to stop him from speaking.

28:19   Any Roman citizen had the privilege of standing trial before Caesar himself in Rome. However, it was very expensive to claim this right.

28:20   the resurrection (Compare Acts 26:6-8; 13:32-37.)

28:29   Some manuscripts have verse 29 "And when he had said these things, the Jews left, having a great argument among themselves."

ROMANS

Chapter 1

Paul says, "Hi"

1 From Paul, a servant of Christ Jesus. I was chosen to be an apostle—especially selected for *telling* God's Good News. **2** God promised the Good News in the Holy Scriptures long ago through His prophets. **3** The Good News is about God's Son who, on the physical side, was a descendant of David. **4** But long ago, it was planned that our Lord Jesus Christ be the Son of God with power in a holy, divine way. How? By rising from death! **5** Through Jesus we have received gracious love and the work of apostles, so that for Jesus' name, we *could try to persuade* all non-Jewish people to believe and obey. **6** You are some of them. You were called by Jesus Christ.

7 To all of you in Rome who are loved by God and called to be holy people.

May gracious love and peace come to you from God our Father and from the Lord Jesus Christ.

Our Faith Helps Others

8 First, through Jesus Christ, I thank my God for all of you. People all over the world talk about your faith. **9** My spirit serves God by telling the Good News about His Son. I never forget you. God is my witness. **10** You are always in my prayers. I ask God for some way that I may come to you—if that is what He wants.

11 I want to see you very much, so that I may give you a spiritual gift; it will make you strong— **12** that is, so that we could encourage each other. My faith would help you and your faith would help me.

13 Brothers *and sisters*, I want you to know that I planned to come to you many times. But, until now, I was stopped. I wanted to win some followers* *for Jesus* among you, too, as I have among other non-Jewish people. **14** I feel I must help the civilized* and the uncivilized, the educated and the uneducated people. **15** So, I am eager to tell the Good News to you in Rome, too.

Right With God

16 I am not ashamed of the Good News, because it is God's power for saving anyone who believes it—Jews first, then non-Jews.* **17** The Good News reveals the way that God makes people right. It begins and ends by faith.* This is written:
"The person who is right with God by faith will live *forever*."   *Habakkuk 2:4*

Plainly Seen

18 God's punishment is being revealed from heaven against all sin and ungodliness of people who use sin to hide the truth. **19** What can be known about God is plain to them, because God made it plain to them. **20** Since the beginning of the world, the unseen qualities of God—His unseen power and His divinity—could be clearly seen and understood from what God made. They have no excuse.

1:13   literally, some fruit
1:14   literally, Greeks
1:16   literally, Greeks
1:17   literally, from faith to faith

231

21 Because, even though they knew God, they didn't give God the glory that He should have. They weren't thankful, either. Instead, their thinking became nonsense and their foolish hearts became dark.   **22** They acted as if they were wise, but they became fools.   **23** They exchanged the glory of an undying God for something else—idols that look like a human being, birds, animals with four feet, or reptiles. All these die.

24 So, God handed them over to the sinful desires of their hearts. They became sexually unclean, degrading their own bodies with one another.   **25** They exchanged God's truth for a lie. Instead of worshiping God, the Maker, they worshiped and served something which was made. (God is praised forever. Amen.)   **26** This is why God handed them over to immoral, unnatural drives. Even their females exchanged their natural sexual drives for unnatural ones.   **27** In the same way, males stopped feeling natural sexual drives for females and burned up in their lust for one another—males with males. They do what is shameful, but they must receive in themselves the consequences for this error.

28 Also, since they didn't want to allow God to stay within their circle of knowledge, God handed them over to worthless thinking, to do things they should never do. **29** They are filled with all kinds of wrong, with evil, greed, and depravity. They are full of jealousy, murder, fighting, tricks, malice, gossiping,   **30** slander, hatred for God, insults, pride, boasting, and new ways to do evil. They don't obey their parents. **31** They always break promises. They are stupid and heartless. They show no pity for others.   **32** They know that what God said is right—that people who practice such things deserve death—but they do them anyway. And they even encourage others who are practicing the same things.

Chapter 2

No Excuses

1 Therefore, if anyone condemns someone else, you are without excuse, sir, because when you condemn someone else, you are only condemning yourself. You are always doing the same things that you are condemning!   **2** We know God is right when He condemns people who always do such things.   **3** But, mister, you are judging people who practice such things—yet you are doing the same things! Will you escape God's condemnation?   **4** Do you look down on the wealth of God's kindness, tolerance, and patience? Surely you know that God's kindness is meant to lead you to a change of heart.

5 But your heart is hard and unchanged. You are storing up punishment for yourself on the Day of punishment when God's righteous judgment will be revealed.   **6** God will pay back each person according to the way that person lived.   **7** Eternal life will go to those who, by patiently doing good things, are looking for glory, honor, and life with no end.   **8** But, punishment and anger will go to those who are following wrong, by being selfish and not obeying the truth.   **9** There will be trouble and pain for every human being who does evil. This is true, first for a Jew, then also for a non-Jew.* **10** Glory, honor, and peace will belong to any person who is doing good—for a Jew first, then also a non-Jew.   **11** God treats everyone alike.

12 All people who sin without law will be destroyed without law. All people who sin with *the* law will be judged by *the* law.   **13** The people who only listen to *the* law are not right with God, but the people who obey *the* law are the ones who are made right

---

2:9   literally, Greek

with God.   **14** Sometimes non-Jews (who do not have *the* law) naturally obey things of the law. So, they are their own law (even though they don't have *the* law).   **15** Their actions show that the law is written in their hearts. Their consciences prove this is true, because their thoughts sometimes accuse them and sometimes even excuse them.   **16** On that Day, God will use this Good News of mine to judge the secret things of human beings through Jesus Christ.

The End Doesn't Justify the Means

17 You call yourself a Jew. You depend on *the* law *of Moses*. You brag about being in God.   **18** You know what *God* wants. You choose what is better, because the law teaches you.   **19** You have persuaded yourself that you are a guide to blind men, a light for people in darkness,   **20** a master over uneducated people, and a teacher of those who are not mature, because in the law, you have all knowledge and truth.   **21** So, you teach others, but surely **you** teach yourself. You tell others, "You must not steal!" but do **you** steal?   **22** You say, "You must not commit adultery!" but do **you** commit adultery? You hate false gods, but do **you** rob temples?   **23** You brag about being in *the* law, but are **you** bringing shame on the law of God by not obeying it?   **24** This is written:

"They say evil things about the name of God among the people of the world because of you."
Ezekiel 36:20

25 True, being circumcised* is important, if you always follow *the* law. However, if you don't obey *the* law, it is as if you had never been circumcised.   **26** Therefore, if a man who is not circumcised obeys the things that the law says are right, God will regard his uncircumcision as if it were circumcision!   **27** The man who is not physically circumcised, but who obeys the law, will condemn you. You are circumcised and you have the law written down, but you don't obey the law.

28 Being Jewish is not just what is on the outside. Circumcision is more than flesh.   **29** No, being a Jew depends on what is on the inside. True circumcision is circumcision of the heart *performed* by *the* Spirit, not the written code.* This person has praise from God, not human beings.

Chapter 3

1 So, what does a Jew have that a non-Jew doesn't have? What good is circumcision?*   **2** It is worth much in many ways! First, Jews were trusted with messages from God.   **3** However, some Jews became unbelievers. Will their lack of faith cancel God's loyalty?   **4 Never!** Even though every man is a liar, God will be true. This is written:
"When You speak, You will be right.
When You judge, You will conquer."
Psalm 51:4
5 Now if our wrong makes God's righteousness look better, what should we say? God would be wrong to punish us, wouldn't He? (I am thinking as a human being.)   **6 Never!** If that were true, how could God condemn the world?   **7** But, if my lie makes God's truth look better and gives God *more* glory, why am I still being condemned as a

---

2:25   literally, circumcision
2:29   literally, in spirit, not letter
3:1   a physical mark; cutting off the foreskin of the male sex organ as a sign of God's agreement with Abraham (Genesis 17:9-14).

sinner?   **8** Perhaps we should say, "Let's do evil things, so that good things will happen"? (Some people are saying awful things about us. They claim that we said this. They deserve to be condemned.)

Who's Good Anyway?

9 What should we think? Are Jews better off? Not at all! We have already proved that all Jews and also non-Jews* are under sin's *power*.   **10** This is written:
"No one is good—not even one person!
11 No one understands.
No one is looking for God.
12 All people have turned away from God
and become completely useless.
No one is kind—not even one person!"

Psalm 14:1-3; Ecclesiastes 7:20

13 "Their throats are like an open grave.
They use their tongues to trick people."

Psalm 5:9

"Like dangerous snakes, poison is under their lips."

Psalm 140:3

14 "Their mouths are filled with cursing and bitterness."

Psalm 10:7

15 "They move quickly to kill someone.
16 After they leave, people are suffering and destroyed.
17 They have not known the peaceful way."

Isaiah 59:7-8

18 "They do not fear God."

Psalm 36:1

19 We know that everything the law says it says to people who are within the law, so that every mouth must be shut. The whole world must be guilty before God.   **20** So, no one will be made right with God by following *the* law, because, through *the* law, we become aware of sin.

Make It Right With God

21 Now, without *the* law, the way God makes people right has been revealed. The law and the prophets point toward this truth: **22** Committing oneself to* Jesus Christ is what makes a person right with God. *Salvation* is for **anyone** who believes! It makes no difference *who you are*,   **23** because everyone has sinned and is far away from God's glory.   **24** But, with God's gracious love, we are made right with God through Christ Jesus who scts us free.* And, all of this is free!   **25** God offered Christ *as a sacrifice*. When Christ died, this became the way that sins are taken away—if we believe. This showed God's justice, too. God passed over sins which had been committed before this time.   **26** God was tolerant, but now, at this present time, to show His justice, He makes a person right who trusts in Jesus, and He is still fair.
27 "So, what room is left for bragging?"
It is shut out!
"How? Through some kind of law? Through deeds?"
No! But through the principle of faith!

3:9   literally, Greeks
3:22   or, faith in
3:24   or, through the release which is in Christ Jesus

28 Because we conclude that a person
      is made right with God by faith—without following
      the law *of Moses.*
29 Is God only a God for the Jews?
      Isn't He a God for non-Jews?
"Yes, He is a God for non-Jewish people, too."
30 Since there is only one God,
      He will make a Jew* right from* faith
      and make a non-Jew* right through faith.
31 "Well then, do we cancel *the* law through faith?"
      Certainly not! On the contrary, we uphold *the* law.

Chapter 4

1 "Then what should we say about Abraham, our ancestor? What did he gain from his human experience?
2 If Abraham was made righteous by human effort, then he would have something to boast about."—**but not with God!**
3 What does the Scripture say?

"Abraham believed God, and so God declared him a righteous
    man."   *Genesis 15:6*

4 Pay does not come to a worker as a favor—he earns it!   **5** But suppose a person doesn't work for it? Instead, he believes in God who makes an ungodly man righteous. Then, his faith is regarded as righteousness.   **6** David talks about the happiness of a man whom God regards as righteous (without human effort):
7 "Sinners who are forgiven are happy.
      Their sins have been covered.
8 If the Lord *God* does not count a man's sin,
      then that man is happy."   *Psalm 32:1-2*

9 Therefore, this happiness is for Jews* **and** non-Jews,* because we are saying that Abraham's faith was regarded as righteousness.   **10** How was it accepted? Did this happen while Abraham was circumcised* or when he was uncircumcised? It was during the time when he was **not** circumcised!   **11** When Abraham received the mark of circumcision, it was a seal to prove that the faith he had (while he was not circumcised) was considered as righteousness by God. So, Abraham is an ancestor to all people who are declared righteous, even though they are not circumcised.   **12** Abraham is an ancestor of Jews,* the circumcised. Not only of them, he is also an ancestor to people who follow the example of the faith which Abraham, our ancestor, had while he was not circumcised.

God's Promise

13 *God's* promise to Abraham and his descendants (that Abraham would inherit the world*) did **not** come through *the* law. Instead, it came through the righteousness which

---

3:30	literally, the circumcision	
3:30	or, because of	
3:30	literally, the uncircumcision	
4:9	literally, the circumcision	
4:9	literally, the uncircumcision	
4:10	literally, in circumcision	
4:12	literally, circumcision	
4:13	See Genesis 17:3-6.	

comes by faith.   14 If we are truly heirs* because of *the* law, faith means nothing and God's promise is worthless,   15 because the law brings punishment *from God*. Where no law exists, there can be no sin.

16 This is why it is by faith, so that it will be a favor—to confirm the promise *that God made* to every descendant, not only for the Jew* but also for the *non-Jew* who has the same kind of faith that Abraham had. Abraham is the ancestor of us all.   17 This is written:

"I have made you to be an ancestor of many nations."   *Genesis 17:5*

In the presence of God, Abraham believed that God could make dead people come back to life, that God could call for things that did not exist, as though they existed.

18 When there was no hope, Abraham believed with hope that he would become an ancestor of many nations, just as God said:

"Your descendants will be like this."   *Genesis 15:5*

19 He understood that his body was practically dead (He was about 100 years old.) and that Sarah couldn't have children, either. But Abraham's faith didn't weaken. 20 He did not doubt God's promise. He believed. His faith made him even stronger. He gave glory to God.   21 He was convinced that God was able to do what He had promised.   22 So, because *of this faith,*

"God declared Abraham a righteous man."   *Genesis 15:6*

23 This *verse* about Abraham's acceptance was written not only for Abraham; 24 it was also written for us. We are going to be accepted, too. We believe in the One who raised our Lord Jesus from death.   25 Jesus was handed over *to die* for our sins. He was raised from death to make us right with God.

Chapter 5

Find Access

1 Since we have been made right with God by faith, we have peace with God through our Lord Jesus Christ.   2 Through Jesus, we have access by faith into this favor where we now stand. We feel good, because now we can hope for the glory of God.   3 Not only that, we can feel good about our troubles, because we know that suffering develops endurance.   4 Endurance develops character. Character develops hope.   5 And, hope never disappoints us, because God's love has been poured into our hearts through the Holy Spirit who was given to us.

6 While we were still helpless and ungodly, Christ died for us—at exactly the right time.   7 It is rare when someone dies for another person—even for a good person. However, some do dare to die for a good man.   8 But God reassures us of His love for us in this way: While we were still **sinners**, Christ died for us!

9 Since Christ's blood has made us right with God, even more we will be saved from God's punishment through Christ.   10 We were God's enemies, but the death of His Son was used to make us God's friends. Now that we have become friends of God, we

---

4:14   These are people who receive what has been promised to them when their loved one dies.
4:16   literally, the one from the law

will be saved even more by Christ's life. **11** Not only that, we feel good about being in God through our Lord Jesus Christ. We now have friendship *with God* through Christ.

Picture Adam; Picture Christ

12 Sin came into the world through one man. And, death came into the world through sin. In this way, death spread to all mankind, because all sinned. **13** Sin was in the world before *the* law *of Moses* came, but because *the* law had not yet come, sin was not thought of as sin. **14** But, from Adam's time to the time of Moses, death ruled over people who did not sin in the same way that Adam did. Adam was a picture of what was going to happen.

15 But the gift *of God* was not like the sin *of Adam*; many people died because of one man's sin. No, God's gracious love and the free gift that comes through one man, Jesus Christ, overflowed even more to many people. **16** Also, the gift *of God* is not like that which came through one man's sin. Following the sin of one man came the verdict of "guilty," but the free gift *of God* followed many sins and made people right with God. **17** Death used one man's sin to rule through one man. Those who receive the overflow of *God's* gracious love and the gift of righteousness will rule even more in life through one man, Jesus Christ!

18 So, when one man* sinned, all mankind became condemned. But, in the same way, through one man* came an act of righteousness. It could bring life and make all persons right with God. **19** Many people were made sinners through the disobedience of one man.* But, through the obedience of one man,* many people will be made righteous. **20** *The* law came in to increase sin. But where sin increased, *God's* gracious love overflowed much more. **21** Sin used death to rule. In the same way, God's gracious love rules through righteousness through our Lord Jesus Christ for eternal life.

Chapter 6

Equipped With Righteous Tools

1 What should our answer be? Should we continue living in sin, so that *God's* gracious love will increase? **2 Never!** How could we live in sin anymore? We died to it!* **3** You know that all of us were immersed into Christ Jesus. Don't you know that we were immersed into his death? **4** So, through immersion, we were buried with him into death. Christ was raised from death through the glory of the Father. In the same way, we will live a new life.

5 Because if we have been planted with Christ, dying as he died, we will also be raised to life *with him*. **6** You know that our sinful selves* were nailed to the cross with Christ, so that the body of sin would lose its power, so that sin will no longer be used to make us slaves. **7** A person who dies has been set free from sin.

5:18	Adam
5:18	Jesus Christ
5:19	Adam
5:19	Jesus Christ
6:2	or, quit living in sin
6:6	or, our old man

8 Since we died with Christ, we believe that we will also live with him. **9** You know that Christ was raised from death, never to die again—death does not rule over him anymore! **10** This was the type of death he died: He died for sin, once for all time, but the kind of life that he now lives is for God. **11** In the same way, think of yourselves as being dead to sin, but alive to God by Christ Jesus.

12 Therefore, don't let sin rule over your dying bodies. Don't obey the desires of your bodies. **13** Don't allow the members of your body to be used as evil tools for sin. Instead, give yourselves to God as people who have come back to life from death. Use the members of your body as righteous tools for God. **14** Sin shall not rule over you, because you are not under *the* law—you are under *God's* gracious love!

Two Choices

15 What does this mean? Should we sin because we are not under *the* law, but under *God's* gracious love? **Never!** **16** Surely you know that you are slaves to whomever you offer yourselves to obey? The one you obey is your master. You could obey sin which leads to death or you could obey *God*. This leads to being righteous. **17** But thank God that, even though you were slaves of sin, you obeyed from your hearts that pattern of teaching* which you were given. **18** And, after you were set free from sin, you became slaves to righteousness.

19 Because of your human weakness, I am speaking as a man: You once gave the members of your body to be slaves to moral impurity, and to more and more sin. Now, in the same way, give the parts of your body to be slaves to righteousness for being holy. **20** When you were slaves of sin, you were people who were free from the control of righteousness. **21** So, what good do you have from that time? You are ashamed of those things now! Those things will end up in death, **22** but now that you have been set free from sin, you are slaves to God. You get something good for being holy—the goal is eternal life! **23** The pay *you get* for sinning is death, but God's gift is eternal life in Christ Jesus, our Lord.

Chapter 7

Released From the Law

1 Brothers, surely you know (because I'm talking to those who understand *the* law) that the law only rules over a person for as long as he lives. **2** A married woman is bound to her husband by *the* law for as long as he lives, but if her husband dies, she is released from the law of marriage.* **3** Therefore, if she were married to a different man while her real husband is still alive, God would call her an adulteress.* However, if her husband dies, she is free from *the* law *of marriage*. She would not be an adulteress if she got married to a different man later.

4 So, my brothers, you also died to the law through Christ's body. You can *marry* someone else—the one who was raised from death, so that you* can produce fruit for God. **5** When we were controlled by our human nature,* the sinful desires which came through the law were working in our bodies. We produced fruit for death. **6** But

---

6:17   See Romans 6:4-7.
7:2   literally, the husband
7:3   a woman guilty of adultery, sexual sin
7:4   literally, we
7:5   what people naturally do if they are not controlled by God's Spirit (See Romans 8:9.)

now we have been released from the law. We died to what bound us before, so that we can serve with a new spirit, not *by following* a strict code.*

Sin Took a Chance

7 What should our answer be? Is the law the same thing as sin? **Never!** Only through *the* law could I have learned what sin was. Without the law, one could not know what evil desire is. It said:

"You must not want things which don't belong to you."   *Exodus 20:17*

8 Sin took the chance to use the command to make me want all kinds of things which didn't belong to me, because without *the* law, sin is dead.   9 I used to be living without *the* law, but when the command came in, sin came to life.   10 Then I died. I found that the same command which was supposed to bring life brought death instead! 11 Sin took the chance to use the command to take hold of me and kill me with the command.   12 For this reason the law is holy. The commands are holy, fair, and good.

13 Did what was for my good become death? **Never!** But, so that sin would look like sin, sin worked through what was for my good *to bring* death! Sin would become very, very sinful through the command.

I Really Don't Want To

14 We know that the law is spiritual, but I am not. I'm human—sold under sin! 15 I don't understand what is happening to me: I don't always do what I really want to do. Instead, I am always doing what I actually hate.   16 Since I am doing what I don't want to do, I am agreeing with the law, that the law is right.   17 But now, I am not the one who is doing this anymore. No, it is sin which is living in me.   18 I know that good does not live in me. (I mean, in my human nature.) I am ready and willing to do good, but I can't do it.   19 I am not doing the good that I actually want to do. Instead, I continue doing something evil that I really don't want to do.   20 Since I am doing what I really don't want to do, it is not me doing it anymore—it is the sin which is living in me that is doing it!

21 So, I find this principle: When I want to do something good, evil is controlling me.   22 My inner self happily agrees with the law of God.   23 However, I see a different law in my body, making war with the law of my mind. It is making me a prisoner to the sinful law* which is in my body.   24 I am a miserable man. Who will help me escape this body of death?   25 Thank God, *I can escape* through Jesus Christ, our Lord. Therefore, I serve God's law with my mind, but I serve the sinful law *of my body* with my human nature.

Chapter 8

No Condemnation Now

1 So, there is no condemnation now for those people who are in Christ Jesus. 2 The law of the Spirit of life in Christ Jesus has set me free from the law of sin and death.   3 The law was weak through human nature. God did what the law couldn't do: He sent His own Son *as an offering* for sin. He came with a nature like man's sinful human nature. And concerning sin, this is how God used human nature to condemn sin.

7:6   literally, in newness of spirit and not in oldness of letter
7:23   desire

4 He wanted to completely satisfy in us what the law says is right. We are living by following the Spirit, not by following human nature.

5 People who follow human nature are thinking about the *evil* things which human nature wants. People who follow the Spirit are thinking about the things that the Spirit wants. 6 The way human nature thinks is death, but the way the Spirit thinks is life and peace. 7 The way human nature thinks is hatred for God. It doesn't want to put itself under the law of God. It can't! 8 People controlled by human nature cannot please God.

9 However, **you** are not being controlled by human nature; you are being controlled by the Spirit—if God's Spirit lives in you. If anyone does not have Christ's Spirit, this person does not belong to Christ. 10 But since Christ is in you, even though your body is dying (because of sin), your spirit is alive (because you have been made right with God). 11 And, if the Spirit of the One who raised Jesus from death lives in you, then the One who raised Christ from death will make your dead bodies live, using His Spirit who is living in you.

12 Therefore, brothers, we shouldn't live by following our human nature. 13 If you do, you will die. If you use the Spirit to kill the evil deeds of the body, you will live. 14 All people who are being led by God's Spirit are sons of God. 15 God did not give you a spirit to make you slaves, to be afraid again. Instead, you received *the* Spirit *who* makes you sons. Through the Spirit, we cry out, "Father, dear Father!" 16 This same Spirit agrees with our spirits, that we are God's children. 17 Since we are children, we are also heirs—heirs of God and co-heirs with Christ. If we suffer together, we will share glory together.

Everything Works Together for Good

18 I consider the sufferings of the present time not worth comparing with the future glory which will be revealed to us. 19 Creation waits eagerly for the time when the sons of God will be revealed. 20 Creation was tied to worthlessness. That was not what it wanted, but God wanted it that way. So, He bound it. However, there is hope! 21 Creation itself will be set free from the slavery of decay *and be brought* into the glorious freedom of God's children. 22 We know, even now, that all creation is groaning with pain. It feels pain, like a woman who will soon give birth. 23 Not only that, but we, who have the first-fruits of the Spirit, groan with pain also. We are waiting to become true sons—when our bodies will be set free! 24 We were saved with this hope. A hope which is seen is not hope. Who hopes for something he can see? 25 But, since we are hoping for something we cannot yet see, we patiently wait for it.

26 We don't know how we should pray, but the Spirit helps our weakness. He personally talks to God for us with feelings which *our* language cannot express. 27 God searches *all men's* hearts. He knows what the Spirit is thinking. The Spirit talks to God in behalf of holy people, using the manner which *pleases* God.

28 We know that all things work together for good for people who love God. They are called for God's purpose. 29 The people whom God knew about long ago were made a part of God's plan long ago. God wanted them to become just like His Son. This is the way Christ would be the firstborn among many brothers. 30 God made them a part of His plan long ago. These are the people whom He called. The people whom God called are the people He made right. Those whom God made right are the same ones who received glory from God.

Jesus on the Right Side

31 What should we think about all these things? Since God is for us, who can be against us? **32** God did not keep His own Son. Instead, God gave him up for all of us. Therefore, wouldn't God give us everything? **33** Who could accuse God's chosen people? God is the One who declares people to be righteous! **34** Who will condemn? Christ Jesus is the one who died and was raised from death. And, he is at God's right side, talking to God for us. **35** Who can separate us from Christ's love? Will trouble, pain, persecution, having no food or clothes, danger, or violence separate us? **36** This is written:

> "All day long we are in danger of dying for You.
> We are treated like sheep which will soon be killed." *Psalm 44:22*

37 But, in all these things, we are more than conquerors through the one who loved us. **38-39** I am sure that **nothing** will be able to separate us from God's love which is *found* in Christ Jesus, our Lord. None of these things:

death,
life,
angels,
rulers,
the present time,
the future,
powers,
heights,
depth.

Chapter 9

Roots

1 I am telling the truth in Christ; I'm not lying. My conscience agrees with the Holy Spirit. **2** I feel great sorrow and constant pain in my heart. **3** I could wish that *I* were condemned—*cut off* from Christ—for the sake of my *Jewish* brothers, my human relatives. **4** They are the people of Israel. *God's* sonship, glory, agreements, law, worship, and promises belong to them. **5** They have the family roots. Christ, in the human sense, came from them. *However*, God is over everyone. Praise Him forever. Amen.

6 God's message certainly did not fail. Not all the people from Israel are truly people of Israel. **7** Not all the people who descended from Abraham are children *of Abraham*, either. No,

> "Your true descendants will come through Isaac." *Genesis 21:12*

8 This means that not all physical descendants are children of God. Instead, the children of *God's* promise are counted as the real descendants. **9** This is what the promise said:

> "At the right time I will come, and Sarah will give birth
> to a son." *Genesis 18:10*

10 Not only that, but Rebekah's two sons came from the same man, Isaac, our ancestor. **11-12** But, before they were born, before they had done anything—good or bad—God told her,

"The older son will serve the younger son."   *Genesis 25:23*

This happened in order to show that the choice came from God,* not from human effort. God wanted His special choice to last.   **13** This is written:

"I loved Jacob
    more than I loved Esau."   *Malachi 1:2-3*

14 What should we conclude? God is not unfair, is He? **Never!**   **15** God said to Moses,

"I will show mercy to the people I want to show mercy to. I will feel sorry for the
    people I want to feel sorry for."   *Exodus 33:19*

16 Therefore, it does not *depend on* what man wants or tries to do. Instead, it is the mercy of God.   **17** Because the Scripture said this about Pharaoh:

"I allowed you to become a leader for a reason—that I might show My power
    through you. My name will spread to the whole world."   *Exodus 9:16*

18 So, God shows mercy to those He wants to show mercy to. And, if God wants to, He makes some people stubborn.

Who Can Resist?

19 Surely you will say this to me: "Then why does God blame us? Who can resist God's plan?   **20** Who are **you**? You are only a human being. You cannot talk back to God. The thing which is made cannot say to the One who made it, "Why did you make me like this?"   **21** Does the potter have the right to use the same clay in two ways? Yes. He may use part of it to make a beautiful pot. Or, he may use part of it for something ordinary.

22 God wanted to show His anger and to make His power clear. So, He was very patient with people who would be punished. They were made ready for destruction. **23** God wanted to make the wealth of His glory clear to people who would receive mercy. Long ago, He prepared them to receive glory.   **24** God called us not only from among Jews but also from among non-Jews.   **25** It is as God says in *the book of* Hosea:

"I will call people who didn't belong to Me 'My People.'
    I will love the *nation* that was unloved."   *Hosea 2:23*

26 "This will happen where they said, 'You are not My people:'

They will be called 'the sons of the living God'
    in that same place!"   *Hosea 1:10*

27 Isaiah cried out for Israel:

"Even if the number of the sons of Israel becomes as
    large as the number of grains of the ocean sands,
    only some of them will be saved.   **28** The Lord *God*
    will close His books* on the whole world quickly
    and completely."   *Isaiah 10:23*

9:11-12 literally, the One who called
9:28   an expression in accounting; it means: "He will finish his business."

29 It is like Isaiah said long ago:

"If Almighty God* had not left us some descendants,
we would have become like the cities of Sodom and
Gomorrah." *Isaiah 1:9*

Don't Chase After Lawlessness

30 What should we conclude? Non-Jews (who were not trying to find righteousness) received righteousness; it was the kind of righteousness which comes from faith. **31** The people of Israel were trying to chase after "law-righteousness" in *the* law, but they did **not** get it. **32** Why? Because that kind of righteousness does not come from faith. Instead, it comes from human effort. They stumbled on the stone for stumbling.* **33** This is written:

"Look! I am putting a stone for stumbling
and a rock for tripping in Jerusalem.*
The person who believes in him will not be ashamed." *Isaiah 28:16*

Chapter 10

1 Brothers, I pray to God that the Jewish people will be saved; that is my heart's desire. **2** I tell you the truth, they have much enthusiasm for God, but they don't understand! **3** They ignored God's righteousness and tried to establish their own type of righteousness. They did not put themselves under God's kind of righteousness. **4** Christ is the purpose of *the* law. Everyone who believes *in Christ* will be made right with God.

Believing in Christ

5 Moses wrote about the type of righteousness which comes from the law:

"A person who wants to find life by following these
things* must **do** the things that the law says." *Leviticus 18:5*

6 But the kind of righteousness which comes from faith says things like this: "You must not say this in your heart, 'Who will go up to heaven?' (This means to bring Christ down.) **7** or 'Who will go down to the bottomless *pit*?' (This means to bring Christ back from death.)." **8** But, what does it say?

"The message is near you;
It is in your mouth and in your heart." *Deuteronomy 30:14*

This refers to the message about faith which we proclaim. **9** If you confess with your mouth that "Jesus is Lord" and if you believe in your heart that God raised Jesus from death, you will be saved. **10** To become right with God a person believes with his heart. Declaring it openly,* that person comes into salvation. **11** The Scripture says:

"Everyone who believes in him will not be ashamed." *Isaiah 28:16*

9:29   literally, Lord of the *heavenly* armies *of angels*
9:32   Jesus
9:33   literally, Zion
10:5   the law
10:10   or, When one uses the mouth to confess,

12 There is no difference between Jews and non-Jews! The Lord is the same Lord of everybody. He richly blesses everyone who trusts* in Him:

13 "Every person who trusts in the Lord will be saved."   *Joel 2:32*

14 But, how could they trust in One in whom they did not believe? How could they believe in One they had never heard about? How can they hear about *God*, if someone doesn't preach *about Him*?   **15** How are they going to be able to preach about Him, if men are not being sent? This is written:

"It is wonderful when men come to tell good news!"   *Isaiah 52:7*

16 However, not everyone has obeyed the Good News. Isaiah said,

"Lord *God*, who believed our report?"   *Isaiah 53:1*

17 Since a person believes something because he hears about it, he should hear the message of Christ.

18 But, I ask, "Didn't they hear?" **Yes!**

"The sound of their voices went out to all the earth.
   Their words went out to the farthest places in the
      world."   *Psalm 19:4*

19 But, I ask, "Didn't Israel know this?" First, Moses said:

"I will use a non-nation to make you jealous.
   I will make you angry with a stupid nation."   *Deuteronomy 32:21*

20 Then Isaiah dared to say:

"The people who were not looking for Me* found Me.
   I appeared to people who were not asking for Me."   *Isaiah 65:1*

21 *God* said this to the people of Israel:

"I have held out my hands* all day long to people
   that is rebellious and won't obey."   *Isaiah 65:2*

Chapter 11

Grace Means Grace

1 So, I ask, "God has not rejected His people, has He?" **Never!** I am a Jew,* too. I am a descendant of Abraham. I come from the tribe of Benjamin.   **2** God did not reject His people whom He knew about ahead of time. You know the Scripture about Elijah when he was pleading to God against the people of Israel:

3 "Lord *God*, they have killed Your prophets.
   They have torn down Your altars. I am the only one left.
   And, they are trying to kill me!"   *1 Kings 19:10*

10:12   literally, calls on the name of the Lord
10:20   God
10:21   a kind invitation from God; it shows continuous patience.
11:1   literally, an Israelite

244

4 What did God tell him?

"I have kept for Myself 7,000 men who have never
worshiped* Baal."   *1 Kings 19:18*

5 So, it is the same today. There is only a small group whom God has chosen through His gracious love.   **6** Since it is by God's mercy,* it is not through human effort anymore. If that were not true, grace would not mean grace.

7 So, what does this mean? The people of Israel tried so hard to get something, but they didn't get it. However, God's chosen few did get it! The rest became stubborn.
8 This is written:

"God gave them a numb spirit.
    They have eyes, but they don't see.
    They have ears, but they don't listen.
This is true even today."   *Deuteronomy 29:4*

9 David said,

"I hope they will be caught
        and trapped at their own table!*
    I hope they will trip
        and be paid back!
10 I hope their eyes will become dark,
        so that they can't see!
    I hope their backs will always break!"   *Psalm 69:22-23*

11 So, I ask, 'When the Jews stumbled, did it ruin them?" **No!** Through their sin, salvation came to people who are not Jewish. Why? To make Jewish people jealous!
12 But, if their sin *brings* rich blessings to the world and their defeat *brings* rich blessings to non-Jews, then including them *would bring* even richer blessings!

Sharing in the Sap

13 Now, I am talking to you non-Jews: Since I am the apostle to non-Jewish people, I will be proud of my ministry.   **14** Perhaps, I can make physical *Israel*, my own people, jealous. Then I can save some of them. **15** If throwing them away means that the world is brought back to God, what would receiving them be? It would be like coming back to life from death!   **16** If the first piece of bread *offered to God* is holy, then all of it is holy. And, if the root is holy, the branches are holy, too.

17 Yes, some of the branches were broken off. You non-Jews are like part of a wild olive tree which has been grafted in among the natural olive branches. You are sharing in the sap of the root of the olive tree.   **18** Don't brag! You are not more important than the natural branches. If you brag, *remember*, you are not holding up the root. The root is holding **you** up!

19 You might say this: "But the natural branches were broken off, so that I could be grafted in!"   **20** True, they were broken off, but it was because they did not believe.

11:4   literally, bowed the knee to
11:6   kindness to one who does not deserve it
11:9   While they are eating, their enemy will catch them by surprise.

But you keep your position by faith. Don't think you are more special. Instead, fear! **21** Since God did not keep the natural branches, He may not spare you, either!

22 So, look at how kind God is and how harsh God is! He was harsh to those who fell, but He is kind to you—if you stay in His kindness. If you don't, you will be cut off. **23** And, if the Jewish people start believing, they will be grafted in! God is able to graft them in again. **24** Because, since you non-Jews were cut from a wild olive tree and grafted in—in an unnatural way, against nature—into a tame olive tree, how much easier it would be to graft in these natural branches into their own olive tree.

All "Israel" Will Be Saved

25 Brothers, I want you to know this secret: (This should make you feel humble.) Part of the people of Israel have become stubborn until the time when the complete *number* of non-Jewish people have come in. **26** And, in this way, all "Israel" will be saved. This is written:
"The Savior will come out of Jerusalem.*
   He will remove all ungodly ways from the people of Jacob.
27 This will be My agreement with them
      when I take their sins away."   *Isaiah 59:20-21*
28 For the sake of you non-Jews, they are enemies of the gospel. But, because of the ancestors, they are dear *friends* by God's choice. **29** God's gifts and God's calling cannot be changed. **30** You *non-Jews* did not obey God in the past, but now you have received mercy because they did not obey. **31** In the same way, the Jewish people are now disobedient to God, so that they can receive God's mercy, too. You have already received His mercy. **32** God has classed all people under the category of disobedience, so that He may show mercy to all of them.

Does God Owe Anyone?

33 O the depth of God's wealth, wisdom, and knowledge! His decisions cannot be searched. His ways cannot be found:
34 "Who understands the Lord's mind?
      Who gives Him advice?"   *Isaiah 40:13*
35 "Who has loaned something to God,
      so that God needs to pay him back?"   *Job 41:11*
   36 Everything *exists* because of Him,
         through Him, and for Him. Let the glory be His
         forever! Amen!

Chapter 12

Body Parts

1 So, brothers, with God's tender feelings, I beg you to offer your bodies as a living, holy, pleasing sacrifice to God. This is true worship from you. **2** Don't act like people of this world. Instead, be changed inside by letting your mind be made new again. Then you can determine what is good, pleasing, and perfect—what God wants.

3 Through God's gracious love which has been given to me, I am telling each one of you, don't think you are better than you really are. Instead, be modest in the way you think. God distributed a measure of faith to each person. **4** In one body we have many

---

11:26   literally, Zion

parts. These parts don't all do the same thing.   **5** In the same way, many people are one body in Christ. Each part is a member of the other parts.   **6** God's gracious love gave us different gifts:

If it is prophesying, then prophesy by degree of faith.

If it is helping other people, then help.

7 If it is teaching, then teach.

8 If it is encouraging people, then encourage.

If it is giving money, then be generous.

If it is leading others, then work hard.

If it is showing mercy, then be cheerful.

9 Love must be sincere. Hate evil. Hold onto good.   **10** Have the same kind of love for one another which brothers have. Give each other more honor than you do yourselves.   **11** Work hard. Don't be lazy. Serve the Lord with a boiling spirit.

12 Rejoice in hope. Be patient during times of trouble. Continue praying. **13** Share things with holy people who need it. Try to bring strangers into your homes. **14** Bless those who persecute you. Bless and don't condemn.   **15** Be happy with those who are happy. Cry with those who are crying.   **16** Get along with one another. Mix with humble people; don't try to be clever. Don't think you are "wise."   **17** If someone does wrong to you, don't pay him back with another wrong. Be sure you do what everyone already knows is right.   **18** If possible, from your part, live in peace with everybody.   **19** Don't avenge yourselves, dear *friends*. Instead, leave room for *God* to punish. This is written:

> "The Lord says, 'Revenge belongs to me
> —I will pay it back'!"   *Deuteronomy 32:35*

20 "If your enemy is hungry, feed him.
> If he is thirsty, give him something to drink.
> By doing this, you will make him burn up with
> shame."*   *Proverbs 25:21-22*

21 Don't let evil defeat you. Instead, use good to defeat evil.

Chapter 13

Under God's Authority

1 Every person must put himself under existing authority. God is over all *human* authority; the government positions are those which God appointed.   **2** So, if someone rebels against authority, he is going against what God appointed. Rebels will receive condemnation.   **3** Rulers don't scare people who do good things; only evil-doers should fear. Do you want to be unafraid of *a man in* authority? Do good things! Then, he will honor you.   **4** He is God's servant for your own good. But, if you commit a crime, you **should** be afraid, because he can use real force!* He is God's servant to give fair punishment to anyone who commits a crime.   **5** So, you must obey, not only because you could be punished, but also for the sake of your conscience.

6 This is why you pay taxes. These men are servants of God, giving all their time to ruling.   **7** Pay them back whatever you owe—tariffs, taxes, respect, or honor.

12:20   literally, pile coals of fire on his head
13:4   literally, He does not carry the sword for nothing.

Dress Yourself With Jesus

8 The only thing you should owe anyone is love. The person who loves another person has made *the* law complete:

9 "You must not commit adultery."
"You must not commit murder."
"You must not steal."
"You must not want something
     which belongs to someone else." *Exodus 20:13-15,17*

And, any other command is covered by this one sentence:
"Love other people the same way you love yourself." *Leviticus 19:18*

10 Love does not hurt other people. So, love is the completion of *the* law.

11 You know this is the right time for you to wake up from sleeping. It's late! The time for our deliverance is now nearer than when we first believed. **12** The night is almost gone; daytime is near! So, put away deeds of darkness.* Put on the weapons of light.* **13** We should live properly, like people do during the daytime, not with orgies or by getting drunk, not committing sexual sin or having wild sex parties, not with fighting or jealousy. **14** Instead, put on the Lord Jesus Christ. Don't think about how to satisfy the *evil* desires of your human nature.

Chapter 14

Stand and Answer

1 Accept the *brother* who is weak in faith, but don't argue about opinions. **2** One person believes that he is allowed to eat anything. But the weaker *brother* eats nothing but vegetables. **3** The one who eats *anything* must not look down on the one who does not eat. And, the one who does not eat *meat* must not condemn the one who eats, because God accepts him, too. **4** Who are you? Can you judge the servant of someone else? That servant's master decides whether he is a good or bad servant, *not you.* He will be successful; the Lord is able to make him successful.

5 One person thinks that one day is *more holy* than another day. But, another man thinks that every day is the same. Each person must be sure in his own mind. **6** When someone is honoring a special day, he is doing this for the Lord. When someone is eating *in a special way*, he is thanking God. And, the *brother* who is not eating *meat* is doing that for the Lord. He also thanks God! **7** None of us lives alone and none of us dies alone. **8** If we live, let's live for the Lord. If we die, let's die for the Lord. It doesn't matter whether we live or die—we belong to the Lord!

9 Christ died and came back to life, so that he could rule over the living and the dead. **10** But, who are you? Can you judge your brother? Also, why do you look down on your brother? Because we will all stand in front of God at the *Judge's* bench. **11** This is written:

"The Lord says, '*As sure as* I am alive:
Every knee will bow to Me.*
Every tongue will declare that *I am* God.' " *Isaiah 45:23*

12 So, each one of us must give an answer to God for the way we live.

13:12   sin
13:12   truth
14:11   This shows submission.

Don't Trip Anyone Up

13 Stop criticizing one another. Instead, do this: Decide not to put anything there which could trip your brother or cause him to sin.   **14** In the Lord Jesus, I know, and I'm sure, that nothing is unholy in and of itself—unless it becomes "unholy" to the person who thinks it is unholy.   **15** If your brother feels upset because of what you eat, you are not living with love anymore. Don't destroy that *brother* with your food; Christ died for him!   **16** So, don't let anyone say something evil about your good.   **17** God's kingdom does not consist of eating and drinking; what's important is being right with God, having peace, and being happy in the Holy Spirit.   **18** The person who serves Christ like this will please God and be liked by people.

19 Therefore, let us try to have peace and build up one another.   **20** Don't destroy God's work for the sake of food. Everything is pure. But, it is wrong for a person to eat anything that might trip someone else.   **21** It is better if you don't eat meat, drink wine, or do anything that might trip your brother.

22 You have your own faith. Keep it between yourself and God! The person who doesn't feel condemned is happy. He *knows* what he is doing.   **23** But the person who has doubts feels condemned, if he goes ahead and eats, because he is not sure. A person must be sure that everything he does is right, or else it is sin.

Chapter 15

Follow Jesus in the Chase

1 We who are strong should help weaker *brothers* with things they cannot do, not to please ourselves.   **2** Each of us should please the other person, building him up. **3** Because even Christ did not please himself. This is written:
"The insults of the people who were insulting you fell
   on me."   *Psalm 69:9*
4 Everything that was written long ago was written to teach us. We should learn that we can have hope through the patience and comfort *we get* from the Scriptures.   **5** The God who gives you patience and comfort will help you agree with one another, as you follow Christ Jesus.   **6** Then, with one voice, all together, you will give glory to the God and Father of our Lord Jesus Christ.

Accept Everyone As Christ Did

7 For God's glory, accept one another, as Christ accepted you.   **8** I tell you, Christ became a servant of the Jewish people* for the sake of God's truth. He did this to confirm *God's* promises to our ancestors.   **9** Then other nations would give glory to God for His mercy. This is written:
"This is why I will acknowledge You among the nations.*
   I will sing to Your name."   *Psalm 18:49*
10 Again *Moses* said,
"You people who are not Jewish,
   celebrate with God's people!"*   *Deuteronomy 32:43*

15:8   literally, circumcision
15:9   or, non-Jewish people
15:10   the Jews, Israel

11 Again,
"All nations, praise the Lord *God*!
Let all people praise Him!"   *Psalm 117:1*
12 Again Isaiah said,
"The descendant* of Jesse will come.
He will rise to rule the nations.*
The nations will place their hopes on him."   *Isaiah 11:10*
13 The God of hope will fill you with every kind of happiness and peace while you trust Him. He will use hope to flood you with the power of the Holy Spirit.

Leading Non-Jewish People to God

14 My brothers, I feel sure about you. You are full of goodness, complete with every kind of knowledge, and able to warn one another.   15 *In this letter* I have written to you about several things. I was very honest with you because of the gracious love that God gave me. I wanted to help you remember.   16 I have been *allowed* to be Christ Jesus' servant to non-Jews. I am performing holy service to God's Good News. Then, after the nations* have been made holy by the Holy Spirit, they will become an acceptable offering to God.

17 So, in Christ Jesus, I take pride in the *offerings that are made* to God. 18 Because I dare not say anything about the way Christ has used me to get something done about leading the non-Jewish people to obey God. He just used my words, my actions,   19 powerful proofs from God, miracles, and the power of the Spirit. I have told the Good News everywhere—from Jerusalem all the way to Illyricum.*   20 I've always wanted to tell it where they didn't know anything about Christ. I didn't want to build on someone else's foundation.   21 This is written:

"The people who were not told about him will learn.
Those who have not heard will *begin to* understand."   *Isaiah 52:15*

Let's Hang Together

22 So, I was stopped from coming to you many times.   23 But now, I have no more places *to preach* in this area. And, I've wanted very much to come to you for many years.   24 So, whenever I travel to Spain, I hope to visit you while passing through. After I've enjoyed my visit for a while, you can help me to continue my trip to Spain. 25 I am going to Jerusalem now to help the Christians.*   26 The *Christians* in the areas of Macedonia and Achaia were delighted to share in doing something for the poor holy people in Jerusalem.   27 They were delighted, because they owe them a lot. Since non-Jews have shared in the spiritual blessings of Jews, they should help them with physical things.   28 When I've finished this and made sure that it does some good, I will come to you on my way to Spain.   29 I know when I get there, I will come with Christ's complete blessing.

30 Brothers, through our Lord Jesus Christ and through the love of the *Holy* Spirit, I beg you to pray to God for me. Help me fight on!   31 Pray that I will be rescued from people in the land of Judea who are not persuaded. Pray that my ministry to Jerusalem

---

15:12   Jesus Christ
15:12   or, non-Jews
15:16   or, non-Jews
15:19   an area along the eastern coast of the Adriatic Sea. Today it is Yugoslavia.
15:25   literally, the holy people

will be acceptable to the holy people there.   **32** Pray that, if God wants this, I will come to you with joy. Then I can be with you and relax.   **33** May the God of peace be with all of you. Amen.

Chapter 16

God Chaser Roll Call

1 I recommend our sister Phoebe to you. She is a servant of the congregation in the town of Cenchrea.   **2** I want you to accept her, as holy people should in the Lord *Jesus*. Help her with anything she might need from you, because she has been very helpful to many people and to me also.

3 Greet Priscilla* and Aquila, my co-workers in Christ Jesus.   **4** They risked their very lives for me. I am not the only one who is thankful for them; all the non-Jewish congregations are thankful, too!

5 Also, greet the group which meets in their house.
Greet my dear Epaenetus, too. He was the first convert to Christ in the land of Asia.

6 Greet Mary. She worked very hard for you.

7 Greet my relatives, Andronicus and Junias. They were in jail with me. The apostles think they are special. They were in Christ before I was.

8 Greet Ampliatus, my dear *friend* in the Lord *Jesus*.

9 Greet Urbanus, our co-worker in Christ, and Stachys, my dear *friend*.

10 Greet Apelles. He was tested in Christ.

Greet the people in the family of Aristobulus.

11 Greet Herodion, my relative.

Greet those in Narcissus' family who are in the Lord *Jesus*.

12 Greet Tryphaena and Tryphosa. These women worked very hard in the Lord *Jesus*.

Greet Persis, my dear *friend*. She has worked very hard in the Lord *Jesus*, too.

13 Greet Rufus,* the one chosen in the Lord *Jesus*. Also, greet his mother; she treats me as her son.

14 Greet Asyncritus, Phlegon, Hermes, Patrobas, Hermas, and the brothers who are with them.

15 Greet Philologus, Julia, Nereus and his sister, and Olympas and all the holy people who are with them.

16 Greet one another with a holy kiss.
All the congregations of Christ greet you.

Wise and Simple

17 Brothers, I beg you, watch out for people who cause splits and do things which cause people to sin. This is against the teaching which you learned from us. Turn away

16:3   literally, Prisca
16:13   His father may have been Simon, the one who carried Jesus' cross (Mark 15:21).

from them.   **18** People like this in Christ our Lord are only serving their own appetites. They fool innocent people with smooth talk and flattery.   **19** Everyone has heard about how you obeyed. I'm proud of you. However, I want you to be wise about good, and simple about evil.

20 The God of peace will crush Satan under your feet soon. May the gracious love of Jesus our Lord be with you.

21 Timothy, our co-worker, greets you. And so do Lucius, Jason, and Sosipater (my relatives).

22 I, Tertius (who copied this letter), greet you in the Lord *Jesus*.

23 Gaius greets you. The whole congregation and I are his guests.
Erastus greets you. He is the city manager.
Brother Quartus sends you his greeting, too.   **24** *

The Secret's Out

25 *I commit you to God* who is able to make you strong with my gospel (the preaching about Jesus Christ) and the secret revelation which has been kept hidden for a long, long time.   **26** This secret has now been made clear through the prophetic writings. The eternal God ordered this, so that when it becomes known, all nations will believe it and obey.

27 Give glory forever to God—who alone is all-wise—through Jesus Christ. Amen.

16:24   Some very early manuscripts omit the last sentence of verse 20 and use it as verse 24.

1 CORINTHIANS

Chapter 1

The First Church of Corinth

1 From brother Sosthenes and from Paul, an apostle of Christ Jesus. God wanted me to be an apostle—He called me.

2 To the congregation of God in the city of Corinth. You have been made holy in Christ. God called you to be holy. This letter is also addressed to people everywhere who trust the name of Jesus Christ. He rules both them and us.

3 May gracious love and peace from God our Father and the Lord Jesus Christ be with you.

God Chasers Are Rich

4 I always thank my God for you. He has given you gracious love in Christ Jesus. **5** In Christ, you became rich in every way—in everything you say and everything you know.

6 The truth about Christ was confirmed in you.   **7** You don't need any more gifts while you are waiting for our Lord Jesus Christ to be revealed *from heaven*.   **8** Jesus will make you strong until the end. On the *Judgment* Day of our Lord Jesus Christ you will be innocent.   **9** God called you into a relationship of sharing with His Son, our Lord Jesus Christ. God is faithful.

Division Is Wrong!

10 Brothers *and sisters*, I beg you, by the authority of our Lord Jesus Christ: All of you must agree. Get together. Have the same attitude and the same purpose. There should be no divisions among you.

11 My brothers, some of Cloe's people told me about you: There are arguments among you.   **12** To each one of you who is saying, "I belong to Paul," "I belong to Apollos," "I belong to Peter,"* or "I belong to Christ," this is what I have to say: **13** Is Christ divided up into pieces? Paul was not nailed to the cross for you, was he? You were not immersed by Paul's authority, were you?

14 I thank God that I immersed none of you—except Crispus and Gaius.   **15** None of you could say you were immersed on **my** authority.   **16** (Oh yes, I did immerse the people in Stephanas' house, too. I don't remember immersing anyone else.)   **17** Christ sent me not merely to immerse people, but to tell the Good News about Jesus. I must not tell it in a way that people regard as "wise." *The meaning of* the cross of Christ must not lose its power.

God-Chasing Power

18 To people who are being lost the message about Jesus' being nailed to a cross sounds silly, but it is God's power to us who are being saved.   **19** This is written:

> "I will destroy the *so-called* 'wisdom' of wise men
> and reject the 'understanding' of people
> of understanding."

Isaiah 29:14

1:12   literally, Cephas.

20 Where does that leave the "wise" man? Where is the "expert"? Where is the man in the world who can argue so skillfully? God has made this world's "wisdom" look foolish. **21** Evil people used their "wisdom," but they could not know the true God. This shows how wise God really is. It pleased God to save people who believe the "silly" message of preaching! **22** Jewish people are always asking for proofs from God. Non-Jewish people are always looking for "wisdom." **23** But we always preach Christ, the one who was nailed to the cross! This is embarrassing to Jews and nonsense to people who are not Jews. **24** To those of us who were called by God, whether we are Jews or non-Jews, this is the true message: Jesus is the Christ, God's power and God's wisdom! **25** God's "nonsense" is still wiser than the "wisdom" of human beings. His "weakness" is still stronger than man's "strength."

26 Brothers, look at the way that God called you: By human standards, not many of you were educated, important leaders, or people with much influence. **27** But God chose things which seem meaningless to people in the world. Why? To make wise men ashamed. God chose things which seem weak to the world to make strong people humble. **28** God chose things which the world thinks are not important, but He destroyed things which they think are important. **29** So, no person can brag in front of God. **30** But, because of God, you are now in Christ Jesus. To us, Christ has become wisdom— the only true wisdom that comes from God. Christ means being right with God, being holy and free. **31** Just as it is written:

> "If anyone wants to be proud, let him be proud of the
> Lord!"
> *Jeremiah 9:24*

Chapter 2

God Chasers Are Backed by the Holy Ghost

1 Brothers, when I came to you, I told you about God's secret. And I didn't use fancy words or man's wisdom. **2** No, I decided to talk about only one subject—Jesus Christ, the one who was nailed to the cross! **3** When I came to you, I was very nervous. I felt weak and afraid. **4** I didn't use the words of educated men to persuade people. Instead, I preached the message. I showed that it was backed up by the Spirit and real power. **5** Why? So that your trust would not depend upon human wisdom, but upon God's power!

God Chasers' Wisdom

6 We are speaking *true* wisdom to people who are *spiritually* mature. We are not talking about what this world calls "wisdom" or the rulers of this world, who are losing their power. **7** No, we are talking about God's secret wisdom, which has been hidden. Since before time began, God planned this glory for us. **8** None of the rulers of this world understood this. If they had known it, they would not have nailed the Lord of glory to the cross. **9** This has been written:

> "No eye has ever seen this and no ear has ever heard this.
> No human being has ever imagined this.
> But this is what God prepared for those who love Him." *Isaiah 64:4; 52:15*

10 God used the Spirit to show this *secret* to you. The Spirit searches everything—even the deep things of God. **11** How many people truly understand what is inside just one person? Only that person's spirit really knows. In the same way, only the Spirit of God knows all about God.   **12** It is not the spirit of the world which we have received. Instead, we received the Spirit who comes from God, so that we may understand the things which God gave to us.

13 These are the things we are saying. We are not using human ideas of wisdom which man taught us. Instead, we are using words which the Spirit teaches. We explain Spiritual things with Spiritual words.   **14** An uninspired person does not receive messages from God's Spirit. To him, they are without meaning; he cannot understand them. They can only be understood in a Spiritual way.   **15** The Spiritual person understands everything, but no one completely understands him:

16 "Who can completely understand the Lord's mind?
Who can give Him advice?"   *Isaiah 40:13*

But **we** have the mind of Christ!

Chapter 3

Jesus Is the Foundation

1 Brothers, I couldn't talk to you as I talk to people who are Spiritual. Instead, you were like worldly people, like babies in Christ.   **2** I gave you milk to drink, not solid food. You were not yet old enough. Even now you are not ready.   **3** You are still worldly. There is jealousy and arguing among you. Are you not worldly then? You are living like *sinful* people, aren't you?   **4** When someone says, "I belong to Paul" and another one says, "I belong to Apollos," you are acting like people *in sin.*

5 Who is Apollos? Who is Paul? We are only ministers. You believed the Good News by *listening to* us. The Lord gave each of us a job to do.   **6** I planted a seed, Apollos watered it, but *God* made it grow.   **7** The person who did the planting is not important. The person who gave it water is not important, but **God**, who made it grow, is important!   **8** The planter and the waterer work together. Each person will receive his own reward for doing his work.   **9** We also work together with God. You are God's farm.

10 Also, you are God's building. With the gracious love that God gave me, I laid the foundation like a skillful worker and another man builds upon that foundation. Each builder must be careful how he builds on it.   **11** It is wrong for anyone to try to lay another foundation. The *true* foundation is Jesus Christ!   **12** Someone may use gold, silver, or precious stones to build upon the foundation. Other people may use wood, hay, or straw.   **13** The results of each person's effort will become plain. The *Judgment* Day will make it clear. Fire will test it to see how solid each person's work really is.   **14** What a man built may last. If it does, he will receive a reward. **15** Even if his efforts are completely destroyed, **he** will be saved, though he will feel hurt. It will be difficult—like going through fire.   **16** You yourselves know that you are God's temple sanctuary. Don't you know that the Spirit of God lives in you?   **17** If someone tries to destroy God's temple sanctuary, God will destroy him, because God's temple sanctuary is holy and **you** are God's temple sanctuary.

18 No one should fool himself! If anyone among you thinks he is "wise" (by this world's standards), he ought to become a "fool"—then, he can become truly wise. **19** This world's "wisdom" is really foolishness to God. This has been written:

"God trapped the *so-called* 'wise' people with their
own tricks."   *Job 5:13*

20 And again:

"The Lord *God* knows how worthless the thoughts of
so-called 'wise' people are."   *Psalm 94:11*

21 So, no person can brag about human '*wisdom.*'
Everything belongs to you:
22 Paul,
Apollos,
Peter,*
the world,
life,
death,
the present,
the future.

Everything is yours!   **23** All of you belong to Christ. And, Christ belongs to God.

Chapter 4

1 So then, a person should think of us as Christ's helpers. We are in charge of God's secrets.   **2** One thing is expected of a manager—he must be faithful.   **3** It doesn't matter to me that you judge me by human standards. I don't even judge myself!   **4** My conscience isn't hurting me, but this does not make me right with God. The Lord is the One who judges me.   **5** You must not pre-judge anything before the Lord *Jesus* comes. He will bring to light the things which are hidden in the dark. He will make clear the motives of the hearts *of people*. At that time, God will reward each individual.

6 Brothers, I have applied these things to myself and Apollos for your sake, so that you may learn from our example. You must not go beyond what the Scriptures say. Don't be more proud of one person than another.   **7** How are you better than anyone else? What do you have that you did not receive *from God*? Since you received it *from God*, then why do you brag, as though you did **not** receive it?

8 You are already satisfied *with yourselves*. You have already become "rich." You have become "kings," ruling without us. I wish you really were kings. Then we could rule with you!   **9** It seems as though God has made us apostles look like the least important of all people, like men condemned to die. We have become a show to people, to the world, and to the angels.   **10** Because of Christ we are fools, but you are such wise men in Christ. We are powerless, but you are strong. You are famous, but we have no honor.   **11** At this moment, we are hungry, thirsty, poorly dressed, beat up, and without a home.   **12** We work hard with our own hands. When people curse us, we bless them. When they persecute us, we endure.   **13** When people say cruel things to us, we encourage. We have become like the world's garbage. At this very moment, we are like the scum of the earth!

14 I'm not writing these things to shame you. I am only warning you like my precious children.   **15** Though you may have 10,000 trainers in Christ, you don't have more than one father. With the Good News **I** fathered you in Christ Jesus.   **16** So, I beg you, be like me.   **17** This is why I sent Timothy to you. He is my precious, faithful child in the Lord *Jesus*. Timothy will help you remember the ways in Christ which I teach in each congregation everywhere.   **18** Some of you are acting proud, thinking I won't come there.   **19** But I will come to you soon, if that is what the Lord wants. I

3:22   literally, Cephas.

will find out not what these proud people can say, but what they can do!   20 Because the kingdom of God is not talk, but real power.   21 Which do you prefer? Should I come to you with a rod *for punishing*, or with a loving, gentle attitude?

Chapter 5

Watch it!

1 It is being told everywhere that there is a terrible sexual sin among you. And, it is the kind of sexual sin that almost never occurs—even among people of the world: Some man is having sexual relations with his stepmother!*   2 But, instead of feeling sorry about this, you seem proud of it! The man who has done this should be put away from your group.   3 Although my body is not there, my spirit is present with you. I have already decided, as if I were present, what you should do about the man who has behaved in this way.   4 When you and my spirit gather together, by the authority of our Lord Jesus and with his power, *this is what should be done*:   5 Turn such a man over to Satan! This may destroy his flesh, so that his spirit may be saved on the *Judgment* Day of the Lord.

6 Your pride is not good. Don't you realize that only a little yeast makes a whole lump of dough rise?   7 Clean out the old yeast *of sin*, so that you may become a new batch of dough. Then you will be pure.* Christ, our Passover lamb, was sacrificed. 8 So, let us celebrate our Passover Festival, but not by using the old yeast of sin and evil. Instead, let us use sincerity and truth.

9 I wrote this to you in another letter: "You must not associate with people who commit sexual sin."   10 But I didn't mean the people from this world who commit sexual sin, or greedy people, or robbers, or people who worship false gods. You would need to leave the earth to get away from them.   11 But in this letter I am telling you not to associate with a person (who calls himself a brother), if he commits sexual sin, or if he is a greedy person, or if he worships false gods, or if he says terrible things about people, or if he is a drunkard, or if he robs people. Don't even eat with such a person!

12-13 It is none of my business to judge people on the outside *of the congregation*. God is the One who will judge outsiders. You are supposed to judge people on the inside. So, put this evil man away from you!

Chapter 6

Stop Fighting!

1 One of you has a serious matter in court against another *brother*. Does this person dare to have himself judged in front of sinners? This should be judged before the holy people.   2 Surely you realize that the holy people are the ones who will judge the world. Since you will judge the people in the world, aren't you worthy to judge small matters *in the congregation*?   3 Don't you realize that we will judge angels? Surely we should *be able to* judge matters in this life.   4 When you have such civil cases, why do you put them before *outsiders* whose *opinion* the congregation does not consider important?   5 I am saying this to make you feel ashamed. Do you not have even one person in your group who is wise? Is there no one who can decide what is right between two of his *Christian* brothers? 6 Instead, one brother is against his brother in court—and this

---

5:1   literally, his father's wife.
5:7   or, clean.

is happening in front of non-believers!   7 You already have lawsuits among you. This shows that you have completely failed! It would be better to allow someone to do wrong to you, wouldn't it? Why not let someone cheat you?   8 Instead, you are doing wrong and you are cheating. And, you are doing this to **brothers**!

9 Surely you must realize that evil people will not enter God's kingdom? Don't be fooled. These are the kind of people I'm talking about:

They commit sexual sin.
They worship false gods.
They commit adultery.
They are perverts.
They are homosexuals.
10 They steal.
They are greedy.
They are drunkards.
They say terrible things about people.
They rob people.

People like this won't enter the kingdom of God.   11 Some of you were like that, but you were washed *of sin* and made holy. You have been made right with God by the authority of the Lord Jesus Christ and with the Spirit of our God.

Our Bodies Belong to the Lord

12 "I may do anything I want to do," but not everything is best for me. Yes, "I may do anything I want to do," but I won't allow myself to be a slave to anything. 13 "Food helps to keep the stomach satisfied. The stomach is supposed to receive food," but God will destroy both the stomach and food. The human body should function for the Lord's purpose. Committing sexual sin is **not** the purpose of the body. It should be used for the Lord.   14 God raised the Lord *Jesus* from death. With the same power He will also raise you.

15 Surely you realize that your bodies are parts of Christ's body. Should the parts of Christ's body be changed to the parts of a whore's body? **Certainly not!**   16 Don't you know that the person who has sex with a whore is one body with her? The Scripture says:

"A man and a woman will become one flesh."   *Genesis 2:24*

17 But the person who joins himself to the Lord is one spirit with Him.

18 Run away from sexual sin! Any other sin which a person might do is outside his body, but if a person commits a sexual sin, he is sinning against his own body. 19 Surely you realize that your body is a temple sanctuary? You have *received* the Holy Spirit from God. The Holy Spirit is inside you—in the temple sanctuary. You don't belong to yourselves.   20 You were bought; you cost something. Use your body to give glory to God!

Chapter 7

God-Chasing Rules for Marriage

1 You have already written to me about *marriage*: It is good for a man not to marry. 2 However, there is so much sexual sin everywhere. So, each man should be married and each woman should be married.   3 The husband should satisfy his wife sexually. In the same way, the wife should satisfy her husband's sexual needs.   4 The wife does not own her body; it belongs to her husband. And the husband does not own his body;

his wife does. **5** Don't cheat one another of sex. You may agree to stop for a while, so that you may pray to God more, but after this time, you should come together again. Otherwise, Satan might tempt you through not having enough self-control.

6 From my own knowledge, and not as a command, I am saying this: **7** I wish everyone could be *single* like me, but God has given each person his own special gift.

8 This is what I say to single people and widows: If you were to stay unmarried as I am, it would be better for you. **9** But, if you don't have self-control, then go ahead and get married. It would be better for you to get married than always to be burning *with sexual desire*.

10 To married people I am giving this order (the command is not mine; the Lord *Jesus* gave this order): A wife must not separate from her husband. **11** If she does, she must stay unmarried—or come back to her husband. A husband must not leave his wife, either.

12 I am saying this to others there (The Lord *Jesus* did not give a *direct* command.): A brother might be married to a woman who is not a believer. Suppose she likes being married to him; he must not leave her. **13** A *Christian* woman might have a husband who is an unbeliever, but he likes being married to her. She must not leave him, **14** because the unbelieving husband is made "holy" by his *Christian* wife. And the unbelieving wife is made "holy" by the *Christian* brother. Otherwise, your children would be *spiritually* unclean; now they are holy.

15 If the unbeliever wants to separate *from his mate*, allow that person to separate. A *Christian* brother or sister is not bound in such cases. God called us *to live* in peace. **16** O wife, who knows—you might convert your *unbelieving* husband? O husband, who knows—you might convert your *unbelieving* wife?

17 The Lord has given a role to each person. He should live his life the way it was when God called him. This is what I tell people to do in all the congregations: **18** If God called someone with the marks of circumcision,* he must not try to remove those marks. If God called someone else without the marks of circumcision, he must not become circumcised. **19** Circumcision is not important; being uncircumcised is not important, either. Obeying God's commands is what's important. **20** Each person should stay in the role he had when God first called him. **21** Were you a slave when God called you? That shouldn't bother you. But if you can get your freedom, get it. **22** The person who was a slave when God called him is now the Lord's free man. In the same way, the person who was a free man when God called him is now Christ's slave. **23** *Christ* paid a price for you; don't be slaves of men. **24** Brothers, stay as you were when God called you.

God-Chasing Rules for Singles

25 *You wrote me a letter* about virgin girls. I don't have a *direct* command from the Lord *Jesus*, but I am giving you what I know. I'm dependable; the Lord has given me mercy. **26** Because of present serious times, I think the best thing a man can do is to remain as he is: **27** Are you bound to a wife? Don't break up the marriage. Are you unmarried? Don't look for a wife. **28** But if you do get married, you haven't done wrong. And, if a virgin girl gets married, she has not sinned.

7:18   cutting off the foreskin of the make sex organ as a sign of God's agreement with Israel (Gen. 17:9-14).

However, married people will have many troubles at this time, and I would like to protect you.

29 Brothers, I am saying this because time is short. Soon men who have wives must act as though they are not married. **30** People who are crying must act as though they are not really crying. Those who are happy must act as though they are not happy. People who buy things must act as though they don't own what they've bought. **31** Those who do business with the world must act as though they don't care. Why? Because this world, as you see it, won't last long.

32 I want you to be free from worry. An unmarried *Christian* man is concerned about the Lord's things and he is trying to please the Lord. **33** A married *Christian* man is worried about worldly things; he is trying to please his wife. **34** He is torn between the two. An unmarried *Christian* woman or virgin girl is concerned about the Lord's things; she wants to be holy in body and spirit. A married *Christian* woman worries about worldly things; she is trying to please her husband.

35 I am saying this to help you. I'm not trying to add an extra burden to you. Do what seems right. Give yourselves completely to the Lord without distraction.

36 Someone may not think he is doing the right thing with his bride-to-be. She may not be getting any younger, either. He may feel he should marry her. Let him do what he wants to; he is not sinning. Let them get married! **37** However, another man may have already firmly decided that he does not need to get married, because he has complete control of his *sexual* will-power. He has decided in his heart that he won't marry her. He'll be doing a fine thing, too. **38** The man who marries his bride-to-be is doing a good thing, but the man who does not marry will be doing even better. **39** A *Christian* woman is bound *by her marriage promise* as long as her husband lives, but if her husband dies, she becomes free from it. She may marry anyone—anyone in the Lord *Jesus*. **40** But I think she would be happier if she stayed a widow. And I think that I, too, have the Spirit of God.

Chapter 8

God Chasers Are Careful

1 *You wrote me* about meat offered to false gods. We know that all of us have *spiritual* knowledge. Knowledge makes a person proud, but love builds up *other people*. **2** Someone may seem to know a lot, but he still doesn't know what he must know. **3** If someone loves God, God knows this person.

4 *You wrote me* about *eating* meat which has been offered to false gods. We know that they really don't exist. There is only one true God. **5** There are "gods" in heaven and on earth—many "gods" and many "lords"—but they are not real. **6** To us, there is only one God—the Father. He is the Source of everything. We *live* for Him. There is only one Lord—Jesus Christ. Everything *was created* through him. We *live* through him.

7 However, not everyone has this *spiritual* knowledge. Some people still have the habit of treating idols* as though they were real when they eat such meat. Their conscience is weak; they feel that the food makes them unclean. **8** Food is not the thing that brings us closer to God. We are not losing anything if we don't eat some things. We are not any better off if we do eat.

8:7   or, false gods.

9 But, be careful! Don't let your freedom cause a weak person to sin.   **10** You have *spiritual* knowledge. Suppose you sit down to eat meat inside the temple of a false god and suppose a person with a weak conscience sees you. His conscience would become bold; he would go inside and eat meat offered to false gods, too!   **11** So, your *spiritual* knowledge would destroy a person with a weak conscience. And, Christ died for that brother!   **12** In this way, you would have sinned against the brothers. You would have hurt their weak consciences and you would have sinned against Christ!   **13** Therefore, if meat causes my brother to sin, I will never eat meat. I don't want to make my brother sin.

Chapter 9

God Chasers Support the Ministry

1 I am free, am I not? I'm an apostle, am I not? I have seen our Lord Jesus, haven't I? You are the result of my efforts for the Lord, aren't you?   **2** Others may not think I truly am an apostle. At least to you, I am an apostle, because **you** are the proof of it in the Lord *Jesus*!

3 When people criticize me, this is my defense: **4** We have the right to receive food and drink *for work*.   **5** Do not each of us have the right to travel with a Christian* wife? We have the same right as the other apostles, brothers of the Lord *Jesus*, and Peter.*   **6** Are we, Barnabas and myself, the only ones who have to work for a living?

7 Soldiers don't pay their own wages. A farmer who plants a vineyard is allowed to eat some of the grapes. A shepherd who takes care of the flock of sheep gets some of the milk from the flock.

8 I am not claiming these things from human examples. The law says the same things.   **9** This is written in the law of Moses:

"Don't cover the ox's mouth while it is walking around
on the wheat straw."   *Deuteronomy 25:4*

Did God say this because He cares about oxen?   **10** God said all this for us; it was written *to teach* us something. The person who is plowing should plow with hope. The man who separates the grain from the straw should hope to share part of the grain. **11** Since we planted spiritual things among you, it should be no big thing to harvest physical things from you.   **12** Other people have the right for support from you. Shouldn't we have it, too? Yes, but we have not used this right. We endure all of these things, because we don't want to do anything to slow down the gospel of Christ. **13** Surely you realize that those priests who work in the temple area eat *some of the food that is offered there*. And, those who work near the altar share *in the food that is offered* there.   **14** In the same way, the Lord *Jesus* commanded that the men who are preaching the Good News should be able to make a living from *preaching* it.

15 I have not used any of these privileges. I am not writing these things so that I can get something from you—I would rather die first! No one will take away what I'm so proud of!   **16** I am telling the Good News, but that is nothing I can brag about. I feel compelled to do it. How awful it would be for me if I were not telling the Good News!

9:5   literally, who is a sister.
9:5   literally, Cephas.

17 If I do it because I really choose to do it, I could get a reward. But if I do it as a duty, I am only doing the job that God gave me. **18** What reward do I get? I tell the story of the Good News free of charge. So, I don't use my privilege when I am telling the Good News.

19 I am my own man; no man owns me. I make myself a slave to everyone, so that I may win many people for *the Good News*. **20** To Jews, I became more Jewish to win them. I obey *the* law for the good of those who *think they* are under its rule. (I am not really under its authority).* I am only trying to win those who obey *the* law. **21** I obey no special rules for the good of non-Jewish people. This doesn't mean that I am free from God's law; I am within Christ's law! I am only trying to win non-Jewish people *for the gospel*. **22** To weak people, I became weak, so that I could win weak people. I have become almost anything for the good of everyone, so that I could save some of them in some way. **23** Everything I do, I do for *the spreading of* the gospel. I want to share in it. **24** Surely you realize that, of all those who are running a race in the stadium, only one of them can receive the prize. In the same way, run your race, so that you may win the prize. **25** Every athlete who is in training must have complete control of his body. He trains to receive a prize; it will not last. But, we do it to receive a prize which lasts forever. **26** So, I am not just running in one spot. I'm not shadowboxing; I really punch! **27** I make my body tough, bringing it under complete control. Otherwise, I might be disqualified, after I have preached to others.

Chapter 10

Warnings for Those Who Are Chasing the Lord

1 Brothers, I want you to realize that all of our ancestors were under the cloud and all of them passed through the *Red* Sea.* **2** All of them were plunged* into Moses' *protection* under the cloud and in the sea. **3** All of them ate the same spiritual food.* **4** All of them drank the same spiritual drink.* They were drinking from the spiritual rock which was following them. (That rock was Christ.) **5** However, God was not pleased with most of them. Their dead bodies were scattered all over the desert.

6 But these things are examples for us. We must not want evil things as our ancestors did. **7** We must not worship false gods as some of them did. This is written:

"The people sat down to eat and drink

and then they got up to play around." *Exodus 32:6*

8 We must not commit sexual sin as some of them did. In one day, *God* destroyed 23,000 people! **9** We must not test the Lord as some of them did. They were killed by snakes. **10** You must not complain, as some of them did. An angel of death killed them.

11 But all of these things happened to them for examples. This was written to warn us—we who are confronted by the end of the ages. **12** The person who thinks he is safe should be careful—he might fall! **13** You have been tempted the same way all people have been tempted, but God is faithful. He will not allow *Satan* to tempt you

---

9:20   Paul treated it as Jewish custom.
10:1   Exodus 14:22.
10:2   literally, immersed (Greek has *baptized*). Exodus 13:21-22; 14:19-22
10:3   Deuteronomy. 8:3; Nehemiah. 9:20
10:4   Exodus 17:6; Numbers 20:11; Psalm 78:15

with more than you can resist. No, when you are being tempted, God will also give you a way to escape, so that you can endure it.

14 So, my dear *friends*, run away from false gods. **15** I am talking the way I would talk to wise men. Weigh what I am saying. **16** The cup of blessing which we bless is the sharing of Christ's blood, isn't it? When we all break off a piece of the bread, it is the sharing of Christ's body, isn't it? **17** Though there are many of us, we are one body. There is one loaf, but all of us share this one loaf.

18 Look at physical Israel: The people who eat what is offered *to God* share in the altar. **19** So, what am I saying? Does something offered to a false god mean anything? Is an idol real? **20** No! The people of the world are offering things to demons, not to the true God. I don't want you to be partners with demons! **21** You must not drink from the cup of the Lord **and** from the cup of demons. You must not share at the Lord's table **and** at the table of demons. **22** Are we trying to make the Lord jealous? Are we stronger than He is?

23 "I am allowed to do anything," but not everything is the best thing to do. Yes, "I am allowed to do anything," but not everything builds up other people. **24** Look for things which are good for someone else, not only for yourself.

25 Eat anything that is sold in the meat market. Don't ask any questions because of conscience. **26** "The earth and everything in it belongs to the Lord."*

27 If an unbeliever invites you *to his home* and you want to go, eat whatever he puts in front of you. Don't ask any questions because of conscience. **28** But if anyone says this to you: "This was offered to an idol!" don't eat it—because of the one who said this and because of conscience. **29** By "conscience" I mean not yours, but his!

But why is my freedom being judged by the conscience of someone else? **30** If I am thankful for what I have, why can someone say evil things about something for which I am thankful to God?

31 If you are eating, drinking, or doing anything, do everything to give glory to God. **32** Don't cause anyone to sin—Jews, non-Jews, or anyone in the community of God. **33** I try to please everyone in every way. I'm not looking for what is best for me, but what is best for most people, so that they will be saved.

Chapter 11

1 Follow my example, as I am following the example of Christ.

Lady and Gentlemen God Chasers

2 I praise you, because you remember me in all things. You are loyal to the teaching that I passed on to you: **3** I want you to understand that God is over Christ. Christ is over every male. And males are over females. **4** Every male who is praying or prophesying with his head covered brings shame to his head.* **5** Any female who is praying or prophesying with her head uncovered brings shame on her head.* This means the same thing as shaving the head.* **6** If a woman's head is not covered, she should cut off all her hair! Since it is shameful for a woman to have her hair cut off or shaved, she should wear a covering. **7** A male ought not to cover his head. He is the image and glory of God; the female is the glory of the male. **8** The male did not come from the female; she came from him. **9** The male was not made for the female; she was made

---

10:26 Psalm 24:1
11:4 Christ
11:5 males
11:5 a very shameful thing to do

for him.   **10** This is why a female ought to show some sign on her head that she is respecting authority. She should also do it because of the angels.

11 In the Lord *Jesus*, she is not independent; she needs the male. But the male is not independent of the female, either.   **12** The female came from the male, but males also come from females. Everything comes from God.   **13** Decide for yourselves: Does it seem right to you that a woman should pray to God without a covering?   **14** Don't you just naturally conclude that it is shameful for a man to wear long hair?   **15** A woman's glory is her long hair. It is given to her for a covering.   **16** If someone wants to argue about it, we don't have a different custom, neither do the congregations of God.

The Supper of the Lord

17 I am not praising you with the following instructions: Your meetings are hurting you, instead of helping you!   **18** First, when you come together as a congregation, I hear that there are divisions among you. I believe part of this is true.   **19** It is *apparently* necessary to have factions among you, so that it will become plain which of you are "true" *believers*.   **20** When you gather together, you are not eating the **Lord's** supper,   **21** because each person takes his own supper. He does not wait for others; he just goes ahead and eats. So, one stays hungry and another gets drunk.   **22** You have houses where you can eat and drink. Do you look down on God's congregation? Do you want to make poor people ashamed? What should I say to you? Should I praise you? I most certainly do not!

23 I received from the Lord what I passed on to you: During the night that the Lord Jesus was betrayed, he took bread.   **24** Then he thanked God for it and broke off some of it. Jesus said, "This bread is* my body *which I am giving* for you. Eat this to remember me."   **25** After supper, Jesus took a cup in the same way. He said, "This cup is* the new agreement *with God* in my blood. Drink this to remember me. Every time you drink this, you will be remembering me."   **26** Every time you eat this bread and drink from this cup, you are telling about the Lord *Jesus'* death, until he returns.

27 So, if anyone eats the bread or drinks the cup of the Lord with the wrong attitude, he will be guilty of sinning against the body and the blood of the Lord *Jesus Christ*!   **28** Each person must look deeply into his own heart. Then he should eat the bread and drink from the cup in the right way.   **29** If someone is eating and drinking without recognizing the meaning of the body *of Christ*, he is condemning himself by eating and drinking!   **30** This is why many of you are weak and sick. A large number of you have died, too.   **31** If we judged ourselves, we would not be judged.   **32** No, the Lord judges us. We are being corrected, so that we will not be condemned with the people of the world.   **33** So, my brothers, when you gather together to eat *the supper of the Lord*, wait for one another.   **34** If *someone comes* only for the food, he should stay home and eat there! Meeting together should not bring condemnation on you. I will give more orders when I come.

Chapter 12

Spiritual Gifts

1 Brothers, I want you to know *the truth* about spiritual *gifts*.   **2** Do you remember when you were people of the world? You were controlled by false gods which couldn't talk; you followed them.   **3** So, I make this clear to you: No one who is speaking by

---

11:24   or, represents, symbolizes
11:25   or, represents, symbolizes

264

God's Spirit can say, "Jesus, be cursed!" And, no one can say, "Jesus is Lord," unless he says it by the Holy Spirit.

4 There are many different *spiritual* gifts, but it is the same Spirit who *gives them.* 5 There are many different ways of serving, but it is the same Lord *Jesus who is being served.* 6 There are many different abilities, but it is the same God who gives them. God gives all of these powers to all of the people *who have them.* 7 The showing of the Spirit is given to each one for the good of everyone:

8 The ability to speak wisely
   is given through the Spirit to one person.
The ability to give knowledge
   is given by the same Spirit to another person.
9 A different person receives
   faith by the same Spirit.
The ability to heal diseases
   is given to another by the one Spirit.
10 The ability to work miracles
   is given to someone else.
The ability to prophesy
   is given to another person.
The ability to see the difference between what spirits teach
   is given to another one.
The ability to speak different *inspired* languages*
   is given to one.
The ability to interpret *inspired* languages*
   is given to someone else.

11 All of these powers are given by one and the same Spirit. He distributes them to each person as he chooses.

Body Language

12 The body is a unit, but it has many parts. All of the many parts of the body make up one body. Christ is the same way. 13 All of us were immersed into this one body *of Christ* by one Spirit—Jews/non-Jews, slaves/free men—we all drink from the same Spirit.

14 The body does not have only one part; it has many parts. 15 The foot might say, "Since I am not a hand, I don't belong with the body," but it still belongs with the body! 16 The ear might say, "Since I'm not an eye, I don't belong with the body," but it still does belong with the body! 17 If the whole body were an eye, how would the body hear? If the whole body were an ear, where would smelling come from? 18 God has now put each member in the body as He chose to do. 19 If everything were just one member, there would be no body! 20 But now, though we are many members, we are one body. 21 The eye cannot say this to the hand: "I do not need you!" Again, the head cannot say to the feet: "I do not need you!" 22 No, the members of the body which seem to be weaker than other parts are truly necessary. 23 There are parts of the body which we think are ugly. We give these parts special care. We treat an unmentionable part of the body with special attention. 24 The more beautiful parts of our body don't need this. But God has joined the parts of the body together. He gives more

---

12:10   with the help of the Holy Spirit
12:10   with the help of the Holy Spirit

honor to the parts that need it. **25** God wants no division in the body. Instead, He wants the members to care about one another. **26** If one member is suffering, all of the members are suffering, too. If another member receives an honor, then all the members are happy for him.

27 Each one of you is part of Christ's body. **28** Among all those whom God called out, He put in these people:

first, apostles;

second, prophets;

third, teachers;

next, those who work miracles;

then, people who heal diseases;

people who help others;

organizers;

those who speak *inspired* languages.*

29 All of them are not apostles, are they? Not all of them are prophets, are they? Are all of them teachers? All of them are not miracle workers, are they? **30** All of them do not have the gift of healing diseases, do they? Not all of them speak *inspired* languages,* do they? All of them cannot interpret *inspired* languages,* can they? **31** Eagerly desire the more important *spiritual* gifts.

True Love

I will now show you the best way of all:

Chapter 13

1 Even if I speak with human languages or the language of angels, but do not have loving concern, I have only become like the noisy sound of a gong or the ringing sound from cymbals. **2** I may have the ability to prophesy, know all secrets, possess all knowledge, and have the kind of faith which can move mountains, but if I don't have concern for others, I am nothing. **3** I could give away everything I own and sacrifice my body, so that I could brag about it, but if I did not have love, I have gained nothing.

4 A loving person

is patient;

is kind;

is not jealous;

is not boastful;

is not proud;

5 is not rude;

is not interested only in himself;

is even-tempered;

does not hold grudges;

6 is not happy when someone else does wrong;

is happy when truth wins;

7 never quits;

always trusts;

always hopes *for the best*;

always keeps on going.

12:28   with the help of the Holy Spirit
12:30   with the help of the Holy Spirit
12:30   with the help of the Holy Spirit

8 Love lasts forever. There are such things as prophecies, but they will disappear. There are such things as *inspired* languages,* but they will stop. There is such a thing as knowledge *from God*, but it will disappear. **9** We only know portions of things *from God*. We prophesy in parts, **10** but when that which is complete comes, the parts will disappear.

11 When I was a child, I used to talk about the things that a child would talk about. I thought and reasoned as a child does, but now that I have become an adult, I have put aside the ways of children. **12** At this time, we see only a blurred image in the *metal* mirror. At the time of maturity, we will see plainly—as one person looking at another's face. Now I know things only partially, but then I will know everything completely, just as God knows me.

13 Now these three things last: faith, hope, and love—but the most important of these is love.

Chapter 14

God Chasers Understand Spiritual Gifts

1 Follow the loving way and eagerly desire the spiritual *gifts*, especially prophesying. **2** Anyone who is speaking in an *inspired* language* is not communicating to men, but to God. No one understands him. He is speaking the secrets *of God* by inspiration. **3** But everyone who prophesies to people is speaking to build them up, to encourage them, and to comfort them. **4** The one who is speaking an *inspired* language* is only helping himself, but the one who is prophesying is helping the congregation. **5** I wish that all of you could speak with *inspired* languages, but even more, I wish you could prophesy. The one who is prophesying is more effective than the one who speaks in *inspired* languages*—unless someone can explain it in such a way that the congregation will get some good from it.

6 Now, brothers, if I come speaking *inspired* languages to you, what good will you get out of it? I may speak to you by revelation, *inspired* knowledge, prophecy, or *inspired* teaching.

7 Lifeless instruments, such as a flute or a harp, produce a sound. This sound must be made clearly or no one can recognize the tune which is being played on the flute or the harp. **8** If the bugle makes a sound which is not clear, no one will prepare for battle. **9** In the same way, if you use an *inspired* language to give your fine message, how will anyone understand what is being said? You will seem to be like a person who talks to himself!* **10** There are many different languages in the world. All of them have meaning. **11** If I don't understand the meaning of the language,* I am a foreigner to the one who is speaking and he is a foreigner to me. **12** Since you are eager for spiritual *gifts*, eagerly desire those which will help the whole congregation the most.

13 So, the one who is speaking in an *inspired* language* must pray that he will *be able to* interpret what he said. **14** When I am using an *inspired* language* in prayer,

---

13:8 with the help of the Holy Spirit
14:2 with the help of the Holy Spirit
14:4 with the help of the Holy Spirit
14:5 with the help of the Holy Spirit
14:9 literally, like one who is talking into the air
14:11 literally, sound
14:13 with the help of the Holy Spirit

my spirit is praying, but my understanding has no part in it.   **15** So, what should I do? I will pray with my spirit and pray with understanding, too. I will sing *to God* with my spirit and sing with understanding, too.   **16** When you are praising God *in an inspired language* only with your spirit, how will the ordinary person know when to say, "Amen"? You are giving thanks *to God*, but that man doesn't know what you are saying.   **17** It is a fine thing that you are giving thanks *to God*, but the other person is not getting any good out of it.

18 I thank God that I speak in *inspired* languages* more than all of you.   **19** However, in the meeting I would rather speak five words with understanding to teach other people than thousands of words in an *inspired* language!*

20 Brothers, be as innocent as children about evil things, but don't be like children in how you think. Be mature!   **21** This is written in the law:

> "I will speak to this nation
>   with different languages
>   and different dialects,
>   but they will not obey me."   *Isaiah 28:11-12; Deuteronomy 28:49*

That is what the Lord *God* said.

22 Speaking *inspired* languages* is a proof from God to unbelievers, not to the people who already believe. The ability to prophesy is proof to believers, not to unbelievers.   **23** Suppose the whole congregation gathers together and everyone is speaking with *inspired* languages.* Then an ordinary person or unbeliever comes into *the room*. Would he not say you are crazy?   **24** But if everyone can prophesy, and an unbeliever or ordinary person comes into *the room*, he will feel convicted of sin by everything *that is happening*. He will feel judged by everyone.   **25** The secret things of his heart will come out into the open. He will bow down his face and begin to worship God, confessing: "God is really among you!"

God Chasers Get in Order

26 Brothers, what should be done? When you gather together, someone may have a song. Someone else may have a teaching to give, a special revelation, an *inspired* language, or an interpretation. Everything should be done for the good *of the whole group*. **27** If someone speaks with an *inspired* language,* let him speak—but only two or three at the most. Let them speak by taking turns, and let only one person interpret.   **28** If no interpreter is there, the person who speaks an *inspired* language* must not speak in the congregation. However, he is allowed to think to himself and worship God silently. **29** Let two or three prophets talk, while others judge carefully what they say.   **30** If a revelation *from God* comes to another person who is sitting down, the first prophet must stop talking *immediately*.   **31** All of you will have an opportunity to prophesy, but it

---

14:14   with the help of the Holy Spirit
14:18   with the help of the Holy Spirit
14:19   with the help of the Holy Spirit
14:22   God gave some of them the miraculous gift of being able to speak inspired languages fluently which they had never learned before.
14:23   with the help of the Holy Spirit
14:27   with the help of the Holy Spirit
14:28   with the help of the Holy Spirit

must be by turn, so that everyone will learn and be encouraged.   32 The people who have the gift of prophecy can control their own spirits.   33 God is a God of peace, not confusion.

This is the way it should be in all of the congregations of the holy people!   34 The women must be quiet in the meetings. They are not allowed to speak. They must be under authority, as the law says.*   35 If the women want to learn *more* about something, they should ask their husbands at home. It is shameful for a woman to speak in the meeting.

36 Did God's message come from you? Are you the only ones it came to?

37 Someone may think he is a prophet or an inspired person. However, that person must acknowledge that what I am writing to you is a command from the Lord!   38 If he doesn't want to listen, he won't be listened to.*

39 So, my brothers, eagerly desire the ability to prophesy. And, don't try to stop people from speaking in *inspired* languages.*   40 Everything should be done properly and orderly.

Chapter 15

Dying to See Him

1 Brothers, I am telling you the Good News which I've already told you. You accepted it and you are still staying with it.   2 If you hold onto the Good News which I told you, then, through it, you are being saved—unless you believed it for nothing!   3 First of all, I passed on to you the same thing which was passed on to me: Christ died for our sins. (The Scriptures told about this before it happened.)   4 He was buried and he was raised from death on the third day. (The Scriptures foretold this, too.)   5 Then Jesus appeared to Peter, and later to all the apostles.   6 Then he appeared to more than 500 brothers at the same time. Most of these people are still alive today, but some of them have already died.   7 Christ appeared to James, and then to all the apostles.   8 Last of all, he also appeared to me. I was like a baby born very late.   9 Of all the apostles, I am the least important. I don't even deserve to be called an apostle; I persecuted the called-out people of God!   10 But I am what I am because of God's gracious love which he pointed toward me. This paid off! I worked harder than all of the other *apostles*. But, it was not really **I** that was working so hard—it was God's gracious love which I have with me!   11 It doesn't matter whether the Good News came through me or through others—we preached it and you believed it!

12 Since it is being preached that Christ has been raised from death, why do some of you claim that, when people die, they do not live again?   13 If people don't rise from death, then Christ has not been raised from death.   14 And if Christ hasn't been raised from death, then what we are preaching is not true. You have believed in something which is false!   15 We are guilty of being liars about God. We told "the truth from God," that God raised Christ from death. But, if people don't rise from death, then God did **not** raise Christ from death!   16 If people don't rise from death, then Christ has not been raised from death, either.   17 And if Christ hasn't been raised from death,

14:34   Genesis 3:16?
14:38   or, If someone is ignorant, let him be ignorant.
14:39   with the help of the Holy Spirit
15:5   literally, Cephas

your faith is worthless. You are still *lost* in your sins!   **18** And, all of those who died in Christ are gone.   **19** If we have put our hope in Christ in this life, *and Christ did not rise from death*, then, of all people, we should be pitied the most.

20 But now, Christ has been raised from death! He was the first one of those who have already died.   **21** Death came *into the world* through one man; rising from death has also come through one man.   **22** Everyone dies because of what Adam did, and everyone will live because of what Christ did.   **23** Each one will rise from death in his proper order. Christ was the first one. The people who belong to Christ will rise from death when Jesus comes *from heaven*.   **24** Then the end will come. Christ will hand over the kingdom to God the Father. Christ will destroy every ruler, every authority and power.   **25** Christ must be the king, until God puts all Christ's enemies under Christ's feet.*   **26** Death is the last enemy to be destroyed.

27 "God will put everything under his feet."   *Psalm 8:6*
(When it says "everything," it is clear that this does not include God, the One who put everything under Christ's authority.)   **28** After God does this, Christ* will put himself under God's authority (the One who put everything under Christ). This is the way that God will be above all things in everything.

29 Some people are immersed on account of people who died. If people don't rise from death, then why do they do this?   **30** Why are we always in danger?   **31** I face death every day. (Brothers, I am proud of you; that is the one thing I have in Christ Jesus our Lord.)   **32** I fought against wild animals in the city of Ephesus. If people don't rise from death, what good did I get from it, if it were for only human reasons?

"Let's eat and drink *today*; we will die
tomorrow!"   *Isaiah 22:13; 56:12*
33 Don't be fooled, "Bad friends will spoil good habits."   **34** Be alert and do what is right.* Some people don't have a true knowledge of God. (I say this to make you feel ashamed.)

How Do We Rise?

35 But someone will say, "How do people rise *from death*? What kind of body do they come back with?"   **36** You are foolish! What you plant does not live, unless it dies *first*.   **37** When you plant something, you are not planting the full-grown plant! No, it is a bare seed, perhaps wheat or some other grain.   **38** God gives it the shape He wants. Each kind of seed has its own shape.   **39** All cell tissue* is different. Human beings have their own kind of flesh. Animals have a different type, as do birds and fish.

40 There are bodies in the universe and bodies on earth, but the beauty of the universe is different from the beauty of anything on earth.   **41** The sun has its own beauty; the moon has another kind of beauty. The stars have still another type of beauty. Even the stars are different from one another in their beauty.

42 So, people **do** rise from death! A dead body is buried in decay, but it will be raised, never to die again.   **43** A dead body will be buried with sadness, but it will be raised *from death* with splendor. A dead body is buried in weakness, but it will be raised

---

15:25   or, under his control
15:28   literally, the Son
15:34   or, Think straight and stop sinning.
15:39   literally, flesh

with power.   **44** A dead body is buried as a physical body, but it will be raised as a spiritual body.

Since there is a physical body, there is also a spiritual body.   **45** This has been written:

"The first man, Adam, was a living soul."   *Genesis 2:7*

But the last Adam* became a life-giving spirit.   **46** The physical body came first, not the spiritual body.   **47** The first man came from the dust of the earth. The second man* came from heaven.   **48** Earthly people are like the one who came from dust. The ones *who go to* heaven will be like the one who came from heaven.   **49** Now we look like the one who came from dust, but we will look like the one who came from heaven.

50 Brothers, I am saying this, because people in their physical form* cannot enter the kingdom of God. That which can decay cannot have a share in what never dies. **51** Listen! I am telling you a secret: We all will not stay in death; we will all be changed.   **52** We will be changed instantly, like the twinkle in someone's eye. That last trumpet will sound. Then people will rise from death, never to die again.   **53** This decaying body must be dressed with immortality. This body, which can die, must be dressed with a body which can never die.   **54** This body, which can be destroyed, will be replaced with a body which cannot be destroyed. This body, which can die, will be replaced with a body which can never die. Then the message which has been written will come true:

"Victory has swallowed up death.   *Isaiah 25:8*

55 Where is your victory, O death?
Where is your power to hurt, O death?"   *Hosea 13:14*

56 Sin is death's power to hurt. Sin gets its strength from its relationship with the law *of God.*   **57** But, thank God, through our Lord Jesus Christ, God gives us the victory! **58** So, my dear brothers, be firm and don't be moved. Always be doing something for the Lord. You must realize that your hard work for the Lord will not be without meaning.

Chapter 16

God Chasers Are Givers

1 *You wrote me* about the special collection for the holy people *in Judea.* I have already given orders to the congregations in the Galatian area. Do the same thing they did: **2** Every Sunday* each one of you must store something aside, saving up from what you have profited. There should be no special collections after I have come. **3** When I arrive, choose the men you want. I will send them to Jerusalem with letters *of introduction.* They will carry your gift.   **4** Perhaps, I should go, too. If so, they will travel with me.

15:45   Jesus Christ
15:47   Jesus Christ
15:50   literally, flesh and blood
16:2   literally, the first day of the week

Paul Made Plans

5 I will come to you after I travel through the Macedonian area. (I am going that way.)   **6** Maybe I will stay with you—even spend the winter there. Then you can send me on ahead to wherever I am going.   **7** I don't want to see you as I am passing through, just for a short while. I hope to stay with you for a long time, if the Lord allows this.   **8** I will stay here in Ephesus until Pentecost Day.*   **9** A very important opportunity has come for me to be effective, though many people are against me.

10 If Timothy comes to you, be sure that he has nothing to worry about while he is with you. Timothy does the Lord's work as I do.   **11** None of you should make him feel as though he is not important. Send him on ahead with your blessing, so that he may come back to me. I am expecting him to come along with the brothers you choose.

12 *You wrote me* about brother Apollos. Many times I encouraged him and some other brothers to come to you. He didn't want to go, so that he may go now. He will come when he has a chance.

God Chasers—Watch Out!

13 Watch out! Stand firm in the faith! Be strong like men! Hold on tight!   **14** All of you should act with love.

15 You know Stephanas' family. They were the first converts* in the Achaian area. They have given themselves completely to help the holy people. Brothers, I beg you **16** to put yourselves under people like them and everyone who likes to work together, under those who work hard *for the Lord*.   **17** I was very happy when Stephanas, Fortunatus, and Achaicus arrived. These men make up for your not being here.   **18** They made my spirit feel refreshed, as I'm sure they did yours, too. You should give special recognition to men like these.

19 The congregations in the land of Asia send you their greetings. Aquila and Priscilla* send you many greetings in the Lord. The group that meets in their house sends you greetings, too.   **20** All of the brothers send you greetings. You should greet one another with a holy kiss.

21 With my own hand I am writing my greeting—FROM PAUL.   **22** If anyone does not love the Lord, he should be condemned! Please, Lord, come!   **23** May the gracious love of our Lord Jesus be with you.   **24** *I send* my love to all of you who are in Christ Jesus.

16:8   A yearly Jewish feast of the wheat harvest celebrated about early June. It was observed 50 days after the Passover feast.

16:15   literally, first-fruits

16:19   literally, Prisca

2 CORINTHIANS

Chapter 1

Let's Get Started

1 From Paul (God wanted me to be an apostle of Christ Jesus.) and from brother Timothy.

To God's congregation in the city of Corinth and to all of the holy people all over the Achaian area.

2 May gracious love and peace *come* from God our Father and the Lord Jesus Christ.

God Chasers Get Help

3 *Give* praise to God, the Father of our Lord Jesus Christ. He is the Father of tender feelings, the God of all comfort.   **4** He encourages us when we have any kind of trouble. This is why we are able to encourage people who are having all kinds of trouble. We use the help which God gives **us**!   **5** Just as the sufferings of Christ overflowed into our lives, in the same way, our help also overflows *to others* through Christ.   **6** If we are having trouble, it is for **your** sake! We want you to receive comfort and be saved. If we receive comfort, it is for **you**! We want you to receive comfort. When you are encouraged, you will be able to endure the same kind of suffering we experience. **7** Our hope for you is firm. Because you share the sufferings, we know that you will also share in the comfort.

8 Brothers *and sisters*, we want you to know about the trouble we went through in the land of Asia. The burdens were heavier than we could carry; we thought we were not going to live anymore.   **9** We felt we had been condemned to die. But, *something happened* to make us put our hope upon God (who raises people from death) and not in ourselves.   **10** God has rescued us from such life and death situations and He will rescue us in the future. We have placed *all* our hopes on Him. He will always rescue us, **11** while you are working together, praying for us. Then many people will be thankful to God for His favor to us. This is an answer to the prayers of many people.

Paul Checks His Motives

12 This is what makes us feel so good: Our conscience is telling the truth. We have lived our lives in this world purely and with the kind of sincerity *which comes* from God, especially toward you. We lived by God's gracious love, not human wisdom. **13** We are writing to you only what you can read and understand. I hope you will get a complete understanding,   **14** as you have understood parts of what we've said before. Then you can be proud of us, as we will be proud of you on the Day when the Lord Jesus *comes*.

15 I was sure of this, so I planned to come to you again. Then you would be helped twice.   **16** I planned to visit you on my way to and from the Macedonian area. Then you could help me on my trip to the land of Judea.   **17** When I make my plans, do you think I often change my mind? Do I plan in a human way, saying yes when I mean no? **18** God is dependable. Our message to you is not saying one thing and meaning something else.   **19** Jesus Christ, the Son of God, was preached among you through us— Silas,* Timothy, and myself. That message was not inconsistent! No, in Christ, it was a

---

1:19   literally, Silvanus

definite yes!   **20** All of God's promises are "yes" in Christ! Through Christ, we *give* glory to God *by saying* "Amen."   **21** God makes all of us—you and us—firm in Christ. God has chosen us.*   **22** He sealed us and gave the *Holy* Spirit as a guarantee in our hearts.

23 I call upon God as my Witness; He knows my motives: I didn't go back again to Corinth, because I didn't want to hurt you.   **24** We are not trying to rule over your faith, because you are standing by faith. No, we are working *with* you, so that you will be happy.

Chapter 2

1 I decided in my own mind that I would not visit you again with sadness. **2** Because, if I make you sad, who will cheer me up? The ones whom I made sad? **3** Why did I write this letter? Because, when I visit, I want you to make me feel happy, as you should, and not sad. I'm sure that all of you are happy when I am happy.   **4** I wrote you from a troubled, heavy heart, with many tears. I didn't want to make you feel sad. No, I wanted to show you the great love which I have for you.

God Chasers Forgive

5 I am not the only one that this person *in your group** has made sad—it's all of you. Well, some of you. (I don't want to be too unkind.)   **6** This man has *suffered* enough punishment from the whole group.   **7** Now, you should forgive and encourage this person, so that he won't be overcome with too much sorrow.   **8** I beg you to show him that you truly love him.   **9** Why did I write you? To find out if you could pass this test: Would you always obey?   **10** If you forgive someone, then I forgive him, too. Christ sees me do it. I forgive, because you do.   **11** Then Satan won't fool us. We know all about his tricks.

Where's Titus?

12 When I came to the city of Troas to tell the Good News about Christ, there was an open door for me in the Lord.   **13** But I was still very worried, because I couldn't find Titus, my brother. So, I told them good-bye and left for Macedonia.

God Chasers Have the Victory

14 Thank God! He always gives us the victory in Christ. God uses us to spread to all places the sweet smell of knowing Him.   **15** To God, we are the pleasant smell of Christ among the people who are being saved and among those who are lost.   **16** To one group, we are the smell of death; to the other group, the smell of life. Are we great enough for these things?   **17** We are not like many people who sell God's message. No, we speak sincerely before God in Christ—as men whom God has sent.

Chapter 3

People Read Your Lives

1 Are we beginning to pat ourselves on the back? Some people need letters of recommendation. We don't need letters like that, from you or to you, do we?   **2** **You** are our letters! You are written on our hearts. Everyone knows you and can read you.

1:21   literally, has anointed us
2:5   See 1 Corinthians 5:1-13.

3 You are the result of our work. You are clearly a letter from Christ. It is not written with ink, but with the Spirit of the living God. It is not on stone tablets, but on the tablets of human hearts!

4 This is the sort of confidence we have toward God through Christ. 5 It's not that we are so great, to think we can do anything on our own. No, our ability comes from God! 6 He made us able ministers of a new agreement, which is spiritual, not literal. The letter *of the law* kills, but the Spirit gives life!

7 *The law* was written on stones, but it came with such splendor that the sons of Israel could not continue looking at Moses' face, though that glory was fading away. And that was a ministry of death! 8 But how much more glorious will be the ministry of the Spirit? 9 Since the ministry which brought condemnation was glorious, how much more glorious will be the ministry which makes a person right with God? 10 Though *the law* was glorious, it is not bright, when compared to a glory which is so much brighter *today*. 11 And the glory that lasts is greater than the glory that faded.

12 So, we are very bold, because we have such a hope. 13 We are not like Moses, who always wore a covering over his face, until the brightness faded away. He wanted to stop the sons of Israel from staring at it.* 14 Their minds were closed. To this day, when they read the Old Testament, the covering is still there! It cannot be uncovered, because it is removed only in Christ. 15 Even today, when they read *the law of* Moses, a covering lies upon their hearts. 16 But, when someone

"turns to the Lord, the covering is removed." *Exodus 34:34*

17 The Spirit is "the Lord." There is freedom wherever the Spirit of the Lord is. 18 All of us have uncovered faces; we reflect the same glory. It comes from the Spirit of the Lord. With one glory after another, we are being changed to look more like him.

Chapter 4

God Chasers Don't Give Up

1 That is why we don't give up. God has given us mercy. We have this ministry. 2 No, we put away secret things of which people are ashamed. We don't live by playing around with God's message or by using it in the wrong way. Instead, we make the truth plain, presenting ourselves to every person's conscience before God. 3 If our gospel is covered, it is covered to those who are lost. 4 The god of this world* is among those people. They don't believe because he has blinded their minds. They cannot see the light of the glorious gospel of Christ who is the image of God. 5 We are proclaiming that Christ Jesus is Lord. We are not proclaiming ourselves. Because of Jesus, we are only your servants.

Shine On, God Chasers

6 God has said,
"From darkness let the light shine!" *Genesis 1:3*
He made light shine in our hearts, too. This brings us the light of knowing God's glory which can be seen in the face of Christ!

7 Why do we have this treasure in clay jars?* To show that this superior power comes from God, not from us. 8 We are being squeezed, but we can still move. Sometimes

---

3:13   See Exodus 34:33-35.
4:4   the Devil
4:7   human bodies

we are in doubt, but we don't doubt the truth.   **9** We are being chased, but God never abandons us. We are knocked down, but never knocked out.   **10** We are always carrying the deadness of Jesus in our bodies, so that, in our bodies, we may make Jesus' life obvious, too.   **11** Because of Jesus, those of us who are still alive are always being given up to die. Then the life of Jesus will be made clear in our dying flesh.   **12** So, death is active in us, but life is active in you.

Speak On, God Chasers

13 This is written:

"I believed, so I spoke."   *Psalm 116:10*

Having that same spirit of faith, we also believe, and that is why we speak.   **14** We know that God raised the Lord Jesus *from death*. He will also raise us *to life* with Jesus. He will present us, along with you, *to God*.   **15** Everything happens for your *good*, so that *God's* gracious love will touch many more lives. They will be thankful and this will overflow for the glory of God.

16 That's why we never give up. Even though our physical bodies are wearing out, our spirits are getting younger every day.*   **17** The troubles we now have will last only a short time. They are working out a far greater eternal glory for us, which is worth so much more than what we are suffering now.   **18** We shouldn't look at things which can be seen. Instead, we should look for things which cannot be seen. What is seen is only temporary, but what is unseen lasts forever.

Chapter 5

1 When the earthly "tent" in which we live* is destroyed, we know that we have another building which comes from God, a house in the heavenly worlds, not man-made. It lasts forever.   **2** That is why we groan, yearning to be clothed with our heavenly house.   **3** Since we will be clothed *with a body*, we will not be a naked *spirit*. **4** While we are in our bodies* now, we are groaning because we feel burdened. That doesn't mean we want to die;* we only want a new life.* Then *eternal* life will swallow up that which can die.   **5** God made us for this very reason and He has given us the Spirit as a guarantee *that we will live again*

Be Cheerful

6 Therefore, we are always cheerful. We know that, while we are at home in our physical bodies, we are not with the Lord—where home is.   **7** We live by believing, not by seeing.   **8** But we are cheerful; we would rather leave our bodies, and be at home with the Lord.   **9** So, whether we stay on earth or go home, we always want to please God.   **10** All of us must appear in front of Christ's judgment bench. Then each person will receive good or bad as a reward—according to what he did while he was in his physical body.

4:16	or, being renewed day after day
5:1	our physical bodies
5:4	literally, tents
5:4	literally, put off (our tent)
5:4	literally, to put on (the heavenly house)

God Chasers Want More People to Join the Chase

11 We know what the fear of the Lord really means. So, we try to persuade people *to live right*. God knows all about us; I hope your consciences know us, too.   **12** Again we are not patting ourselves on the back in front of you. No, we are only giving you a good reason to be proud of us. Then you will have something to say to people who are proud of outward things, and not proud of what is in the heart.   **13** If we are crazy, then we are crazy for God! If we are in our right mind, then it is for your sake. **14** Christ's love controls us. One man died for everyone. So, everyone died. We are sure of that!   **15** Christ died for everyone, so that people who are alive won't live only for themselves anymore. Instead, they will live for the one who died and came back to life for them.

16 So, from now on, we really don't know a person by merely looking at his physical body. At one time, we knew about Christ from a human viewpoint, but we do not know him in that way anymore.   **17** So, if anyone is in Christ, he is a new creation. Old things have passed away. Listen, everything has become new.   **18** Everything comes from God. He uses Christ to bring us back to Himself. God gave us the work of bringing people back *to Himself.*   **19** When God was bringing the people of the world back to Himself in Christ, He was not counting their sins against them. God gave us the message about how He brings people back to Himself.

20 We are representing Christ. It is as though God is encouraging you through us. We beg you, for Christ's sake, come back to God!   **21** Christ never sinned, but God caused him to become sin for us, so that we could be right with God in Christ.

Chapter 6

God Chasers Have a BIG JOB to Do

1 As God's co-workers, you have received God's gracious love. We beg you, don't waste it!

2 *The Scripture* says:

"At the right time I listened to you.
    I helped you on the day of salvation."   *Isaiah 49:8*

Listen! **Now** is the right time. Listen! **Now** is the day of salvation!

3 We are always careful not to do anything which might hurt someone. We don't want anyone to blame the ministry.   **4** Instead, in everything, we try to conduct ourselves as God's ministers
    when we must endure much,
    when we are suffering,
    during hard times,
    when we are having problems,
5 when we are beaten,
    when we are in jail,
    during riots,
    while working hard,
    in sleepless nights,
    when we are hungry.
6 We try to do this with purity,
    with understanding,

> with patience,
> with kindness,
> with the Holy Spirit,
> with sincere love,
> 7 with a true message,
> and with God's power.

We have used the weapons of good to attack and to defend.* 8 Through glory and disgrace, sometimes having a good reputation, and sometimes having a bad one. *We are treated* as men who fool people, but we tell the truth. 9 *We are treated* as if no one knows who we are, but we are well known. *We are treated* as if we are dying, but, look, we are still alive! *We are treated* as if we are beaten men, but we're not dead yet. 10 *We are treated* like men who are supposed to be sad, but we are always happy. *We are treated* as beggars, yet we make many people rich *in faith*. *We are treated* as men who own nothing, but we have everything!

11 We have spoken plainly to you Corinthian people. We opened wide our hearts. 12 We are not holding back our tender feelings from you. **You** are the ones who are holding back! 13 I am talking to you as if you were *my* children: Open your hearts wide. Love us back!

Wrong and Right Won't Mix

14 Don't be mismatched with unbelievers! How can right and wrong be partners? What do light and darkness share? 15 How can Christ and Satan* agree? What does a believer have in common with an unbeliever? 16 How can God's temple sanctuary exist next to false gods? **We** are the sanctuary of the living God! It is as God said:

> "I will live in them and move among them.
>> I will be their God.
>> They will be my people."   *Leviticus 26:12*

> 17 " 'So, come away from them!
>> Be separate!' says the Lord.
> 'Don't touch what is not pure.
>> Then I will accept you.' "   *Isaiah 52:11*

> 18 " 'I will be your Father.
>> And, you will be my sons and daughters,'   *2 Samuel 7:14*

says Almighty God."*

Chapter 7

1 Dear *friends*, since we have these promises, we should make ourselves clean from anything which might pollute the body or the spirit. Let us be completely holy, showing respect for God.

Paul's Letter

2 Open up to us! We haven't done wrong to anyone; we ruined no one. We never took advantage of anybody. 3 I am not saying this to condemn you. I have told you

---

6:7   literally, on the right and on the left
6:15   literally, Beliar (without worth)
6:18   literally, Lord Almighty. A traditional Jewish reading to avoid pronouncing the name of God.

before that you have a place in our hearts. We are together in life or death.   4 I have a lot of confidence in you. I'm very proud of you. Even though we have been through all kinds of trouble, I feel greatly encouraged and my joy is overflowing.

5 When we went into the Macedonian area, our bodies had no rest at all. We had all sorts of trouble. Outside, there were fights; inside, we had fears.   6 However, God comforts people who are down; He comforted us when Titus came.   7 Not only that, we felt encouraged by the comfort you gave him. He told us about how much you yearned *to see me*, how deeply sorry you were, and about your enthusiasm for me. So I felt even happier.

8 Even though I made you sad with my letter, I am not sorry about it now. However, I could have regretted it. (I see that that letter made you sad for a while.)   9 I am glad now, not because you were sad, but because you were sad enough to change your hearts! You became sad, and that is what God wanted. So we didn't need to discipline you at all.   10 The kind of sorrow which God uses brings a change of heart that leads to salvation. There are no regrets. But the kind of sorrow in the world leads to death. 11 Look at what God's type of sorrow has produced in you! You are now eager. You wanted to defend yourselves. It made you upset. You were alarmed. You yearned to do something. You were excited. You wanted to make it right! You proved that you were innocent in every way in this matter.

12 So I did not write you because of the person who did wrong or because of the person who was wronged. It was to find out how loyal you are to us before God. 13 That is why we are encouraged.

Besides that, we are especially glad to see Titus happy. All of you made him feel very good.   14 I had bragged about you to him, and you didn't let me down. Just as everything we told you was true, what we told Titus about you was also true.   15 He loves you even more when he remembers that all of you obeyed. You welcomed him with fear and trembling.   16 I am happy that I can be completely confident of you.

Chapter 8

The Macedonian Brothers

1 Now, brothers, we are going to tell you about the gracious love which God has shown to the congregations in Macedonia: 2 These believers suffered hard testing. However, even though they were very poor, they gave very generously. They were so happy.   3 I tell you the truth, they gave as much as they could—even more than they should—because they really wanted to.   4 They begged us again and again for the privilege of having a part in helping the holy people *in the land of Judea*.   5 They did not do as we expected. No, the first thing they did was to give themselves to the Lord. Then they gave themselves to us to be used in whatever way the Lord wanted.   6 That is why we begged Titus to finish *collecting* your special gift of love. (He was the one who started it.)   7 You are rich in everything: You have faith; you can tell *God's* message; you have a lot of knowledge; you are very eager to help; you love us. Now, be rich with this special gift of love!

8 I am not giving this as an order. (Other believers are eager to help, too.) I am only testing to see if your love is true.   9 You know the gracious love of our Lord Jesus Christ. Even though he was rich, he became very poor for your sake. Why? So that **you** could become rich—because he was poor.

10 This is the advice I am giving; this is what's best for you: A year ago, you were the first to do something—even the first to want to do something.   **11** So, finish doing it now! You planned it eagerly; be just as ready to complete it! Do whatever you can.   **12** If someone is ready *to give*, God accepts what that person has, not what he doesn't have.

13 We don't want to make you suffer, just to give them some relief. Everyone should have the same amount.   **14** At this time, you have more than you need, while they are in need. Some day, you may be in need and they will have more than they need. There should be a balance.   **15** It is like this Scripture:
"The man who gathered much did not have too much.
And the man who gathered a small amount
did not have too little." *Exodus 16:18*

Need Some Help?

16 I thank God. He put the same eagerness in Titus' heart which I have for you. **17** When we asked Titus to help you, he welcomed it. He is enthusiastic. He is coming to you, because he really wants to.   **18** Along with Titus, we are sending the brother who is respected among all of the congregations for preaching the Good News. **19** Not only that, he was appointed by the congregations to travel with us, when we take this special gift of love.* We will use this to give glory to the Lord. *It shows* how ready we are to help.
20 We want to stay away from any criticism of the way we use this generous gift. **21** We are trying to plan ahead for what looks right to man and to God.
22 Along with them, we are also sending our brother. We've often found him to be ready to help in many ways. But now, because he is so sure of you, he is even more enthusiastic.   **23** *I will say this* for Titus: He is my partner. We work together for you. Our brothers* are messengers of the congregations. They are Christ's glory.   **24** So, show your love. Show why we are so proud of you. Then it will be clear to the *other* congregations.

Chapter 9

God Chasers Plant Seeds

1 I don't need to write you about helping the holy people *in the land of Judea.* **2** Because I know you are ready, I have been bragging about you to the Macedonian believers: "The believers in Achaia were prepared a year ago!" Your excitement has made most of them start giving.   **3** But I am sending these brothers, so that our pride in you about this matter will not be empty words. Then you will be prepared, as I was saying all along.   **4** What if some Macedonian believers come with me? They might find that you are not prepared. Then we will be ashamed of you, because we were so sure! You will be ashamed, too.   **5** Therefore, I thought I must ask these brothers to come to you ahead of time. They can help collect the money which you promised long ago. Then, as a true gift, it will be ready, not something I forced you to do.

6 *Remember* this: The person who plants only a few seeds will harvest very little, but the man who plants a lot of seeds will gather a great harvest.   **7** Each person *should give* as he planned ahead of time in his heart. He should not be sorry *that he gave* or

8:19   money
8:23   It is not known who they were.

280

feel forced *to give*. God loves a cheerful giver.   **8** God is able to give you everything you need. You will always have more than enough to do any good deed well. **9** It is like what this Scripture says:

"God gives freely to the poor people.
His righteousness lasts forever."   *Psalm 112:9*

10 God gives seed to the man who plants, and He will give him bread to eat. God will also give you plenty of *spiritual* seed and make your righteousness grow into a fine harvest.   **11** He will make you rich in every way, so that you may always be generous. This will cause the people to thank God for what came through us.

12 You are helping them. It is like a serving ministry which does two things: *(1)* It takes care of the needs of the holy people. *(2)* Many people will thank God, like an overflowing *river*.   **13** When you help them, it is proof that you put yourself under Christ's authority and that you agree with his gospel. Sharing with them or anyone else shows that you are generous.   **14** When they pray for you, they will yearn *to see* you, because of God's unusual favor toward you.   **15** Thank God for His gift. It is too much for words.

Chapter 10

Our Weapons Come From God

1 I, Paul, appeal to you through the gentleness and kindness of Christ. (*Some people say that* I am humble when I am with you, and that I am bold when I am not with you.) **2** Please don't force me to be blunt with you when I come there. I'm quite sure I'll have to challenge those who think we live like people in this world.   **3** We live in this world, but we don't fight like people in this world.   **4** For our fight we are not using weapons which come from this world. No, our weapons come from God. They are powerful enough to break down strong forts.   **5** We break down false logic and anything which rises up against what we know is true about God. We capture every thought to make it obey Christ.   **6** After you have completely obeyed, we are ready to punish anyone who has broken *God's* law.

7 You are looking only at the way things seem to be. If anyone is sure he belongs to Christ, he should think twice about himself. We belong to Christ just as much as he does!   **8** The Lord gave us authority for building you up, not for tearing you down. Even if I take great pride in our authority, I won't let anyone put us down.   **9** I don't want you to think I'm trying to scare you with letters.   **10** Some people say, "Paul's letters are strong and heavy, but when he comes in person, he is weak. He is not a good speaker."   **11** Such a person should consider that what we say in letters, while absent, we will prove in deed when we are present!

12 We dare not take ourselves too seriously or compare ourselves with those people who pat themselves on the back. When they use themselves to measure by, and compare themselves with themselves, they are foolish.   **13** But we will not boast beyond what God allows. Instead, we will stay within the limit which God has set for us; that includes you.   **14** Since you were included, we didn't go too far when we came to you, bringing the Good News about Christ.   **15** And we are not going too far, when we are proud of the hard work which others have done. As your faith grows, we hope that all of our work among you will increase.   **16** We want to tell the Good News in areas beyond where you are. We don't want to brag about work done by another person in a different country.

17 "If anyone wants to be proud,
     let him be proud of the Lord." *Jeremiah 9:24*

18 Who is approved? It is not the one who pats himself on the back. It's the one whom the Lord pats on the back!

Chapter 11

Paul Preached at Zero Cost

1 I hope you'll put up with a little of my foolishness. You're already doing that. **2** I'm jealous for you with a jealousy *that comes* from God. I promised to present you as a pure virgin to one man—Christ. **3** With a clever trick the snake fooled Eve.* I'm afraid that your minds might be polluted, too. You might leave the simplicity and purity which is in Christ. **4** Someone might come preaching about another Jesus who is different from the Jesus we preached to you. You welcome a different kind of spirit that you did not receive *before*. How can you put up so easily with a gospel that is different from the first one you accepted?

5 I think I am just as good as any of those "super" apostles! **6** I may use common words, but I know what I'm talking about. We have always made this very clear to you.

7 I preached the Good News to you at no cost. Did I do wrong when I lowered myself to lift you up? **8** I "robbed" other congregations, taking pay from them, to help you. **9** While I was with you, when I needed something, I didn't ask any of you for anything. The brothers who came from the Macedonian area filled my needs. I never allowed myself to be a burden to you, and I never will. **10** The truth of Christ is in me: I'm proud of this. Nobody in the whole Achaian area can take that away from me! **11** Why? Is it because I don't love you? No, God knows that I **do** love you!

12 I will continue doing what I'm doing. There are some *"apostles"* who are looking for a chance to brag that they are just like us. I want to cut off any chance of this happening. **13** These men are false apostles. They try to look like true apostles of Christ, but they are lying about their work. **14** And, it's no wonder, because Satan himself can make himself look like an angel of light. **15** So, it isn't any big thing, when the servants of Satan try to look like servants of righteousness. However, Satan's servants will end up the same way they lived.

Paul's Braggin' a Little

16 Again I'm saying, no one should think of me as a fool. But, if you do, bear with me, as you would a fool. Then I can brag a little *as fools do*. **17** When I confidently brag like this, I am not talking as the Lord would have it. I am only talking like a fool. **18** Many men are bragging in a human way. So I will brag, too. **19** You are wise— you gladly put up with fools. **20** They make slaves of you. Anyone can take your money. Anyone can take advantage of you. Anyone can treat you as though you are not important. You will let anyone slap your face! **21** I'm ashamed to say it, but we were too weak to do that.

If someone dares *to brag*, I can too. (I'm talking foolishly.) **22** Are they Hebrews?* So am I! Are they sons of Israel? I'm one too! Are they descendants of Abraham? So am I! **23** Are they servants of Christ? (I'm talking like a madman.) I am

---

11:3   See Gen. 3:1-13.
11:22   Aramaic-speaking Jews

more of a servant than they are! I have worked much harder than they have. I've been in jail more often than they have. I have been beaten more times *than I can remember*. Many times I've been close to dying.   **24** On five different occasions the Jewish leaders whipped me 39 times.*   **25** Three different times I was beaten with rods. Once they tried to stone me to death.* I was on three different ships that wrecked; once I was in the ocean for about 24 hours.   **26** I'm always traveling. I'm in danger of floods, bandits, Jews,* non-Jews, in danger in cities, in deserts, in the ocean, and in danger from false brothers.   **27** I have worked so very hard. I've often gone without sleep, food, or drink. I have been hungry many times. I've been cold and without enough clothes.   **28** On top of everything else, every day I feel the pressure of my concern for all the congregations.   **29** When someone is weak, I feel weak too. When someone falls into sin, it really upsets me.

30 If I must brag, I will brag about things which show how weak I am.   **31** The God and Father of the Lord Jesus knows that I am not lying. (He should be praised forever.)   **32** The governor under King Aretas was watching the city of Damascus. His men were trying to arrest me.   **33** But I was lowered in a basket through a window of the city walls. I got away from him.*

Chapter 12

Depending on God

1 It doesn't do any good, but I must continue bragging. I will now move on to visions and revelations from the Lord.   **2** I knew a man in Christ 14 years ago. This man was caught up to the third heaven. I don't know whether he was in his physical body or not—God knows.   **3** But I know such a person. Again, I don't know if he was in or out of his physical body—God knows.   **4** This man was caught up to Paradise.* He heard things which cannot be re-told; a man is not allowed to tell such things to other men.   **5** I will brag about such a man. I won't brag about myself—only about my weaknesses.   **6** Even if I wanted to brag, I would not be foolish, because I'm speaking the truth. However, I don't want to do that, or else someone might think more of me than he does when he sees me or hears me *in person*.

7 I've seen some very unusual revelations. God gave me something, so that I would not become too proud—a thorn in the flesh, a messenger of Satan. It always tortures me, stopping me from becoming too proud.   **8** I begged the Lord about this three times. I wanted it to go away from me.   **9** He said this to me: "My gracious love is enough for you. Power is made perfect in weakness." So I will be very happy to brag about my weaknesses, so that the power of Christ will rest upon me.   **10** This is why, for Christ, I can take pleasure in weaknesses, insults, hardships, persecutions, and disasters. Because when I am weak, that's when I am really strong.

Paul, a Fool for God

11 I have become a fool, but **you** forced me to do it. You should have been patting **me** on the back. Even if I am nothing, I'm just as good as any of those "super"

11:24   Deuteronomy 25:3 limits a beating to 40 lashes. The practice was to stop at 39 lashes for fear of giving too many, and then be punished themselves.
11:25   See Acts 14:19.
11:26   or, my own nation, kind, people, or race
11:32-33   See Acts 9:24-25.
12:4   Compare Revelation 2:7.

apostles. **12** The signs of a true apostle have been done among you very patiently—proofs from God, miracles, and powers. **13** Did I treat you as if you were less important than the other congregations? No, I didn't burden you. Was that wrong? Please forgive me!

14 Listen, I'm ready to visit you for the third time. I won't be a burden. I want **you**, not your money! Parents should save up *to help* their children, not the other way around. **15** I will gladly spend my money and my energy for your souls. It seems that the more I love you, the less you love me.

16 Nevertheless, I've not been a burden to you. But, am I a clever man? Did I use a trick to catch you? **17** I sent some men to you. Did I use any of them to take advantage of you? **18** I begged Titus *to go to you* and I sent the brother with him. Titus didn't take advantage of you, did he? We lived with the same attitude. We set the same example, didn't we?

19 Throughout this letter have you been thinking that we are trying to defend ourselves to you? Dear *friends*, we are doing everything to help build you up. We speak in Christ before God. **20** When I visit you, I'm afraid you will not be as I want to find you. Then I won't be as you want me to be! You might be jealous, angry, too proud, divided, in confusion, talking against one another, gossiping, or fighting. **21** When I visit you again, I'm afraid my God will humble me in front of you. I will cry over many people who have already sinned, because they have not changed their hearts about the evil things they have done—indecency, sexual sin, and wild parties.

Chapter 13

I'll Be Back!

1 This is the third time I am coming to you. *If someone is going to accuse me,*

"The testimony of two or three people is true." *Deuteronomy 19:15*

2 When I was with you the last time, I told you ahead of time. Now that I am not with you, I am warning you again: When I come there the next time, I will punish those people who have already sinned and all the others. **3** You are looking for proof that Christ speaks through me. Christ is not weak toward you; he is powerful among you. **4** Though Christ was nailed to the cross when he was weak, he now lives by the power of God! In Christ, we are weak, but we will live with Christ for you by the power of God.

5 Test yourselves to find out if you are *truly* in the faith. Prove it to yourselves. Unless you fail, surely you know that Christ Jesus is among you? **6** I hope you know we are not failures. **7** We pray to God that you won't do something wrong. We are not trying to look like winners. No, we want you to do what is good, even though it looks as if we failed. **8** We can do nothing against the truth; we can only do something for the truth. **9** We are happy whenever we are weak while you are strong. And we are praying that you will be perfect. **10** That is why I write these things while I am away from you. Then, when I come, I will not need to be harsh, when I use the authority that the Lord gave me for building up, not for tearing down.

11 Finally, brothers, good-bye! Try to be whole. I beg you, agree with each other. Be at peace. The God of love and peace will be with you.

12 Greet one another with a holy kiss. All of the holy people here are greeting you.

13 May the gracious love of the Lord Jesus, the love of God, and the sharing of the Holy Spirit be with all of you.

GALATIANS

Chapter 1

Hi, Galatians!

1-2 From Paul, an apostle, and from all of the brothers who are with me.

I was not *chosen* by human beings to be an apostle, neither was I *sent* from a human being. No, it was through Jesus Christ and God the Father who raised Jesus from death.

To the congregations in the Galatian area:

3 May God our Father and the Lord Jesus Christ be kind to you and give you peace. **4** Jesus sacrificed himself for our sins, so that we might escape from the evil in this world. This is what God our Father wanted. **5** To God be the glory forever and ever. Amen.

There Is Only One Chase

6 Not long ago, God called you through His gracious love *which came through Christ*, but now I am surprised at you people! You are already turning away toward a different gospel.* **7** There is actually no other true gospel. However, some people are disturbing you; they want to distort the gospel of Christ. **8** If we ourselves—or even an angel from heaven—tell you a different gospel than the true gospel which we told you, then we should be condemned! **9** I said this before; I am saying it again: If anyone preaches a gospel to you that is different from what you received, let that person be condemned.*

10 Do you think I'm now trying to win man over? No! **God** is the One whom I am trying to please. Am I trying to please man? If I were, I would not be a servant of Christ.

How Paul Began His Chase

11 Brothers *and sisters*, I am letting you know that the gospel which I preached to you was not man-made. **12** I did not receive the gospel from a human being; no man taught it to me. No, Jesus Christ revealed the gospel to me.

13 You have heard about my past life in the Jewish faith. I violently persecuted God's called-out people. I tried to destroy them. **14** In the Jewish faith I was becoming a leader, doing better than most Jews my own age. I tried harder than anyone else to follow the traditions which came from our ancestors.

15 But **God** called me through His gracious love. Even before I was born, He had special plans for me. God wanted me **16** to tell the Good News about Jesus to non-Jewish people. So He revealed His Son in me. I didn't receive advice or get help from any human being.* **17** I didn't go up right away *to see* the apostles in Jerusalem. (These men were apostles before I was.) No, I went away to Arabia. Afterward, I went back to the city of Damascus.

18 Three years later, I went up to Jerusalem to meet Peter* and for 15 days I stayed with him. **19** I saw no other apostles—only James,* the brother of the Lord *Jesus*.

1:6   Some Jews who believed in Christ were teaching non-Jewish people that they could not be saved unless they were first circumcised (became Jewish). See Acts 15:1-5.

1:9   or, If anyone tells you another way to be saved, that person should be condemned!

1:16   literally, flesh and blood

1:18   literally, Cephas

1:19   not the apostle James

20 God knows that the things which I am writing to you are true. **21** Later I went to the areas of Syria and Cilicia.*

22 In Judea, the congregations in Christ did not know my face. **23** They had only heard this about me: "This man used to persecute us, but now he is preaching the same faith he once tried to destroy!" **24** They were praising God because of me.

Chapter 2

Two God Chasers Go Out

1 After **14** years, I went with Barnabas up to Jerusalem again, and I took Titus along with me. **2** I went up because God showed me that I should go. I went to those men who were the leaders. When we were alone, I explained to them about the gospel which I proclaim to non-Jewish people, so that my past work and the work I do now would not be wasted. **3** Titus was with me. Although he was not Jewish,* these leaders did **not** force him to be circumcised.* **4** *It was very important for us to talk*, because some false brothers had secretly come into our group. Like spies, they came in to find out about the freedom which we have in Christ Jesus. They wanted to make us slaves. **5** But not for one moment did we give in to what those false brothers wanted! We wanted the truth of the gospel to continue with you.

6 Those men who seemed to be important did not change the gospel which I preach. (It doesn't matter to me whether they were "important" or not; God treats all people alike.) **7** Those leaders saw that God had entrusted me with *the work of* telling the Good News to non-Jewish people,* just as God had given Peter *the work of* telling the Good News to Jews.* **8** God gave him the power to work as an apostle for Jewish people.* God also gave me this power—for people who are not Jews! **9** James, Peter, and John seemed to be the main leaders. They knew that God had given me grace. So, they accepted Barnabas and me. They said, "We agree. You should go to non-Jewish people. We will go to the Jews."* **10** They asked us to do only one thing—to remember to help the *Jewish* poor people. This was something I really wanted to do anyway.

What's the Truth?

11 Peter* came to Antioch *in Syria*. Because he was wrong, I opposed him. **12** *This is what happened*:

When Peter first came to Antioch, he always ate with non-Jewish people. But then, some Jewish men were sent from James.* When they came, Peter stopped eating with those who were not Jewish and separated himself from them. He was afraid of the Jews

---

1:21   where Paul's home was (Tarsus). See Acts 21:39.
2:3   literally, a Greek
2:3   a physical mark, cutting off the foreskin, which sealed the agreement that God made with Abraham. See Genesis 17:9-14.
2:7   the uncircumcision
2:7   the circumcision
2:8   the circumcision
2:9   the circumcision
2:11   literally, Cephas
2:12   James was a leader in the Jerusalem congregation (Acts 21:18). He did not approve of this false teaching (Acts 15:24).

who believed that all non-Jewish people must be circumcised.* 13 Peter was two-faced.* The other Jewish believers joined Peter. They were two-faced, too. Even Barnabas was influenced by the things which those Jewish believers did. 14 I saw what they did. They were not following the truth of the gospel. So, I spoke to Peter* in such a way that all the other Jews could hear what I said: "Since you are a Jew, but do not live as a Jew, why do you now force non-Jewish people to live as Jews? **You** live like non-Jewish people do."

God Chasers Get Right With God

15 We Jews were not born non-Jewish or sinners; we were born as Jews. 16 We know that a person is not made right with God by following *the* law. Committing oneself to Jesus Christ is what makes a person right with God. So, we made a commitment to Christ Jesus, because we wanted to be made right with God. We are right with God because we made that commitment, not because of following *the* law. Nobody will ever be made right by following *the* law.

17 We Jews came to Christ to be made right with God. So, it is clear that we were sinners, too. Does this mean that Christ makes us sinners? 18 But I would truly be wrong to begin teaching again those things which I gave up. 19 I *stopped living* for *the* law. I died to the law, so that I may now live for God. I* was killed on the cross with Christ. 20 So, the life which I now live is not really me—it is Christ living in me! I still live in my body, but I live by faith in the Son of God. He is the one who loved me; he sacrificed himself for me. 21 This gift is from God, and it is very important to me. Because if *the* law could have made us right with God, then Christ died for nothing!

Chapter 3

Christ Is the Source

1 You people in Galatia were told very clearly about the death of Jesus Christ on the cross. However, you were very foolish; you let someone trick you. 2 Tell me this one thing: How did you receive the *Holy* Spirit? Did you receive the Spirit by following *the* law? No! You received the Spirit because you heard *the Good News* and believed it. 3 You began *your life in Christ* with the Spirit. Are you trying to continue it by your own power? You are so foolish! 4 Many things have happened to you. Was it all a waste of time? I hope not! 5 Does God give you the Spirit because you follow *the* law? Does God work miracles among you because you follow the law? It is because you heard *the Good News* and believed it.

6 *The Scriptures say* the same thing about Abraham:

"Abraham believed God, and so God declared him a righteous man."

Genesis 15:6

7 So, you should know that the *true* children of Abraham are those who have faith.
8 The Scriptures told what would happen in the future. These writings said that God

---

2:12   The Jews who taught this doctrine were called Judaizers, i.e. the ones who wanted to be believers in Jesus.
2:13   literally, a hypocrite. A hypocrite is a person who acts as if he is good, but he is not.
2:14   literally, Cephas
2:19   my old life

would make non-Jewish people right—through their faith. The Good News was told to Abraham long ago:

"*Abraham*, God will use you to bless all people on earth."   *Genesis 12:3*

9 All people who believe are blessed in the same way that Abraham was blessed for his faith,   **10** but people who depend on following *the* law *to make them right* are under condemnation, because it is written,

"A person must do everything which is written in the book of the law. If he does not always obey those things, then that person is under condemnation!"
Deuteronomy 27:26

11 So, it is clear that no person may be made right with God by *the* law. *The Scriptures say*,

"The person who is right with God by faith will live *forever*."   *Habakkuk 2:4*

12 The law is not based on faith. Instead, *the law says*,

"A person who wants to find life by following these things* must **do** the things the law says."
Leviticus 18:5

13 The law put us under condemnation, but Christ took that condemnation away. He changed places with us; he put **himself** under that condemnation. It is written,

"When a person's body is hung on a tree,* *it shows that* the person has been condemned."
Deuteronomy 21:23

14 Christ did this, so that God's *promised* blessing to Abraham could be given to all people. This blessing comes through Christ Jesus. God wanted us to receive the promise of the *Holy* Spirit through believing.

Abraham—a Great God Chaser

15 Brothers, let me give you an example: A man writes a will. After the will is made legal, no one else may change that will or add to it, and no one can ignore it.   **16** God made promises to Abraham and his descendant. God did not say "and to your descendants." That would mean many people. But God said, "and to your descendant." This means only one person—Christ.   **17** That is what I mean: God made out a will to Abraham, promising to do the things which He told Abraham. *The* law came 430 years after the will was made, but it did not change God's promise to Abraham.   **18** Can following *the* law give us the things which God promised? If we could receive those things by following *the* law, then it is not God's promise which brings us those things. But God freely gave *His blessings* to Abraham through the promise He made.

Lay Down the Law

19 Therefore, what was the purpose of the law? The law was given *to show people* the difference between right and wrong. It continued until the *special* descendant* *of Abraham* came. God's promise was about this descendant. The law was given through angels. The angels used *Moses* as a go-between *to give the law to people.*   (**20** A go-between is not needed when there is only one side; God is only one side.)

21 Therefore, does this mean that the law is against God's promises? If there were a law which could give men life, then we could truly be made right by following *the* law.

3:12   the law of Moses
3:13   meaning, the cross of wood where Jesus was crucified
3:19   Jesus

22 However, *this cannot be true*, because the Scriptures *showed that* all people are bound by sin, so that the promise would be given to people through faith—to those who believe in Jesus Christ!

23 Before this faith came, we were all held in check by *the* law. We had no freedom until God revealed to us the way of faith which was coming.   **24** So, the law was our trainer,* until Christ came, so that we could be made right with God through faith. **25** The way of faith has come. Therefore, we do not live under law* anymore.

26-27 You were all immersed into Christ. So, you were all clothed with Christ. You are all children of God through faith in Christ Jesus.   **28** Now, in Christ, there is no difference between Jew and non-Jew,* between slave and free, between male and female. You are all the same in Christ Jesus.   **29** You belong to Christ. Therefore, you are Abraham's descendants. You receive all of God's blessings because of the promise *which God made to Abraham.*

Chapter 4

God Chasers Are God's Kids

1 I am telling *you* this: While the heir is still a child, he is no different from a slave. It doesn't matter that the heir owns everything,   **2** because while he is a child, he must obey the people *chosen* to take care of him until the child reaches the age which his father set.   **3** It is the same for us. We were once *like* little children, slaves to the standards of this world,   **4** but when the right time came, God sent His Son. God's Son was born from a woman; he lived under *the* law.   **5** God did this, so that He could buy back the freedom of those who were under *the* law. God's purpose was to make us His children.

6 You **are** *God's* children. That is why God sent the Spirit of His Son into your hearts. The Spirit cries out, "Father, dear Father."   **7** So, now you are no longer a slave—you are God's child, God's heir.

God is REALLY Real

8 In the past, you didn't know God. You were slaves to gods which were not real,   **9** but now you know the true God. Actually, it is God who knows you! So, why do you turn back to those weak and useless standards which you followed before? Do you want to be slaves to those things again?   **10** You are still observing special days, months, seasons, and years.*   **11** I am afraid for you. I am afraid that my work for you has been wasted.

12 Brothers, I, too, was *once* like you. So, please, become like me *now*. You were very good to me before.   **13** Do you remember why I came to you the first time? It was because I was sick. That was when I preached the Good News to you.   **14** My

---

3:24	literally, schoolmaster. This was a person who took care of a child on his way to and from school. A schoolmaster did **not** teach; he only delivered the child to the teacher safely, like a school bus driver today.
3:25	literally, schoolmaster. This was a person who took care of a child on his way to and from school. A schoolmaster did **not** teach; he only delivered the child to the teacher safely, like a school bus driver today.
3:28	literally, Greek
4:10	rules from the law of Moses

sickness was a burden to you, but you didn't look down on me or make me go away. Instead, you welcomed me as if I were an angel from God. You accepted me as if I were Christ Jesus himself! **15** Where is your happiness now? I tell you the truth, you would have plucked out your own eyes and given them to me, if that were possible. **16** Now, have I become your enemy, because I am telling you the truth?

17 Those people* are working hard to persuade you to turn against us, but this is not good for you. They want you to follow only them and no one else. **18** It is good for people to show interest in you, but only if their purpose is always good. This is true whether I am with you or not. **19** My little children, again I feel pain for you, such as a mother feels when she gives birth to her child. I will feel this, until Christ is fully formed in you. **20** I wish I could be with you now. Then perhaps I could change the tone of my voice. I don't know what to do with you!

Two Chasers—Only One is Chasing God

21 Since some of you people still want to be under *the* law *of Moses*, tell me, won't you listen to what the law says? **22** It is written that Abraham had two sons. The mother of one son was a slave woman. The mother of the other son was a free woman. **23** Abraham's son from the slave woman was born in the normal human way, but the son from the free woman was born because of the promise *which God made to Abraham.*

24 This true story is an example for us: The two women are like the two agreements *between God and men.* One agreement is *the law which God made* on Mount Sinai.* The people who are under this agreement are like slaves. The mother, named Hagar, is like that agreement. **25** So Hagar is like Mount Sinai in Arabia. She represents the city of Jerusalem today. This city is a slave, and all of its people are slaves *to the law,* **26** but the heavenly Jerusalem which is above is like the free woman. This is our mother.

27 It is written:

"Be happy, O woman who cannot have children!
You never gave birth.
Shout and cry out *with joy*!
You never felt the pain of giving birth.
The wife whose husband has left her*
will have more children than the wife who has a husband."　　　　*Isaiah 54:1*

28-29 One son *of Abraham** was born in the normal way. *Abraham's* other son, Isaac, was born by *the power of* the Spirit because *of God's promise.* My brothers, you are also children of promise, just as Isaac was then. Ishmael persecuted Isaac. It is the same way now. **30** But what does the Scripture say?

"Throw out the slave woman and her son! The son
of the free woman will receive everything that his

4:17　　literally, schoolmaster. This was a person who took care of a child on his way to and from school. A schoolmaster did **not** teach; he only delivered the child to the teacher safely, like a school bus driver today.

4:24　　a mountain on the Sinai peninsula where God gave the law of Moses (Exodus 19:20)

4:27　　She is all alone.

4:28-29 Ishmael

father has, but the son of the slave woman will receive nothing." *Genesis 21:10*

31 Therefore, my brothers, we are not children of the slave woman. We are children of the free woman.

Chapter 5
Keep the Faith

1 We have freedom now. Christ made us free. So stand firm. Don't turn and go back into slavery.* **2** Listen! I, Paul, am telling you this: if you allow yourselves to be circumcised, then Christ does you no good. **3** Again, I warn every man: If you allow yourselves to be circumcised, then you must follow the entire law. **4** If you try to be made right with God through *the* law, then you are cut off from Christ—you have fallen from grace! **5** But we have a *true* hope: We wait for it eagerly. We will be made right with God through the Spirit. How? By faith! **6** When a person is in Christ Jesus, it doesn't matter whether he is circumcised or not. The only thing which is important is faith—the kind of faith which works through love.

7 You were running a good race. You *were obeying* the truth. Who persuaded you to stop? **8** That persuasion does not come from God who called you. **9** *Be careful*! "Just a little yeast makes the whole batch of dough rise."* **10** Somebody is disturbing you *with different ideas*. Whoever that person is, he will certainly be punished. I trust in the Lord that you will not believe those ideas.

11 Brothers, I still don't preach that people must be circumcised.* If I did, why am I still being persecuted? Then the embarrassment of the cross would be neutralized. **12** I wish those people who are upsetting you would add castration* *to their circumcision*!

13 Brothers, although God called you to be free, don't use your freedom as an excuse to do all of the things which your physical body wants. Instead, serve each other through love. **14** The entire law is made complete in this one command:

"Love other people the same way you love yourself." *Leviticus 19:18*

15 Be careful! If you continue hurting each other and tearing each other apart, you might completely destroy one another!

16 So, I tell you: Live by following *the* Spirit. Then you won't do *the selfish and evil things* which you want in your human nature. **17** The human nature wants things which are against the Spirit. The Spirit wants things which are against our human nature. These oppose each other. Because of this, you cannot do the things that you really intend to do. **18** But, if you let *the* Spirit lead you, then you are not under *the* law.

19 Human nature does things which are wrong. These are clear:

committing sexual sin,

not being pure,

having orgies,

20 worshiping false gods,

practicing witchcraft,

5:1   the slavery of the law

5:9   The meaning is: Something small can become a very big problem.

5:11   a physical mark, cutting off the foreskin. This sealed the agreement that God made with Abraham. See Genesis 17:9-14.

5:12   literally, would cut themselves off

> hating people,
> making trouble,
> being jealous,
> becoming too angry,
> being selfish,
> making people angry with each other,
> causing divisions,
> 21 envying others,
> getting drunk,
> having wild parties,
> and other such things.

I warn you now, as I warned you before: The people who do these things will not inherit God's kingdom. **22** But the Spirit produces:

> love,
> joy,
> peace,
> patience,
> kindness,
> goodness,
> faithfulness,
> 23 gentleness,
> self-control.

There is no law against things such as these. **24** Those who belong to Christ Jesus have nailed their own human nature to crosses, along with *its* feelings and selfish desires. **25** Since we get life from *the* Spirit, we should follow *the* Spirit. **26** We must not be conceited or make trouble for each other. Neither should we be jealous of one another.

Chapter 6

Help Each Other

1 Brothers, a person *in your congregation* might fall into a particular sin. You people who are spiritual should repair such a person with a gentle spirit. But watch yourself! You also might be tempted to sin. **2** Help carry each other's burdens. In this way, you truly satisfy the "law" of Christ. **3** If someone thinks that he is important (when he really is not), he is only fooling himself. **4** A person should not compare himself with someone else. Each person should judge his own actions. Then he may take pride in what he himself has done. **5** Each person must shoulder his own responsibility.

6 The one who is learning about *God's* message should share all of the good things *he has* with the one who is teaching him.

Never Give Up

7 Don't be fooled! You cannot mock God. A person harvests only the things which he plants.* **8** If a person lives* to satisfy his human nature, then his selfish ways will bring* eternal death to him. But, if a person lives* to please the Spirit, he will receive

---

6:7 Life is like a farmer who gets only what he plants.
6:8 literally, plants
6:8 literally, harvests
6:8 plants

eternal life from the Spirit.   9 We must never become tired of doing good. We will receive our harvest *of eternal life* at the right time. We must never give up!   10 Therefore, when we have the chance to do good to anybody, we should do it, but we should give special attention to those who are within the family of believers.

The Cross, the Cross

11 I AM WRITING THIS MYSELF; LOOK AT THE LARGE LETTERS I AM USING!   12 Some men are trying to force you to be circumcised.* They do these things, so that *the Jewish people* will accept them, fearing they will be persecuted, if they follow only the cross of Christ.*   13 These men who are circumcised do not obey *the* law themselves, but they want you to be circumcised, so that they may brag about your flesh.   14 I hope that I will never brag about something like that! The cross of our Lord Jesus Christ is my only reason for bragging. Through the cross of Jesus, my world has died and I died to the world.   15 It doesn't matter whether a person is circumcised or uncircumcised. All that is important is being a new creation.   16 Peace and mercy to the people who follow this rule—to God's Israel.

17 So don't give me any more trouble. I carry scars on my body which show that I belong to Jesus.

18 Brothers, may the gracious love of our Lord Jesus Christ be with your spirit. Amen.

6:12   a physical mark, cutting off the foreskin. This sealed the agreement that God made with Abraham. See Genesis 17:9-14.
6:12   a picture of the gospel—the death and resurrection of Christ, God's way of salvation
6:14   literally, has been crucified (nailed to the cross)
6:17   When Paul preached Christ, some people beat him; this left scars.

EPHESIANS

Hi, Ephesians!

1 From Paul. God wanted me to be an apostle of Christ Jesus.

To the holy people who *live* in the city of Ephesus,* those who are faithful to Christ Jesus.

2 May gracious love and peace *come* to you from God our Father and the Lord Jesus Christ.

God Chasers Are Blessed

3 Praise God! He is the Father of our Lord Jesus Christ. In Christ, God blessed us with every spiritual blessing in heaven.   **4** In Christ, God chose us before the world began. He wanted us to be holy and spotless before Him in love.   **5** God planned long ago that we become His own sons through Jesus Christ. This would please God; it is what He wanted.   **6** *We* praise God for His glorious, gracious love that He gave us in Christ. God loves him.   **7** We have something in Christ—his blood has set us free. We have the forgiveness of sins! God's gracious love is so rich!   **8** It overwhelms us with all kinds of wisdom and understanding.   **9** To us God made clear the secret of what He wanted. He was pleased to plan this in Christ.   **10** God's plan is to bring everything together in Christ—in heaven and on earth—under Christ as Head. When the right time arrives, He will do this.

11 We were chosen in Christ. God planned this long ago for His purpose. He works out everything. God decides what He wants.   **12** We were the first to pin our hopes on Christ. This happened so that we could become praise to God's glory.

13 You are in Christ, too. You heard the true message, the Good News about your salvation. After you believed, you were sealed* in Christ with the Holy Spirit whom *God* promised.   **14** The Spirit is the guarantee that we will receive the inheritance. God will set His own people free for the praise of His glory.

15 I have heard about your faith in the Lord Jesus Christ and the love you have for all the holy people.   **16** So, I never stop thanking *God* for you. I always mention you in my prayers.   **17** I want the God of our Lord Jesus Christ, the glorious Father, to give you insight and a wise spirit. Then you will know Him better.   **18** *I pray that* the eyes of your heart will receive light. Then you will know the meaning of the hope of God's invitation. You will know the riches of His glorious inheritance among the holy people. **19** You will know God's great power which is available to us who believe. It is like the exercising of His mighty strength,   **20** when He raised Christ from death and put him at His own right side in the heavenly world.   **21** There Christ is far above any ruler, authority, power, lord or title which can be given, not only in this world, but also in the next world.   **22** God put everything under Christ's feet. God appointed him to be *the* Head over all things among the people called out by God.*   **23** This community is Christ's body. It is the totality of Christ; he completes everything everywhere.

1:1   Some manuscripts do not have "at Ephesus."
1:13   A seal shows that an agreement has been approved.
1:22   The Greek word is *ekklesia*, which is often translated "church."

Chapter 2

Salvation From Sin

1 You were *spiritually* dead in your sins and violations.

2 In the past you lived in those things. You followed the *evil* ways of this world and the ruler of the power of the air—that *evil* spirit who is now working in those who disobey God. **3** We all used to live among people like that, with the evil desires in our human nature. We satisfied the impulses of our bodies and minds. We were like all other people—naturally deserving punishment.

4 However, God was rich in mercy, because of His great love which He had for us. **5** While we were *spiritually* dead in sins,* God made us alive with Christ. (You have been saved by *God's* gracious love.) **6** And God raised us from *spiritual* death and seated us in the heavenly world with Christ Jesus. **7** God wanted to show the superior riches of His gracious love for all time. He did this by using Jesus to be kind to us. **8** You have been saved by *God's* gracious love through faith. Salvation does not come from you; it is God's gift. **9** It does not come from human effort. If that were true, someone could brag about *earning* it. **10** We are what God made. In Christ Jesus we have been created for doing good deeds. God prepared these good deeds long ago, so that we could live by them.

God Chasers Have Hope

11 Physically you are not Jewish. Those who have been physically circumcised called you "the uncircumcised."* Do you remember? **12** At that time you were without Christ. You were foreigners. You could not be part of Israel. You were strangers to the agreements of *God's* promise. You had no hope. You were in the world without God. **13** You used to be far away, but now, in Christ Jesus, you have come near. This was *made possible* by the blood of Christ.

14 Christ himself is our peace. He has made Jews and non-Jews one. He used his own body to break down the fence of hate which separated them. **15** Christ cancelled the law which had commands in strict orders. He wanted to create one new man from two, making peace between them. **16** Then he could make them friends of God with one body through the cross. He used the cross to kill the hate. **17** When Jesus came, "He preached peace to you who were far away and peace to those who were near."* **18** Because, through Christ, both Jews and non-Jews have a way to get to the Father— by one Spirit!

19 So, you are not strangers and visitors anymore. Instead, you are co-citizens with the holy people and members of God's family. **20** You have been built on the foundation of the apostles and prophets. Christ Jesus is its most important stone.* **21** The whole building is joined together in Christ. It becomes a holy temple sanctuary in the Lord *Jesus.* **22** In Christ you, too, are being built up for God, so that He may live in you by *His* Spirit.

Chapter 3

God's Plan

1 This is why I, Paul, am Christ Jesus' prisoner for you non-Jews.

2:5 or, violations
2:11 literally, foreskin. Non-Jews
2:17 Isaiah 57:19; 52:7; Zechariah 7:10
2:20 literally, cornerstone

2 Surely you have heard about the plan of God's gracious love which was given to me for you.   3 God used a revelation to make this secret clear. (I wrote a little bit about it before.)   4 As you read this, you will be able to grasp my understanding of the secret of Christ.   5 People of other generations were not told this, but now it has been revealed to God's holy apostles and prophets by *His* Spirit: 6 Jewish people and non-Jewish people are now partners; they will inherit together. And through the Good News, they share *God's* promise in Christ Jesus.

7 I became a minister of this gospel. God's free gracious love was given to me by exercising His power.   8 This gracious love was given to me, even though I am the least important of all the holy people. God wanted to preach the unsearchable riches of Christ to non-Jewish people.   9 He wanted to teach everyone about the meaning of the secret plan. It was hidden in God a long, long time ago. (He created everything.) 10 Why was it hidden? So that, through the people whom God called out, His many kinds of wisdom could be made clear to rulers and powers in the heavenly world. 11 This happened for God's eternal purpose which He accomplished in Christ Jesus, our Lord.   12 In Christ and by believing in Christ, we have boldness and confidence to come near to *God*.   13 So, I am asking you not to give up. I am suffering for you; this is glory for you.

Christ's Love

14 This is why I bow down* to the Father.   15 Every family in heaven and on earth gets its name from the Father.   16 *I pray* that God will use His Spirit to give you power from the riches of His glory to make the person inside you strong.   17 Then, through believing in Christ, he will live in your hearts. You will have your roots and foundation in love.   18-19 Then you and all of the holy people will be able to completely understand the meaning of Christ's love—how wide it is, how long it is, how high it is, and how deep it is. It goes beyond knowing, but you will know it. Then you will be filled with the totality of God.

20 Glory to God! He is able to do so much more than we can even think of or ask for. God uses the power that is working in us.   21 Glory to God among all the people He has called out and in Christ Jesus for all generations forever and ever. Amen.

Chapter 4

God Chasers Are Invited

1 So I, the prisoner in the Lord *Jesus*, beg you to live as though you were worthy of God's invitation.   2 Be completely humble, gentle, and patient. Put up with one another in love.   3 Try hard to keep the Spirit's unity; use peace to tie it together.   4 There is one body and one Spirit. You were called to one hope, when God called you.
5 There is one Lord *Jesus*. There is one faith. There is one immersion.   6 There is one God. He is the Father of everyone. God is above everything, through everything, and in everything.

7 Each one of us has received God's gracious love. Christ gave it by measure.
8 *The Scripture* says:
  "When he went up high, he captured everything.
   He gave gifts to human beings."

Psalm 68:18

3:14   literally, bend my knees (in worship)

(9 When it says "he went up," it could only mean that Christ came down to the lower parts of the earth. **10** The one who came down is the same one who went up—above all the heavens. He wanted to fill the universe.) **11** Christ appointed apostles, prophets, evangelists,* *spiritual* shepherds, and teachers **12** to prepare the holy people for a ministry of service, for building up the body of Christ. **13** How long? Until we are all together. We must be united in our faith and knowledge of the Son of God. We must become *like* a full-grown man, reaching for the greatest potential of Christ.

14 Then we will not be little children anymore. The waves will not throw us back and forth. We won't be blown away by the winds of *false* teaching which clever men invent to trick people into following error. **15** When we speak the truth with love, we will grow up into Christ in every way. He is the Head. **16** He is the Source. The whole body is joined and held together with each joint that helps it. It grows with love and builds itself up. Each part does its job.

God Chasers Think Differently

17 I am telling the truth in the Lord *Jesus*: Live no longer as the people of the world live. Their thinking is worthless. **18** Their minds have become dark. The life of God is foreign to them. They don't know about it, because their hearts are stubborn. **19** When they lost all feeling of shame, they gave themselves over to sensuality, so that they could try every kind of unclean sex, wanting more and more of such things.

20 However, this is not the way you learned about Christ. **21** You heard about him. Then you were taught in him. (The truth is in Jesus.) **22** You were taught to put away your old way of living. It will destroy you. Those evil desires can fool you. **23** You were taught to develop a new way of thinking. **24** You were taught to be clothed with a new personality like that of God. It was created with true righteousness and holiness.

25 Therefore, put away lying. Let each one speak the truth to the other person. We are all parts of each other. **26** You are allowed to become angry, but don't sin. And don't let any day end without getting rid of your angry feelings. **27** Don't give the Devil a chance. **28** The person who steals must not steal anymore. Instead, he must work hard, using his own hands to do good, so that he may have something to share with someone who needs it. **29** Don't let any rotten word come out of your mouth. Instead, say something good to build up what is missing. Then it will be a blessing to those who hear it. **30** Don't make God's Holy Spirit sad. You were sealed* with the Spirit for the Day of freedom. **31** May all bitterness, anger, grudges, yelling, and cursing—every kind of evil—be taken away from you. **32** Have tender feelings and be kind to one another. Forgive one another just as God, in Christ, forgave you.

Chapter 5

God Chasers Live Love

1 Try to copy God, as precious children do. **2** Live a life of love, just as Christ loved us. He gave himself for us. He was an offering and a sacrifice that smells sweet to God.

4:11   preachers of the Good News (Acts 8:5; 21:8)
4:30   A seal shows that an agreement has been approved.

3 No type of impurity, sexual sin, or greed should be mentioned among you. That isn't proper for holy people.   4 You should not use obscene or foolish words. Dirty jokes are out of line. Instead, you should be thankful.   5 You can be sure of this one thing: no sexual sinner, no immoral or greedy person (He is the same as one who worships a false god.) will have a share in the kingdom of Christ and God.

6 Don't let anyone fool you with empty words. This is why God's punishment is coming against people who won't obey.   7 So, don't take part in these things with them.

8 In the past you were *in* darkness,* but now, you are *in* light, in the Lord *Jesus*. Live like children of light,   9 because the light produces all kinds of goodness, righteousness, and truth.   10 Test *everything* to see if it would please the Lord.   11 Don't share in those deeds of darkness.* They are not productive. Instead, prove that they are wrong.   12 The things which happen in secret are too shameful to talk about. 13 Everything that the light exposes will become clear. 14 Light makes everything clear. This *song* says:

"Get up, you sleeper!
   Rise from death!
and, Christ will shine on you."

15 Therefore, be very careful how you live. Don't live like foolish people; live like wise people.   16 Take advantage of every opportunity, because these are evil times. 17 This is why you should not be fools. Instead, try to understand what the Lord wants.

18 Don't get drunk with wine; this leads to wildness. No, be filled with the Spirit. 19 Use psalms, songs of praise, and spiritual songs to talk to one another. Strum your heart and sing to the Lord.   20 Always thank God the Father for everything with the name of our Lord Jesus Christ.

Husbands and Wives

21 Put yourselves under each other to show respect for Christ.   22 Wives, you must put yourselves under your own husbands' authority as you do for the Lord. 23 A husband* is to be the leader of *his* wife* like Christ is the Leader of the people called out by God. He is the Savior of the body.   24 Wives should put themselves under their husbands' authority in everything, as Christ's people put themselves under his authority.

25 Husbands, love your wives, as Christ loved those called out by God. He gave his life for them.   26 He used a washing of water through the message to make God's people holy.   27 He wanted to give to himself a glorious group of people called out by God—a community that does not have stain or wrinkle or any such thing. Instead, he wanted them to be holy and spotless.   28 Husbands ought to love their wives as their own bodies. The man who loves his wife loves himself.   29 No man ever hated his own flesh. No, he feeds it and takes care of it. Christ does the same thing for *his* community.   30 We are members of Christ's body.   31 *The Scripture says*:

"This is why a man will leave his father and mother
   and be joined to his wife. The husband and wife will
become one flesh."

Genesis 2:24

5:8	sin
5:11	sin
5:23	literally, male, man
5:23	or, woman

32 This is a great secret. (I am talking about *the relationship* between Christ and the people whom God has called out.)   **33** Each one of you must love his wife, just as he loves himself. And *each* wife must show respect for her husband.

Chapter 6

Kid God Chasers

1 Children, in the Lord, obey your parents, because this is right.   **2** The first command with a promise is this:
"You must show respect for your father and mother.
3 Then you will be fine. You will live
a long time on the earth."   *Exodus 20:12*
4 Fathers, don't push your children to the point of rage. Instead, take care of them, using the Lord's warning and discipline.

Servant God Chasers—Read This

5 Slaves, obey your human masters with fear and trembling—but sincerely, just as you would obey Christ.   **6** Don't be a servant only while your master is looking, like slaves who only want to be people-pleasers. Instead, from your soul, do what God wants—as slaves of Christ.   **7** Serve cheerfully, as if it were for the Lord *Jesus* and not for people.   **8** Each one of you knows that, if a slave or free man does something good, the Lord *Jesus* will give him a reward for doing that.

9 Masters, treat your slaves the same way. Don't try to scare them. You know that the Lord *Jesus* is in heaven. He is their Lord and your Lord. God treats everyone the same.

All of God's Armor

10 Last of all, be clothed with the Lord *Jesus* and the power of his strength.   **11** Put on all of God's armor. Then you will be able to stand against the evil tricks of the Devil. **12** Our fight is not against human beings.* No, it is against rulers, against authorities, against world powers of this darkness, and against evil spiritual beings in the heavenly world.   **13** This is why you must take up all of God's armor. Then, when the time for battle comes, you will be able to resist. And, after you have fought your best, you will stand.

14 So stand *firm*, using truth as a belt around your waist. Put on the chest-plate of righteousness.   **15** With shoes on your feet, be ready to tell the Good News about peace.   **16** And, along with everything else, take up faith for a shield. With this, you will be able to put out all the burning arrows of the evil one.*   **17** Take the helmet of salvation. And, *use* the sword of the Spirit. (This is the message of God.)   **18** Pray with the Spirit at all times. Use all kinds of prayers and requests. Be on guard! Always pray for all the holy people.

19 Pray for me, too! Then, when I open my mouth *to speak*, the message will be given to me. With boldness I will make clear the secret of the Good News.   **20** I am a representative in chains* for this gospel. Pray that I will speak boldly about it, as I should.

See Ya, Ephesians

21 Tychicus, *my* dear brother and faithful servant in the Lord *Jesus*, will tell you all about things here. Then you will know what is happening to me and what I am doing.

6:12   literally, flesh and blood
6:16   the Devil
6:20   Paul was in prison in Rome when he wrote this letter.

22 That is why I sent him to you. Then you will learn about how we are. He will encourage your hearts.

23 Peace to the brothers *there*. Love with faith from God the Father and the Lord Jesus Christ. **24** May gracious love be with all those people who love our Lord Jesus Christ with a love that never dies.

PHILIPPIANS

Chapter 1

Hi, Philippians!

1 From Paul and Timothy, servants of Christ Jesus.

To all of the holy people (including the overseers and servants) in Christ Jesus, who *live* in the city of Philippi.

2 May gracious love and peace *come* to you from God our Father and the Lord Jesus Christ.

God Chasers Share Love

3 Every time I think of you, I thank my God.   **4** In all prayers for all of you, I always pray with joy.   **5** You shared in *preaching* the Good News from the very first day until now.   **6** I feel sure of this one thing: The One who began a good work among you will continue it until it is finished, when Christ Jesus *comes*.   **7** I have you in my heart. So, it is right for me to feel like this about all of you. Whether I am in chains or giving a defense of the Good News and confirming it, all of you share with me in this gracious love.   **8** My God knows that I am telling the truth: With the tender feelings of Christ Jesus I yearn for all of you.

9 This is what I am praying for: I want your love to overflow more and more with a fuller knowledge and all insight.   **10** Then you will be able to test what is best, so you will be pure and without guilt when Christ *comes*.   **11** You will be filled with what righteousness produces through Jesus Christ for the glory and praise of God.

Paul, the God Chaser Behind Bars

12 Brothers *and sisters*, I want you to know that the things which have happened to me have really helped the gospel to go forward.   **13** So, the fact that I am in chains for the cause of Christ has become clear to the whole palace guard* and to all the other *soldiers*.   **14** And, because of my chains, most of the brothers in the Lord have become more confident. They dare to speak the message with *almost* no fear.

15 Some people are proclaiming Christ with motives of jealousy and bickering, but others proclaim with a good heart.   **16** They do it from love, knowing that I am ready to defend the gospel.   **17** But some preach Christ from selfish ambition, not sincerely. They think they can cause trouble for me while I am in prison.   **18** So what? The only important thing is that Christ is being preached! I am happy about this, whether it comes from true or false motives.*

Yes, and I will be happy in the future too,   **19** because I know I will be saved. You are praying and the Spirit of Jesus Christ is also helping.   **20** I am hoping and expecting that I will never be ashamed. Instead, may I have all courage, so that my body will be used to make Christ more important now and always, whether I am alive or when I die.   **21** Because, to me, living is Christ and dying is even better.   **22** But suppose I go on living in my body? This could mean productive work. Which should I choose? I don't know.   **23** I am torn between living and dying. I have a strong desire to die and be with Christ. That would be so much better *for me*,   **24** but staying alive is more

---

1:13   literally, Praetorian, the imperial Roman guard; prison
1:18   literally, by pretense or in truth

important for your sakes.   **25** Being sure of this, I now know that I will stay on. I will continue with all of you, so that you may grow and have a happy faith.   **26** Then when I come to you again, you will be proud of me and this will overflow in Christ Jesus.

27 Live as though you were worthy of the Good News. I might come and visit you, but if I don't get there, I want to hear *good* things about you—that you stand *firm* with one spirit, with one heart, fighting for the faith of the gospel.   **28** Don't let those who are against you scare you. This will show them that they will lose, but you will be saved. This comes from God.   **29** You not only have the privilege of believing in Christ, but also the privilege of suffering for Christ.   **30** You saw the struggle I've had and you hear about the one I'm having now. Now, you have the same thing.

Chapter 2

God Chasers: Be Like Christ!

1 Are you encouraged in Christ? Are you comforted by *his* love? Do you share with the Spirit? Do you have any tender feelings or compassion *for others*?   **2** Make me truly happy; I want you to agree among yourselves and to have the same love *for one another*. Be united in soul and mind.   **3** Do nothing from selfish ambition or conceited pride. Instead, humbly treat others better than yourselves.   **4** Look for what is important to others, not just what is important to you.

5 Have the same attitude among you that Christ Jesus had:
6 Though Christ was divine by nature,
> He did not think that being equal with God was
> > something to hold onto.
7 Instead, he emptied himself, taking on the very nature
> of a slave.
> He became like human beings, appearing in human
> form.
8 He humbled himself.
> He obeyed, though it meant dying,
> > even dying on a cross!
9 So, God made him the most important.
> God gave him a name that is above every name.
10 God wanted every knee to bow,* when the name of
> Jesus is mentioned;
> those in the heavenly world, on earth, and under
> the earth.
11 And every tongue will confess that "Jesus Christ is
> Lord" for the glory of God the Father.

Work Out Your Own Salvation

12 So, dear *friends*, you have always obeyed me when I was with you, but it is even more important that you obey while I am gone. Work out your own salvation with fear and trembling,   **13** because God is the One who is working in you. How? He causes you to want to do what pleases Him.

14 Do everything without complaining or arguing about it.   **15** Then you will be pure and innocent. You will be God's children, spotless in the middle of a dishonest, evil

---

2:10   showing submission. Compare Isaiah 45:23; Romans 14:11.

generation of people. You will shine among them like stars in the universe. **16** Hold out the message of life. Then, when Christ *comes*, I can boast that my past work was not wasted, or the work I do now, either. **17** No, even if it is true that I am poured out like a drink offering for the sacrifice and service of your faith, I am glad. I am happy for all of you. **18** You should be happy for the same reason. Be happy with me!

Timothy, a God Chaser, Is Coming

19 In the Lord Jesus, I hope to send Timothy to you soon. Then I will be cheered up when I find out about what is happening with you. **20** Timothy is the only one who has the same attitude I have. He really cares about what happens to you. **21** Everyone else looks out for himself—not for the things of Jesus Christ— **22** but you know that Timothy has passed the test. Timothy has served with me for the Good News, as a son working for his father. **23** So, I hope to send him, whenever I see how things go here. **24** I am sure in the Lord that I, too, will come soon.

Epaphroditus, Another God Chaser, Is Coming Later

25 But I think I need to send back Epaphroditus, my brother, co-worker, and fellow-soldier. He is your messenger and he has helped me with whatever I needed. **26** He yearns for all of you. He feels depressed, because you heard that he was sick. **27** He was so sick that he almost died! However, God gave him mercy, and not just him, but me too! I would have become sadder and sadder. **28** So, I am very eager to send Epaphroditus. When you see him again, you will be happy. And I will not feel so sad. **29** Welcome him in the Lord with great joy. Give glory to men like him. **30** For Christ's work, Epaphroditus almost died. He risked his life to make up for what was missing in your service to me.

Chapter 3

The Dogs Are on the Loose

1 Last of all, my brothers, be happy in the Lord. It doesn't bother me to write the same things to you again, but it is safe for you.
2 Watch out for dogs.* Watch out for men who do evil. Watch out for mutilators.* **3** We are the true circumcision, not they.* We worship with God's Spirit. We boast in Christ Jesus. Our trust is not *based* on flesh!
4 I could trust in flesh. If someone thinks he can trust in the flesh, I have more reason to do that: **5** I was circumcised eight days *after I was born*. I come from the people of Israel. I am from the tribe of Benjamin. My Hebrew parents gave me a Hebrew education. I *learned the* law as a Pharisee. **6** I tried so hard that I even persecuted the people in God's community. I had law-righteousness. I felt no guilt.
7 The things which I used to think were good for me are now worthless to me because of Christ. **8** Not only that, I think everything is worthless except what is so much more valuable—knowing Christ Jesus, my Lord. I have thrown everything else away because of him. It's all garbage! I want to have Christ. **9** I want to be in him,

---

3:2   Judaizers, i.e. those who tried to force non-Jews to become Jewish before they were allowed to be Christians. See Acts 15:1-5.

3:2   the Judaizers who "butchered" the flesh of non-Jews. They seemed to care more about flesh than souls.

3:3   not the mutilating Judaizers

not having "my" righteousness (the kind that comes from *the* law) but having the righteousness which comes through believing in Christ (the kind of righteousness which comes from God based on faith).   **10** Then I will know Christ and the power he had when he came back to life. I want to share in Christ's suffering and become like him when he died, that   **11** somehow I may reach the resurrection from death.

God Chasers Press On

12 I have not yet made the resurrection my own. And I have not already become perfect, but I press on to win what Christ Jesus won for me.   **13** Brothers, I don't think I've already won it, but I'm doing one thing: I am reaching out—forgetting about what is behind me.   **14** I am pressing on toward the goal to win the prize to which God called me. It is above in Christ Jesus.

15 Those who are *spiritually* mature will think like this, but if you think in a different way, God will reveal this to you.   **16** However, we should live by the same standard we have followed until now.

17 Brothers, be like me! We gave you a *good* example. Pay attention to the people who follow it.   **18** Because—as I was often telling you and I am now saying this with tears—many people are living as enemies of the cross of Christ!   **19** They will end up in hell.* Their god is their stomach. Their glory is in their shame. They think only about earthly things,   **20** but we are citizens of heaven. We are expecting a Savior, the Lord Jesus Christ, to come from heaven.   **21** Using the power that allows him to put everything under his control, Christ will change our humble bodies to be like his glorious body.

Chapter 4

Don't Worry; Be Happy

1 So, my brothers, I love you and yearn for you. You are my crown and joy. Dear *friends*, stand in the Lord!

2 Euodia and Syntyche, I beg you, agree with one another in the Lord.   **3** Yes, I am asking you, faithful Suzygus,* help these women. They both fought next to me for the Good News. Clement and my other co-workers did, too. Their names are in the Book of Life.

4 Always be happy in the Lord. Again I say, be happy!

5 Show a gentle spirit to everyone. The Lord is near.   **6** Don't worry about anything. Instead, let God know what you are asking for in prayer. Tell Him all about what you want. And, be thankful.   **7** God's peace, which goes far beyond all *human* understanding, will guard your hearts and minds in Christ Jesus.

8 Finally, brothers, think about good things and things that will bring praise—whatever is true, noble, right, pure, lovely, and honorable.   **9** Practice the things you learned from me, received from me, heard from me, or saw in me. The God of peace will be with you.

God Chasers: Be Helpful

10 I am very happy in the Lord that, after all this time, you are *still* concerned for me. You were always concerned, but you didn't have the chance *to give*.   **11** I am not

3:19   literally, destruction
4:3   or, partner

saying this because I need something now. I have learned to be satisfied in any situation. **12** I know what it is to go without and I know what it is to have plenty. At all times, I have learned the secret of being full or going hungry, of having plenty or very little. **13** I can do anything—by the one who gives me the power. **14** But it was good of you to share with me in my troubles.

15 When I left the Macedonian area after the Good News first came *to them*, not one congregation helped (in giving or receiving things). **You** were the only ones—and you Philippians know this! **16** Even while I was in the city of Thessalonica, time and again when I needed help, you sent something to me. **17** I am not looking for gifts. I only want to see "credit" added to your account. **18** I have gotten everything. It is more than enough. I have plenty, since I received the things you sent with Epaphroditus. It is an acceptable sacrifice, a sweet smell that pleases God. **19** My God will fill all of your needs with His wealth in glory in Christ Jesus.

20 Give glory to our God and Father forever and ever. Amen.

'Bye for Now

21 Greet every holy person in Christ Jesus. The brothers here with me send you their greetings. **22** All of the holy people here greet you, especially those in Caesar's household.*

23 May the gracious love of the Lord Jesus Christ be with your spirit.

4:22   probably referring to Nero's soldiers and the palace guards whom Paul had converted to Christ (See Philippians 1:13.)

COLOSSIANS

Chapter 1

Hi, Colossians!

1 From Paul (God wanted me to be an apostle of Christ Jesus.) and from brother Timothy.

2 To the holy people and faithful brothers *and sisters* in Christ in the city of Colossae.

May gracious love and peace *come* to you from God our Father.

The Good News Is Spreading

3 For you we thank God, the Father of our Lord Jesus Christ. (We are always praying.)   **4** We have heard about your faith in Christ Jesus and the love that you have for all of the holy people   **5** because of the hope that is hidden away in heaven for you. You heard about this hope long ago in the true message—the Good News.   **6** It came to you as it is now all over the world. It is producing fruit* and increasing *its influence.* It has been doing the same thing among you ever since you first heard and learned about God's gracious love in *the* truth.   **7** You learned it from Epaphras, our dear co-slave. He is a faithful servant of Christ for us.   **8** He has also told us about your love in *the* Spirit.

9 Since the day we heard about you, we haven't stopped praying for you. We ask that you may be filled with the knowledge of what God wants, with all kinds of wisdom and spiritual understanding.   **10** We want you to live as if you were worthy of the Lord *Jesus.* Please him in every way. Produce the fruit of good deeds. Grow in your knowledge of God.   **11** Be strong! Have all the strength of His glorious power. Then you will be able to endure anything. You *will learn* patience with joy.   **12** Give thanks to the Father who entitled you to have a part of what holy people will receive. The holy people are in the light.   **13** He rescued us from the power of darkness* and moved us into the kingdom of His dear Son.   **14** We have freedom in Christ—the forgiveness of sins.

Christ

15 Christ is the image of God who cannot be seen. Christ is superior to everything that was made,   **16** because, in Christ, everything was created: everything in the heavenly world and everything on earth, things that can be seen and things which cannot be seen—thrones, lords, rulers, and powers. Everything was created through Christ and for Christ.   **17** Christ is before everything and everything holds together in Christ. **18** Christ is the Head of the body, the people called out by God. Christ is the Source— the first one to rise from death so that he could be first in everything,   **19** because it pleased *God to have* the totality live in Christ,   **20** and, through Christ, to bring everything back to Him. God used the blood of the cross of Christ to make peace with everything on earth and everything in the heavenly world.

21 In the past, you did evil things. You were strangers and enemies *of God* in your mind.   **22** But now, Christ's physical body has brought you back *to God* through

---

1:6   converts
1:13   sin

death. He wanted to present you holy, spotless, and without guilt before Him.   **23** But, you must stay rooted and grounded in the faith. Don't be moved away from the hope of the Good News that you heard. It was proclaimed to every person under heaven. I, Paul, am a minister* of this gospel.

Paul Takes Christ's Message On

24 I am happy even though I am now suffering for you. Christ did not finish the suffering. I am completing the suffering which was left over. I am doing this in my body for Christ's body, the community.   **25** I was made a minister of that community by God's plan which was given to me for your sakes. God wanted me to complete His message.   **26** This is the secret that was kept hidden from generations and for ages, but now it has been made clear to God's holy people.   **27** God wanted them to make clear the meaning of the glorious wealth of this secret in people who are not Jewish. The secret is Christ in you; he is the hope of glory.

28 We preach Christ. We use every kind of wisdom to teach and warn every person. We want to present every person *to God* perfect in Christ.   **29** This is what I am working for. Using all the energy that he exercises so powerfully in me, I am struggling to do this.

Chapter 2

1 I want you to know how hard I have fought for you and for the people of the town of Laodicea and for all of those who have not met me face to face.   **2** Then their hearts will be encouraged and bound together with love. They will have all the wealth of complete understanding, knowing God's secret—Christ.   **3** All of the treasures and hidden wisdom are *found* in Christ.

4 I am telling this, so that no one will fool you with false reasonings.   **5** Even though I am physically not there with you, I am with you in spirit. It makes me feel happy when I see how orderly and how strong your faith in Christ is.

Christ Is the Answer

6 So, continue living in Christ, just as you did when you accepted Christ Jesus as Lord.   **7** Be rooted and built up in him. Be firm in faith, as you were taught. Overflow with thankfulness.

8 Be careful! Don't let anyone capture you with philosophy or misleading theories that can fool you. These come from human tradition and worldly standards, not from Christ!

9 The totality of divinity lives embodied in Christ.   **10** You are completed in Christ. He is above* every ruler and authority.

The Cross

11 In Christ, you were circumcised* with a non-human circumcision. With Christ's circumcision, you stripped away the human nature of your bodies.   **12** You were buried with Christ by immersion. You were also raised with Christ through believing in the power of God who raised Christ from death.

1:23	or, servant
2:10	literally, the head of
2:11	cutting off the foreskin of the male sex organ as a sign of God's agreement with Israel. (See Genesis 17:9-14.)

13 When you were *spiritually* dead in your sins and your human nature was not circumcised, God brought you back to life with Christ. He forgave all of our sins. **14** God wiped away the written code with its strict orders. It was negative; it was against us. He took it out of the way. He nailed it to the cross. **15** After God stripped away *the power of* the rulers and authorities, He showed this openly, using the cross to show His victory over them.

16 So, don't let anyone condemn you for what you eat or drink, or a religious festival, or the new moon holiday, or Sabbaths. **17** These are only a shadow of the future; Christ is real. **18** Don't let anyone who likes to act "humble" and to worship angels disqualify you from the race. He talks in detail about what he has "seen." His unspiritual mind makes him boastful—for no real reason. **19** He is not holding onto the Head.* The whole body grows the way God made it grow, held together by its joints and ligaments, getting its support from the Head.

God Chasers Have New Standards

20 If you truly died with Christ, leaving behind the standards of the world, why are you living as if you were still in the world? You are making strict rules:

21 "Don't handle it!"
"Don't taste this!"
"Don't touch that!"

22 None of these things will last after they have been used for a while. They are human commands and teachings. **23** These things look like there is wisdom behind them. They have forced worship, false humility, and harsh treatment of the human body, but, they don't help control physical desires at all!

Chapter 3

God Chasers Appear

1 So, since you were raised with Christ, search for things that are above,* where Christ is sitting at God's right side. **2** Think about things that are above, not things on the earth. **3** Since you have died,* your life has been hidden away with Christ in God. **4** When Christ (your life) appears, then you will appear with him in glory, too.

God Chasers Kill Sin

5 So, kill the earthly parts: sexual sin, that which is dirty, lust, evil desire, and greed. (Greed is the same thing as worshiping a false god.) **6** Because of these things, God's punishment will come upon people who will not obey. **7** In the past, **you** used to live that way!

8 But now, you must put away all of those things: anger, grudges, feelings of hate, cursing, and dirty words. **9** Do not lie to one another. Strip away that old personality, along with its habits. **10** Put on the new personality, which is being renewed, by learning to be like the image of its Creator. **11** Here there are no Greeks or Jews, no circumcision or uncircumcision, no foreigners, no Scythians,* no slaves or free men. Christ is everything and in everything.

2:19	Christ
3:1	Heaven
3:3	See Colossians 2:11-12.
3:11	Scythians were savages, animal-like barbarians.

12 So, clothe yourselves with tender feelings, kindness, humility, gentleness, and patience—like God's chosen, holy people whom He loves.   **13** Put up with one another. If someone has a problem with somebody else, forgive each other as the Lord forgave you.   **14** Add love to all of these things. Love binds them all together in perfect unity.   **15** Let the peace of Christ direct your hearts. God called you in one body to peace. Be thankful.   **16** Let the teaching of Christ live among you in an abundant way. Use all wisdom to teach and warn one another with psalms, songs of praise, and spiritual songs, singing to God with your hearts.   **17** Everything you say or do should be done by the authority of the Lord Jesus. Thank God the Father through Christ.

How to Treat Others

18 Wives, put yourselves under your husbands' authority. This is what the Lord wants.   **19** Husbands, love your wives. Don't be harsh with them.

20 Children, in everything obey your parents. This is pleasing to the Lord.

21 Fathers, don't make your children bitter, or they will give up.

22 Slaves, in everything obey your human masters. Don't serve them only when they are looking, like slaves who are trying to be people-pleasers. Instead, serve with a sincere heart, showing respect for the Lord.   **23** Whatever you do, work at it—really try hard—as if it were for the Lord, not men.   **24** Be a slave to Christ, the master. You know you will receive a reward from the Lord; it will be an inheritance.   **25** Anyone who does wrong will be paid back *for his wrong*. And, to God, everyone is the same.

Chapter 4

1 Masters, treat your slaves well and fairly. Remember, **you** have a Master in heaven, too.

God Chasers Share the Message

2 Continue in prayer. Be alert. Be thankful.   **3** Pray for us, too. Pray that God will give us an opportunity *to share* the message, to talk about the secret of Christ. That is why I am tied up in chains.*   **4** I want to make the message clear, as I should.

5 Live wisely in front of outsiders. Take advantage of every opportunity.   **6** Your message should always be beautiful, flavored with salt.* You should learn how you must answer each person.

On a Personal Note

7 Tychicus will tell you all of the news about me. He is *our* dear brother, faithful servant, and co-slave in the Lord.   **8** That is why I sent him to you. Then you will find out everything that is happening to us. He will encourage your hearts.   **9** With him is Onesimus,* the dear, faithful brother. He is one of your own number. They will tell you everything that is happening here.

10 Aristarchus, my cellmate, greets you. Mark, the cousin of Barnabas, greets you, too. You have already received instructions about him. If he comes to you, welcome him.   **11** Jesus (the one called Justus) sends his greetings. These are the only Jews who are my co-workers in the kingdom of God *here*. They have been very helpful to me.

4:3   Paul was in prison, bound by chains, when he wrote this letter.

4:6   Salt makes things taste good. Your language should make the gospel more attractive and appealing.

4:9   Onesimus was the runaway slave of Philemon (see the Philemon letter) who lived in Colossae. Onesimus became a Christian.

12 Epaphras* greets you. He is one of your own and a servant of Christ Jesus. He is always wrestling in his prayers for you. He wants you to stand complete, totally sure of everything that God wants.   **13** I'll tell you the truth about him—he works very hard for you and the *believers* in the towns of Laodicea and Hierapolis!   **14** Luke,* the dear doctor, greets you. Demas does, too.

15 Greet the brothers in Laodicea. Greet Nympha and the group that meets in her home.

16 After this letter has been read to all of you, see that it is read to the congregation in Laodicea. Then you can read the letter which they received.

17 Tell this to Archippus:* "Be sure that you finish the work you received in the Lord!"

18 I write this with my own hand: "GREETINGS FROM PAUL. Remember my chains."*
Gracious love be with you.

4:12   Epaphras was a member of the congregation at Colossae. He was with Paul in prison while Paul was writing this letter. (See Colossians 1:7; Philemon 23.)
4:14   Luke was one of Paul's traveling companions. Luke wrote Luke and Acts.
4:17   Archippus was a servant of the Colossian congregation and may have been a member of Philemon's family. (See Philemon 2.)
4:18   Paul was in prison at the time he wrote this letter. (See Acts 28:30.)

1 THESSALONIANS

Chapter 1

Hi, Thessalonians!

1 From Paul, Silas,* and Timothy.

To the congregation of the Thessalonians in God the Father and in the Lord Jesus Christ.

Gracious love and peace to you.

God Chasers Keep the Faith

2 We always thank God for all of you. We continually mention you in our prayers. **3** Before our God and Father, we remember the effort that *came* from your faith, the hard work that *came* from your love, and your endurance which *comes* from the hope in our Lord Jesus Christ.

4 Brothers *and sisters*, God loves you. You know He has chosen you. **5** How did our gospel come to you? It came not only with talk, but also with power, the Holy Spirit, and with much conviction. You know how we lived among you for your sake. **6** You copied us and the Lord *Jesus*. Even during much suffering, you accepted the message with the joy that comes from the Holy Spirit. **7** So, you became an example to all of the believers in the areas of Macedonia and Achaia. **8** The Lord's message rang out from you. *The news about* your faith in God has gone out, too. Not only did it go to Macedonia and Achaia, it went everywhere! We don't have to talk about it, **9** because people tell us about how we came in among you and how you turned away from false gods to God. Now you are serving the true, living God **10** and waiting for His Son to come from heaven. Jesus, whom God raised from death, will rescue us from the punishment that is coming *from God.*

Chapter 2

God Chasers Are Like Moms

1 Brothers, you know that our stay among you was a success. **2** Before *we arrived there*, as you know, we had suffered and had been insulted in the city of Philippi.* But with our God's *help*, we dared to tell you God's Good News, even when some people strongly opposed us. **3** Our plea does not come from false, impure, or tricky motives. **4** No, we talk like men who have been tested by God. He trusted us with the Good News. We don't talk like men who are trying to please people. No, God tests our hearts. **5** In the past, you know we never used flattery. We didn't try to look good, only to get your money. God knows this is true! **6** We were not looking for glory from human beings—not from you or anyone else.

7 As Christ's apostles, we could have been hard on you, but we were gentle among you, like a mother taking care of her children. **8** We loved you very much. It was a pleasure to share with you not only God's Good News, but also our lives. You had become precious to us. **9** Brothers, do you remember our hard work? We were

---

1:1   literally, Silvanus
2:2   See Acts 16:11-39.

311

exhausted. We worked night and day; we didn't want to be a burden to you while we preached God's Good News to you.

10 We were pure, righteous, and without guilt among you believers. You know it and God knows it! **11** You know that we treated each one of you as a father treats his own children. **12** We encouraged you, comforted you, and told you to live your lives worthy of God who called you into His kingdom and glory.

13 This is why we continually thank God: When you received God's message that you heard from us, you accepted it as the *true* message of God, not a human message. It is working in you believers. **14** Brothers, be like God's congregations which are in Christ Jesus in the land of Judea. Your own countrymen make you suffer in the same way that the Judeans make them suffer. **15** They killed the Lord Jesus and the prophets. They drove us out. They are not pleasing God and they are against all people. **16** They try to stop us from talking to non-Jewish people to keep them from being saved. They are always piling up their sins. *God's* punishment has finally come upon them.

Paul Misses the Thessalonians

17 Brothers, we were forced to leave you for a short time. (This was in body, not in spirit.*) With a strong desire, we tried very hard to see you face to face. **18** Several times, even I, Paul, wanted to come to you, but Satan stopped us. **19** What are we hoping for? What would make us happy? What is the crown we will take pride in before our Lord Jesus when he returns? It is **you**! **20** You are our glory, our joy.

Chapter 3

Why Timothy Was Sent

1 We decided to stay behind alone in Athens. But, when we could wait no longer, **2** we sent Timothy. He is our brother and God's co-worker for the gospel of Christ. We wanted him to help your faith and make you strong. **3** We didn't want anyone to be shaken by these troubles. You know that we must be ready for this. **4** When we were with you, we told you ahead of time: "We are about to be persecuted." And, as you know, it happened. **5** That is why I couldn't wait any longer; I sent *Timothy* to find out if your faith *was strong*. The tempter* could have tempted you and our hard work would have been wasted.

6 But Timothy has just now come back from you to us. He has told us the good news about your faith and love; that you always have good memories of us and yearn to see us, just as much as we want to see you. **7** Brothers, this is why your faith encouraged us, even though we are in trouble and suffering. **8** If you stand in the Lord, we feel alive now. **9** We cannot thank God enough. Can we repay our God for all of the happiness we have before Him because of you? **10** Day and night we are praying very hard that we will see your faces and supply anything that is missing in your faith.

11 May God Himself, our Father, and our Lord Jesus prepare a way for us to come to you. **12** May the Lord make your love grow and overflow to one another and everyone else, just as our love does toward you. **13** May the Lord make your spirits* strong, without guilt, and holy before God, our Father, when our Lord Jesus returns with all his holy ones.

2:17   literally, in face, not in heart
3:5   Satan
3:13   literally, hearts

Chapter 4

God Chasers Are God Pleasers

1 Finally, brothers, we gave you instructions about how you must live to please God. You are living that way now. We are asking, yes begging, you in the Lord Jesus to do even more!   2 You know some of the orders we gave you through the Lord Jesus. 3 This is what God wants: You must be holy. Stay away from sexual sin.   4 Each one of you should know how to control his own body,* with holiness and honor.   5 This should not be with a lustful desire, like people of the world who don't know God. 6 No one should take advantage of or cheat his brother in business. The Lord will punish those who do such things, as we told you before and warned you.   7 God did not call us to be unholy, but to be holy.   8 So, the person who rejects this is not rejecting man, but God. God gives His Holy Spirit to you.

9 We don't need to write you about loving your brothers. God has already taught you how to love one another;   10 you are doing this. You love all the brothers throughout Macedonia. Brothers, we beg you, love them even more!

11 Try to live a quiet life. Mind your own business. Work with your own hands, as we told you.   12 Then outsiders will respect the way you live. You will not be dependent on anyone.

When Jesus Comes Back

13 Brothers, I want you to know *the truth* about the people who have already died. Then you will not be sad like others who have no hope.   14 Since we believe that Jesus died and came back to life, through him, in the same way, God will bring along with Jesus those who have died.

15 We are telling you the Lord's teaching: When the Lord *Jesus* returns, we who are still alive on earth will not go ahead of those who have already died.   16 The Lord himself will come down from heaven with a command, with the voice of the angel leader, and with the sound of God's trumpet. The dead people in Christ will be the first to rise from death.   17 Then we who are still alive on earth will be gathered up with them in the clouds to meet the Lord in the air. And so, we will always be with the Lord. 18 Therefore, comfort one another with these words.

Chapter 5

We Should Be Ready

1 Brothers, we don't need to write you about dates and times,   2 because you know very well that the Day of the Lord will come *suddenly*, like a robber in the night. 3 People will say, "Things are peaceful and safe." That's when destruction will suddenly hit them. It will be like when the birth pain *comes* to a pregnant woman. They won't be able to run away.

4 But, brothers, **you** are not in the dark. That Day will not surprise you as a robber does.   5 All of you are sons of light and sons of daytime. We do not belong with the night or darkness.*   6 So, we should not be asleep like others are. No, we should be awake and alert.   7 Sleepers sleep at night; drinkers get drunk at night,   8 but we belong with the daytime. We should be alert. Put on faith and love for your chest-plate,

---

4:4   literally, container
5:5   sin

313

and for your helmet put on the hope of salvation.   **9** God did not plan for us to be punished, but to have salvation through our Lord Jesus Christ.   **10** Whether we are awake or asleep, Christ died for us, so that we will live together with him.   **11** So, comfort one another. Continue building each other up, just as you are doing now.

By the Way— Don't Forget

12 Brothers, we beg you to respect those who are working hard among you. They are leading you in the Lord and warning you.   **13** Because of their work, treat them with the greatest honor in love. Be at peace with one another.   **14** Brothers, we beg you, warn those who are lazy. Comfort people who are afraid. Help the weaker ones. Be patient with everyone.   **15** Be sure that no one pays back wrong with a wrong. Instead, always try to do good to one another and to everyone.

16 Always be happy.   **17** Pray continually.   **18** Thank God at all times. This is what God wants for you in Christ Jesus.   **19** Don't put out *the fire of* the Spirit. **20** Don't think prophecy is unimportant.   **21** Test everything; keep what is good. **22** Stay away from every kind of evil—even from what looks like evil.

23 The God of peace Himself will make you completely holy. May He keep your spirit, soul, and body whole without guilt until our Lord Jesus Christ comes.   **24** And, he **will** come. God is the One who calls you. He is faithful.

25 Brothers, pray for us also.

26 Greet all the brothers with a holy kiss.

27 *Before* the Lord, I order you to have this letter read to all the brothers.

28 May the gracious love of our Lord Jesus Christ be with you.

2 THESSALONIANS

Chapter 1

Hi Again!

1 From Paul, Silas,* and Timothy.

To the congregation of the Thessalonians in God our Father and in the Lord Jesus Christ.

2 May gracious love and peace *come* to you from God the Father and from the Lord Jesus Christ.

We Know You Are Suffering

3 We should always thank God for you, brothers *and sisters*. We really should, because your faith is growing fast. The love that each of you has for one another is also becoming stronger. **4** So, among God's congregations, we are proud of you. You are going through persecutions and troubles. We tell them how you still believe and endure.

5 This shows that God's judgment is right. You are suffering for the kingdom of God. So, you are worthy of it. **6** God is fair. He will give trouble to those who make trouble for you. **7** But, to those of you who are having trouble, He will also give you— and us—rest! The Lord Jesus will be revealed from heaven with his powerful angels. **8** *He will come* with a flaming fire. He will punish the people who do not acknowledge God and those who don't obey the gospel of our Lord Jesus. **9** They will be punished with eternal destruction—away from the Lord and from the glory of his strength. **10** Why will Jesus come? So that his holy people may give him glory. All believers will be amazed. On that day, you will be there, too, because you believed our story. **11** This is why we always pray for you. Our God called you; we want Him to make you worthy of that! May God also accomplish in a powerful way all of the good *you** want to do and every action that comes from your faith. **12** In this way, the name of our Lord Jesus will be honored by you and you will be honored by him. All this *was made possible* by the gracious love of our God and the Lord Jesus Christ.

Chapter 2

The Day of the Lord

1 Our Lord Jesus Christ is coming. And we will be gathered together with him. But, brothers, we beg you **2** not to allow your minds to be alarmed or quickly upset. Perhaps some spirit, message, or letter said, "The Day of the Lord has already come!" We sent no such letter. **3** Don't let anyone fool you like that, because "the falling away" must come first. The lawless man, the son of destruction,* will be revealed then. **4** He will be against everything that people worship or think is divine. He will lift himself above all of these things. He will even sit in God's temple sanctuary, claiming that he is God.

1:1   literally, Silvanus
1:11   or, God
2:3   Hell

5 Surely you remember when I was still with you that I always told you these things. 6 And now, you know what is holding the lawless man back—he must be revealed at the proper time. 7 The secret of lawlessness is already working. Someone is holding it back. Until that changes, nothing will happen. 8 Only then will the lawless man be revealed. The Lord Jesus will kill him with a blast from his mouth. When Jesus comes with splendor, Jesus will destroy him. 9 The lawless man will come with Satan's power. He will use all kinds of false powers, proofs, and miracles. 10 There will be every kind of evil to fool the people who are being destroyed. Why? Because they did not accept the love of the truth, so that they could be saved. 11 This is why God sends them a deceiving power, so that they will believe the lie. 12 Then all people who did not believe the truth will be condemned. They enjoyed sin.

God Chasers Take A Stand

13 But we should always thank God for you, brothers. The Lord loves you. God planned for you to be saved. You are *His* first crop. You believed the truth, and the Spirit made you holy. 14 Using our gospel, God called you into this. He wanted you to have the glory of our Lord Jesus Christ. 15 So, brothers, stand *firm*! We have spoken to you and written a letter.* Hold onto the things we taught you.

16-17 Our Lord Jesus Christ himself and God our Father will encourage your hearts and make you strong in every good word and deed. He loved us and, with gracious love, gave us eternal comfort and good hope.

Chapter 3

Pray, So the Gospel Will Spread Like Fire!

1 Finally, brothers, pray for us. Pray that the Lord's message will spread fast and be honored just as it was with you. 2 Pray that we will be rescued from unfair, evil men. Not all people are believers. 3 But the Lord is faithful; He will protect you from the evil one.* The Lord will make you strong. 4 We trust the Lord that you are doing—and will do—the things we order you to do.

5 May the Lord guide your hearts into the love of God and the endurance of Christ.

God Chasers: Get to Work!

6 Brothers, by the authority of the Lord Jesus Christ, we order you to withdraw from any brother who is a lazy person, a troublemaker. He is not living the way we taught you to live. 7 You know how you ought to act—like us! We were always busy among you. 8 We never ate the food of anybody, unless we paid for it! No, night and day, we worked hard to the point of exhaustion. Why? So we wouldn't be a burden to any of you. 9 We have the right *to be paid*, but we wanted to be an example for you to follow. 10 Even when we were with you, we gave you this order: "If a person doesn't want to work, then don't let him eat!"

11 We hear that some men among you are living lazy lives; they are not working. Instead, they keep other people from working. 12 By the Lord Jesus Christ, we order—even beg—you people, "Get to work! Quietly earn your own living."

2:15   First Thessalonians
3:3   the Devil

13 Brothers, never get tired of doing good. **14** If someone won't obey our teaching in this letter, give him notice. Don't associate with him! Then he will feel ashamed. **15** Don't think of him as an enemy; warn him as you would a brother.

Good-bye

16 May the Lord of peace Himself always give you peace in every way. May the Lord be with all of you.

17 This is the way I write: "GREETINGS FROM PAUL! This was with my own hand."* It is my signature on every letter. **18** May the gracious love of our Lord Jesus Christ be with all of you.

3:17   Before this, someone was copying down what Paul said to write. (Compare Romans 16:22.)

1 TIMOTHY

Chapter 1

One God Chaser to Another

1 From Paul. I am an apostle of Christ Jesus. God our Savior and Christ Jesus our hope ordered this.

2 To Timothy, *my* true son in *the* faith.

May God the Father and Christ Jesus our Lord give you gracious love, mercy, and peace.

God Chasers Follow From the Right Plan

3 While I was traveling to the Macedonian area, I begged you to stay in the city of Ephesus. Some men there are teaching a different teaching. I want you to order them to stop doing this. **4** They should not hold onto myths* or endless lists of ancestors. These cause arguments. They are not helping God's plan *which comes* by faith. **5** Love is the real reason for this command. It comes from a pure heart, a good conscience, and honest faith. **6** Some of them have wandered away. They are lost in empty talk. **7** They want to be teachers of *the* law, but they don't understand what they are talking about or the things they are so sure of.

8 We know that the law is good if a person uses it rightly. **9** We also know this: *The* law was not made for a good man, but for people who are lawless, rebels, ungodly, sinners, unholy, not religious, father-killers, mother-killers, murderers, **10** sexual sinners, homosexuals, slave traders, liars, and those who break promises. These and other things are against the healthy teaching **11** as found in the glorious gospel of the blessed God which He trusted to me.

Jesus Saved Even Me

12 I am thankful to Christ Jesus our Lord who gave me power. He thought I was faithful, so he appointed me for this work. **13** In the past, I said evil things against God. I was a persecutor and a man of violence. But I received mercy because, when I was an unbeliever, I didn't know what I was doing. **14** Then the kindness of our Lord came upon me like a flood, with the faith and love which are in Christ Jesus.

15 This statement is something you can trust; it is worth complete acceptance: "Christ Jesus came into the world to save sinners." I am the worst one, **16** but, because of this, I received mercy. Christ Jesus wanted to show all his patience in me, the worst sinner. This was an example for those who were about to believe in him for eternal life. **17** *Give* honor and glory forever and ever to the eternal King who cannot die or be seen, the only God. Amen.

18 Timothy, my son, I give you this instruction. It is like the prophecies which were made earlier about you. Use them to fight the good fight. **19** Hold onto the faith and a good conscience, which some people have rejected. They wrecked their faith, like a ship *at sea*. **20** Some of them are Hymenaeus and Alexander. I gave them to Satan, so that they could be corrected and not say evil things against God *anymore*.

1:4   or, legends, fables

Chapter 2

God Chasers Pray and Pray and Pray

1 First of all, I beg you to pray for all people. Ask for things. Speak for them. Be thankful to God for them. 2 Pray for kings and all those who have authority, so that we may lead peaceful, quiet lives. We want to be godly and serious. 3 This is good and acceptable before God, our Savior. 4 God wants all persons to be saved and to begin understanding the truth. 5 There is one God. There is one go-between between God and human beings—the man Christ Jesus. 6 Christ gave himself for everyone. He was the price. That was God's proof given at the right time. 7 This is why I was made a preacher, an apostle (I speak the truth; I'm not lying.), and a teacher of people who are not Jewish. I use faith and truth.

8 Everywhere I want the men to do the praying, lifting up holy hands.* No anger. No arguing.

Words for Female God Chasers

9 In the same way, I want the women to dress modestly. They should use good sense and be proper, avoiding fancy hairdos and gold, or pearls, or expensive clothes. 10 Instead, use good deeds *to be beautiful*. Do what religious women think is right.

11 A woman must learn quietly and put herself completely under authority. 12 I don't allow a woman to teach over a man or have authority over him. No, she should be quiet. 13 Adam was made first. Eve was made next. 14 Also, Adam was not seduced; the woman was. She fell into sin. 15 But a woman may be saved through motherhood,* if she continues with faith, love, and holiness with good sense.

Chapter 3

Qualifications to Be an Overseer

1 This is something you can trust: "If a man wants to be an overseer, he desires a good work."

2 An overseer
   must be above suspicion,
   must be a faithful, married man,*
   must be sensible,
   must have self-control,
   must be organized,
   must love people enough to invite them into his home,
   must be a good teacher,
3 must not be addicted to wine,
   must not be a violent man,
   must be gentle,
   must be peaceful,
   must not love money,
4 must lead his own family well,

2:8   the customary manner of praying to God
2:15   giving birth to children
3:2   literally, the husband of one wife

must have children who put themselves under his authority with all respect. **5** (If a man doesn't know how to lead his own family, he would not know how to take care of the congregation of God.)

6 He must not be a new convert. (He might become boastful and fall into the Devil's condemnation.)

7 He must have good things said about him by outsiders. (Then he will not fall into shame and a trap of the Devil.)

Learn to Serve

8 In the same way, servants*

must be respectable,

must be sincere,

must not drink too much wine,

must not be greedy for dirty money,

9 must hold onto the secret of faith with a clear conscience.

10 These men must be tested first. If no one accuses them, then let them serve as servants.

11 *Their* wives must be the same way—respectable, not gossips, sensible, and faithful in all things.

12 Servants* must be faithful, married men. They must lead their children and their homes well. **13** The men who serve well as servants will win for themselves a very good position. And they will be more confident about the faith of Christ Jesus.

We Are Family

14 As I write these things to you, I am hoping to come to you soon. **15** But if I'm late, you will know how *we* must live in God's family, the community of the living God. We are the pillar and foundation of truth. **16** We must agree that the secret of our faith is great:

Christ appeared in a human body.

He was shown to be right by the Spirit.

He was seen by angels.

He was preached among the nations.

He was believed in the world.

He was taken up to heaven.*

Chapter 4

1 The Spirit clearly says that some people will pull away from the faith in later times. They will follow lying spirits and teachings of demons. **2** Like hypocrites* they will tell lies. Their consciences feel nothing, as though they have been branded with a hot iron. **3** They try to stop people from getting married. They tell people to stay away from *certain* foods. God created these foods to be eaten by thankful believers and people who know the truth. **4** Everything that God created is good. If anything is received with thanksgiving, it should be accepted. **5** It is made holy through God's message and prayer.

3:8   literally, deacons

3:12   literally, deacons

3:16   literally, glory

4:2   those who act as if they are good, but they're really not

God Chasers Are Examples

6 If you present these things to the brothers, you will be a good minister* of Christ Jesus. You are being fed by the words of faith and good teaching which you have followed.   **7** Stay away from unholy stories and old wives' tales. Train yourself to be godly.   **8** Physical training has some importance, but being godly is much more important for everything else. It promises life for now and in the future.

9 This statement is something you can trust; it is worth complete acceptance: **10** We have put our hope on the living God. He is the Savior of all persons, especially believers. This is why we work hard and try so hard.

11 Order that these things be done. Teach them.   **12** Don't let anyone think that just because you are young what you say is not important. Instead, be an example for believers by what you say and how you live, with love, faith, and purity.

13 Until I come, spend time reading *the Scriptures publicly*, comforting people, and teaching them.   **14** Don't neglect the *spiritual* gift that is inside you. It was given to you through a prophetic message, when the group of elders put their hands on you.*

15 Care about these things. Stay with them, so that your progress will be clear to everyone.   **16** Watch yourself and what you teach. Stay with them, because if you do these things, you will save yourself and the people who listen to you.

Chapter 5

Do's and Don'ts

1 Don't criticize an older man. Instead, comfort him like a father. Treat younger men like brothers.   **2** Treat older women like mothers and younger women like sisters, with all purity.

3 Honor widows who are truly widows.   **4** But, if a widow has children or grandchildren, then they should learn to be godly first with their own family. They should repay what they owe to their grandparents, because this is acceptable before God. **5** The widow who is truly a widow and who is all alone has put her hope in God. Day and night she continues praying and asking God *for help*.   **6** But the widow who lives for pleasure has already died (while she is still living).   **7** Give these orders, so that they will not be accused.   **8** If a man does not support his relatives—and especially his own family—he shows that he does not believe; he is worse than an unbeliever.

9 Don't put a widow on the list *for help* if she is under 60 years old. She must have been faithful to her husband.   **10** It should be clear to all that she has done good deeds: Did she raise children? Did she welcome strangers? Did she wash the feet of holy people? Did she help people who were suffering? Did she practice all kinds of good deeds?

11 Don't put the young widows on the list, because after their sexual desires become strong again, they want to marry and leave Christ.   **12** They become condemned, because they reject their first faith.   **13** Also, they learn to be lazy. They go from one house to the next. Not only are they lazy, but they are gossips and meddlers. They talk about things they shouldn't talk about.   **14** I want the young *widows* to get married again, have children, and make a home. This will not give the enemy a chance to say bad things about us. (**15** Some have already turned away to follow Satan.)   **16** If a believing woman has widows *in her family*, she should support them. Don't let the congregation get this burden. Then the congregation can support widows who are truly widows.

4:6   or, servant
4:14   Here it does not mean violence; it means to appoint. (Compare Acts 13:3.)

17 The elders who are good leaders deserve double the pay. This is especially true for those who work hard at preaching and teaching. **18** The Scripture says,
 "Don't put something over the ox's mouth while it
  is walking around on the wheat straw."   *Deuteronomy 25:4*
and
 "A worker should be given his pay."   *Luke 10:7*
19 When someone accuses an elder, don't accept it unless two or three people are saying the same thing. **20** There are some people who continue to sin. Prove them wrong publicly. Then the others will show respect. **21** Before God, Christ Jesus, and the chosen angels, I order you to obey these things. Don't pre-judge or give any special favors to anyone.

22 Don't confirm* someone too quickly. Don't share in the sins of others. Keep yourself pure.

23 You are often sick. Do not drink water only. Instead, use a little wine, because of your stomach.

24 The sins of some people are clear. They are punished now. The sins of others appear later. **25** In the same way, good deeds are clear. Even secret good deeds cannot be hidden.

Chapter 6

1 All slaves should feel that their masters deserve all honor. Then no one can say something evil about God's name or the teaching. **2** Slaves who have believing masters should not look down on their masters, because they are brothers. Instead, these slaves should serve them even better, because the masters are getting some good from their help. These masters are dear believers.

God Chasers Teach

Comfort people. Teach these things. **3** Someone may teach a different teaching. If he doesn't hold onto healthy words (the words of our Lord Jesus Christ) and godly teaching, **4** he is boastful. He doesn't understand anything; he is sick. He likes arguments and fights about words. Jealousy, fighting, words against God, and evil thoughts occur. **5** There is always trouble with people who have polluted minds. They don't have the truth anymore. They think that religion* is a way of making money. **6** If one is godly and content, there **is** great profit! **7** We brought nothing into the world and we can't take anything out of it. **8** If we have food and clothes, we will be satisfied with these things. **9** But the people who want to be rich fall into temptation, a trap, and many foolish desires that hurt them. These things drown people in ruin and destruction.* **10** Loving money is the root of all kinds of evil. Some people want money so badly that they have wandered away from the faith. They have so painfully wounded themselves.

Fight the Good Fight

11 But you, O man of God, run away from these things. Follow after faith, love, endurance, what is good, godly, and gentle. **12-13** Fight the good fight of the faith. Hold onto eternal life. (God gives life to everything.) You were called into this life when

---

5:22 literally, put your hands on (someone)
6:5 godliness
6:9 hell

you made the good confession in front of many witnesses. Before God and Christ Jesus who made the good confession to Pontius Pilate,* I command you   14 to be pure and clear from all shame, to obey this order until our Lord Jesus Christ appears.   15 God will show this at the right time. God is happy. He is the only Ruler, the King of kings, and the Lord of lords.   16 Only God never dies. He lives in light. No one can come near it. No human being has seen Him. No human being is able to see Him. Honor and power belong to Him forever. Amen.

17 Tell the rich people ("rich" in this world) not to brag. They shouldn't place their hope upon wealth. That is not a sure thing. Instead, they should put their hope on God who abundantly gives us everything to enjoy.   18 Rich people should do good things. They should be "rich" in good deeds. They must be generous and want to share. 19 They will store up a good foundation for themselves in the future. Then they can get hold of real life.

20 Timothy, guard what you were given! Turn away from unholy stories, old wives' tales, and the opposition of so-called "knowledge."   21 Some believers have claimed to have this "knowledge," but they have strayed away from the faith.

Gracious love be with you.

6:12-13 See John 18:36-37; 19:11.

2 TIMOTHY

Dear Friend

1 From Paul. I am an apostle of Christ Jesus because this is what God wanted. This was by the promise of life that is in Christ Jesus.

2 To Timothy, my dear son.

May gracious love, mercy, and peace come from God the Father and Christ Jesus our Lord.

Chasers Ashamed? I Think Not!

3 Like my ancestors, I serve God with a clear conscience. I thank Him. Day and night I always mention you in my prayers. **4** I yearn to see you. That would make me so very happy. I remember your tears. **5** I remember the true faith that is in you. It lived first in Lois, your grandmother, and then in Eunice, your mother. I'm sure it is *still* in you, too. **6** This is why I am reminding you to keep the fire of God's *spiritual* gift burning. It is in you because I put my hands on you.* **7** God did not give us a cowardly attitude. No, God gave us one of power, love, and good sense.

8 So, don't be ashamed to tell the truth about our Lord *Jesus* or about me, his prisoner. Instead, suffer for the Good News by God's power.

9 God saved us and called us with a holy calling. This was not by our efforts. Instead, it was by God's own purpose and gracious love which was given to us in Christ Jesus before time began. **10** Now it has been made clear since Christ Jesus, our Savior, appeared. He destroyed death. Through the gospel, he has made it clear that we will live and never die.

11 I was made a preacher, an apostle, and a teacher *of the gospel.* **12** This is why I am now suffering these things. But, I'm not ashamed, because I know the One I have believed in. And I'm sure that He is able to guard what I have trusted to Him until that Day.

13 The healthy words you heard me speak should be kept as an example with the faith and love that is in Christ Jesus. **14** Guard what you were trusted with through the Holy Spirit who lives in us.

15 I know this: Everyone in the land of Asia abandoned me, including Phygelus and Hermogenes. **16** May the Lord give mercy to Onesiphorus' family. He often made me feel better. My being in jail did not make him feel ashamed. **17** No, when he was in Rome, he searched and searched until he found me. **18** May the Lord *Jesus* allow him to find mercy from the Lord *God* on the *Judgment* Day. You know exactly how much he helped me in the city of Ephesus.

Chapter 2

God Chasers Are Good Soldiers

1 So you, my son, be strong in the gracious love that is in Christ Jesus. **2** Along with many witnesses, you heard some teachings from me. Pass these things on to faithful men who will be able to teach other men.

1:6   This showed that Timothy was appointed. To observe the practice of hand-laying see Acts 8:18, 19; 19:6.

3 Suffer like a good soldier of Christ Jesus. 4 No soldier gets mixed up with the world of business; he wants to please his superior officer. 5 If someone competes as an athlete, he will not win the prize, unless he follows the rules. 6 The farmer, who works hard, must be the first person to have a share of the crop. 7 Think about what I'm saying, because the Lord will give you an understanding of everything.

8 Don't forget the Descendant of David, Jesus Christ, who was raised from death. This is the Good News I tell. 9 Like a criminal I suffer for the gospel—even if it means prison! But, God's message has not been confined. 10 Why do I endure all of these things? It is for the people chosen *by God*. I want *them* also to receive the salvation which is in Christ Jesus with eternal glory. 11 This is a *song* you can believe in:

"If we died with Christ, we will also live with him.
12 If we endure, we will also rule with him.
If we say no to him, he will say no to us.
13 If we are not faithful, he is always faithful,
because he must remain true to himself."*

God Chasers Are Good Examples

14 Continue reminding the people about these things. Warn them before God not to have fights about words, for that is useless. It destroys the people who are listening. 15 Do your best to present yourself to God as one who has passed the test. Be a worker who has nothing to be ashamed of. Interpret the message of truth in the proper way. 16 Stay away from unholy stories and empty talk. Those who continue doing this will only become more ungodly. 17 Their message spreads like cancer.* Some of them are Hymenaeus and Philetus. 18 They have wandered away from the truth. They claim that the resurrection of the dead has already come! And they have turned some people away from the faith. 19 But God's solid foundation stands firm. It has this stamp:

"The Lord *God* knows who belongs to him."   *Numbers 16:5*

and

"Every person who wears the name of the Lord *God*
must pull away from wrong."   *Numbers 16:26*

20 In a large house there are different bowls. Some are made of gold or silver, but some are made of wood or clay. Some are for nice things, but some are for ugly purposes. 21 So, if a person cleans himself up from these *evil* things, he will be *like* a bowl for nice things. He is special and useful for the Master, ready to do any good work.

22 Run away from the evil desires which some young people have. Follow righteousness, faith, love, and peace. Do this with people who trust in the Lord with a pure heart. 23 Stay away from foolish and silly arguments. You know they cause fights. 24 The Lord's servant must not fight. No, he should be kind to everyone. He should be a good teacher. He shouldn't want to pay somebody back with evil. 25 He must gently correct people who are against him. Perhaps God will allow them to have a change of heart, leading them to know the truth. 26 Then they will wake up and get away from the Devil's trap. The Devil has captured them to do what he wants them to do.

2:13   literally, He cannot deny himself.
2:17   or, gangrene, a disease that spreads throughout the body, decaying the flesh

Chapter 3

The Last Times

1 Know this: There will be hard times during the last days.   **2** People will be self-ish,* greedy, boastful, proud, blasphemers, disobeying their parents, unthankful, unholy,   **3** without natural love, unforgiving, gossips, violent, mean, hating good, **4** traitors, wild, and conceited. They will love pleasures more than they love God. **5** They will hold the outer form of religion, but they say no to its *inner* power. Stay away from these people.   **6** Some of these men move into homes and "capture" women who are heavy with sins and *easily* led into many types of evil desires. **7** These people are "always learning," but they are never able to come to truth. **8** They are like Jannes and Jambres, the men who were against Moses.* In the same way, these people are against the truth. Their minds are completely polluted. They have failed the faith.   **9** But, they will not make much progress because their stupidity, like that of Jannes and Jambres, will become clear to everyone.

God Chasers Get Crowned

10 You have followed my teaching, my life, my purpose, my faith, my patience, my love, and my endurance.   **11** You know my persecutions, the kinds of things I suffered in the cities of Antioch *in Pisidia*, Iconium, and Lystra.* I put up with all kinds of per-secutions, but the Lord rescued me from all of them.   **12** Everyone who wants to live a godly life in Christ Jesus will be persecuted.   **13** Evil men and cheaters will become worse and worse. They will fool people and others will fool them.   **14** But you must stay with the things you trust, the things you were taught. You know the people you learned them from.   **15** You have known the Holy Scriptures* since you were a child. The Scriptures are able to make you wise for salvation through believing in Christ Jesus.   **16** Every Scripture is inspired by God and useful for teaching, for proving *sin-ners* wrong, for correcting errors, and for training people to be right with God. **17** Then the man of God will be right, prepared for any good work.

Chapter 4

1 In the future, Christ will judge people who are now alive and people who have died. Because of the nearness of his appearance and his kingdom, I warn you before God and Christ Jesus: **2** Preach the message! Be ready in good times and times that are not so good. Prove *sinners* wrong. Correct and comfort, with all kinds of patience and teaching.   **3** The time will come when people will not put up with healthy teach-ing. Instead, following their own evil desires, they will gather to themselves many, many teachers to say what they want to hear.   **4** And, they will turn away from listen-ing to the truth. They will go after myths.   **5** Use self-control in everything. Endure. Do the work of one who preaches the Good News. Finish your ministry.

6 I am already being poured out *like a drink offering*. The time has come for me to die.*   **7** I have fought a good fight. I have finished the race. I have kept the faith.

3:2	literally, lovers of themselves
3:8	See Exodus 7:11,12.
3:11	a town near where Timothy had lived when he was a young man (Acts 16:1)
3:15	the Old Testament, the only ancient writings from God available at that time
4:4	or, legends, fables
4:6	literally, depart

8 At last, there is a crown of righteousness waiting for me. The Lord *Jesus* will reward me on that *Judgment* Day. He is a fair judge. Not only will he reward me, but he'll reward all people who have longed for his appearance.

Only Luke Is With Me

9 Do your best to come to me soon.   **10** Demas abandoned me; he loved today's world. He went to the city of Thessalonica and Crescens left for the land of Galatia. Titus went to the Dalmatian area.   **11** Only Luke is with me. Bring Mark along with you, because he is useful for the work.*   **12** I sent Tychicus to the city of Ephesus. **13** I left a heavy coat with Carpus in the city of Troas. When you come, bring the coat, the books, and especially the leather scrolls.

14 Alexander, the copper-worker, hurt me very much; the Lord will pay him back for what he did.   **15** You should be on guard, too. He was very much against our teachings.

16 No one came to *help* me at my first defense trial; they all abandoned me. (May the Lord not hold this against them!)   **17** But the Lord stood beside me. He made me strong, so that the message would be fully preached through me and so that all the non-Jewish people would listen. The Lord rescued me from the lion's mouth.*   **18** The Lord will rescue me from every evil attack. He will save me for His heavenly kingdom. *Give* glory to Him forever and ever. Amen.

See Ya Later

19 Greet Priscilla* and Aquila. Greet the family of Onesiphorus.   **20** Erastus stayed in the city of Corinth. I left Trophimus in the city of Miletus. He was sick.

21 Do your best to come before winter.

Eubulus, Pudens, Linus, Claudia, and all of the brothers here send their greetings.

22 May the Lord be with your spirit. May gracious love be with you.

4:11   Compare Acts 13:13; 15:36-41.
4:17   certain death
4:19   literally, Prisca

327

TITUS

Hi, Titus

1 From Paul, a servant of God and an apostle of Jesus Christ for *helping* God's chosen ones believe and fully understand the truth of godly living.   **2** This is based on hope—hope for eternal life. God promised this before time began; and God does not lie! **3** At the right time, God made His message clear. It was entrusted to me. By order of God our Savior I proclaim it.

4 To Titus, my true son by the faith we share. May gracious love and peace *come to you* from God the Father and from Christ Jesus, our Savior.

Some God Chasers Must Qualify

5 I left you on the island of Crete because I wanted you to straighten out things that still needed to be done and to confirm elders in each town as I told you.   **6** An elder

must be above suspicion,
must be a faithful, married man,*
must have faithful children
 who could not be accused of being wild or disobedient,

7 must have a good reputation, since he watches over God's work,
must not be overbearing,
must not be hot-tempered,
must not be addicted to wine,
must not be a violent man,
must not be dishonest in money matters,

8 must love people enough to invite them into his home,
must love what is good,
must be wise,
must be fair,
must be a holy man,
must have control of himself,

9 must hold onto the faithful message
 as it has been taught, so that he can be strong, encouraging people with healthy teaching and correcting those who are against *the truth.*

10 There are many people who won't obey, especially Jewish believers who claim that non-Jewish believers must be circumcised.* They have nothing to say, but they talk anyway. They lead other people the wrong way.   **11** Their mouths **must** be shut. They are upsetting entire families, teaching things they must not teach. Why? To make money!   **12** One of their own teachers said:

"Cretan people are always liars, mean brutes, and lazy—but they love to eat."*

1:6 literally, husband of one wife
1:10 to cut off the foreskin of the male sex organ as a sign of God's agreement with Israel (Genesis 17:9-14)
1:12 Epimenides wrote this in *de Oraculis.*

13 This is true. That is why you must always be correcting them sharply. Then they will have a healthy faith.   **14** They must not hold onto Jewish legends* or the commands of men who are turning away from the truth.   **15** Everything is clean to those who are clean, but nothing is clean to those who are polluted and unfaithful. Their consciences and the way they think are both polluted.   **16** They claim they know God, but their actions show that this is not true. They are rotten, disobedient, and worthless for doing anything good.

Chapter 2

Training Camp

1 But you must continue to speak proper things for healthy teaching.   **2** Tell the older men to be serious, worthy of respect, self-controlled, healthy in their faith, loving, and enduring.

3 In the same way, tell the older women to live the way holy women should live and not to be gossips or slaves to wine. They should be teachers of good things.   **4** Then they can train the younger women to love their husbands and children,   **5** to control themselves, to be pure, to keep house, to be good, and to obey their husbands. Then no one can say evil things about God's message.

6 In the same way, encourage the younger men to control themselves.   **7** You yourself must set an example in everything by doing good things. When you teach, be serious and be sincere.   **8** Offer a healthy message that cannot be criticized, so that an enemy will feel ashamed, having nothing bad to say against us.

9 Slaves must obey their own masters in everything. They must please them and not talk back.   **10** They must not steal from them. Instead, slaves must show that they are good and can be trusted completely. Then the teaching of God, our Savior, will look beautiful in every way.

11 The gracious love of God has appeared to save all mankind.   **12** It trains us to say no to ungodly ways and worldly desires and to live self-controlled, upright, and godly lives in this world.   **13** We are waiting for the blessed hope and the glorious appearance of our great God and Savior, Jesus Christ.   **14** He gave himself for us, so that he could buy us back from every kind of sin. He wanted to make a nation clean for his very own, a nation eager to do good deeds.   **15** Continue saying these things. Keep on encouraging and correcting with full authority. Don't let anyone look down on you!

Chapter 3

No Division Problems

1 Remind the people to put themselves under rulers and those in authority, to obey them, to be ready to do any good work,   **2** not to say evil things about anyone, to be peaceable, to be considerate, and to show true humility toward every person.
3 We, too, were disobedient, foolish, and fooled. We were slaves to all kinds of human desires and pleasures. We lived our lives being mean to and jealous of others. People hated us and we hated them.   **4** But then, the kindness and love of God our

---

1:14   myths, fables

Savior appeared. 5 He saved us by a washing of rebirth and renewal of the Holy Spirit. Salvation did not come from any good deeds that **we** ourselves did. No, it came by God's mercy! 6 Through Jesus Christ, our Savior, God generously poured out the Holy Spirit upon us. 7 This is how we have been made right with God. This is how we have become heirs: By *God's* gracious love we have the hope of eternal life. 8 That statement is something you can trust.

I want you to stress these matters, so that those who have committed themselves to God may be careful to devote themselves to doing good deeds. These things are good and useful for people. 9 But stay away from foolish issues, long lists of ancestors, arguments, or disputes about the law *of Moses*. These are useless and without purpose. 10 After the first and second warnings, have nothing to do with a person who causes divisions. 11 You know that such a person is always sinning and corrupt; he knows he's wrong.

So Long for Now

12 When I send Artemas or Tychicus to you, do your best to come to me in the city of Nicopolis, because I have decided to spend the winter there. 13 Do your best to help Zenas the lawyer and Apollos on their way, so that they have everything they need. 14 Our people must learn to devote themselves to doing good deeds. They must learn to be productive, providing for real needs.

15 Those who are here with me send their greetings. Send our greetings to those in *the* faith who love us. May gracious love be with all of you.

PHILEMON

Hi, Philemon!

1 From Paul, a prisoner* of Christ Jesus, and from brother Timothy.
To
    Philemon, our dear *friend* and co-worker,
2 the group that meets in your home,
    sister Apphia,
Archippus, our co-soldier.
3 May God our Father and the Lord Jesus Christ give you gracious love and peace.

Philemon Gets a Lift

4 I always thank my God for you. I always remember you in my prayers. **5** I hear about the love and faith you have for the Lord Jesus and for all of the holy people. **6** *I pray that* you will actively share your faith with a real understanding of every good thing which we have in Christ. **7** I feel very happy and encouraged because of your love. Brother, you have lifted up the hearts of the holy people.

Onesimus Is a God Chaser—He Really Is

8 And so, in Christ, I have plenty of freedom to order you to do what you should do. **9** But, because of love, I would rather encourage. I, Paul, am an old man and also now a prisoner* for Christ Jesus. **10** I appeal to you for my child, Onesimus.* I "fathered"* him in prison. **11** Before this, he was not useful to you, but now, he **is** useful to you and me.

12 I send him—my very heart—back to you. **13** I was wanting to keep him for myself. While in prison for the Good News, he could have helped me as your servant.* **14** But I didn't want to do anything, unless you knew about it. Then your goodness would not be forced. It would be because you really wanted to do it.

15 Perhaps this is why Onesimus was separated *from you* for a while. Now you can have him back forever. **16** Onesimus is not really a slave anymore. No, he is more than a slave; he is a dear brother—especially to me. But this is even more true for you, both as a man and as a brother in the Lord.

17 If you think of me as your partner, accept Onesimus as you would accept **me**. **18** If he did anything wrong toward you or if he owes you money, put that on **my** bill. **19** I, Paul, am writing this with my own hand: "I will pay you back." (I won't mention that you owe me your very life.*) **20** Yes, brother, I hope in the Lord that you will lift up my heart in Christ.

21 As I write this letter, I'm sure you will obey. I know that you will do even more than I'm asking for. **22** Oh yes, prepare a guest room for me. I hope to be given back to you, because you are praying for this.

1:1   When Paul wrote this letter, he was in prison in Rome.
1:9   When Paul wrote this letter, he was in prison in Rome.
1:10   The Greek name Onesimus means "useful."
1:10   Paul converted Onesimus to Christ.
1:13   Onesimus was Philemon's slave.
1:19   Paul had converted Philemon to Christ earlier.

Fond Farewells

23 Epaphras,* my cellmate in Christ Jesus, sends greetings to you. **24** My co-workers—Mark, Aristarchus, Demas, and Luke—send you their greetings, too. **25** May the gracious love of the Lord Jesus Christ be with your spirit. Amen.

1:23   Epaphras had helped the Colossian congregation (Colossians 1:7).

HEBREWS

Long, Long Ago

1 Long ago, God used the prophets to speak to *our* ancestors many times and in many ways; **2** but, during these last times, God used *His* Son to speak to us. God appointed him to inherit everything. Through him God made the universe. **3** The Son is the shining brightness of God's glory and the exact picture of God's real being. The Son holds up the universe with his powerful word. After he had provided a cleansing from sin, he sat down at God's* right side in heaven.

Just How Great Is Jesus?

4 Jesus has received a title—Son. This is better than any of the angels. He is so much more important than angels.

5 God never said this to an angel:

    "You are My Son.

      I have fathered you today."   *Psalm 2:7*

and again,

    "I will be his Father

      and he will be My Son."   *2 Samuel 7:14*

6 Again, when God brought His first Son into the world, He says:

    "All God's angels must worship him!"   *Psalm 97:7*

7 God was talking about angels here:

    "God makes His angels winds

      and His servants flames of fire."   *Psalm 104:4*

8 But God said this about His Son:

    " Your throne, O God, *lasts* forever and ever.

      You rule your kingdom fairly.

9 You have loved what is right and hated what is wrong.

    This is why God, your God, has made you king

      over your friends with the oil of gladness."   *Psalm 45:6-7*

10 *God* also *said this about His Son*:

    "Lord, in the beginning, you laid the foundation of the earth.

      The heavens are the result of your work.

11 The heavens and the earth will be destroyed, but **you**

    will continue.

      Like a robe, they will get old.

12 They will be rolled up like an overcoat;

    they will be changed like a robe.

      But **you** are *still* the same.

        You will never get old."   *Psalm 102:25-27*

13 God never said this to any of the angels:

    "Sit at My right side until I put your enemies under your feet for a

      footstool."   *Psalm 110:1*

14 All angels are serving spirits sent to help those who will receive salvation.

1:3   literally, the Majesty; Jewish people often avoided direct references to God because of their deep respect for Him.

Chapter 2

Pay Attention!

1 This is why we must really pay attention to the things we have heard. If we don't, we might drift away. **2** The message that *God* spoke through angels was firm. Every person who broke *God's law* or disobeyed it received fair punishment. **3** If we don't care about so great a salvation, we will not escape *punishment*. In the beginning, the Lord *Jesus* told about this salvation. Later, the people who heard *him* showed us that it was true. **4** Also, God proved that it was true with miracles, amazing things, and different kinds of powers and *spiritual gifts* from the Holy Spirit which were distributed the way God wanted.

Under Foot

5 God did not put the future world (which we are talking about) under the angels.
6 Someone has said somewhere *in the Scriptures*:
"What is man, that You should care about him?
What are his children,* that You should take care
of them?
7 You made man a little lower than angels.
You crowned him with glory and honor.
8 You put everything under his control." *Psalm 8:4-7*
When God "put everything" under man, this meant everything! But, today, we see that everything has not yet been put under man. **9** We see Jesus. He was made "a little lower than angels." But when Jesus suffered and died, he was "crowned with glory and honor." By God's gracious love he did this to taste death for every person.

10 God made everything for Himself. When He brought many sons to glory, it was only right for Him to use suffering to make the Leader* of their salvation perfect.

11 The people who were made holy and the one who made them holy all come from one *Father*. That is why Jesus is not ashamed to call them "brothers." **12** *The Scripture says*:
"I will announce Your name to my brothers.
I will sing to You in the middle of the congregation." *Psalm 22:22*

13 Again, *the Scripture says*:
"I will trust Him." *Isaiah 8:17*
Again:
"Look! I am with the children whom God gave me." *Isaiah 8:18*
14 The "children" are human.* So, Jesus also shared in their humanity. He wanted to use death to destroy the Devil who has the power of death. **15** Jesus also wanted to set all people free from the slavery of fearing death all their lives. **16** It is clear that he is helping Abraham's descendants, not angels. **17** This means that Jesus had to become like his brothers in every way. Then he could become a faithful, merciful high priest, *offering himself* to God for the forgiveness of the sins of the people. **18** Before Jesus suffered, **he** was tempted. That is why he is able to help people who are being tempted now.

2:6 literally, a son of man
2:10 Jesus
2:14 literally, flesh and blood

Chapter 3

Jesus Is Greater Than Moses

1 Therefore, holy brothers *and sisters*, you who share in God's* calling, think about Jesus—the one whom we confessed was the Apostle and High Priest.   **2** Jesus was faithful to God who appointed him, as Moses was faithful among all of God's family.*   **3** A builder deserves more praise than the house he built. So, Jesus deserves more honor than Moses.   **4** Every house is built by someone, but God built everything.   **5** Moses was faithful like a servant in all God's family, (He told the truth about what God would say in the future.)   **6** but Christ is like a Son over God's house. We are that house, if we hold on to the confidence and the hope we are proud of.

Don't Have Stubborn Hearts

7 Therefore, the Holy Spirit says:
"If you hear God's voice today,
8 don't let your hearts become stubborn,
    as you did during the rebellion
    in the time of testing in the desert.
9 Your ancestors put Me to the test,
    though they saw My deeds for 40 years.
10 So, I was angry with that generation.
    I said, 'Their hearts always wander away.
    They have not known My ways.'
11 So, while I was angry, I made a vow:
    'They will never go into My place of rest.' " *Psalm 95:7-11*

12 Brothers, be careful! If you're not, some of you might develop an evil, unbelieving heart that pulls away from the living God.   **13** Instead, every day comfort one another while it is still "today," so none of you will become stubborn because sin has fooled you.   **14** If, to the very end, we hold tightly to the confidence we had at the beginning, we are partners with Christ.

15 Again:
"If you hear God's voice today,
    don't let your hearts become stubborn,
    as you did during the rebellion." *Psalm 95:7-8*
16 Who heard God's voice and rebelled? It was all of the people whom Moses brought out of Egypt!   **17** With whom was God angry for 40 years? It was with those people who sinned! Their dead bodies lay in the desert.*   **18** God vowed that they would never enter His place of rest. Who would never go? Those who did not obey God!   **19** We can see that they couldn't go in, because they did not believe.

Chapter 4

The Rest Is for You

1 The promise of going into God's place of rest is still open, but we should be afraid. If you're not, some of you might not make it.   **2** We were told good news, as they

---

3:1   literally, a heavenly calling
3:2   literally, house
3:17   literally, The corpses fell in the desert. (See Numbers 14:32.)

were, but the message they heard didn't help them, because they didn't believe it.
3 We believe. So, we are entering that place of rest. God said:

> "While I was angry, I made a vow:
>> 'They will not enter My place of rest!' "　　　　　　　　　　　　　　*Psalm 95:11*

But God's works were finished at the time He created the world!　4 Somewhere *in the Scriptures* God has said this about the seventh day:

> "God rested on the seventh day from all His works."　　　　　　　　*Genesis 2:2*

5 *But listen* again to the same *Scripture*:

> "They will not enter My place of rest."　　　　　　　　　　　　　　*Psalm 95:11*

6 The people who were first told the good news did not enter, because they did not obey God. However, that place of rest is still open for some people to enter.　7 God planned for a day *called* "today." A long time *after Moses*, God used David to say this (as was mentioned before):

> "If you hear God's voice **today**,
>> don't let your hearts become stubborn."　　　　　　　　　　　　*Psalm 95:7-8*

8 If Joshua had given them rest, then later God would not have talked about another day.　9 So, there is a keeping of sabbath* still open for God's people.　10 A person who enters God's place of rest also rests from his works, as God rested from His works.　11 We must do our best to enter *God's* place of rest, so that no one will fall away, following the example they set by not obeying God.

12 God's message is alive and active. It is sharper than any sword with two sharp edges. It can slice between the soul and the spirit or between the joints and bone marrow. It can tell the difference between the desires and the intentions of the human mind.　13 Nothing in creation is hidden before God. To His eyes everything is naked and bare.* We must give an answer to God.

Jesus, Our High Priest

14 So, we have a High Priest who has gone through the heavens. He is Jesus, the Son of God. We must hold on to what we said we believed.　15 Our High Priest can sympathize with our weaknesses. He was tempted in every way, as we are, but he never sinned!　16 Let us come near *God's* throne of gracious love with confidence. Then we can receive mercy and we can find gracious love to help us when we need it.

Chapter 5

1 Every high priest is chosen from among men. He is appointed to serve God for them. They want him to offer gifts and sacrifices to God for sins.　2 Since, in many ways, he himself is weak, he can gently handle people who are ignorant or those who wander away.　3 That is why he must offer something for his own sins, as well as for the sins of the people.

4 No one, on his own, can take this honor; God must call him, just as He called Aaron.*　5 In the same way, Christ did not give himself the glory of being a high priest. No, God said this to him:

4:9　　or, Sabbath rest
4:12　　literally, heart
4:13　　exposed, i.e. all things lie open, nothing is hidden.
5:4　　See Exodus 28:1.

"You are My Son.
I have fathered you today."

Psalm 2:7

6 And God said this in another Scripture:

"You are a priest forever
in the category of Melchizedek." *Psalm 110:4*

7 During Jesus' human life, he offered prayers to God. Once, with strong cries and tears, Jesus asked God to save him from death. (God could have done it, too, *but He didn't.*) God listened to Jesus because Jesus was devoted to God. 8 Even though Jesus was *God's* Son, Jesus learned to obey from the things he suffered. 9 After Jesus was made perfect, he became the Source of eternal salvation for everyone who will obey him. 10 God appointed Jesus to be High Priest, in the category of Melchizedek.

11 Since you have become *spiritually* hard-of-hearing, the teaching about Melchizedek is very hard to explain. 12 You should have become teachers a long time ago, but you need someone to teach you again the first principles of God's sayings. You need milk, not solid food. 13 Anyone who lives on milk is still a baby. He has not experienced the teaching of righteousness. 14 But solid food is for grown-ups— people who have trained their senses by using them to tell the difference between right and wrong.

Chapter 6

Keep On Keeping On

1 So, we should leave the basic things we learned about Christ and go on to more mature things. We should not lay again the foundation of turning away from *depending on* dead human efforts, of believing in God, 2 teaching about immersions, putting hands on people,* rising from death, and eternal judgment. 3 And, if God allows, we will go on.

4 Some people once had the light. They tasted some of the heavenly gift and shared in the Holy Spirit. 5 They tasted how good the word of God is and the powers of the future world, 6 but they have fallen away. It is impossible* to bring them back to a change of heart. In their lives, they nail the Son of God to the cross again, shaming him publicly.

7 God blesses land which drinks in the rain that often falls on it. This land produces a good crop for the people who farm it. 8 But land which produces thorny weeds and thorn bushes is not good and it is near condemnation. It will end up being burned.

9 But, dear *friends*, even though we talk like this, we are sure of better things for you—things that go with salvation. 10 God is fair. He will remember what you did and the love you showed toward His name. You have helped *God's* holy people and continue to do so. 11 We want each one of you to continue doing your best until the very end. Then you can make sure of your hope. 12 We don't want you to become lazy. Be like people who will receive *God's* promises through faith and patience.

6:2   This was the usual way to appoint men. It does not mean to do violence.
6:6   "It is impossible" has been moved from verse 4.

What a Promise!

13 When God vowed to Abraham, He could not make a vow by anyone greater than Himself. So, God made the vow by Himself.   14 He said:

> "I will surely bless you, and I will surely give you
>   many descendants."

Genesis 22:17

15 Abraham was patient and later he received what God promised.

16 People make vows by someone who is greater than they are. This confirms agreements and stops all arguments among them.   17 God wanted to show very clearly that His plan would not change. So, He made a vow to confirm it to the people who received the promise *made to Abraham.*   18 It is impossible for God to lie about these two actions.* God wanted to use these two things (which cannot change) to give us much comfort. We have run for safety to take hold of the hope that is in front of us.   19 This hope that we have is like an anchor for the soul. It is safe and sure. It goes behind the curtain inside the *heavenly* temple sanctuary   20 where Jesus has already entered for us. He has become High Priest forever, in the category of Melchizedek.

Chapter 7

Old Makes Way for New

1 This Melchizedek was king of the city of Salem and priest of the Most High God. When Abraham was coming back from defeating the kings,* Melchizedek met him and blessed him.   2 And Abraham shared ten percent of everything with him. First, Melchizedek means "king of what is right." He was also king of Salem (which means "king of peace").   3 We don't know who his father or mother was. We don't have a list of his ancestors or descendants. And we don't know when he was born or how long he lived.* Melchizedek is like the Son of God—he continues as a priest for all time.

4 Look how great Melchizedek was! Even Abraham, our father, gave him ten percent of the treasures from the battle.   5 The law *of Moses* orders that the people *of Israel* must give ten percent to the sons of Levi, who were the priests. The Levites are their brothers even though they came from Abraham.   6 But Melchizedek was not a descendant of Levi. And yet, even though Abraham had *God's* promises, Abraham gave **him** ten percent. Melchizedek blessed Abraham!   7 Everyone would agree that a more important person blesses one who is less important.   8 Levites are men. They receive ten percent and die, but Melchizedek received ten percent and (we are told) still lives!   9 One could even say that Melchizedek received ten percent from Levi through Abraham,   10 because when Melchizedek met Abraham, Levi was still inside Abraham's body.*

11 The people received the law through the Levites. If a person could become perfect through the group of Levite priests, why was a different kind of priest needed to come through the Melchizedek type of priesthood, instead of through Aaron's priesthood?   12 Since there was a change in the kind of priests, there must also be a change

---

6:18   The two unchangeable things are: (1) God's spoken word (the promise); (2) God's oath (unnecessary).

7:1   See Genesis 14:17-20.

7:3   Only the tribe of Levi was appointed to serve as priests. See Numbers 3:5-10.

7:10   Levi was the great-grandson of Abraham.

of the law. **13** The one we are talking about belonged to a different tribe. No one from that tribe could serve at the altar.* **14** It is very clear that our Lord *Jesus* came from the tribe of Judah. Moses said nothing about anyone in this tribe becoming a priest. **15** Now, it becomes even plainer: a different priest has come; he is like Melchizedek. **16** Christ became a priest, not because of human rules and laws, but by the power of a life that cannot be destroyed.

17 This truth is told *in the Scriptures*:

"You are a priest forever

in the category of Melchizedek." *Psalm 110:4*

18 The old rule was done away with because it was weak and useless. **19** The law made nothing perfect, but we can now come close to God through a better hope.

20 This happened with *God's* vow. The others became priests without a vow, **21** but Christ became a priest with *God's* vow. This is what was said to him:

"The Lord *God* made a vow.

He will never change it:

'You will be a priest forever.'" *Psalm 110:4*

22 Because of a promise like this, Jesus has become the guarantee of a better agreement.

23 One priest *of Levi* could not live forever. Many priests were needed to continue the line. **24** Jesus lives forever. He never passes on his priestly work to others. **25** So, Christ can completely save the people who come to God through him. Christ always lives to plead for them.

26 Jesus is the High Priest we need. He is holy, good, and without sin. He is lifted high above the heavens, separated from sinners. **27** Jesus is not like the other high priests. He doesn't need to offer sacrifices every day for his own sins and later for the sins of the people, because Jesus offered **himself** *for our sins* once for all time. **28** The law appoints men as high priests; these men are not perfect. But, after the law, *God's* vow came. It appointed the Son* as High Priest. He has been made perfect forever.

Chapter 8

The Better Agreement

1 This is the point of what is being said: We have such a High Priest. He sat down in heaven at the right side of God's* throne. **2** He is a minister in the most holy place, the tent which is real. God, not man, put up this tent.

3 Every high priest was appointed to offer gifts and sacrifices. Our High Priest also needed something to offer. **4** If Jesus were on earth *today*, he would not be a priest *of Levi*.* They offer gifts as the law *commands*. **5** They worship *at a temple* which is only a copy of what is in heaven. It is not the original. When Moses was about to build the holy tent, God warned him:

"Be careful! You must make everything like the

pattern which I showed you on the mountain." *Exodus 25:40*

6 But now, Jesus has received a ministry that is better than theirs. He makes a better agreement between God and man. It is based on better promises.

7:13 See Numbers 8:5-26. Only the Levites were allowed to do this.
7:28 Jesus
8:1 literally, the throne of the Majesty in the heavens
8:4 because Jesus was from the tribe of Judah (See Matthew 1:2; Luke 3:33.)

The Best Agreement

7 If nothing had been wrong with the first agreement, then there would have been no room for the second agreement.   **8** But God found something wrong with the people. He said *through Jeremiah*:

"Listen! The Lord *God* says,
 'The time is coming when I will make a new agreement
   with the family of Israel
     and the family of Judah.
9 It will not be like the agreement which I made with their ancestors
   when I took their hand and led them out of the land of Egypt.
 They did not continue with My agreement.
 So I paid no attention to them.
10 This is the *new* agreement that I will make
   with the family of Israel
     in the future.
I will put My laws in their minds.
 I will write them upon their hearts.
I will be their God.
 They will be My people.
11 No one will ever teach his neighbor
   or his brother like this:
    " You must know the Lord *God!*"
Everyone will *already* know Me,
 from the most important person to the least
     important person.
12 I will show mercy to their wrongs.
 I will forget about their sins forever.' "

Jeremiah 31:31-34

13 When God said, "a new agreement," He made the first agreement old. What is old and worn out is almost gone.

Chapter 9

A New Agreement

1 The first agreement had rules for worship and a holy place in this world.   **2** The sanctuary was built. In the first room,* there were the lampstand, the table, and the holy loaves of bread. This room was called "the holy place."   **3** The second room behind the curtain was called "the most holy place."   **4** This room contained the golden altar and the chest of the agreement. The chest was completely covered with gold. Inside the chest, there were three things: the golden jar of manna,* Aaron's rod which had started to grow,* and the stone tablets of *God's* agreement.   **5** *Two* glorious angel-like statues stood above the chest. Their wings were spread over the place where sins were taken away. But now is not the time to talk about every detail of these things.

6 After everything was ready, the priests were always going in and out of the first room to perform their worship services.   **7** But, once each year, the high priest went

---

9:2   literally, tent
9:4   Manna is food which God gave Israel in the desert. (See Exodus 16:13-21; Numbers 11:7-9.)
9:4   sprouted, budded, or blossomed

alone into the second room. He had to have blood with him. He offered this blood to God for himself and for the sins which the people did without knowing about them. **8** While the first room is still standing, the Holy Spirit uses this to show that the way into the most holy place had not yet been opened. **9** This is symbolic for today: It shows that gifts and sacrifices, which are being offered to God, cannot clear the worshiper's conscience. **10** These were only physical rules about food, drink, and different kinds of washings.* They were to last until the time when everything would be made right.

The Blood of Christ

11 But Christ has come as High Priest over good things which already exist. He went through the greater and more perfect sanctuary.* It is not man-made. (This means that it is not a part of this world.) **12** Once for all time, Christ went into the most holy place and secured *for others* everlasting forgiveness* from sin. He used his own blood, not the blood of goats or calves. **13** The blood of goats, bulls, or the ashes from a young cow are sprinkled upon unholy people. This makes them separate and clean on the outside. **14** But, how much more will the blood of Christ make our consciences clean from dead human efforts, so that we can worship the living God! Through the everlasting Spirit, Christ offered himself to God as a perfect sacrifice.

15 This is why Christ can make a new agreement between God and man. The people broke God's law while they were living under the first agreement. But the death *of Christ* was the price to set them free from sin. Now those people who have been called by God may receive the eternal inheritance that God promised.

16 When a person wants his property to go to others after he dies, he makes a will. That will is worthless, unless someone can prove that a person died, **17** because a will is not in effect until someone dies. The will does not take effect during the life of the person who made the will. **18** That is why even the first *agreement* was not in effect until blood *sealed it.* **19** Moses told all of the people every command of the law. Then he took some water and some blood from calves. He used a hyssop branch and red wool to sprinkle the book *of the law* and all the people. **20** Moses said,

"This blood *seals* the agreement
that God commanded you to obey." *Exodus 24:8*

21 In the same way, Moses used blood to sprinkle the holy tent and all the things used for a worship service. **22** Yes, the law says that almost everything must be made clean with blood. Unless blood is poured out, sins are not forgiven.

A Better Sacrifice

23 The copies of the things in heaven had to be made clean with the sacrifices, but the original things in heaven needed better sacrifices than those. **24** Christ did not enter the most holy place which was man-made, a copy of the real one. No, he went into heaven itself to appear before God for us. **25** The high priest goes into the most holy place every year with blood, but it is not his own blood. Christ did not enter heaven to offer himself again and again. **26** If he had done that, he would have had to suffer over and over since the world began. But now, at the end of the ages, Christ has

---

9:10   literally, immersions
9:11   literally, tent room
9:12   eternal release from sin

appeared to get rid of sin once for all time by sacrificing himself.   **27** It is certain that all persons die one time. And, the Judgment *Day* comes after death.   **28** In the same way, Christ was sacrificed once for all time to take away the sins of many people. Christ *will come* again. Why? Not to get rid of sin, but to save the people who are waiting for him. They will see him.

Chapter 10

The Best Sacrifice

1 The law was only a copy* of good things in the future. It was not the real thing. The same sacrifices, offered year after year, could never make worshipers perfect. **2** Otherwise, they would have stopped making sacrifices, because the worshipers would have been made clean once for all time. They would not feel guilty.   **3** But every year, when the sacrifices were made, the people remembered their sins. **4** Goat's blood or bull's blood could never take away sin.
   5 So, when Christ came into the world, this is what he said:
     "You did not want a sacrifice or an offering.
       But You prepared a body for me.
   6 You were not pleased
      with burnt offerings or sin offerings.
   7 Then I said,
     'Look! I have come to do what You want, O God!'
     This is written about me in the first part of the scroll."   *Psalm 40:6-8*
8 He said this above: "You did not want a sacrifice, an offering, burnt offerings, or sin offerings. You were not pleased with these things." But the law said that these must be offered.   **9** Then he said, "Look! I have come to do what You want." God took away the first *group of sacrifices*, so that He could set up the second *sacrifice*. **10** Because God wanted to do that, we have been made holy once for all time through *the sacrifice of* the body of Jesus Christ.
   11 A priest serves at the worship service every day. He offers the same sacrifices again and again, but these things can never take away sin.   **12** But after Jesus offered one sacrifice for sin forever, he sat down at God's right side.   **13** Now he is waiting for his enemies to be put under his feet.*   **14** There are people who have become holy. With one sacrifice Christ made them perfect forever.
   15 The Holy Spirit tells us the truth. He tells us: **16** "The Lord *God* says,
     'This is the agreement I will make with them in the future:
     I will put My laws on their hearts.
     I will write My laws on their minds.
   17 I will forget about their sins and their wrongs.' "   *Jeremiah 31:31-34*
   18 When these people are forgiven, sacrifices for sin are no longer *needed*.

God Chasers Deal Direct

   19 So, brothers, with the blood of Jesus we have confidence to go into the most holy place.   **20** His body is the new living way that made an opening through the curtain. (This is his body.) **21** We have a great Priest *serving* over God's house, too.   **22** So, let us come with a true heart and be sure of our faith. Our hearts should be made pure*

10:1   literally, shadow
10:13   in his control
10:22   literally, sprinkled

from a guilty conscience. Our bodies should be washed with pure water. **23** Let us hold tightly to the hope we said we believed in. God promised and He is dependable. **24** And let us think about how we may cause one another to love and to do good things. **25** Do not quit meeting together, as some people are in the habit of doing. Instead, encourage *one another* even more, since you see the day* coming closer.

26 We have received the truth; we know it. If we continue sinning on purpose, there will be no more sacrifices for sin, **27** only a terrible waiting for judgment and for the great fire to burn up the enemies *of God*. **28** If someone did not want to obey the law of Moses, and two or three people said that this was true, then that person died without mercy. **29** Who deserves even more punishment than that? The person who walks all over the Son of God, who thinks that the blood which made him holy is unholy, who insults the loving *Holy* Spirit. **30** We know who said this:

"Revenge belongs to Me; I will pay it back." *Deuteronomy 32:35*

Again,

"The Lord *God* will judge His people." *Deuteronomy 32:36*

31 It is a terrible thing to fall into the hands of the living God!

32 Do you remember those days when you first received *God's* light? You won a great contest of suffering. **33** Sometimes you suffered and they called you bad names. When others were treated like that, you also suffered with them.

34 You felt sorry for people they put in jail. When they took over your property, you accepted this gladly, because you knew you owned better things which last.

35 So, don't throw away your confidence! It will be greatly rewarded. **36** You need to have endurance. Then, when you have done what God wants, you will receive what God promised. *The Scripture says this*:

37 "In a very short time, God* will come.

He will not be late.

38 The person who is right with God by faith will live *forever*.

But if that person moves back, I will not be pleased with him." *Habakkuk 2:3*

39 We are not like the person who moves back and is destroyed. We are like the person who believes and is saved!

Chapter 11

Faithful God Chasers

1 Faith is the title-deed* to the things we hope for. Faith is being sure of things we cannot see. **2** The elders had this *kind of* faith long ago. It pleased God.

3 By faith, we understand that the universe was put together by God's word. What we see was made from what we cannot see.

4 By faith, Abel offered God a better sacrifice than Cain did. Abel was a good man, through faith. God was pleased with his gifts.* Abel is dead, but, through faith, he still speaks *to us*.

5 By faith, Enoch was taken up to God. He did not die:

"No one could find Enoch

because God had taken him to heaven." *Genesis 5:24*

10:25 or, Day

10:37 literally, the coming one will come

11:1 or, substance, nature

11:4 See Genesis 4:3-10.

Before Enoch was taken up, it was said that he pleased God.   **6** If someone doesn't believe *in God*, he cannot please God, because the person who comes to God **must** believe that He lives.* That person must also believe that God will give rewards to the people who are searching for Him.

7 By faith, when God warned Noah about some future things which could not be seen yet, Noah built a ship* to save his family.* He respected God. Through his faith, Noah showed that the world was wrong. He received the kind of righteousness that comes from faith.

8 By faith, when God called Abraham to go away to a place that he would later receive as an inheritance, Abraham obeyed.* He left, not knowing where he was going. **9** By faith, Abraham lived as a foreigner in the promised land. He lived in tents. Isaac and Jacob did too. They were to receive the same promise *from God*.   **10** Abraham was waiting for a city with foundations that God would design and build.   **11** By faith, Abraham was able to become a father; he was really too old. Sarah couldn't have children, but Abraham believed in God who promised *that Abraham would have descendants*.   **12** Although Abraham was almost dead, many descendants came from this one man *in his old age*—like "the number of stars in the sky and the sand on the ocean beaches."*

13 All of these people died having faith. They had not yet received the things which God had promised. They saw that those things were far in the future, but they welcomed them. They admitted that they were strangers on earth. It was not their home.   **14** When people say that sort of thing, it shows that they are looking for a home country.   **15** They had come from another country. They were not trying to remember what it was like. They could have gone back there,   **16** but they were yearning for a better country—a heavenly one. So, God prepared a city for them. He is not ashamed to be called "their God."

17 By faith, when God tested Abraham, Abraham offered Isaac as a sacrifice.* Abraham had received promises *from God that he would have many descendants*, but Abraham still offered his only son.   **18** Abraham was told this:

"Your descendants will come through Isaac."   *Genesis 21:12*

19 Abraham thought that God was able to raise Isaac from death. In a way, he *did* get Isaac back from death.*

20 By faith, Isaac talked about sure things when he blessed Jacob and Esau.*

21 By faith, when Jacob was dying, he blessed both of Joseph's sons.* Jacob "worshiped, *leaning* on the top of his walking cane."*

22 By faith, when Joseph was near death, he remembered that *God said* that the sons of Israel would leave *Egypt*. And he gave orders about burying his bones.*

11:6   or, exists
11:7   ark
11:7   literally, household (See Genesis 6:13-22.)
11:8   See Genesis 12:1-4.
11:12   See Genesis 15:5-6; 22:17.
11:17   See Genesis 22:1-12.
11:19   See Genesis 22:13.
11:20   See Genesis 27:24-40.
11:21   See Genesis 48:1-20.
11:21   See Genesis 47:31.
11:22   See Genesis 50:24-26.

23 By faith, after Moses was born, his parents hid him for three months. They were not afraid to disobey the king's order.* They saw that he was no ordinary baby.

24 By faith, when Moses had grown up, he said no to being called "Pharaoh's daughter's son." **25** God's people were being mistreated. Moses chose to be mistreated also, instead of having fun for a while doing sinful things.

26 *Suffering* shame for the Messiah* was more important to Moses than the rich treasures of Egypt. He was looking ahead to the reward.

27 By faith, Moses left Egypt behind. He was not afraid of making the king angry. Moses kept going toward the unseen One, as though he could see Him.

28 By faith, Moses ate the Passover meal. He made them put blood *over their doors.* Then the destroyer would pass over* their houses and not kill their oldest sons.

29 By faith, the people went through the Red Sea,* as if it were dry ground. When the Egyptian soldiers tried to do it, they were drowned.*

30 By faith, the walls of the city of Jericho fell down, after it had been surrounded for seven days.*

31 By faith, Rahab the prostitute gladly welcomed the spies.* She was not killed along with the people who did not obey.

32 What more can I say? Time does not allow me to tell about Gideon, Barak, Samson, Jephthah, David, Samuel, and the prophets. **33** By faith, they defeated kingdoms. They did what was right. They received promises *from God*. They shut the mouths of lions. **34** They put out a great fire. They escaped from people who were trying to kill them with swords. Their weakness became strength. They became powerful in war. They completely defeated foreign armies.

35 Some women received their *sons* back from death. Other people *were told to turn against God*, but they refused. So, they were not set free. Instead, they were tortured to death. They chose to have something better—when they rise from death. **36** Some people were beaten and laughed at. Others were tied up and thrown in jail. **37** Some people were stoned to death. Others were sawed in two. Some were murdered with swords. Others went around in sheepskins and goatskins. They really needed help. They suffered. They were mistreated. **38** They wandered in deserts, mountains, caves, and holes in the ground. The world was not worthy of having these people!

39 Through faith, all of these people have gained respect. But they did **not** receive *God's* promise! **40** They would not be made perfect without us, because God had planned something better for us.

Chapter 12

Keep Your Eyes on Jesus

1 We are surrounded by such a large number* of witnesses! We must put aside anything that might slow us down. Sin can easily tie us up. Let us run with endurance the

---

11:23   See Exodus 1:22; 2:2.
11:26   See 1 Corinthians 10:4; 2 Corinthians 1:5.
11:28   See Exodus 12:1-13.
11:29   Sea of Reeds
11:29   See Exodus 14:23-28.
11:30   See Joshua 6:15-20.
11:31   See Joshua 6:22-25.
12:1   literally, a cloud

race that is ahead of us.   2 Jesus endured when he had to suffer shame and die on a cross. Why? Because of the happiness that lay ahead for him. He didn't mind the way he had to die.

Keep your eyes on Jesus. He is the beginning and the goal of our faith. Now he sits at the right side of God's throne.   3 Think about what Jesus had to endure from sinners— they were all against him. Then you will not get tired and give up.

God Loves = God Disciplines

4 In your fight against sin, you have not fought so hard that you had to die.   5 You have forgotten these words of comfort which speak to you as sons:

"My son, when the Lord punishes you, don't take it lightly.
    Don't be discouraged when God corrects you,
6 because the Lord *God* disciplines the one He loves.

He whips every person He accepts as a son."   *Proverbs 3:11-12*
7 So, endure discipline; God is treating you like sons. Every father disciplines his son.   8 Everyone has to go through that. If you didn't, then you would not be true sons. You would be illegitimate.   9 All of us had human fathers. They disciplined us and we respected them for doing it. So, we should put ourselves under the Father of spirits even more. Then we will live.   10 For a short time, our fathers disciplined us, whenever they thought they should, but God disciplines us for our own good. He wants us to share His holiness.   11 All punishment seems terrible at the time. It is painful. But, for people who have been trained by it, it pays off with a peaceful crop of righteousness.

God Chasers: Be Holy

12 Lift up your sagging arms and make your weak knees strong!   13 Walk only on flat roads. Then your lame foot won't hurt so much. It will get well.

14 Try to be at peace with everyone. Try to be holy. If you are not holy, you will never see the Lord.   15 Be sure that no one leaves God's gracious love. Don't let anyone become like a bitter root that grows up to make trouble and pollute many people. 16 Don't let anyone become a sexual sinner or an ungodly person like Esau. Although he was the oldest son, he sold his inheritance rights for just one meal!   17 Later, you know, he wanted to receive the blessing, but he was turned away. Even though he cried, trying to find a way to change it, he could not.

18 *Unlike the people of Israel*, you have not come to a Mount *Sinai* which can be touched. It was on fire. There were storms. It was dark and gloomy.   19 You have not come to the blast of a trumpet and a Voice speaking words. The people who heard this Voice begged *Moses* that nothing more be said to them.   20 They could not stand what was ordered:

"Even if an animal touches the mountain,
    it must be stoned to death!"   *Exodus 19:12-13*
21 This was such a terrible sight that even Moses said:

"I am so afraid that I'm trembling."   *Deuteronomy 9:19*
22 No, you have come to Mount Zion; to the heavenly Jerusalem, the city of the living God. You have come to thousands upon thousands of angels happily gathered together.   23 You have come to the congregation of the firstborn. Their names have been written in heaven. You have come to God, the Judge of all people. You have come

to the spirits of good people who have been made perfect.   24 You have come to Jesus. He made a new agreement between God and man. And, you have come to blood for sprinkling. It is saying better things than Abel's blood.*

What Can Be Shaken Will Be Shaken

25 Be careful! Be sure you listen to the One who is talking to you. God warned the Jewish people, but they didn't listen. They did not escape on earth. If we turn away from God who speaks from heaven, we will be punished even more.   26 At that time, God's voice shook the earth, but now He has promised this:

"Once again, I will shake not only the earth, but also
    heaven!"   *Haggai 2:6*

27 The words, "once again," clearly show that things which can be shaken will be taken away. (This means things that were made.) Then what cannot be shaken will remain.

28 Therefore, we should be thankful, because we are receiving a kingdom which cannot be shaken. We must worship God in a way that will please Him—with reverence and fear—   29 because our God is like a fire which destroys everything.*

Chapter 13

God Is There for You

1 Continue loving your brothers.   2 Don't forget to welcome strangers into your home. By doing this, some people have had angels visit them and they didn't know it.*
3 There are people in jail. Remember them as if you were there too. There are people who are being mistreated. Remember them as though you were suffering with them.

4 Marriage should be treated with respect by everyone. The marriage bed must be kept pure. God will judge all sexual sinners and all people who commit adultery.

5 Don't love money. Be satisfied with what you have.

God Himself has said this:
    "I will never leave you.
        I will never abandon you."   *Deuteronomy 31:6*

6 So, we can cheerfully say this:
    "The Lord *God* is my Helper.
        I will not be afraid.
    What can man do to me?"   *Psalm 118:6*

7 Don't forget your leaders. They told you God's message. Look at the way their lives have turned out! Live lives of faith like them.   8 Jesus Christ is the same yesterday, today, and forever.   9 Don't get carried away with different kinds of strange teachings. Our hearts are made strong by God's gracious love, not by food. Special foods haven't helped the people who make rules about them.

10 The men who serve at the holy tent have no right to eat at our altar.

11 The high priest carries animal blood into the most holy place for sins, but the bodies of the animals are burned outside the city walls.   12 Jesus also suffered and died outside the city, so that he could make the people holy with his blood.   13 Let us

---

12:24   mercy not vengeance. Abel's blood was the blood of a righteous man. Jesus' blood was the blood of
            a perfect man.
12:29   literally, a consuming fire
13:2   See Genesis 18:1-8; 19:1-3.

go to him out there—outside the city walls! Let us carry his shame!   **14** We don't have a city here on earth which will last forever, but we **are** looking for that type of city in the future!

15 Therefore, let us always offer, through Jesus, the sacrifice of praise to God—the fruit of our lips, telling the truth about His name.   **16** Don't forget to share and to do good. God is pleased with sacrifices like these.

17 Allow yourselves to be persuaded by your leaders, and yield. They keep watch over your souls; they must give an answer *to God.* Yield, so that they will have a happy job, not a burden. Being a burden doesn't help you, either.

18 Pray for us. We are sure we have a good conscience, because we want to live right toward everyone.   **19** I especially beg you to do this, so that I may soon be with you again.

God Chasing Is God Pleasing

20 God brought our Lord Jesus back from death. Jesus is the great Shepherd of the sheep. Using Jesus' blood of the eternal agreement, the God of peace   **21** will give you whatever good things you need, so that you can do what He wants. Through Jesus Christ, God will do what pleases Him in us. *Give* God the glory forever and ever. Amen.

Sincerely, Paul

22 Brothers, I beg you, put up with my message of comfort, because my letter to you is not long.

23 I want you to know that Timothy, our brother, has been released *from jail.* If he comes here soon, we will come together to visit you.

24 We send greetings to all of your leaders and to all of the holy people. The *believers* from Italy greet you.   **25** Gracious love be with all of you.

JAMES

Chapter 1

James says, "Hi."

1 From James, a servant of God and of the Lord Jesus Christ:
Greetings to the twelve tribes *of Israel* which are scattered everywhere in the world.

This Is a Test

2 My brothers *and sisters*, you should be very happy when you experience many kinds of troubles, **3** because you know that the testing of your faith will develop more endurance. **4** Endure, so that your actions will be truly complete. Then you will be mature. You will have everything; you will need nothing. **5** But if any one of you does need wisdom, just ask God. It will be given to you. God is the One who gives freely to all people, and He does this without complaining. **6** So, when you ask God, ask with confidence, without doubting, because the person who doubts God is as unstable as a wave of the sea during a storm. **7** A person who wavers like this must not think that his prayer will be honored by the Lord. **8** His heart is divided into two parts, and no one can depend on anything he does.

Riches Are Only Temporary

9 Let the brother who is poor feel good that *God* lifted him up **10** and the rich brother should feel good that *God* lowered him. For *man* is like the flower of the field—here for only a short while. **11** The sun rises and gets hotter and hotter. As it burns the grass, its flowers dry up. The sun's heat destroys their beauty. They die. It is the same with a rich man. Even when business is good, he may die and be worth nothing.

Enduring Tests

12 Therefore, happy is the man who, though tested, endures. When he endures tests, God will give him the reward* of *eternal* life which God has promised to those who love Him. **13** When someone is being tested, he shouldn't think that God is tempting him to do wrong. Evil cannot tempt God and God does not tempt anyone with evil. **14** When someone desires things *which he knows are wrong*, he is tempting himself. His selfish desire pulls him away *from God* and holds him. **15** After that desire has been conceived, it produces sin. Then the sin grows and results in death. **16** Make no mistake about it, my dear brothers, this is true!

Gifts for God Chasers

17 Every good and perfect gift comes down to us from God, the Source of truth. The Father of lights is always consistent and changeless.* **18** God decided to give us life again through the message of His truth, so that we may be the first-fruits of His creation.

Got the Word

19 So, my dear brothers, you should know this: Every person should be more willing to listen than to speak. Be slow to get angry. **20** A man's anger doesn't show

---

1:12   literally, crown
1:17   literally, . . . Father of lights, with whom there is no variation or shadow of turning.

God's goodness. **21** Remove every evil and overpowering evil influence from your life. And, humbly accept *God's* message which has been planted in you. It is able to save your souls.

Just Do It

22 Do what *God's* message says; don't just listen *and do nothing*. When you merely sit and listen to the message, you are only fooling yourselves. **23** Suppose a person hears the message *of God* and does nothing. This is like a man who gazes at his face in the mirror. **24** He "sees" himself *for a moment*, but he walks away, soon forgetting what he looked like. **25** But the person who looks closely into the law (the perfect law of freedom) and holds on to it is not *like* the one who hears it and forgets about it. He is the one who really practices the law. He finds happiness in doing it.

26 If any of you thinks he serves God, but does not control what he says, then he fools his own heart. His "service" to God is worth nothing. **27** What God the Father accepts as pure unpolluted service are *things like* this:

Take care of children who have no parents.

Help widows in trouble.

Keep yourself *pure* from the filth* of the world.

Chapter 2

Respect for Other People

1 My brothers, you are believers in our glorious Lord Jesus Christ. So, don't treat people differently: **2** Suppose someone comes into your congregation and that person is dressed in fancy clothes and is wearing rings of gold. Then suppose a beggar also comes in, wearing ragged old clothes. **3** Do you give special attention to the one who is wearing the fancy clothes? Do you seat him in the best place? Then do you say to the beggar, "Stand over there!" or "Sit here near my feet!"? **4** Are you not contradicting yourselves? You have become critics with evil motives!

5 Listen to me, my dear brothers! Was it not the poor people in the world whom God chose to make rich in faith and to receive the kingdom which He promised to all who love Him? **6** But **you** have dishonored the beggar! Do not the rich people oppress you and drag you into court? **7** Aren't they the ones who say awful things about the precious name that you wear?

8 The royal command is found in Scripture:

" You must love other people the same way you love
yourself."   *Leviticus 19:18*

If you obey *this command*, you are doing fine, **9** but if you treat anyone differently, your deeds are sinful! So, according to the law, you will be judged as wrongdoers.
10 The person who "obeys" the whole law and yet breaks only one of its commands is as guilty as if he broke all of the commands! **11** The One who said,

"You must not commit adultery."   *Exodus 20:14*
also said,
"You must not commit murder."   *Exodus 20:13*

1:27   or, sin

If you have not committed adultery, but you have murdered someone, then the law says that you are a wrongdoer.   **12** So now, you should speak and act as people who know that they will be judged by a law of freedom.   **13** At the Judgment, *God* will show no mercy to the person who did not show mercy to others. Mercy triumphs over judgment.

So, You Believe In God?

14 My brothers, if a person claims he has faith, but he will not serve *God*, what good is *that kind of faith*? Can a "faith" like that save him?   **15** Suppose a brother or sister needs clothing or daily food.   **16** And you say, "Go in peace. I hope you will find enough clothes to keep you warm and will have plenty to eat!" Unless you give them what they need, what good have you done?   **17** So, even faith is dead,* when it is alone and will not act.   **18** But someone might say this: "You have faith, but I'm a man of action!" How can you show me your faith without your actions? From my actions, you can **see** my faith!   **19** You say that you believe there is one God? That's fine! The demons also believe this and shake with fear.   **20** You empty person, must you be shown that faith without actions is worth nothing?   **21** Abraham is our father. Isaac was Abraham's son. Abraham offered Isaac to God on the altar. Yet, it was by the things which Abraham did that he was made right with God.*   **22** Don't you see how Abraham's faith and his actions worked together? His faith was made perfect because of the things he did.

23 The Scripture was fulfilled which says:
"Abraham believed God, and so God declared him
a righteous man."   *Genesis 15:6*
Abraham was even called "God's beloved."*   **24** Don't you see that a person is righteous *before God* because of his actions? He cannot be made right by "faith" alone.

25 And, in the same way, wasn't Rahab, the prostitute, also made right *with God* because of what she did? She welcomed the messengers *of Joshua* and helped them get away.*

26 So, just as the human body is dead without the spirit, the type of "faith" which does not act is dead, too!

Chapter 3

Taming the Tongue

1 My brothers, not many of you should become teachers, because you know that those of us who teach will be judged very carefully.   **2** We all make many mistakes. Who is so perfect that he hasn't made a mistake—said something he shouldn't have? Which one of you is able to control his whole body?   **3** We put bits into the mouths of horses, so that we can make them obey us. When we control their mouths, we can control their whole body.   **4** It is the same with ships. Although a ship is very large and is moved by strong winds, yet only a tiny rudder guides the ship's course, and the

---

2:17   or, without life, useless
2:21   See Genesis 22:1-18.
2:23   or, friend. Compare Genesis 18:17 with John 15:15. Also see Second Chronicles 20:7 and Isaiah
            41:8.
2:25   See Joshua 2:1-21.

captain's wish controls the rudder. **5** It is the same with our tongue. Though it may be small, it brags about great things.

A big forest fire can be started by only a little flame. **6** The tongue is *like* fire! Even though it is small, it can be a world of evil among other members of the body; it pollutes the entire body. It can set the whole world on fire; hell starts the fire. **7** Mankind tames and has tamed every kind of animal in nature—beasts, birds, reptiles, and fish. **8** However, man has not tamed the tongue; it is wild and evil, full of poison which can kill. **9** How can we, with our tongues, praise the Lord *God, our* Father, and yet curse human beings who were made in the image of God? **10** How can it be that praises and curses come from the same mouth? No, my brothers, it shouldn't be like this! **11** Does good water and bitter water flow from the same fountain? **12** My brothers, can a fig tree produce olives? Can a grapevine yield figs? In the same way, it is impossible to have salt water and fresh water coming from the same spring!

True Wisdom Comes From God

13 Is there a person among you who is truly wise? Is he also intelligent? Then he should show his wisdom by living right. He should do good things wisely and humbly. **14** But if you are selfish and full of bitterness in your hearts, don't brag about it and don't make the truth look like a lie. **15** That kind of "wisdom" does not come down from God; it is the wisdom of the world, the wisdom which is not spiritual, the wisdom of demons. **16** And if there is jealousy and selfishness, then confusion and every other kind of evil will be present, too. **17** However, the wisdom which comes from God is first pure, then peaceful, gentle, willing to obey, full of mercy and good deeds, without doubts or hypocrisy.* **18** And the fruit of righteousness grows peacefully within the people who make peace.

Chapter 4

Inner Wars

1 Do you know why there are wars and struggles among yourselves? They come from within, from your own selfish desires which make war inside your bodies. **2** You desire something, but you don't get it. So you are jealous and commit murder. And you still don't get it! You argue and you fight for it. *Why don't you have what you want*? It is because you don't ask for it *from God.* **3** And even if you do ask, you don't receive, because you ask, so that you may use it in an evil way for your own selfish desires. **4** You *spiritual* adulterers! Don't you know that loving this world is hating God? The person who wants to be in love with the world becomes God's enemy. **5** The Scripture says that there is a spirit living in you that makes you want to do wrong.* Do you think the Scripture says this for nothing? **6** God will give you strength to overcome. That is why the Scripture says,

"God is against those who are proud,
but He gives help to humble people."

Proverbs 3:34

Resist and Submit

7 So, put yourselves under God's authority. Resist the Devil and he will run away from you. **8** Get close to God, and God will get close to you. Wash your hands *of sin*, you

---

3:17   being two-faced; acting as if you are good, when you are not
4:5   See Exodus 20:5.

sinners. Make your hearts pure, you who have divided hearts. **9** Be sad, be sorry, and cry. Change your laughter into crying. Turn your joy into sadness. **10** Be humble before the Lord and He will lift you up.

Here Comes the Judge

11 Brothers, don't say evil things against each other. A person who speaks against his brother or judges him is also criticizing *the* law and judging *the* law. Now if you judge *the* law, you are not a follower of *the* law. Instead, you are a judge. **12** There is one Law-giver and Judge. *Only* He is able to save or to destroy. Who are you to pass judgment on your fellow man?

To Do or Not to Do (THAT Is the Question)

13 Come on now, you who say: "Today or tomorrow we will go to such-and-such a city. We will stay there a year, do business, and make money." **14** You don't know what will happen tomorrow! Your life is like a fog. It appears for a short time and then it disappears. **15** You should have said, "If God wants, we will live and do this or that." **16** But now, you are boasting in your pride. All such bragging is evil! **17** A person sins when he knows he should do something good, but doesn't do it.

Chapter 5

Poor Rich People

1 Come on now, you rich people. Cry out and be very sad, because much trouble will come upon you. **2** At that time, your valuables will become worthless! The moths will eat up your clothes. **3** Your gold and your silver will rust. That rust will become a witness against you and it will eat at your flesh like fire, because you have kept treasures to yourself in the last days. **4** Men harvested your fields, but you cheated them out of the pay that they deserved, and their pay is screaming against you for justice. God Almighty* hears this. **5** You have lived a life of luxury on earth; you've enjoyed yourselves. Your hearts have grown fat *like an animal* ready for the killing. **6** You have condemned and murdered an innocent man, and he did not resist you.

Patiently Have Patience

7 So, brothers, be patient; the Lord will come. The farmer is patient. He waits for his precious crop to grow up from the earth. He does not harvest until the first rain and the last rain have passed.* **8** In the same way, you also must be patient. Make your hearts strong; the Lord is coming again soon.

9 Brothers, don't complain against one another, or God will judge you. The Judge is standing just outside the door. **10** Brothers, take, for example, the trouble the prophets had and their patience when they spoke with the authority of the Lord *God*. **11** As you can see, we admire those who have patience.* Remember how patient Job was? And do you remember how the Lord was tender* and merciful to him?

5:4   literally, the Lord of the *angelic* armies *of heaven*
5:7   The farmer must wait patiently for both rains (Deuteronomy 11:13,14; Joel 2:23,24).
5:11   or, endurance. Compare James 1:3,4.
5:11   or, affectionate, sympathetic, compassionate

12 More than anything else, my brothers, don't swear by God—not by heaven nor by earth nor by anything! Your yes should be "yes," and your no should be "no." Otherwise, you will fall into condemnation.

Prayer Power Like Elijah

13 If one of you is in trouble, he should pray. If one of you is happy, he should sing. **14** If one of you is sick, he should call for the elders of the congregation. They will pray for him and put oil on him* in the name of the Lord. **15** Prayer *to God* made in faith will make the sick person well. The Lord will raise him up. If this person has sinned, then God will forgive him. **16** Admit your sins to one another. Pray for each other. God will make you well. When a person is right with God, the power of his sincere prayer is tremendous! **17** Elijah was a human being with feelings just like ours. He prayed that it would not rain, and for 3 $\frac{1}{2}$ years it did not rain. **18** Again, Elijah prayed that it would rain. Then it rained, and things grew on the earth again.

Rescue Wanderers

19 My brothers, if one of you wanders away from the truth, someone else should help bring him back to the truth. **20** Remember this: The person who brings that sinner back from the wrong way will save his soul from death. Many sins will be covered.

5:14   The oil seem to have been used for medical purposes (Isaiah 1:6; Luke 10:34).

1 PETER

Chapter 1

Greetings From Peter

1 From Peter, an apostle of Jesus Christ.

To *God's* chosen, homeless people scattered throughout the areas of Pontus, Galatia, Cappadocia, Asia, and Bithynia. **2** God the Father knew about you long ago. The Spirit has made you holy, to obey Jesus Christ and to be sprinkled* with his blood.

May you have complete peace and gracious love.

For Heaven's Sake, Go for the Gold

3 Praise the God and Father of our Lord Jesus Christ! Because of God's great mercy, He raised Jesus Christ from death, to give us new life. This leads to hope that lives on. **4** It also leads to an inheritance which is kept in heaven for you. That inheritance will never decay, spoil, or fade away. **5** Through your faith, God's power protects you for salvation, which is ready to be revealed at the end of time.

6 You should be glad about this, even though many kinds of struggles may have made you sad for a little while. **7** The purpose of these struggles is to test your faith. Your faith is more precious than gold. Gold will be destroyed, but after your faith is tested through fire, it will last. When Jesus Christ is revealed, your faith will be praise, glory, and honor *for him*. **8** Though you never saw Jesus, you love him. You don't see him now either, but you believe and you're glad. You don't know how to express just how happy you are—it is glorious! **9** You are receiving the salvation of your souls, the goal of believing.

10 What about this salvation? The prophets spoke about this gracious love which was *meant* for you. They searched very carefully **11** for the time and the way that things would happen. The Spirit of Christ was in them, showing them. Long ago, they told the truth about the sufferings of Christ and the glories that came later. **12** It was revealed to them that they were serving **you**, not themselves! Now, men who preach the Good News have told you these things by the Holy Spirit who was sent from heaven. Even angels want to bend down to look into these things.

Be Holy; Be Intensely Holy

13 So, get your minds ready.* Be alert. Put your hope completely upon the gracious love that you will receive when Jesus Christ appears. **14** Like children who always obey, don't be controlled by the evil desires you used to have when you didn't know any better. **15** Instead, in all your life be holy, as God is holy. He called you. **16** This is written:

"You must be holy because **I** am holy!" *Leviticus 11:44*

17 You call upon the Father. He is fair to each person. God will judge you by the way you lived. You should live your lives with respect *for God*. You are only here for a short time. **18** You know the worthless kind of life you got from your ancestors. You were not purchased from this with something that doesn't last, like silver or gold. **19** No, it was with the precious blood of Christ, like that of a perfect lamb; nothing is

---

1:2   cleansed
1:13   literally, gird up the loins of your mind

wrong with it. **20** Before the world was made, God chose Christ; but now, in the last times, Christ has appeared for **you**. **21** Through Christ, you believe in God. God raised Christ from death and gave him glory. Now your faith and hope can be toward God.

22 When you obeyed the truth, you made your souls pure. This led you to loving your brothers *and sisters*. That love must be sincere. Love one another intensely from your hearts. **23** You have been born again. The seed that caused this will never die. It is God's message that lives and lasts. **24** *This is written*:
"All human flesh is like grass.
Its glory is like a grass flower.
The grass burns up and the flower falls off,
25 But the Lord's message remains forever."
This is the message which was preached to you.

Isaiah 40:6-8

Chapter 2

God Chasers Are Living Stones

1 Therefore, put away all evil, every trick, hypocrisy, jealousy, and any kind of evil talk. **2** Be like little babies who have just been born: Yearn for pure, spiritual milk, so that you may use it to grow up for salvation. **3** *The Scripture says*,
"You have tasted that the Lord is kind."

Psalm 34:8

4 You are coming to the living Stone.* Human beings did not think this Stone was important, but God chose him; he is precious. **5** **You** also are like living stones. God is using you to build a spiritual house, so that you will be a holy group of priests, offering spiritual sacrifices which God will gladly accept through Jesus Christ. **6** A section in the Scriptures says this:

"Listen! I am putting a stone in Jerusalem.*
He is a chosen, precious cornerstone.*
The person who believes in him
will never be made ashamed."

Isaiah 28:16

7 To you believers this Stone is precious, but to unbelievers, it is "the Stone that you builders did not think was important. This Stone has become the Cornerstone."*

Another *Scripture says*:

8 "It is a stone that will make people stumble
and a rock that will make them fall."

Isaiah 8:14

They stumble, because they have not been persuaded by the message. (This was supposed to happen.)

9 But **you** are a chosen race, a royal group of priests, a holy nation, and a special people. You must tell about the wonderful things that God has done. He called you from darkness* into His amazing light.

2:4 Jesus
2:6 literally, Zion
2:6 the most important stone in the building
2:7 Psalm 118:22
2:9 sin

10 *The Scripture says*:
"Those who were once not a people
     are now God's people.
Those who had not received mercy
     now have received mercy."

Hosea 2:23

Do Good

11 Dear *friends*, I beg you, you are only visitors here *on earth* for a short time. Put away human evil desires. These things make war with the soul.   **12** You should live good lives among the people of the world. They might say evil things against you, as if you were doing wrong. But when they see your good deeds, they will give glory to God on the Day when He returns to take care of us.

13 Because of the Lord, put yourselves under every human authority that has been set up. This means the Emperor* (who has the most authority) or governors.   **14** They are sent by the Emperor to punish people who do wrong and to praise people who do right.   **15** In this way, by doing good, you will silence foolish, ignorant men. This is what God wants.   **16** You should be like free men, but don't use your freedom as a cover-up for evil. Instead, be like servants of God.   **17** Give honor to everyone. Love the brotherhood. Respect God. And, honor the Emperor.

Suffer As Christ Did

18 Family servants must put themselves under their masters' authority, showing all respect. Do this for the good and kind masters, as well as the dishonest ones!   **19** If you suffer pain unfairly, but you take it because your conscience is *controlled* by God, then that will be to your credit.   **20** Suppose some servants do wrong and they endure a beating. Should they get credit? No! But, if you servants do right, yet you endure suffering, then God will bless you for this.   **21** This is why you were called: Christ suffered for you! Christ left you an example. He wants you to follow in his steps.   **22** *The Scripture says*:
"Nothing false was ever found in his mouth."

Isaiah 53:9

23 When they insulted Christ, he did not insult them back. While he was suffering, he wasn't trying to get even. Jesus gave himself over to God who judges fairly.   **24** In his body he carried our sins on the wooden cross. He wants us to quit sinning* and live right. His wounds were used to heal us.   **25** You were like wandering sheep, but now, you have come back to the Shepherd,* the one who watches over your souls.

Chapter 3

Attention: All Ladies

1 In the same way, you wives must put yourselves under your own husbands' authority. Some of them may not obey the message, but through the *good* lives of you wives, these husbands will be won over without having to say a word.   **2** They will see the kind of pure life you live, which shows respect *for God*.   **3** Your beauty must not be the outer beauty of fancy hairdos, wearing gold jewelry, or expensive clothes.   **4** Instead, it should be the hidden personality of the heart with a gentle and quiet spirit that lasts and lasts. This

---

2:13   Caesar
2:24   put away sin
2:25   Jesus

is very valuable before God.   **5** In the past, holy women put their hope in God. They put themselves under their own husbands' authority. This is the way they made themselves beautiful.   **6** *Be* like Sarah. She obeyed Abraham; she called him "Mr." If you do good things, you can become her "daughters." Don't be afraid of anything.

7 In the same way, you husbands, as you live with your wives, you must understand that they are not as strong as you are. Treat them with honor. They will also receive the gift of life. You must not allow your prayers to be blocked.

Bless and Be Blessed

8 Finally, all of you must be together in your thinking. Try to feel the same thing that others feel. Love your brothers. Take pity on people who need your help. Be people who are humble.   **9** Don't pay back any wrong with another wrong. Don't insult someone when they insult you. Instead, bless them! This is why you were called. God wants you to receive a blessing.

10 The *Scripture says*:
"The person who wants to love life
  and see good days
 must keep his tongue from speaking an evil thing
  and his lips from saying something false.
11 He must turn away from evil and do right.
  He must look for peace and follow it.
12 The Lord *God* is watching good people
  and He is listening to their prayers.
 The Lord is against those who do wrong."   *Psalm 34:12-16*
13 If you truly desire to do right, who will hurt you?   **14** But even if you do suffer because you are doing right, you should be happy. Don't be upset. Don't be afraid like they are afraid.   **15** Make a special holy place in your hearts for Christ, the Lord. Always be ready to give an answer of defense to anyone who asks you why you have hope inside you.   **16** But, do this with gentleness and respect, having a clear conscience. Then those who say evil things about your good life in Christ will be ashamed of the things they said.   **17** If God wants you to suffer, then suffering for doing right is better than suffering for doing wrong.   **18** Christ died for your sins once for all time. He was a good man dying for bad men. Why? To bring you to God. Although his body was put to death, his spirit was alive.   **19** In the spirit, Christ went and preached to spirits in prison.   **20** They did not obey in the past, when God waited patiently during Noah's time. This was when the ship* was being built. A few people (eight people) were saved in it through water.   **21** Today, this is a picture of how immersion saves us through the raising of Jesus Christ from death. Immersion is not getting rid of body dirt. No, it is an appeal to God for a clear conscience.   **22** Christ has gone to heaven. He is at God's right side. Angels, authorities, and powers have been put under his authority.

Chapter 4

Lifestyle of the God Chaser

1 Since Christ suffered in his human body, you should take this same attitude as your weapon, because the person who suffers in the human body has nothing to do with sin.

3:20   ark

2 From now on, though you will live the rest of your lives in the human body, you will not be doing the evil desires of people anymore. Instead, you will be doing what God wants. **3** You've already spent enough time doing what people of the world like to do: living in sexual excess, having evil desires, getting drunk, wild sex parties, drinking contests, and forbidden worship of false gods. **4** They think you are strange if you don't run with them after the same wild way of living. Then they say terrible things about you. **5** But they must give an answer to God who is ready to judge people who are alive and people who have died. **6** This is why the gospel was preached to those who are now dead. They could be judged in the body with *all* persons, but they would live with God in the spirit.

Do Everything for Him

7 The end of all things is near. Keep a clear head and be alert, so that you will be able to pray. **8** The most important thing is loving one another with all your heart, because love covers many, many sins. **9** Invite one another into your homes without complaining about it. **10** Each person should use the *spiritual* gift he has received to help other people, like a good manager of the many kinds of God's gracious love. **11** If someone speaks, he should use God's sayings. If someone serves, he should do it with the strength that God supplies. Then, in everything, God will be given the glory through Jesus Christ. *Give* God the glory and power forever and ever. Amen.

Here Comes the Judge

12 Dear *friends*, don't be surprised because of the fierce struggle you're in, as if something strange were happening to you. **13** Instead, be glad that you are sharing in the sufferings of Christ. Then, when his glory is revealed, you will be very, very happy. **14** If someone insults you because of Christ's name, you should be happy, because the Spirit of glory and the Spirit of God is resting upon you. **15** If one of you suffers, it shouldn't be because you are a murderer, a robber, a criminal, or a meddler. **16** But if you must suffer as a Christian, you shouldn't be ashamed. Use this name to give glory to God.

17 The time for judging starts with God's family. Since we are to be *judged* first, what will happen to people who don't obey the gospel of God? **18** *The Scripture says*:

"If a good man will barely be saved,
then where will the ungodly sinner be?" *Proverbs 11:31*

19 So, the people who are suffering by God's will must commit their souls to a faithful Creator by doing good things.

Chapter 5

Oversee God's People

1 I saw Christ suffer many things. And I will share in the future glory which will be revealed. I am also an old man. So, I beg the older men among you **2** to shepherd* God's flock among you. Watch over them as God wants you to, not because you have to. Don't be in it for the money, but be eager. **3** Don't act like lords over the people.*

5:2   or, take care of God's people, as a shepherd takes care of his sheep
5:3   literally, portion

Instead, be examples for the flock. **4** When the Chief Shepherd* appears, you will receive the glorious crown* which will never fade away.

5 In the same way, younger men, put yourselves under *the influence of* older men. Everyone should be humble with one another. Wear humility like a covering, because *the Scripture says*:

> "God is against those who are proud,
>> but He gives help to humble people."   *Proverbs 3:34*

6 So, make yourselves humble under God's powerful hand. Then, at the right time, He will lift you up. **7** Throw all your worries onto God, because He cares for you.

8 Be alert! Watch! The Devil is your enemy. He is like a lion. He walks around, roaring and looking for someone to eat. **9** Those of you who are strong in faith must resist him. You know that the brotherhood in other parts of the world is experiencing the same suffering as you are.

10 God called you into His eternal glory in Christ. After you have suffered a little while, the God of all gracious love will make you complete, strong, firm, and solid. **11** Power belongs to Him forever. Amen.

Final Greetings

12 I wrote you these few things through Silas,* a faithful brother whom I respect very much. I wanted to comfort you and tell you that God's gracious love is real. Stand in it!

13 The congregation* in Babylon sends you greetings. *God* chose them also. Mark, my son, greets you, too.

14 Greet one another with a loving kiss.

Peace to all of you who are in Christ.

5:4   Jesus
5:4   prize
5:12   literally, Silvanus. Silvanus copied down what Peter said to write.
5:13   literally, the elect

2 PETER

Chapter 1

More Greetings From Peter

1 From Simon* Peter, a servant and an apostle of Jesus Christ.
To the people who have received a faith which is like our precious faith. *It came* through the righteousness of our God and of our Savior, Jesus Christ.
2 Gracious love to you and may peace greatly increase by a full knowledge of God and Jesus, our Lord.

Live Like God

3 God's divine power has given us everything we need for living a godly life. We know God. He called us to His own glory and goodness, **4** which He used to give us great and precious promises. Through these things God wants us to share in His divine nature. And, we must escape from the pollution which is in the world in evil desire.
5 This is why you must do your very best to add:

goodness to your faith,
  knowledge to your goodness,
  6 self-control to your knowledge,
    endurance to your self-control,
      godliness to your endurance,
        7 brotherly love to godliness,
          unselfish concern to brotherly love.

8 If you have these qualities and they are improving,* then they will make you active and productive in knowing Jesus Christ, our Lord. **9** But, if these things are not part of someone, then that person cannot see very far; he is blind. He has forgotten that he was made clean from his old sins.
10 So, brothers *and sisters*, do your best to make *God's* calling and choice of you a sure thing. If you are doing these things, you will never fall away. **11** In this way, you will get a warm welcome into the eternal kingdom of our Lord and Savior, Jesus Christ.
12 So, in the future, I will always help you remember these things even though you know them and you are firm in the truth at this time. **13** While I am still in this body,* I think it is right for me to refresh your memory. **14** I know I will soon put my body* aside. (Jesus Christ, our Lord, has made this clear to me.) **15** I want to do my best to be sure that, after I die, you will always be able to remember these things.

We Told the Truth

16 When we told you about the power and coming of Jesus Christ, our Lord, we were not following clever myths. No, we **saw** his greatness! **17** When the Voice came to Christ from majestic glory, he received honor and glory from God the Father:

1:1	literally, Simeon
1:8	or, growing
1:13	literally, tent
1:14	literally, tent

"This is My Son, and I love him.
I am very pleased with him."   *Matthew 17:5*

18 We heard this Voice come from heaven! We were with Jesus on the holy mountain.

19 We *apostles* have the prophetic message which is made sure. You would do well to pay attention to it. It is like a lamp shining in a dark place until dawn, and the Morning Star* rises in your hearts.   **20** This is the most important thing you should know: No prophecy of Scripture ever came about by a prophet's own ideas,   **21** because prophecy never came from what man wanted. No, those men spoke from God while they were being influenced by the Holy Spirit.

Chapter 2

It Won't Be Long Now

1 There will be false teachers among you just as there were false prophets among the people *of Israel*. They will secretly bring in destructive opinions, even rejecting the Master who purchased them. But they will bring sudden destruction upon themselves!   **2** Many people will follow them into sexual excess. Because of these men, people will say evil things about the way of truth.   **3** Because of greed, they will use invented teachings to make money off you. Long ago condemnation was waiting for them. They will be destroyed; it won't be long now!

4 God punished angels who sinned. He sent them to hell.* They were put in chains in the dark. They will be guarded there until the time for judgment.   **5** God also punished the old world. God struck the world of ungodly people with a flood, but He protected eight people in Noah's family. Noah proclaimed what was right.

6 God condemned the cities of Sodom and Gomorrah; He burned them up. This was an example of what will happen to ungodly people.   **7** But God rescued Lot, a good man. Lot was very upset about the wild sex life of the people *in Sodom*.   **8** Lot was living among them day and night. When he saw and heard their lawless deeds, he felt tortured in his righteous soul.   **9** The Lord *God* knows how to rescue a godly person from temptation. The Lord also knows how to reserve evil people for the Judgment Day and still punish them now.   **10** This is especially true for the people who follow the filthy desires of their human nature. They look down on *God's* authority.

These false teachers are daring and boastful. They are not afraid of saying evil things against glorious beings.   **11** Angels are far stronger and more powerful than these false teachers, but even the angels do not say evil things against them before the Lord.   **12** These men are speaking evil of things they know nothing about. They are like dumb animals, *guided* only by instinct. They were born to be caught and killed. Like animals, they will die.   **13** They will be paid a reward of hurt for the people they hurt. They think that pleasure is carousing in the daytime. When they eat love feasts with you, they are like ugly spots and sores; they stuff themselves.   **14** They can't look at women without wanting to go to bed with them. They never stop sinning. They lead weak people away and then trap them. Their hearts are trained in greed. They are children of hell.*   **15** They have left behind the right way* and wandered off, following the way

---

1:19   Jesus
2:4   Tartarus
2:14   literally, cursed children
2:15   literally, straight way

of Balaam (the son of Beor).* Balaam loved the money he received for doing wrong, **16** but Balaam was proven wrong for not obeying God. Donkeys don't talk, but a donkey spoke with a man's voice to Balaam! The donkey stopped the foolish thing that the prophet *Balaam was planning to do.*

17 These false teachers are like wells which have no water. They are like fog blown by a storm. The blackest part of darkness has been reserved for them, **18** because they say stupid, boastful things. They use evil sexual desires of human nature to lead people into a trap. Those people almost got away from those who are living in error. **19** These false teachers promise those people "freedom," but **they** are slaves of pollution. (A person is a slave to whatever has defeated him.) **20** They got away from the pollution of the world through knowing our Lord and Savior, Jesus Christ. But they got involved again and were defeated. Since they did this, they ended up worse than they were before they started. **21** It would have been better if they had never known the right way. But they knew it and then turned away from the holy command which was passed down to them. **22** The truth of these old sayings has happened to them:

"The dog went back to his own vomit." *Proverbs 26:11*
and
"The pig that was washed *clean* went back to roll in the mud."

Chapter 3

Refresh Your Memory

1 Dear *friends*, this is the second letter I have written to you. I used both letters to refresh your memory to do pure thinking. **2** I want you to remember the words that the holy prophets spoke long ago and the command that our Lord and Savior gave through your apostles.

3 This is the first thing you should know: In the last days, some people will make fun, laughing as they do it. They will follow their own desires. **4** They will ask, "When is Jesus coming back as he promised? Where is he? Since our ancestors died, from the beginning of time,* everything continues in the same way!" **5** But they forgot (on purpose) that the heavens existed long ago and God's word used water to make the land come from water. **6** It was with water (a flood) that the old world was destroyed. **7** Today's heavens and earth have been reserved for fire by the same word *of God*, kept for the Judgment Day to destroy ungodly people.

8 Dear *friends*, don't forget this one thing: One of the Lord's days is like 1,000 years. To Him 1,000 years is like one day. **9** The Lord is not slow to keep His promise (as some people think of "slow"). No, He is patient with you. He wants everyone to find room for a change in their hearts. He doesn't want anyone to be lost.

10 The Day of the Lord will come *suddenly*, like a robber. The heavens will pass away with a whizzing noise. The elements will be destroyed with heat. The earth and every force in it will be gone.*

11 In this way, everything will be destroyed. So, what kind of people should you be? You must live holy and godly lives **12** while you are expecting the Day of God to

---

2:15   Some manuscripts have "Bosor"; See Numbers 22–24; Deuteronomy 23:3-4.
3:4   literally, beginning of creation
3:10   There is great uncertainty about the precise meaning here. A wide variety of different readings arose in early copies: "will be found (dissolved)"; "will disappear"; "will be burned up"; and it was even omitted altogether in some manuscripts.

come. You should want it to come sooner. On that Day, the heavens will be destroyed by fire. Because of the heat, the elements will melt.   **13** We are expecting new heavens and a new earth, as *God* promised. Righteousness will live there.

14 So, dear *friends*, while you are waiting for these things *to happen*, do your best to be *spiritually* clean* and at peace with God.   **15** Think about this: The delay* of the Lord's *coming* means *more time* for people to be saved. It is like what our dear brother Paul wrote you with the wisdom that God gave him.   **16** In all of his letters, he writes the same way about all these things. There are some things in those letters which are hard to understand. Some weak and uneducated people twist those things just as they do the other Scriptures. When they do this, they destroy themselves.

17 So, dear *friends*, since you already know these things, guard them. Then you won't fall away from your safe position. You could be carried away by the error of lawless people.

18 Grow in the gracious love and knowledge of our Lord and Savior, Jesus Christ. *Give* him glory now and forever. Amen.

3:14   spotless and without blemish (See Exodus 12:5.)
3:15   literally, longsuffering, patience

1 JOHN

Chapter 1

John says, "Hi."

1 About the Message of life:* What has existed since the beginning
    we heard,
    we saw with our own eyes,
    we watched,
    we touched with our hands.
2 That life was shown *to us*. We saw it. We can prove it. We are telling you about that eternal life that was with the Father. This life was shown to us.   **3** Now to you also we are telling the things we have seen and heard, because we want you to share with us. What we share is with God the Father and with His Son, Jesus Christ.   **4** We are writing you these things, so that you may be full of joy with us.

Light

5 This is the message that we have heard from him and which we are now telling you: God is light;* there is no darkness* in God at all.   **6** Therefore, if we say we are friends with God, yet we continue living in darkness, then we are liars. We are not following the truth.   **7** God is in the light.* We should also live in light. If we live in the light, then we have a relationship of sharing with each other, and the blood of Jesus, God's Son, continues to cleanse us from all sin.
8 If we say, "We have no sin!" then we are only fooling ourselves. The truth is not in us.   **9** However, if we admit our sins, then God will forgive us. We can trust God; He does what is right. He will cleanse us from every evil thing.   **10** If we say, "We have not sinned!" then we are calling God a liar. God's *true* teaching is not in us.

Chapter 2

You Oughta Obey

1 My little* children, I write these things so that you will not sin. But when any person does sin, we have Jesus Christ—the righteous one—to help defend us before God, the Father.   **2** Jesus is the way our sins are taken away—the way all people may have their sins taken away.
3 If we obey what God has commanded us to do, then we are sure that we really do know God.   **4** Someone may say, "I know God!" but if he does not obey God's commands, then that person is a liar, the truth is not in him.   **5** When someone obeys *God's* teaching, then God's love has become complete in that person. This is how we know we are in God: **6** If a person claims that God lives in him, then he ought to live as Jesus lived.

1:1   or, the living Message (Jesus)
1:5   righteousness
1:5   sin
1:7   righteousness
2:1   or, dear. John was a very old man when he wrote this letter; he affectionately referred to everyone as his "little children."

The Same Commandment

7 My dear *friends*, I'm not writing you a new command. No, it is the same command you have had from the beginning. This old command is the teaching that you have heard. **8** And yet, I write you this command as a new command. It is true in Jesus and in yourselves. The darkness* is passing away and the true light is already shining.

9 A person may claim, "I am in the light," but if he hates his brother *or sister*, he is still in the darkness.*

10 The person who loves his brother *or sister* lives in the light, and there is nothing in that person which will cause *him* to fall into sin. **11** The person who hates his brother *or sister* is in darkness. He walks around in darkness. He doesn't know where he's going, because the darkness has blinded him.

12 I am writing to you, dear children,
> because your sins are forgiven
>> because of the authority of *Jesus*.

13 I am writing to you, fathers,
> because you know the one who existed
>> from the beginning.

I am writing to you, young men,
> because you have conquered the evil one.*

14 I wrote to you, children,
> because you know the Father.

I wrote to you, fathers,
> because you know the one who existed
>> from the beginning.

I wrote to you, young men,
> because you are strong;
> God's message lives in you,
>> and you have conquered the evil one.

Who Are We Pleasing?

15 Don't love the world or the things in the world. If someone loves the world, the Father's love is not in that person. **16** These are the *evil* things in the world:
> wanting sinful things to please our bodies
> wanting the things that we see
> being too proud of the things that we have.

None of those things come from the Father; each one of them comes from the world. **17** The world is passing away and everything in the world which men want is passing away too, but the person who does what God wants lives forever.

God Chasers Belong

18 Little children, the time of the end is near! You have heard that the enemy of Christ* is coming. And now, many enemies of Christ are already here. Therefore, we know that the time of the end is near. **19** Those enemies of Christ *were in our group*, but they left us. They didn't really belong with us. If they had really been part of our

---

2:8 sin
2:9 sin
2:13 the Devil
2:18 or, Anti-Christ

group, they would have stayed with us, but they left. This shows that none of them really belonged with us.

20 You have the gift* that the Holy One gave you. This is why you all know the truth. **21** Why did I write you? Did I write because you don't know the truth? No, I wrote this letter because you **do** know the truth! And you know that no lie comes from the truth.

22 So, who is the liar? It is the one who claims that Jesus is not the Christ! This person is the enemy of Christ. He does not believe in the Father or in His Son. **23** Everyone who denies the Son does not have the Father, but the person who confesses the Son also has the Father.

24 Be sure you continue to follow the teaching which you heard from the beginning. If you continue in what you heard from the beginning, then you will stay in the Son and in the Father. **25** This is what God promised us: He promised us eternal life.

26 I wrote these things about those people who are trying to fool you. **27** *God* gave you a gift.* You still have this gift inside you. You don't need anyone to teach you. The gift that He gave you teaches you about everything. This gift is true; it is not false. Because of this, continue to live in God, just as His gift taught you.

28 Yes, my little children, live in Him. If we do this, we can have confidence and not be ashamed on the Day when Christ appears. **29** You know Christ is righteous. You know that every person who does what is right is God's child.

Chapter 3

Do Right, God Chasers

1 Look at the kind of love that the Father has given us: We are called children of God. And, we really **are** God's children! The people in the world don't understand it, because they have not known Him.

2 Dear *friends*, we are now children of God. It does not yet appear what we will be in the future. We know when Christ comes again, we will be like him. We will see him as he really is. **3** Christ is pure and every person who has this hope *based* on Christ makes himself pure like Christ.

4 Every person who sins is breaking *God's* law. Sin is breaking *God's* law. **5** You know that Christ appeared to take away the sins of people. There is no sin in Christ. **6** So, the person who lives in Jesus does not make a practice of sinning. Every person who continues to sin has never really understood Jesus or known him.

7 Little children, don't let anyone fool you. Jesus is righteous. To be righteous like Jesus, a person must do what is right. **8** Since the beginning, the Devil has been sinning. The person who continues to sin belongs to the Devil. Why did the Son of God appear? To destroy the Devil's works.

9 When God makes a person His child, that person does not continue to sin, because God's seed remains in him. That person is not able to continue to sin, because he has become a child of God. **10** This is how we can clearly *see* who God's children are. Also, *we can know* who the Devil's children are. The person who doesn't do what is right is not a child of God. The person who does not love his brother is not a child of God.

2:20   literally, an anointing
2:27   literally, the anointing

You Must Learn to Hate Hate

11 This is the message that you have heard from the beginning: We must love one another. **12** Don't be like Cain.* Cain belonged to the evil one.* He killed his brother *Abel*. Why did Cain kill his brother? Because the things which Cain did were evil, but the things which his brother did were right.

13 Brothers, don't be surprised when the people of this world hate you. **14** We know we have moved away from death and come into life, because we love the brothers. The person who doesn't love stays in death. **15** Every person who hates his brother is a murderer.* And you know that no murderer has eternal life in him. **16** This is how we know what real love is: Jesus gave up his life for us. So, we ought to give up our lives for the brothers. **17** Suppose a brother is rich enough to have all the things he needs. And, he sees another brother who doesn't have the things he needs. What if the *rich* brother doesn't help the *poor* brother? How can God's love stay in him? **18** My little children, our love should not be mere words or talk. No, our love must be true love in action. **19-20** That is how we know we belong to the truth. And when our conscience makes us feel guilty, we still may have peace before God, because God is greater than our conscience. God knows everything.

21 My dear *friends*, if our consciences do not make us feel guilty, then we can have confidence when we come to God. **22** God gives us the things for which we ask. We receive these things because we obey God's commands and we do what pleases Him. **23** This is what God commands—that we believe in the name of His Son, Jesus Christ, and that we love each other, just as He commanded. **24** The person who obeys God's commands lives in God and God lives in that person. How do we know that God lives in us? We know it because of the Spirit whom God gave us.

Chapter 4

Test the Spirits

1 My dear *friends*, many false prophets are now in the world. So, don't believe every spirit. Test the spirits to see whether they are from God. **2** This is how you can recognize God's Spirit: One Spirit says, "I believe that Jesus is the Christ. Jesus came to earth and became a human being." That Spirit is from God. **3** Another spirit refuses to say this about Jesus. That spirit is not from God. This is the spirit of the enemy of Christ. You have heard he was coming and now he is already in the world!

4 My little children, you belong to God. You have conquered the *false prophets*, because the One who is in you is greater than the one who is in the people of the world.* **5** Those *false prophets* belong to the world. The things they say are also from the world. The world listens to what they say. **6** We are from God. The people who know God listen to us, but the people who are not from God don't listen to us. That is how we can recognize the Spirit who is true and the spirit who is false.

God Is Love

7 Dear *friends*, we should love one another, because love comes from God. The person who loves has become God's child; he knows God. **8** The person who doesn't

---

3:12   See Genesis 4:1-8.
3:12   the Devil
3:15   See Matthew 5:21-26.
4:4   God is much more powerful than Satan.

love does not know God, because God is love.   9 This is how God showed His love to us: God sent His one and only* Son into the world that we may live through him. 10 Real love (God's love for us, not our love for God) is this: God sent His Son to be the way that God takes away our sins.

You Must Learn to Hate Hate

11 Since God loved us that much, dear *friends*, we ought to love each other, too. 12 No person has ever seen God, but if we love each other, then God lives in us and God's love is made perfect in us.

13 We know we live in God and God lives in us. He gave us His Spirit.   14 We have seen that the Father sent His Son to be the Savior of the world. That is what we are telling people.   15 If someone confesses, "I believe that Jesus is the Son of God," then God lives in that person and that person lives in God.   16 We know the love that God has for us and we trust that love.

God is love. The one who lives in love lives in God and God lives in that person. 17 Love is made perfect in us. So, we can have confidence on the Judgment Day, because we are like Him in this world.   18 Love does not contain fear; perfect love pushes out fear. Love has not been perfected in the person who *still* has fear; he is afraid of being punished.

19 We love, because God first loved us.   20 If someone claims, "I love God," but that person hates his *Christian* brother, then that person is a liar! One who does not love his brother (whom he has seen) **cannot** love God (whom he has not seen)!   21 God gave us this command: The person who loves God must love his brother, too.

Chapter 5

God Chasers Conquer

1 Every person who believes that Jesus is the Christ is God's child. Every person who loves the Father also loves the Father's children.   2 We know that we love God's children when we love God and we obey His commands.   3 Loving God means obeying His commands. God's commands are not too hard for us.   4 Everyone who is a child of God conquers the world. It is our faith which conquers the world.   5 Who is the person who conquers the world? Only the one who believes that Jesus is God's Son.

Three Agree

6 Jesus Christ is the one who came. He came with water* and with blood.* Jesus did not come by water only. No, Jesus came by both water **and** blood. The *Holy* Spirit tells us this is true. The Spirit is the truth.   7 So, there are three witnesses which tell us *about Jesus*:   8 the Spirit, the water, and the blood. These three witnesses agree. 9 We believe human beings when they say something is true, but what God says is more important. This is what God told us: He told us the truth about His own Son. 10 The person who believes in the Son of God has the witness in him. The person who does not believe God is really calling God a liar, because he doesn't believe what God told us about His Son.   11 This is what God told us: He has given us eternal life. This

---

4:9   or, only begotten
5:6   immersion by John
5:6   dying on the cross (John 19:34)

369

eternal life is in His Son.   **12** The person who has the Son has life, but the person who doesn't have the Son of God does not have life.

God Listens to Our Prayers

13 I wrote these things to you people who believe in the authority of the Son of God. I wanted you to know that you have eternal life now.   **14** This is the *kind of* confidence we have toward God. If we ask God for something (and it agrees with what God wants *for us*), God listens to what we say.   **15** Since God listens to us every time we ask Him, we know He has already given us the things we have asked for from Him.

16 Suppose a person sees his *Christian* brother sinning a sin which does not lead to *eternal* death. He should pray to God for that brother. Then God will give life to that brother. *I am talking about* people whose sin does not lead to *eternal* death. There is a sin which leads to death. I don't mean that a person should pray about that sin. **17** Doing wrong is always sin, but there is a sin which does not lead to *eternal* death.

18 We know that anyone who has become a child of God does not continue to sin. The Son of God* keeps God's child *safe*. The evil one* cannot touch him.   **19** Though the evil one is everywhere in the whole world, we know we belong to God.   **20** We know that the Son of God has come. He has given us understanding. Now, we may know the true God and our lives are in that true God—and in His Son, Jesus Christ. He is the true God, and he is eternal life.   **21** So, little children, keep yourselves away from false gods.

5:18   literally, the one born of God (Jesus)
5:18   the Devil

2 JOHN

John Says, "Hi." Again

1 From the elder.

To the chosen lady* and to her children.

I truly love all of you. All of those people who know the truth love you, too. **2** We love you because of the truth—the truth that stays in us. This truth will be with us forever.

3 Gracious love, mercy, and peace will be with us from God the Father and from His Son, Jesus Christ, through truth and love.

Love Each Other

4 I was very happy to find out about some of your children. They are following the way of truth, just as the Father told us. **5** And now, dear lady,* I beg you: Let us all love each other. (This is not a new command; it is the same command that we had from the beginning.) **6** Loving means living the way He commanded us to live. This is God's command: that you live a life of love. You heard this from the beginning.

Reject False Teachers

7 Many false teachers are now in the world. They won't admit that Jesus Christ came *to earth* and became a human being. A person like that is a false teacher and an enemy of Christ. **8** Be careful! Don't lose the reward you have worked for. Be sure you receive **all** of it.

9 A person must continue to follow only the teaching of Christ. If anyone goes beyond Christ's teaching, then he does not have God. But if a person continues to stay within the teaching, then he has both the Father and the Son. **10** If someone comes to you, but that person does not bring this teaching, don't receive him into your home. Don't welcome him. **11** If you do, then you are helping him do his evil work.

I Want to See You

12 I have much to write you, but I don't want to use paper and ink. Instead, I hope to come visit you. Then we can talk face to face. That will make us very happy. **13** The children of your chosen sister* send their greetings to you.

1:1   This letter could have been written to a woman or to a congregation.
1:5   This letter could have been written to a woman or to a congregation.
1:13   This may refer to another congregation of the Lord's people.

3 JOHN

John Says "Hi" One More Time

1 From the elder.

To my dear *friend*, Gaius, whom I truly love.   **2** My dear *friend, I know that* your soul is doing well. I pray that you are doing well in every other way and that you are feeling all right.   **3** Some brothers came and told me about the truth in your *life*, that you continue to follow the way of truth. This made me very happy.   **4** It always gives me the greatest joy when I hear that my children are living by the way of truth.

Friends in Need

5 My dear *friend*, it's good that you continue to help the brothers—even brothers you don't know!   **6** In front of the whole congregation these brothers told us about the love you have. Please help them continue their trip in a way that will please God.   **7** They went out on behalf of Jesus.* They accepted no help from unbelievers.   **8** We ought to help such people, so that we may be co-workers for the truth.

God Chasers Tell the Truth

9 I wrote a letter to the congregation, but Diotrephes rejected us. He always wants to be number one.   **10** If I come, I will talk about what he is doing. He tells lies and says bad things about us. But he's not satisfied with that! He rejects those brothers and tries to stop those who want to help the brothers; he throws them out of the congregation.

11 My dear *friend*, don't copy what is bad; copy what is good. The person who does what is good is from God, but the person who does wrong has never known God.

12 All of the people and the truth itself say good things about Demetrius. We do, too. You know that what we say is true.

I'll Be Seein' You

13 I have many things that I want to write you, but I don't want to use pen and ink.   **14** I hope to visit you soon. Then we can talk face to face.   **15** The friends here with me send their greetings. Please give our greetings to each one of the friends there. Peace to you.

1:7   literally, the Name

JUDE

Jude Says "Hi."

1 From Jude, a servant of Jesus Christ and a brother of James.

To the people who are loved by God the Father, the chosen ones protected by Jesus Christ.

2 May you have mercy, peace, and love—abundantly.

Danger, Danger, Danger!

3-4 Dear *friends*, I was always very eager to write you about the salvation we share. But, I felt forced to write you because some men have come in secretly. I am begging you to fight for the faith which God passed on to the holy people once for all time. These men don't want God. Long ago it was written that they would be condemned. They are turning away from the gracious love of our God to orgies,* rejecting Jesus Christ, our only Lord and Master.

5 You once knew all about these things, but I want to remind you of them: The Lord *God* saved the people *of Israel* from the land of Egypt, but later, He destroyed those who did not believe. **6** Some angels did not keep their first *position*. Instead, they left their home. They have been kept in darkness below in chains forever, until the great Day of Judgment. **7** Just like the cities of Sodom and Gomorrah and the towns around them, the people gave themselves over to sexual sin, even perversion. They provide us with an example of people who receive justice—eternal fire.

8 The men *with you* are like that, too. They have *false* visions. They pollute their own bodies. They reject authority and they say evil things about glorious beings. **9** Once, Michael, the angel leader, was arguing with the Devil about Moses' *dead* body. But not even Michael dared to condemn *the Devil* for the evil things he was saying against God. Instead, Michael said, "The **Lord** *God* will rebuke you!" **10** These men *with you* are saying awful words about things they don't understand. They are like dumb animals, following only what they understand by instinct. And they use this knowledge to destroy themselves.

11 How terrible it will be for them! They are traveling the same road that Cain did.* They have hurried to make money, as when Balaam *tried to* fool *Israel*,* but they will be destroyed like Korah's rebellion.* **12** These men are ugly spots at your love feasts. They eat with you; they feel no embarrassment. They shepherd themselves. They are like clouds carried along by the wind—but they have no rain. They are like autumn trees that have no fruit, pulled up by the roots and twice as dead. **13** They are like wild waves of the ocean, foaming up their own shame. They are like wandering stars. God has forever reserved for them the darkest darkness.

14 Six *generations* after Adam, Enoch prophesied about these men: "Look! The Lord *God* comes with 10,000 of His holy *angels*. **15** He will judge everyone and condemn all people who don't want God, for all their ungodly deeds that they did and for all the harsh things these ungodly sinners said against Him."

1:4   wild, drunken, sex parties
1:11   See Genesis 4:1-16.
1:11   See Numbers 22:7.
1:11   See Numbers 16:1-3, 31-35.

16 These men are complainers, blaming others, living by their own evil desires, bragging about themselves and flattering other people, so that they can get ahead.

Be Built

17 But, dear *friends*, you should remember the words which the apostles of our Lord Jesus Christ spoke not too long ago. **18** They were telling you, "In the last times, there will be men who will make fun of you. They won't want God; they will follow their own desires." **19** These are the men who are making trouble. They are only physical; they have no spirit.

20 But, dear *friends*, build up your lives on your holy faith, praying with the Holy Spirit. **21** Keep yourselves inside God's love while you are waiting for the mercy of our Lord Jesus Christ *to give you* eternal life.

22 Show mercy to those who are doubting, **23** but save them by plucking them out of the fire. With fear, show mercy to others, but hate even the clothes which are stained with their evil nature.

Be Blessed

24 Now, to the One who is able to keep you from falling and to help you be spotless with gladness before His glory, **25** to God our only Savior, through our Lord Jesus Christ, be great glory, power, and authority—before all time, now, and forever. Amen.

REVELATION

Chapter 1

1 This book is what Jesus Christ revealed. God gave this revelation to Jesus to show his servants the things which must happen soon. Jesus revealed it to John, his servant, sending it through his angel.   **2** John told the truth about the things he saw—the testimony of Jesus Christ and the message of God.   **3** Happy is the person who reads the words of this prophecy, listens to them, and obeys the things written here, because the time is near.

Seven Congregations

4 From John.

To the seven congregations in the land of Asia.*

The One who is, who was, and who will be *sends* you gracious love and peace; so do the seven spirits who are before God's throne.   **5-6** Gracious love and peace from Jesus Christ, too. He is the faithful Witness, the first one to rise from death, and the Ruler of the kings of earth.

May glory and power be his forever and ever. Amen! Jesus loved us. He bled, setting us free from our sins. He formed us into a kingdom. We are priests to God, his Father.

7 "Look! He is coming with the clouds."   *Daniel 7:13*

"Every eye will see him;

even those who wounded him."   *Zechariah 12:10,12,14*

Because of him, all people on earth will cry.

Yes, amen!

8 "I am the A and the Z"* says the Lord God. He is the One who is, who was, and who will be. He is all-powerful.

Island Revelation

9 I am John, your brother. In Jesus I share with you the trouble, the endurance, and the kingdom. I was on an island called Patmos. *They put me there*, because *I preached* the message of God and the evidence about Jesus.   **10** During the Lord's day, I was in the Spirit. I heard a loud voice *speaking* behind me. It was like the sound from a trumpet.   **11** It said, "Write what you see in a scroll. Send it to these seven congregations:

Ephesus,
Smyrna,
Pergamum,
Thyatira,
Sardis,
Philadelphia,
Laodicea."

12 I turned around to look at the voice which was talking to me. After I turned around, I saw seven golden lampstands.   **13** There was one like the Son of Man* among them. He was dressed with a very long robe. He wore a golden belt around his

---

1:4	modern Turkey
1:8	literally, the Alpha and the Omega (the first and the last letters of the Greek alphabet.) Here it means the beginning and the end.
1:13	See Daniel 7:13-14. This refers to Jesus, the Messiah.

waist.   **14** His head and his hair were white, white like wool or like snow. His eyes were like the flame of a fire.   **15** His feet were like brass, glowing in an oven. His voice was loud, like *the rushing of* much water.   **16** He had seven stars in his right hand. A sword, sharp on both edges, was coming out of his mouth. His face looked like the sun, when it shines its brightest.

17 When I saw him, I fell down at his feet as if I were dead. Then he put his right hand on me and said, "Don't be afraid! I am the first and the last.   **18** I am the one who is alive. I was dead, but, look, I am alive forever and ever! I have the keys to death and Hades.*   **19** So write the things which you saw, the things that are now and the things that are about to happen after the present time.   **20** This is the secret of the seven stars in my right hand and the seven golden lampstands which you saw on my right: The seven stars are the messengers of the seven congregations. The seven lampstands are the seven congregations."

Chapter 2

To the God Chasers at Ephesus

1 "Write this to the messenger of the congregation in Ephesus: The one who is holding the seven stars in his right hand, the one who is walking among the seven golden lampstands, says this: **2** 'I know what you have done, how hard you have worked, and how patient you have been. I know that you cannot tolerate evil people. You have tested those men who call themselves apostles. They are not apostles. You found out that they are liars!   **3** You have endurance. Yet you have carried on because of my name; you've not become tired.   **4** But I have something against you—you no longer love me as you did in the beginning.   **5** Therefore, remember from where you have fallen. Change your heart! Do the things you did in the beginning. If you won't change your heart, I will come and take your lampstand from its place.   **6** However, you **do** have this—you hate what the Nicolaitan people* are doing. I hate those things, too.   **7** The person who has an ear should listen to what the Spirit is saying to the congregations. To the person who conquers I will give something to eat. It will come from the Tree of Life, which is in the Paradise* of God.' "

To the God Chasers at Smyrna

8 "Write this to the messenger of the congregation in Smyrna: The one who is the first and the last, who was dead and came back to life, says this: **9** 'I know your troubles and how poor you are (but you are actually rich) and I know about the slander of those who call themselves Jews. (They are not Jews; they are a synagogue of Satan!)   **10** Don't be afraid of anything you are about to suffer. Look, the Devil is about to throw some of you into prison. He wants to test you. You will have trouble for ten days. Be faithful, even if you must die. I will give you the crown* of life.   **11** The person who has an ear should listen to what the Spirit is saying to the congregations. The person who conquers will never be hurt by the second death.' "

1:18   the Greek word for the unseen world of the dead
2:6   followers of Nicolas. It may be the same person in Acts 6:5.
2:7   See Genesis 2:8-17.
2:10   reward

To the God Chasers at Pergamum

12 "Write this to the messenger of the congregation in Pergamum: The one who has the sword which is sharp on both edges says, **13** 'I know where you live (It is Satan's throne.), but you are holding onto my name. You did not leave my faith, even during the time of Antipas, my faithful witness. He was taken from you and killed. Satan lives where you are. **14** But I have a few things against you: You have some people there who are holding onto Balaam's teaching.* Balaam was teaching Balak to put a temptation in front of the sons of Israel to make them sin, to eat food offered to false gods and to make them commit sexual sin. **15** In the same way, you have some people there who are also holding onto the teaching of the Nicolaitans. **16** So, change your hearts! If you don't, I will come soon. I will make war against them with the sword which comes from my mouth. **17** The person who has an ear should listen to what the Spirit is saying to the congregations. I will give some of the hidden manna* to the person who conquers. I will also give him a little white stone. A new name* will have been written on the stone. The only person who knows the name is the one who gets it.' "

To the God Chasers at Thyatira

18 "Write this to the messenger of the congregation in Thyatira: The Son of God, whose eyes are like the flame of a fire and whose feet are like shining brass, says, **19** 'I know your deeds, your love, your faith, your service, and your endurance. You are doing more now than you did in the beginning. **20** However, I have something against you: You are tolerating that woman, Jezebel.* She calls herself a prophetess. She fools my servants and teaches them to commit sexual sin and to eat food offered to false gods. **21** I gave her time to change her heart, but she didn't want to stop committing sexual sin. **22** Look! If she and the men who are committing adultery with her are not sorry for what they have done, I will throw them on a bed of great trouble. **23** I will kill her children.* Then all of the congregations will know that I am the one who searches the deepest human thoughts and feelings. The way you live is the way I will reward each one of you. **24** Some of you in Thyatira do not hold to this teaching. You don't know "the deep things of Satan." I am not putting another burden upon you. **25** Hold onto what you have until I come. **26** I will give authority over the people of the world to the person who conquers and always obeys me. **27-28** I have received this *authority* from my Father. He will take care of His enemies like a shepherd does—with an iron rod, shattering them like clay pots.* I will also give him the Morning Star.* **29** The person who has an ear should listen to what the Spirit is saying to the congregations.' "

Chapter 3

To the God Chasers at Sardis

1 "Write this to the messenger of the congregation in Sardis: The one who has the seven spirits of God and the seven stars says this: 'I know what you have done. People

---

2:14	See Numbers 22—24; Deuteronomy 23:3-4.
2:17	Perhaps this is explained by John 6:31-36.
2:17	Compare Exodus 28:36-38; 1 Peter 2:9; Revelation 14:1.
2:20	A vengeful, merciless, pagan queen. See 1 Kings 16:31–21:23; 2 Kings 9:7,30-37
2:23	This probably refers to her followers.
2:27-28	Clay pots are very brittle; they cannot stand against iron which is very hard and strong.
2:27-28	Jesus. See Revelation 22:16.

may think you are alive, but you are dead! **2** Wake up! Make strong the things which remain and are about to die. I have not found your actions complete before my God. **3** So, remember what you have received and heard. Then obey it. Change your heart! If you don't wake up, I will come like a robber. You will never know precisely when I will come upon you. **4** However, you have a few individuals in Sardis who have not polluted their clothes.* They will walk with me *dressed* in white;* they are worthy people. **5** In the same way, the person who conquers will wear white clothes. His name will never be erased from the Book of Life. I will speak for him in front of my Father and in front of His angels. **6** The person who has an ear should listen to what the Spirit is saying to the congregations.' "

To the God Chasers at Philadelphia

7 "Write this to the messenger of the congregation in Philadelphia: The one who is holy and true says, 'He has David's key. He opens, and no one closes; he closes, and no one opens. **8** I know what you have done. Listen! I have put a door in front of you. It is open. No one can close it. Though you don't have much strength, you have obeyed my teaching and have not denied my name. **9** Look, I will handle those from the synagogue of Satan. They call themselves true Jews, but they are not. They are lying. Listen! I will make them come and bow down at your feet. Then they will know that I have loved you. **10** You obeyed my teaching about endurance. Now, I will keep you from the time of testing which is about to come upon the whole world. All people on earth will be tested. **11** I am coming soon. Hold onto what you have, so that no one can take away your crown.* **12** I will make the victorious person a pillar in the temple sanctuary of my God. He will never leave there. On him I will write my new name, my God's name, and the name of the city of my God. That city is the new Jerusalem, which is coming down from heaven from my God. **13** The person who has an ear should listen to what the Spirit is saying to the congregations.' "

To the God Chasers at Laodicea

14 "Write this to the messenger of the congregation in Laodicea: The Amen, the faithful and true Witness, the Source of God's creation says: **15** 'I know what you've done. You are not cold; you are not hot. I wish you were either cold or hot! **16** Instead, you are lukewarm—not hot, not cold. So, I am going to vomit you out of my mouth. **17** You say, "I am rich." You *think* you have been rich and you don't need anything. Don't you realize that you are miserable, pitiful, poor, blind, and naked? **18** I advise you to buy refined gold from me, so that you may truly be rich. Buy white clothes from me, so that you will be dressed and you won't see the shame of your nakedness. Buy medicine from me to rub into your eyes, so that you may see. **19** I correct and punish those whom I love. Be serious. Change your heart! **20** Listen, I stand at the door. I am knocking. If anyone hears my voice and opens the door, I will come inside with him. We will have dinner together. **21** I will give *the right* to sit with me at my throne to the person who conquers as I conquered, and as I sat down beside my Father at His throne. **22** The person who has an ear should listen to what the Spirit is saying to the congregations.' "

3:4   They have lived good lives. See 1 Corinthians 6:11.
3:4   White symbolizes purity.
3:11   reward

Chapter 4

Throne Room Worship

1 Later I looked and there was an open door in heaven. The voice which I had heard before was talking to me. It sounded *loud*, like a trumpet: "Come up here! I will show you things which must happen later." **2** Immediately, I was in the Spirit. Look, a throne was put there in heaven. One was sitting on it. **3** He looked like jasper and carnelian—precious jewels. There was a rainbow around the throne. It looked like an emerald. **4** There were 24 thrones around the throne and 24 elders were sitting on the thrones. They were dressed in white clothes.* They had golden crowns on their heads, too. **5** Lightning, thunder, and rumblings came from the throne. Seven lamps were burning in front of the throne. (They are the seven spirits of God.) **6** In front of the throne there was something like a glass lake; it looked like crystal.

There were four beings next to the throne and all around it. They had eyes everywhere—in front and behind. **7** The first being was like a lion. The second being was like a bull. The third being had a face like a man's face. And the fourth being was like an eagle flying. **8** Each of the four beings had six wings and each one was covered with eyes—inside and outside. Day and night they never stopped saying this:

"Holy, holy, holy is the Lord God,
the all-powerful One;
the One who was, who is, and who will be."

9 The four beings give glory, honor, and thanks to the One who is sitting on the throne and who lives forever and ever. **10** Then the 24 elders fall down in front of the One who is sitting on the throne. They worship the One who lives forever and ever. They lay their crowns before the throne, saying:
11 "O Lord, our God, You are worthy
to receive glory, honor, and power,
because You made everything.
All things were created because of Your will."

Chapter 5

Lion and Lamb

1 I saw a scroll* on the right of the One who was sitting on the throne. The scroll had writing on both sides of it. It was sealed with seven seals. **2** And I saw a strong angel. He was announcing this loudly: "Who is worthy to open the scroll, to open its seals?" **3** But there was no one in heaven, on earth, or under the earth who could open the scroll. No one could look inside it. **4** I was in tears, because no one could be found. No one was worthy to open the scroll. No one could look inside it.

5 One of the elders said to me, "Don't cry! Look, the Lion from the tribe of Judah has been victorious. He is the Descendant* of David. He will open the scroll and its seven seals."

6 Then I saw a Lamb standing there. It looked as though it had been killed. It was very close to the throne and the four beings, surrounded by the elders. It had seven horns and seven eyes. (These are the seven spirits of God sent to the whole earth.)

4:4   White symbolizes purity.
5:1   a long roll of leather or papyrus used for writing on a book
5:5   Jesus

7 It came and took the scroll from the right hand of the One who was sitting on the throne. **8** When it did this, the four beings and the 24 elders fell down in front of the Lamb. They had harps and golden bowls full of incense.* (These are the prayers of the holy people.) **9** They sang a new song:

> "You are worthy to take the scroll
>   and to open its seals,
> because you were killed; you used your blood
>   to buy back some people for God
>   from every tribe, language, people, and nation.

10 You changed them into a kingdom and priests for our God.
    They will rule over the earth."

11 I looked, and I heard the sound of many angels, the four beings, and the elders around the throne. The number of them was thousands of thousands and ten thousands of ten thousands. **12** They shouted:

> "The Lamb who was killed is worthy to receive
>   power, wealth, wisdom, strength, honor, glory, and
>   praise!"

13 And I heard every creature in heaven, on earth, under the earth, and in the ocean, and everything that is in them. They said this:

> "Praise, honor, glory, and power belong to the One
>   who is sitting on the throne and to the Lamb
>   forever and ever."

14 The four beings said again and again, "Amen!" And the elders fell down and worshiped.

Chapter 6

The Seven Seals: Who Will Stand?

1 I watched as the Lamb opened one of the seven seals. Then I heard one of the four beings say with a voice as loud as thunder, "Come!" **2** I looked, and there was a white horse. The person riding it had a bow. He was given a crown. As a conquerer, he rode out to conquer.

3 And when the Lamb opened the second seal, I heard the second being say, "Come!" **4** And another horse came out. It was red like fire. The person riding it was told to take peace away from the people of the earth, so that they would kill one another. He was given a great sword.

5 And when the Lamb opened the third seal, I heard the third being say, "Come!" I looked, and there was a black horse. The person who was riding it had weighing scales* in his hand. **6** I heard something like a voice come from among the four beings. It said, "A quart of wheat for a silver coin,* three quarts of barley for a silver coin,* but don't hurt the olive oil or the wine."

5:8   A special powder used in Jewish worship (Luke 1:9). It smelled good when it was burned. Compare
        Numbers 16:46-47; Psalm 141:2.
6:5   Bread was sold by weight. This shows how precious even a little food was.
6:6   Normally, a silver coin would buy eight to twelve times more. Inflation hurts poor people much more
        than the rich.

7 And when the Lamb opened the fourth seal, I heard the voice of the fourth being say, "Come!" **8** I looked and there was a pale-colored horse. The rider was named Death. Hades* was following him. They were given authority over one-fourth of the earth. They could kill with the sword, with famine, with disease, or use wild animals from the earth.

9 And when the Lamb opened the fifth seal, I saw under the altar the souls of those who had been killed because *they had preached* the message of God and because of the testimony that they had *given.* **10** They pleaded loudly, "How long, holy and true Master? Will you ever judge the people on earth and pay them back for killing us?"

11 Each of them was given a white robe. They were told to rest a little while longer, until everything was complete. (Their co-slaves and their brothers were also about to be killed, as they had been killed.)

12 And when the Lamb had opened the sixth seal, I observed a great earthquake. The sun became black like sackcloth made of goat hair. The whole moon became *red* like blood. **13** The stars of the sky fell to earth, as a fig tree drops its figs when it is shaken by a strong wind. **14** The sky disappeared like a scroll which is rolled up. Every mountain and island was moved from its place. **15** The kings of the earth, the important men, commanders, rich men, strong men, all slaves and free men hid themselves in caves and among the rocks of the mountains. **16** And they said to the mountains and to the rocks, "Fall on us. Hide us from the face of the One who is sitting on the throne. Hide us from the Lamb's punishment." **17** The great Day of his anger has come. Who will be able to stand?

Chapter 7

These Are Standing

1 Later I saw four angels standing at the four corners of the earth. They were holding back the four winds of the earth, so that no wind could blow upon the earth, upon the ocean, or upon any tree. **2** I saw another angel coming up from the east. He had the seal of the living God. He shouted to the four angels who were told to hurt the earth and the ocean, **3** "Don't hurt the earth, the ocean, or the trees until we put a seal on the foreheads of the servants of our God." **4** I heard the number of those who had been sealed. It was 144,000 from every tribe of the sons of Israel:*

5 12,000 sealed from the tribe of Judah,
12,000 sealed from the tribe of Reuben,
12,000 sealed from the tribe of Gad,
6 12,000 sealed from the tribe of Asher,
12,000 sealed from the tribe of Naphtali,
12,000 sealed from the tribe of Manasseh,
7 12,000 sealed from the tribe of Simeon,
12,000 sealed from the tribe of Levi,
12,000 sealed from the tribe of Issachar,
8 12,000 sealed from the tribe of Zebulun,

6:8   the Greek word for the unseen world of the dead
7:4   Twelve was a complete number to the Jews. 12,000 X 12 symbolized all of God's people.

12,000 sealed from the tribe of Joseph,
12,000 sealed from the tribe of Benjamin.

No More Tears

9 Later I looked and there was such a large crowd of people that no one could count them. They came from every nation, tribe, people, and language. They were standing in front of the throne and in front of the Lamb. They were dressed in white robes. Palm branches were in their hands. **10** They shouted, "Salvation belongs to our God, the One who is sitting on the throne! Salvation belongs to the Lamb, too!"

11 All the angels stood around the elders and the four beings, around the throne. They fell down on their faces in front of the throne and worshiped God. **12** They said, "Amen! Praise, glory, wisdom, thanks, honor, power, and strength belong to our God forever and ever! Amen!"

13 One of the elders asked me, "Who are those people dressed in white robes? Where did they come from?"

14 I answered him, "Sir, **you** know!"

He said to me, "They are the ones who came through the great trouble *safely*. Using the Lamb's blood, they washed their robes to make them white. **15** This is why they are before God's throne. They worship God day and night in His temple sanctuary. The One who is sitting on the throne will live with them. **16** They will never be hungry or thirsty. No heat or sun will burn them. **17** The Lamb in the middle of the throne will take care of them, like a shepherd does.* He will lead them to springs of fresh* water. God will wipe away every tear from their eyes."*

Chapter 8

Silence and Thunder

1 And when the Lamb opened the seventh seal, there was silence in heaven for about half an hour. **2** I saw seven angels, who always stand in front of God. They were given seven trumpets.

3 Another angel came and stood at the golden altar. He had a golden censer.* He was given much incense,* so that he could offer it with all the holy people's prayers on the altar before the throne. **4** The smoke from the incense went up from the angel's hand before God, with the prayers of the holy people. **5** The angel took the censer and filled it with fire from the altar. Then he threw it on the earth. Thunder, rumblings, lightning, and an earthquake took place.

The Seven Trumpets

6 The seven angels who had the seven trumpets prepared to sound them.

7 The first angel sounded his trumpet. There was hail and fire, mixed with blood. This was thrown on the earth. One-third of the earth was burned up. One-third of the trees were burned up. And, all of the green grass was burned up.

7:17   See Psalm 23:1; Ezekiel 34:23; John 10:11,14.
7:17   literally, living
7:17   See Isaiah 25:8; Revelation 21:4.
8:3   a container in which incense was burned
8:3   A special powder used in Jewish worship (Luke 1:9). It smelled good when it was burned. Compare Numbers 16:46-47; Psalm 141:2.

8 The second angel sounded his trumpet. Something like a great burning mountain was thrown into the ocean. One-third of the ocean was changed into blood. **9** One-third of the living creatures in the ocean died. One-third of the ships were destroyed.

10 The third angel sounded his trumpet. A great star fell from the sky. It was burning like a torch. It fell on one-third of the rivers and on the springs of water. **11** The name of that star is Bitterness.* It changed one-third of the water into bitter water. Many people died because of the water; it was poison.

12 The fourth angel sounded his trumpet. He struck one-third of the sun, one-third of the moon, and one-third of the stars. One-third of them became dark. The day was only one-third as bright as usual. And the night was two-thirds darker.

13 I looked and I heard an eagle flying in the middle of the air. It was shouting, "How horrible! How horrible! How horrible it will be for people who live on earth! There will be three more such blasts of trumpets in the future by three more angels."

Chapter 9

1 The fifth angel sounded his trumpet. I saw a star which had fallen to the ground from the sky. He was given the key to the bottomless pit. **2** He opened it. Smoke came up from the pit like the smoke from a great oven. The smoke from the pit made the sun and the air dark. **3** Grasshoppers came from the smoke and went into the world. They were given power, like that of scorpions on earth. **4** They were told not to hurt the grass of the earth, any green plant, or any tree. They could only hurt those who did not have God's seal on their foreheads. **5** They were not allowed to kill them—only to torture them for five months. The pain they suffered was like that of a scorpion when it stings someone. **6** During that time, people will look for death, but they won't find it. They will want to die, but death will run away from them.

7 The grasshoppers looked like horses prepared for war. They had crowns like gold on their heads. Their faces looked like the faces of people. **8** They had hair like the hair of women. Their teeth were like lion's teeth. **9** They had chests like iron breastplates. The sound of their wings was like the roar of many horses and chariots running into battle. **10** Their tails were like scorpions' tails. They had stingers in them, with the power to hurt human beings for five months. **11** They had a king over them. He was an angel from the bottomless *pit*. In Hebrew his name is Abaddon.* In Greek it is Apollyon.*

12 One horror has gone. But listen, there are still two more to come!

13 The sixth angel sounded his trumpet. I heard a sound coming from the corners* of the golden altar, which is in front of God. **14** It said to the sixth angel with the trumpet, "You must release the four angels! They have been bound at the great river Euphrates." **15** So the four angels were released. They had been prepared for this *exact* hour of this *exact* day of this *exact* month of this *exact* year to kill one-third of mankind. **16** The number of soldiers on horses was 200 million (I overheard the number.). **17** In the same way, in my vision I saw the horses and their riders. They had fiery red, yellow, and blue armor. The heads of the horses were like the heads of lions.

8:11   literally, Wormwood
9:11   a Hebrew name meaning "destruction"
9:11   a Greek name meaning "destruction"
9:13   Blood was often placed on the corners (horns) of the incense altar (Leviticus 4:7). Compare Revelation 8:3-5.

Fire, smoke, and sulfur came out of their mouths.   **18** One-third of mankind was killed by these three plagues—the fire, the smoke, and the sulfur that came from their mouths. **19** The power of the horses was in their mouths and in their tails. Their tails had heads on them like snakes. They could use them to hurt people.

20 Some people were not killed by these plagues. They did not change their hearts about the things they had made with their hands—false gods made of gold, silver, brass, stone, and wood—things which cannot see, hear, or walk. These people did not stop worshiping demons.   **21** They were not sorry about their murders, their evil magic, the sexual sin they had committed, or their robberies.

Chapter 10

A Strong Angel

1 Then I saw another strong angel coming down from heaven. He was dressed with a cloud. A rainbow was above his head. His face was *shining* like the sun, and his legs were like columns of fire.   **2** He had a little scroll in his hand; it was not rolled up. He put his right foot in the ocean and his left foot on land.   **3** He shouted very loudly, like when a lion roars. After he shouted, the seven thunders *answered* with rumblings. **4** After the seven thunders spoke, I was just about to write this down. But I heard a voice from heaven say, "Seal up what the seven thunders said. Don't write those things!"

5 The angel that I saw standing in the ocean and on land raised his right hand to heaven.   **6** He vowed by the One who lives forever and ever, by God who made heaven and everything in it, the earth and everything on it, and the ocean and everything in it. He said, "There will be no more time!"

7 But, during the time when the seventh angel is about to sound his trumpet, God's secret plan will be finished, just as He announced to His servants, the prophets.

8 The voice that I had heard from heaven was speaking to me again. It said, "Go, take the scroll which is unrolled in the angel's hand. He is standing in the ocean and on land."

9 I went to the angel and asked him to give me the scroll. He said to me, "Take it and eat it! It will be sweet as honey in your mouth, but it will be sour in your stomach." **10** So, I took the little scroll from the angel's hand and ate it. And it tasted as sweet as honey in my mouth, but when I ate it, it made my stomach sour.   **11** Then they said to me, "You must prophesy again to the peoples, nations, languages, and to many kings."

Chapter 11

Measuring Up

1 I was given a long measuring stick. It was like a rod. He said, "Get up! Measure God's temple sanctuary and the altar, and count the people who are worshiping there. **2** But don't measure the court outside the temple sanctuary, because it is for non-Jews.* They will trample the holy city for 42 months.   **3** I will give my two witnesses *power*. They will prophesy for 1,260 days, while they are dressed in sackcloth.*   **4** (These

---

11:2   or, the nations
11:3   This was a very rough kind of cloth. It was worn by people who mourned a death or who felt very
        sorry or sad about some other serious trouble. Compare Matthew 11:21.

men are the two olive trees and the two lampstands that stand before the Lord of the earth.)   **5** If any enemy wants to hurt them, a fire comes out of their mouth and burns them up. Any person who tries to hurt them will die like this.   **6** They have the authority to shut the sky. It won't rain while they are prophesying. They also have the authority to change all water into blood. They can strike the earth with any plague as often as they wish.   **7** When they finish giving their evidence, the wild animal that comes up from the bottomless *pit* will fight them and he will defeat them. He will kill them. **8-9** Their dead bodies *will lie exposed* in the streets of the great city. (Spiritually, it is named Sodom and Egypt, where their Lord was nailed to the cross.) They won't allow their bodies to be buried. People from every nation, tribe, language, and race will look at the bodies for three and a half days.   **10** The people who live on earth will be very happy. They will have a party. They will exchange gifts, because the two prophets *died*. They had made the people who live on earth suffer.   **11** But, after the three and a half days, the breath of life* from God will come* into them. They will stand up. The people who will be watching them will become very afraid.   **12** Then the two prophets will hear a loud voice speaking to them from heaven, "Come up here!" They will go up into heaven in a cloud. Their enemies will watch them.   **13** At that moment, there will be a great earthquake. Ten percent of the city will fall. 7,000 persons will be killed in the earthquake. The other people will be frightened. They will give glory to the God of heaven.

Reign and Rain

14 The second horror is gone. Listen! The third horror is coming soon.

15 The seventh angel sounded his trumpet. There were loud voices in heaven. They said, "The kingdom of the world has become the kingdom of our Lord *God* and of His Christ. He will rule forever and ever!"   **16** The 24 elders were sitting on their thrones in front of God. They fell down on their faces and worshiped God.   **17** They said, "We thank you, Lord God, the all-powerful One, the One who is and the One who was. You have used Your great power and have begun to rule.   **18** The people of the world were angry, but Your punishment has come. The right time has come to judge people who have died, to give rewards to Your servants, the prophets, to the holy people, and to those who respect Your name—the unimportant people and the important people—and to destroy those people who destroy the earth."   **19** God's temple sanctuary was opened in heaven. The holy chest which holds God's agreement appeared in His temple sanctuary. There were flashes of lightning, rumblings, thunder, an earthquake, and large hailstones.

Chapter 12

A Woman, a Child, and a Dragon

1 A great sign appeared in heaven. It was of a woman dressed with the sun. The moon was under her feet. A crown of twelve stars was on her head.   **2** She was pregnant. Because she was about to give birth and suffer, she cried out in pain.

3 Then another sign appeared in heaven. Look! It was a large red dragon. It had seven heads and ten horns. Seven crowns were on its seven heads.   **4** Its tail dragged

---

11:11   or, the Spirit of life
11:11   or, enter

one-third of the stars from the sky and threw them toward earth. The dragon stood in front of the woman who was about to give birth. He wanted to eat up the child as soon as it was born.   5 She had a baby boy who would rule all of the people of the world with an iron rod. But her child was taken away to God, to His throne.   6 The woman ran away into the desert. She had a place there which God had prepared for her. She could be cared for in that place for 1,260 days.

7 There was a war in heaven. Michael and his angels fought against the dragon. The dragon and his angels fought back.   8 But the dragon was not strong enough. There was no place left for the dragon and his angels in heaven anymore.   9 The large dragon was thrown out. (This is the old snake who is the same as the one called the Devil, Satan. He is the one who fools the whole world.) He was thrown down to the earth. He and his angels were thrown out.   10 I heard a loud voice in heaven say, "Now have come the salvation, the power, the kingdom of our God, and the authority of His Christ, because the accuser of our brothers has been thrown out. He always accuses them in front of our God day and night.   11 But they have defeated him because of the Lamb's blood and because of the message of their testimony. Even when they were about to die, they did not love their lives *more than God.*   12 This is why you should celebrate, O heavens and those of you who live there. How horrible it will be for the earth and the ocean, because the Devil has come down to where you are. He is very angry. He knows that he only has a short while."

13 When the dragon saw that he was thrown *down* to the earth, he hunted for the woman who had given birth to the boy.   14 Two wings from a large eagle were given to the woman, so that she could fly to her place in the desert. There, away from the presence of the snake, she would be taken care of for a time, times, and half a time. 15 Behind her the snake vomited up a lot of water, like a river. He wanted to sweep her away with the flood.   16 But the earth helped the woman. The earth opened up its mouth and swallowed the river of water which the snake had vomited.   17 The dragon was very angry at the woman. The dragon left to make war against the rest of her children. They obey the commands of God and they hold the testimony of Jesus. 18 The dragon stood on the beach.

Chapter 13

God Chasers Must Endure

1 I saw a wild animal coming up out of the ocean. It had ten horns and seven heads. There were ten crowns on its ten horns. And there was a filthy name on each head. 2 The wild animal that I saw looked like a leopard. Its feet were like the feet of a bear, and its mouth was like a lion's mouth. The dragon gave his power, his throne, and his great authority to the wild animal.   3 One of its heads seemed as though it had been seriously wounded, but the death wound had been healed. The people of the whole world were so amazed that they followed the wild animal.   4 They worshiped the dragon, because he gave the wild animal authority. They also worshiped the wild animal, saying, "Who is like the wild animal? Who could fight it?"

5 It was given a mouth to talk big and say evil things against God. It could use its authority for 42 months.   6 It opened its mouth to say evil things against God, against God's name, God's tent, and those who live in heaven.   7 It was allowed to start a war against the holy people and to defeat them. It received authority over every tribe,

people, language, and nation, **8** but not over the people who have their names written in the Lamb's Book of Life. Before the world was created, *God planned for* the Lamb to be killed. All of the other people who are living on earth will worship the wild animal.

9 If someone has an ear, he should listen:

10 "If anyone is supposed to be captured,
then he will surely be captured.
If anyone is supposed to be killed with a sword,
then he will surely be killed with a sword."

This means that holy people must endure and be faithful.

11 I saw another wild animal coming up out of the earth. It had two horns like a lamb's horns. It was talking like a dragon. **12** On his behalf, it used the complete authority of the wild animal that had already come. It forced the earth and the people there to worship the first wild animal whose death wound had been healed. **13** It performed great proofs. It made fire come down to earth from the sky in front of human beings. **14** It used their miracles to fool the people who were living on the earth. These powers had been given to it in the presence of the *first* wild animal. It told the people living on earth to make an idol for the *first* wild animal. (This was the one that had been killed with a sword, but it had come back to life.) **15** It was allowed to give the breath of life to the wild animal's idol. It talked and forced everyone to worship the idol or to be killed. **16** It forced everyone to receive a mark on his right hand or upon his forehead—unimportant people and important people, rich and poor, free men and slaves. **17** No one was allowed to buy or sell, if he didn't have the mark (the wild animal's name or number of the name).

18 This is *true* wisdom: The person who has understanding should figure out the number of the wild animal. (It is the same way that men count.) Its number is 666.

Chapter 14

Spotless

1 I looked and there was a Lamb. He was standing on Mount Zion.* 144,000 people were with him. They had his name and his Father's name written on their foreheads. **2** I heard a sound coming from the sky. It sounded like the roar of much water and like the sound of thunder. The sound I heard was also like the music coming from harps. **3** They were singing a new song in front of the throne, the four beings, and the elders. No one could learn that song—only the 144,000. They had been purchased from the earth. **4** They are virgins.* *Evil* women have not made them *spiritually* unclean. They follow the Lamb wherever he goes. They were bought from among human beings. They are the first ones to be offered to God and to the Lamb. **5** They never tell a lie. They are spotless.

Rest for God Chasers

6 I saw another angel flying in the middle of the air. He had the eternal Good News to tell those who are living on the earth—every nation, tribe, language, and people. **7** He said with a loud voice: "Respect God and give Him glory! The time has come for God to judge. Worship the One who made the sky, the earth, the ocean, and the springs of water!"

14:1   Zion was symbolic of the holiest place on earth to the Jews—God's temple in Jerusalem. The temple was built on this mountain. See Micah 4; Isaiah 40; Hebrews 12:22-23.

14:4   They were spiritual virgins. They kept themselves pure, faithful to God.

8 A second angel followed. He said, "It has fallen! The great city of Babylon has fallen!" She had forced all of the nations to drink the punishing wine of her sexual sin.

9 A third angel followed the first two angels. He said with a loud voice: "If anyone worships the wild animal and his idol and receives a mark on his forehead or on his hand, **10** he must drink from God's punishing wine. It has been poured full strength into God's cup of punishment. That person will be tortured in front of the holy angels and the Lamb with fire and sulfur. **11** The smoke will rise forever and ever from torturing those who worship the wild animal and its idol or anyone who receives the mark of its name. Day or night they will have no rest *from suffering*."

12 This means that holy people must endure. They must obey God's commands and hold onto the faith of Jesus.

13 Then I heard a voice coming from heaven. It said, "Write this: 'From now on, the people who die in the Lord are happy. The Spirit says that they will enjoy rest after they have worked so hard. Their *good* deeds follow them.' "

In the Crowd

14 I looked and there was a white cloud. There was one sitting on the cloud. He looked like *the* Son of Man.* He had a golden crown on his head and a sharp sickle in his hand. **15** Another angel came out of the temple sanctuary. This angel shouted very loudly to the one who was sitting on the cloud, "Send out your sickle! Harvest! The time for the harvesting has come! The earth harvest is ready!" **16** So the one who was sitting on the cloud swung his sickle across the earth and harvested the earth.

17 Another angel came out of the temple sanctuary in heaven. He had a sharp sickle, too. **18** And another angel came from the altar. He had power over fire. He called loudly to the angel with the sharp sickle, "Send out your sharp sickle! Gather the bunches of grapes in the vineyard of the earth. Its grapes are ripe!" **19** So, the angel swung his sickle to earth and gathered the grapes from the vineyard of the earth. Then he threw them into the winepress of God's anger. **20** Outside the city, the grapes were crushed down in this tank. All around for 180 miles the blood flowed out of the tank. It came up as high as the mouth of a horse!

Chapter 15

The Seven Plagues

1 I saw another great and amazing warning in heaven: There were seven angels with the last seven plagues. With them God's punishment will be finished.

2 I saw something which looked like a glass lake mixed with fire. Some people had defeated the wild animal, its idol, and the number of its name. They were standing on this glass lake. They had the harps of God. **3** They were singing the song of Moses, God's servant, and the song of the Lamb:

"Your actions are great and amazing,
     Lord God Almighty.
 Your ways are fair and true,
     O King of the nations.
4 Lord, who would not respect You
     and give glory to Your name?
 Only **You** are holy.

14:14   See Daniel 7:13-14. This refers to Jesus, the Messiah.

All of the nations will come and
  worship before You.
Your righteous deeds have become clear."

5 Later I saw this: The special tent of the temple sanctuary in heaven was open. **6** The seven angels with the seven plagues came out of the temple sanctuary. They were dressed in clean, bright linen and they wore golden belts around their waists. **7** Then one of the four beings gave the seven angels seven golden bowls of the punishment of God who lives forever and ever. **8** The temple sanctuary was filled with smoke which came from the glory and power of God. No one could go into the temple sanctuary until the seven plagues of the seven angels were finished.

Chapter 16

Sin Is Punished

1 I heard a loud voice coming from the temple sanctuary. It was saying this to the seven angels: "Go and pour out the seven bowls of God's punishment on the earth!"

2 The first angel left and poured out his bowl on the earth. This caused terrible ugly sores on the people who had the wild animal's mark and who worshiped its idol.

3 The second angel poured out his bowl in the ocean. The ocean changed into something like the blood of a dead man. Every living thing in the ocean died.

4 The third angel poured out his bowl in the rivers and springs of water. They changed into blood.

5 I heard this angel say this:

"You are fair, O Holy One, who is and who was,
  because You have decided *to do* these things.
6 They made *Your* holy people and prophets bleed.
  So, You gave them blood to drink.
They deserve this."

7 I heard someone at the altar say this:

"Yes, Lord God Almighty, Your decisions* are true and fair!"

8 The fourth angel poured out his bowl on the sun. He was allowed to use fire to burn people. **9** They were burned by the intense heat. They said evil things against the name of God, who had the control of these plagues, but they wouldn't change their hearts and give glory to God.

10 The fifth angel poured out his bowl on the throne of the wild animal. The wild animal's kingdom became dark. Because of the pain, people chewed on their own tongues. **11** They said evil things against the God of heaven, because they had sores and they were in pain. But they wouldn't change their hearts about the *evil* things which they were doing.

12 The sixth angel poured out his bowl into the great river, Euphrates. The water in it was dried up to prepare the road for the kings of the east. **13** Then I saw three evil spirits that looked like frogs. They came out of the mouths of the dragon, the wild animal, and the false prophets. **14** They are spirits of demons; they perform miracles. They go out to the kings of the whole world, to bring them together for Almighty God's great day of battle.

16:7   literally, judgments

15 Listen! I am coming *suddenly*, like a robber. The person who is awake and holds onto his clothes will be happy. He will not walk around naked and be ashamed in front of people. **16** He gathered them to a place called Armageddon in the Hebrew language.

17 The seventh angel poured out his bowl into the air. A loud voice came from the throne from the temple sanctuary: "It is done!" **18** There were flashes of lightning, rumblings, thunder, and a great earthquake. There has never been such an earthquake since man has been on earth. It was tremendous! **19** The great city broke into three parts. The cities of the people of the world fell down. God did not forget the great city of Babylon; He gave her the wine cup filled with His punishment. **20** Every island disappeared. Even mountains could not be found. **21** Giant hailstones rained down on people from the sky. Each of the hailstones weighed about 100 pounds! Because of the hailstone plague, the people said evil things against God. This plague was awful.

Chapter 17

Filthy Things

1 One of the seven angels who had the seven bowls came. He spoke with me, "Come, I will show you the condemnation of the famous whore.* She sits on much water. **2** The kings of the earth have committed sexual sin with her. The people who live on the earth have gotten drunk from the wine of her sexual sin."

3 In the Spirit, the angel carried me away to a desert. I saw a woman sitting on a wild animal. It was red. It had ungodly names written all over it. It had seven heads and ten horns. **4** The woman was dressed in purple and red clothes. She was covered with gold, precious jewels, and pearls. She had a golden cup in her hand. It was full of obscene and filthy things which came from her sexual sin. **5** This name, which has a secret meaning, was written on her forehead:

BABYLON THE GREAT
THE MOTHER OF WHORES
AND
THE FILTHY THINGS OF THE WORLD

6 I could see that the woman was drunk from the blood of holy people and the blood of Jesus' witnesses.

I was amazed when I saw this great sight. **7** The angel asked me, "Why are you amazed? I will tell you the secret about the woman and the wild animal that she is riding. It has seven heads and ten horns: **8** The wild animal that you saw existed at one time, but does not exist now. It is about to come up out of the bottomless *pit* and go to destruction.* There will be people who live on earth whose names have not been written in the Book of Life, since the beginning of the world. They will be amazed when they see the wild animal, because he existed one time. He does not exist now, but he will come back.

9 "The person who has wisdom will understand this: The seven heads are seven hills. The woman is sitting on them. They are seven kings, too. **10** Five kings have fallen, one king is now ruling, and another king has not yet come. When he does come, he must last for a little while. **11** The wild animal that existed at one time, but does

---

17:1   prostitute—a bad woman. She sold her body to men to use for sex.
17:8   Hell

not exist now, is an eighth king. He belongs with the seven kings. He is going off to destruction.* **12** The ten horns that you saw are ten kings. They have not yet received their kingdoms. But, along with the wild animal, they will get the power of kings for one hour. **13** They have one goal—they must give their power and authority to the wild animal. **14** They will fight against the Lamb. But the Lamb will defeat them, because he is Lord of lords and King of kings. The people with the Lamb are the called, the chosen and the faithful."

15 Then the angel said this to me: "The waters that you saw, where the whore sits, are peoples, crowds, nations, and languages. **16** The ten horns and the wild animal that you saw will hate the whore. They will abandon her, leaving her naked and ruined. They will eat her flesh and destroy her by fire. **17** God has put this *desire* into their hearts—to accomplish His purpose and to give their kingdom to the wild animal, until the words of God come true. The woman whom you saw is the great city which has a kingdom *ruling* over kings of the world."

Chapter 18

The Glory Light

1 Later I saw another angel coming down from heaven. He had great authority. His glory lighted the earth. **2** He shouted this with a strong voice:

"It has fallen! The great city of Babylon has fallen!
She has now become a home for demons
and a place for every evil spirit,
for every spiritually unclean, hated bird.
3 She has forced all of the nations to drink
from the raging wine of her sexual sin.
The kings of the earth committed sexual sin with her.
The businessmen of the earth became rich
from her lust for power."

4 I heard another voice coming from heaven. It said:

"Come out of her, my people!
You must not share in her sins!
Get away from the plagues which come upon her!
Don't get caught with her!
5 Her sins are piled up all the way to heaven.
God has not forgotten her crimes.
6 Treat her as she treated others!
Pay her back double for the *evil* things she did.
She mixed a cup *of suffering* for others;
mix it double for her!

7 She gave herself glory and luxury.
Pay her back with torture and pain.
In her heart she boasts,
'I am a queen sitting here.

17:11   Hell

> I am not a widow.
> I will never feel pain.'

8 This is why plagues will come on her in one day.
> There will be death, sorrow, and no food.
> Fire will burn her up.
> The Lord God is strong; He judges her."

9 When the kings of the earth see the smoke from her burning, they will cry over her. They had committed sexual sin with her and shared luxury with her.   **10** She is being punished. They will be afraid. So they will stand far away, saying, "How horrible this is! How horrible this is for you, O great, strong city of Babylon! Your condemnation came in one hour!"

11 The businessmen of the earth will cry over her and feel sorry. No one will buy their cargoes anymore:

12 cargoes of gold and silver;
> of precious jewels and pearls;
> of fine cotton, purple dye, silk, and scarlet cloth;
> of all kinds of citron wood, ivory articles,
> and expensive woods;
> of brass, iron, and marble;
13 of cinnamon, spice, incense, perfume, and precious spices;
> of wine and olive oil;
> of fine flour and wheat;
> of cattle, sheep, horses, and wagons;
> and of the bodies and the souls of men.
14 All things that you wanted are gone.
> All of your wealth and glamor have disappeared.
> No one will ever be able to find them.

15 The men who did business with these things stood far away. They had gotten rich because of her, but now they were afraid. She was being punished. They were crying and feeling sorry.   **16** They said:

> "How horrible this is! How horrible this is for you,
> > O great city!
> You were dressed with fine cotton, purple, and scarlet cloth.
> > You wore gold, precious jewelry, and pearls.
17 Such wealth was destroyed in only one hour!"

Every ship captain, sea traveler, sailor, and sea merchant stood far away.   **18** They saw her going up in smoke. They were shouting, "What city was ever like this city?" **19** They began to throw dust on their heads.* They were yelling and feeling sorry. They said:

> "How horrible this is! How horrible this is for the
> > great city!
> All those who owned ships in the ocean became
> > rich because of her.
> But, in only one hour, it was all destroyed!

18:19   This was a way of showing extreme anger.

20 O heaven, celebrate over her!
> You, too, holy people, apostles, and prophets,
because God condemned her for the way she treated you."

21 Then a strong angel lifted up a large stone and threw it into the ocean. (It was the size of a grinding stone.) He said:
> "The great city of Babylon will be thrown down with
> > this kind of force.
> It will never be found again.

22 The sound of musicians who play the harp, the flute,
> and the trumpet
> will never be heard there again.
Not one of the skills of any kind of worker
> will ever be found there again.
The sound of a grinding stone
will not be heard there again.

23 The light from a lamp
> will never shine there again.
The sound of a bride and groom
> will never be heard there again.
Your businessmen were very important on earth.
> The nations were fooled by your tricks of magic.

24 The blood of prophets, holy people, and everyone on earth who was killed was found in her."

Chapter 19

The Roar of Worship

Later, I heard something in heaven. It sounded like the roar of a large crowd. The people were saying:
> "Hallelujah!*
> Salvation, glory, and power belong to our God
> **2** because His decisions* are true and fair.
> God has condemned the famous whore
> > who used her sexual sin to spoil the world.
> She killed the servants of God,
> > but He has avenged their blood."

3 Again they said:
> "Hallelujah!
> *She is burning and* her smoke will go up forever and ever."

4 The 24 elders and the four beings fell down and worshiped God who was sitting on the throne. They said, "Amen! Hallelujah!"

A Wedding Invitation

5 A voice came out from the throne:
> "Let all of God's servants,

19:1   A Hebrew expression meaning "Praise Yahweh," i.e. "Praise the Lord."
19:2   literally, judgments

those who respect Him,
unimportant and important people,
praise our God."

6 Then I heard something like the sound of a large crowd. It was like the roar of lots of water and loud thunder:
"Hallelujah!
The Lord our God rules.
He is all-powerful.
7 Let us be happy and glad
and give God the glory,
because the wedding of the Lamb has come.
His bride has prepared herself *for him.*
8 She was given clean, bright, fine linen to wear." (The fine linen means the good things which holy people did.)

9 Then the angel said to me, "Write this down: 'The people who have been invited to the Lamb's wedding are happy.' These are the true words of God."

10 I fell down at the angel's feet to worship him, but he said to me, "Don't do that! Worship **God**! I am only a servant, like you and your brothers who have the truth that Jesus gave. The truth that Jesus gave is what inspires prophets."

Come to Dinner

11 I saw heaven opened. Look! There was a white horse! The person who was riding on it was called Faithful and True. He judges fairly. He makes war. **12** His eyes are like the flame of a fire. There are many crowns on his head. He has a name written on him. He is the only one who knows it. **13** He is dressed with a robe dipped in blood. His name is The Message of God. **14** The armies in heaven are following him on white horses. They are dressed in pure, white, fine linen. **15** A sharp sword comes out of his mouth. He uses it to hit the nations. **He** will shepherd them with an iron rod. **He** will crush down *the grapes* of Almighty God's angry punishment in the winepress. **16** He has this name written on his robe and on his thigh:

KING OF KINGS AND LORD OF LORDS

17 I saw an angel standing in the sun. He shouted very loudly to all the birds flying around in the middle of the air, "Come, gather at God's great dinner! **18** You will eat the flesh of kings, of commanders, of strong men, of horses and their riders, of all free men, of slaves, and of unimportant and important people."

19 Then I saw the wild animal, the kings of the earth, and their armies gathered to fight against the one who was riding the *white* horse and against his army. **20** The false prophet had performed miracles in the presence of the wild animal. The false prophet had used these miracles to fool the people who received the mark of the wild animal and who worshiped the wild animal's idol. But both the wild animal and the false prophet were captured and thrown alive into the fiery lake which burns with sulfur. **21** The one who rode the *white* horse used the sword that came from his mouth to kill the other soldiers. All the birds ate up their flesh.

Chapter 20

The Thousand Years

1 I saw an angel coming down from heaven. He had a key to the bottomless *pit* and a big chain in his hand. **2** He grabbed the dragon (that old snake, the Devil, Satan) and tied him up for 1,000 years.   **3** Then the angel threw him into the bottomless *pit*. Then he shut *the door* and sealed it, so that the dragon could not fool the nations until the 1,000 years were finished. After these things, the dragon must be set free for a short time.

4 I saw thrones, too. People sat on them. These were the souls of people who had been killed, because they had told the truth about Jesus and because *they had preached* the message of God. They had not worshiped the wild animal or its idol. They had not received the mark upon their foreheads or on their hands. They were given the power to judge. They lived and ruled with Christ for 1,000 years.   **5** (The other dead people did not come back to life until the 1,000 years were finished. This is the first rising from death.   **6** The person who has a part in this first resurrection is happy and holy. The second death does not have any power over these people. Instead, they will be priests of God and Christ. They will rule with Christ for 1,000 years.)

7 When the 1,000 years is finished, Satan will be set free from his prison.   **8** He will go out in all four directions of the earth to fool the nations—to Gog and Magog*— to gather them for war. There will be many, many soldiers. It will be like the number of the grains of sand on the beaches.   **9** They will come across the surface of the earth and surround the camp of the holy people and the city which *God* loves, but fire will come down from heaven and burn them up.   **10** The Devil who fooled them will be thrown into the lake which burns with sulfur. That is where the wild animal and the false prophet are. They will be tormented day and night, forever and ever.

The Fiery Lake

11 And I saw a great white throne and the One who was sitting on it. The earth and the sky ran away from His face, but they could not find any place *to hide*.   **12** I saw dead people—important and unimportant. They were standing in front of the throne. Books were opened. And another book—the Book of Life—was opened. The dead were judged from the things which had been written in the books, according to the way they had lived.   **13** The ocean yielded the dead people who were in it. Death and Hades* yielded the dead people who were in them. Each person was judged by the way he had lived.   **14** Death and Hades were thrown into the lake of fire. (The second death is the same thing as the lake of fire.)   **15** If someone's name was not found in the Book of Life, he was thrown into the lake of fire.

Chapter 21

A New City

1 Then I saw a new sky and a new earth. The first sky and the first earth were gone. The ocean didn't exist anymore, either.   **2** I saw the holy city, the new Jerusalem, coming down out of heaven from God. It was like a bride prepared for her husband-to-be; she was beautiful.   **3** And I heard a loud voice coming from the throne. It said, "Look! God's sanctuary* is among human beings. God will live with them. They will be His people. God Himself will be with them, and He will be their God.   **4** And

---

20:8   The location is not certain. It may have the spiritual meaning of "all people what are against God." Compare Revelation 11:8; Ezekiel 38:2.

20:13   the Greek word for the unseen world of the dead

21:3   literally, tent

God will wipe away every tear from their eyes. None of these things will exist: death, sorrow, crying, pain. (Old things have passed away.)"

5 The One who was sitting on the throne said, "Listen, I am making everything new. Write this down, because these words are dependable and true: **6** It is done! I am the A and the Z,* the Beginning and the End. From the Spring of Life I will freely give water to the thirsty person. **7** The person who is victorious will receive all these things. I will be his God. And, he will be My son. **8** However, people who are cowards, unbelievers, perverts, murderers, sexual sinners, those who follow occult practices, idol-worshipers, and all liars will be in the lake which burns with fire and sulfur. This is the second death."

Like Jewels

9 One of the seven angels came. (These angels were the ones who had the seven bowls which had been full of the last seven plagues.) He spoke with me, "Come, I will show you the bride of the Lamb." **10** In the Spirit, he carried me to a very tall mountain. He showed me the holy city, Jerusalem. It was coming down out of heaven from God. **11** It had God's glory. It was shining like a very valuable jewel—like crystal-clear jasper. **12** The city had a very high wall, with twelve gates and twelve angels at the gates. Each gate had the name of one tribe of Israel. **13** There were three gates on the east side. There were three gates on the north side. There were three gates on the south side. And, there were three gates on the west side. **14** The wall of the city had twelve foundations. Each foundation had the name of one of the Lamb's apostles.

15 The angel who was speaking to me had a golden measuring stick for measuring the city, its gates, and its wall. **16** The city was square-shaped; its width was the same as its length. The angel measured the city with the stick. The city was 12,000 stadia* long. It was 12,000 stadia high and 12,000 stadia wide. **17** The angel measured the wall of the city. It was 144 cubits* thick. (The angel was using the same measurement that a man *would use.*) **18** The wall was made of jasper. The city was made of pure gold. (It was like pure glass!) **19** Precious jewels were used to make the foundations of the city walls look more beautiful:

The first foundation jewel was jasper.
The second foundation jewel was sapphire.
The third foundation jewel was chalcedony.
The fourth foundation jewel was emerald.
20 The fifth foundation jewel was onyx.
The sixth foundation jewel was carnelian.
The seventh foundation jewel was yellow quartz.
The eighth foundation jewel was beryl.
The ninth foundation jewel was topaz.
The tenth foundation jewel was chrysoprase.
The eleventh foundation jewel was turquoise.
The twelfth foundation jewel was amethyst.

21:3   literally, tent
21:6   literally, the Alpha and the Omega (the first and last letters of the Greek alphabet). Here it means the beginning and the end.
21:16   About the distance from Rome to Jerusalem. The number is probably a symbol of perfection.
21:17   About 70 yards. A cubit was about the length of a man's forearm (measuring from the point of the elbow to the tip of the longest finger).

21 The twelve gates were twelve pearls. Each gate was made of one pearl. The city's street was made of pure gold, but you could see through it—like pure glass!

22 I didn't see a temple sanctuary in the city, because the Lord God Almighty and the Lamb are its temple sanctuary! **23** The city had no need for the sun or moon to shine on it—God's glory gives it light and the Lamb is the lamp of the city. **24** The nations use its light to guide them. The kings of the earth add their splendor to it. **25** Its gates will never be shut, because there is no night there. **26** The glory and honor of the nations will be brought into it. **27** Not one unholy thing will enter the city. No person who is perverted will go in. Liars will not get in. The only people who will enter are the ones whose names are written in the Lamb's Book of Life.

Chapter 22

Coming Home

1 The angel showed me a river of fresh water.* It sparkled like crystal. It flowed from God's throne and from the Lamb's throne. **2** The Trees of Life were in the middle of the city's street and on both sides of the river. They made fruit twelve times *per year*, producing their fruit once each month. The leaves of this kind of tree were for healing the nations. **3** Nothing that God has condemned will be found there. God's throne and the Lamb's throne will be in the city.

God's servants will worship Him with service. **4** They will **see** God's face! His name will be *written* on their foreheads. **5** There will be no night anymore. They will not need the light from a lamp or the light from the sun, because the Lord God will shine on them. They will rule as kings forever and ever.

Come!

6 The angel said to me, "These words are dependable and true: The Lord, the God of the spirits of the prophets, has sent His angel to show His servants what must soon happen. **7** Listen! I am coming soon. Happy is the person who obeys the words of the prophecy of this book."

8 I, John, was the one who was hearing and seeing these things. When I heard them and saw them, I fell down at the feet of the angel who was showing me these things. I wanted to worship him, **9** but he said to me, "Don't do that! Worship God! I am only a servant like you, like your brothers, and like the people who obey the words of this book. **10** Don't seal the words of the prophecy of this book. The right time is near. **11** Let the person who does wrong continue to do wrong. Let the person with a dirty mind continue to think in a filthy way. Let the person who does right continue to do good things. Let the person who is holy continue to be holy."

12 Jesus said, "Listen! I am coming soon. The reward I have is with me. I will pay back each person according to the way he lived. **13** I am the A and the Z,* the first and the last, the beginning and the end."

14 The people who wash their robes are happy. They will have the right to *eat from* the Tree of Life and the right to enter the city. **15** But, outside the city, there are wild dogs, occult people, sexual sinners, murderers, idol-worshipers, and every person who always likes to tell a lie.

22:1   or, of living water; of *the* Water of Life

22:13   literally, the Alpha and the Omega (the first and last letters of the Greek alphabet). Here it means the beginning and the end.

16 "I, Jesus, sent my messenger to tell the *seven* congregations the truth about these things. I am the Descendant from the family of David, the bright Morning Star."*

17 The Spirit and the bride are saying, "Come!" Let the person who is listening say, "Come!" Let the person who is thirsty come. Let him take as much of the living water as he wants.

Don't Change a Word

18 I am telling the truth to every person who is listening to the words of the prophecy of this book. If anyone adds more words to these words, God will add to him the plagues that are written in this book.   **19** And, if anyone takes away from the words of this prophetic book, God will take away that person's share of the Tree of Life and the holy city, which are written about in this book.

20 The Witness says these things, "Yes, I am coming soon!"

Amen! Lord Jesus, come!

21 May the gracious love of the Lord Jesus be with everyone.

22:16   Jesus. He brings on a new day.

THE GOD CHASER'S
ROAD MAP TO GOD

The first step that a God Chaser must take is to go through the door of salvation. Jesus says, "I am the gate. If anyone will go through Me, he will be saved. He may come and go as he pleases and find plenty to eat" (John 10:9).

To begin the chase, you must begin by taking the right road. There are many roads that one can take, but there is only one way that will lead the God Chaser to his ultimate destiny—God. "Go through the narrow door which leads to eternal life. The door is wide and the road is broad which leads to destruction. Many people are entering through it" (Matt. 7:13).

The door of Christ will lead you to the narrow road. "The door is small which leads to life and the road is narrow. Only a few people are finding it" (Matt. 7:14).

Sin is a major roadblock. It keeps you from entering through that gate and walking down that road. You must get past this first major obstacle, if you are going to begin your journey. Sin is missing the mark, and we are all guilty "because everyone has sinned and is far away from God's glory" (Rom. 3:23).

To be a God Chaser, you must first learn that sin cannot be covered or controlled by your own works and power—no matter how hard you try. "He saved us by a washing of rebirth and renewal of the Holy Spirit. Salvation did not come from any good deeds that we ourselves did. No, it came by God's mercy!" (Titus 3:5)

God's great desire for you is that you might discover Him at the end of the chase. However, that ancient problem of sin must be dealt the *fatal* blow. Sin creates a great chasm between God and man (Isa. 59:2), and we must find a way to bridge that gap.

But there is **AWESOME NEWS** for you!

God has already provided that Way (Jesus, John 14:6) to get past the barrier and cross the chasm that sin creates. In Rom. 5:8 the apostle Paul says, "But God reassures us of His love for us in this way: While we were still **sinners**, Christ died for us!" (Also see John 3:16; Rom. 4:25; and 2 Cor. 5:21.)

You see, the Provision (Jesus Christ) is there for you. All you have to do is say "yes" to God's Way, and then the chase can begin. You simply must receive Jesus as God's *only* Way of dealing with your sins. "He gave the right to become God's children to those who did accept him, to those who believe in his name" (John 1:12).

So, here are the steps you must take to begin your journey:

1. Recognize that **you** have sinned. And, you are unable to stop the sin in your life. You have no power within yourself to resist the power of temptation all around you. But, you've got to start somewhere! The rebellious son said, "I will get up and go to my father. I will say to him: 'Father, I sinned against God and in front of you' " (Luke 15:18).
2. Repent of your sins. Prepare yourself to abandon the road that you are on. It is time to turn around and take the road that God has provided for you (Jesus). "So, change your hearts! Come back to God, so that He may wipe out your sins" (Acts 3:19). Perform the actions that *show* that you have really changed (Matt. 3:8), including following the Lord Jesus in everything you say or do (Col. 3:17)—continuing in prayer, fasting, baptism, and true discipleship.
3. Rest in God's Provision (Jesus). The Bible calls this rest "trust" (faith). Faith means that I choose to trust God for my whole life. Rather than retaining selfish control of my life, I place my life in His loving hands. I am hereby choosing to believe that God's Way is better than my way. "If you confess with your mouth that 'Jesus is Lord' and if you believe in your heart that God raised Jesus from death, you will be saved" (Rom. 10:9).

Why don't you take time to pray **right now** and seal your commitment to Him?

Dear God, I have sinned against **You** by choosing to live in my own way. **Today**, I am willing to turn around. I know that I do not have the power to change my life; I choose to let **You** be that power in me from now on. I now open the door of my heart to **You**. Come in **right now** and take control of my life. Please forgive me of my sins and change my life. I accept **JESUS** this day as my Savior and my loving Lord. **Thank You** for Your great love for me! Amen.

LET THE CHASE BEGIN!

Now, your chase can really begin. Remember, this is *only* the beginning. A whole life of spiritual adventures awaits you as you chase after Him. Now you need to start reading the Bible, God's Book.

Tommy Tenney's Biography

Tommy Tenney has been chasing God in active ministry for over 30 years, sharing his passion for the presence of God with countless churches in many nations. The founder of the God-Chasers.network, he has authored several best-selling books, including *The God Chasers*, *God's Dream Team*, *God's Favorite House*, *Answering God's Prayer*, *Secret Sources of Power*, and *God's Secret to Greatness*.

Tommy is no stranger to the miraculous, but his heart's desire is to spend time in the secret, quiet place of intimacy with the Father and his family. Tommy and his wife, Jeannie, reside in Louisiana with their three daughters. A Yorkie, Little Romeo, rounds out the Tenney household.

Run With Us!

When you join the **GodChasers.network** we'll send you a free teaching tape!

If you share in our vision and want to stay current on how the Lord is using GodChasers.network, please add your name to our mailing list. We'd like to keep you updated on what the Spirit is saying through Tommy. We'll also send schedule updates and make you aware of new resources as they become available.

Sign up by calling or writing to (U.S. residents only):

Tommy Tenney
GodChasers.network
P.O. Box 3355
Pineville, Louisiana 71361-3355
USA

318-44CHASE (318.442.4273)
or sign up online at
http://www.GodChasers.net/lists/

We regret that we are only able to send regular postal mailings to U.S. residents at this time. If you live outside the U.S. you can still add your postal address to our mailing list—you will automatically begin to receive our mailings as soon as they are available in your area.

E-mail Announcement List

If you'd like to receive information from us via e-mail, join our E-mail Announcement List by visiting our web-site at www.GodChasers.net/lists/.